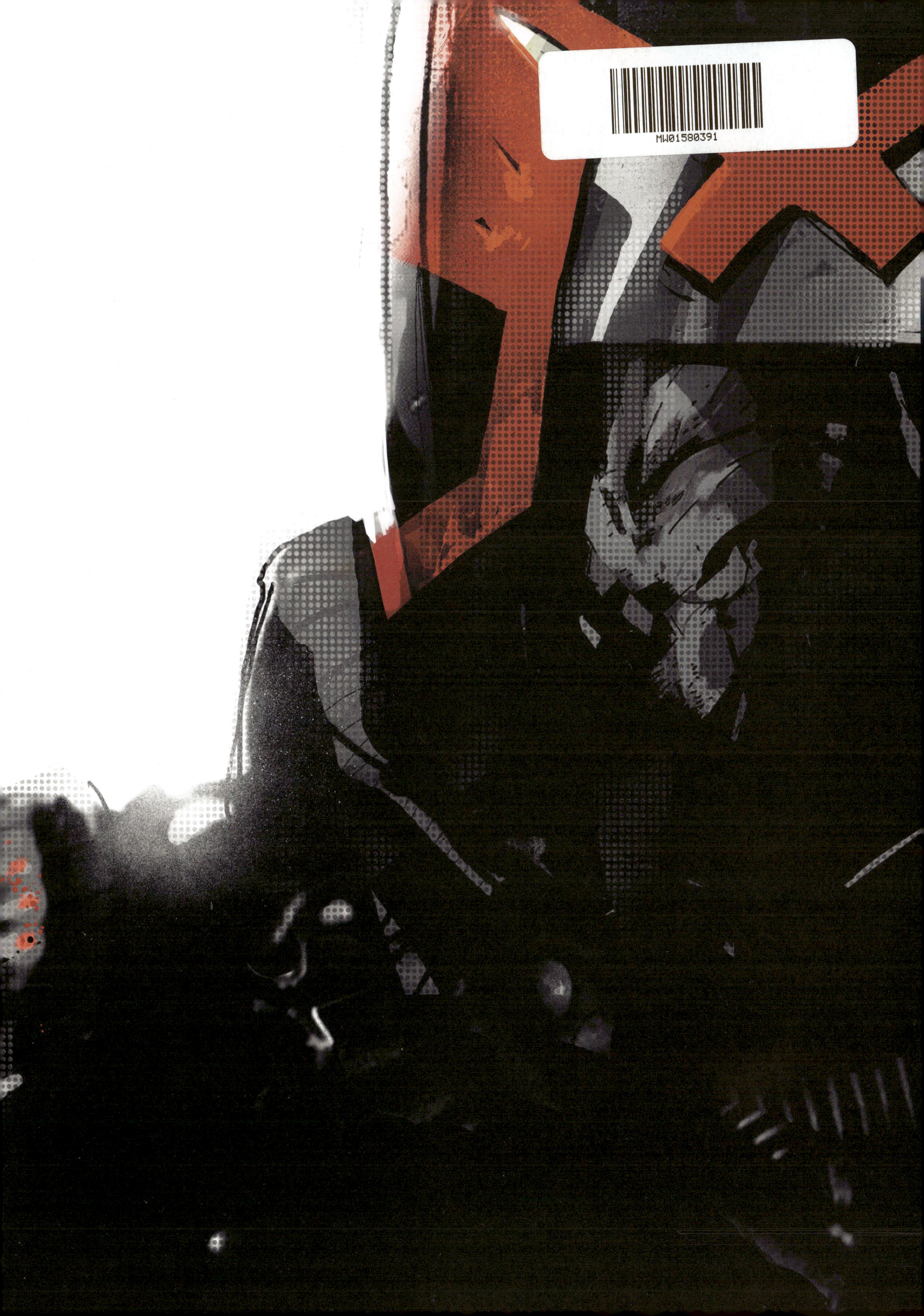

Endpapers: DREDD 2012 3D poster, 2012
This spread: Judge Dredd Card Game sketch, 1999

Judge Dredd created by
JOHN WAGNER and CARLOS EZQUERRA

Rebellion

Creative Director and CEO: Jason Kingsley
Chief Technical Officer: Chris Kingsley
Head of Publishing: Ben Smith
Publishing Director: Beth Lewis
2000 AD Brand Manager: Michael Molcher
2000 AD & Graphic Novel Marketing Manager: Steve Morris
Trade and Special Sales Manager: Owen Johnson
Production Manager: Dagna Dlubak
Rights Manager: Sam Birkett
2000 AD Editor in Chief: Matt Smith
Senior Graphic Novels Editors: Keith Richardson & Oliver Pickles
Graphic Novels Editor: Jonathan Stevenson
Junior Graphics Novel Editor: Chiara Mestieri
Graphic Design: Sam Gretton & Gemma Sheldrake
Reprographics: Joseph Morgan, Scarlett Willow & Richard Tustian
Archivists: Charlene Taylor & Alex Habgood

All contents copyright © Rebellion 1999-2025, unless otherwise stated.
All Rights Reserved.
Judge Dredd, Tor Cyan, Missionary Man, Lenny Zero, Shako and all related characters, their distinctive likenesses and related elements featured in this publication are trademarks of Rebellion 2000 AD Ltd. 2000 AD is a registered trademark. The stories, characters and incidents featured in this publication are entirely fictional.

Published by Rebellion, Riverside House, Osney Mead, Oxford, OX2 0ES, UK
www.rebellion.co.uk

Retail ISBN: 978-1-83786-538-3
Exclusive slipcase edition ISBN: 978-1-83786-625-0

Printed in China
First published: July 2025
10 9 8 7 6 5 4 3 2 1

To find out more about 2000 AD, visit www.2000AD.com

Curated by JOCK
Designed by GEMMA SHELDRAKE
Edited by OLIVER PICKLES and CHIARA MESTIERI
Special thanks to MONDO

THE ART OF JUDGE DREDD

JOCK

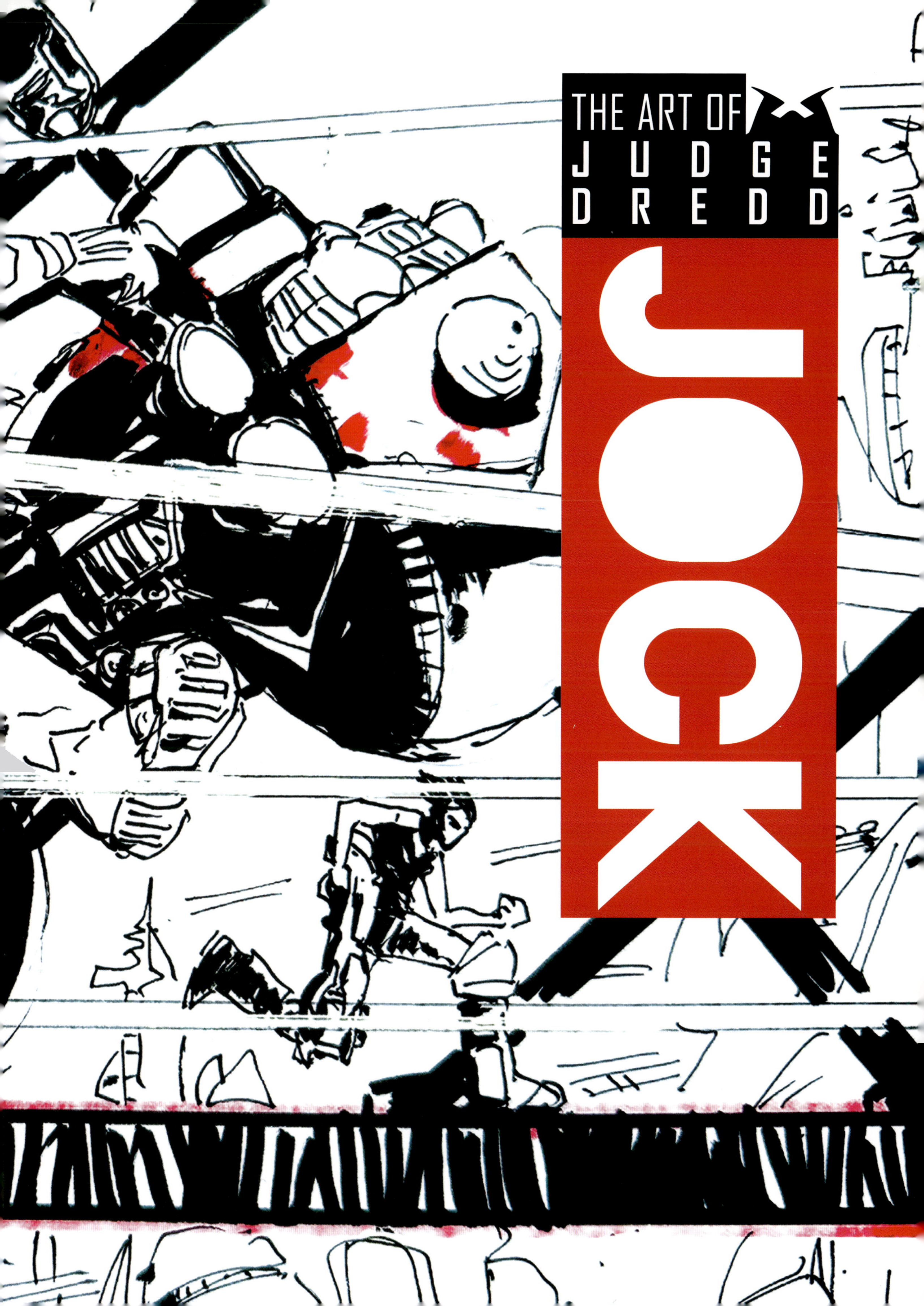

JOCK – 25 YEARS IN THE ISO-CUBE

BY MICHAEL MOLCHER

EVERYTHING MUST BEGIN SOMEWHERE. FOR KANDINSKY, EVERYTHING STARTED 'FROM A DOT'. FOR JOCK, IT'S A LINE.

Mark Simpson, better known by his teenage nickname, is one of the most fascinating artists to emerge from the British comic book **2000 AD**. In less than a year, he entered the acclaimed weekly anthology's pantheon of notable creators, before beginning a rapid ascent into the 'mainstream' of comics, and is now one of the industry's most recognisable and high-profile creators.

Yet every fresh page must begin somewhere.

'It's about putting the line on the page and making it mean something,' he says. Within that line is possibility, the myriad of choices that are going to have to be negotiated. That alone can make that first mark daunting.

'It's the hardest thing, to just begin. There's a Stanley Kubrick quote: "Sometimes the truth of the thing is not so much in the *think* of it, but in the *feel* of it." That seems to be the right way for me to approach it, to feel it out.

'Back in the day my drawing might have been more meditative or intense, but now it's part of my day-to-day. I'm still pretty good at following my instincts – I don't think it's any less for it – but with the reality of drawing daily, you learn to do it effectively and regularly.'

Despite the endless rigours of deadlines, there is something instinctive and reflexive about Jock's work. It all blooms from that first mark on the page: lines given heavy meaning by both the forms they trace and their placement on the page, their simplicity or complexity, the presence or absence of blocks of black ink. An ingrained understanding of dead space and shadow, streaking lines and nib splatters that create a cutting, chiaroscuro-like contrast, focusing the eye and channelling the action.

It embodies the graphic sensibility of Klimt's secessionists, the expressive lines – thin and thick – of Egon Schiele and Jon J. Muth, Ansel Adams' vast but human American landscapes, the explosive energy of Bruce Lee movies, and the sinewed bodies of Mick McMahon – a mix unique in comics and one that began in the pages of **2000 AD.**

The cradle of multiple 'British invasions' that have mauled, reshaped, and influenced the 'mainstream' of American comics since the 1980s, if the weekly anthology has been a nursery for creators then *Judge Dredd* is its proving ground, the character on which reputations are built. An authoritarian future cop patrolling the soaring streets and teeming towers of the dystopian metropolis of Mega-City One, Dredd was created in 1977 by John Wagner and Carlos Ezquerra, but left their hands before he even first appeared in **2000 AD**'s second issue, as dozens of writers and artists then spent decades putting their own stamp on the taciturn lawman and his outlandish world. Brian Bolland, Steve Dillon, Mick McMahon, Ron Smith, Brendan McCarthy – so many have blazed so brightly in this grim, neon future city that they have gone on to leave an indelible mark on comics and, beyond it, on the wider cultural landscape.

In his own turn, Jock's influence on *Judge Dredd* of the post-millennium is almost inversely proportional to his time as a regular contributor to **2000 AD** – arguably, no other artist since the 1980s has made such an immediate impact on the character, yet he drew just 132 comic pages and 21 covers between 1999 and 2007. And it may have felt that no sooner had he appeared than he was 'snapped up' by American comics giant DC Comics, but any dismissal of his time at **2000 AD** as a mere 'springboard' to the American mainstream is to do it an injustice. Readers of the weekly **2000 AD** and monthly **Judge Dredd Megazine** had front row seats to a rapid burst of artistic evolution.

'We were always going to meet,' old friend and fellow **2000 AD** artist Dom Reardon grins. 'This guy! This guy! He's a drummer, he also likes **2000 AD**! The word came through the grapevine that *this* was the guy to know.'

With his now long-gone remnant of a Scottish burr, eight-year-old Mark had been dubbed 'Scotty' by his schoolmates after his family moved south (later, walking through Glasgow to a comic convention, he would keep his East Kilbride heritage in the back pocket of his homemade trousers 'like a weapon') but by the time he reached his teenage years he had switched to his future identity, an old English joke that had been applied to his brothers and was now a badge of pride: Jock.

Having moved around Dorset as a child, he had finally found himself nestled between the moor and the sea. If Totnes did not exist it would be necessary for the tourist board to invent it: once a year they remember an Elizabethan pirate by rolling oranges down a hill, they fought off the behemoth of Costa Coffee, and even had their own currency for a brief time. There's drugs and homelessness next to boutiques and organic grocers. It has been a counterculture cradle since the old arts college at Dartington opened in the '60s – the ruins of a medieval hall, filled with art, music, dance, theatre and a dream that radical 'contextual arts' could change the world.

That dream closed, bitterly and controversially, in 2010.

It was a girl who was studying at the college that drew Jock there in 1992. She left, he stayed. But then, a year later, he met Reardon at a gig; Reardon was sixteen, Jock nineteen. An event so momentous, he can remember the exact day: 'It was October 8th, 1993, I was about to move in with a mutual friend of Dom's, so we went to a gig that Dom's band were playing that night. He had big bow-tied hair, playing bass brilliantly and he just looked fucking bad ass, I knew I wanted to meet him.'

Jock had returned from the fabled United Kingdom Comic Art Convention (UKCAC) in Glasgow with the Holy Grail that so entranced Reardon: a sample script from DC imprint Vertigo – then already at the height of its cultural impact. This pair immediately shared an infectious, bubbling enthusiasm that continues to this day, one firmly rooted in art.

'We became friends because we both wanted to draw and just used to hang out all the time drawing,' remembers Jock. 'Dom's parents had a beautiful big farmhouse with a cellar, and we'd stay up all night drawing and painting. I was signing on, had no money and I put all my energy into drawing, we used to immerse ourselves completely.'

'At that point all kinds of things emerged,' says Reardon. 'It was ideas passing back and forth, ideas taken from the books and the comics we had and were exposed to. We'd be sat in a room, we'd read them, discuss them, and then try to draw like them. It was an amazing thing.'

'It *was* an amazing thing,' Jock smiles. 'We were at a point in our lives where we were thinking "What are we going to do with our lives?", "What's possible with our lives?", "There are these great artists that we love, making a living drawing and painting – can we do that with ours?" Yes, we can.'

The way they talk about this time is heady: staying over on a Friday night, drawing in front of episodes of **Rock Power Telly**, bouncing off one another, channelling everything they were reading and seeing and absorbing into teenage dreams of making art. For anyone of a similar age, their cultural diet will come as no shock.

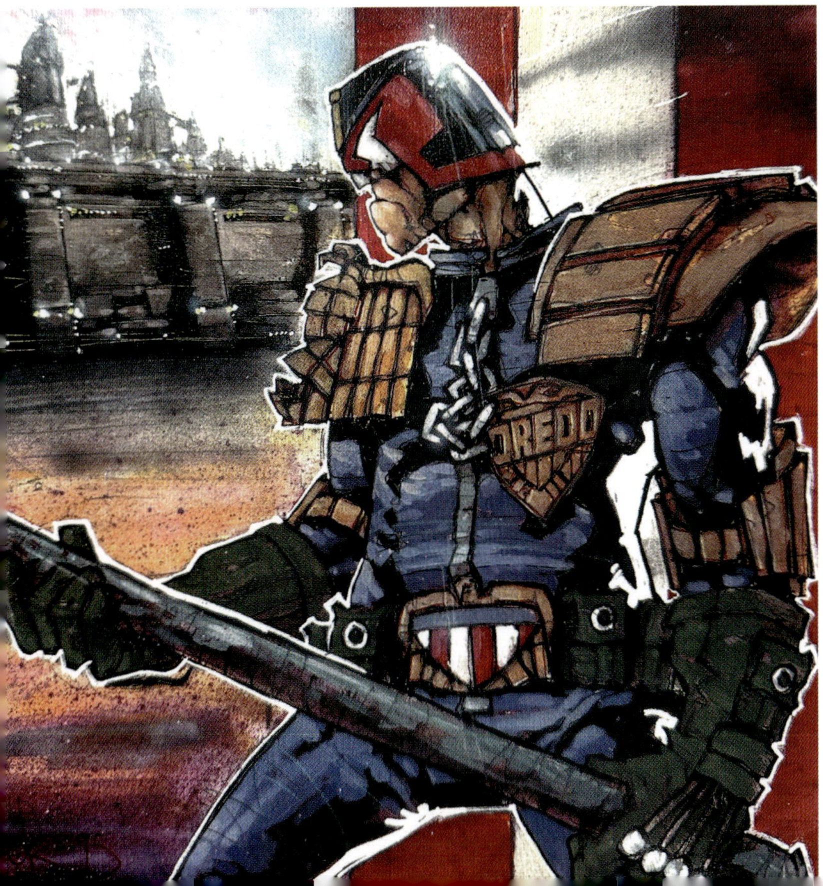
DREDD

Pre-published artwork
1995

'Jesus, this is not the rich history of someone living in the French Bordeaux region,' he laughs, recalling the passions of the 'really nerdy' teenage Jock. 'It was literally Spectrum games and Oliver Frey paintings, covers for [ZX Spectrum] **Crash** magazine – they were magic because his paintings represented what the games felt like, even though the games were super basic. I remember copying a Rambo poster with his big bazooka. I used to paint **Warhammer** figures on a Friday night instead of going out: **Call of Cthulhu**, fantasy roleplay, **Star Wars** role-playing games.

'I wanted to be an artist – that's what I wanted to do, from as early as I can remember. I now realise how lucky that was, as well, because I thought everyone knew what they wanted to do, that they had a thing they'd ideally love to do. When I realised not everyone does, I felt very lucky that I had.'

And then **2000 AD** happened.

'I think it was just luck or chance that I hadn't discovered it before then,' he says. 'I remember seeing an issue at a friend's house, it was issue 500. It had a Brendan McCarthy double-page centre spread in orange and it was really dark, lots of shadows – I didn't really know what I was looking at and didn't even know if I liked it.

'And then, maybe a month later, I saw an **Eagle Comics** reprint of a Brian Bolland cover where Dredd is clinging on to the front of a van jumping over a highway, and he's got his gun out saying "You're under arrest". It's a ridiculous proposition but that slightly over-the-top stuff really appealed. And then after that I went to my newsagents and realised it was a thing I could buy, and I bought it every single week after that.

'I'd have been fifteen, so quite late coming to it, but when I saw **2000 AD**, I didn't realise quite what it was, but I realised that it was the channel that I wanted to put my drawing into. **2000 AD** was like the catalyst, I suppose, it felt like an appropriate channel I could put all that stuff into.

'When I was about 16 I started going out, meeting girls and that sort of stuff – but I still drew all the time, most of my evenings were spent in my bedroom, on my cabin bed, with **2000 AD**s laid out around me with all my favourite art, hip hop music playing on my little turntable... and trying to draw.'

There was an intensity to Dredd at the time that was clearly intoxicating to a teenage mind, not least in a collection of the *Judge Dredd* newspaper strip, which had been appearing in the **Daily Star** newspaper for five years by that point. 'What an introduction that was,' says Jock, thinking over John Wagner, Alan Grant and Ron Smith's concentrated doses of compressed storytelling, even summing up entire multi-part mega-epics in just a few panels. 'Every page is packed with some Mega-City lore... there was so much content in those, I dread to think how they pulled it off, week after week. I remember there's one story with a mutant – I didn't know what a mutant was! It just blew my mind. It was the imagination of it all; the art was amazing, but also this exaggerated form of reality. I loved that.

'That's what I always love about art, how it should represent an inspirational element. **2000 AD** is huge for that, it's so full of massive ideas. I'd copy movie posters – Drew Struzan was the first person whose style I recognised – and then **2000 AD** again because it's all about the strength of the creators' style.

'The unique thing when we were growing up was that every

Pre-published artwork
1996

single strip looked completely different, a completely different take on it – what the hell is this? It's amazing. And then I got into comics more generally, there were American guys I was into, but most US comics had this kind of pedestrian quality to it where they were all similar, in a house style. I realised – to this day – that I'm so grateful to **2000 AD** because it made me think "Well, I can do this my way". It's one of the few things, like music, where it's your currency – you either try and fit in or do it a different way, that can have mixed results, but all my favourite creators are specifically them, they have their own style, their own unique quality. I'm not very objective about what I do but people do say I have my own style, and I've got **2000 AD** to thank for that.'

His teenage art is a riot of his favourite movies, books, art: self-conscious attempts at life drawing, Bruce Lee high-kicking a lightning bolt fired by a hooded wizard in a fantasy desert. Juvenile, but charming. Picking things apart, peeling away the surface to try and understand what makes them work. It was a process of inquiry with comics at its heart, which is not surprising given how at the time **2000 AD** and Vertigo – through artists such as Simon Bisley, Bill Sienkiewicz, and Dave McKean – were challenging the medium's relationship with art.

'We were looking at what we lovingly refer to as "inspiration templates",' says Reardon, 'and they might have been Duncan Fegredo cover art, or it might have been a Degas painting. But they were all inspiration templates for us and balanced in the same category, so we were looking at a whole bunch of different things – which may have been Egon Schiele or may have been Kent Williams or Dave McKean or Monet, they were an eclectic bunch of inspirations. We saw Simon Bisley on *Sláine: The Horned God* and thought "Hang on, can I be a painter AND do comics?" Do both those things?'

'I got very into painting, basically. To the point where I almost wasn't interested in **2000 AD** anymore, because I had lofty aspirations – McKean and Sienkiewicz and Kent Williams were raising the bar for what comics were; that's absolutely still relevant, but that was a little phase that I had,' says Jock.

'At that point, Dom drew in a way that I just didn't understand, and I found it fascinating. It was really thoughtful and considered, and up to that point I'd tried to draw and tried to present things in a way that I thought would look good,

but I wasn't really considering what I was doing as much as I could have done. Dom taught me, or rather, I got that from him... I remember sitting there and we were drawing these aliens for a role-playing game, the Shaktar for SLA Industries, which was our first ever commission after going to our first convention and scoring some work. Dom had an airbrush and was drawing this weird alien lizard's stomach and there was so much going on in the way he rendered the stomach that it blew my mind. I remember looking over his shoulder as he was doing it thinking how amazing it was – it was brilliant.

'It's just those little marks. I will never forget watching him as he did that, and my mind expanded with possibilities. That's incredible, you've said so much with so little, how does he do that? And it made me think about that and how I might try and do that myself.'

What made this process revelatory was not just the external influences they were picking apart, but the different mindset, the different way of doing things that Jock was exposed to. Rather than just *seeing*, he was *thinking*.

'I wasn't wise enough to understand my own workings or how to draw well, how to make something. I was good at drawing at school, but I didn't understand what it takes to do something interesting that people respond to. The time that I had with Dom, and what I learnt from him was his approach to drawing is really thoughtful and slow and that side of my character wasn't as obvious to me at the time.

'He talked about "Be sure you really, really think about what you're doing". Really just stop, slow down, think about what you're doing, see it on this blank bit of paper, start to see what you're about to draw – that comes with empathy, that I was lacking at the time. When you draw a comic, you need empathy to make the characters act so you're seeing the world or the environment you're about to draw even before you put pencil to paper; you're thinking about it and the cogs are working about how you're going to approach it, why are you going to show this thing? What's my camera angle? What's the lens? What's the point?

'By looking at other people and not really comprehending how you can do that, you just have to start chipping away at things like anatomy, layout, the way colour works, and design, and you start to then see the building blocks, how anything that's impressive is made. Then it becomes more transparent to you as your understanding gets better and better; and when I was with Dom that's what we did – we were just getting so into it.

'We'd do a painting and fail, but there'd be a little element that you'd learn, and then you'd do another one – it's not exactly rocket science that the more you do the more you learn, but it was more specifically trying to unravel how you do it, how do you make it good? But also, going back to putting your heart into it, we had delusions of grandeur; we were trying to be "real" artists, trying to be honest and thoughtful and expressive and all those things that make art interesting. We didn't even think about it.'

For a teenager into art, the assumption – at least at the time and *especially* living in the shadow of Dartington – was that years at art college beckoned. But while Jock's life is one defined by the starting and following of lines, they are not always *straight*. Even though Jock completed a foundation year, he didn't get a place on the degree course. So, after all this time swimming in a sea of influences and questions, a decision had to be made: where to go from here?

'The only touchstones I had when I didn't get into art college were comics,' he says. 'So, I went into my local comic book shop and thought "Okay, well maybe I'll give comics a go". I looked at what was on the shelves, completely objectively – what would be the sort of thing I would be interested in doing?

'And I picked out a **Kid Eternity** from Sean Phillips and an **Enigma** issue from Duncan Fegredo ... so you can see how my early stuff is influenced by them. They seemed to have a unique way of approaching things. I'm glad I chose pretty well.

'It was around the time I made the decision to completely commit to art, to not just think "This is something that I do". I'd left college and thought I was going to try and do it, but I wasn't really engaging with what it takes to do it properly.

'I always felt that if I had got into doing a degree course, I wouldn't be doing what I'm doing now, I'd just be more like everyone and, probably, not as good. I feel like that would have done it for me.

'So even though I'd left college and thought I wanted to do it, it wasn't until spending time with Dom that I really fully committed – and by that I mean in myself – to really try and make this work. It wasn't even like a calculated career choice, it was "No, I'm going to put everything I've got into this, and I really hope it works out". It was like jumping off a cliff, like I'm teetering on the edge and am I going to jump off or step back onto the relative safety of dry land? I decided to jump in and – touch wood – maybe that's what it takes.'

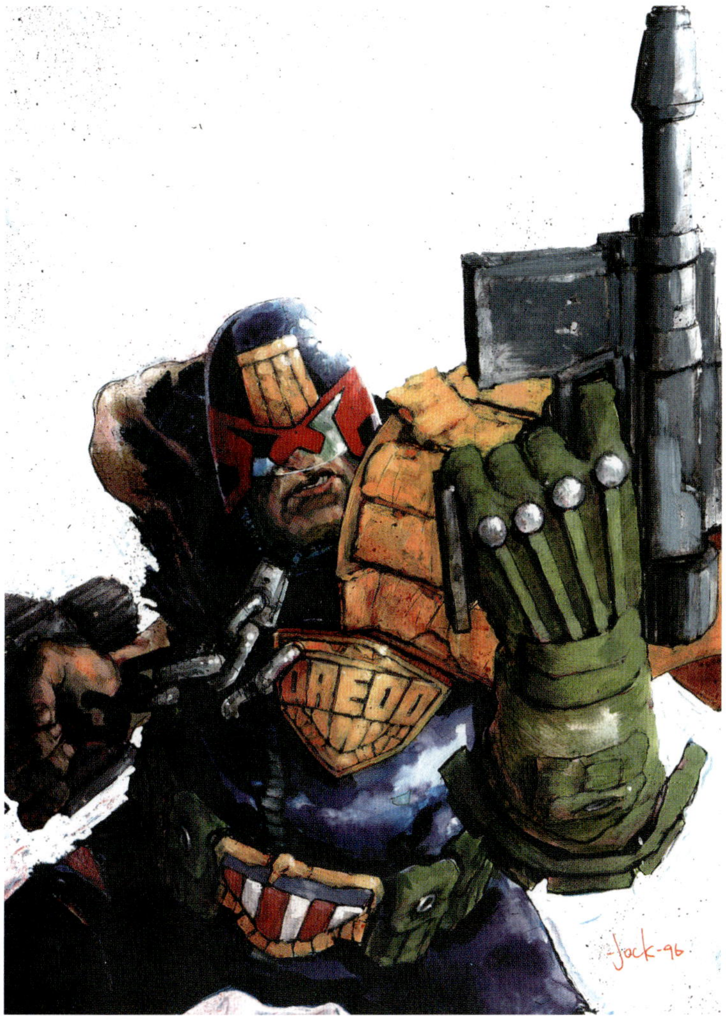
DREDD
Jock-96

Pre-published artwork
1996

Months followed of signing on to the dole, completely immersing themselves in drawing, trying to figure out how this would work. How *they* would work. Before long, it was time for the 1995 UKCAC in Glasgow, at the time virtually the sole comic book convention in the country and the one that attracted the most editors.

The line on the map between Totnes and Scotland's biggest city is 470 miles long. Jock and Reardon had no money. So, they decided to hitchhike the entire way. In a day.

'People don't believe us when we say this, but it did happen,' laughs Jock. 'It was pushing 11:30 in the morning and we had hundreds of miles to go, and we were stood on a motorway slip road. We both had really long hair and I was wearing home-made trousers, both of us with big portfolios under our arms. We were full of the joys of spring, but it was beginning to dawn on us that time was getting on and we were still in bloody Exeter.

'Then one of us, God's honest truth, said "We could do with, like, a red sports car to come along and pick us up". And I kid you not, two minutes later a little two-seater Mazda with this business guy from London pulled up and Dom squeezed in the back and we drove at a hundred and fifty miles an hour up to Bath, and from that point on every time we stopped and needed another lift we'd say something like, "Well, we're in Carlisle and it's getting dark, wouldn't it be great if a car came along that was going straight to Glasgow". Then this car would turn up, the driver would ask us where we were going, we'd say Glasgow, and he'd say, "Me too". It was really quite weird. It was quite magical; we were young, and it was all going to plan.'

Once there, fortune continued to smile. 'Why are you showing this to me?' **2000 AD** artist Glenn Fabry told Jock after viewing his portfolio. 'Fuck off and make some money!'

'David Bishop was there very specifically looking for **Lawman of the Future** [*Judge Dredd* movie tie-in title for kids] samples and I showed him my *Judge Dredd* portfolio and he said, "This is pretty good but you don't really want to draw for us, do you?" and I was like "N...no", so there was a real sense that we were aiming for something. We weren't there by any stretch at all, we weren't ready yet, we weren't good enough, but Steve MacManus saw something in us, he saw potential.

'There was a point, because we had delusions of grandeur, having been inspired by Monet and Schiele and all the masters, – joking aside – I didn't want to draw for **Lawman of the Future** because I didn't want to do something that was anything less than *Judge Dredd* itself.'

Their presence created enough of a stir that Steve MacManus, former **2000 AD** editor but still working in publisher IPC's comics group, sought them out. Though impressed, he told both of them that they weren't ready… yet.

Just two weeks later, they were at a band practice at Reardon's parents' house on a Sunday. 'Dom's mum comes down and says there's a phone call for him, Dom puts his bass down and nips upstairs. Then he comes back down again and says, "Jock, it's Steve MacManus on the phone for you, mate",

Jock's first published 2000 AD work
Sci-Fi Special 1995

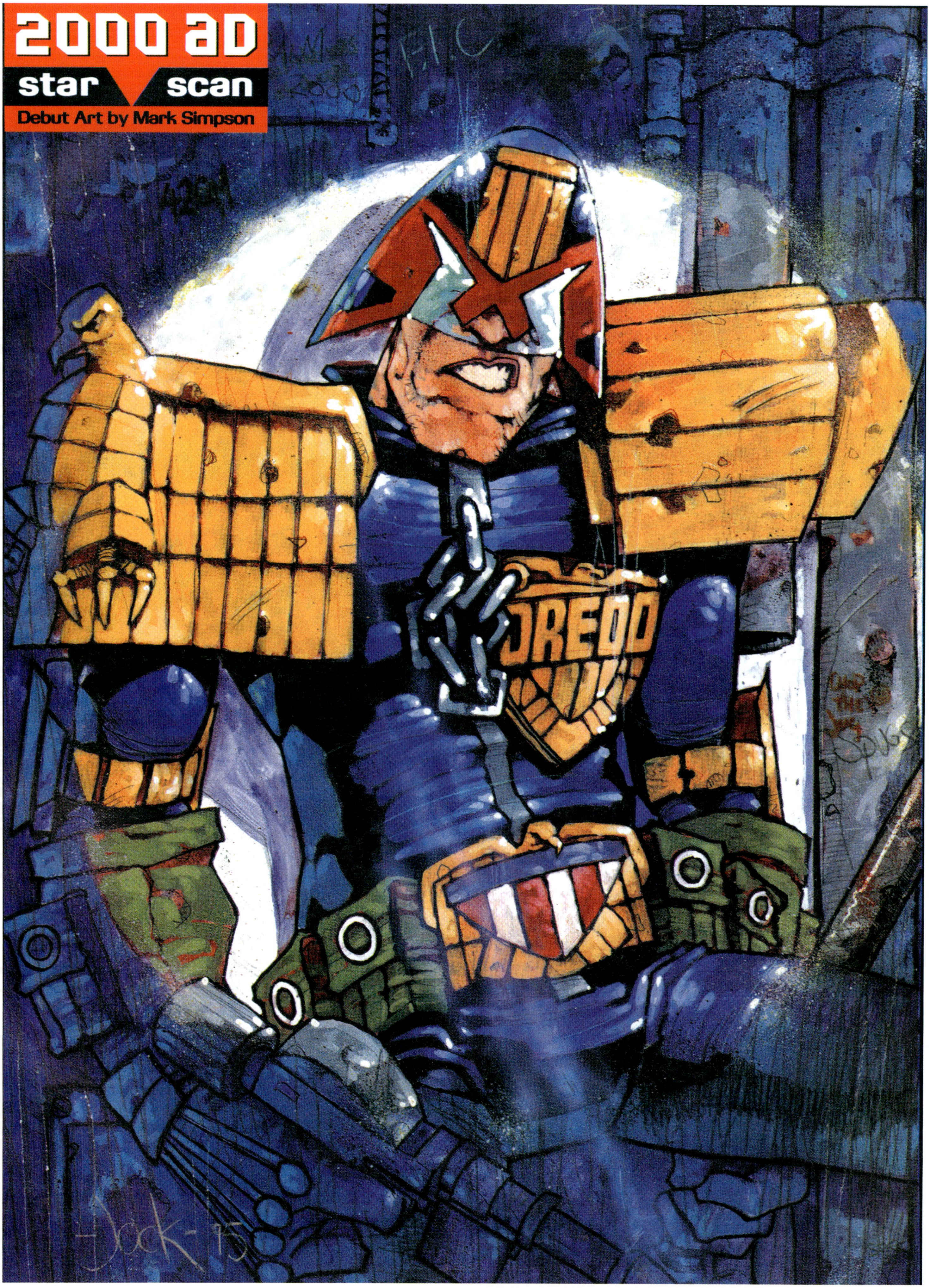
2000 AD
star scan
Debut Art by Mark Simpson
DREDD
Jock-95

and I'm like "What?!". Steve said he wanted me to do a pin-up, and I asked if it could be Dredd.

'It was just all a bit too good to be true, we were just on cloud nine,' he says, only years later realising how unusual and personal making such a call was for an editor.

This first pin-up, credited to Mark Simpson, is a remarkable document of a nascent talent. It is, of course, of Judge Dredd. The page is crowded, every surface covered with thick textures, each trying to evoke the bold, solid colours Sean Phillips had used on *Judge Dredd* a few years prior, or the speckled, unsettling paints of Duncan Fegredo's covers for 1993's **Enigma**.

Dredd's pose, however, betrays a deeper influence – he seems to be leaning back against a wall, his right arm curving around to the Lawgiver in his hand, as if cradling it; his legs are spread and his head cocked at an angle. It reminds the reader of nothing less than Mick McMahon's iconic title page from 'Block Mania', the 1981 story that led to the long 'The Apocalypse War' storyline.

It is the work of a teenager, plucking elements that excite but without the experience to know how and why they worked, or how they should work *together*. This attempt to merge two eras of *Judge Dredd* is typical of Jock's head-long search for a way to both evoke the past he loved and also to make it his own. MacManus wasn't wrong – there was obvious potential. But it wasn't quite ready.

Most artists will have a similar story – that first flush of affirmation, the fizz of possibility. The line of the future seems to run off into the distance as the gamble of committing to a life in art seems ready to pay off. Yet as so often the case, it came under pressure from real life almost immediately.

Despite a smattering of work after this – the odd pin-up, some art for Wizards of the Coast's popular tabletop card game **Magic: The Gathering** – the high faded away, to be replaced by frustration as the line forward seemed to fade. Five years later, Jock had a young son and a part-time job to make ends meet. The prospect offered by that shining moment in Glasgow seemed more and more like a dream.

'We didn't really keep up the momentum with Steve [MacManus] that we should have,' Jock admits. 'He did phone a couple of years later, just to see what I was up to, again a really cool thing to do. I met [then-**2000 AD** deputy editor] Andy Diggle at a convention in Bristol, he looked through my stuff and said it was good but not good enough for **2000 AD**.

'By this point I wasn't letting go. I asked "Okay, well, what am I good enough for; covers, pin-ups?" So, he gave me a sample script. He said he liked my stuff and might have work for me in the future, but I took it with a pinch of salt.

'Anyway, after having my son, Dom and I tried to revisit those magic times of staying up all night. I went up to his new house and stayed in the garage, on my hands and knees doing a painting. I remember walking home at six in the morning and I wasn't happy with what I'd done; it was getting light, and I had a son at home and thought, "What am I doing?!"

'I've got a family, enough is enough, I've got responsibilities. It was the first time I really, really thought, in all honesty to myself, about just getting a normal job.

'I got up about midday the next day and went into my studio and looked at the painting; the sun was shining in, and it didn't look *too* bad. I went downstairs and, I kid you not, I flicked on the answerphone and there was a message from Andy Diggle with my first work for **2000 AD**. And I've not been out of work since.

'I felt really lucky but at the same time I felt like I could do it, in the pit of my stomach,' he says about his decision to pursue art as a career, a choice that had been, in his own words, like 'jumping off a cliff'. But fortune will only get you so far, so it is moments like this where one must stick or twist.

'I was probably a bit naive, but I felt like I could do it. That's what kept me at it, motivated me after all of the rejections just to keep doing it. I don't believe in fate, but I do think you make your own luck and that was strange timing, and it's still just chance.'

Judge Dredd is a challenge to any artist. With only the lower half of his face exposed to the viewer, they are either forced to evoke whatever emotion (or lack thereof) they can out of only half a face, or make his physicality do the talking. For Jock – like so many who went before him – this is a feature, not a bug.

His Dredd is implacable, monolithic, yet lithe and sinuous. When designer Jan Shepheard crafted the strip's original logo in 1977, she created a visual metaphor – not only are the letters craggy and rock-like, but the inside edge of the first letter of 'Judge' is a subtle side profile of Dredd's face. In the strip, other Judges nicknamed him 'Old Stoney Face' and no other artist has so embodied that nickname in their portrayal of Wagner and Ezquerra's lawman.

The chin of Jock's Dredd is a cliff face, a pitted and lined escarpment cut with sharp shadows and rivulets. It bulges with solidity, enlarged almost to ridiculous proportions. ('That did happen once,' Jock laughs, discussing his cover for the **Judge Dredd Megazine** in 2001, where a craggy-faced Dredd glances over his shoulder at the reader. 'I sent the prelims and David Bishop, who was editor, dropped me a line and said, "That's far too big". So, you *can* take it too far.') But those folds and crags contain all the authoritarian lawman's pent-up emotion, rage and control. He becomes, for Jock, a force of barely contained nature.

It was this chin that attracted Andy Diggle's attention.

'My first clear memory of seeing Jock's work is in the submissions pile of **2000 AD**,' says Diggle. 'I was basically just the office assistant and one of the first things that David Bishop asked me to do was to tackle the unsolicited submissions pile, which he just hadn't got the time or staff or resources to deal with.

'We had a big plan chest full of **2000 AD** artwork, on top of which was piled was a, I guess, two-foot-high pile of scripts and artwork – all unsolicited submissions that nobody had looked at in months. It was literally a teetering pile, and the mission was basically "Go through that and find out if there is anybody good in there".

'It's easy with artwork to tell if somebody's got it or not, you can tell at a glance and I specifically remember the image that sold me on his work – it was just a Dredd headshot, very bold, stark headshot, black and white line art headshot of Dredd, and I just thought it was amazing, it looked like Mount Rushmore; this kind of gravitas, the kind of sternness, the kind of weight to it, a heft. And I loved it, and it's not often I have a visceral reaction to artwork.'

By 1999, the boom of painted comics sparked by **X-Men** artist Kent Williams, **Arkham Asylum** artist Dave McKean and **Elektra: Assassin** artist Bill Sienkiewicz, and by Simon Bisley's work on **2000 AD**'s *Sláine: The Horned God*, had come to a muddy halt, to be replaced by a new breed of painter artist, exemplified by Sean Phillips, Duncan Fegredo, and Dermot Power. Theirs was a fresher amalgam of painting, inks and pencils, less in thrall to the fantasy art of Frank Frazetta and more influenced by impressionism, graphic design, and pop culture. With paints full of fizzing energy, Fegredo's **Enigma** for Vertigo, Phillips' *Devlin Waugh: Swimming in Blood* for **2000 AD**, and Power's *Sláine: Treasures of Britain* were redefining how paint and the comics medium could work while exerting a powerful influence on a young Jock.

That influence was on full display in 'Reapermen', Jock's first printed work in **2000 AD**. Written by Gordon Rennie, this 'Pulp Sci-Fi' story – one of the variations on **2000 AD**'s by then venerable Future Shock format – was published in **2000 AD** Prog 1170 and featured five pages of art by Jock, all of it painted.

In hindsight, each page feels like a chrysalis, crammed with recognisable elements of what would become his style, yet all nearly hidden beneath layers of thick paint, as the lofty desire to emulate comics painters and capture the excitement of youthful experimentation wrestles with the very real practicalities of producing full pages to a deadline.

'It's just not very good,' Jock admits, with a laugh. 'It was totally the limitations thing. It was a five page story and by page five, I was starting to get somewhere … but then it was done. I was trying to be Kent Williams and paint **Wolverine**, probably, though that wasn't where I was at.'

It was enough for Diggle to commission a **Judge Dredd Megazine** cover featuring Armitage, Dave Stone and Sean Phillips' Inspector-Morse-meets-Judge-Dredd character. It has never seen print.

'That was likely due to me panicking and wanting it to be really good,' admits Jock. 'Whenever you say to yourself "I am going to knock this one out of the park", you don't – if anything you stifle it. I find you just have to let it go and then if you've got something it'll come out. I find it much easier to just be myself with my work and people seem to respond to it.'

Regardless, it was not enough to dissuade Diggle. The deputy editor had been coming up against editor David Bishop's ambivalence towards the samples that Jock had been sending to **2000 AD**'s offices in London. Although Bishop's tenure at the helm was marked by its openness to allowing radically different artists to develop in print, Diggle found himself as lone cheerleader for the potential he saw in Jock's work.

The 1990s had been rough for the self-styled 'Galaxy's Greatest Comic'. Successive editorial regimes struggled in the shadow of its 1980s 'golden age' as key creators left. Demographics and cultural mores shifted out of its favour. Several bold – or foolhardy – attention-grabbing gambits flopped. The lightning-in-a-bottle seemed to have gone.

The turning point, if there was a single one, came when Diggle – who stepped into the editor's chair in June 2000 – penned a famous memo for creators in which he astutely defined what the ideal **2000 AD** story should represent: 'A shot glass of rocket fuel'.

Although his turbulent two-year tenure was short, the effects of the return to what he deemed to be **2000 AD**'s 'core values' of action-first storytelling proved to be profound – not least because he gave Jock his first comics work.

'In November 1999 I remember doing a Dredd painting and I made sure it spanned the millennium by deliberately finishing it in the year 2000. I quite liked it and sent it to Andy; he rang up and said he loved it, and could I do twelve pages of black and white Dredd in a month? I hadn't done any black and white artwork for ages, but I just said, "Yeah, course I can!" Internally, I thought I had no idea how I'd do it but I just said yes. And I just had to do it.

'And about halfway through the *Dredd* for Andy I got a call from David asking if I could do a four-part Dredd for **2000 AD**. It really pissed Andy off actually – he was assistant editor to David at the time and had been trying to get me work, but David kept saying no. I think he said about one of my pages that I looked like Brendan McCarthy, to which Andy said, "How is that a bad thing?".'

The first of these stories to see print was Diggle's – 'Dead Ringer' in the **Judge Dredd Megazine**, written by Judge Dredd co-creator John Wagner and beginning in April 2000. After an assassination attempt on a foreign dignitary visiting Mega-City One, the Judges try to replace him with a citizen who happens to be an exact clone, only for the citizen – the hapless Jefferson Jiggs – to flee in fear. In a series of increasingly comedic events, Wagner parodies his and Alan Grant's epic 1980s storyline, 'The Judge Child Quest' (**2000 AD** Progs 156–181,

1980, with art by Brian Bolland, Ron Smith & Mick McMahon, and lettering by Tom Frame), as Dredd pursues Jiggs across the stars to try and avoid a diplomatic incident.

'That was a bit of surprise,' Jock laughs, recalling Diggle's offer. 'Diggle said "Duncan Fegredo's drawn part one, you draw part two" – I was like, "Are you kidding me?". And then he said, "Cam Kennedy's drawing part three". C'mon, really? To say "no pressure" was an understatement.

'I feel like I've always thought, "Okay, I guess it's my turn". I was *so* aware of the situation; I was getting sketches and designs sent through from Duncan and thinking "I can't match this at all. But okay, I'm going to try".'

While Kennedy ended up not drawing one of the story's seven parts, the roster of those who did was no less impressive: Duncan Fegredo, Wayne Reynolds, Simon Coleby, Anthony Williams, Ben Oliver, Richard Elson… and Jock. Along with Sean Phillips, Fegredo had been one of the touchstones to which Jock had turned when he'd interrogated the shelves of his local comic book store for inspiration and whose work had clearly influenced his first pin-up, which did not go unnoticed.

'John McCrea actually contacted Sean Phillips and Duncan Fegredo, thinking that this strip was a combination of the two of them working together under a pseudonym,' he laughs. 'That tells me I was wearing my influences on my sleeve a little bit, but also it was quite a compliment on my first strip.

'That was the only time I've thought about style, about how to handle the rendering; the thing I noticed about them was that they used a lot of black, a lot of white, there was a nice balance in the quality of the design, on top of the great art — Sean's covers were really design-led and that really appealed. So I chose to use a lot of black in my inking.

'I was a few pages in, and I faxed a black and white page to Andy. He replied and said, "I think you're giving Duncan a run for his money"; I didn't believe him for one second, but maybe I was doing alright. So, I blindly just carried on. Looking at the pages now, they feel a bit amateurish to me, they could be more consistent, but I can see there's a bit of juice in them. You can see I'm trying – and, often, with any creative work, that's really an important part, that you care about it, and you try.'

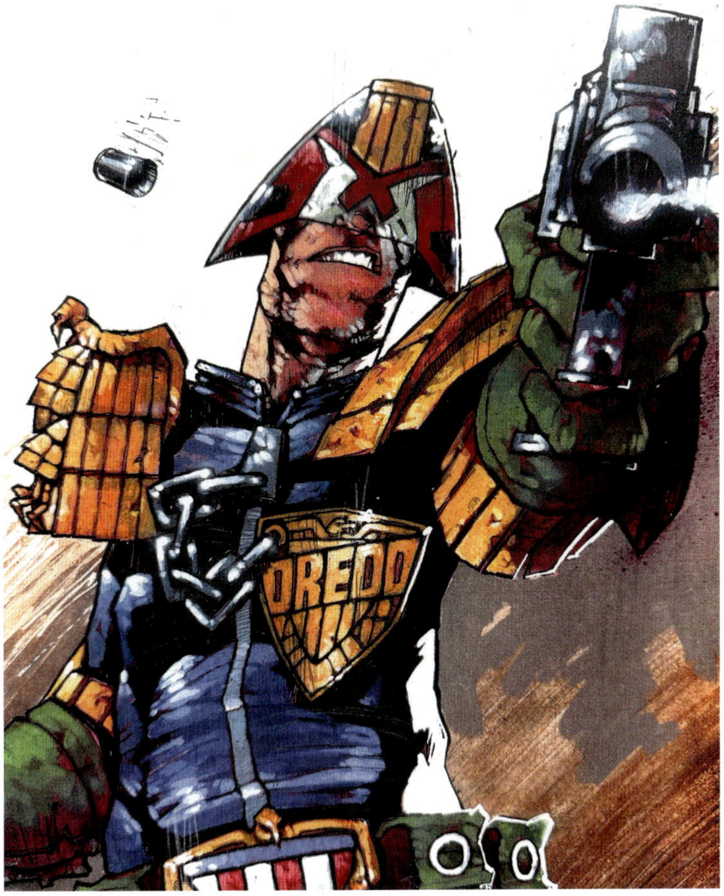
DREDD

Pre-published artwork.
1994.

There are acres of dead space, which leaves a significant field for long-time *Dredd* colourist Chris Blythe to play with, and there are the unmistakable corners that any freshman artist cuts to cover up the flaws they know – consciously or unconsciously – are there in their work. But it is striking, looking at these pages at a distance of twenty-five years, how what could be thought of as Jock's 'style' is already there on the page, and how easily he slips into esteemed company.

'By that point I'd been trying to get work for seven years,' he says. 'I'd done a lot of sample pages and it's arguable whether the 'Dead Ringer' pages were good enough, but there are some nice little touches.'

Jock entered **2000 AD**'s artist roster at the critical turning point where Diggle was trying to steady the ship and, in many ways, his work was the exemplar of Diggle's 'rocket fuel' manifesto (it is no coincidence that the pair went on to partner on **The Losers** for Vertigo, a swaggering, bombastic, violent spy romp through the post-9/11 political landscape): Jock's Dredd seems constantly in movement, the chunky shapes of his uniform almost jostling and grinding in ill-disguised impatience.

Getting two Dredd stories (and being ready for them) after years of trying and almost giving up vindicated every choice to that point.

'He's still my favourite,' he says. 'It's funny, I first discovered Dredd when I was fourteen or fifteen – it represented possibilities, ideas, and a bigger world. You think they're childish ideas, but as I've got older, I still hold on to those things... they become your ammunition. Feeling inspired by ideas and concepts.

'Dredd still represents that to me – even though it's twisted and the character and the world have a real dark satire element to it, there's more to it; it's not been reduced to the fascist state that some stories suggest. My favourite stories were always about the city and the citizens, and how the human spirit would flourish within the oppressive Judge system. That's always been the thing I've loved about it most. Dredd — how can you love that guy? But I still do, because he's the hero and the villain, he's what the story needs him to be. But it was always stories like 'Supersurf' and 'Chopper' that I loved, 'Over the Wall' where the kid risks stealing a flower to give to the girl he loves, 'The Graveyard Shift' where the Judges are in the background.

'When I think about the character it still represents, like the best science fiction does, more than we have now. And not always in a good way, but it represents possibilities and imagination and larger-than-life qualities, which I think is a lovely thing so I – weirdly – still think of Dredd and his world warmly.

'You've got to be careful with nostalgia but I still – slightly romantically – believe that we can be better, that no matter

what the system does to you there'll always be that kid climbing over a wall.'

Perhaps the reason that Jock's spell on *Dredd* – brief as it was – feels evocative is that it acts as synthesis of so many of the strip's definitive artists: there's the solidity of Brian Bolland, the perspectives of Ron Smith, the blocky, distorted figures of Mick McMahon, and the action of co-creator Carlos Ezquerra. Each element locks into place early in his portrayal of the monolithic lawman, the proportions of his outlandish uniform almost a weapon in and of themselves, lithe limbs stretched to breaking point in athletic reach, and the grim, implacable chin and the grimace balanced above it.

'When I first started buying the comic and I was a little younger, I was more impressed by the more decorative stuff, like Bolland for example. He had a detailed, impressive style. And when I was younger, I found Mick's stuff slightly odd, slightly harder to swallow in some ways. It was only when I was getting a bit older that I started realizing what Mick was doing was building a 3D world within the panels.

'Other artists do it too, but people do it to different levels. People can take that incredibly far and some take it more 2D and more kind of graphical – which Mick has also done brilliantly.

'But there was something about that particular era of 'Block Mania', 'Sky Chariots' – I'd put that in the top three comic art of all time, easily – if you look at it with a slightly knowing eye, you start to understand how much he put into his art. So, at the time Brian and Mick are running side-by-side with two completely different approaches. With Mick, it was also his cartooning and exaggeration, but it really was the form in 3D space that he did amazingly well. Mick even said that the reason he left 'Block Mania' is because there were all these crowds, and he had reached the point where each person had to be realised, and it was just too much.

'Someone like Ron Smith will do – brilliantly – something quite impressionistic with dashes and marks, and the eye just reads the busyness of it, and I love that as well. His Mega-City One feels really vibrant and alive, but Mick's stuff was honed in a very particular way and I think that's why he couldn't do 'Block Mania', because it was just too much. Whereas Ron, for example, had this brilliant easiness about the way that he drew and – I would argue – some of his form could be a bit janky sometimes, but overall it was impressionistic rather than being very exacting, and at the time I needed to understand that about comic art, about representing and telling the story as well as you can. He really, really, really influenced me in that way.

'By the time I was working for **2000 AD** I was fully invested in McMahon. Earlier on it was Bolland as I say - but McMahon's art had that strangeness to it that I appreciated more as I got older, along with his world-building and consistency. I was transfixed by him.'

But there's also something *more* to his style: rather than a pure homage, it draws on elements from beyond **2000 AD** and comics. The switch to ink work, rather than painting, exposes perhaps the clearest of artistic influences – early 20th Century Austrian painter Egon Schiele.

'What I love about those guys is they draw the human figure so, so well and it looks so fragile and real, bony and skeletal, yet coupled with brilliant design. Klimt is obvious but Schiele is the same – his drawings are so bold, and design-led. You do that and couple it with the human element, that's a really powerful combination.'

Surrounding him with more established talents, 'Dead Ringer' was a bold debut for Jock, and spoke to a level of maturity beyond his years. But his next story, commissioned by David Bishop, almost immediately exposed his lack of experience. Again written by John Wagner, 'Shirley Temple of Doom' (**2000 AD** Progs 1193–1196, 2000, with colours by Gary Caldwell and lettering by Tom Frame) was a four-part story about an undercover Judge operation against a city block protection racket which goes horribly wrong. The story's different tempo, along with more prosaic pressures, conspired to produce what Jock claims to be his 'worst Dredd work'.

'It was the reality of turning in weekly strips,' he admits. 'I got two weeks for an episode – which is plenty, I'd have no trouble with that now – and David gave me so much advice and help. He'd spend a long time on the phone with me, giving practical advice. I really wanted to show I could get it in on time, and unfortunately I rushed the pages.

'So suddenly that's full-time work for two or three months, and at that point you're doing the job. I was adjusting to what that really meant, not managing my time very well – not for want of trying.

'I think I had one thirty-five-hour stint at the drawing board without getting any sleep, which is easier when you're starting out but it's no way to handle doing the job regularly. I was more focused on getting it in on time rather than on whether it was any good, and I'm rather embarrassed about it. John Wagner's script was fantastic, but talk about being thrown in the deep end! I had to figure out how I was actually approaching this job.'

By this point, Wagner had perfected the slow-burn *Dredd* story, and 'Shirley Temple of Doom' called for character and action in equal parts. There are flashes of confidence and style on the page, and the art remains resolutely consistent, but suddenly the limitations of what Jock could then achieve were in front of him. It's no cliché to call this a learning experience: throughout, faxes filled with sketches and page layouts continued to arrive at Diggle's desk, each one a plea for advice and reassurance.

'I don't know whether that's healthy or not,' Jock laughs. 'It's been interesting digging out work for this book because I can see what my mindset was and I recognise it, but I realise how much I've moved on from there. Maybe it's one of the reasons I've had the career that I've had – I knew this wasn't good enough and I was trying to figure out how to make it better. I still am, to this day.'

What 'Shirley Temple' does show is his inspirations shining through. The figures may need work, but his vision of Mega-City One as a three-dimensional space had already popped into being – his use of forced perspective and backgrounds recalls Ron Smith's lived-in metropolis, while the shape of his city blocks evokes the classic 'pepper shaker' style of Mick McMahon's buildings. This is most evident in the opening

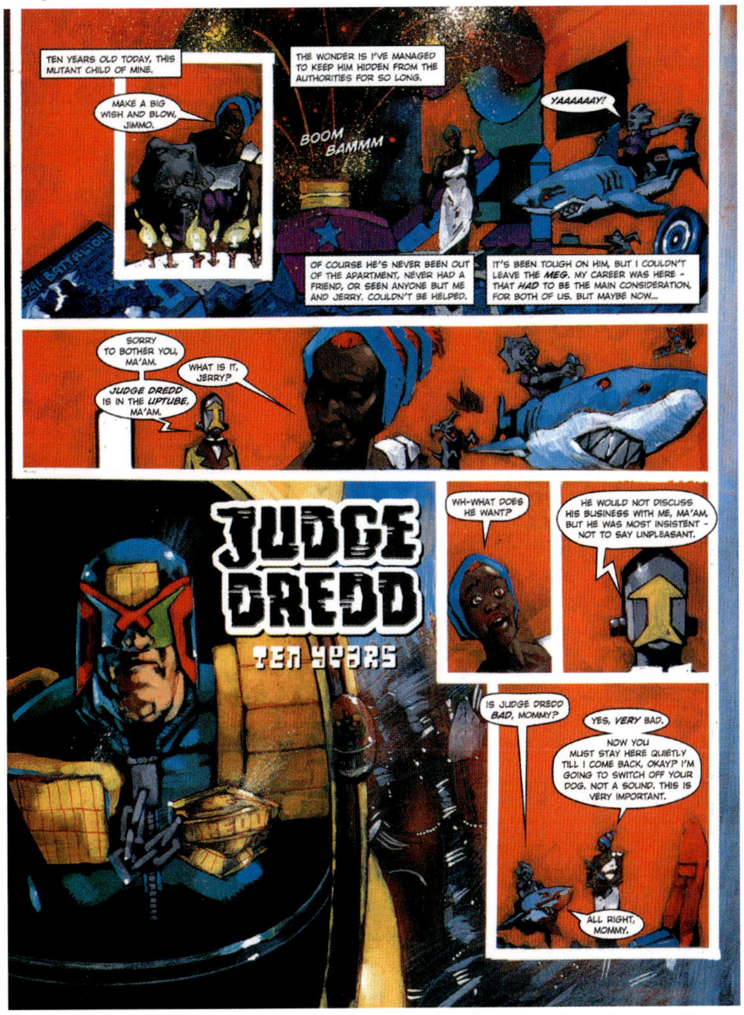
TEN YEARS OLD TODAY, THIS MUTANT CHILD OF MINE.
MAKE A BIG WISH AND BLOW, JIMMO.
THE WONDER IS I'VE MANAGED TO KEEP HIM HIDDEN FROM THE AUTHORITIES FOR SO LONG.
BOOM BAMMM
YAAAAAAY!
OF COURSE HE'S NEVER BEEN OUT OF THE APARTMENT, NEVER HAD A FRIEND, OR SEEN ANYONE BUT ME AND JERRY. COULDN'T BE HELPED.
IT'S BEEN TOUGH ON HIM, BUT I COULDN'T LEAVE THE MEG. MY CAREER WAS HERE - THAT HAD TO BE THE MAIN CONSIDERATION, FOR BOTH OF US. BUT MAYBE NOW...
SORRY TO BOTHER YOU, MA'AM.
WHAT IS IT, JERRY?
JUDGE DREDD IS IN THE UPTUBE, MA'AM.
JUDGE DREDD
TEN YEARS
WH-WHAT DOES HE WANT?
HE WOULD NOT DISCUSS HIS BUSINESS WITH ME, MA'AM, BUT HE WAS MOST INSISTENT - NOT TO SAY UNPLEASANT.
IS JUDGE DREDD BAD, MOMMY?
YES, VERY BAD.
NOW YOU MUST STAY HERE QUIETLY TILL I COME BACK, OKAY? I'M GOING TO SWITCH OFF YOUR DOG. NOT A SOUND. THIS IS VERY IMPORTANT.
ALL RIGHT, MOMMY.

Jude Dredd: Ten Years.
Judge Dredd Megazine 3.70, 2000

page of episode three, in which five tight panels of narration are placed on top of a view of the city with Dredd on his Lawmaster bike in the foreground, echoing McMahon's layouts for the epic 'Block Mania' story and Smith's on the 'Mega Rackets' and 'The Graveyard Shift' serials, which did so much to flesh out Dredd's city.

'Even though 'Shirley Temple' isn't my favourite story I relished the opportunity to cut loose a bit on the city,' he says. 'I guess I wanted to make Mega-City One broader and give it more visual scope, which sounds really arrogant, but you'd catch glimpses of when Ron Smith would show the incredible depth down to the bottom of the city, and I adored that. I wanted to flesh that out.

'I had the art book of the Sylvester Stallone [*Judge Dredd*] movie and [concept artist] Kev Walker had some really lovely city shots, and the scope and the scale was much larger because it was a movie. I thought the comic could benefit from that, and I loved trying to do it.

'Again, thanks to discovering **2000 AD**, even though I had these influences I thought it was my job to do it my way. I can see this younger version of me trying things out, a bit of a wonky face here, missing the mark there, but I can still see what I was shooting for. I'm glad that I was thrown into the deep end, because it meant I had to figure it out.'

Originally titled **Judge Dredd: The Megazine**, **2000 AD**'s first sister title launched in 1990. Sparked by the success of Brett Ewins and Steve Dillon's **Deadline**, which had also led to Fleetway's **Crisis** and **Revolver**, the **Megazine** was designed to give more space for stories about and around **2000 AD**'s biggest character. Its first issue, arriving in September 1990, featured the beginning of what would quickly become a defining Judge Dredd story – John Wagner and Colin MacNeil's 'America'. Discarding his trademark dark humour, Wagner penned a story full of pathos and tragedy, which used the story of a doomed freedom fighter called America Jara to reaffirm the fascistic nature of Justice Department's regime.

A decade later, Diggle hoped to mark the anniversary with another Wagner story, for art he turned to his newest talent. 'America' had been fully painted by MacNeil and Jock decided, in defiance of the difficulties he'd found making painted comics work, that this story needed something special.

'I was quite proud to be given the tenth anniversary story, and I was probably thinking I wanted to make it look more impressive, so I decided to paint it,' he says. 'There's always a little moment of surprise – sometimes good, sometimes bad – when you receive colours from a colourist, you know. And with it being the anniversary strip, I wanted more control over it.

'But at the time I was also trying to have a career as a drummer playing in bands, and 'Ten Years' came about just as I was hired to go on tour around Europe. So, I was painting some of those pages – not just drawing them, *painting* them – on the tour bus driving around Europe, which I do not recommend. So, there was that thrown into the mix, and my head might have been in a bit of a different space.'

'Ten Years' is a moving story about Dredd's attempted deportation of a mutant child whose genetics exclude him from citizenship. His distraught mother then has to watch as a monstrous brute murders several people and, despite his inhuman cruelty, is consigned to the isolation cubes – yet her son faces exile in the deadly Cursed Earth.

Jock's implacable Dredd is there, again brandishing his Lawgiver until it almost bursts out of the page, but here his paints fill the dead space around panels with alternating monotone backgrounds of vivid vermilion, white, and sky blue, and his panels increasingly switch between colour and greys to create visual depth. But it is where the paints are at their thinnest that his work shines through, especially in the faces of the mother and son, which bear the story's emotional heft.

By contrast, that same month **2000 AD** ran another of his stories – in what were becoming his style-defining inks. In 'Crossing Ken Dodd' (published in **2000 AD** Prog 1214, 2000, with colours by Chris Blythe and lettering by Tom Frame), it was clear that, in just a handful of months, he had figured out the lessons from 'Dead Ringer' and 'Shirley Temple'.

A Wagner-penned one-parter packed with humour and bombast, 'Crossing Ken Dodd' played to Jock's strength by being full of action while also being set in a tight three-dimensional space. The Judges deploy vast amounts of manpower into protecting a single man crossing the eponymous Ken Dodd Boulevard – named after the famous Liverpudlian comedian and variety star – as every conceivable kind of armament tries to kill him: gunships, missiles, even a thermal charge melting the road.

In a classic Wagnerian twist, after the Judges finally get him

Pre-published artwork
1995

safely across the road, it is revealed that the citizen is not an unpopular politician or an informant on his way to court – he is the chief inspector of taxes on his way to work … and it is returns season.

Jock is in his element: each panel filled with stylish action, his Judges rendered as a **Keystone Cops** jumble, an image of a shouting Dredd dominating a double-page spread, his style now working in comfortable simpatico with Chris Blythe's colours. There is even room for self-referencing in-jokes, with the six Judges helping the tax officer across the road – Grainger, Roberts, Childs, Moore and Simpson – based on Elevator Suite, the band Jock was playing with at the time, while a background hoarding reads Head-On, the name of their management company.

'It's probably my favourite,' he smiles. 'It was one of those brilliant John Wagner one-offs, it had a larger-than-life precedent with a funny payoff at the end. It was just the madness of the city, the scale of it, it was all in there. And by this point I was excited about what I was doing, there was a big double-page spread with a massive Dredd, just this huge image with him screaming, his mouth wide open.

'I really enjoyed it; I was cooking by then – I was getting to draw Dredd. I don't mean this in an arrogant way – there are a lot of problems I can now pinpoint, but I knew it looked alright. I wasn't particularly overconfident, but you do get these moments when you know you're doing okay, that you're doing something that you're enjoying and that tends to be when the better work happens.'

Jock's original page layouts, unearthed for this book, reveal not just a new self-assured storytelling that was absent from 'Shirley Temple', but also just how confident he had become in emulating McMahon and Smith in creating a palpable sense of *place*.

'It was fully in the flow, but now that would be a nightmare to draw! Looking back on these stories, I realise Mega-City One demands a lot from an artist. If I drew 'Crossing Ken Dodd' now it'd be a nightmare because there are so many flying vehicles, explosions, and groups of Judges, but back then I had a bit of a carefree attitude, which meant that it was quite fun.'

If there is a point at which everything clicks into place, it's on 'Ken Dodd'. The awkward hesitancy of 'Shirley Temple' gives way to an infectious confidence. After the years of trying and not *quite* making it, tenacity – and a willingness to instantly learn from experience – had gotten him through the door and, in crossing that previously unassailable barrier, he seems unleashed.

There is no better example of this than his first cover for **2000 AD**. Bursting from the front of Prog 1203 in the middle of 2000, Dredd falls towards the reader through a shower of bottle-green glass, lips pursed in a shout as he fires an all-too-phallic bullet from between his splayed legs. 'In hindsight, that was probably a bit much,' Jock laughs. 'Originally the line of the bullet went off the page!' The image owes much to the contemporary work of Fegredo and Phillips, not least the striking and contrasting lack of background, but importantly it is a *painted* cover. Gone are the layers of paint masking fear, stripped back to reveal an assertive use of colour and form.

This cover and 'Crossing Ken Dodd' hum with *confidence*; Jock is apparently unfazed by working on the character he'd dreamed of drawing since he was a child, sitting on his bed surrounded by copies of **2000 AD**. It is the confidence of someone engaging with a character on both an artistic, even unconscious, level.

There is a moment in 'Dead Ringer', probably the most assured in Jock's instalment, when Dredd angrily shoots down at a group of 'Stookie Glanders', who have been harvesting a harmless alien race to produce an illegal youth drug. *'I'll be back! You'll pay for your crimes!'* he shouts, colourist Chris Blythe encircling the muzzle of Jock's blocky version of the Lawgiver with glowing fire. *'The name is Dredd – I am the law!'*

A jaw almost unhinged with the force of a righteous roar is a hallmark of Jock's portrayal of Dredd. It is inspired by Brian Bolland's 1985 cover for Issue 22 of Eagle Comics's **Judge Dredd** series, and is a motif that repeats in 'Shirley Temple', 'Crossing Ken Dodd', and later 'Rampots' and 'Safe Hands'. By then, Jock's rendition outdoes even Bolland's in its force and drama.

'I tried it out in 'Shirley Temple', perhaps a little too much I think because I drew his chin so big,' he says. 'In 'Crossing Ken Dodd' it was just right. We'd seen art of him shouting, with every fibre of him screaming, I enjoy those extremes, trying to push that stuff with characters in general. By that point I was drawing my favourite character, and it was really good fun.'

Similarly, his Dredd is often shown from below, as if he is towering over the reader. Fellow **2000 AD** artist Leigh Gallagher once commented that Jock draws Dredd 'like a tank', and the Dredd on his covers for Progs 1258 (2001) and 1304 (2002) is a brute that has more in common with Frank Miller's thick-set, aging Batman in **The Dark Knight Returns** (1986) than McMahon's lithe figures. In the former, his 'daystick' baton is already bloody, his uniform damaged, his helmet dented, a scowl of contempt on his face as he lumbers towards the reader. An unstoppable force.

Where the comparison to McMahon works best is his rendering of Ezquerra's unique design for Dredd's uniform. By the time of the former's swan song on 'Block Mania' in 1981, the pads on Dredd's shoulders had grown from protective clothing into armour, huge and bulky, projecting authority and solidity. In keeping with this, Jock's Dredd also wears his authority on his shoulders – the iconic eagle on one and the ribbed pad on another, simultaneously armour and munition. His elbow pads, his knee pads, his gloves: all are colossal and weighty. By contrast, Jock's iteration of Dredd's helmet leaves little accommodation for comfort – it seems almost to mould to Dredd's head, chrome and cranium one and the same. Fitting headgear for a man who never removes it.

All of these come together to project a single truth – Dredd is unique. In Jock's Mega-City One, he creates a kind of gravity that seems to warp the world around him, carrying an air of indomitable authority, a physical being embodying the monopoly of violence defined by sociologist Max Weber as the defining quality of the modern state.[1] And, as the avatar of a police state that openly detests its own citizens, he brims with barely-contained rage.

'Part of what makes Jock's work great,' argues Andy Diggle, 'is he knows when to say, "This is not a normal person, this is Judge fucking Dredd" and he'll draw him like he's carved out of solid granite. He's not supposed to look like a real person, he's supposed to look *amazing*.

'I always describe Mega-City One as being like a giant pinball machine and Dredd's the bumper. He's this kind of immovable point in the middle of it, and everything else just ricochets off him, everything reacts around him and he's the kind of point of stillness in the middle of it all, and I think Jock's art really encapsulates that, he's this kind of monolithic presence.

'It's not just that there's a weight, there's enough black on the page, enough weight of a line. A lot of comic art seems a little surface, there's no kind of depth to it. But his stuff, it's got heft, there's a solidity to it and it's rough enough and feels a little scrawly, a little edgy, it's not overproduced which I think allows his own voice to come through somehow. It's somehow more personal, more individual.'

This portrayal also betrays something deeply personal: a child's relationship with the kind of authority that is implacable, domineering, and cannot be argued with.

'I think that's probably a good point,' he admits, 'I draw him very strong and people in my life were like that. The upshot I seem to favour with him – when you're a kid and you're looking up... that slightly child-like, looming, monolithic,

---

1 Max Weber, **Politics as a Vocation** (1919)

Line art for Star Scan published in 2000 AD Prog 2003

scary, strong, immovable force – it's a Judge, isn't it.'

Although he insists he was no teenage rebel, that Dredd represents both his relationship with and rejection of authority, his father's profession as a police officer suddenly hits home. 'I hadn't put two-and-two together,' he says. 'Because of course it is. That's the character, he is that force. You cannot do what you want, you have no free will under me, you're going to do what I tell you to do. That's Dredd.

'Becoming an artist was my own act of rebellion. I wanted to prove I could do something 'my way' and do the thing that I loved - it was very important to me. And that was a deliberate choice – "I'm going to show you." Dredd helped me feel beyond the limitations of my world. **2000 AD** was the big dream, the big horizon. That's what the *Dredd* strip represented to me, my kind of wonderland.'

Fittingly, it was rebellion that defined not just his next step, but so much of what came afterwards.

With the tenth anniversary approaching for the **Megazine**, Bishop and Diggle had also looked to commission a birthday cover from Frank Miller, the high-profile writer-artist behind **The Dark Knight Returns**, **Sin City**, and **300**. In an attempt to save up his meagre commissioning budget, Diggle decided to cut scripting costs by writing something himself.

'I wrote this ten page story, 'Lenny Zero', which was a kind of crime story set in the word of Dredd, in which Dredd does not appear, and I was thinking at the time, I could get one of my favourite artists to draw this, I could ask Cam Kennedy to do it, I could ask Colin Wilson or Carlos Ezquerra.

Pre-published artwork
1998

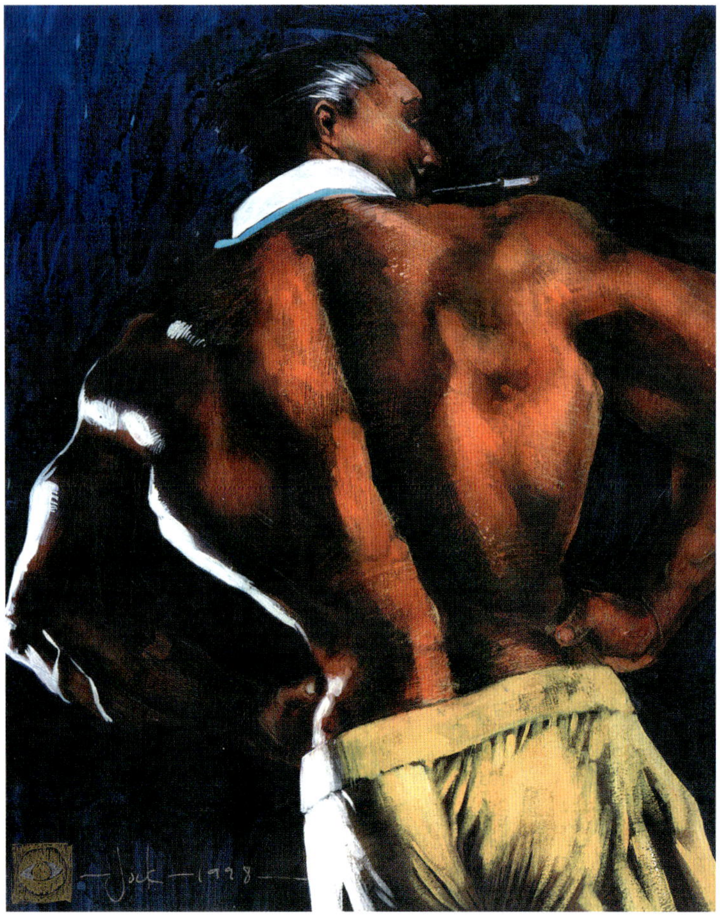

Jock –1998

'I'll admit that was a temptation, but I felt that would be, I don't know, cheating somehow. I'm sort of trying out myself here to see if I'm any good as a writer, see how people react to my stuff, and I'm giving myself a break. I should give somebody else a break too, so I offered it to Jock. And he did a brilliant job, he did a really great job on it.'

'Andy's done this twice now,' laughs Jock. 'It's like a back-handed compliment – he asked me to do his wedding invite with a picture of him and Angela "taking the plunge" but he 'pitched' it to me as "Can you do a picture for my wedding invite?" and I said yes of course, then he added "I was going to ask Brian Bolland to do it, but obviously he's going to say no". Aw, thanks mate! Still, second to Brian Bolland – I'll take that one.

'Then he did it again with 'Lenny Zero'. He was really into [Vertigo series] **Jonny Double** – Jonny Double/Lenny Zero, see? – by Brian Azzarello and Eduardo Risso, so he phoned me and said, "We've got this Frank Miller cover and we're paying him so much that I've had to write something myself. I've got this little story and was going to ask Ed Risso to draw it, but he'll say no ... so will you do it?" You bastard! But again, second to Ed Risso.'

For years in *Judge Dredd*, the 'Wally Squad' had been a running joke – the derisive name given to Justice Department's undercover Judges. Portrayed as a wild contrast to the reserved conservatism of street Judges, these weirdos and misfits have 'gone native' and been tainted by the craziness of the city they infiltrated.

Debuting in the **Megazine** in August 2000, Lenny Zero was a member of the Wally Squad who quit after trying to steal from mob boss 'Little Caesar' Piccante to fund a new life with his lover, Mona, who turned out to be a member of the Judges' internal affairs department, the Special Judicial Squad. With its lead now a professional criminal disenchanted with Justice Department but hated by the Mega-City One underworld, 'Lenny Zero' is an energetic burst of a story, one-part **Serpico** and another **Ocean's Eleven**. For Jock, the strip represents a benchmark.

'It was our own thing, set in a world that we loved, and people really seemed to respond to that,' he says. 'That first script of Andy's was just fantastic, ten pages and so many twists and turns, and I got to show the city, but it had our own take on it. When I look at it now, that probably feels more like 'me', I'd started to figure it out by then. In the second series – I did some Dredds in between – 'Dead Zero', Dredd even turned up, so it all came together, and I still like the splash of Dredd looming over Lenny, that authoritative figure, that monolith showing up in our own strip – brilliant. I knew it was cooking by then.'

Freed from the need to consider colour, he also unlocked a new working method: 'I didn't have a Mac at the time, so I did the greyscales with brushes on acetate and got [friend and fellow artist] John Spelling to scan them in, make them grey, and put them behind the line art. So even with that, I was trying something. On reflection, I didn't necessarily need to do that, but I was interested in figuring out a cool way of doing it that maybe made it its own thing.'

This approach of brush marks on acetate combined with spot colour is where everything clicks into place – the influences, the experiences, the effects, the evolution. The apotheosis of this rapid development seemed to come with the cover to **Judge Dredd Megazine** in November 2001 – even though Bishop had asked for a reduction in the size of Dredd's chin, it is still megalithic, a rocky edifice of brimming frustration and anger; even the eyes of the eagle on his shoulder glare at the reader.

The only colour is that of the thick red band around the edges of Dredd's helmet. Originally the tones were to be red, rather than grey, but the slash of flat contrasting colour gives the glowering tones a vibrancy that leaps from the page. He repeated this grey and red motif on the **Megazine** for August 2002 – another 'Lenny Zero' cover where a simple red strip down the centre of the page cunningly unites the headshot of Lenny in the foreground and the shadowed line-up of gangsters behind and above him.

This visual energy perfectly matched Diggle's scripts, which fizzed with ideas, and Jock said it was clear from the beginning that they sparked off each other.

'There was something about me and Andy working together, I don't know what it is,' says Jock. 'We're different in many ways but I think we balance each other out; he's got a really strong grasp of stories and structure, and I think I wasn't very clean – his scripts are very clean, very sharp and quick, and my stuff isn't so much like that.

'My approach is always to have some dirt... some grit. Give the images a bit of heft when a story beat demanded it, which suits Andy's scripts really well. His stories are full of those moments and we clicked. Lenny was our first thing together, and it was ours,' he says, 'and we did it our way.'

And it was noticed.

A world of espionage, assassination and achingly cool,

wisecracking characters seeking revenge by blowing up things against the backdrop of the "War on Terror" – there isn't a series that really captures the vitality and essence of the Jock and Diggle partnership quite like **The Losers**.

Described by Diggle as 'simultaneously a love letter to Shane Black movies, and hate mail for George Bush', the 32-issue series about a CIA-controlled Special Forces team betrayed by its handler debuted in 2003, earned them both 'exclusivity' deals with DC before it had even seen print, an Eisner Award nomination, and a 2010 Hollywood adaptation starring future Captain America, Chris Evans.

Having left editing behind and having already written for Vertigo, Diggle pitched the series to editor Will Dennis. After the dominance of Neil Gaiman's **Sandman** and Garth Ennis' **Preacher** in the 1990s, the DC imprint was entering a second decade that would be marked by a flowering of new talent. Dennis was initially reluctant to select an artist with so little experience; it was a vote of confidence from imprint editor Karen Berger and Jock's preliminary work that sealed the deal.

'He started putting together these amazing concept designs, like amazing character designs and covers,' says Diggle. 'As much as anything it was like movie poster designs and yeah, there's something going on there – he's got the bit between his teeth, and I think that's probably what clinched it.'

In the post-9/11 world, its brand of gung-ho comic action laid over political reality felt intoxicating, and the sheer bombastic energy of the series was a significant factor. Jock's cover for the first issue was bestrode, in extreme forced perspective, by loose cannon Aisha al-Fadhil, while the rest of this misfit team were wreathed in heavy shadows behind her.

It was not his first use of this low-angled 'worm's eye' view, which would soon become such an important part of his portrayal of Dredd – on a **Judge Dredd Megazine** cover for Gordon Rennie and Frank Quitely's **Missionary Man** in May 2001, a heavily-shadowed Preacher Cain stands in much the same wide-legged stance. It is a pose of immediate and obvious power, a cunning trick for a young artist to use to grab the attention of readers, and of editors. It is as bold a calling card as any American comics had seen.

This attention-grabbing knack for combining high-concept designs with extreme perspectives exposes perhaps the most vital element of his work.

'I think the word 'swagger' is a really good one,' says Jock. 'If you look at the work of a lot of the best people, it all has a bit of an attitude and a swagger; even Cam Kennedy with 'Midnight Surfer', when the Judge is giving a briefing and his hips are slightly bent, he's leaning on one leg – there's just character and swagger in the work, and I've always tried to have some of that. I think that's an element that people respond to. So even though I was an amateur learning on the job, I still tried to put all I had into it.'

Jock's first work for Vertigo had come earlier in 2003 – a single issue of **Hellblazer**, written by Mike Carey, in which John Constantine has to run across London to escape demons sent to hunt him down. For all of its dynamism – the story's conceit pulls the action forward, and Jock walked the actual route through London for reference – there is a nervousness to 'The Game of Cat and Mouse', the style that worked so well on Dredd leaving his characters buried beneath inks. It's clear the pressure of this next step proved unsettling.

'I got a batch of DC board and the first time I put it on my drawing board was a nightmare,' he says. 'It's always easier to chase and want something than to have it, because once you're there you've got to do it. It's easier to imagine what it might be like doing these things you've dreamt of, and hope for, and try and move towards, but when you get there, there's nowhere to hide... "Oh, I've actually got to do this".

'And I was staring at this bit of board and thinking of all the names who've drawn on the same kind of board, and now it was going to be me. I did throw away a lot of pages to begin with, I just redrew them loads and loads. Now, I'm comfortable with it, so I don't worry about it anymore… in a nice way; it's terrible when you stress about it because the drawing suffers.

'There's that quote, isn't there – "Inspiration has to find you working". You've got to be doing the work for those little moments where you're then able to do what you intended all along. You've got to be in the fire. Even looking back over my early work, I can see the weaknesses, but I can also see what I was shooting for.'

One of most striking elements of **The Losers** remains Jock's covers, each one graphically and visually arresting in a way that mainstream US comics sometimes struggle to be, with the overtly political elements of the series providing ample inspiration – one cover showed a giant syringe filled with the American flag 'injecting' itself into a map of Iraq, a startlingly political statement.

'Will [Dennis] didn't want me to do the covers, originally, because he'd seen my **2000 AD** covers,' he says. 'I said, "Well, I've got some ideas", because with 'Lenny Zero', I started trying to bring a bit of '60s design influence, Blue Note Records kind of stuff, which doesn't really work in **2000 AD** because there's always so many cover lines and logos – you need control of the whole thing to really do that well.

'But I was hungry to try something different. And the painted version of the 'Lenny Zero' cover just feels dead, but the line version feels far more alive to me.'

It may seem obvious to the point of banality to assume that the cover of a comic book should be unique or eye-catching, but in an industry in which covers can either be an afterthought or easily fall into bland genericism, Jock's focus on appealing visuals easily made him a breath of fresh air. Part of this is an awareness of graphic design, but also of influences and ideas from outside of the cloistered world of comics. It is notable that one touchstone for this desire to speak to the world outside of comics stretches all the way back to that visit to his local comic shop, and selecting **Kid Eternity** by Ann Nocenti and Sean Phillips as an inspiration.

'One of the reasons I love Sean Phillips is because I always felt that his covers were really nicely designed,' he explains. 'There was always an understanding of more traditional design in his comic covers, in a really smart way. It didn't look like anything else!

'When I was painting early on, his painted stuff was a big

inspiration in how I approached the painting style, which is basically putting down a wash, tone, and then apply opaque paint. The *Killer* cover for **2000 AD** Prog 1266 (2001) is a good example of that – big, deliberate areas of negative space and colour and solidity, and then focus on richer areas with more information and detail – your eye will be drawn there. You can push the eye to a hot-spot. Simple design ideas like that can be really effective on a cover.'

On June 2007's cover for **2000 AD** Prog 1540 Dredd arrests a drunk Scotsman, very much in the vein of those portrayed by fellow Scot Cam Kennedy – dressed in stereotypical tam o' shanter, dirty vest, and kilt, the image dominated by a huge Scottish Saltire, its crossing bands of white against a sea of deep blue. It is markedly different to all his previous **2000 AD** covers; the experience on **The Losers** had a profound effect on his style that bled through to the increasingly rare occasions he returned to work on **2000 AD**, but also meant he was ideally positioned for his next major cover work – **Scalped**.

Dredd had been where he quickly learnt the basics, **The Losers** was bombastic and self-aware, but the covers he produced for Jason Aaron and R.M. Guéra's long-running Vertigo title had a much narrower focus. Debuting in 2007 and set on the fictional Prairie Rose Indian Reservation in South Dakota, **Scalped** pulled no punches in its portrayal of the lives of the Oglala Lakota against a backdrop of crime, poverty, politics, addiction, and social malaise. Guéra's visceral art owed more to Hugo Pratt's **Corto Maltese** or Jean 'Mœbius' Giraud's work on French cowboy saga **Blueberry**, creating a different challenge for Jock, who drew covers for all but four of the series' sixty issues.

'With **Scalped** it was pretty instinctual and a lot of them were done very quickly,' he says, 'a couple of sketches, get the okay, make the art and then it's all completed in just one or two days. I find that's when I'm at my best. Coming from a painterly background, it's a good example of where the art was digital, yet they're more textual and have a more painterly look than **The Losers,** which was much more graphic.

'My primary feeling was that I had to do it justice – every month. Jason and Guéra were doing such an incredible job with this story... if I could match that with the covers then that was a good day for me. It was a really challenging, but a good challenge.'

Taking the lessons from his work on **The Losers** and **2000 AD**, Jock's covers for **Scalped** are at one moment multilayered and thoughtful, the next lashing out at the reader with strong graphical elements and bold social metaphors. In many ways it represents a distilling down of the previous seven years of professional experience, that killer instinct for a striking design now being delivered with both barrels.

'**The Losers** had taught me a lot as I was learning in print, every month, so the **Scalped** covers had that design element and I wanted them to have that visual hook; but they were also able to support a more painterly approach.'

He was brought on by Will Dennis, who – despite the buzz surrounding **The Losers** – says there was, once

Judge Dredd Card Game art
1999

again, resistance to the idea of pairing Jock with the book. This hesitation about his work speaks to how Jock's style challenges ideas around how 'mainstream' comics should look.

'That was a hard sell, internally,' admits Dennis, 'and I knew it was going to be a hard sell externally too. Jock has a very urban quality to his art, so here you have this high concept, this weird setting, rural and dirty and not particularly pleasant, so we'd need to find somebody who's got a slightly more urbane quality or can make it a little sexier. Guéra's art, for me, is sexy, but it's sexy in a very down and dirty way.'

While the covers evolved over the course of the series, the first issue set the tone from the off: like Aisha on the cover of **The Losers**, lead character Dashiell "Dash" Bad Horse dominates the scene, glaring down at the reader while wearing a Native American headdress. There is the trademark Jock swagger but with a coolness, an angry splash of red and the icons of social degradation picked out against his white vest. Capturing the tender cultural scars the series explored so well, Dashiell embodies a kind of brash, mournful suspicion.

'There were a few different versions of that cover,' says writer Jason Aaron. 'Jock ran through a lot of different layouts and ideas before he finally hit on the cover we know. And looking over those other ideas, there are some really great covers in there. It's not that they were misses. It's just that Jock kept pushing until he got to the one that was absolutely perfect. The first perfect piece of work anyone contributed to **Scalped** was that first issue cover.'

Working on covers four months in advance – issues are solicited to comic stores that far ahead – meant Jock was often working on nothing more than a vague paragraph of description from Aaron.

'Out of the fifty-six covers I did, I'd seen script and art beforehand for maybe two and a half issues. Almost all of the covers were based on a paragraph in an email from Jason describing what was going to be happening. And that was it. I kinda like that - you've got to be on your game, it forced me to find a solution that was thematic. The covers weren't literal covers, they were conceptual.

'That was really interesting and challenging. Sometimes I'd be concerned about what was happening in an issue, but when that information isn't there, you can come up with really creative solutions - I think that happened quite a lot.'

'Jock never needed anybody to tell him what to draw,' adds Aaron. 'Jock was the first one out of any of us working on **Scalped** to absolutely nail his contribution. Just look at that first issue cover – Guéra and I were both still finding our way at that point, I think, and would be for a few more issues. But Jock was already firing on all cylinders.

'I've got one of the very first images Jock ever drew of Dash Bad Horse hanging on the wall of my office. It's a promo image that predates the first issue cover. And everything is already there. The action. The attitude. The look and feel. The tone. That image made it easier for me to write the character. And I can say that about a lot of Jock's covers that came after it.'

As well as the obvious influences of Schiele and McMahon, there is a scale to Jock's covers that brings together his desire to showcase the environment of Mega-City One and his growing design sensibility.

The 'Zone System' was developed by the pioneering twentieth century photographer Ansel Adams, famed for his epic photos of the American West. Confronting the problem of capturing both vast landscapes and quotidian detail, his Zone System highlighted foreground detail that would otherwise be swamped by breaking photos into zones, providing a sense of scale in a two-dimensional image. It is striking how much of Jock's work also breaks images down into zones, from his earliest work to now.

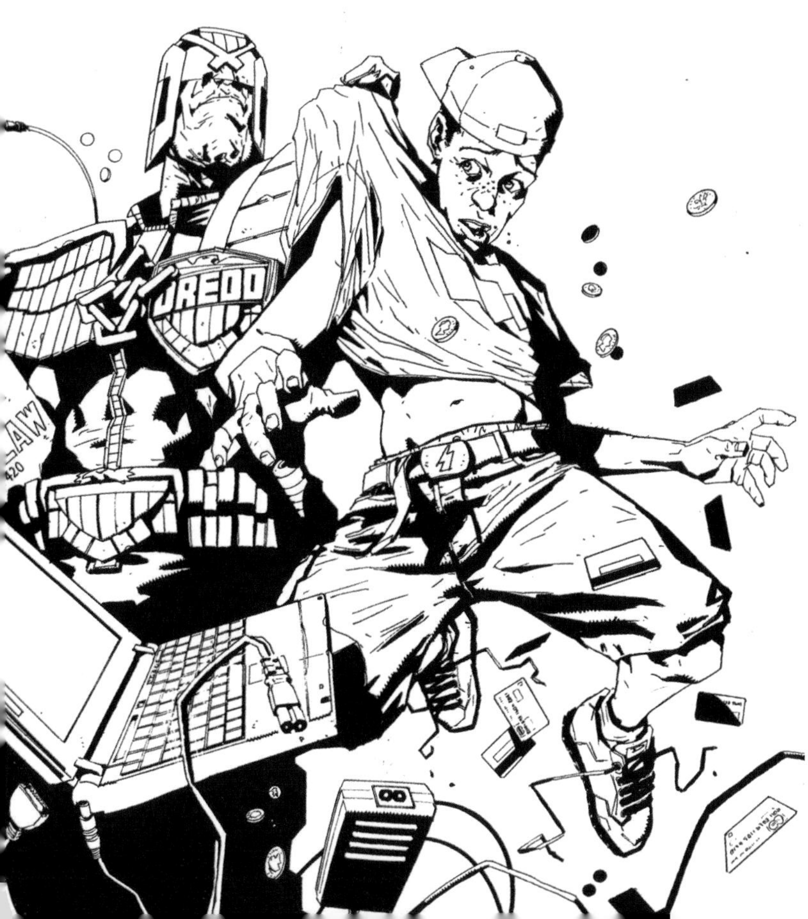
DREDD

'I remember years ago, just after me and Andy did 'Lenny Zero' we were talking about doing a Western,' he says. 'It was before I had a computer and I bought this book called **Cowboy Dreams** that had lots of photos of cowboys from the turn of the century… they were really stark, the landscapes were huge big textures and if there was a figure or a horse they were very dark, almost a silhouette against this sort of big, awesome landscape.

'I really poured over that book because we were thinking about this Western, because I wanted to get it right. I really liked the tone of it and I didn't necessarily reference **Cowboy Dreams** directly, but it definitely would have influenced my approach with **Scalped** because it has that landscape. It's the environment that the characters are in, it's the environment that the characters are a part of.'

There are always layers to Jock's work, both figuratively and in the construction of his work. As Photoshop unleashed the skills he'd learned as a painter, so he began to push the boundaries of cover design to their limits. By using negative space, large empty spaces of opposing colour, bold silhouettes, or scale-inducing foreground detail, Jock's covers produce the same effect – placing characters in their environment, both rendering them tiny and dominating in the same moment.

'I think that's probably a good metaphor for **Scalped** because the characters are physically and mentally caught in an environment that's out of their control. Having that huge landscape is quite interesting. One of the covers has the reservation on top of a pile of poker chips, which are creating the foundation for this society to function. It's a very direct, simple design idea that gets across the concept easily.'

But the evolution of this painterly approach had not come smoothly. While **The Losers** had announced him as a major new talent – a **Green Arrow** mini-series with Diggle followed, before Jock began his era-defining run on **Batman** with writer Scott Snyder – he continued working for **2000 AD**, mostly on covers and *Tor Cyan*, a spin-off from space medical series *Mercy Heights* that was being absorbed into the continuity of **2000 AD**'s classic character Rogue Trooper. Yet while his inking had a newfound maturity, his desire to find a way to merge comics and painting persisted – right up until it hit hard reality.

Created by writer John Smith and artist Sean Phillips, Devlin Waugh is a flamboyant exorcist for the Dredd-world Vatican. His first appearance, 'Swimming in Blood' (**Judge Dredd Megazine** #2.01–2.09, 1992, with lettering by Steve Potter), was a watershed moment not just for Phillips but also for the post-Bisley age of painted comics; combining paints, inks, pencils and even collage, Phillips' work is stylish, eclectic, and vivid.

After a series of one-offs, 'Red Tide' was the long-awaited long-form sequel – with Jock stepping in to replace *Judge Dredd* artist Peter Doherty. A text piece from former **Megazine** editor David Bishop titled 'The Curse of Devlin Waugh' accompanied the first episode, which was drawn by Colin MacNeil (**Judge Dredd Megazine** #202–213, 2003, script by John Smith and lettering by Annie Parkhouse).

British Airways in-flight magazine illustration
2002

'The truth is that I wanted to paint comics but the times I've tried it – on 'Reapermen', 'Ten Years' and [the later *Devlin Waugh* story] 'Red Tide' – it just took so long. *Devlin*, in particular, just took so long and it's not very good.'

Jock produced just seven finished pages, all of them vivid examples of how he struggled to combine his desire to paint with the practicalities of making comics, with linework struggling to stand out against backgrounds of vivid colour.

'Painting sequential comics is so hard,' he admits. 'And, normally, my work has some energy and movement, and I think in that story, the energy and movement just turned into looking a bit scruffy. So, I didn't do it again. With *Devlin*, I was following Sean Phillips, and 'Swimming in Blood' is a really good example of how you paint comics really, really well. There's a real energy and vitality in the pages. It's clear, it's concise, it's sharp.

'I've been very lucky, and I've achieved an awful lot, but there's something about painting sequential pages that I couldn't get right.'

By the time **The Losers** had begun to take off, the demands of producing over twenty pages a month for the North American direct market forced an economy of effort in which he began to trust what he had learnt during those long-ago late night painting sessions. His attempts to merge painting and comics had brought him only frustration, but the lesson that had to be learnt was that paint wasn't the answer – it was what painting had taught him about how his art could *work*. Painting was not an alternative to inking or an impediment to it, it was the key to understanding it.

'Learning to paint makes you understand values on a page – lights and darks, and balancing,' he says. 'Painting is harder, I think. So then getting to be reductive in black and white is really cool because you can cherry pick. If painting teaches you how to do an image with a full range of values, then when you're doing the whites and the blacks you choose with the awareness of knowing how to do the full value range, and you can do it very effectively.

'I just love putting massive slabs of black onto a page and creating strong shadows, little pinpoints of highlights on faces while the rest of it is just black. I've always loved that as it makes the black and white effect more effective.'

Under the pressure of a monthly book, this balancing of light and dark began to come through. It's easy to see the influence of McMahon's stark black and white work here; in the early '80s McMahon began to lay down blocks of black onto his pages before inking around them, the black anchoring each figure with shadows that seemed to hum with solidity. For Jock the lines are less clear-cut than McMahon's stark chiaroscuro, but their relationship to shadow and the balance of light and dark on the page became central to his style.

As his confidence increased, so a new, more febrile energy began to emerge from his pages, based around this notion of layering his work, rather than there being a single layer of inks.

'I was more into opaque painting, which is laying down a wash first and then putting paint over the top – it's actually a completely standard way of painting in oils or acrylics.

Dom [Reardon] was really into watercolour and, for me, good watercolour has everything that I was missing but Dom taught me to have; a good watercolour is really subtle and rich.

'What makes watercolour so good is the freshness of it - it's just one mark and that's it. If you work over it too much it becomes muddy, there's no texture, there's no life, there's no vibrancy. Watercolours were what Dom was really into and I thought it was amazing.

'We used to spend so much time trying to get the paints to be as rich as possible. I can't express enough how a great painter will bring out the rich tones and colour out of paint, whereas someone less skilled will struggle. Understanding how paint works and how opaque paint will sit on top of certain types of underpainting you do and how they react to each other to create a certain texture – I was completely lost in that process.

'And then I got a Mac and Photoshop, which acts in just the same way and uses layers, which is exactly how I painted, and suddenly I could do all these rich textures I had been striving to get when I was painting. So, then it becomes "Why would you do them?", when it's a physical act you're trying to hone the craft, but then the Mac and Photoshop were so powerful the textures became just another tool for me, it was like having another brush or another set of paints. I love the marks of paint and ink, but there has to be more to that – design, composition, and all those things that the Mac really frees you up to play around with.'

So, textures appear, lines seem to vibrate and splinter, patches of grainy brushstrokes complement his lines rather than obfuscate them. Most importantly, inking became where Jock did the bulk of his work – in the do-or-die moment of certainty that comes with that first dash of indelible ink.

'I was still pencilling quite considerably,' he says of his transitional work around 2003. 'And my layouts were much more involved, with fixing, tweaking and redrawing on the layouts to get them closer to the final page. Now I would just do all of that in the final inks.'

Moving the instinctual work to the inking stage, with minimal pencilling, fundamentally changed Jock's work. All of a sudden, the line on the page, pregnant with meaning and possibility, spurs him forward; every line has a purpose because it is laid down in relation to everything around it with an efficient rationality.

Also noticeable since his early days is his awareness of the whole page. So often, artists can overfocus on individual panels, producing disconnected vignettes. In early stories, like 'Crossing Ken Dodd', action crashes against the borders of the next panel as if it has nowhere to go. But by the time Jock moved to American comics, his work had a maturity: he could now see the whole page as a single design, was able to consider the nuts and bolts of storytelling, how a page is built out from a single element or moment of action and how the eye is drawn across it.

'I think it was Frank Miller who said something to the effect of a comic isn't a single page, it's the rhythm of all the pages together, what you're creating as a whole, because that's what people will sense. When you start thinking in those terms, the individual panels mean something very different.'

TAP
TAP
Pre-published artwork
1996

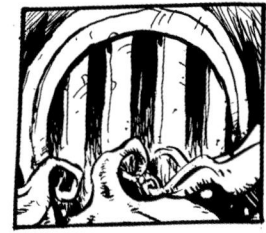

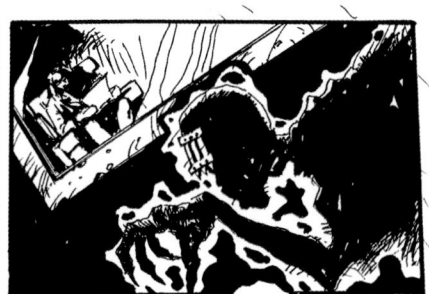

It's a rapid maturing of style and storytelling – and the instincts that drive them – that made his work stand out in the rush of new talent that emerged from the Bishop and Diggle era of **2000 AD**. It's all the more startling given how quickly this process occurred from those first, tentative, nervous pages of 'Lenny Zero' in 2000.

'I used to spend a lot more time on a page,' he says. 'I remember the first time I completed a page in one day was on 'Dead Zero', the second 'Lenny Zero' story, and I couldn't believe I'd done a whole page in a day.

'And then you start working for the American market – and the pages breathe a lot in the American format, what would be a half page conversation in **2000 AD** is suddenly five pages. People complain about decompression, but I actually really like that, how it can breathe a little more.

'Those were the days where I'd take some photos for reference and then go into town to get them developed, get home and start pencilling – that'd be my day. I just don't have the luxury of that now.

'Comics are about rhythm, so if you have a story you've got to work up a speed and then the pages flow easily. The only time I think my pages really work are when I'm in a sort of last-minute panic and I'm piling through them, so they have a cohesive rhythm to them, whereas if I have too much time to think about it they don't flow, they're dead, as if too much over-thinking stifles the storytelling.

'That's the only way I can work. The only way I think readers are going to respond to something you draw is – what were you putting into it at the time? What is the point of this story? That's what good storytelling is, and drawing should reflect the script, and the script should have emotion.'

So much of this focus is thanks to another central pillar of Jock's emergent style – graphic design.

'It's weird,' he laughs, 'so many comic book artists don't seem to put much importance in good design. I get it, they're artists, but design is so important to making things work.

'That was one of things when I started getting published. I loved design, I loved skateboarding magazines with the wide-angled lens photos, I loved the film intros of Pablo Ferro and Saul Bass. When I did covers for **The Losers**, I got to indulge that more than I was able to at **2000 AD**, but a lot of my early 'Lenny Zero' cover sketches are all that stuff. I was trying to shoehorn that stuff in while forgetting that, with the greatest of respect, **2000 AD** – particularly in David Bishop's time – would place multiple cover lines all over the art. It was a hold-over from magazines in the '90s with **Loaded** and lad mag culture, and they were told this would apparently sell a comic. I've got a sketch with David's notes saying "cover lines, cover lines, cover lines" all over it.

'On reflection, I was trying to bring some of that design stuff into comics, because I loved it and didn't see much of it in comics, so I thought it might be a strength that I could bring to my work. And it still serves me well doing covers – even on the early covers – with minimal colours; if you're ever in any trouble on a cover, strip it down to black, white, grey and red, and you're in business, it'll at least look okay. There's been many-a-time I've tried to do a full colour cover and it's just not working, so I'd literally desaturate it and put a red background in. It's a safe bet. When you take stuff away, you put more in.

'For me, it's about being more fluid. Things can happen by mistake – you can put a grey tone over an image, and it suddenly works – and being open to that happening tends to lead to your best work because there's been many times when a happy accident has led to something being effective.

'What I don't like about a lot of comic art is that it can look really impressive, it can be beautifully rendered, but when you read it, it's dead and nothing's really happening. As I've got older I really respond to art where you can feel the artist's hand in the pages, you can feel what person they are. A lot of comic art is guilty of referencing lots of other comic art and lacking that character.'

That desire and ability to integrate elements from beyond comics, and the way it has imbued his art with a degree of 'swagger', has created a demand for his work outside the medium – in the movie industry.

Jock's work on the **DREDD** movie came about almost by accident.

In 2009, Jock heard that work had begun on Alex Garland's adaptation of his favourite character; emboldened by six weeks he had just spent on concept work for a later-abandoned adaptation of Frank Herbert's **Dune** by director Peter Berg (who had originally been in line for the **The Losers** adaptation), Jock put together a series of concept pieces – based purely on the direction he thought the film could go – which he then posted on his social media.

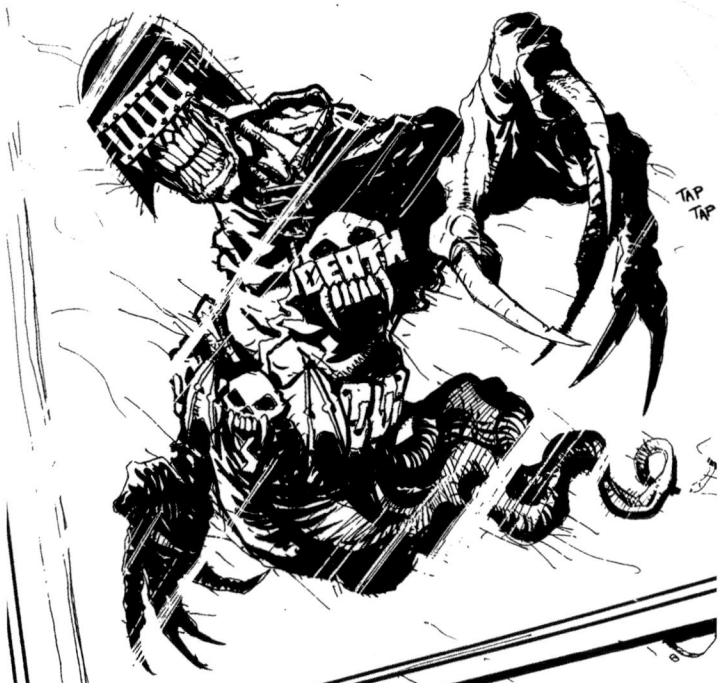

'It was just something I thought would be fun,' he says. 'There was nothing official about it and it was entirely what I thought you could do with a Dredd film. But then all of a sudden it was getting picked up by news sites, all claiming it was official concept art.

'I got contacted by DNA Films, who were Alex Garland's production company, and I thought "Oh no, I'm in trouble here", because I didn't want them thinking I was going around claiming this was something official.'

Fortunately, Garland had been impressed – and asked Jock to work on the film, creating images that would embody the look and feel of **DREDD**, and act as a visual template that the art and costume departments could draw inspiration from. He also ended up turning the storyboards for the film into a comic book, which was bound up and used by the producers.

'They'd had some concept work done already when I first met Alex and [producers] Andrew MacDonald and Allon Reich. It was immediately obvious how practical their approach was going to be – there was nothing fanciful. I took some of my **2000 AD** work, Andrew looked at a page from 'Shirley Temple of Doom' – with the first shot of the crazy funfair with robots and all sorts – and he went "Yeah, none of this, there's no flying cars, there's no robots. This is a very grounded, realistic approach". And that appeals to my sensibilities. I love Mega-City One's zaniness but I was completely on board with Alex's take on the material.'

Being sent location shots from South Africa, Jock painted over them with ideas for world-building and the broader environment. In the world of movies, 'gritty' is often a mere synonym for violent, and while **DREDD** is unashamedly, even viscerally violent – thanks to the psychedelic slow-motion scenes and intended to take advantage of the film's bespoke 3D cinematography – the film's 'grittiness' stems from its incorporation of sci-fi concepts into a world that feels lived in and real.

'It's a film that doesn't compromise,' says Jock. 'It was Alex's very specific vision, and he stuck to it. It's very violent and has an extreme side to it, but I think the world we built has integrity. It just works. There's a tangible sense that this is a world that we, as a society, could end up with. It's hard to be truly objective about it because I worked on it, but it's one of those films that, for me, gets better with every viewing. That's quite a rare thing.'

He details how, throughout the project, there was a rejection of the fanciful, even whimsical science fiction that had defined the comics.

'Alex surprised me in a lot of ways. He was quite demanding in the best possible way and the whole approach requires you to bring really good work to it. A lot of Alex's films are like "What would it really be like if zombies were running around?" and so you get **28 Days Later**. And that was the approach they were bringing to **DREDD**. And I was really excited by that.'

Most of his work on **DREDD** has a frenetic quality. The storyboarded comic is rough, some panels fleshed out, others little more than scribbles, but the urgency of the process breaks up any hesitation in his work – he must react, immediately and instinctively. They give such an impression of movement and speed that it's not difficult to show how that translated onto the screen.

In addition, his images of the centre of Peach Trees Block, where the majority of the film takes place, capture that sense of scale in his environments, a skill he so admired of Mick McMahon and Ron Smith: tiny figures, including Judges, gaze upwards at the dwindling shaft of the block's courtyard. Again, there is that skill at placing the small narrative element next to the epic scene, a comic book tribute to Ansel Adams.

'You're presenting something larger than life in a very realistic, grounded way, and all film work is like that to a degree. But it's more that when you work on comic strips – and particularly on a science fiction strip like *Dredd* – you have little shortcuts. But Alex said no to the clichés you can end up with. Hexagonal corridors are a great example – they can look terrific, but they're just a shortcut that doesn't work in real life. You have to think about what you're doing in a different way to comics work and it's really rewarding in a very different way.

'So, in terms of how my work evolved because of working in movies, and Dredd specifically, it made me really think about what I was doing and what I was presenting.'

DREDD was a watershed moment for Jock, not least because – even though the hoped-for sequel never materialised – it began a long working relationship with Garland. He went on to work on 2014's BAFTA and Oscar-winning **Ex Machina** and 2018's **Annihilation**.

'The **DREDD** movie was my first proper film and if I had done no more after that, I would still have been thrilled because I got to work on Dredd, a character that I love more than any other. Alex has said that he can "feel Jock's fingerprints all over this film" and that is such a lovely thing for me because the love I have for Dredd is weirdly unnatural. It was a landmark moment, I'm so proud of having worked on that film.'

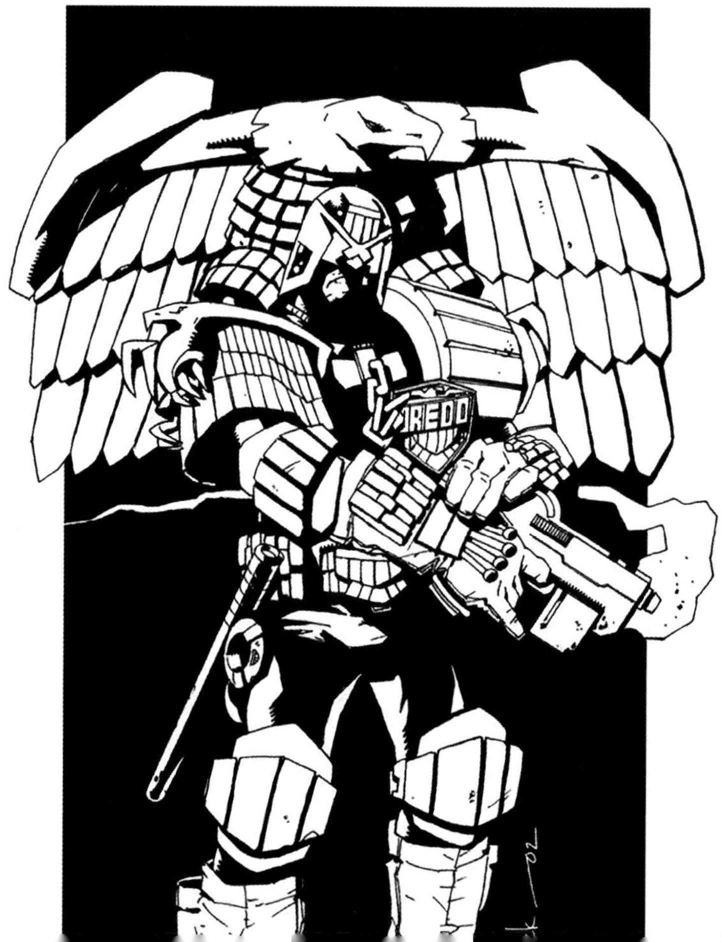
DREDD

Art for Dreddcon 3
2002

Thanks in no small part to his connection with Garland, Jock's film work went on to include **Children of Men**, **Batman Begins**, **X-Men: Days of Future Past**, and **Star Wars: The Last Jedi**. 'Working in films, and the poster work I've done, forces you to think about the image you're presenting in a different way, and inevitably that will inform your work in comics,' he says. 'I came back, and I was better off, I was more aware. To me, good design means there's an idea behind an image, it's not just a drawing of something like Dredd. I've always loved covers that have more of a theme behind them, like McMahon's giant Dredd sat in a chair that's as big as a city from Prog 204.

'I've loved working in different mediums and processes – comics, film and posters, they're all different and it feels like a good thing to do. I took some of my comics tricks to **Star Wars** and the costume designer didn't know what he was looking at 'cause it was all in black,' he laughs. 'He went "What's going on down here? It's all in shadow", so I realised I needed to communicate better with my drawing.

'That's a brilliant challenge to have, because you do rest on your laurels and learn tricks that work in comics but that isn't actually what the discipline is, that's just little shortcuts that can get the job done but they're not always the best thing to do.'

Throughout his career, there has been a demonstrable *cool* to Jock's work. There remains the manic, even feverish energy of his comics, from his collaborations with Scott Snyder on **Batman** and the creator-owned **Wytches**, as well as the titles he has written and drawn, **Batman: One Dark Knight** for DC Comics and space opera **Gone** for DSTLRY; but his success is thanks to that eye for the strong idea, the inventiveness that sees his iconic image of Batman's adversary The Joker – in which his head morphs into a colony of bats – plastered on everything from posters to beach towels. His movie poster designs for Mondo are just as wildly popular.

Regardless of the industry or medium, Jock's style is one that has evolved under pressure, learning from each mistake and every success, in pursuit of the moment when something feels *right*. The closest analogy he can find for that – one he returns to repeatedly – is music.

'You don't think about it. From playing drums, you learn that about music – if you can turn yourself off, that's the best way to play. That's when you surprise yourself. If I have something to offer then whatever it is comes out in those moments – I'm not being logical, I'm being honest and that's always seemed to have worked best for me.

'So, I've got to the point where I try not to think about it, where my thoughts just get in the way of it. I can't stress that enough – the minute I start theorising or I start thinking it should look a certain way then I've lost it, it's gone, and it starts to stress me out.

'When I was young, the goal of being in a band was to get a record deal because you thought that once you got that, you'd made it. But of course, in the real world, if you get the record deal that's when the work actually starts. That's the moment when you sink or swim. And drawing for a living, in print, would be the same – the analogy would be, I was doing demo tapes for seven years, but the minute you get in print it's ... okay, well, this is it!

'It's much easier to chase something; lots of people do this, I think, where they like the idea of doing something and they'll forever chase it because if you don't ever have to do it, your imagination of what you might do when you get there is much larger than the reality of what you do when you get there, if that makes sense. So, when I finally got that DC paper on my drawing board and my skills and experience were at the level they were at... I couldn't pretend anymore. I was not as fully accomplished as I would like to have been – but you've got to do it.

'Doing the job, it goes out into the world and that's the exciting part and the scary part and the revealing part – all of it, it becomes very real at that point.

'There have been a lot of moments for me where it would have been easy to not feel up to the task. Arriving at Pinewood Studios to work on **Star Wars** for the first time, my assignment was to design a new costume for Luke Skywalker, and part of my rational brain said "I can't do this". But I've always had the mentality, in those moments, to say to myself "Well, if I don't then someone else will, so now's my time". If I have a sort of little superpower, it's that I've been lucky with my opportunities and the projects that I've worked on, and I'm able to have those moments. "Wow, I get to do this." It would be easy to feel intimidated by it. But you just have to let that go and go for it.

'Even with music, I played my first gig three weeks after starting playing the drums and I've never stopped gigging since. I just think that's the best way, 'cause you've got nowhere to hide. So much time we spend procrastinating and overthinking everything, you've just got to do it and I've just been really lucky that I've been given the opportunity to do it.'

It comes down to that first act of putting the line on the page, with everything flowing from that, because that is where the pen, guided by intuition and experience, operates on an almost unconscious level as the image works itself out on the page.

What is most striking is that, from that first pin-up in the 1995 **2000 AD Sci-Fi Special** to the concluding page of **Gone** in 2024 – and regardless of the industry or medium – Jock's work has always been clearly, identifiably, unabashedly... *his*. His version of Dredd, brief as it was, remains era-defining, and his profile in the wider comics medium and beyond has not dulled his enthusiasm or gratitude for those beginnings. The line had to start somewhere, and the gradient was steep, but it started in the pages of **2000 AD** on *Judge Dredd*.

'The fact that Dredd has given me my life, that I loved the strip so much and now he's provided the springboard for everything that I've done... it's too much, I'd be a fool not to appreciate it.

'I feel so lucky with everything that I've worked on and the places where it's taken me. The thought that it originated from the spark of the idea that you should follow your own path and have your own take on things, that thing that I learnt when I first picked up **2000 AD**...that's pretty special.

'I can't quite put my finger on what it is, and I don't think I want to know. It is what it is, and I'll just keep going.'

CONTENTS

SECTION ONE — 024
JUDGE DREDD

SECTION TWO — 126
DREDD (2012)

SECTION THREE — 158
2000 AD

JOCK UNDERSTANDS THE ASSIGNMENT.

That much was immediately apparent the moment I first saw his work. It's not just about being able to draw. It's about taste, influence, value judgements. The sum of a million little choices that makes the work add up to something... *more*.

You can teach craft, technique, the do's and don'ts of visual storytelling. But you can't teach taste, and judgement, and gut instinct, and raw talent, and drive. You just know it when you see it. And there it was, in stark black and white – blunt, bold, and brutal – staring up at me from **2000 AD**'s slush pile in 1997. A raw Dredd-head with a chin like a slab of granite, and a helmet reduced almost to abstraction. It felt like a statement; a challenge; a gauntlet thrown down.

You got a problem with that, creep?

I knew right there and then, this Jock guy gets it. He belongs in Mega-City One.

2000 AD never really had a "house style", of the kind that made so many American comics of that era feel so bland and samey. Sure, Mike McMahon was initially asked to mimic Carlos Ezquerra's style on those early *Judge Dredd* strips; but McMahon cannot be so easily constrained, and watching his art style mutate and evolve was one of the great joys of early **2000 AD**. On stories like 'The Judge Child Quest' and 'Block Mania', we saw McMahon riffing with artists as diverse as Ron Smith, Brian Bolland and Steve Dillon, each bringing to life a unique vision of Dredd and his world. Wildly different art styles, yet all equally valid.

That kind of artistic, free-for-all jam session can only work because *Judge Dredd* – the comic, not the man – is so many things at once. It's gritty sci-fi action, and bleak political satire, and absurdist comedy, and slice-of-life kitchen sink drama, and splatterpunk gore all at the same time. That's what the movies could never quite get right – they'd try to pick a lane, set a tone – but the comic has always been everything at once.

That's the madhouse pressure-cooker pinball machine of Mega-City One, and it takes a special kind of artist to bring it to life. They have to be able to spread their arms wide enough to embrace all of those elements – sometimes contradictory – that make *Judge Dredd* what it is. Which is what I mean by understanding the assignment. Knowing when to go big for the cool tough-guy moment, when to move in close and intimate to catch the look in that poor broken citizen's eye, when to turn it up to 11 with lunatic bombast... and when to just play it straight.

By the late '90s, a whole new generation of artists had grown up inspired by **2000 AD**. You can see those influences in Jock's early work – Ezquerra's grit and swagger, McMahon's page design and chunky abstraction, Dillon's peerless composition and flow – but he was also channelling inspiration from beyond the insular world of comics, from Saul Bass to Egon Schiele. Back then it set him apart, raised him above. And even now, after all these years, he's still hungry, still learning, still striving to push himself past the edge of his comfort zone.

That's the kind of artist a writer wants to work with. So I did. Worked out pretty well.

It's been too long.

ANDY DIGGLE
Lancaster, March 2025

Andy Diggle is a comics writer and former editor of **2000 AD**.

He is best known for collaborating with Jock on **The Losers**, **Snapshot**, *Lenny Zero* and **Green Arrow: Year One**. He also wrote the creator-owned graphic novels **Cold Iron**, **Rat Catcher** and **Silent Dragon**; and co-wrote *Judge Dredd Vs Aliens* with John Wagner.

Andy's other work includes **Batman: Gotham by Gaslight**, **Superman**, **Hellblazer** and **Swamp Thing** at DC Comics; **Daredevil** and **Thunderbolts** at Marvel; **James Bond** at Dynamite; **Doctor Who** at IDW; **The Expanse** at Boom! Studios; **Shadowman** at Valiant; **Thief of Thieves** and **Hardcore** at Skybound; and the Eisner-nominated **Prométhée 13:13** at Delcourt.

He lives in Lancashire with his family, two cats and a dog, and he's still learning how to use the Oxford comma.

JUDGE DREDD

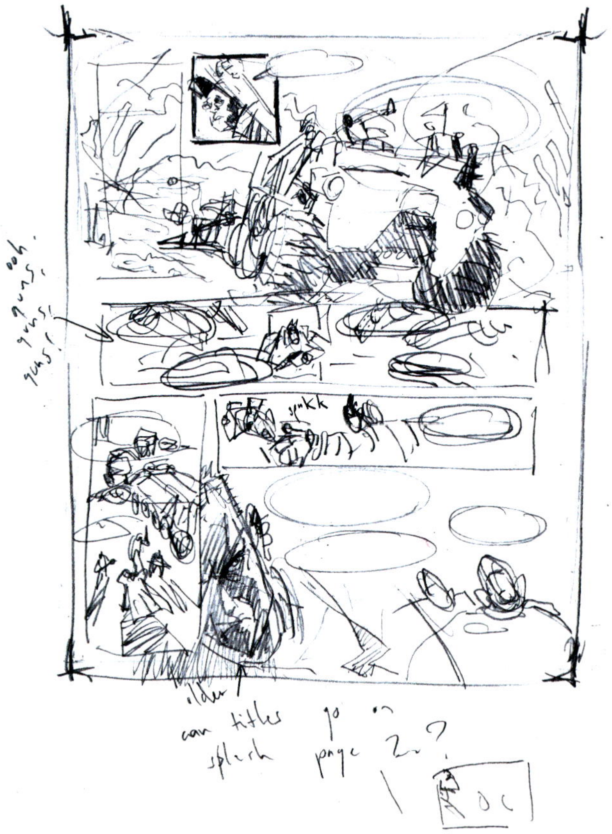

ooh, guns, guns, guns!
yukk
can titles go on splash page 2..?

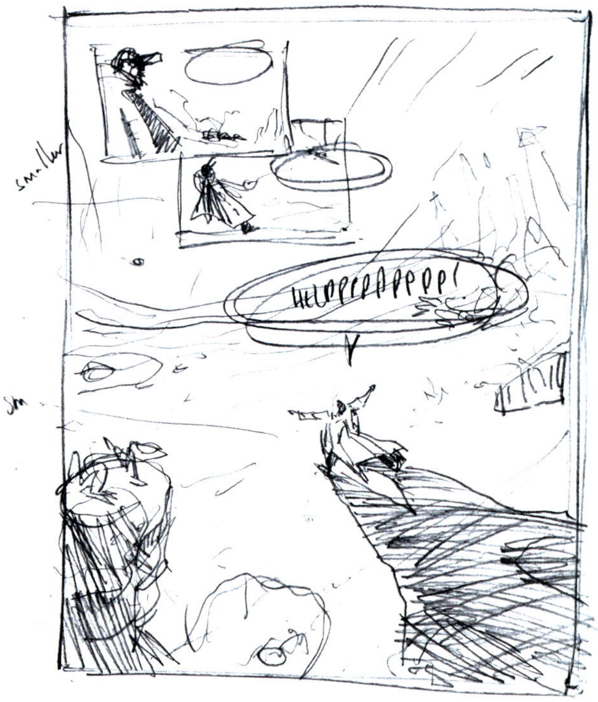

smaller

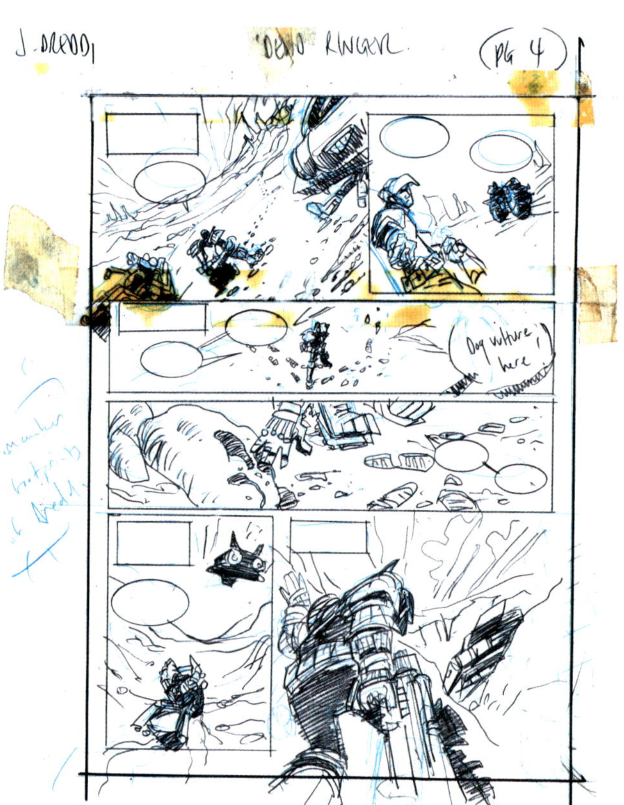

J. DREDD
'DEAD RINGER'
PG 4
Dog vulture here!

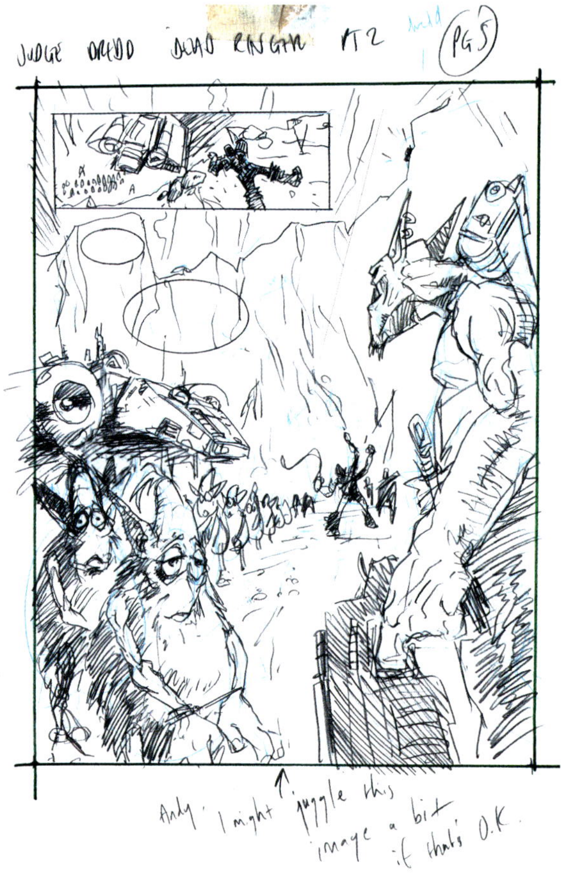

JUDGE DREDD DEAD RINGER PT 2
PG 5
Andy. I might juggle this image a bit if that's O.K

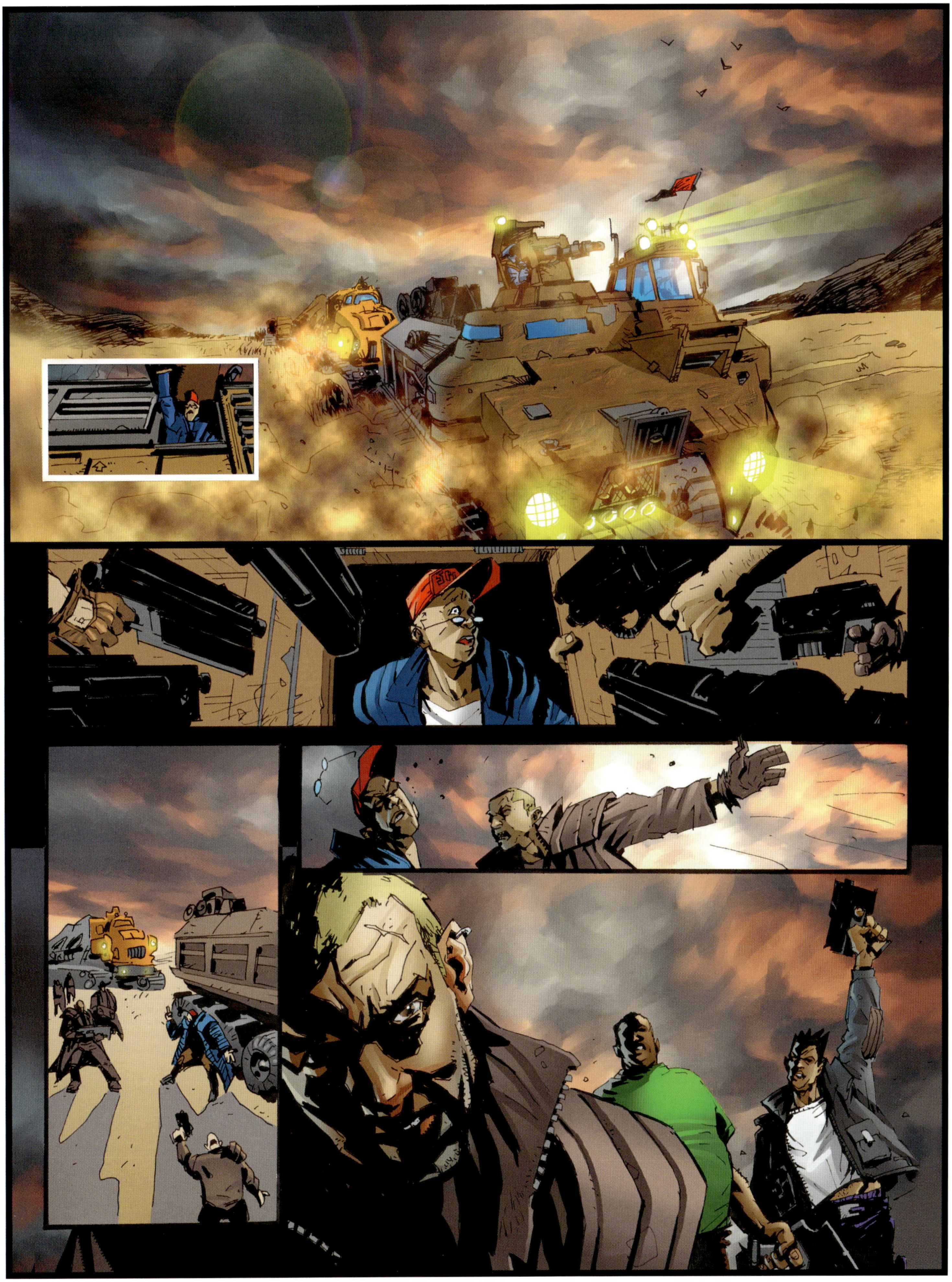

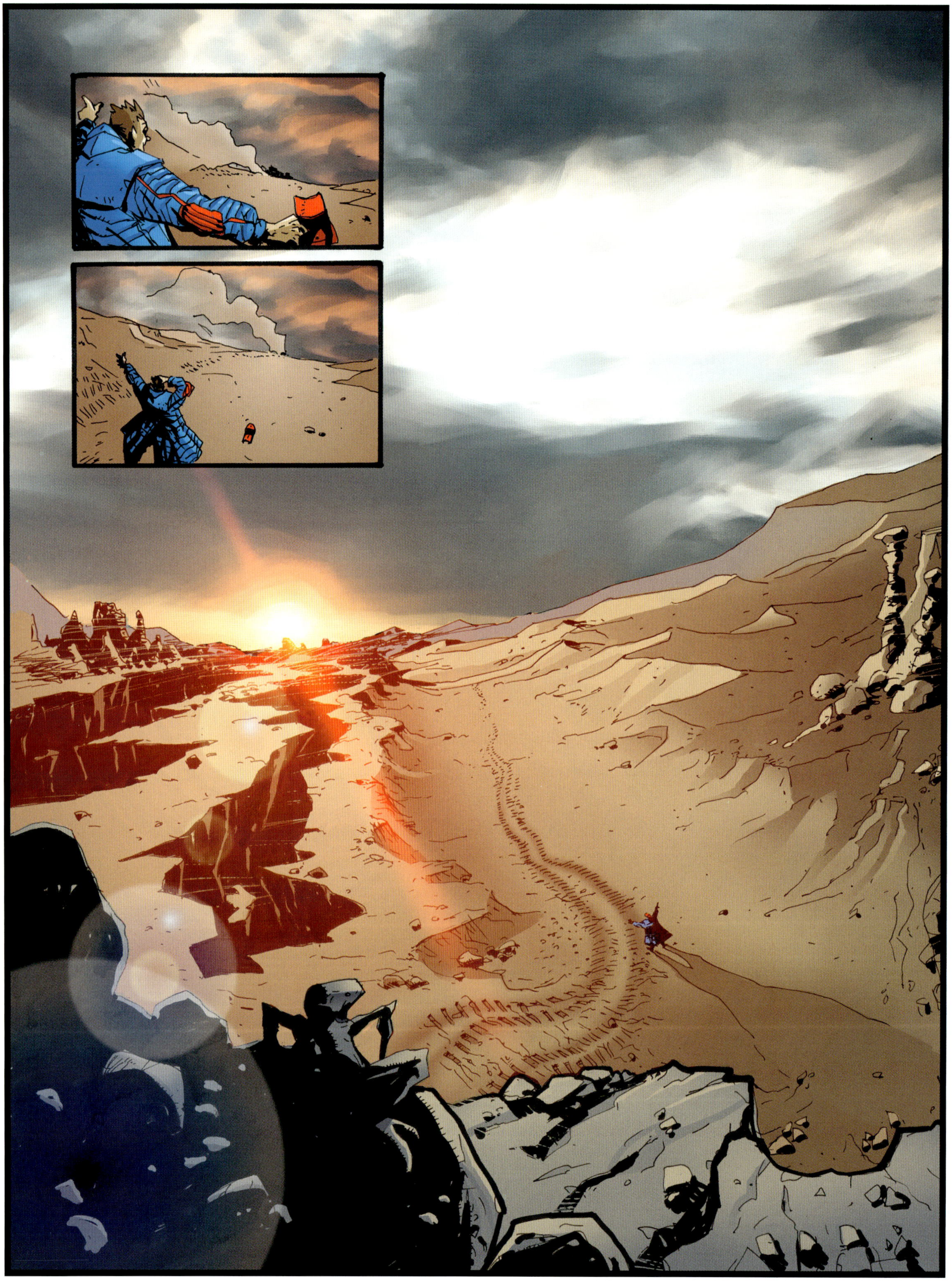

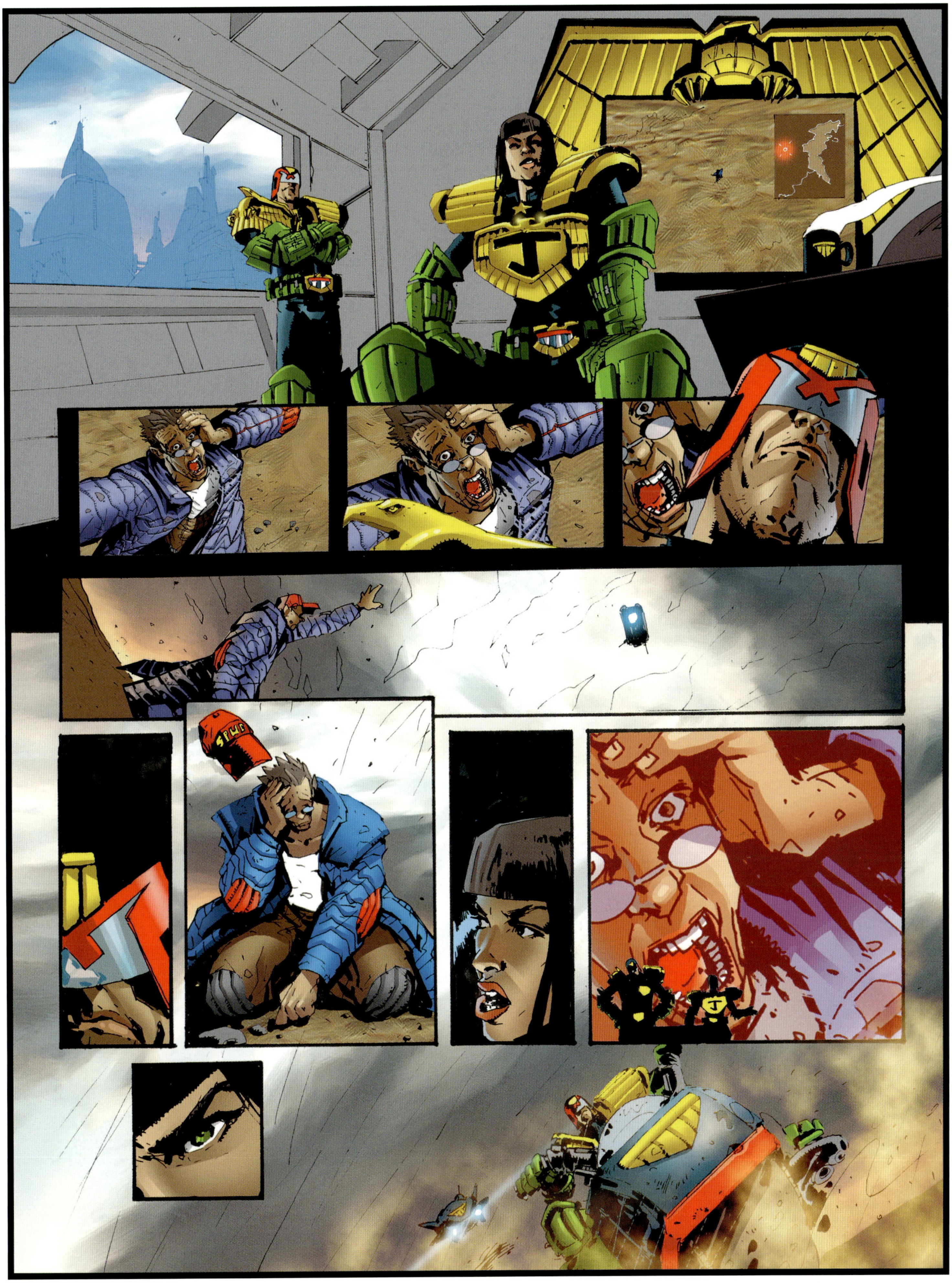

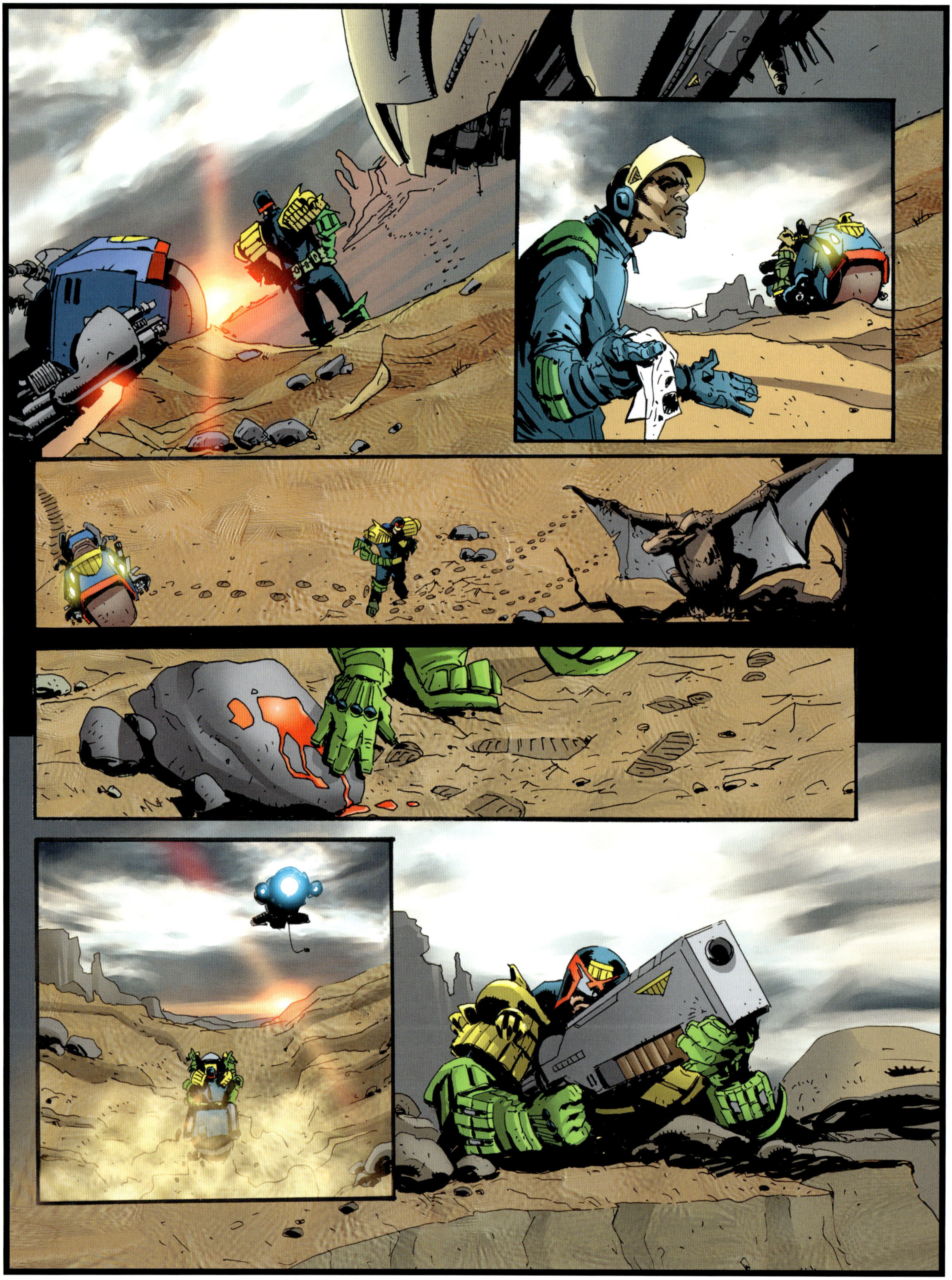

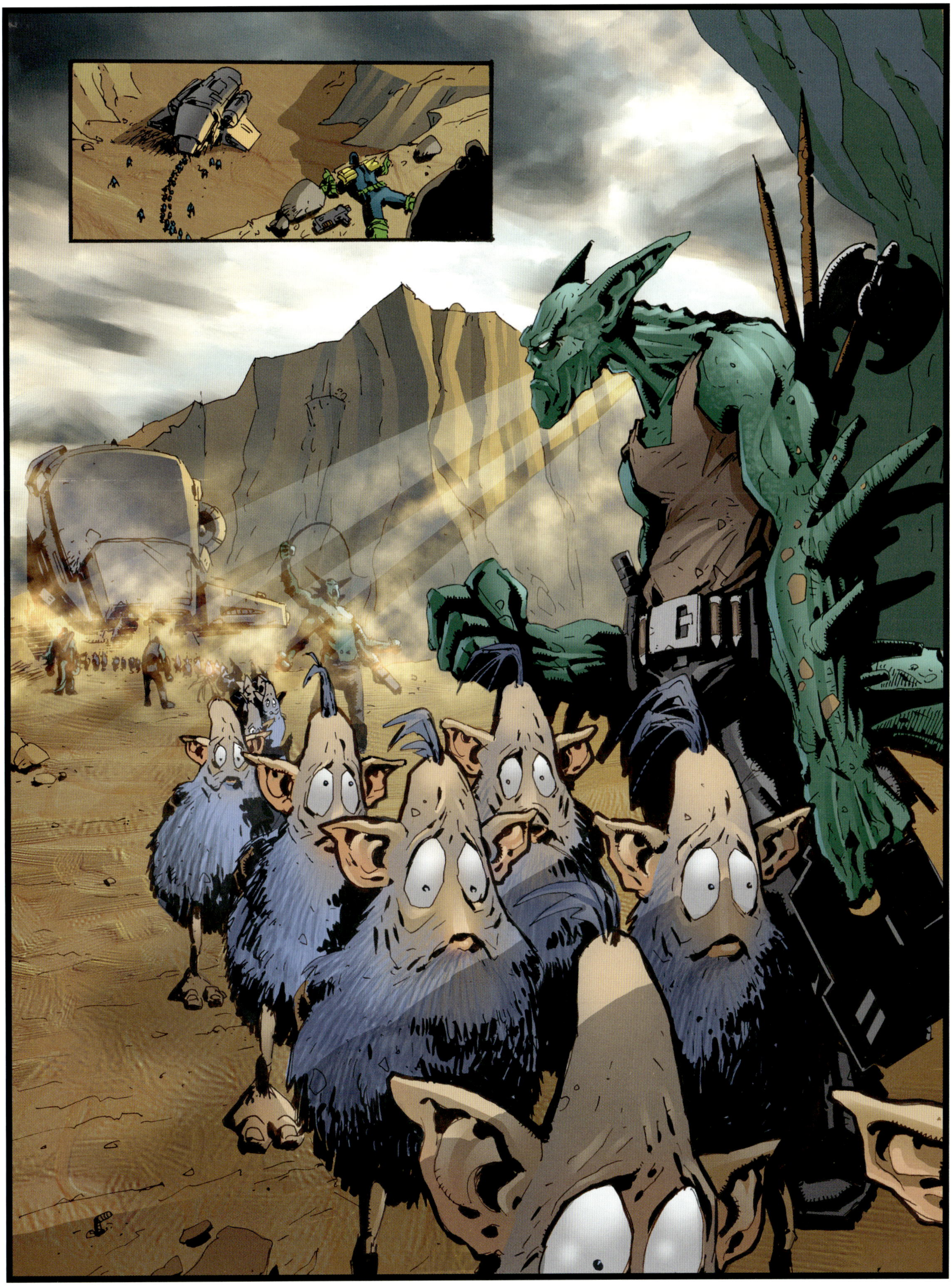

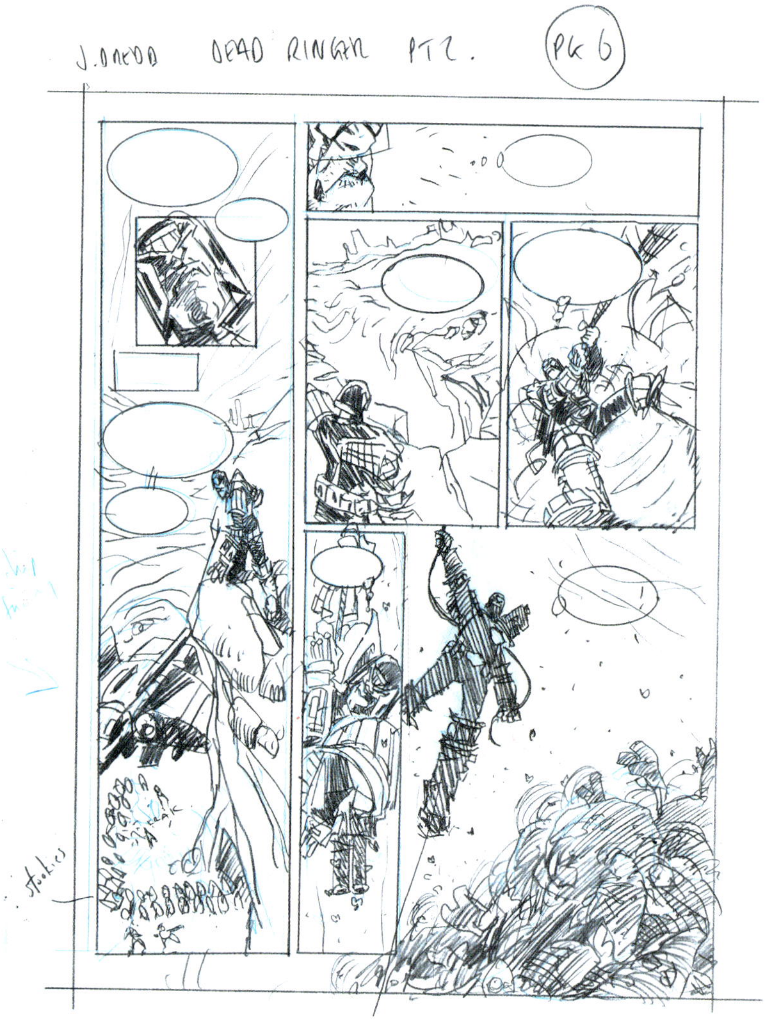
J.DREDD DEAD RINGER PT2. PG 6
stookies
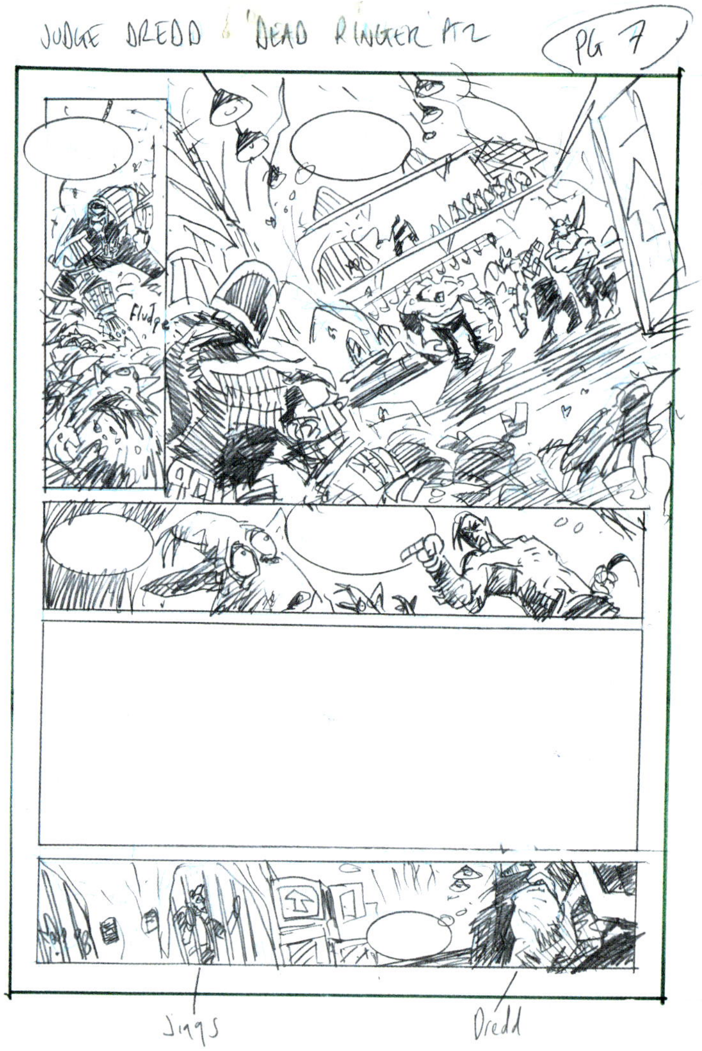
JUDGE DREDD 'DEAD RINGER' PT2 PG 7
Dredd
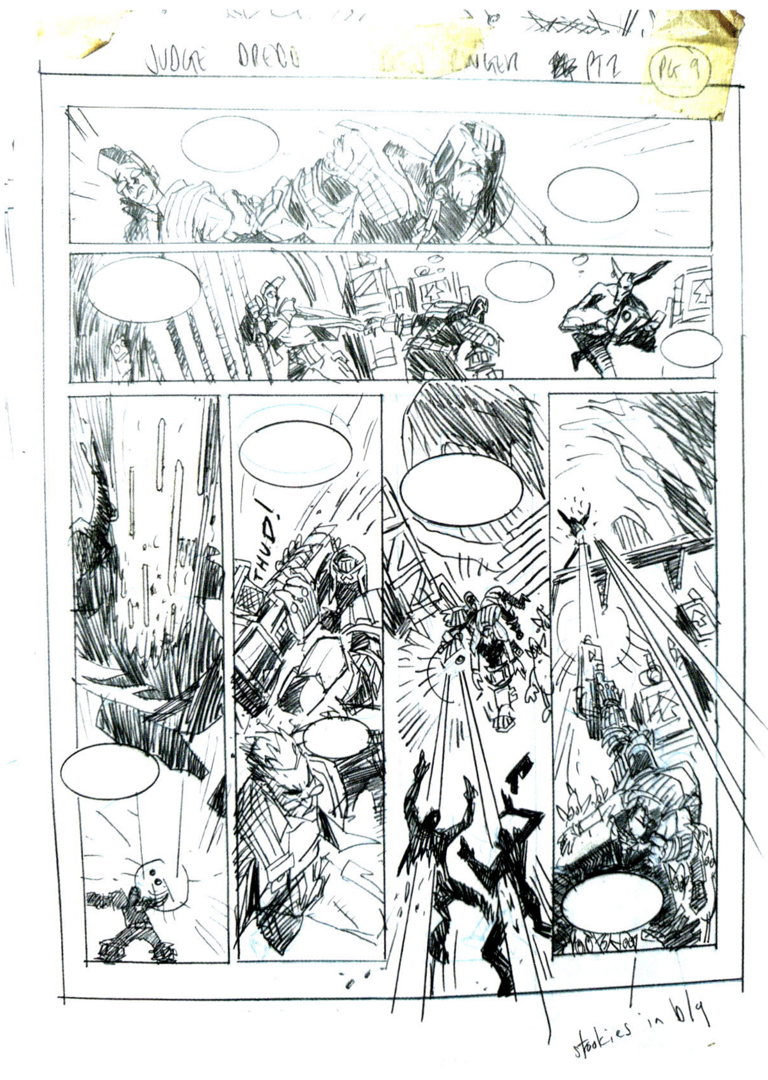
JUDGE DREDD
PT2 PG 9
THUD!
stookies in b/g
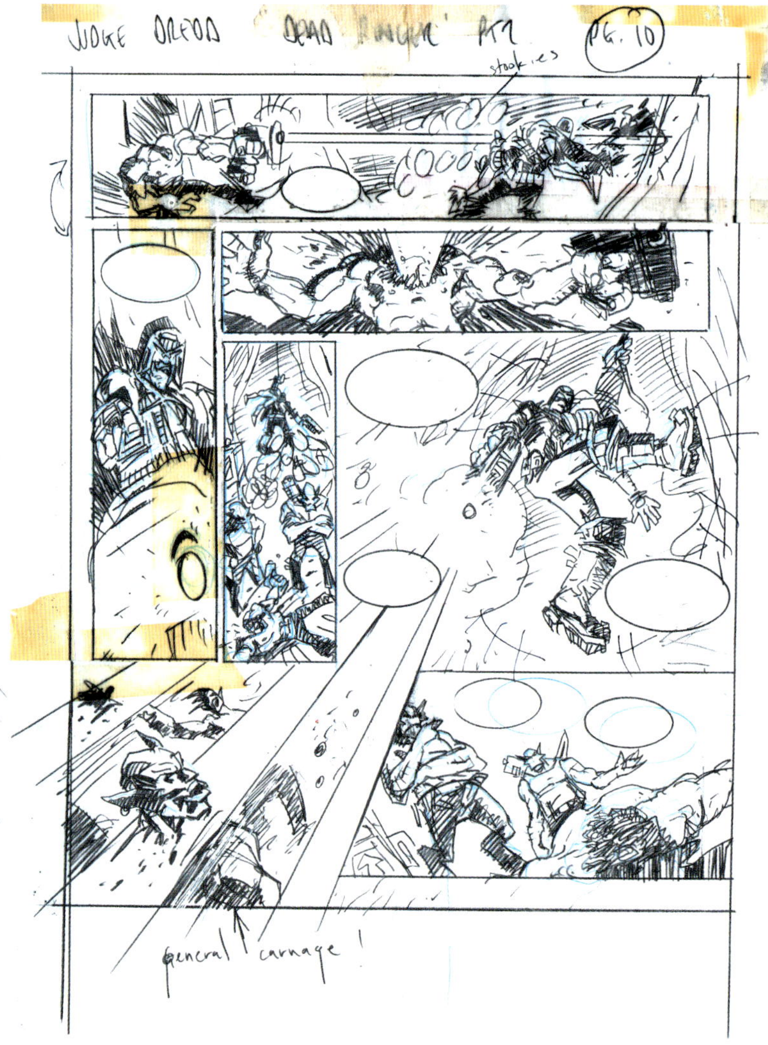
JUDGE DREDD 'DEAD RINGER' PT2 PG. 10
stookies
general carnage!

 JUDGE DREDD: DEAD RINGER LAYOUTS, 2000

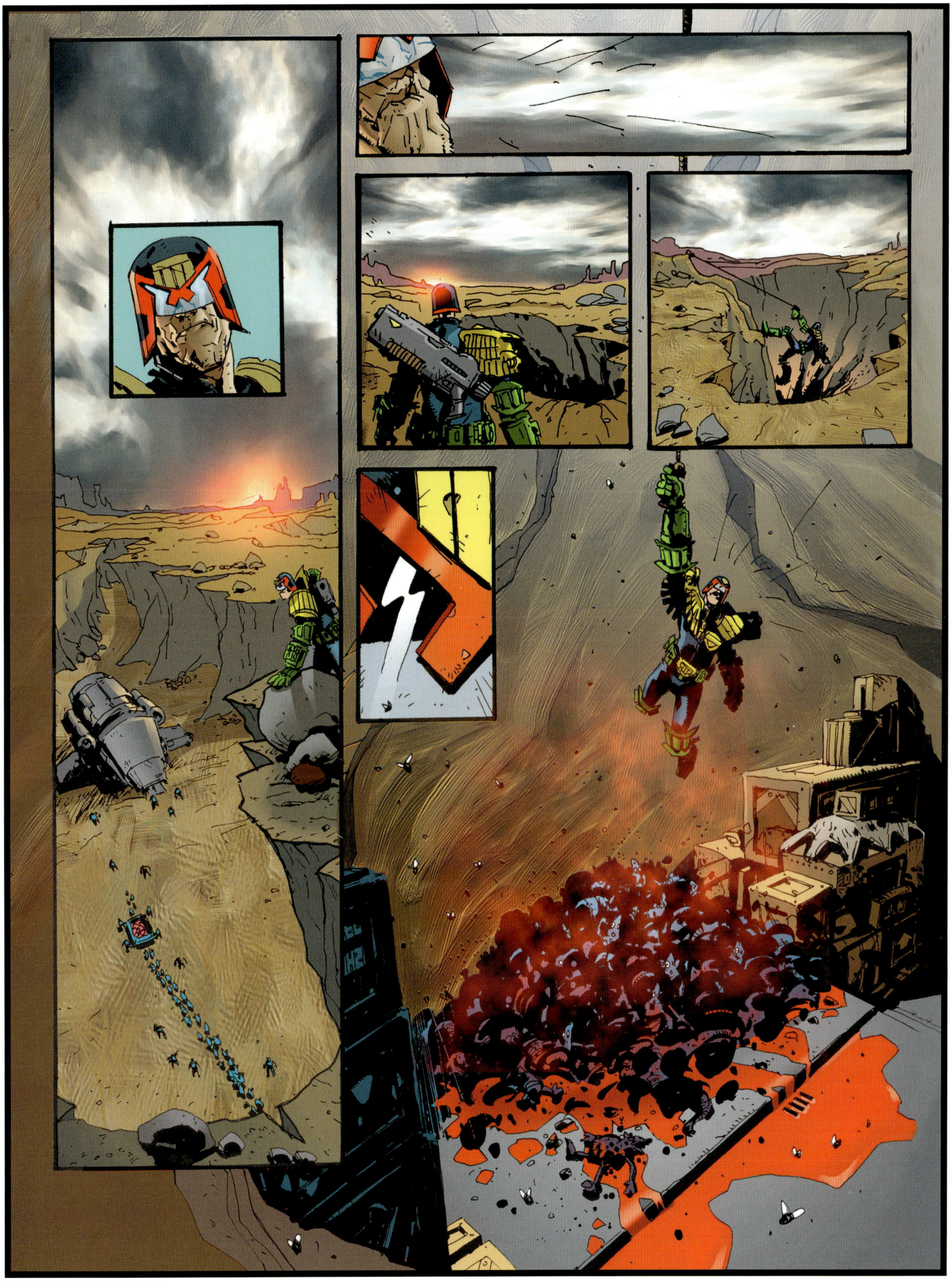

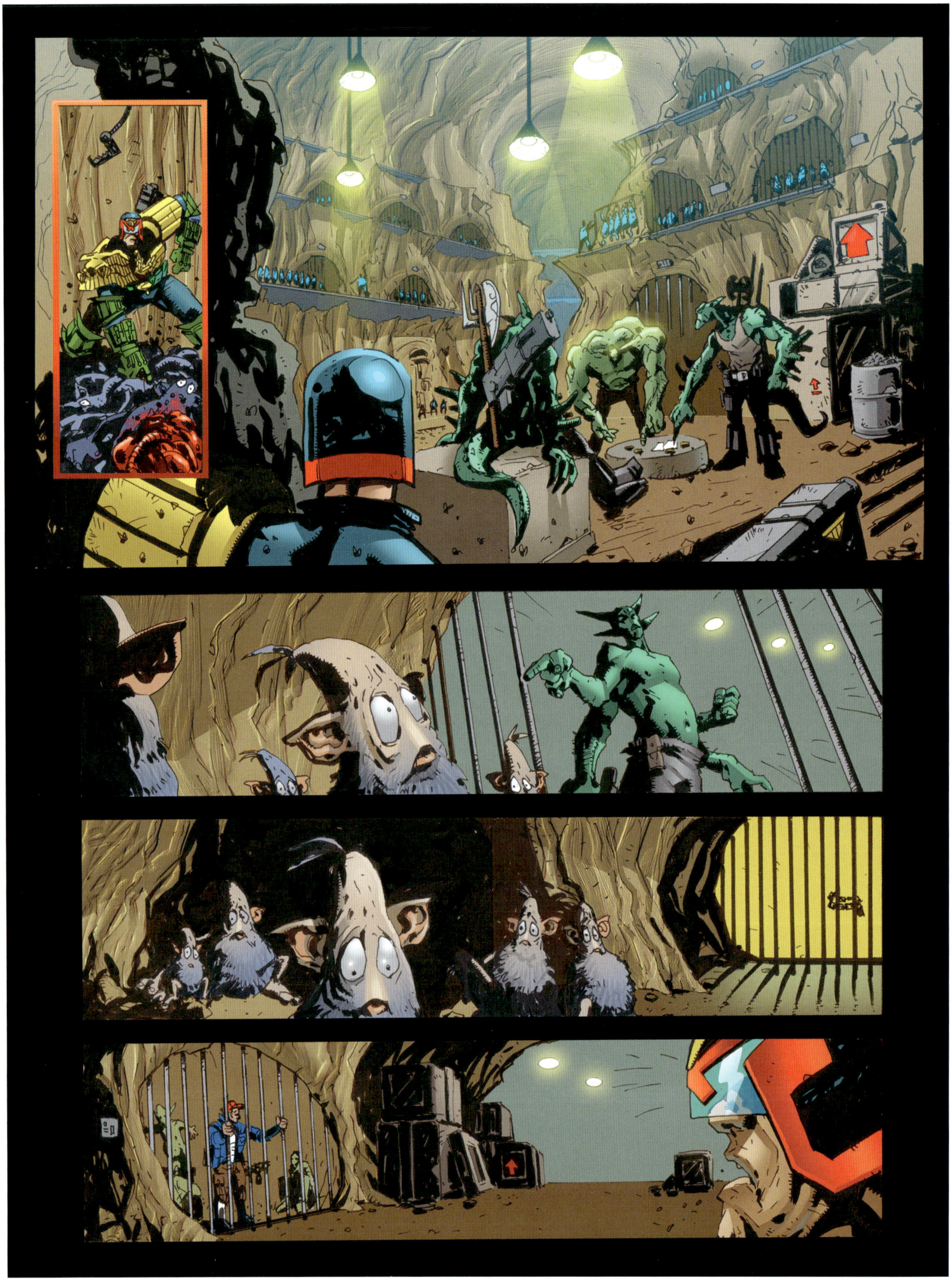

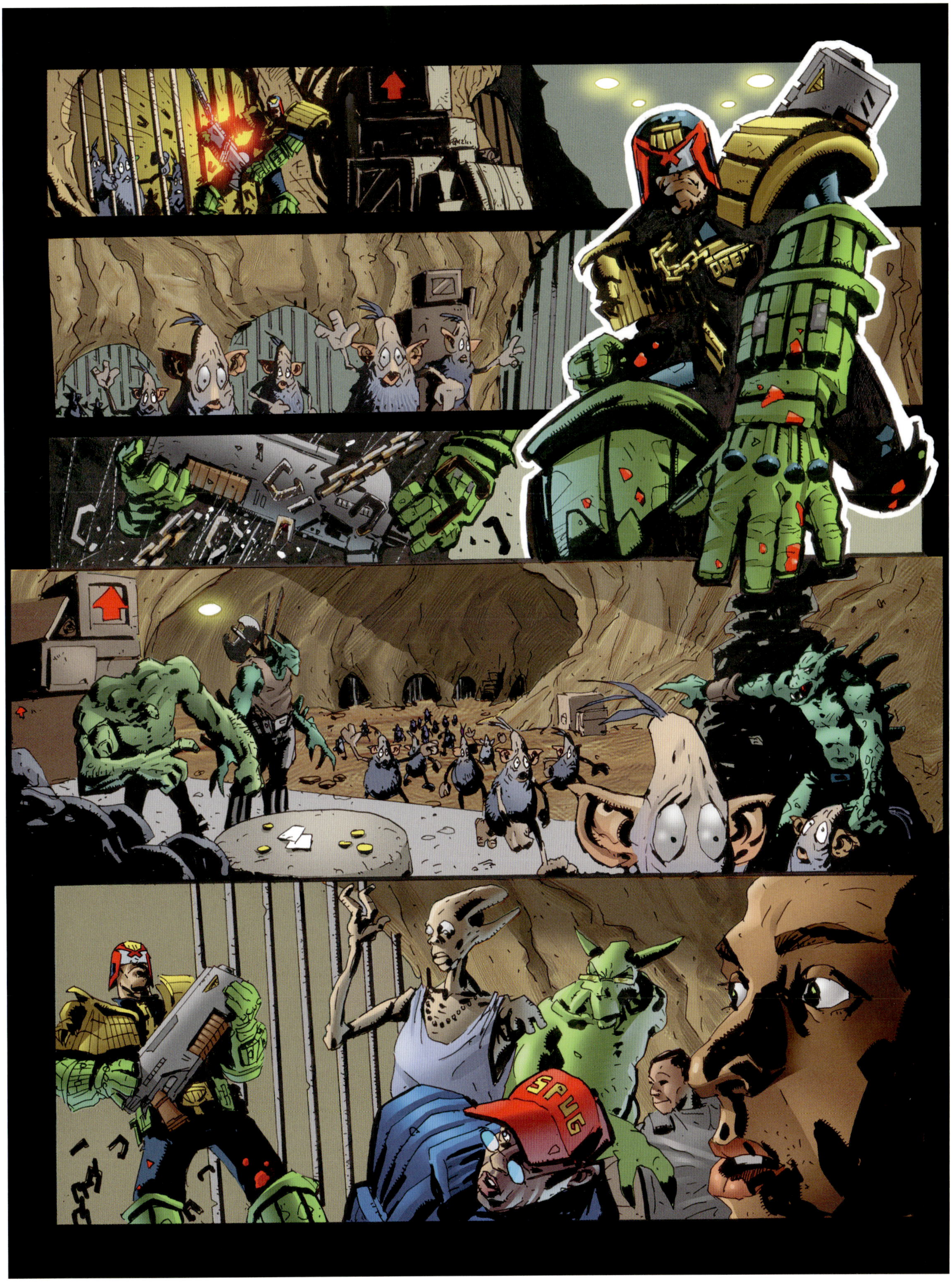
SPUG

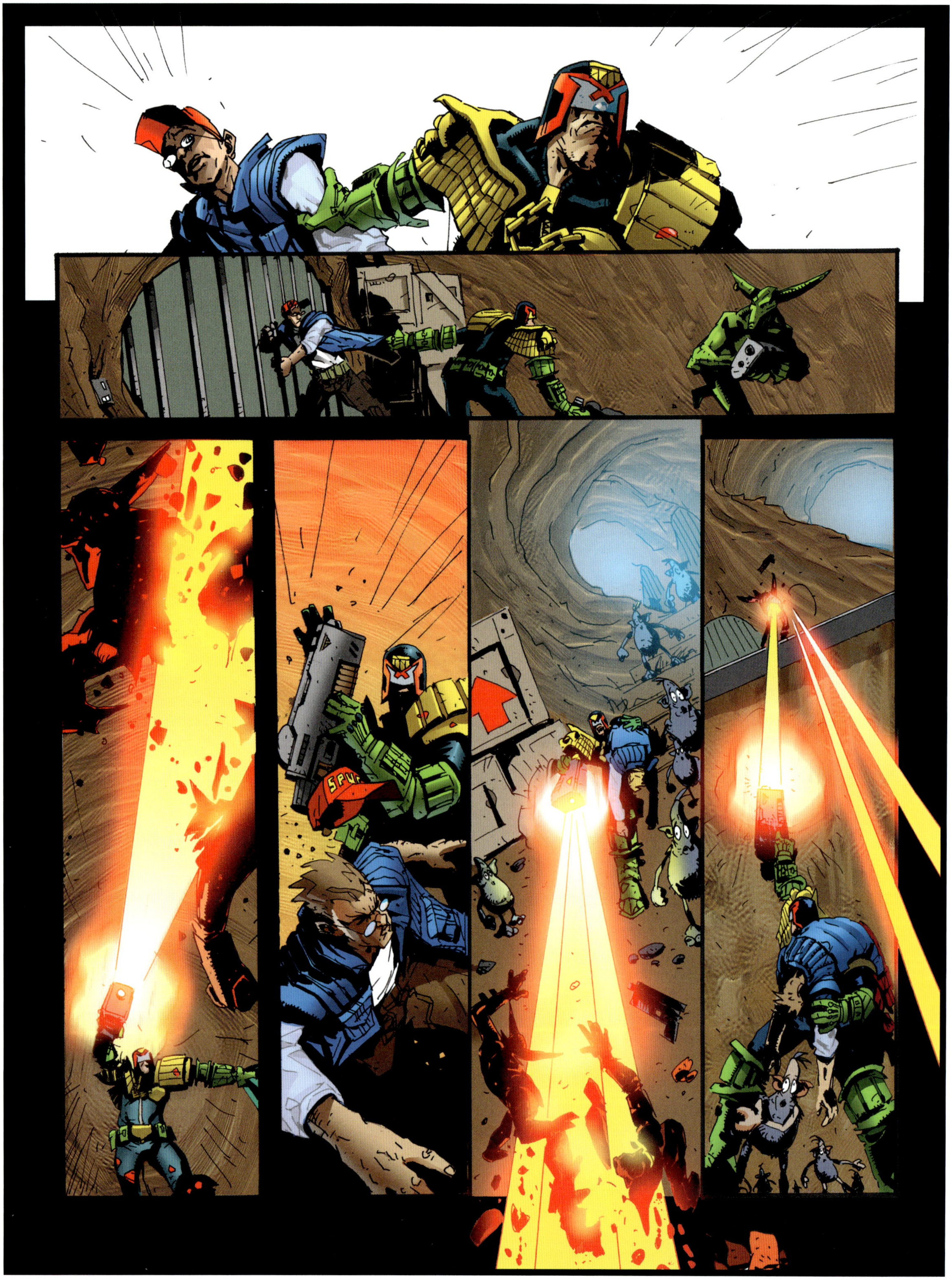
SPUR

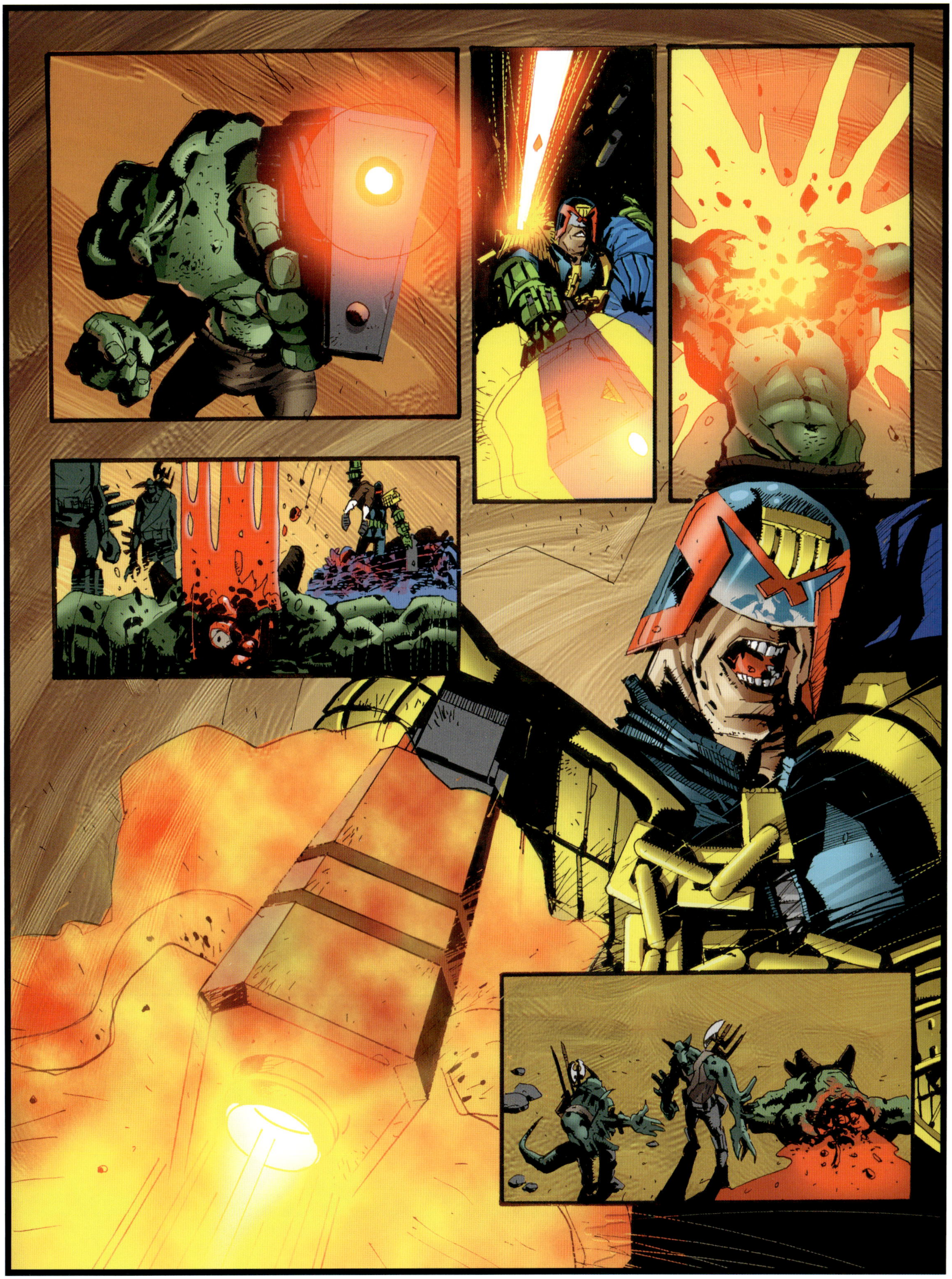

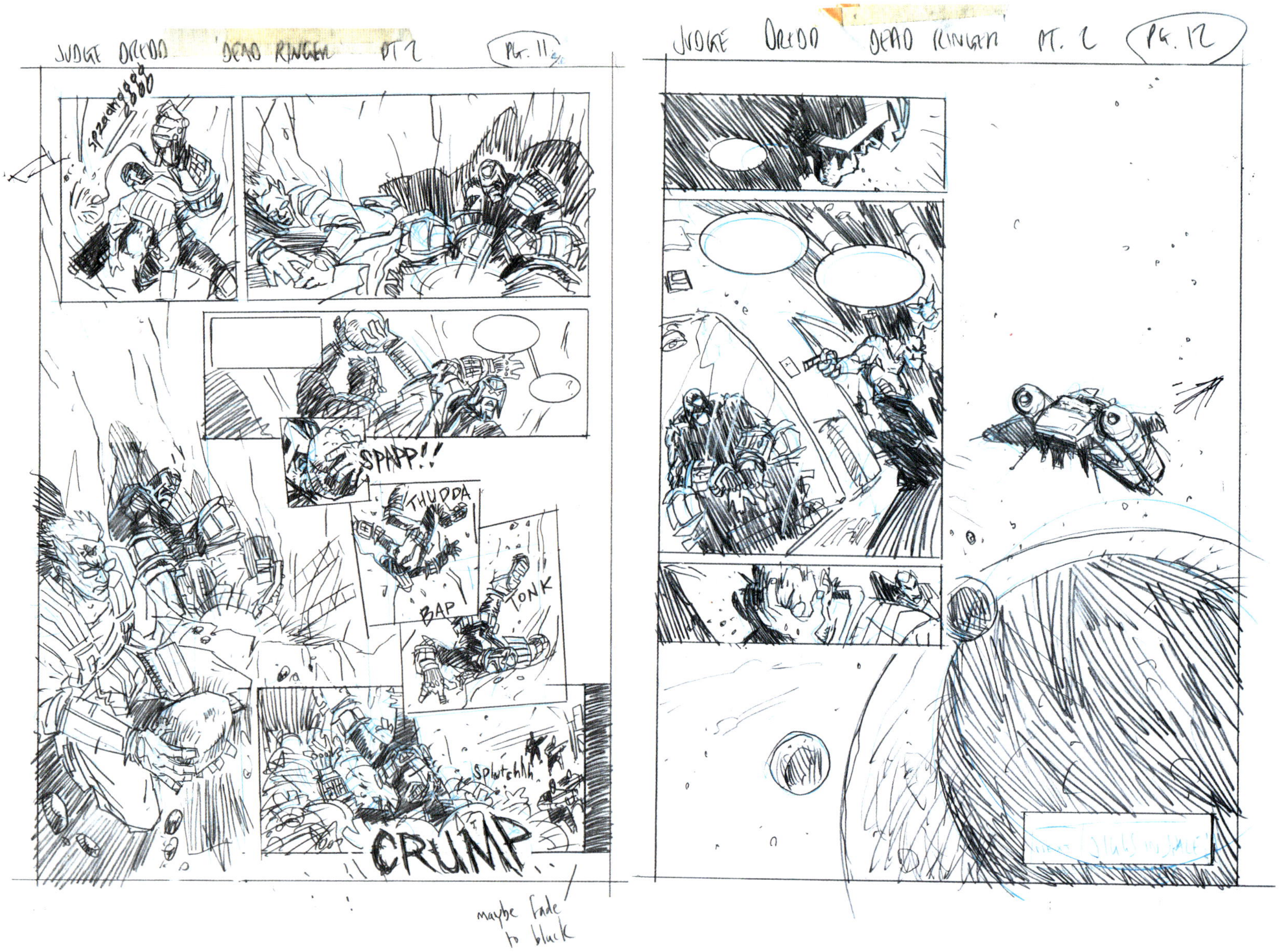
JUDGE DREDD DEAD RINGER PT 2 PG. 11
SPAPP!!
THUDDA
BAP
TONK
Splutchhh
CRUMP
maybe fade to black
JUDGE DREDD DEAD RINGER PT. 2 PG. 12

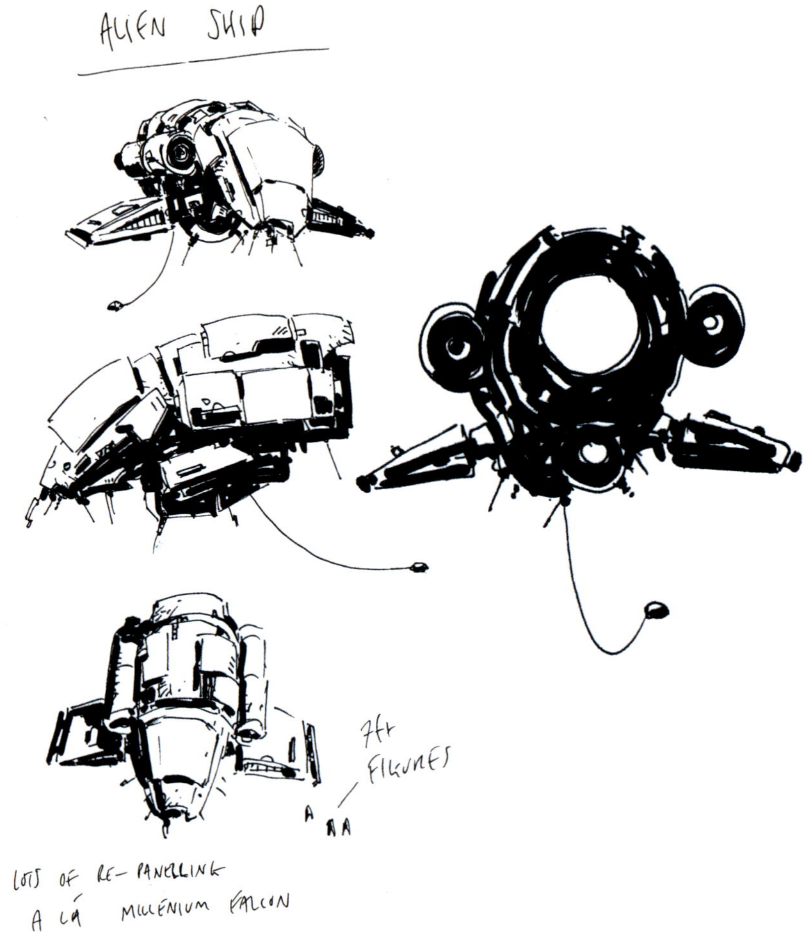
ALIEN SHIP
7ft FIGURES
LOTS OF RE-PANELLING A LA MILLENIUM FALCON

DEAD RINGER

'My first published comic strip, and it was Dredd... talk about being thrown in at the deep end. Seeing all these faxes of sketches and layouts, I was really struck that the things I was asking Andy Diggle at the time that just didn't matter, but they mattered to me, starting out and learning on the job. I can remember the very first time that happened was on 'Dead Ringer' – on the last page, there's a space shuttle, and I asked Andy if it was too small, and should it be more epic? And I remember he just said, "Well, it's not important". And he was absolutely right – it doesn't matter. So long as it's drawn okay and it's telling the story, it's absolutely fine. Starting out, I think I was trying to impress; I was trying to show what I could do; that's part of the journey, I think, part of how you figure it all out for yourself.'

—JOCK

JUDGE DREDD: DEAD RINGER LAYOUTS, 2000
SHIP SKETCHES, 2000

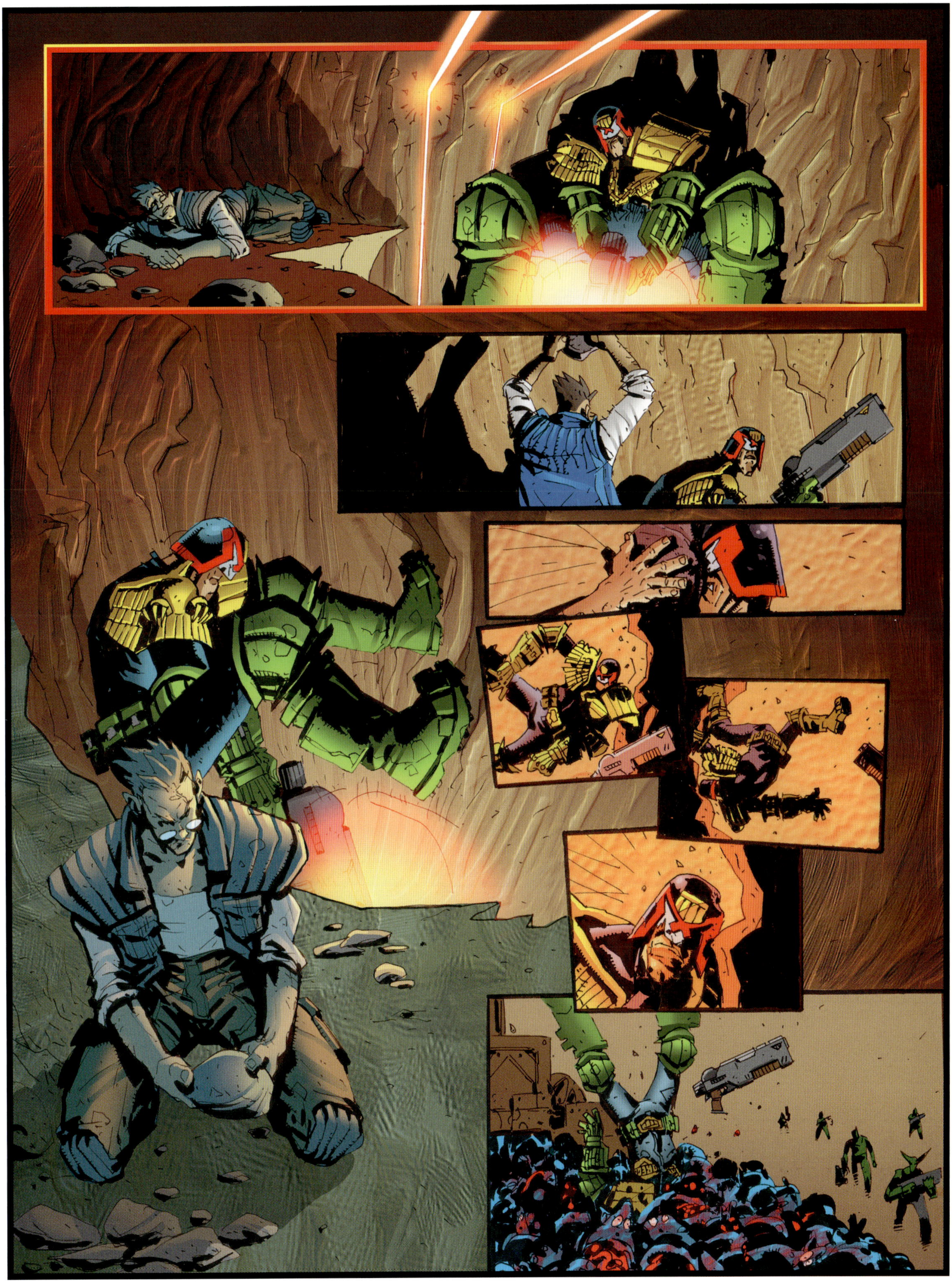

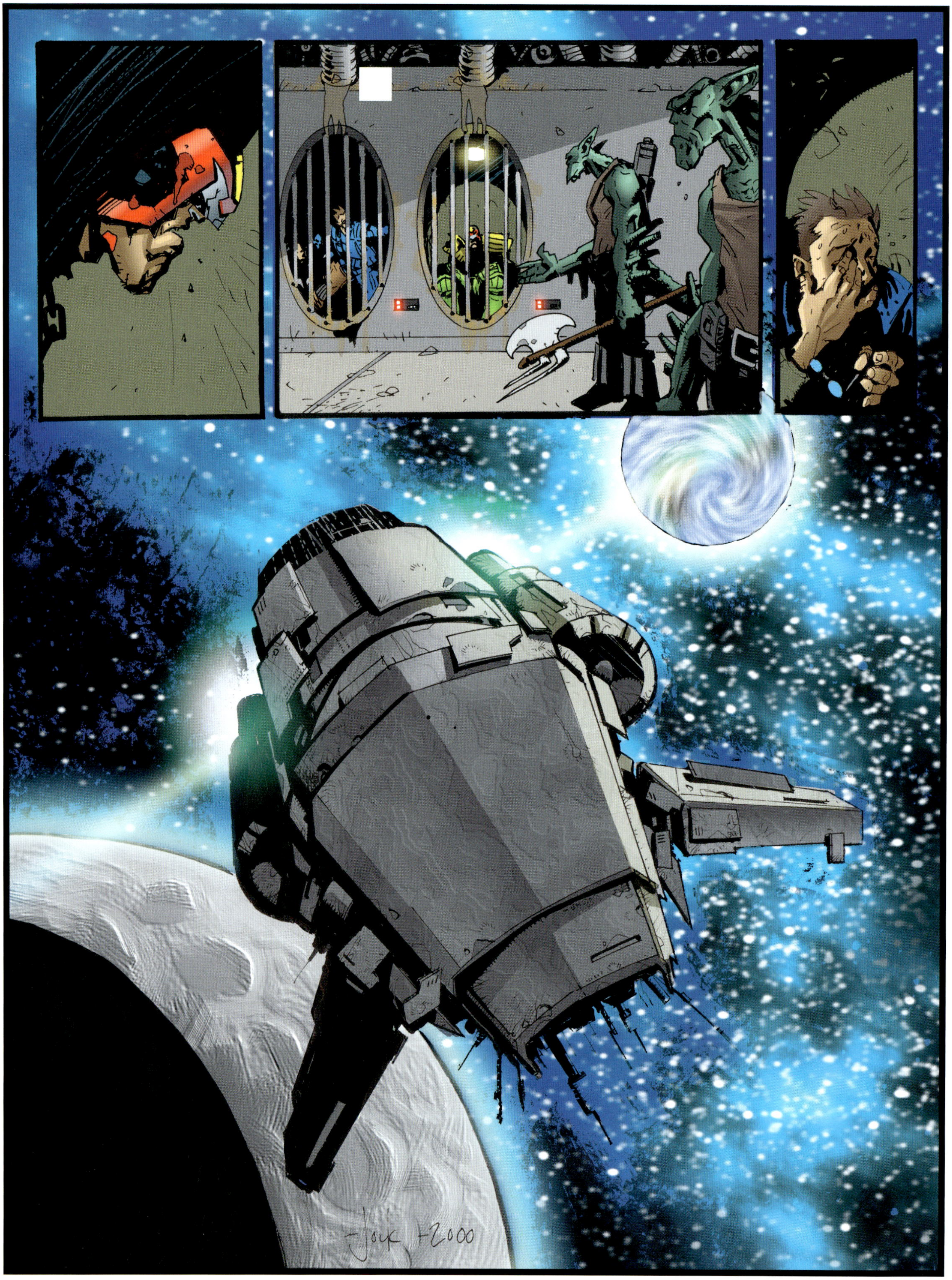

JUDGE DREDD: DEAD RINGER PAGE 12, JUDGE DREDD MEGAZINE 3.65, 2000

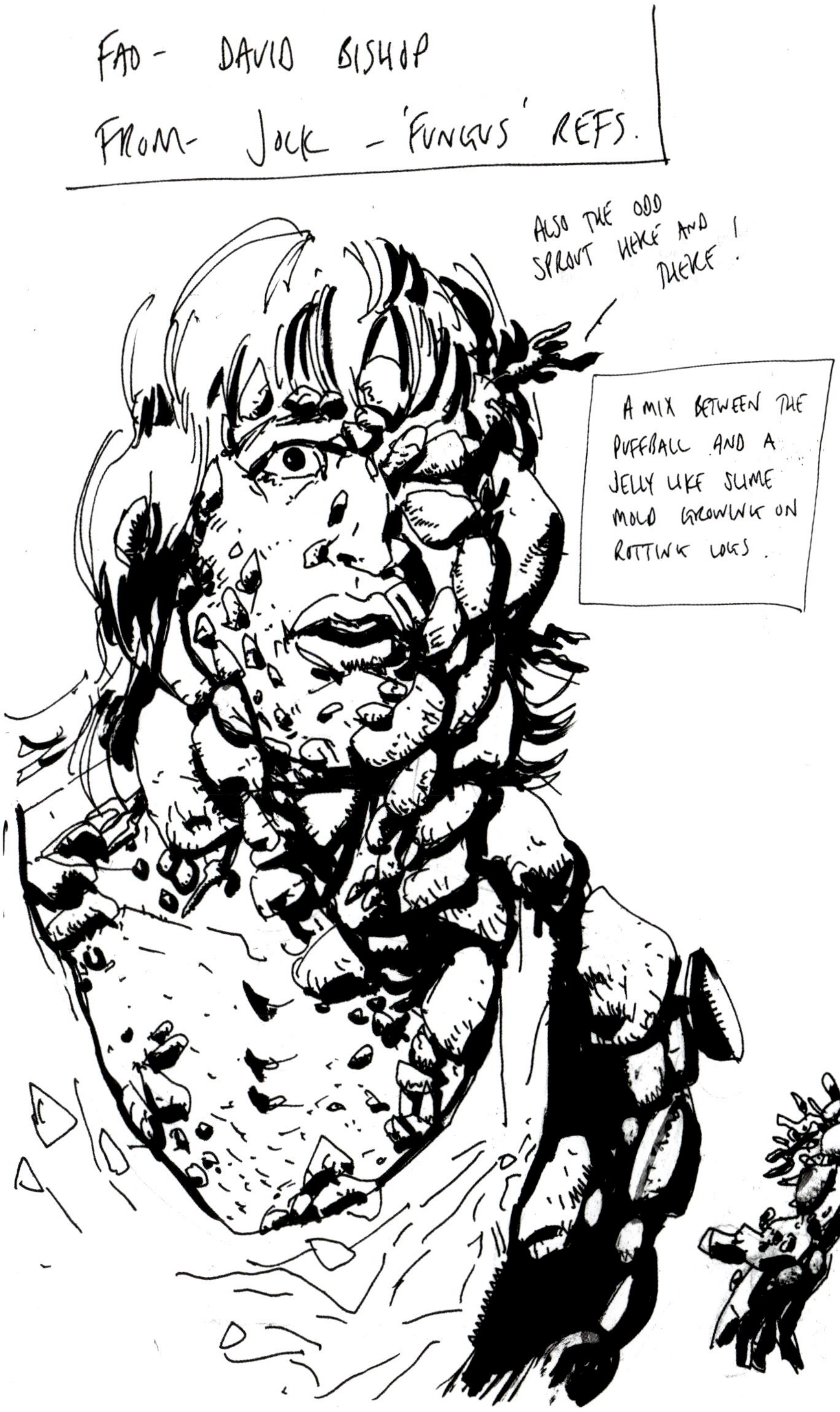
FAO - DAVID BISHOP
FROM - JOCK - 'FUNGUS' REFS.
ALSO THE ODD SPROUT HERE AND THERE!
A MIX BETWEEN THE PUFFBALL AND A JELLY LIKE SLIME MOLD GROWING ON ROTTING LOGS.

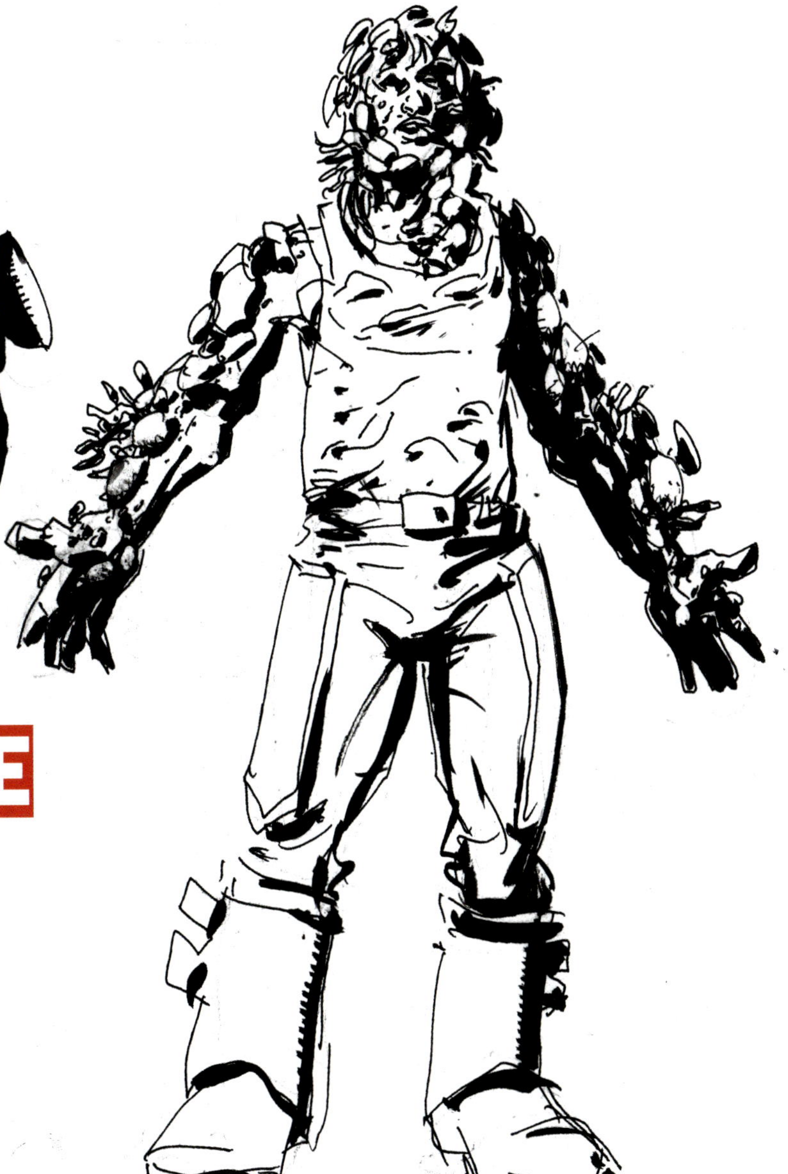

SHIRLEY TEMPLE

'With 'Dead Ringer' it was, "Do you want to get up on stage tonight?" and then with 'Shirley Temple' it was, "You've now got to get on that stage every day for 10 weeks". That's the reality of suddenly having this full-time job. Shirley Temple was me really trying to get to grips with the day-to-day schedule of it. In the story I'm trying to work with exaggerated camera angles and trying to make it dynamic, but I don't think it's very successful as a whole. It's not scruffy, but there's a kind of crass feel to some of the line work, and it looks more amateur to me… more so than on my first assignment, 'Dead Ringer'. I didn't manage my time so well, and I remember pulling a 35-hour non-stop shift to get the last pages in.'

—JOCK

SHIRLEY TEMPLE OF DOOM, CHARACTER ART, 2000

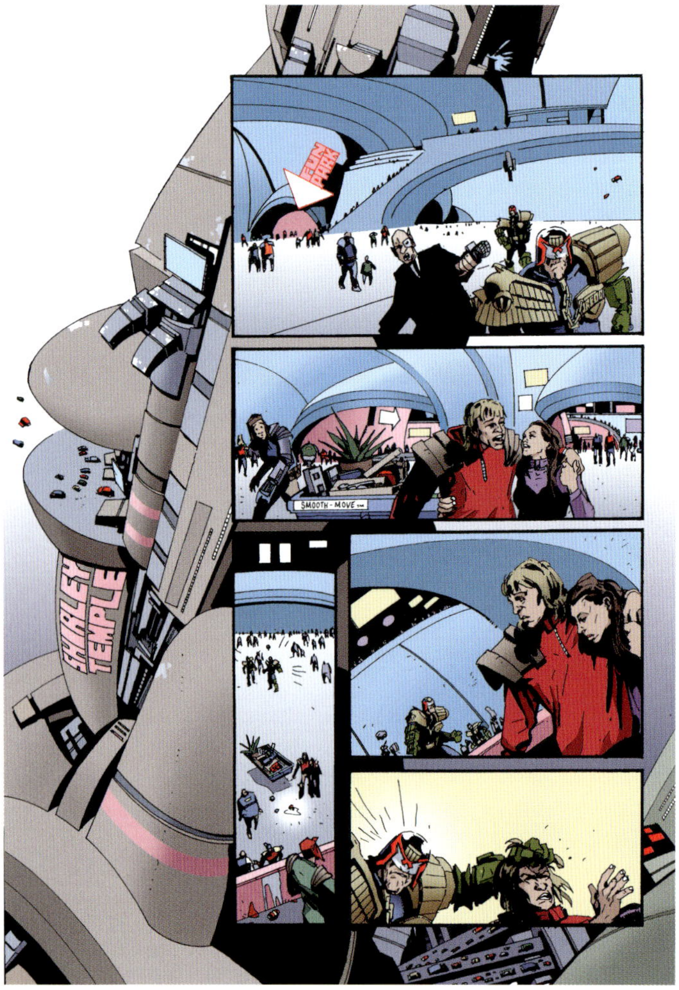
SMOOTH-MOVE
SHIRLEY TEMPLE

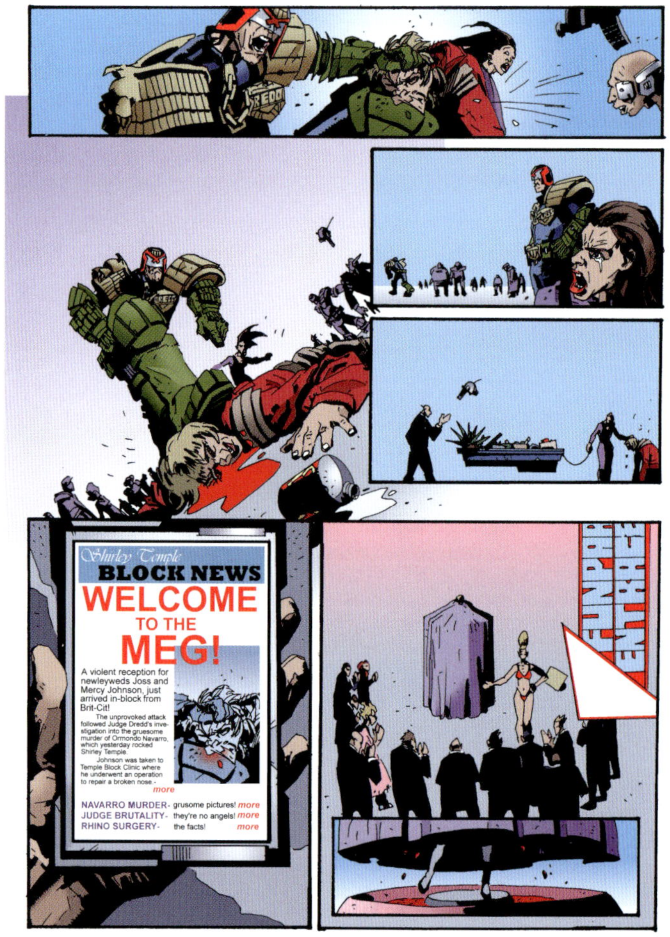
Shirley Temple
BLOCK NEWS
WELCOME TO THE MEG!
A violent reception for newleyweds Joss and Mercy Johnson, just arrived in-block from Brit-Cit!
The unprovoked attack followed Judge Dredd's investigation into the gruesome murder of Ormondo Navarro, which yesterday rocked Shirley Temple.
Johnson was taken to Temple Block Clinic where he underwent an operation to repair a broken nose.- more
NAVARRO MURDER- grusome pictures! more
JUDGE BRUTALITY- they're no angels! more
RHINO SURGERY- the facts! more

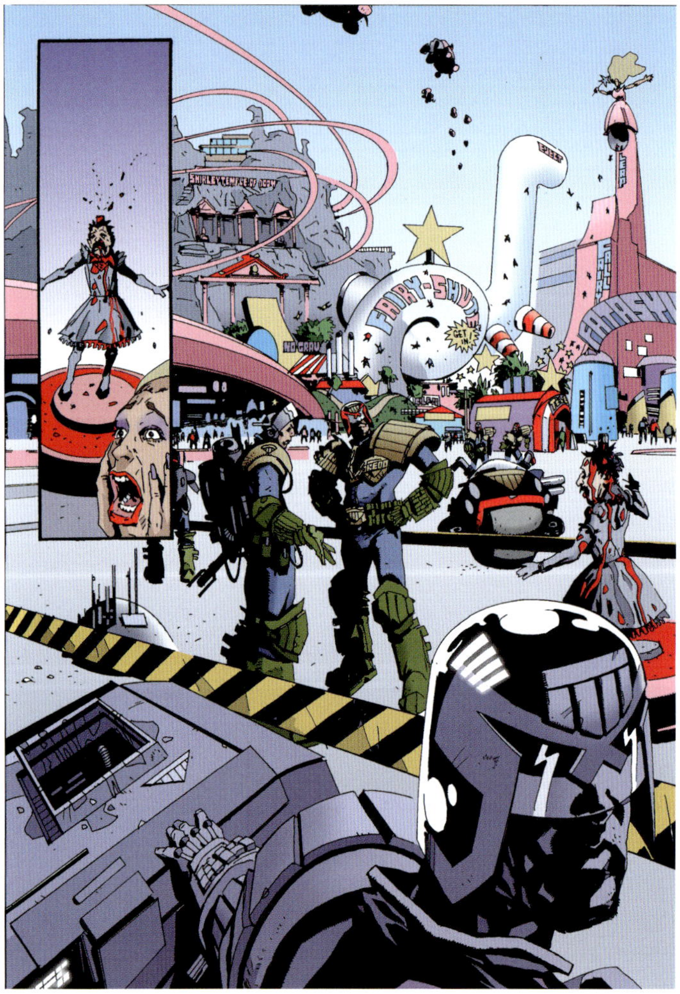
FAIRY-SHUTE

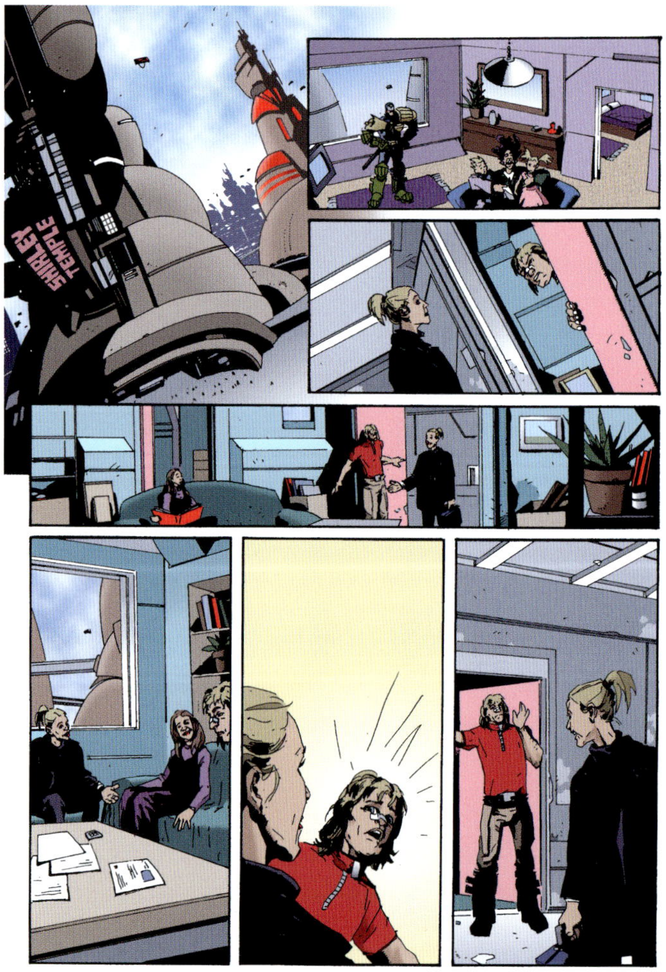
SHIRLEY TEMPLE

JUDGE DREDD: SHIRLEY TEMPLE OF DOOM, 2000 AD PROG 1193-1196, 2000
COLOURS BY GARY CALDWELL

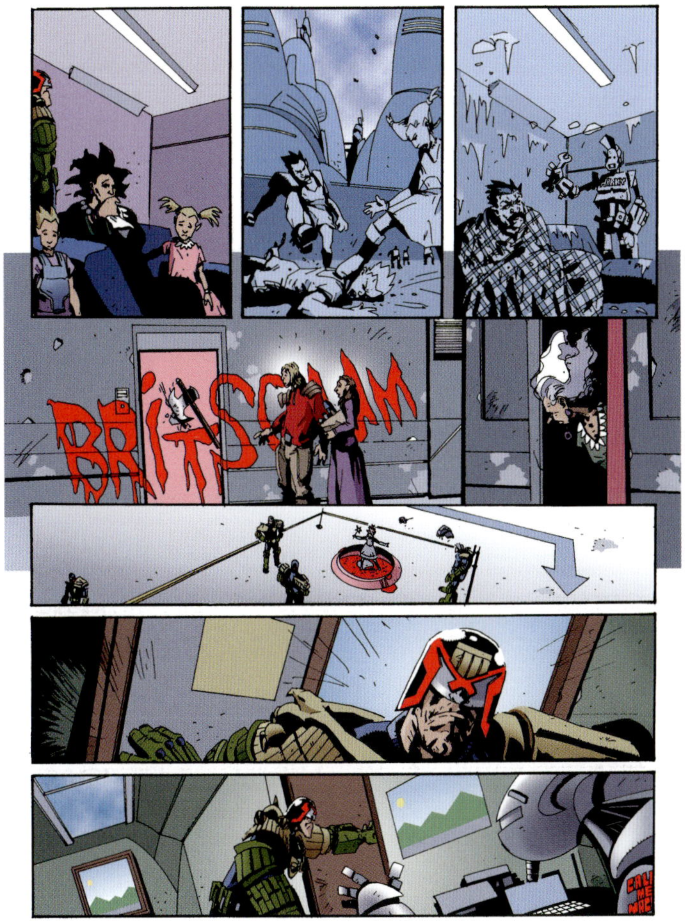
BRITSCAM

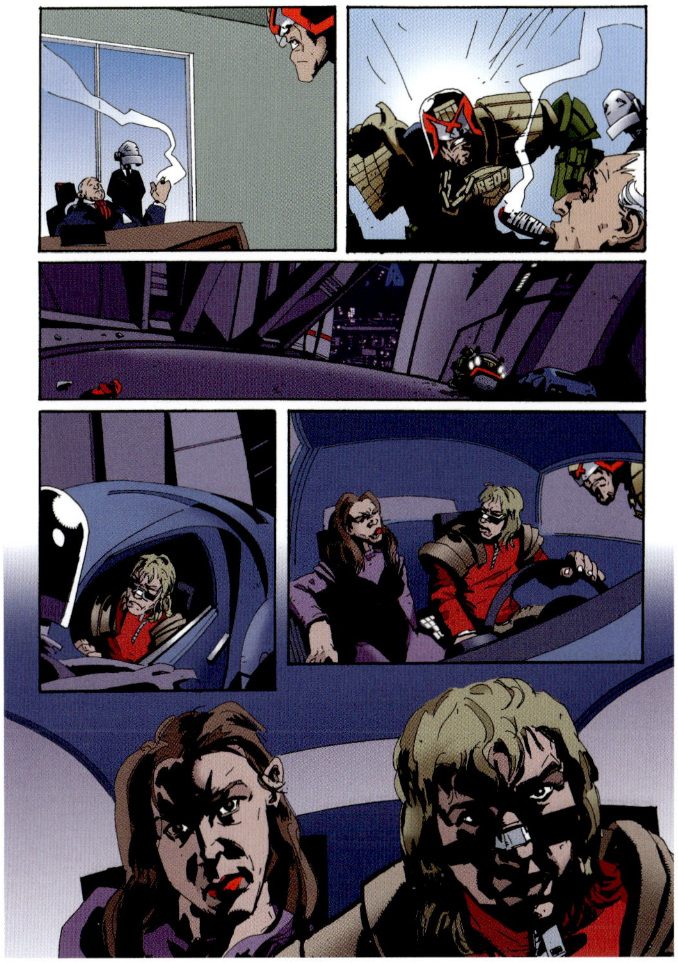

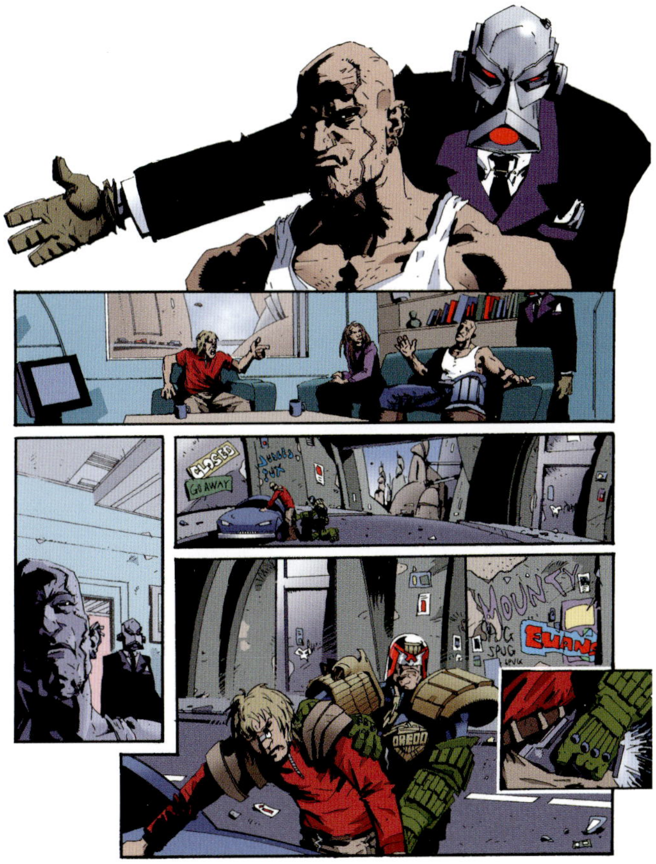
CLOSED
MOUNTY

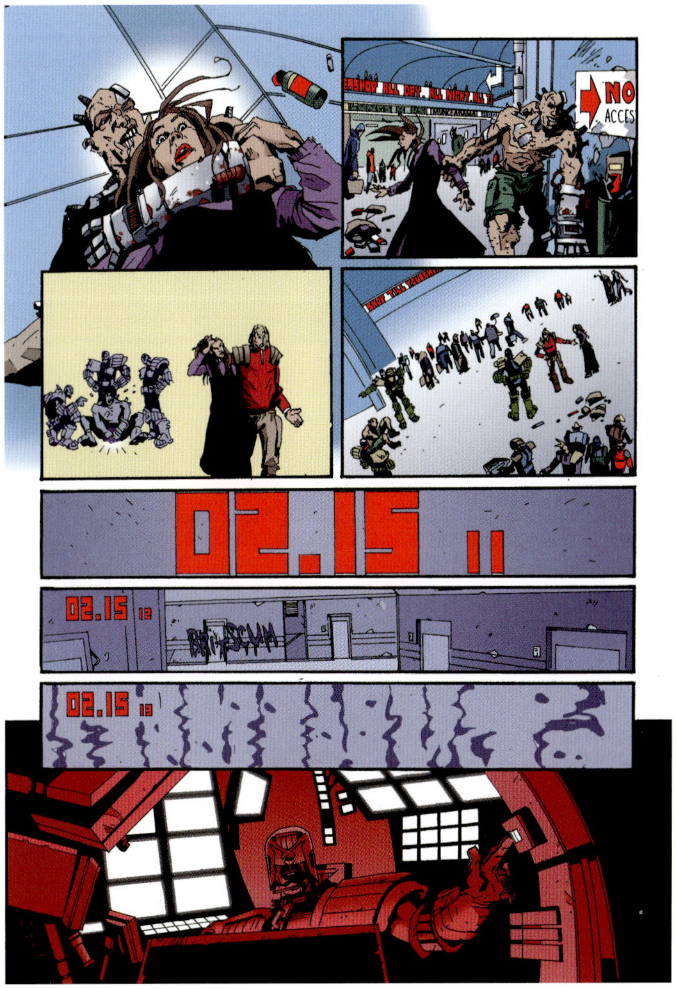
NO
02.15 11
02.15
BRITSCAM
02.15

JUDGE DREDD: SHIRLEY TEMPLE OF DOOM, 2000 AD PROG 1193-1196, 2000
COLOURS BY GARY CALDWELL

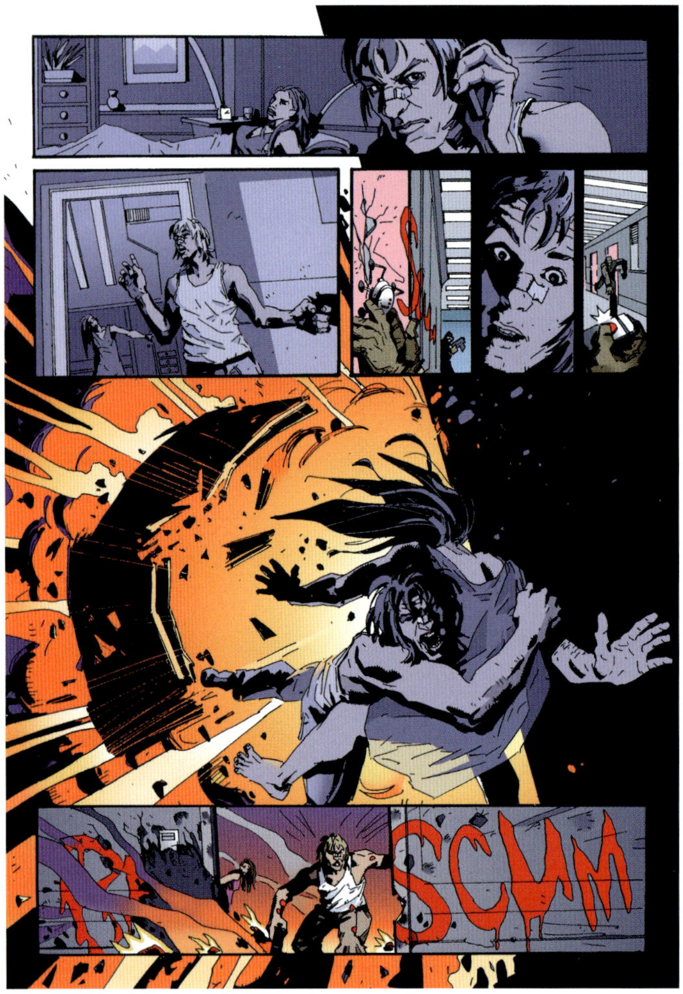
SCUM

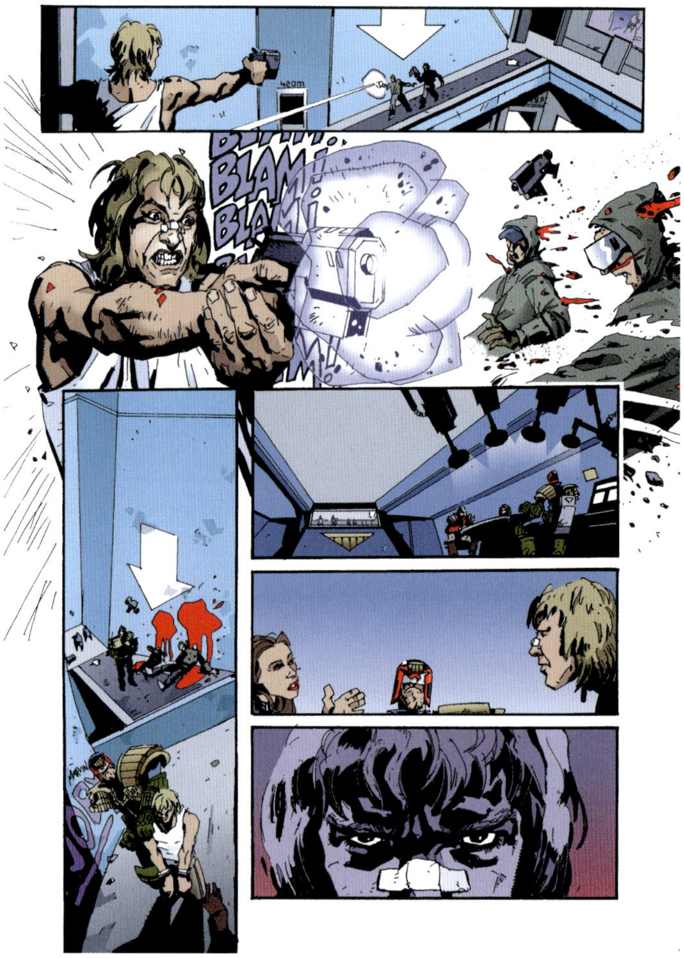
BLAM!
BLAM!

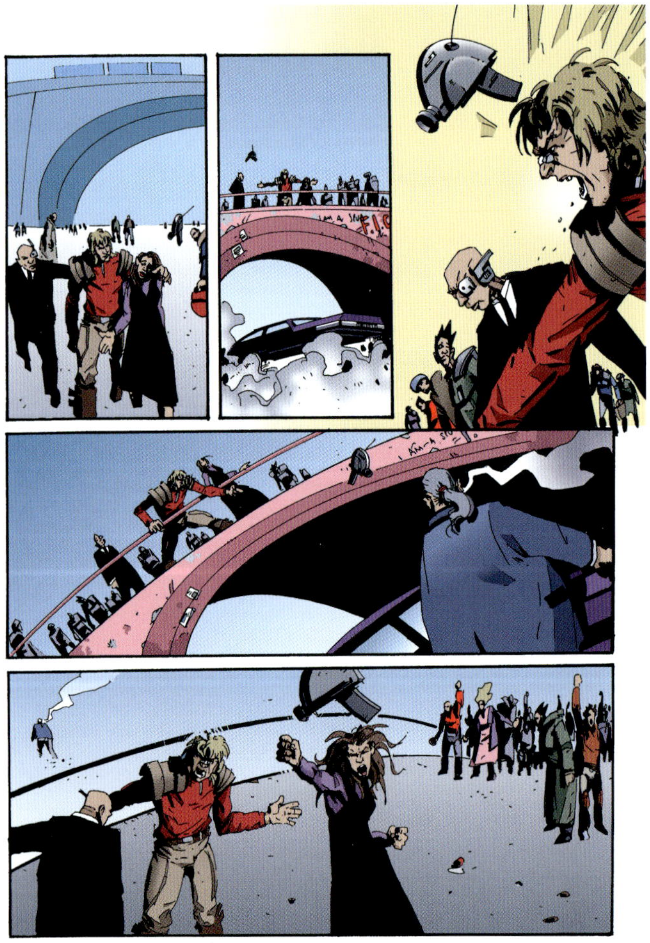

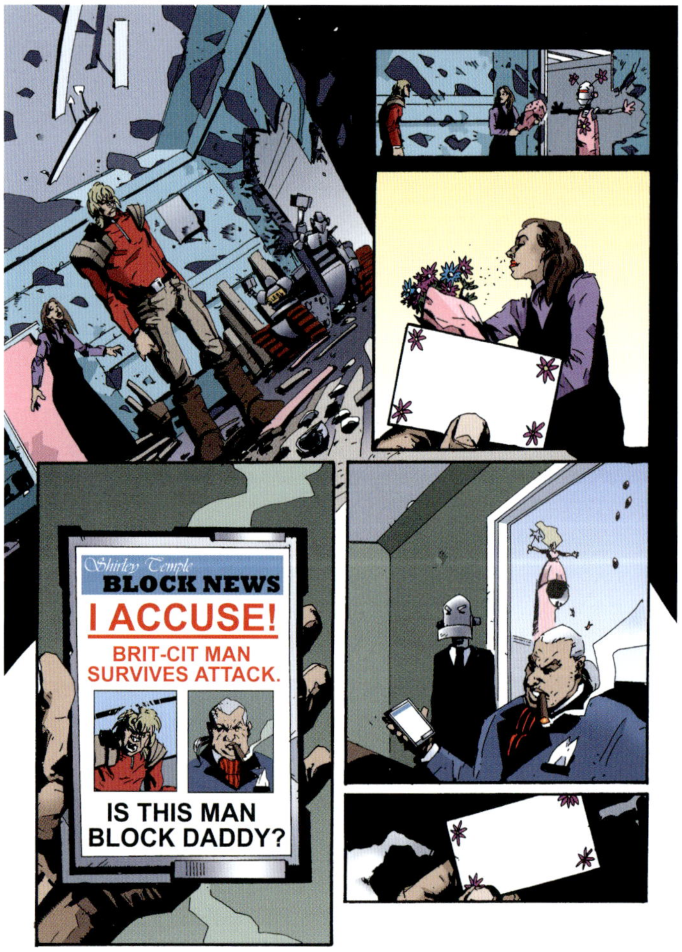
Shirley Temple
BLOCK NEWS
I ACCUSE!
BRIT-CIT MAN SURVIVES ATTACK.
IS THIS MAN BLOCK DADDY?

JUDGE DREDD: SHIRLEY TEMPLE OF DOOM, 2000 AD PROG 1193-1196, 2000
COLOURS BY GARY CALDWELL

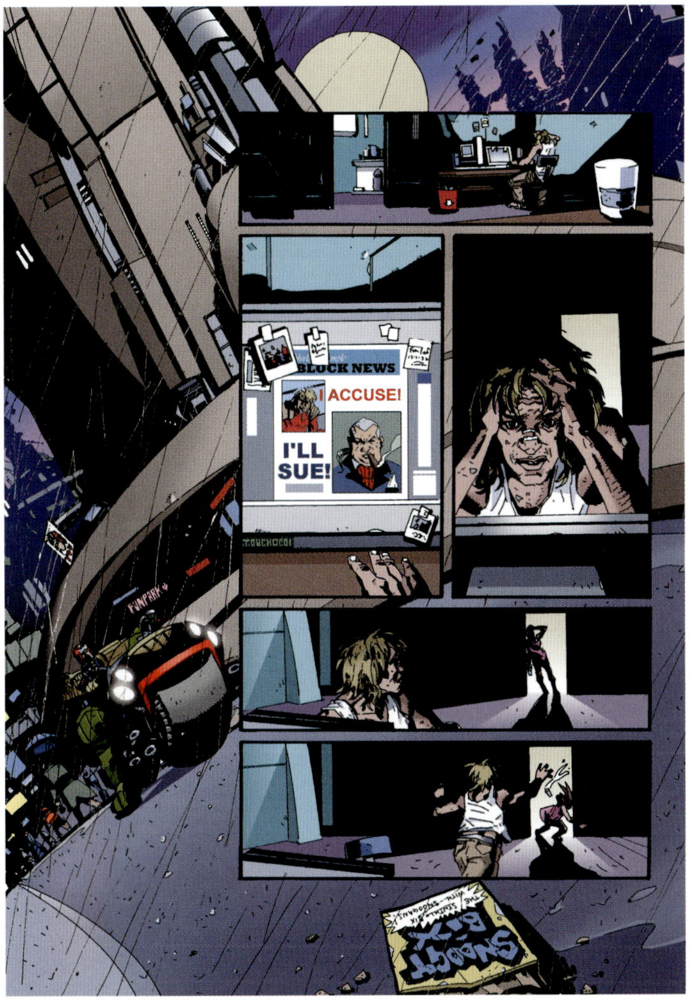
BLOCK NEWS
I ACCUSE!
I'LL SUE!

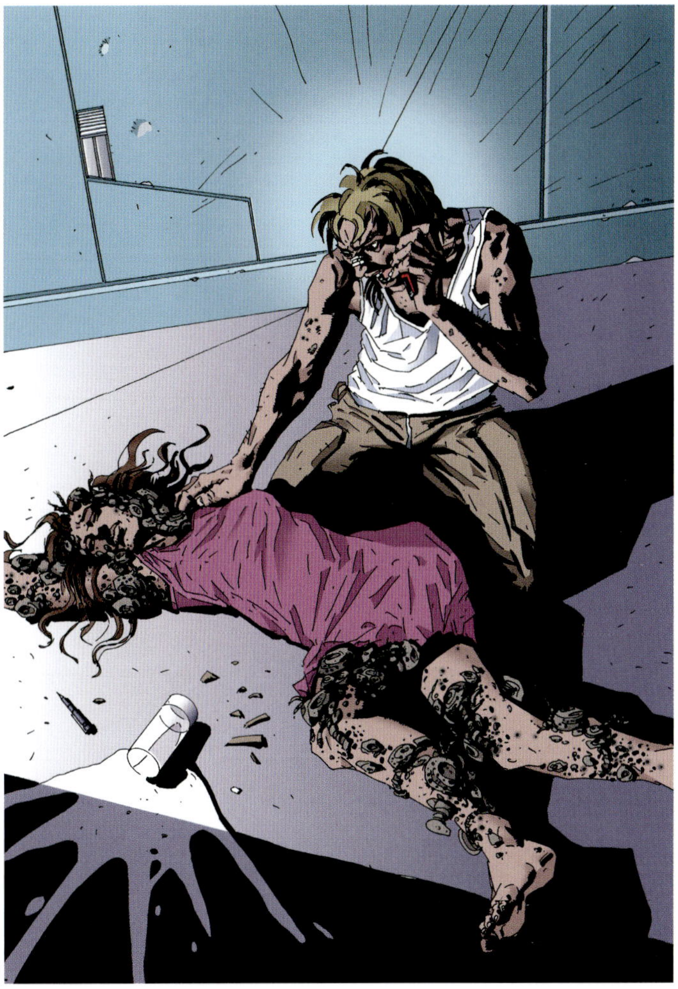

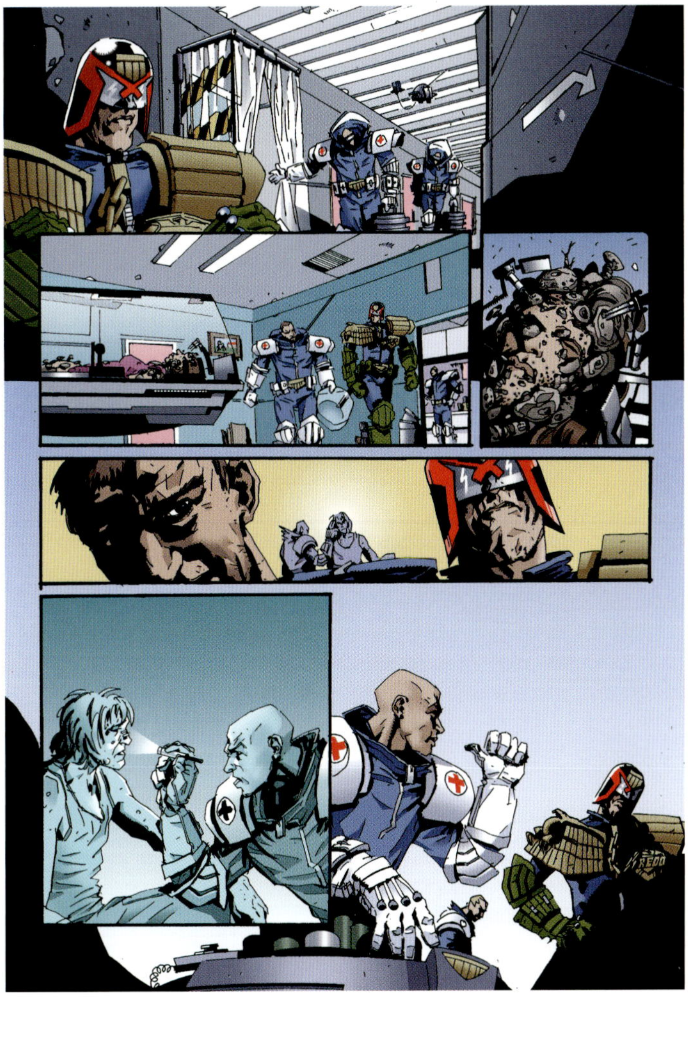

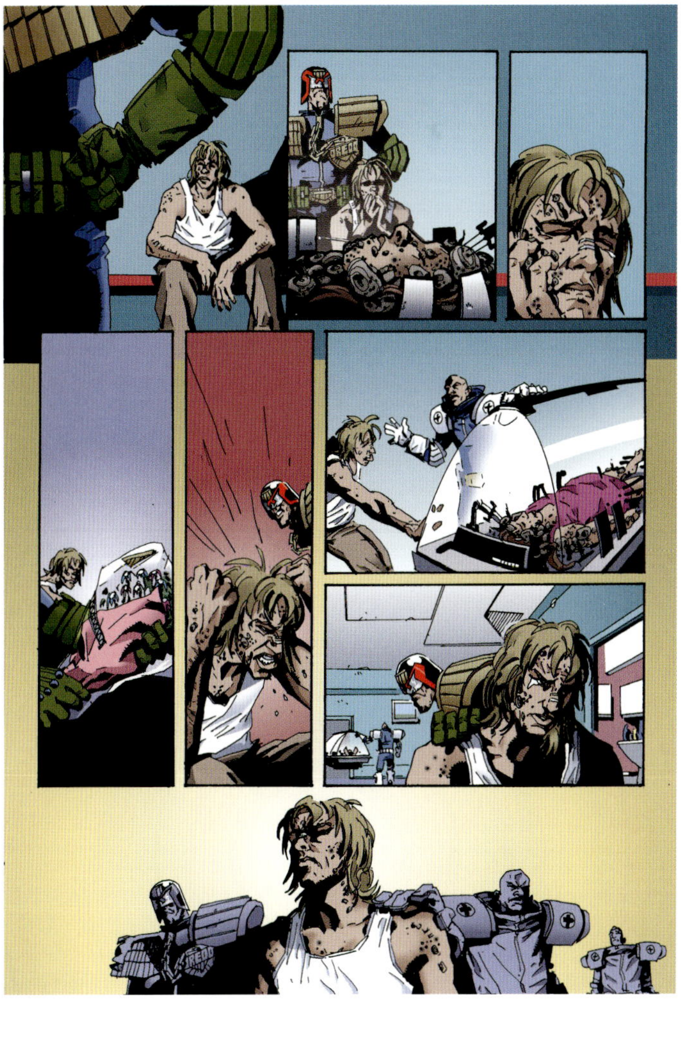

JUDGE DREDD: SHIRLEY TEMPLE OF DOOM, 2000 AD PROG 1193-1196, 2000
COLOURS BY GARY CALDWELL

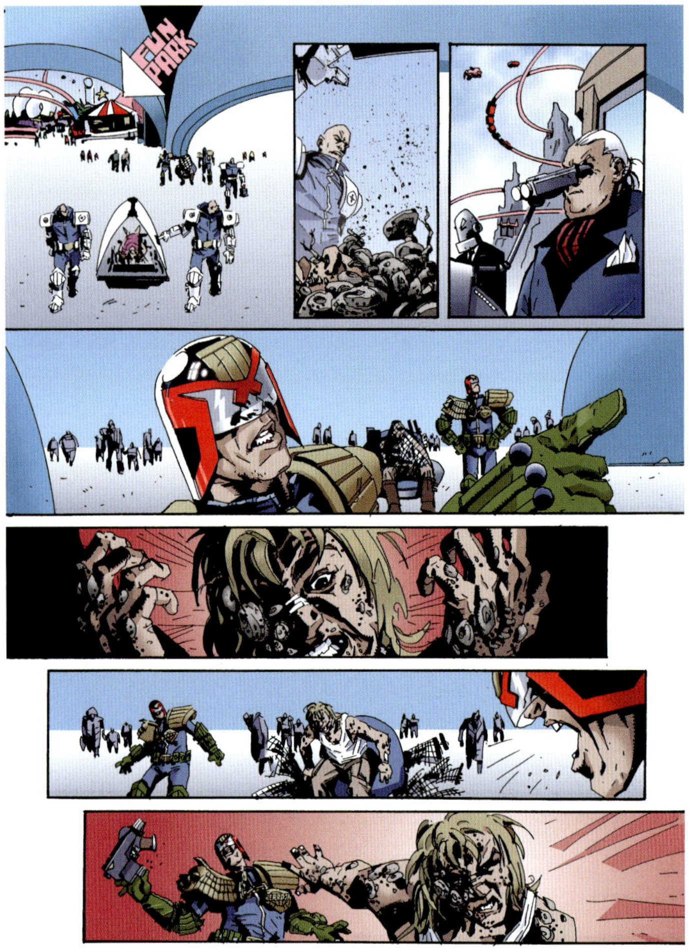
FUN PARK

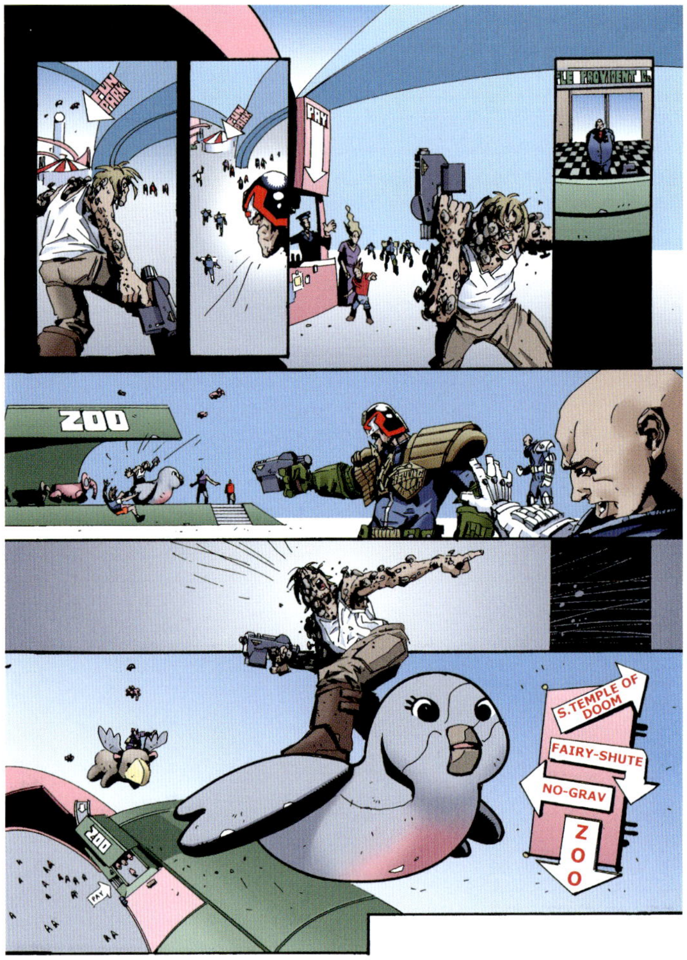
FUN PARK
PAY
ZOO
S.TEMPLE OF DOOM
FAIRY-SHUTE
NO-GRAV
ZOO

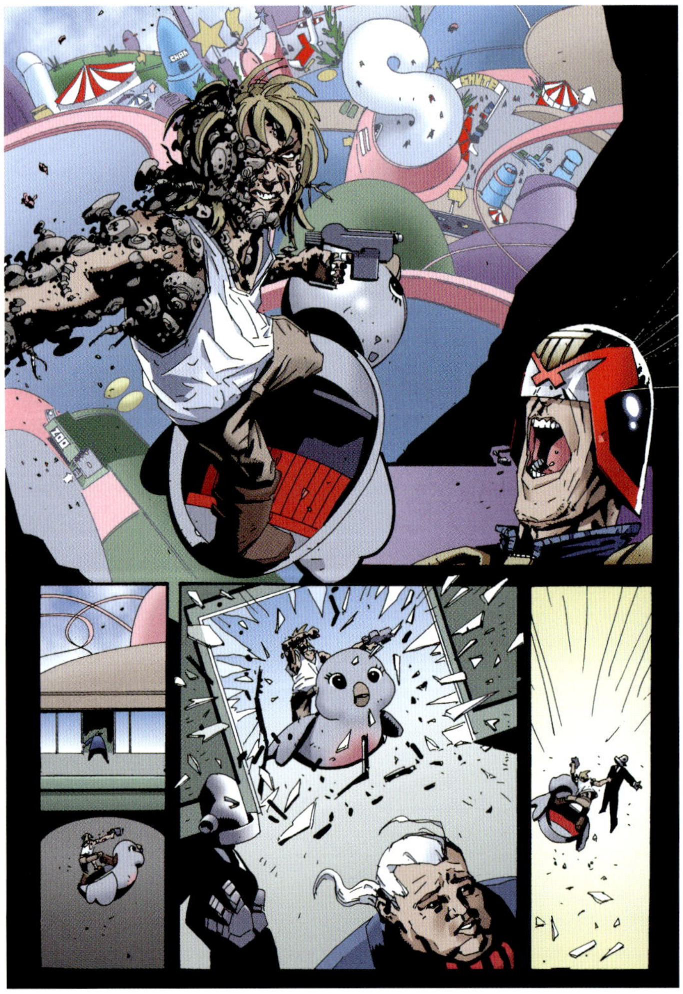

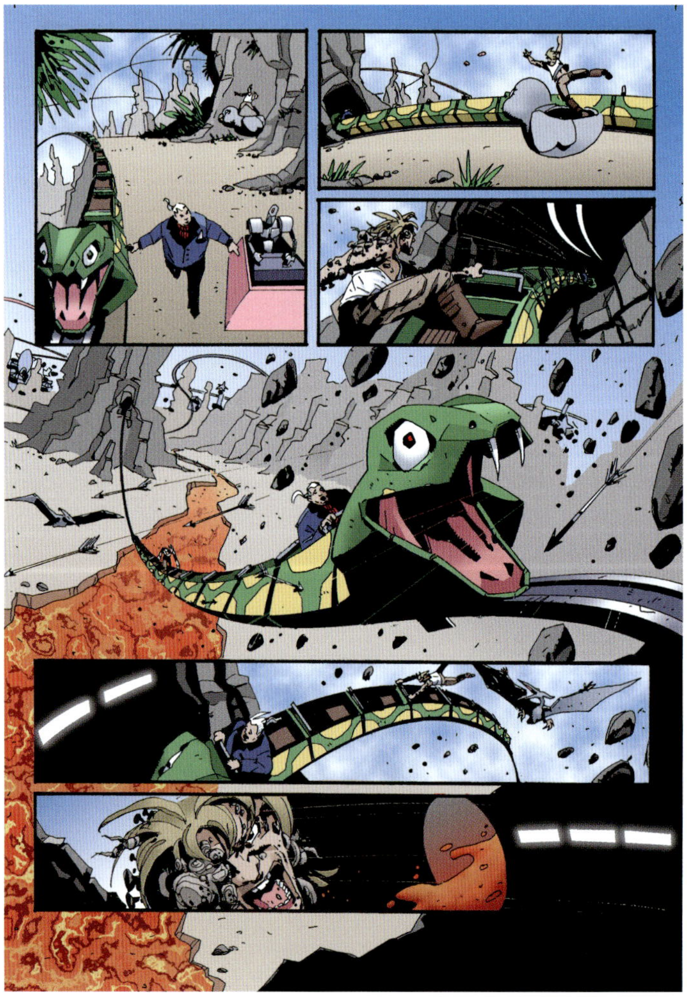

JUDGE DREDD: SHIRLEY TEMPLE OF DOOM, 2000 AD PROG 1193-1196, 2000
COLOURS BY GARY CALDWELL

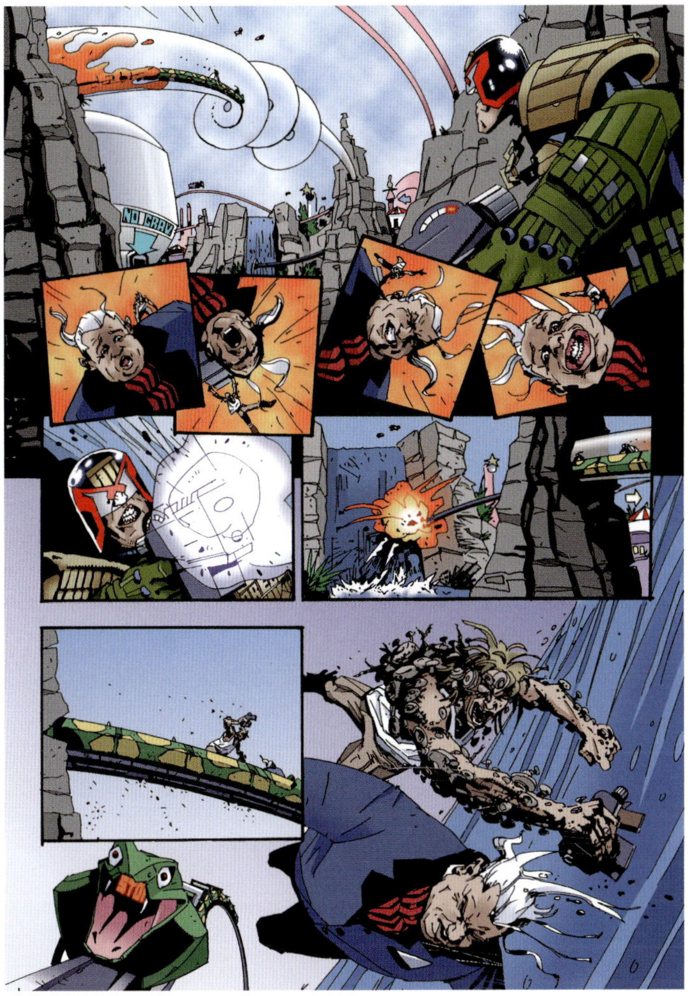

NO GRAV

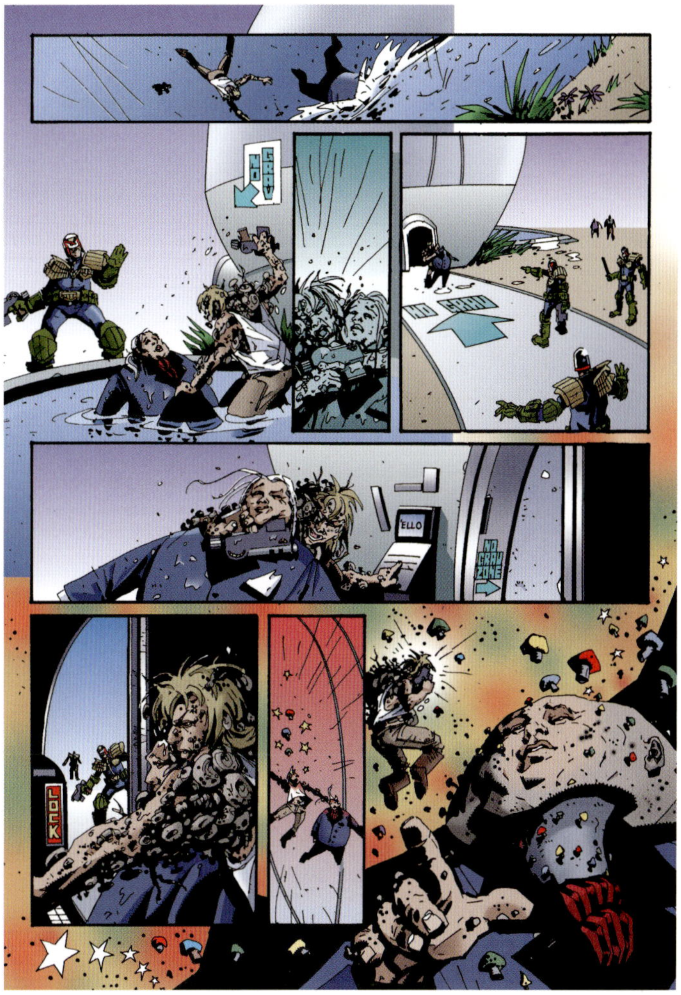

NO GRAV
ELLO
NO GRAV ZONE
LOCK

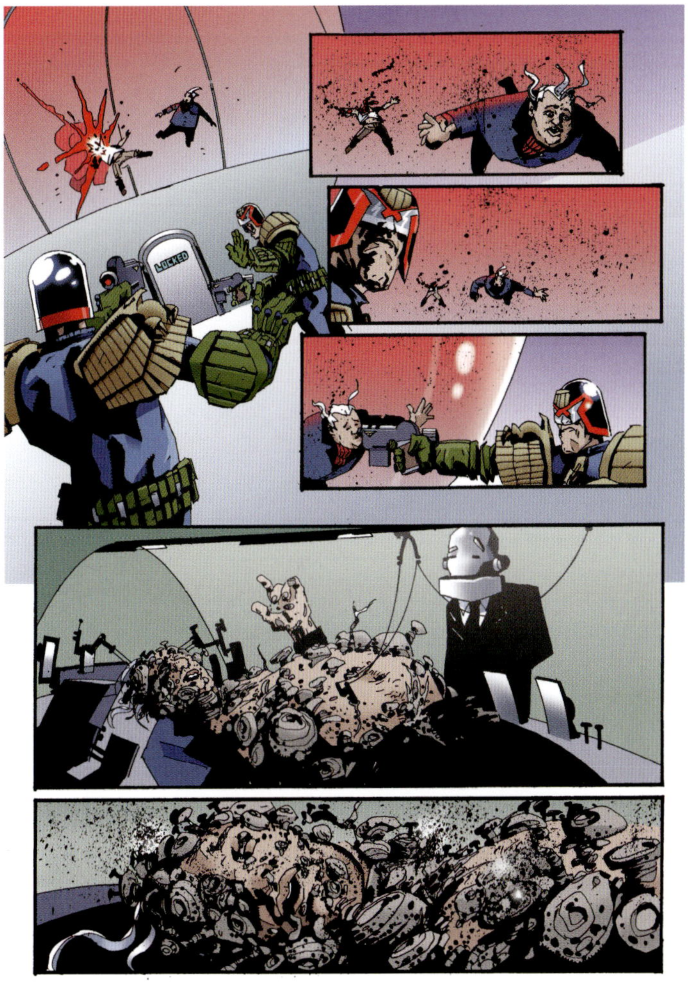

LOCKED

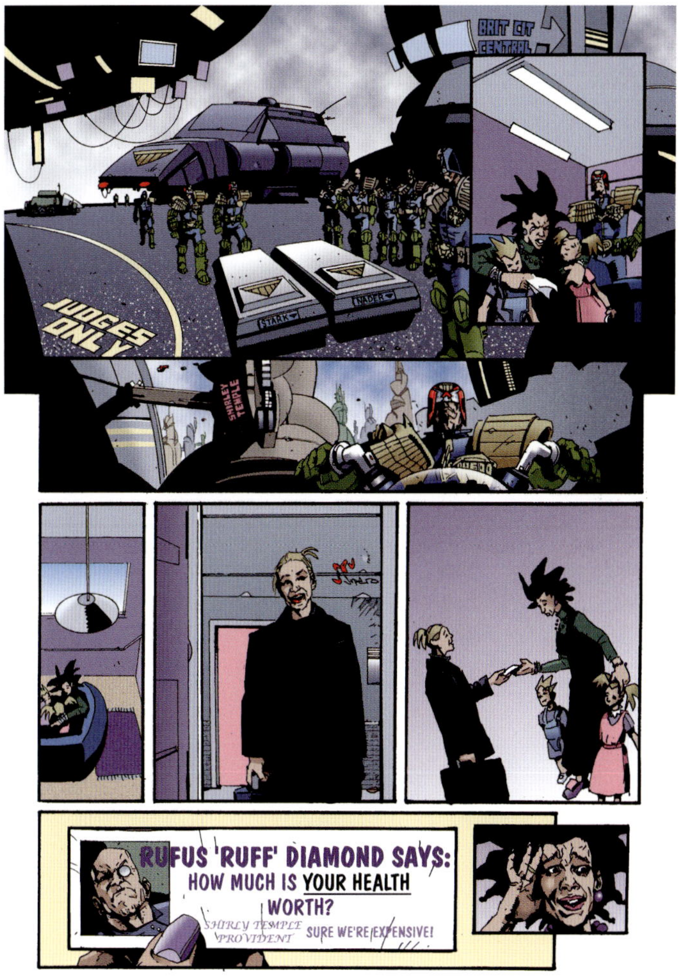

BRIT CIT CENTRAL
JUDGES ONLY
STARK
NADER
SHIRLEY TEMPLE
RUFUS 'RUFF' DIAMOND SAYS:
HOW MUCH IS YOUR HEALTH WORTH?
SHIRLEY TEMPLE PROVIDENT
SURE WE'RE EXPENSIVE!

JUDGE DREDD: SHIRLEY TEMPLE OF DOOM, 2000 AD PROG 1193-1196, 2000
COLOURS BY GARY CALDWELL

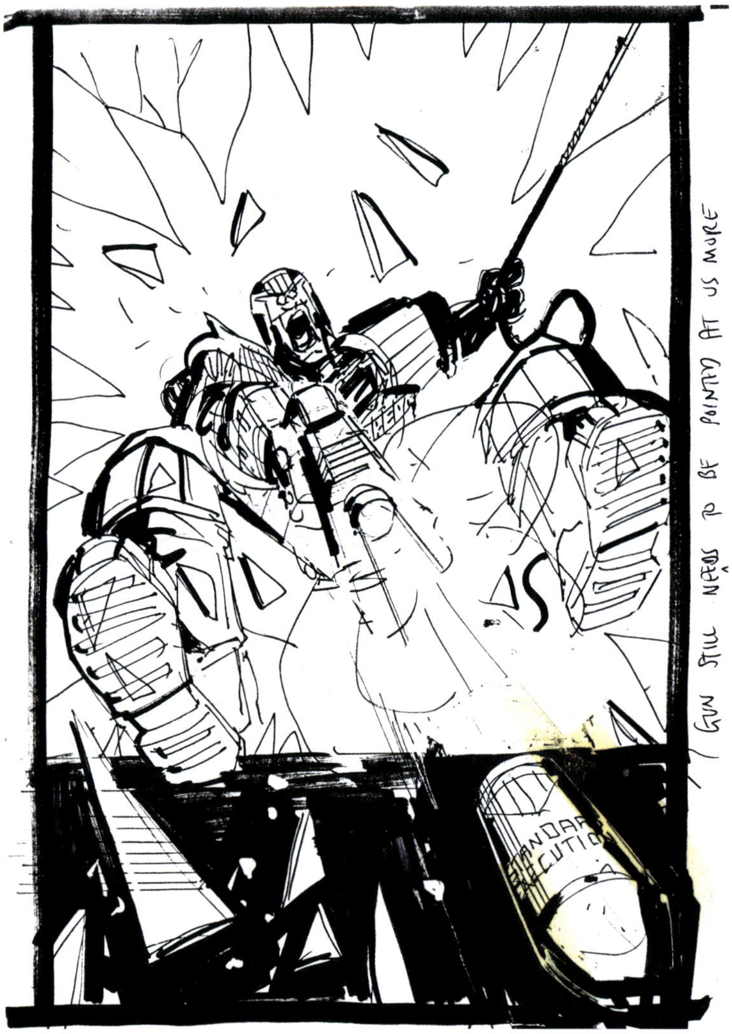
GUN STILL NEEDS TO BE POINTY AT US MORE

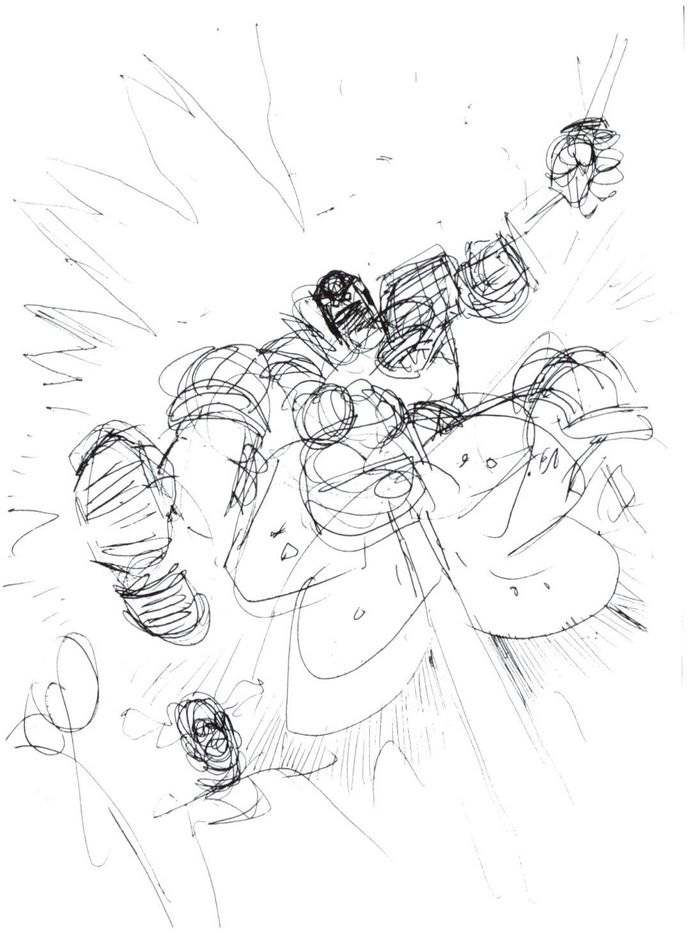

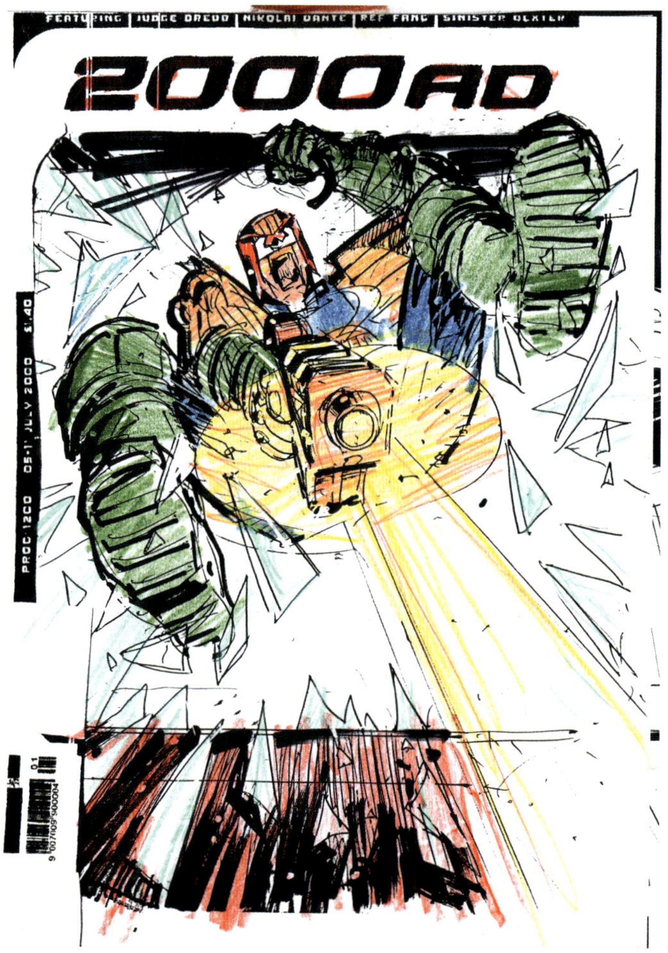
2000 AD

 2000 AD PROG COVER 1203, 2000

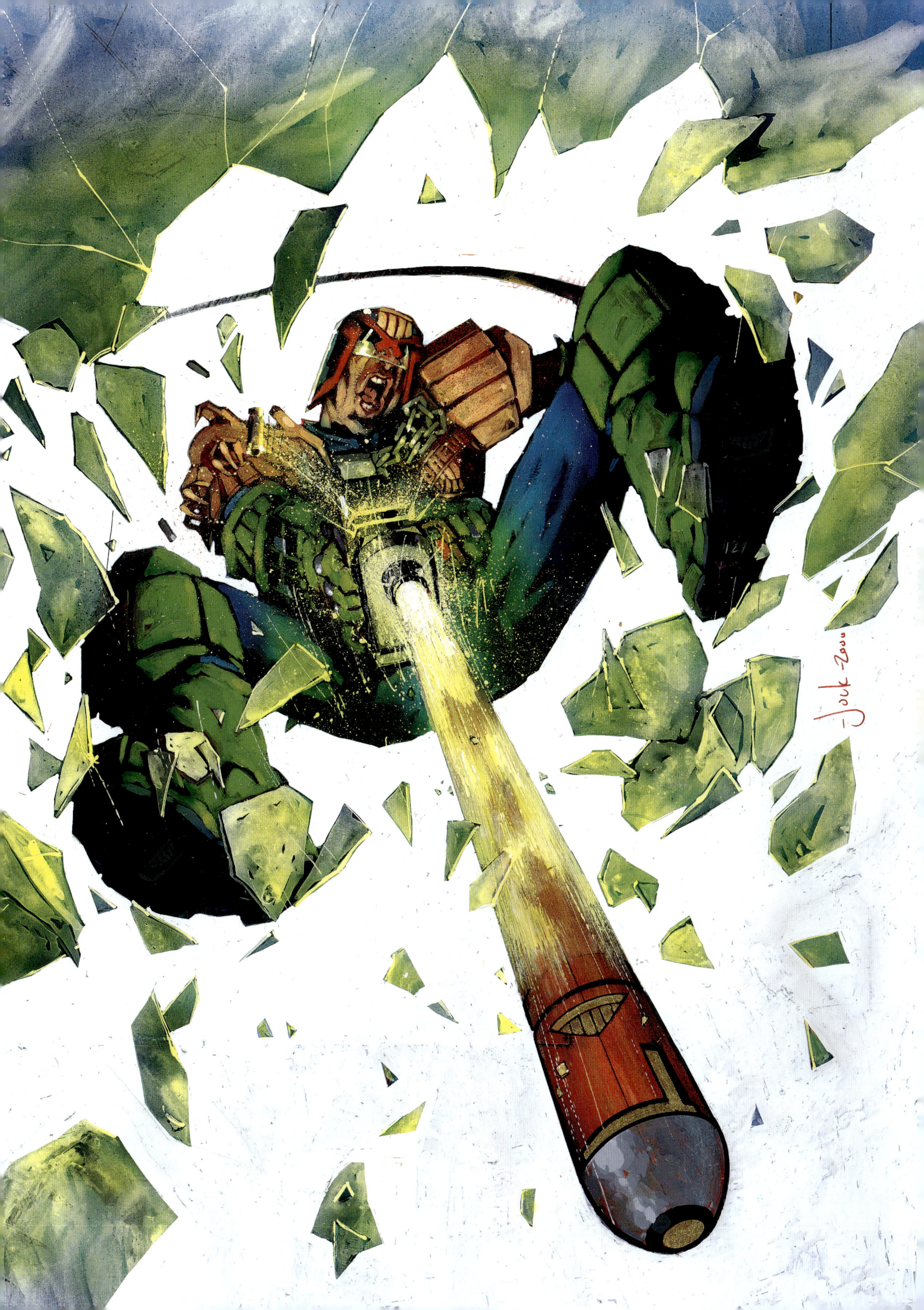
Jock 2000

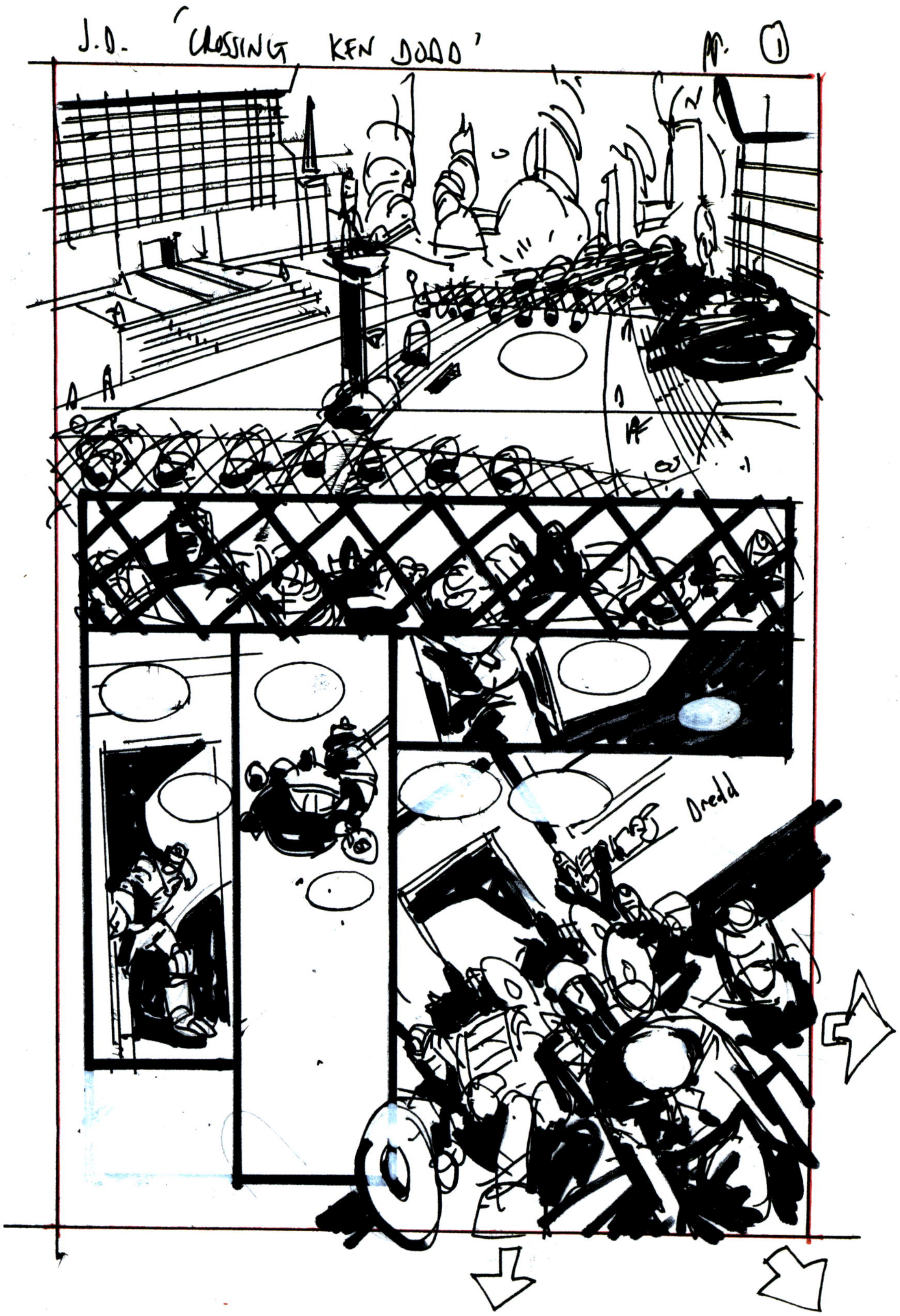
J.D. 'CROSSING KEN DODD'
P. 1
Dredd

 JUDGE DREDD: CROSSING KEN DODD LAYOUT, 2000 AD PROG 1214, 2000

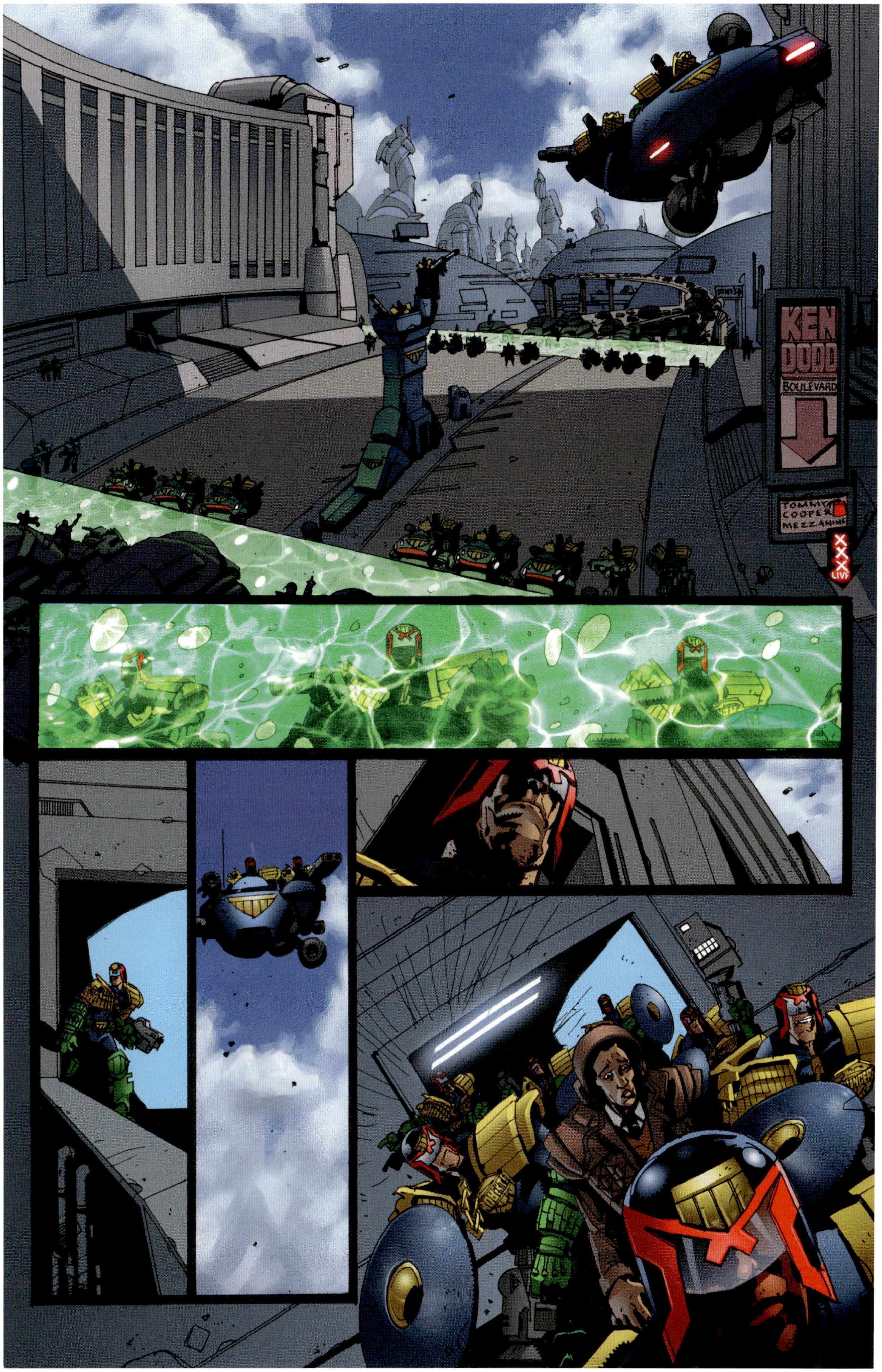
KEN DODD BOULEVARD
TOMMY COOPER MEZZANINE
XXX LIVE

JUDGE DREDD: CROSSING KEN DODD PAGE 1, 2000 AD PROG 1214, 2000
COLOURS BY CHRIS BLYTHE

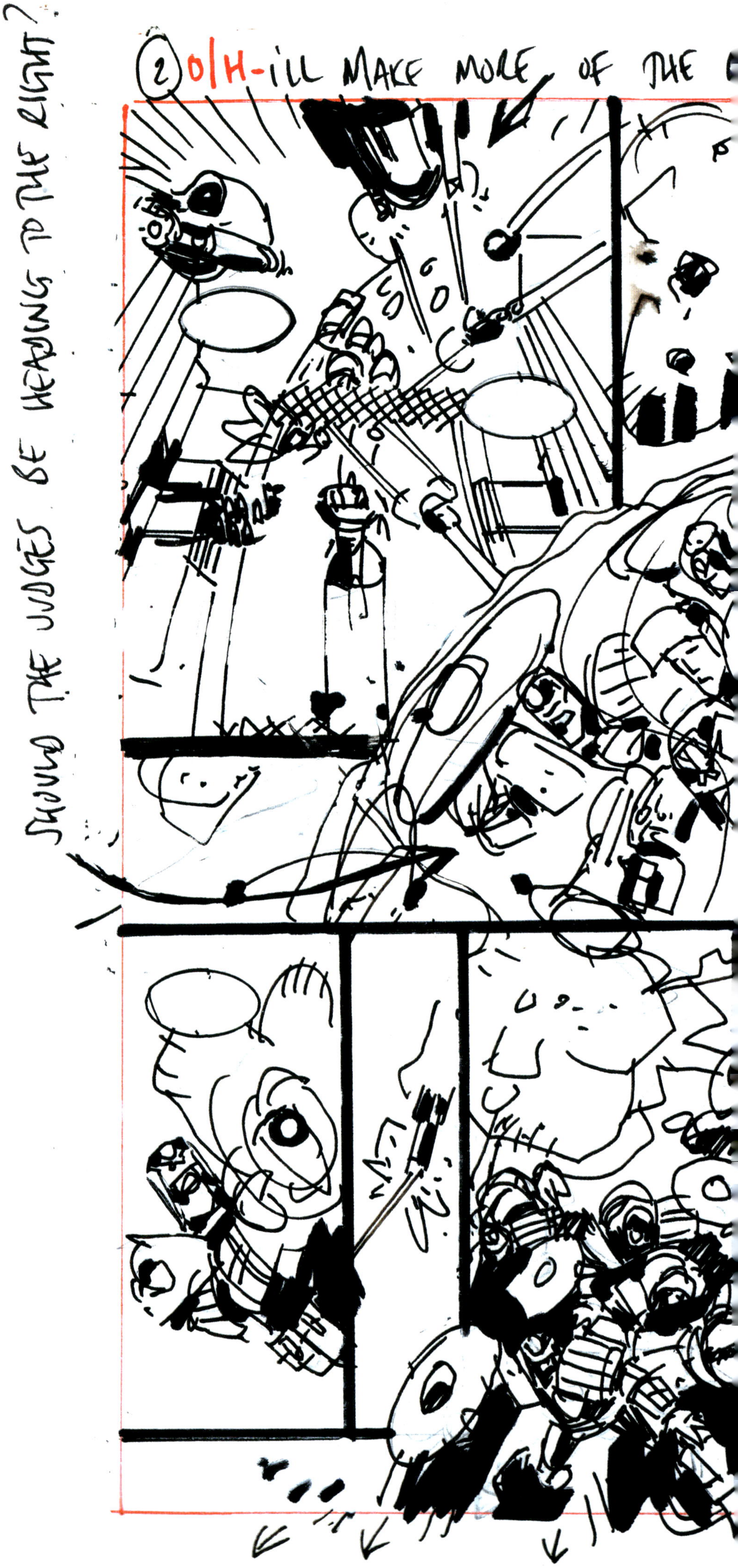
SHOULD THE JUDGES BE HEADING TO THE RIGHT?
2 O/H - ILL MAKE MORE OF THE

JUDGE DREDD: CROSSING KEN DODD LAYOUT, 2000 AD PROG 1214, 2000

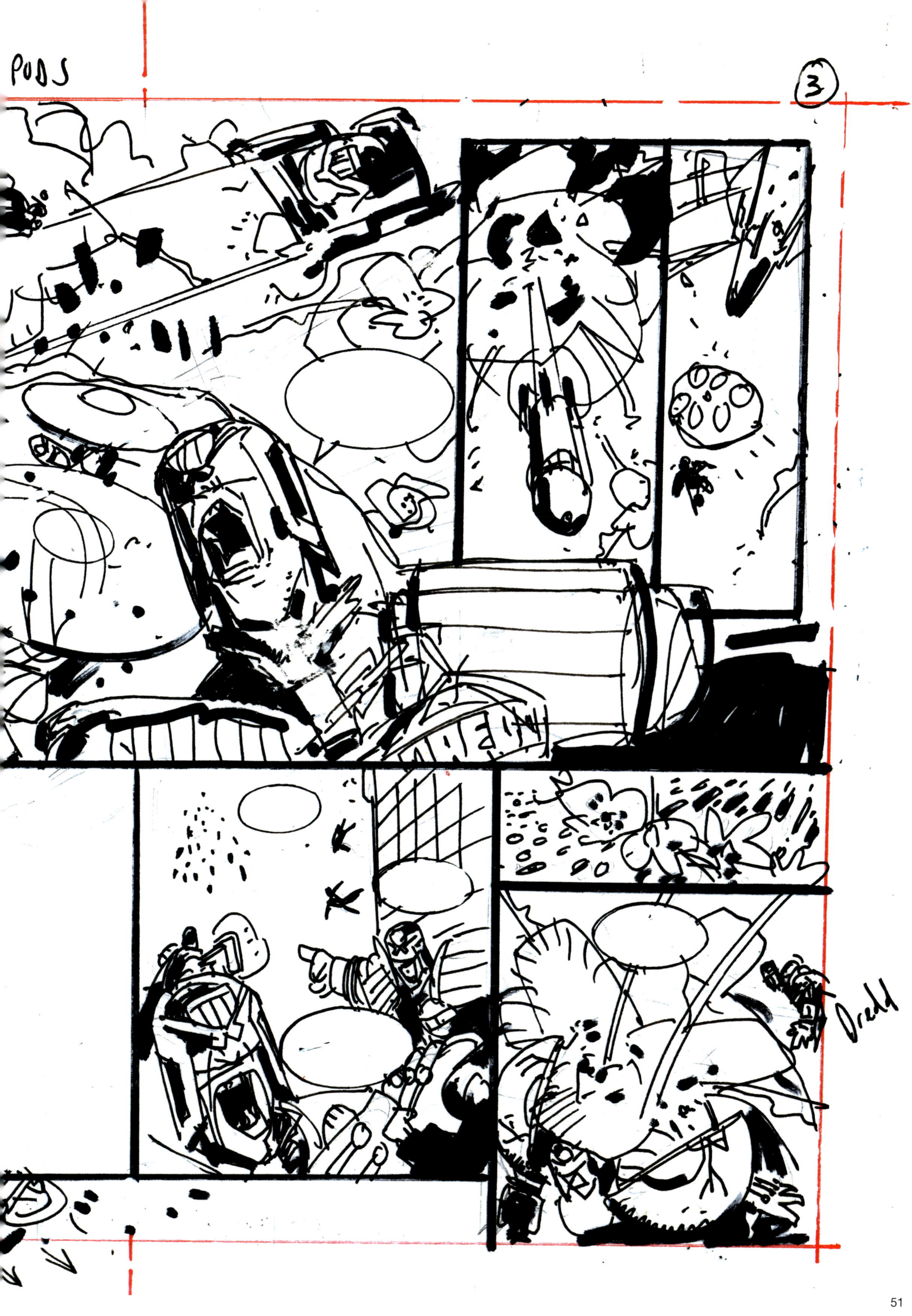
PODS
3
Dredd

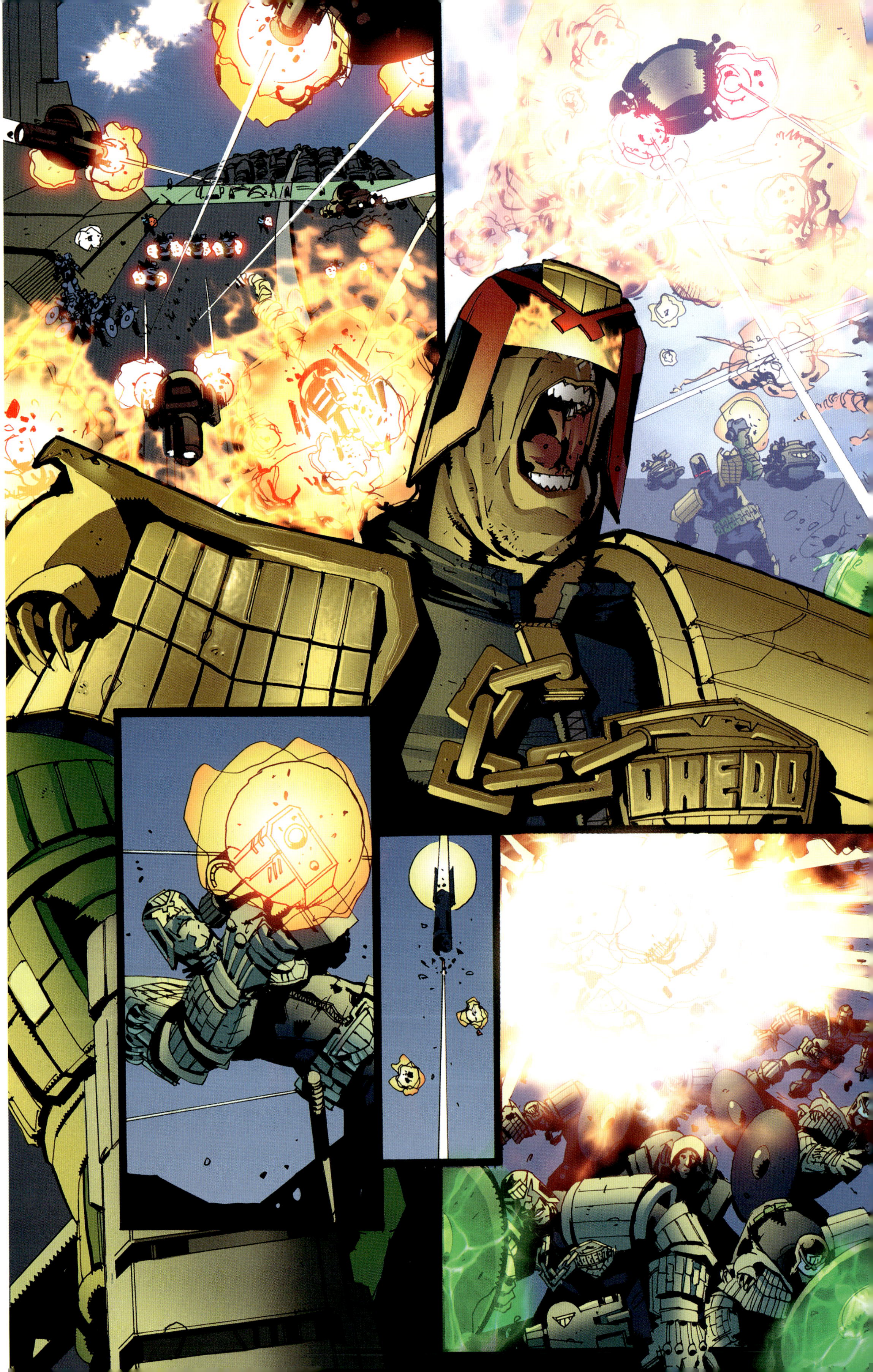
DREDD

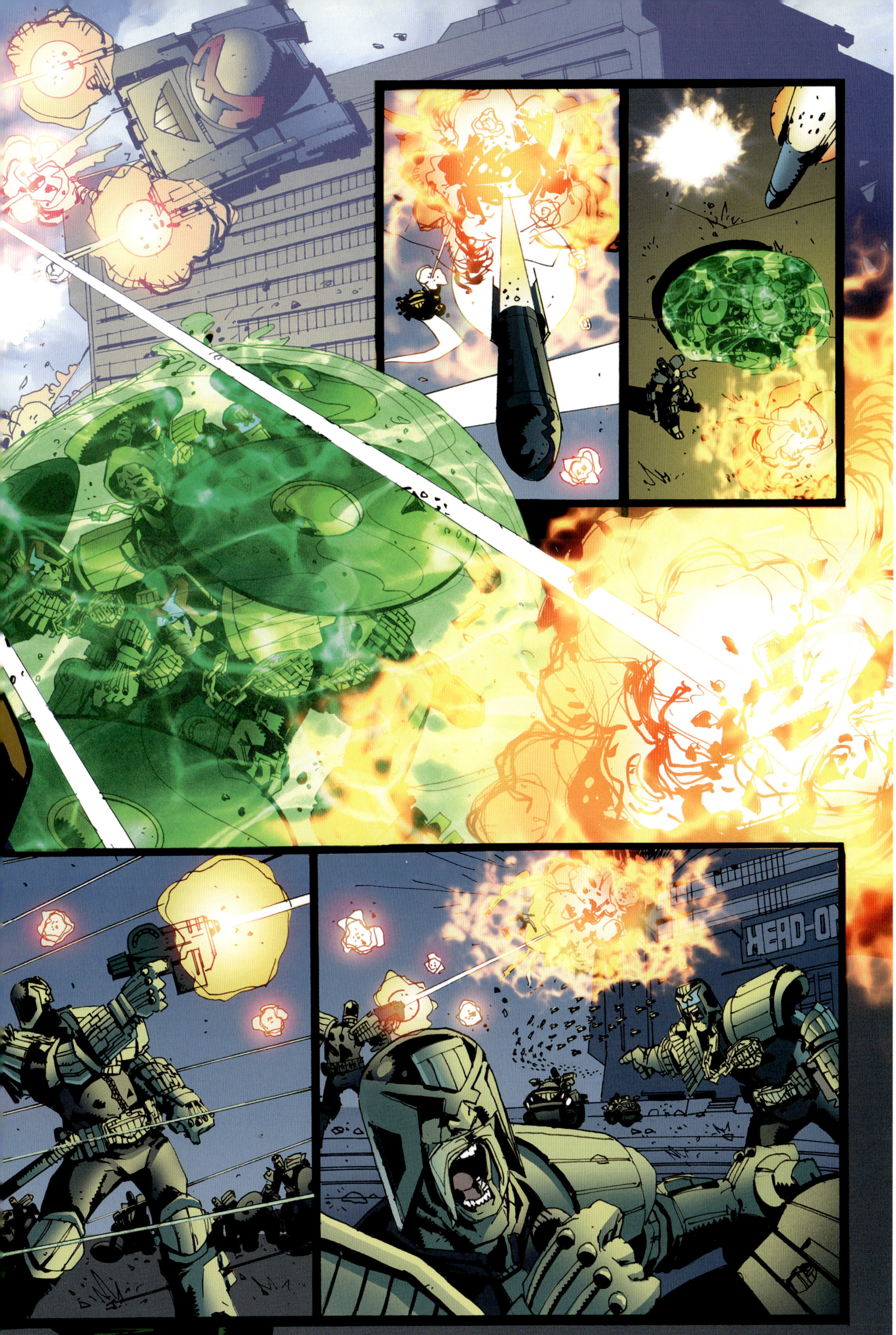

JUDGE DREDD: CROSSING KEN DODD PAGES 2 & 3, 2000 AD PROG 1214, 2000
COLOURS BY CHRIS BLYTHE

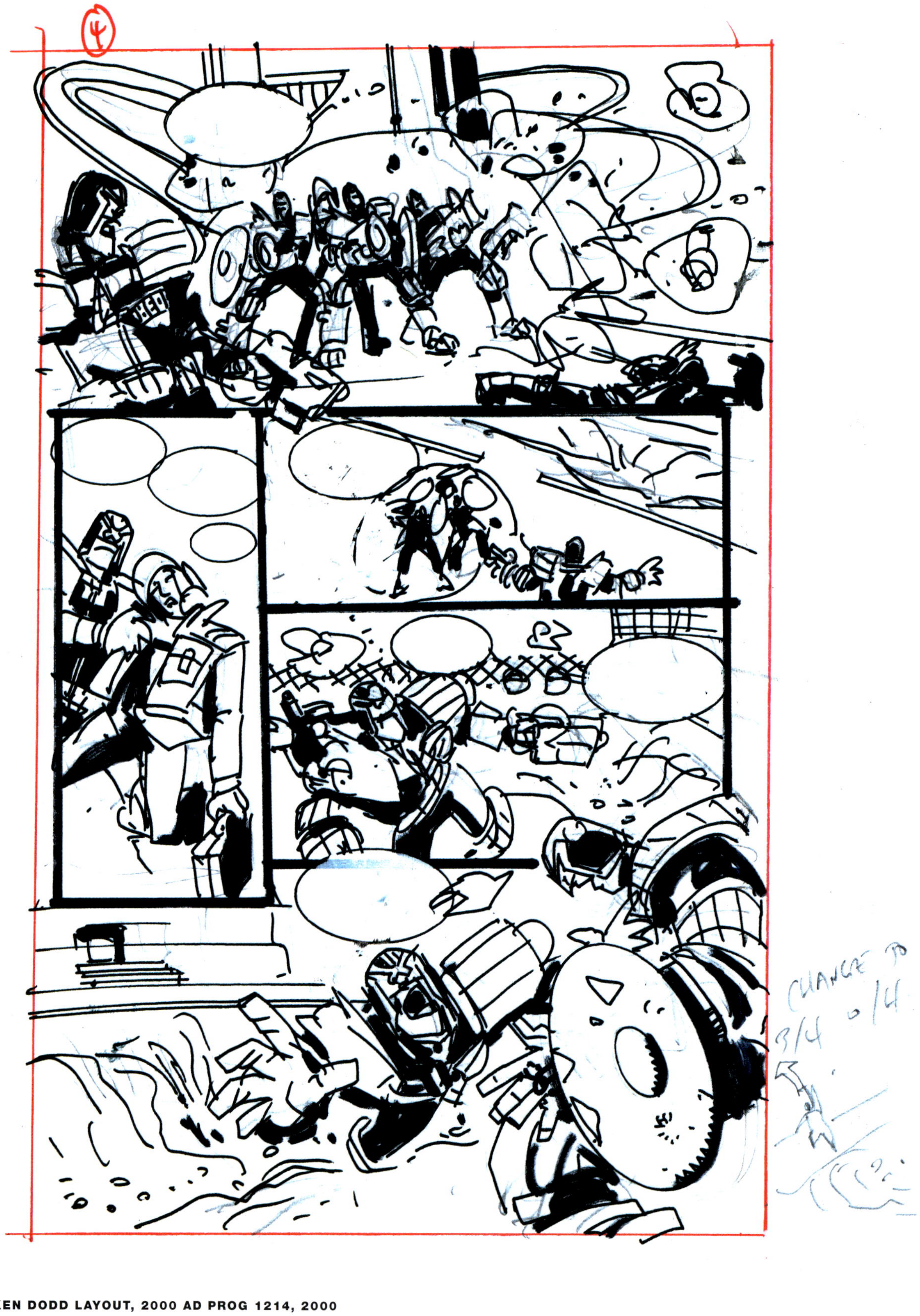
4
CHANGE TO 3/4 o/4

 JUDGE DREDD: CROSSING KEN DODD LAYOUT, 2000 AD PROG 1214, 2000

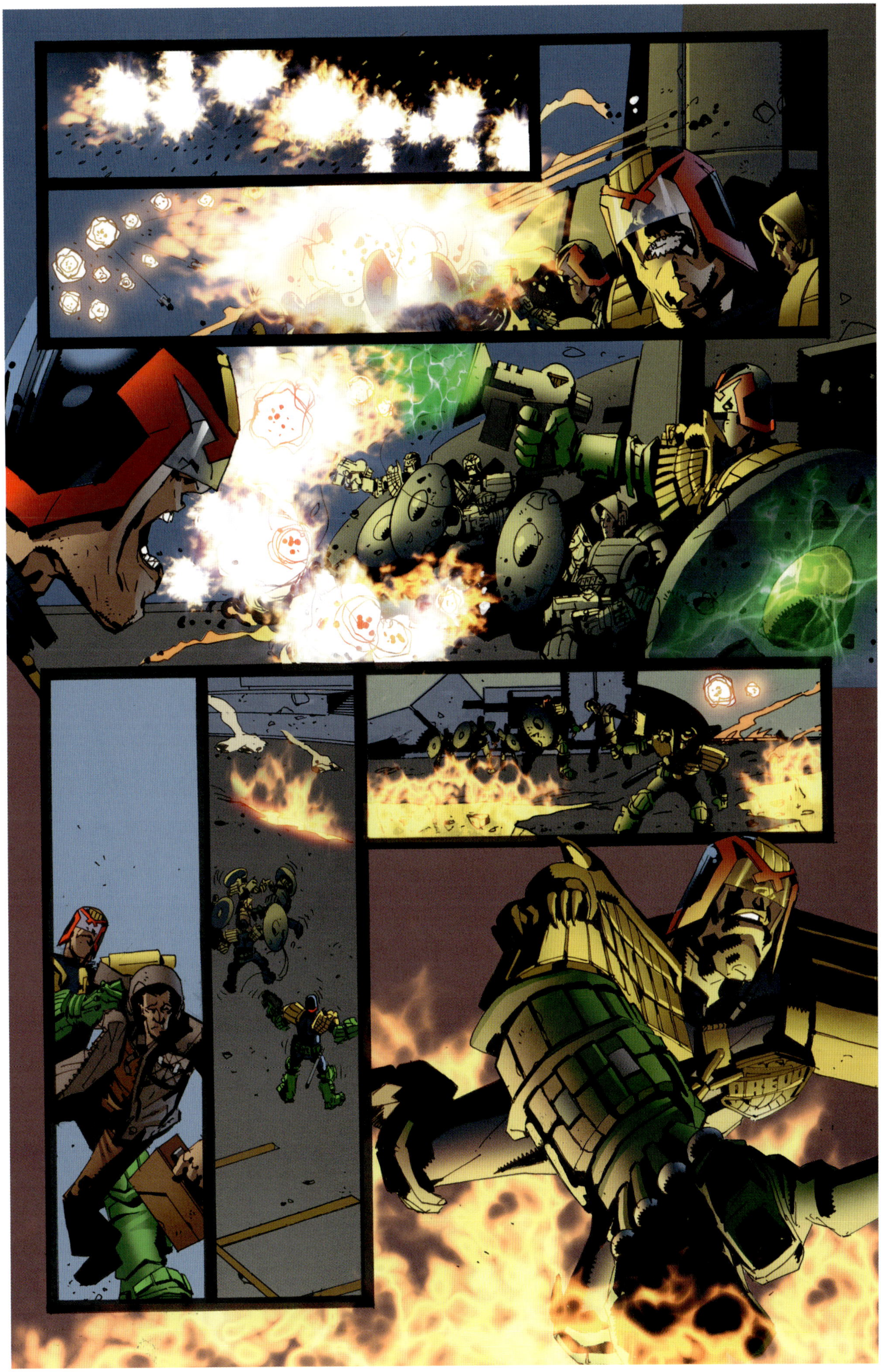

JUDGE DREDD: CROSSING KEN DODD PAGE 4, 2000 AD PROG 1214, 2000
COLOURS BY CHRIS BLYTHE

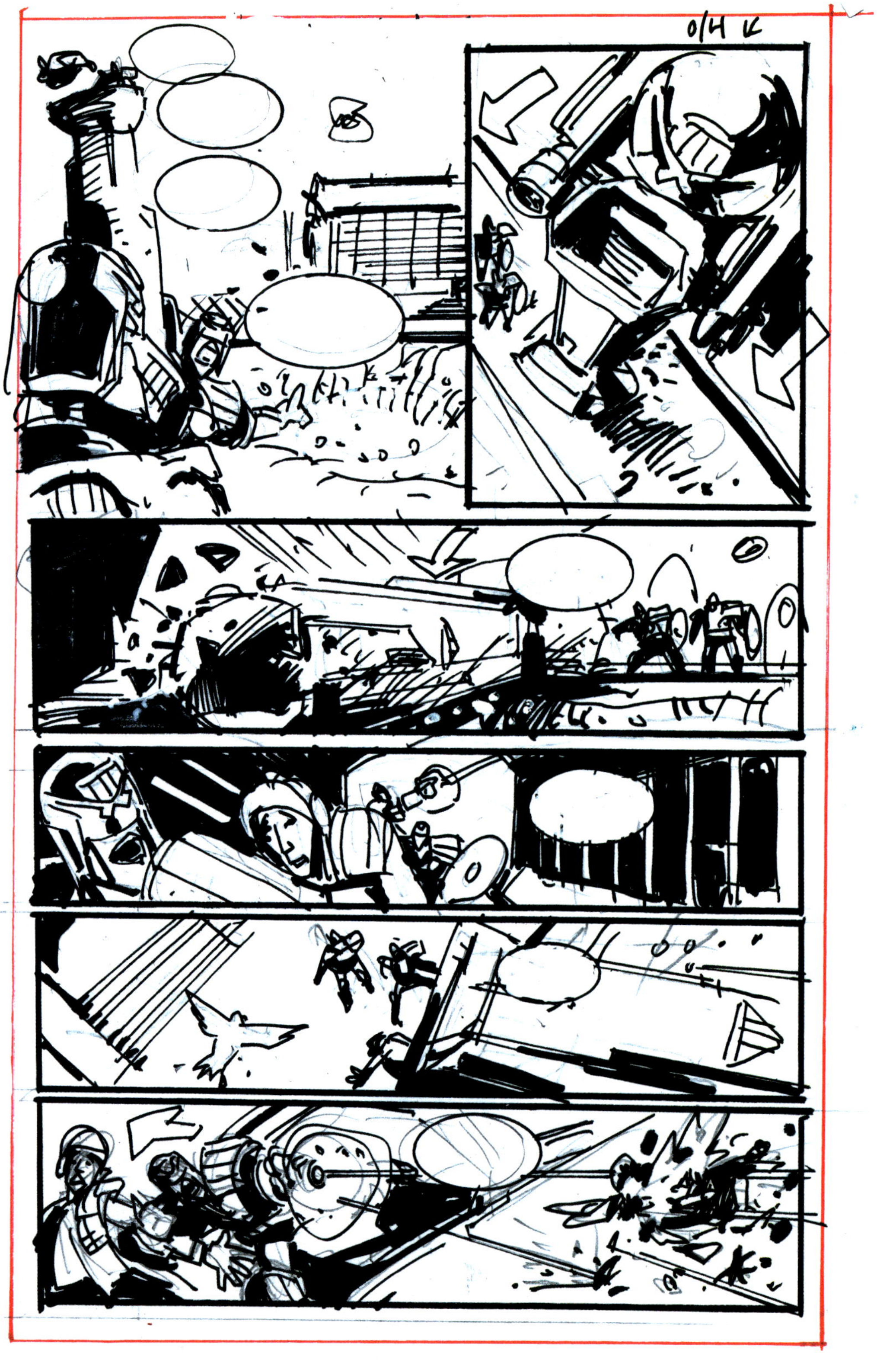

JUDGE DREDD: CROSSING KEN DODD LAYOUT, 2000 AD PROG 1214, 2000

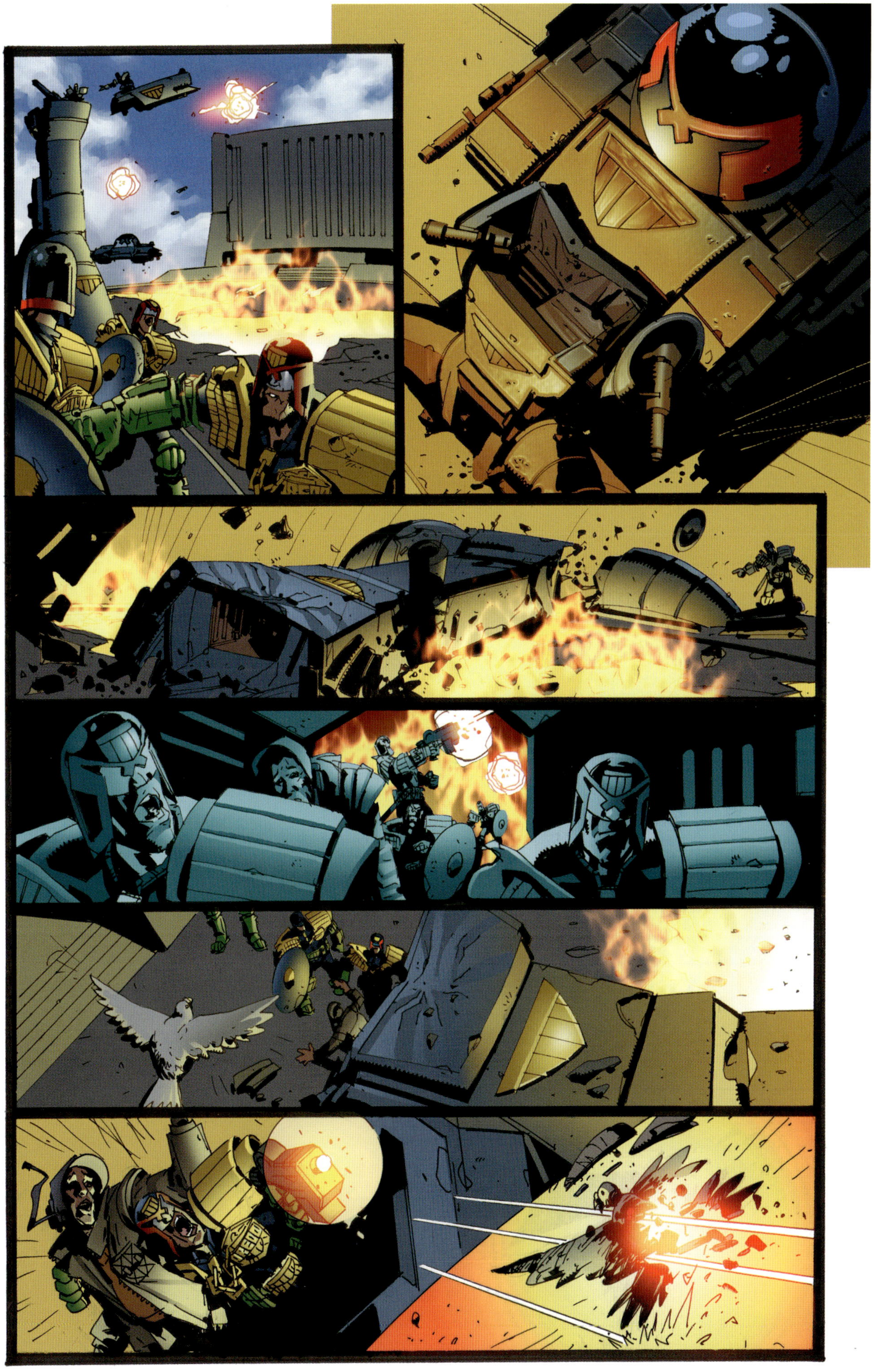

JUDGE DREDD: CROSSING KEN DODD PAGE 5, 2000 AD PROG 1214, 2000
COLOURS BY CHRIS BLYTHE

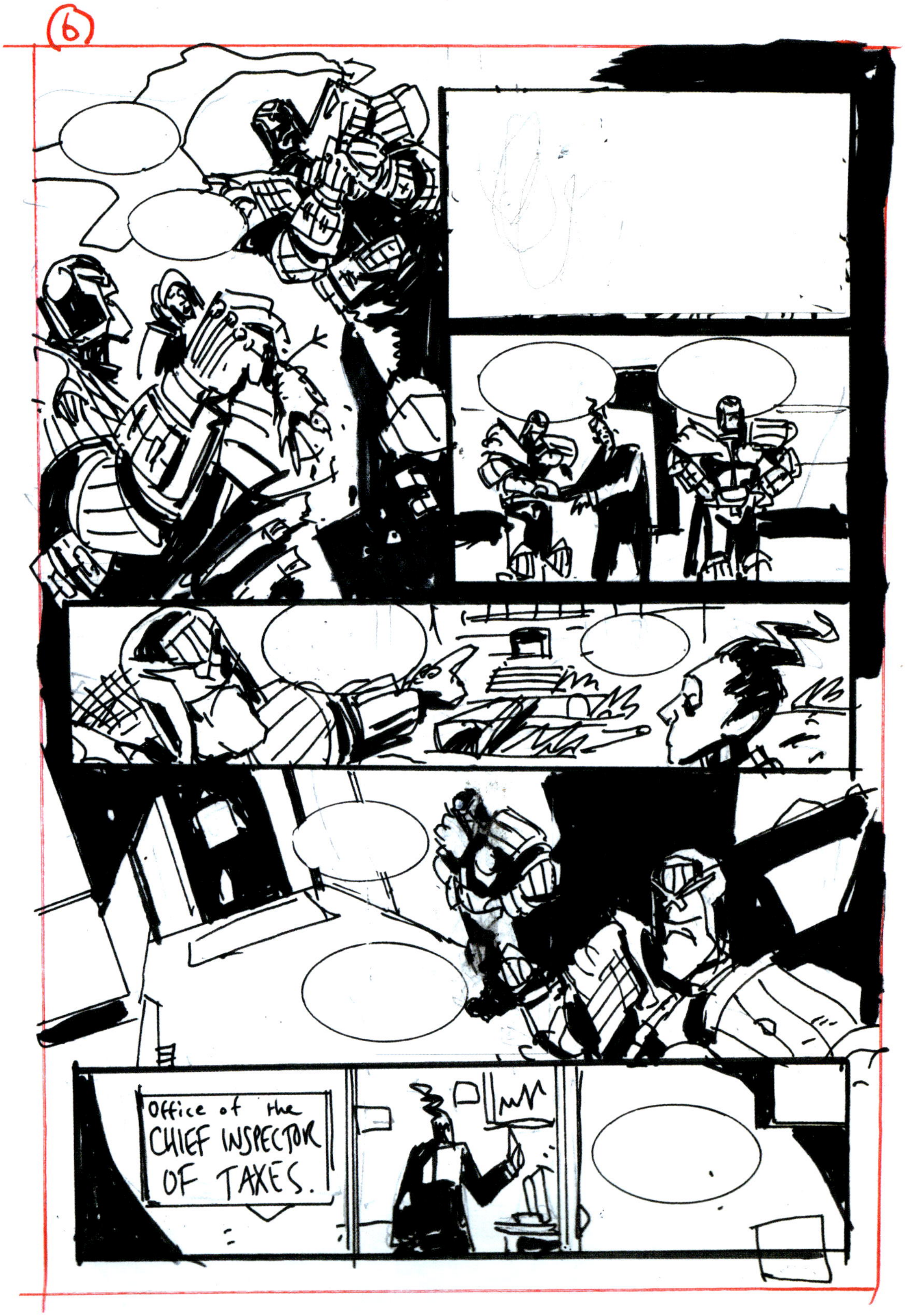
6
Office of the
CHIEF INSPECTOR
OF TAXES.

 JUDGE DREDD: CROSSING KEN DODD LAYOUT, 2000 AD PROG 1214, 2000

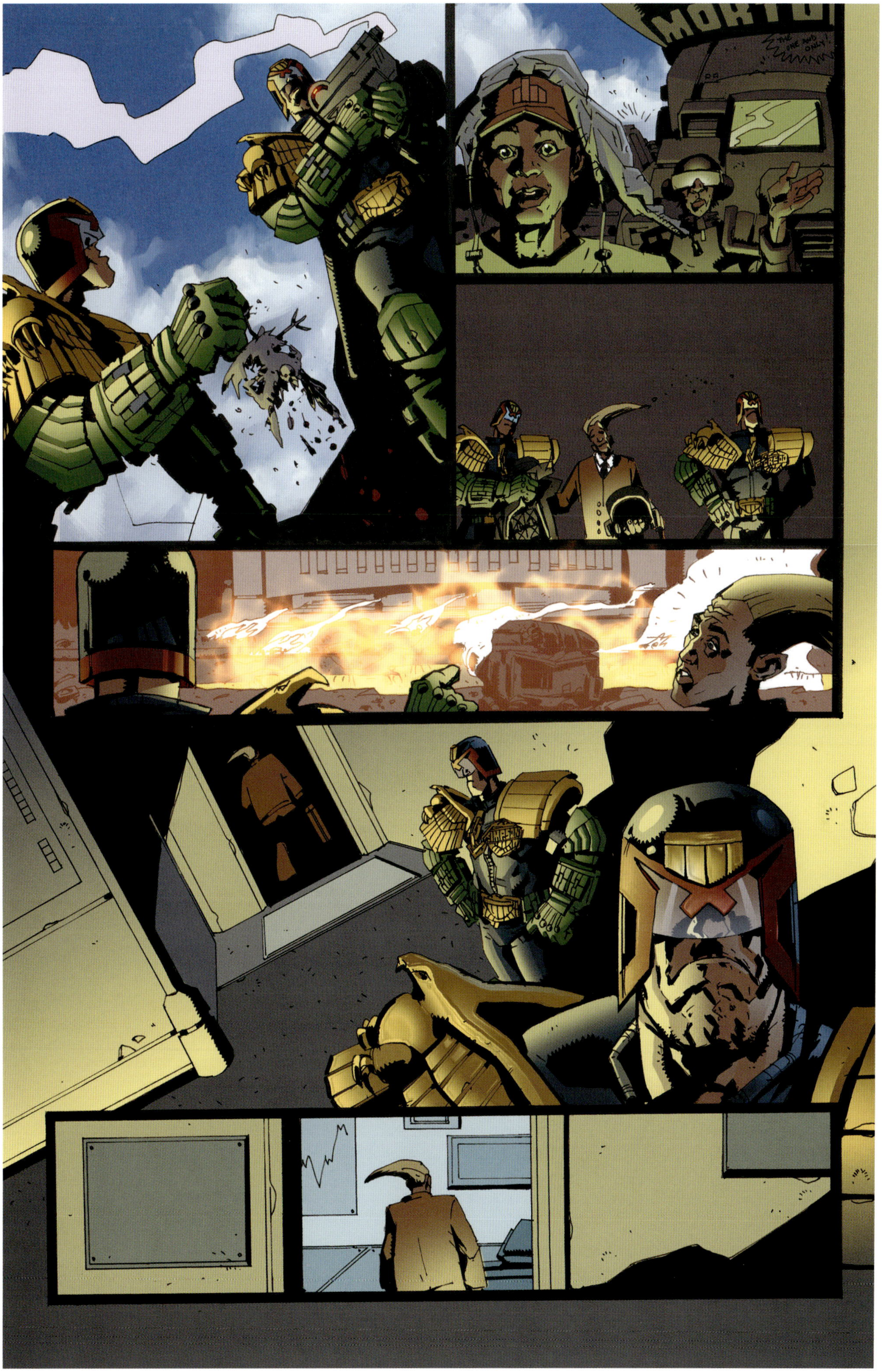
MORTO
THE ONE AND ONLY!
SIMPSON

JUDGE DREDD: CROSSING KEN DODD PAGE 6, 2000 AD PROG 1214, 2000
COLOURS BY CHRIS BLYTHE

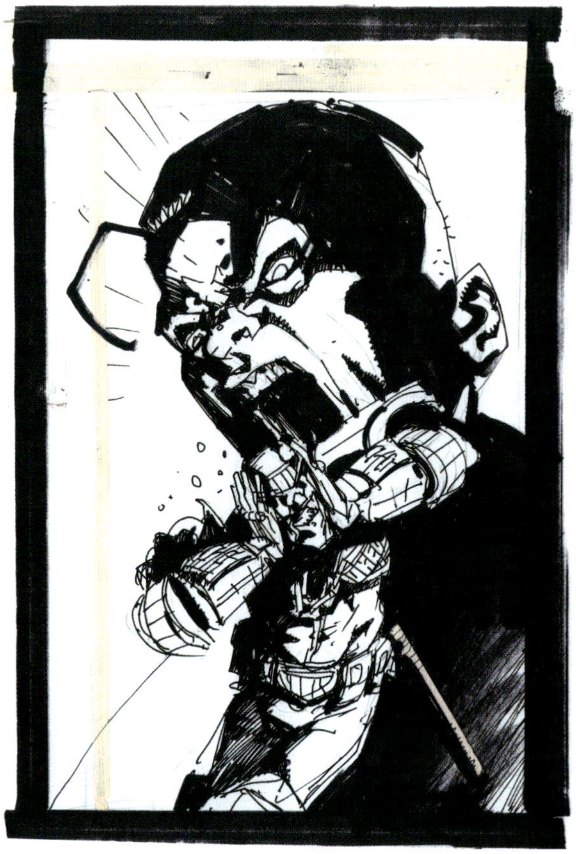

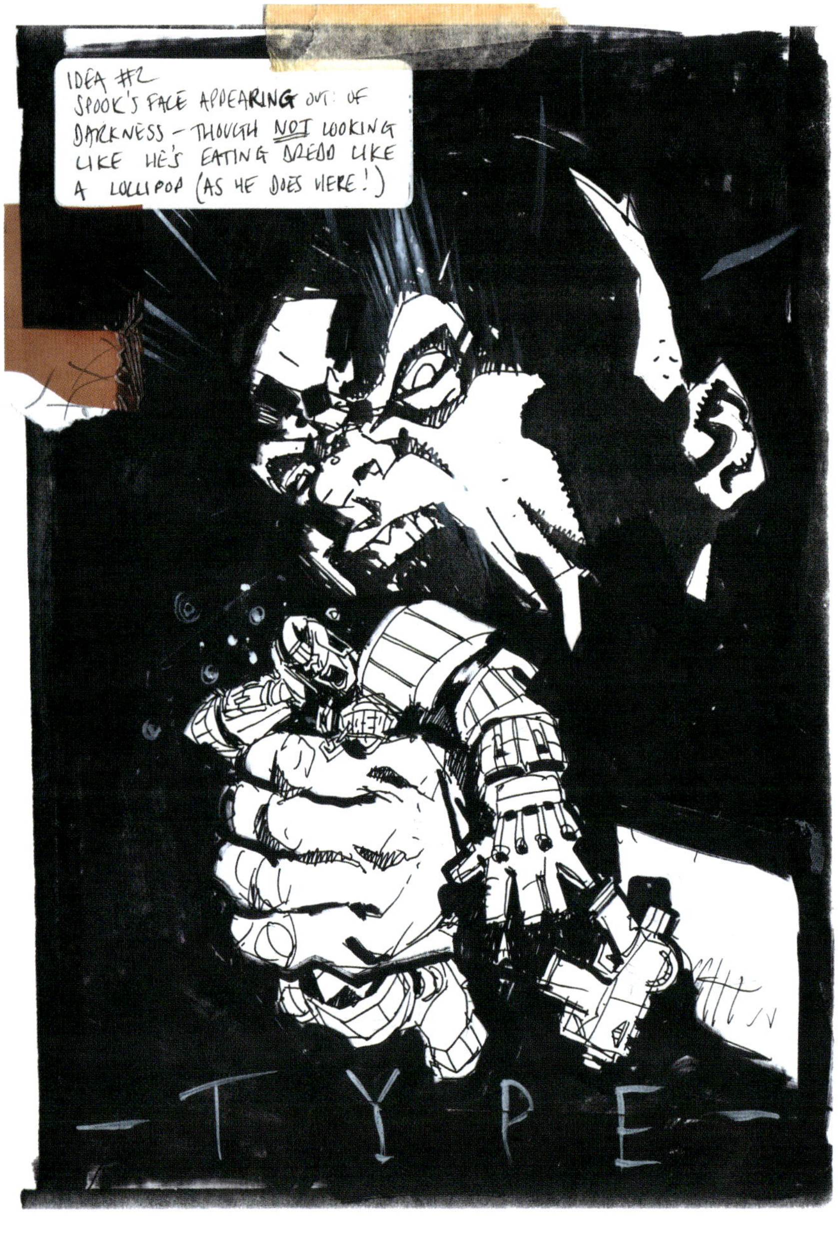
IDEA #2
SPOOK'S FACE APPEARING OUT OF
DARKNESS – THOUGH NOT LOOKING
LIKE HE'S EATING DREDD LIKE
A LOLLIPOP (AS HE DOES HERE!)
TYPE

 2000 AD PROG 1227 COVER, 2001

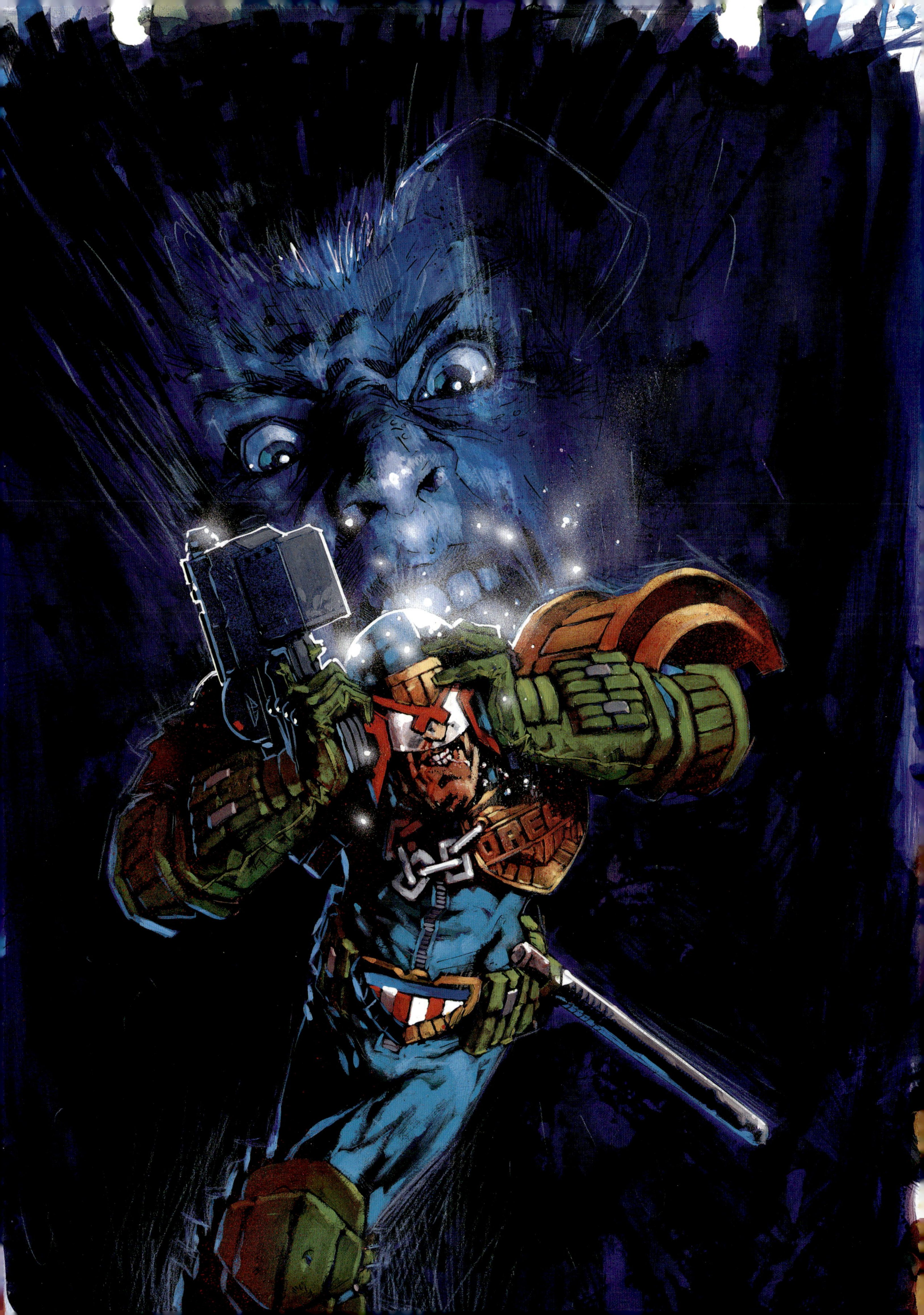

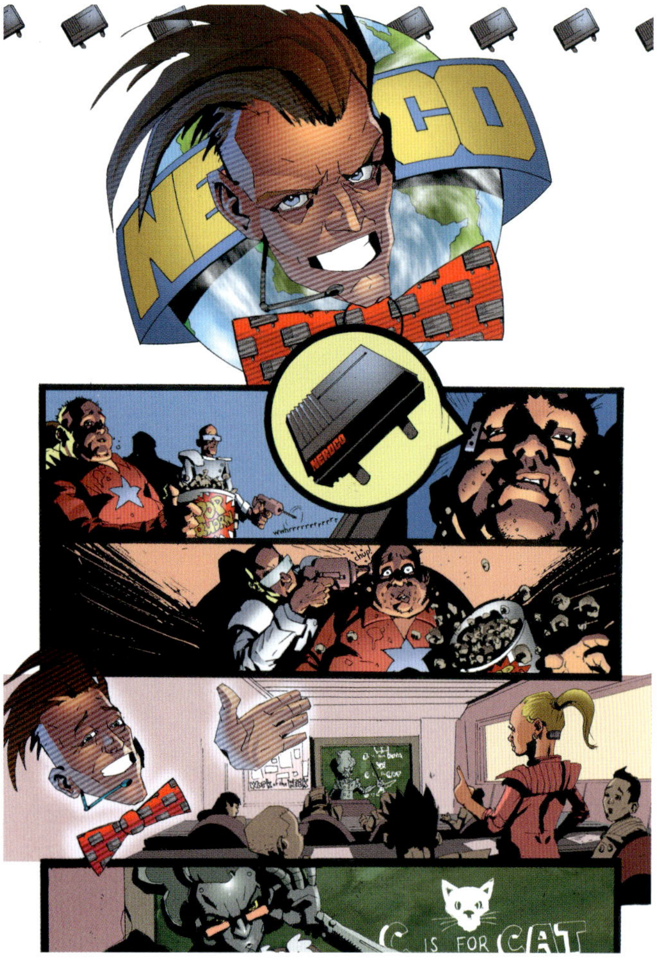
NERCO
C IS FOR CAT

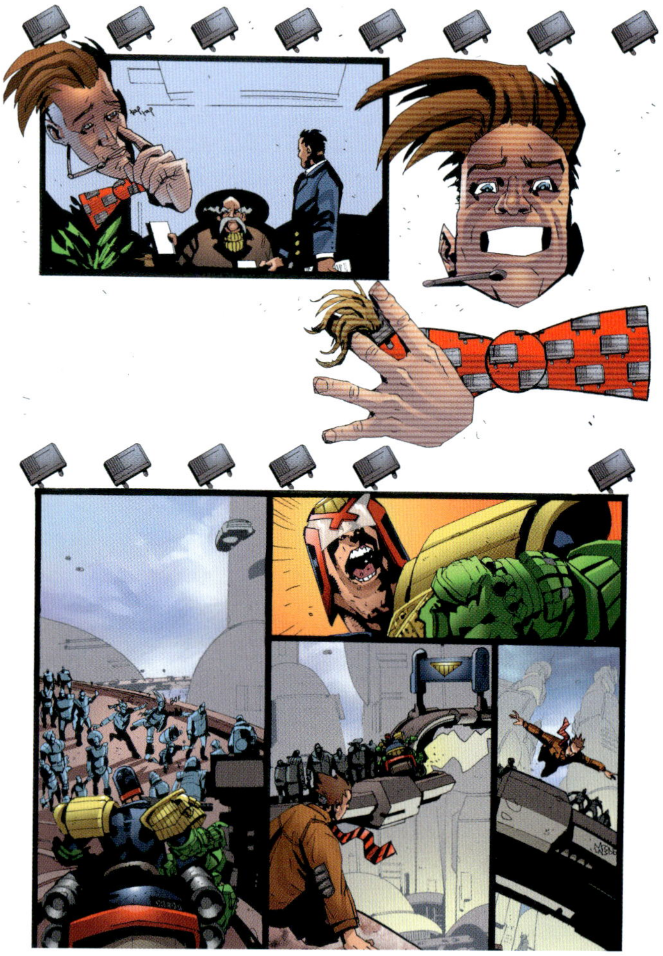

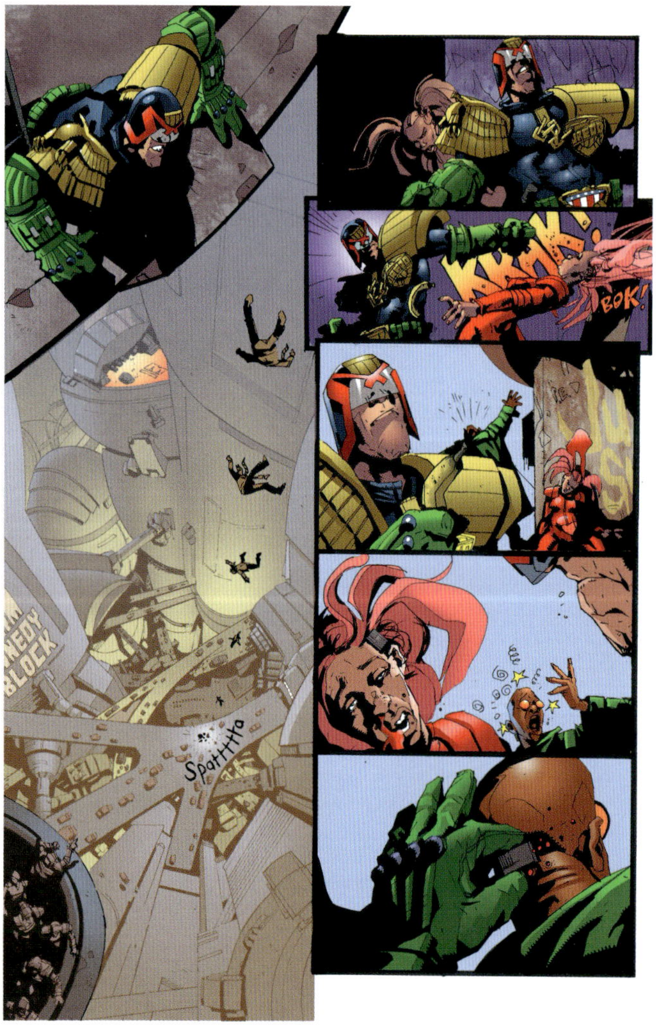
BOK!

JUDGE DREDD: RAMPOTS PAGES 1, 2, 3, 2000 AD PROG 1231, 2001
COLOURS BY CHRIS BLYTHE

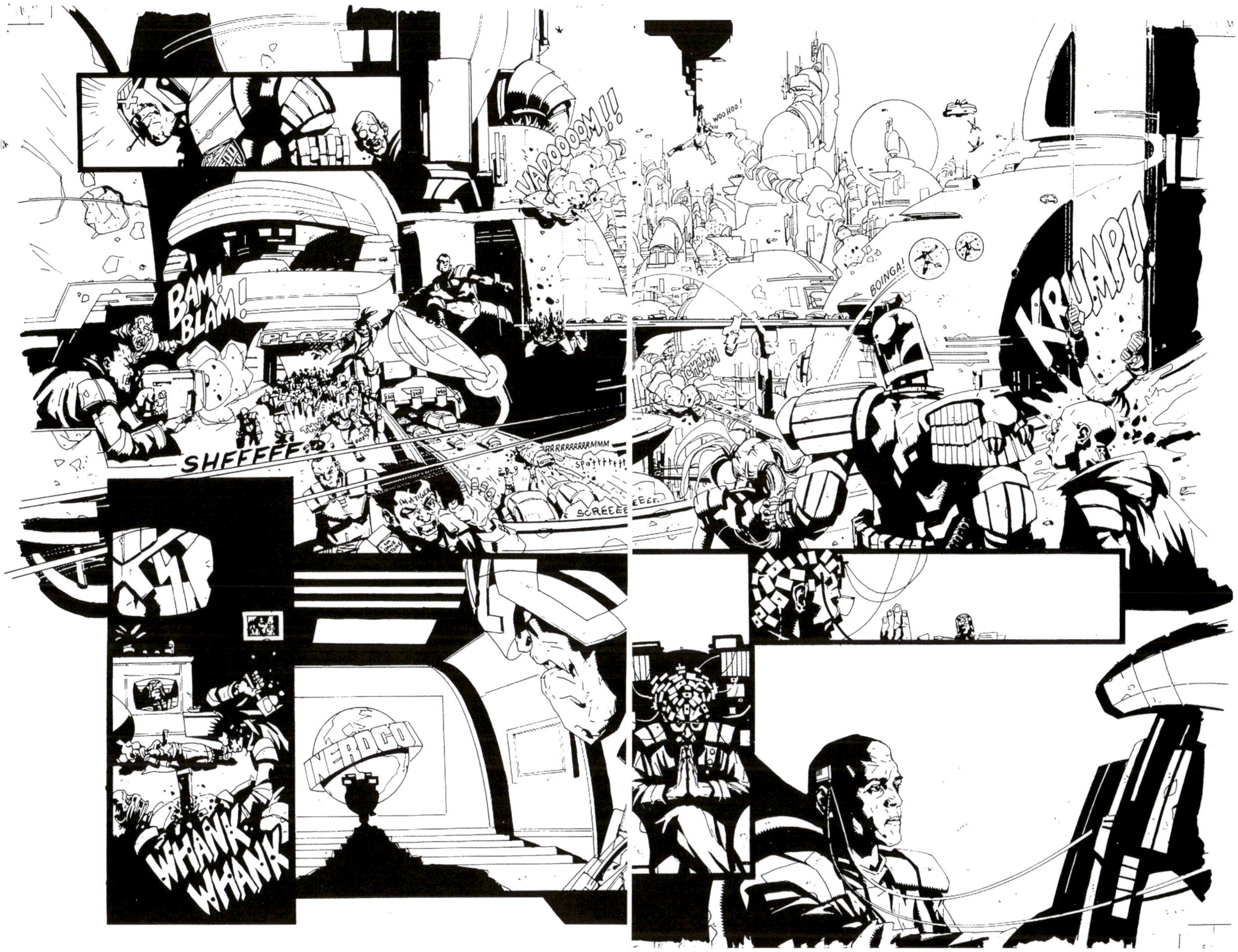
BAM!
BLAM!
VADOOOOM!!
SHFFFFF
BOINGA!
KRUMP!!
NERDCO
WHANK
WHANK

RAMPOTS

'Every single comics page has been drawn with a Rotring Art Pen. We talk about how every image starts with a line – every line on every page has been drawn with one of those. It's a fountain pen so you can see the ink sit on the paper just for a second before it soaks in- it feels more alive and vibrant to me. A lot of artists in comics use technical pens with tiny fine nibs, but I can't bear them. The only thing that's changed is, more recently, I've started using fat marker pens, which bring more texture rather than the more solid blacks and whites I've used in the past. I also use a dry brush, where the gradiated lines bring a bit more depth to the images, which I really enjoy.'

—JOCK

JUDGE DREDD: RAMPOTS INKS PAGES 4 & 5, 2000 AD PROG 1231, 2001

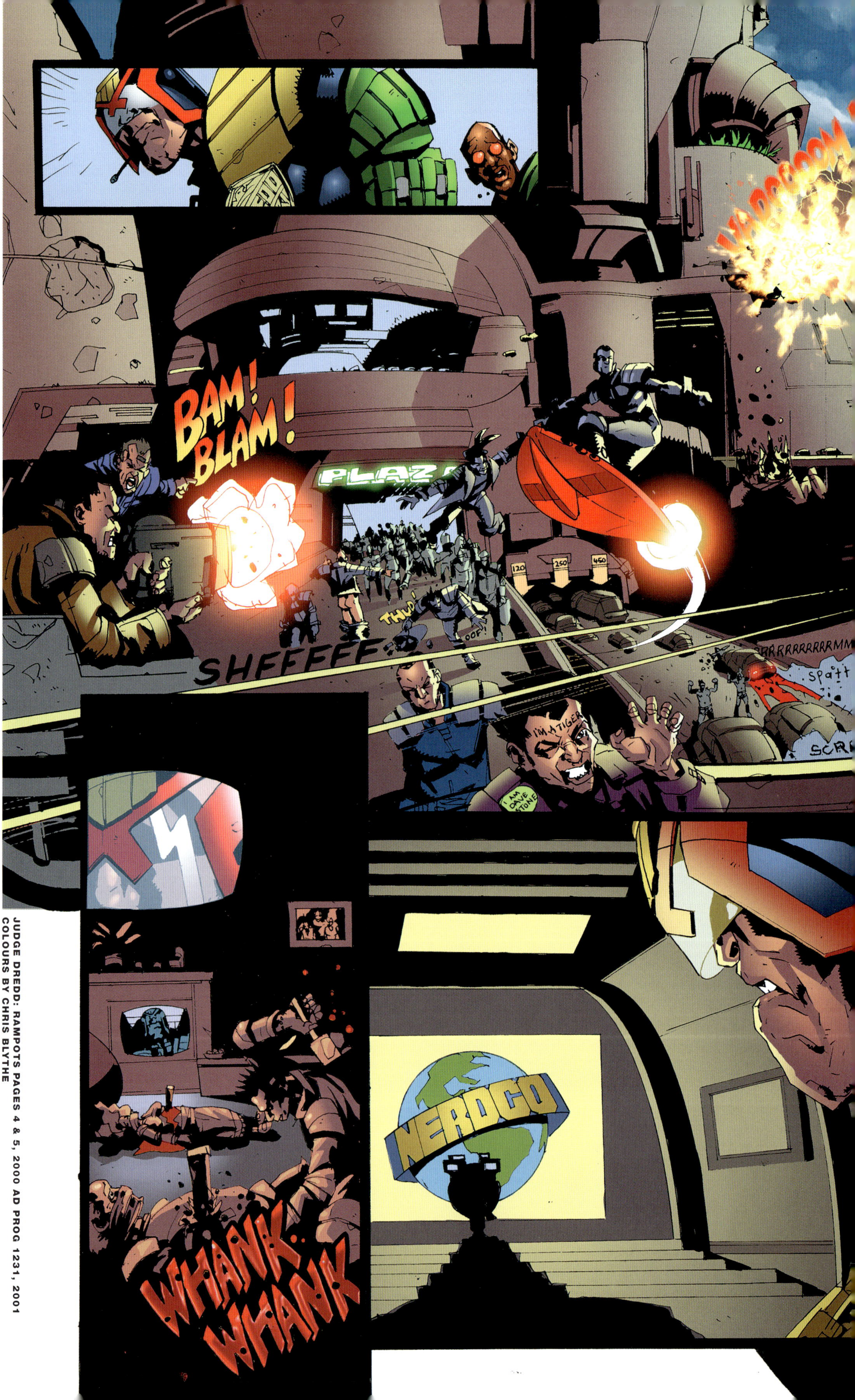
BAM! BLAM!
120
250
450
THUD!
OOF!
SHFFFFF
spatt
I'M A TIGER
I AM DAVE STONE
NERDCO
WHANK WHANK

JUDGE DREDD: RAMPOTS PAGES 4 & 5, 2000 AD PROG 1231, 2001
COLOURS BY CHRIS BLYTHE

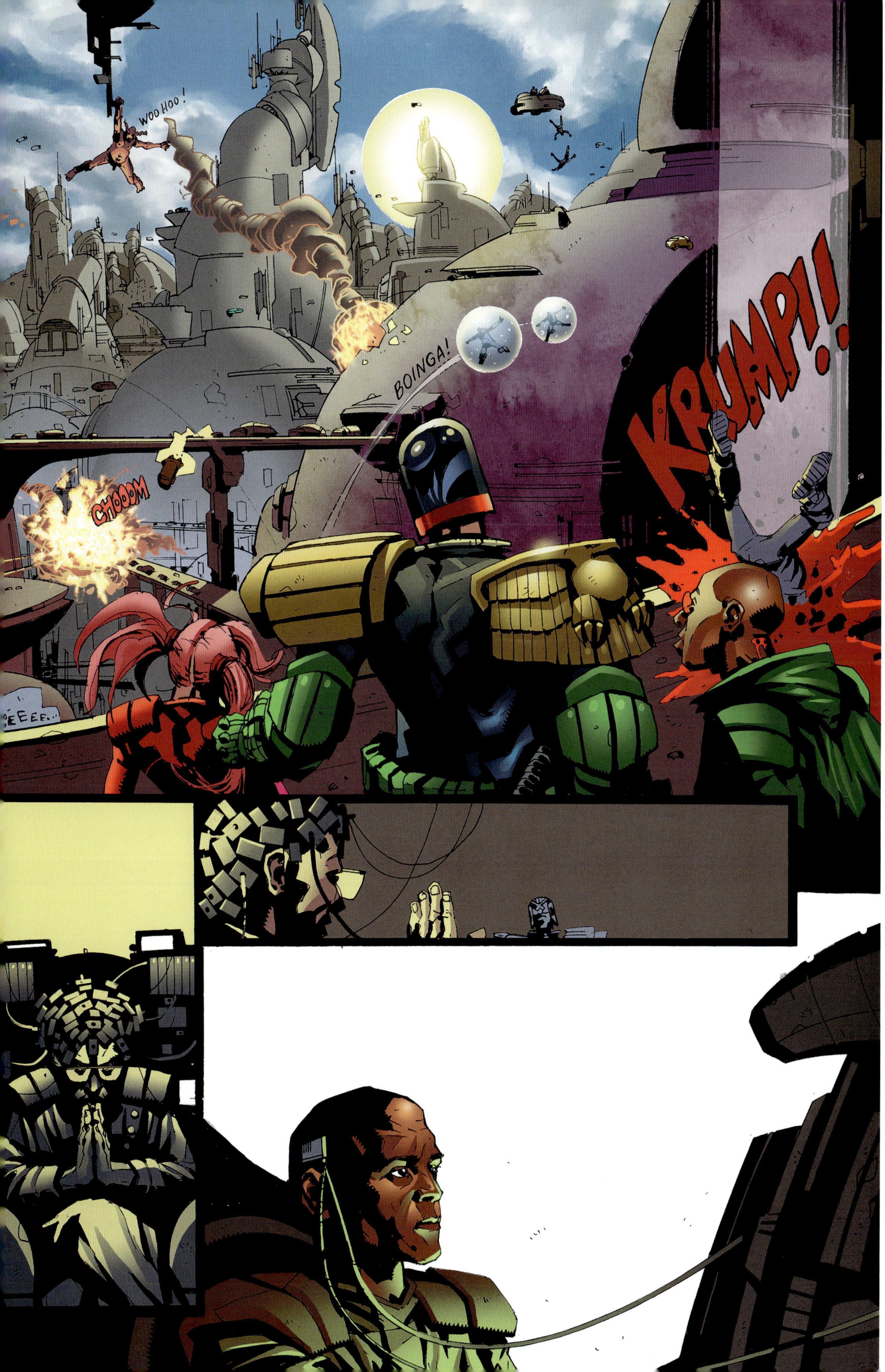
WOO HOO!
BOINGA!
KRUMP!!
CHOOOM
EEEE..

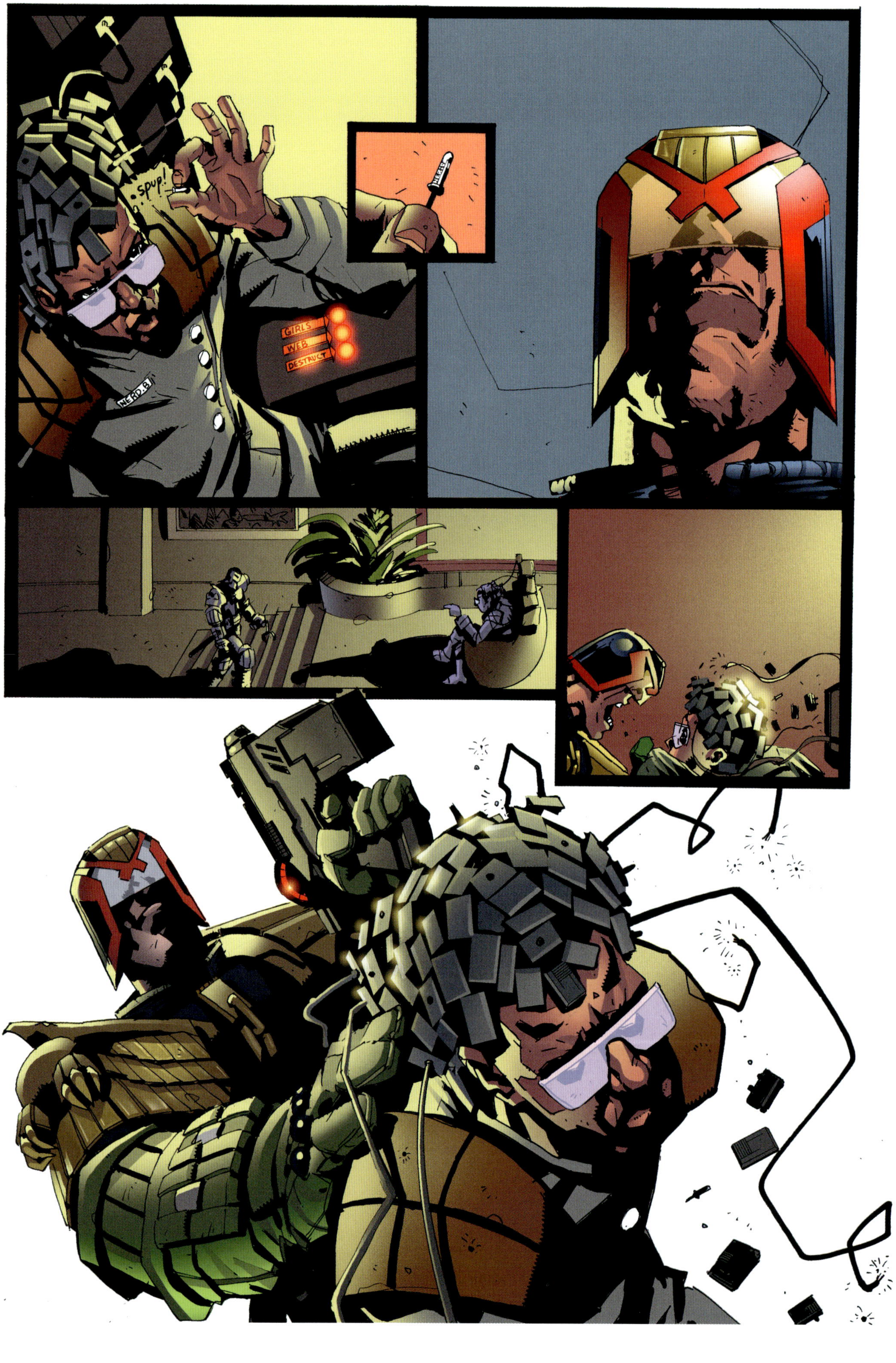

spup!
GIRLS
WEB
DESTRUCT

JUDGE DREDD: RAMPOTS PAGE 6, 2000 AD PROG 1231, 2001
COLOURS BY CHRIS BLYTHE

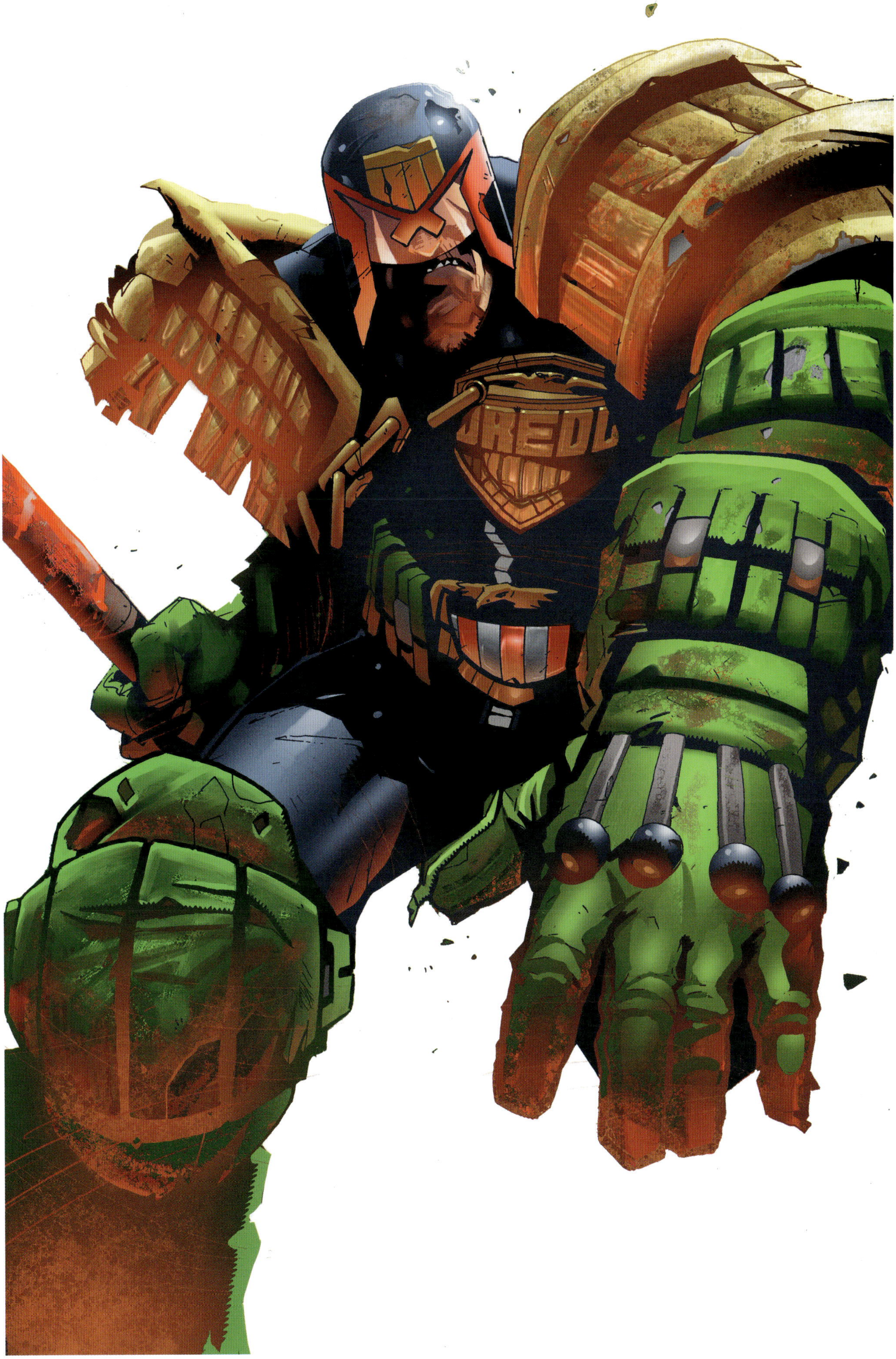

2000 AD PROG 1258 COVER, 2001

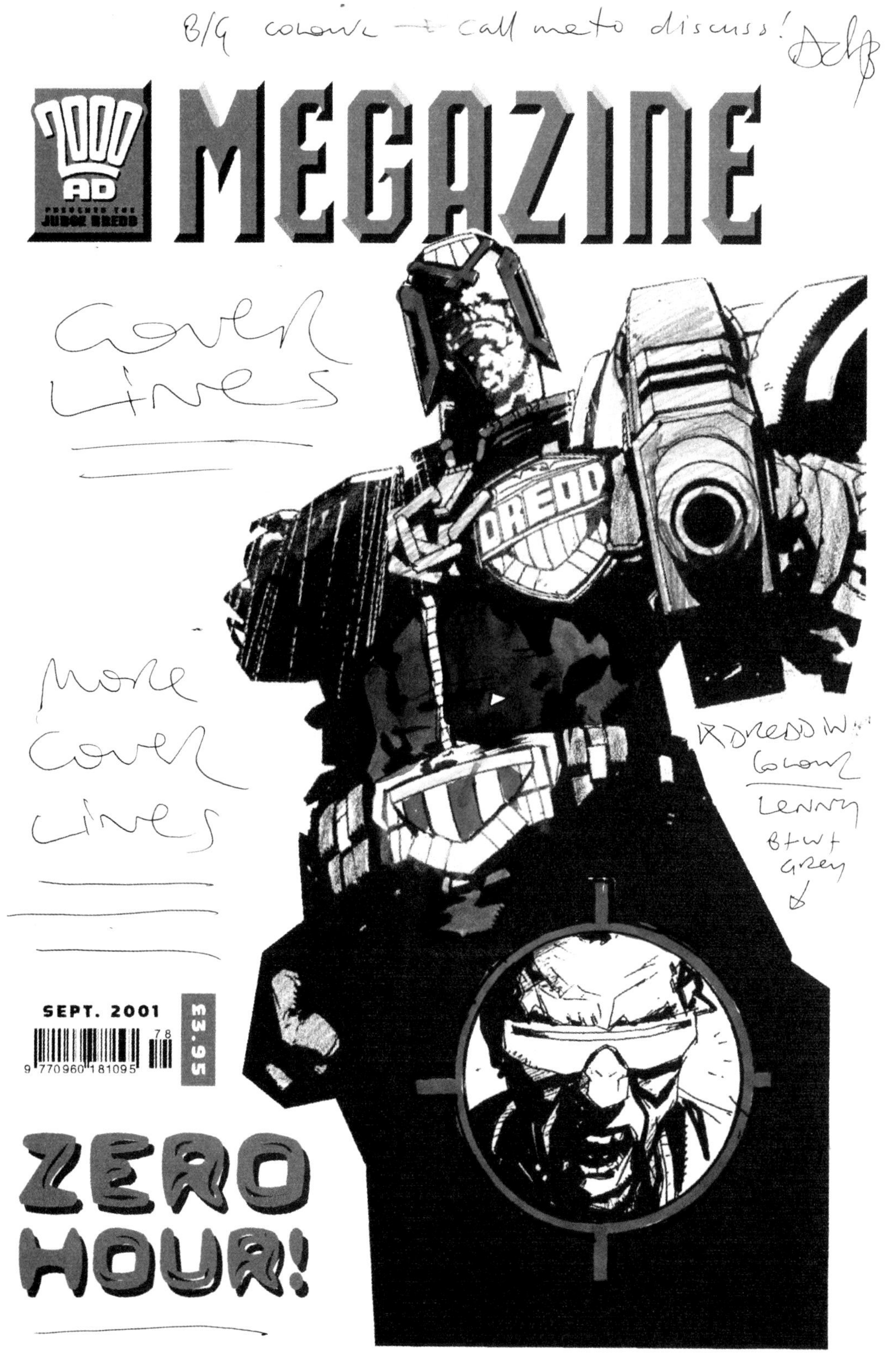
2000 AD
MEGAZINE
COVER LINES
MORE COVER LINES
DREDD
SEPT. 2001
£3.95
ZERO HOUR!

 JUDGE DREDD MEGAZINE 4.02 COVER, 2001

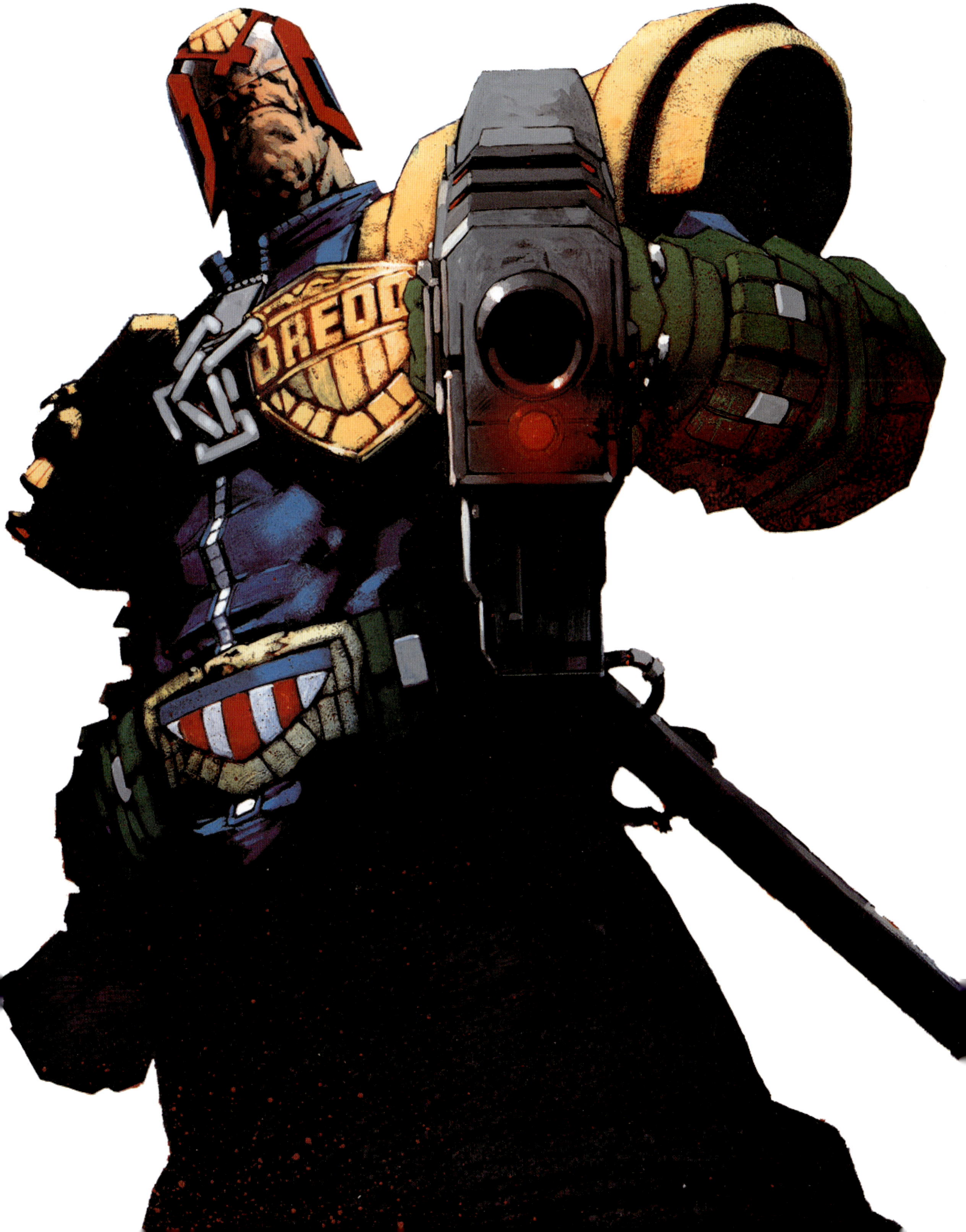
DREDD

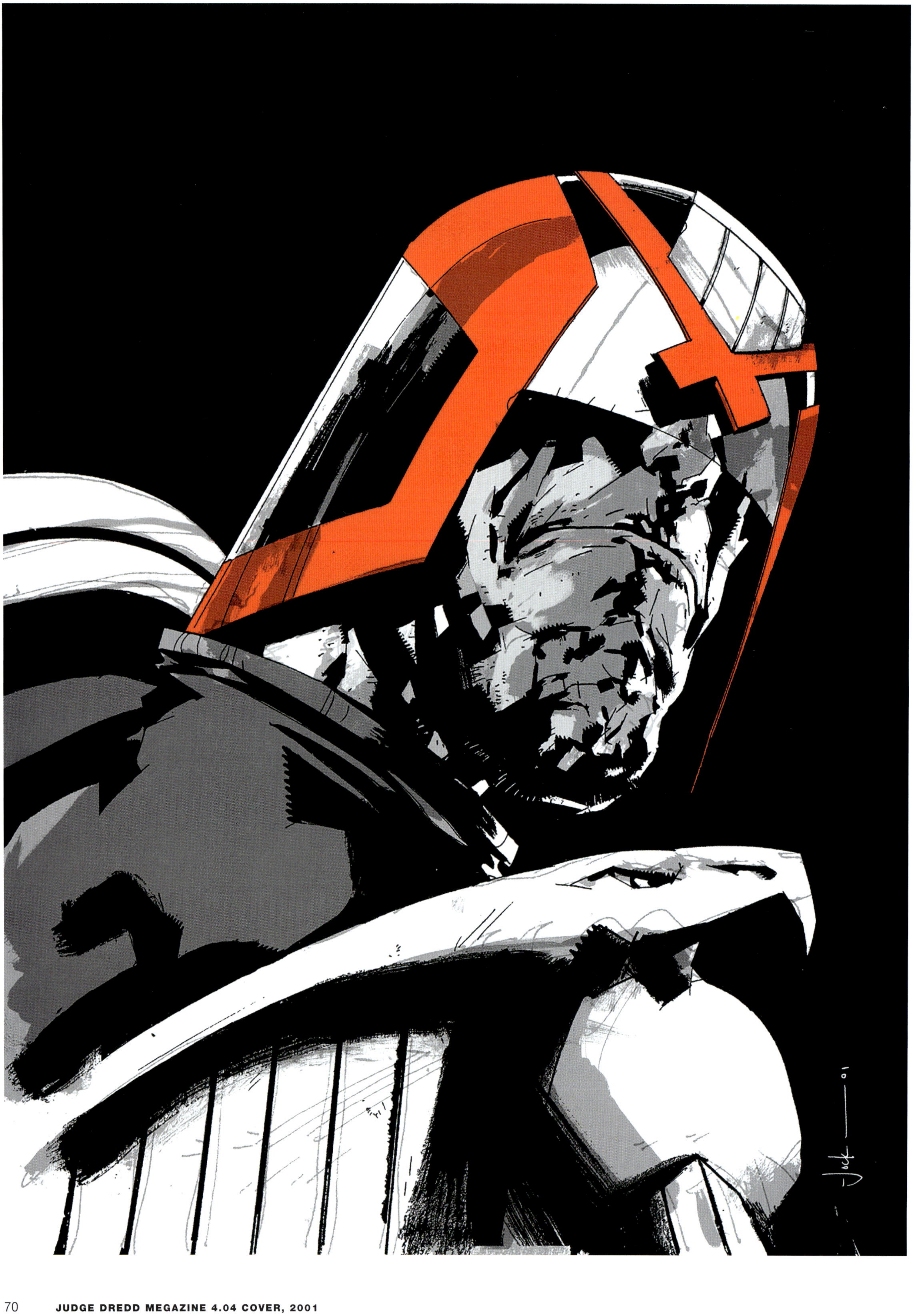

 JUDGE DREDD MEGAZINE 4.04 COVER, 2001

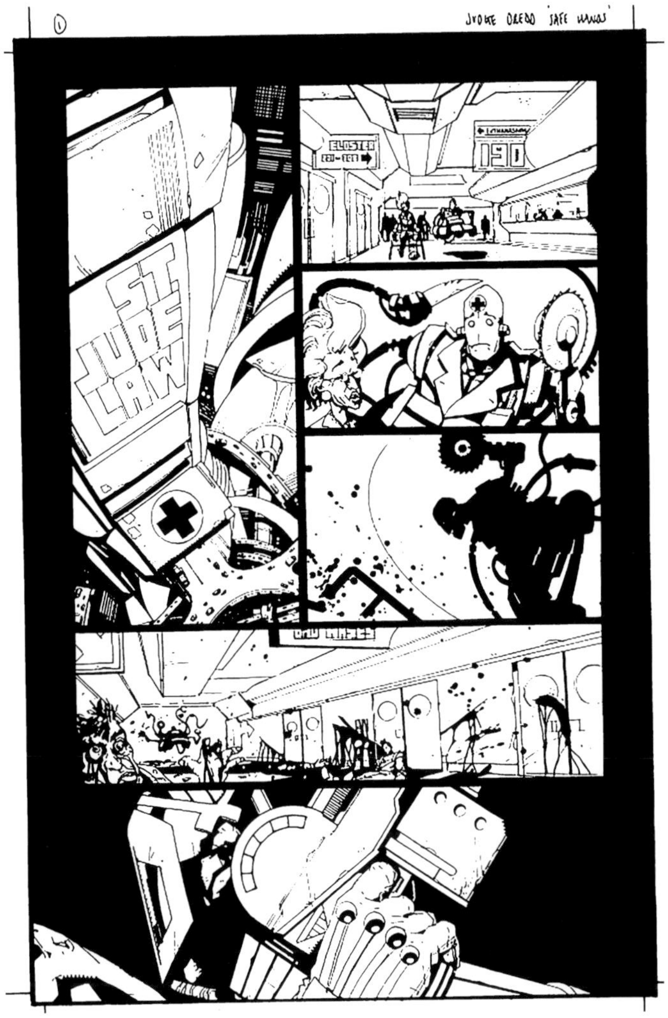
JUDGE DREDD 'SAFE HANDS'
190
ST JUDE LAW

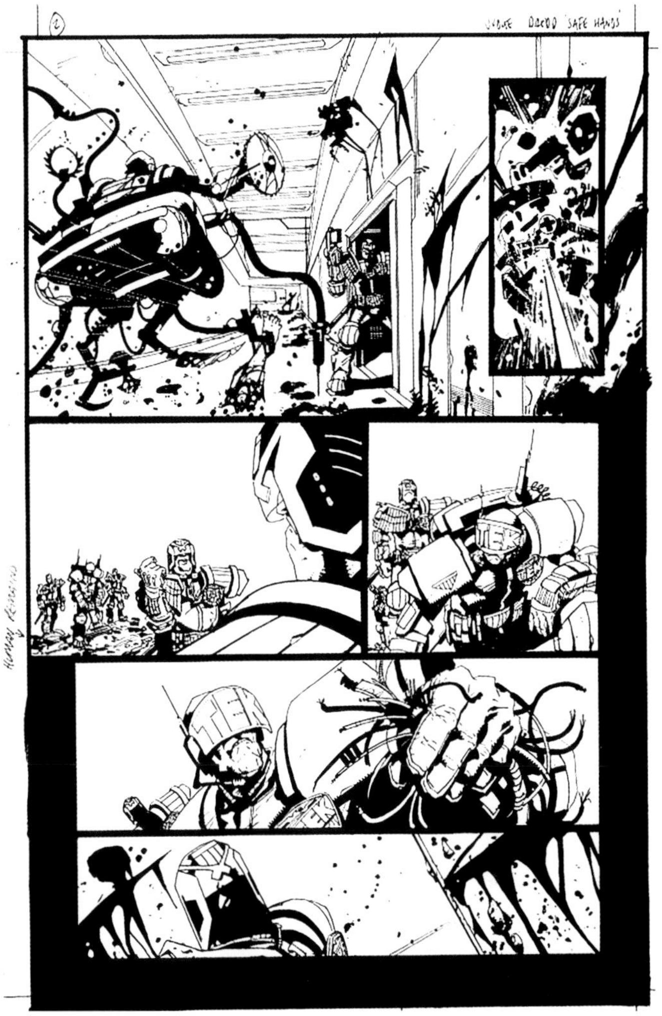
JUDGE DREDD 'SAFE HANDS'

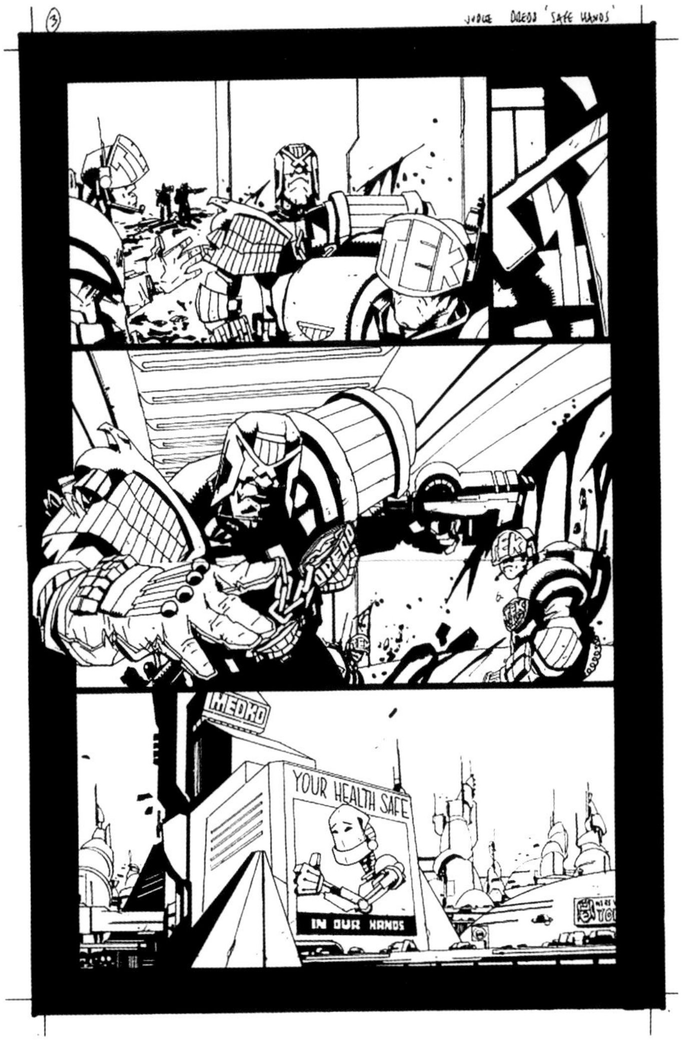
JUDGE DREDD 'SAFE HANDS'
HEDKO
YOUR HEALTH SAFE
IN OUR HANDS

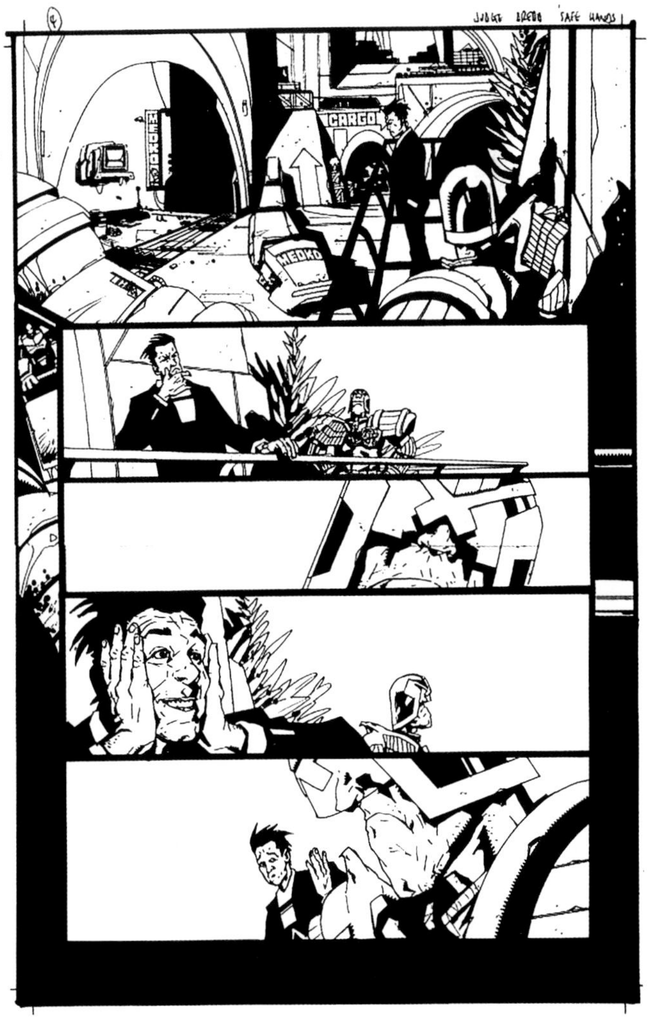
JUDGE DREDD 'SAFE HANDS'
CARGO
HEDKO

JUDGE DREDD: SAFE HANDS INKS, 2000 AD PROG 1273, 2002

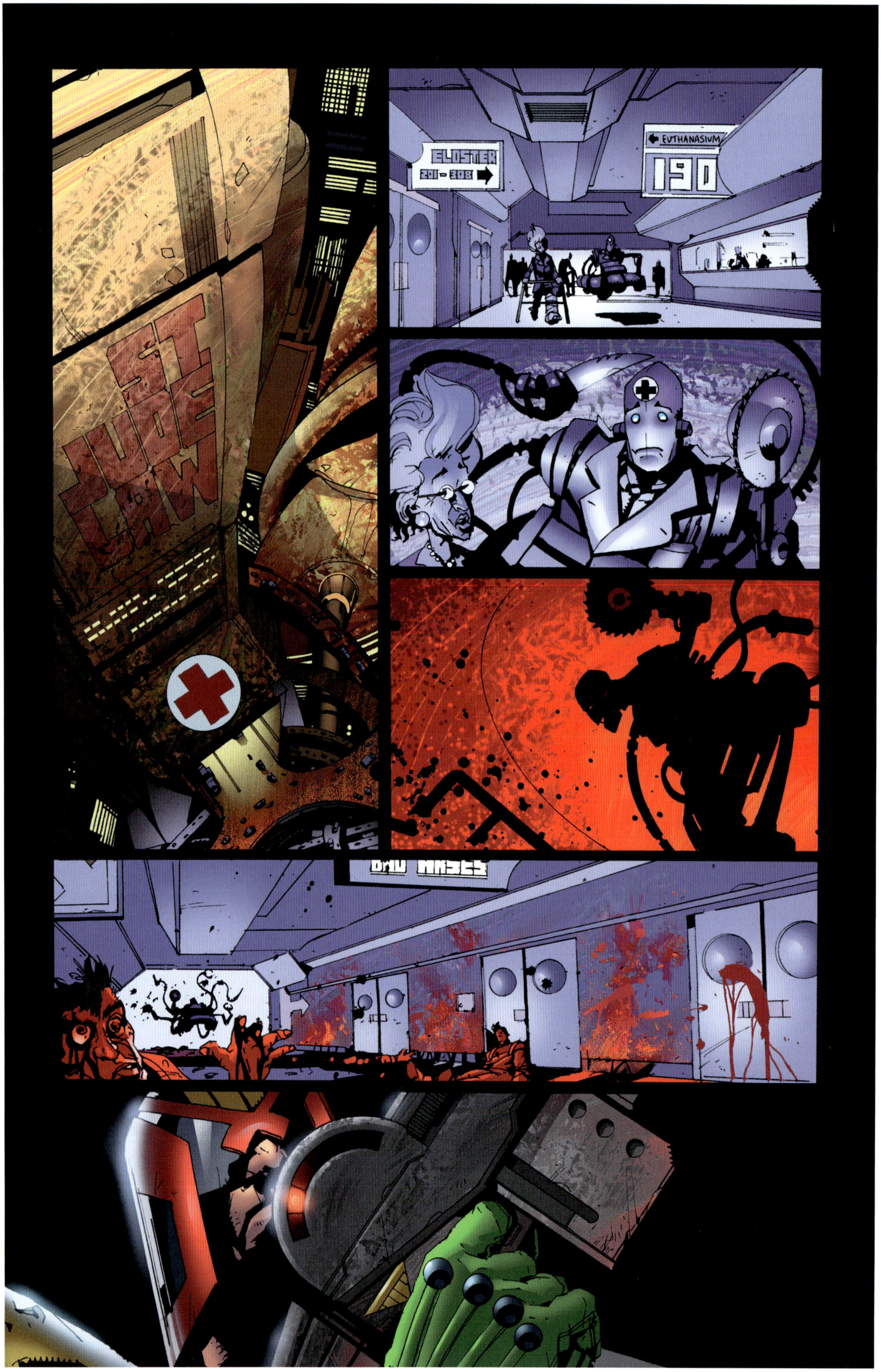
ELOSTER
201 - 308
EUTHANASIUM
190
ST. JUDE LAW

JUDE DREDD: SAFE HANDS PAGE 1, 2000 AD PROG 1273, 2002
COLOURS BY CHRIS BLYTHE

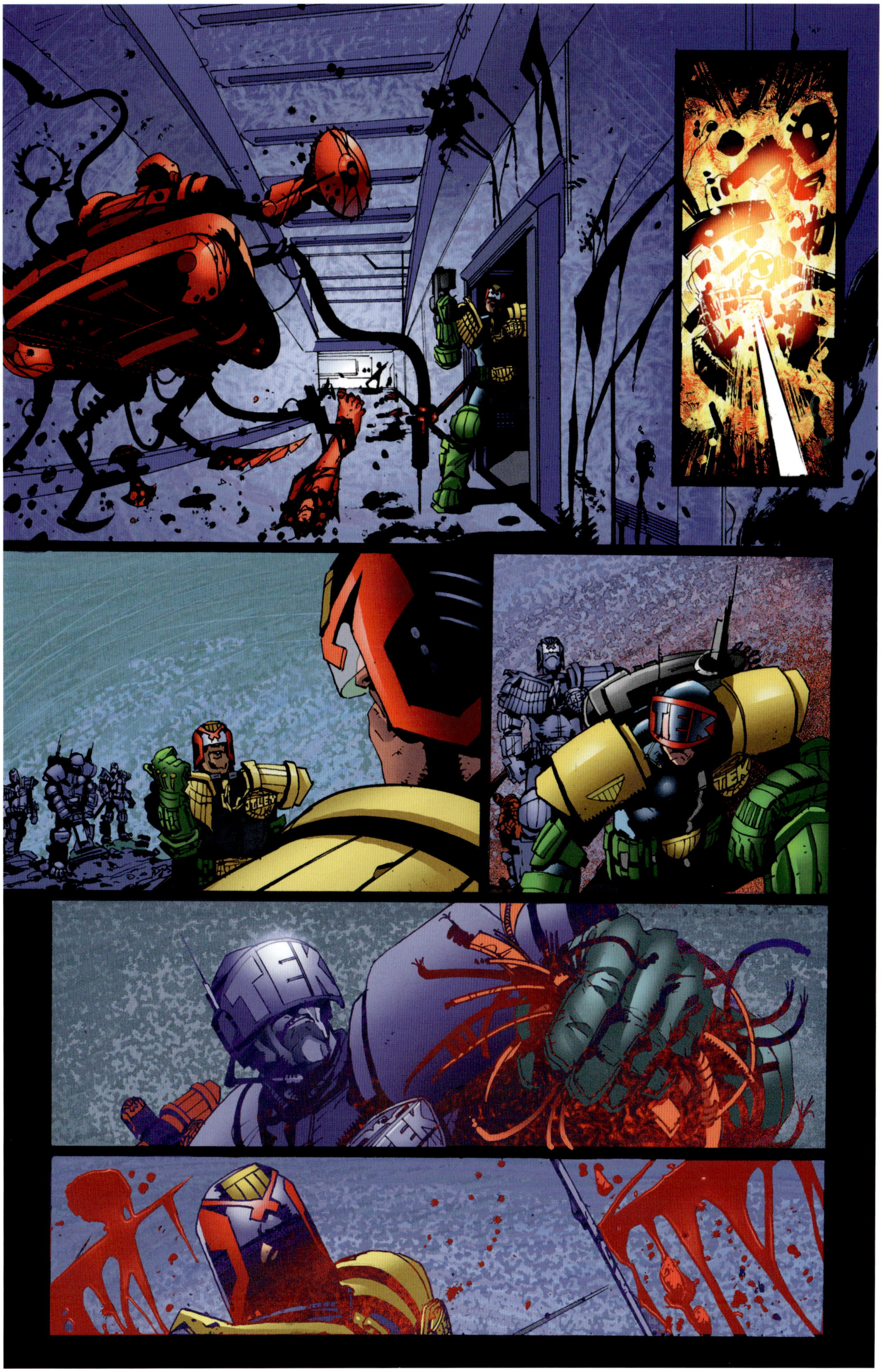
TEK

JUDGE DREDD: SAFE HANDS PAGE 2, 2000 AD PROG 1273, 2002
COLOURS BY CHRIS BLYTHE

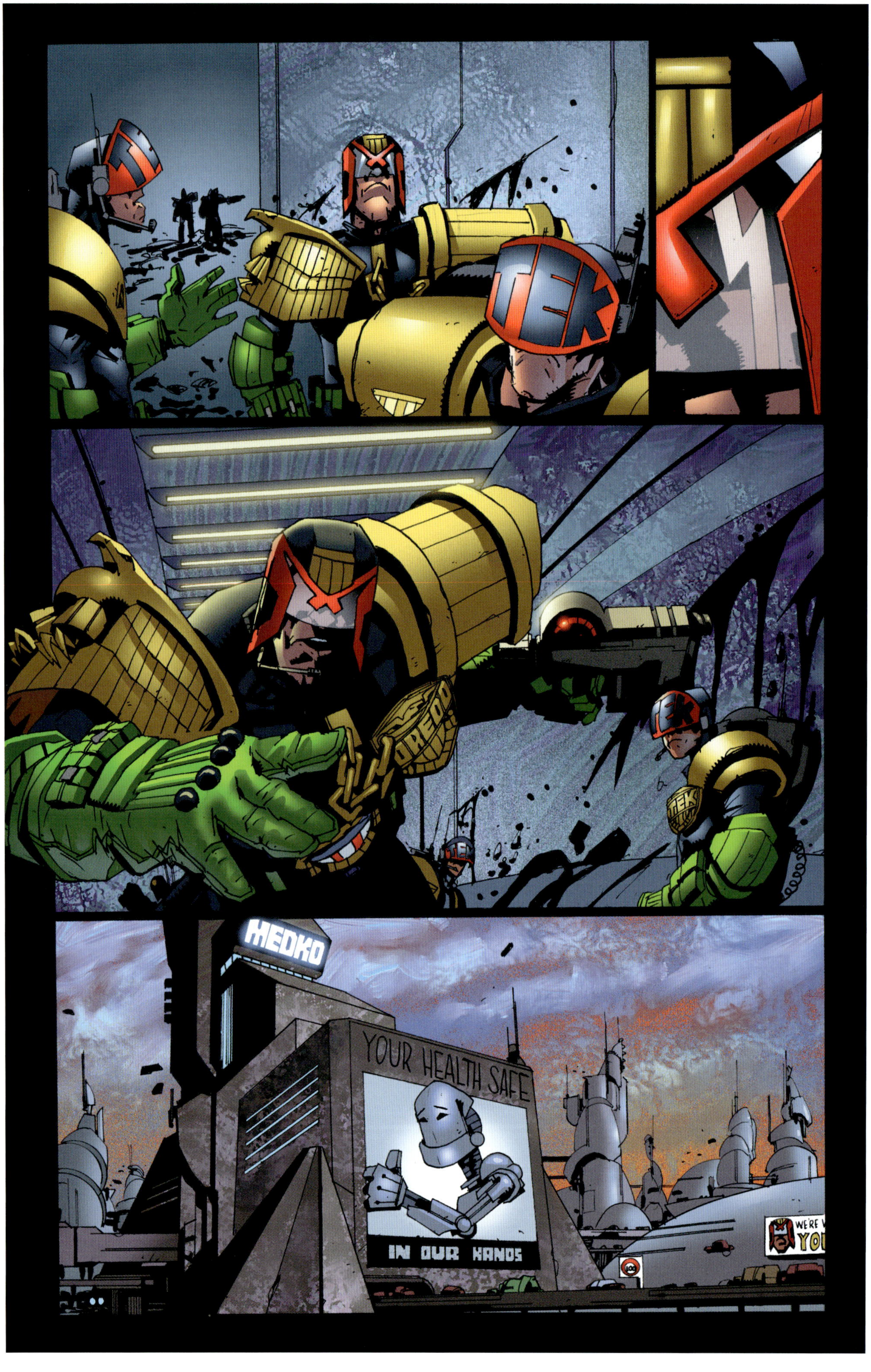
TEK
DREDD
MEDKO
YOUR HEALTH SAFE
IN OUR HANDS

JUDGE DREDD: SAFE HANDS PAGE 3, 2000 AD PROG 1273, 2002
COLOURS BY CHRIS BLYTHE

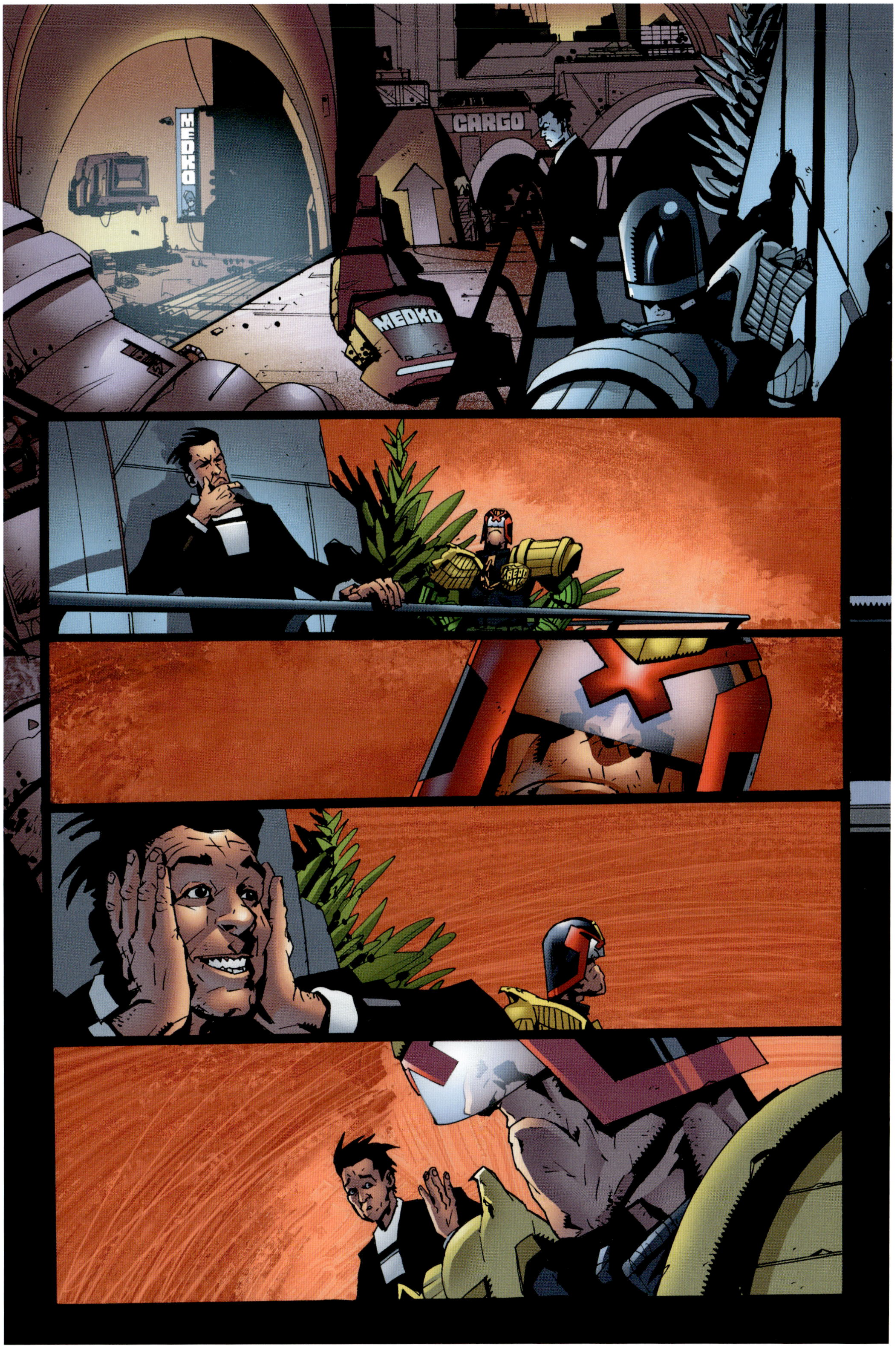
MEDKO
CARGO
MEDKO

JUDGE DREDD: SAFE HANDS PAGE 4, 2000 AD PROG 1273, 2002
COLOURS BY CHRIS BLYTHE

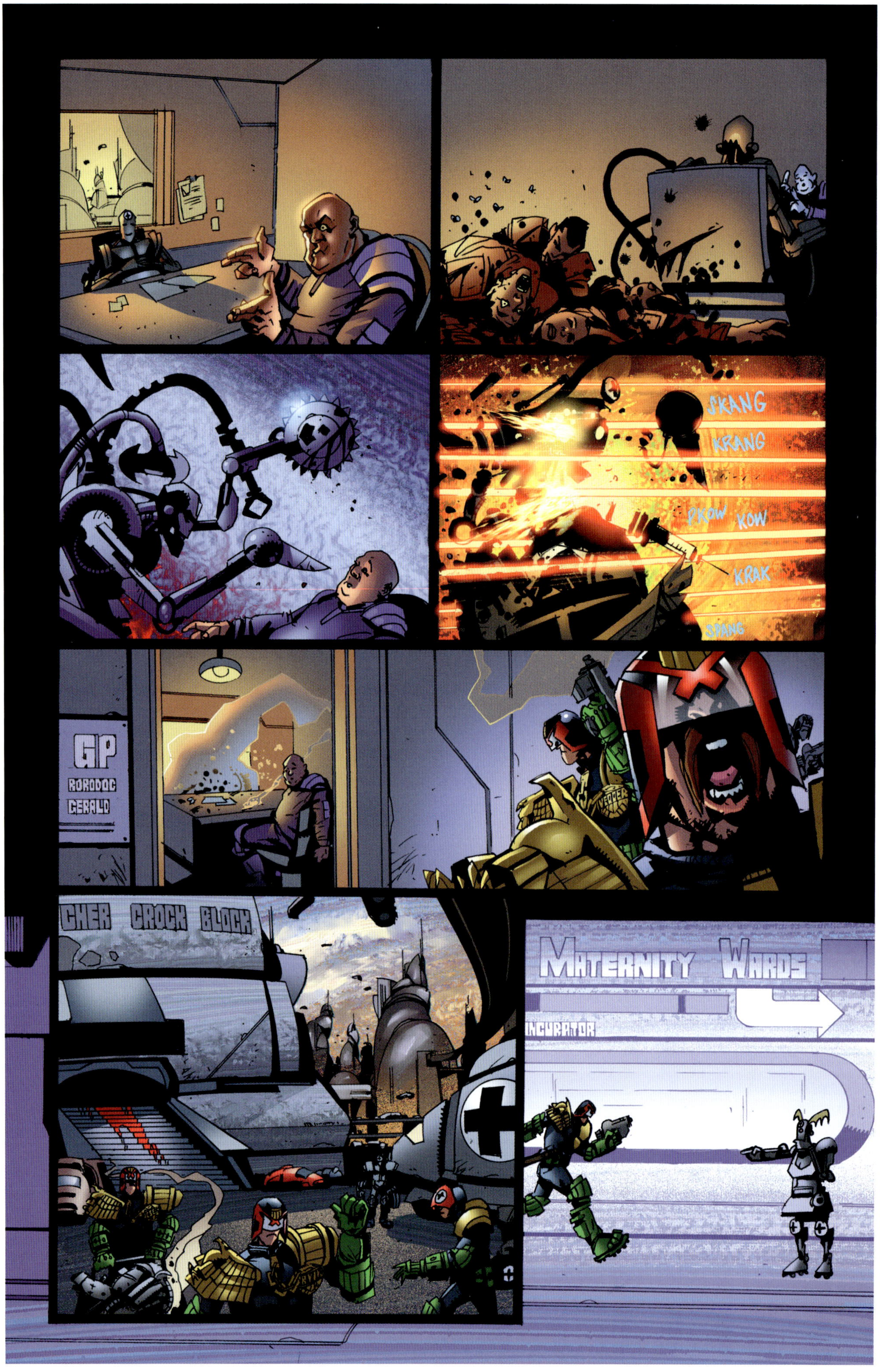
SKANG
KRANG
PKOW KOW
KRAK
SPANG
GP
RORODOC
GERALD
CHER CROCK BLOCK
MATERNITY WARDS
INCUBATOR

JUDGE DREDD: SAFE HANDS PAGE 5, 2000 AD PROG 1273, 2002
COLOURS BY CHRIS BLYTHE

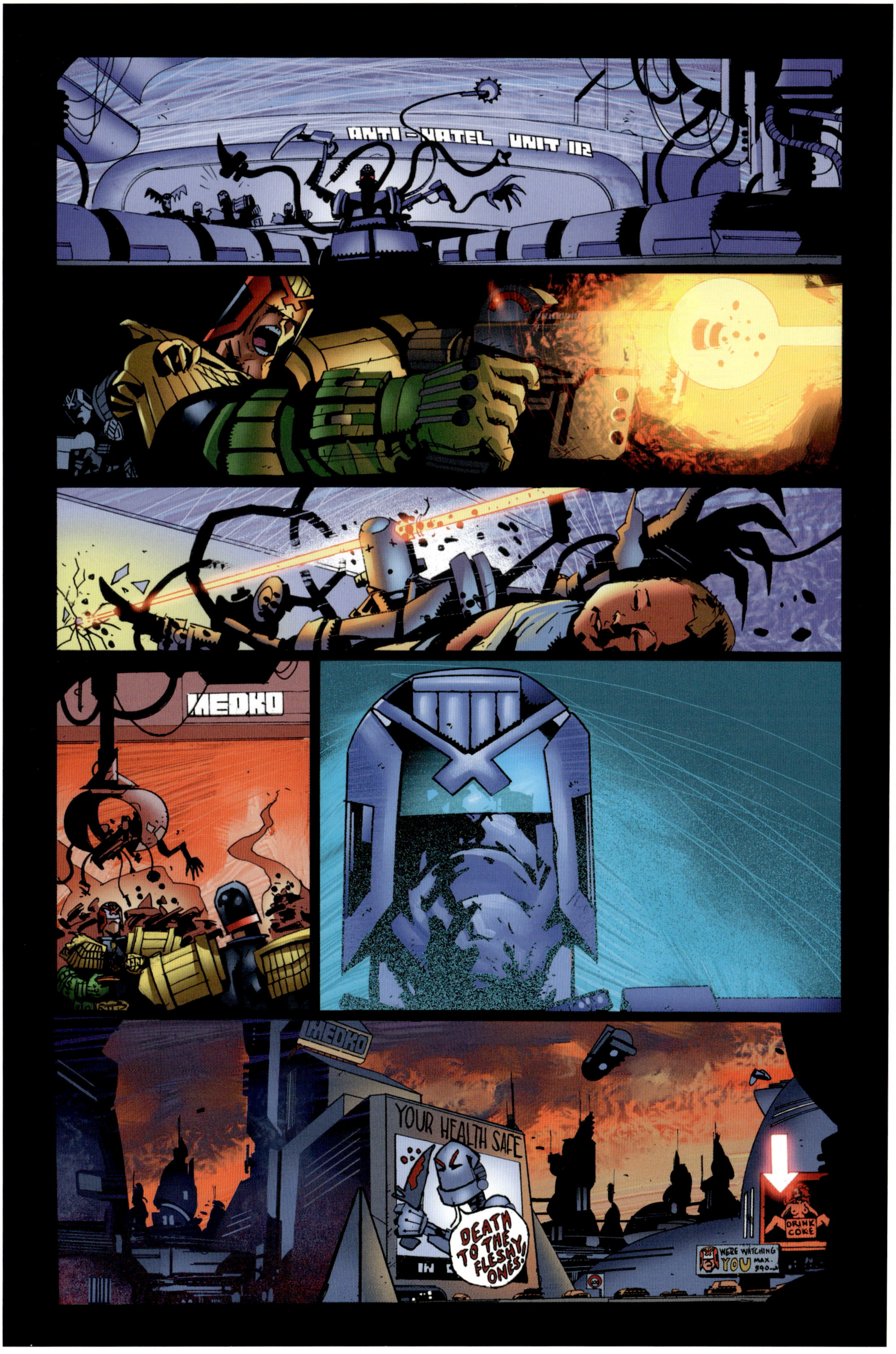
ANTI-HATEL UNIT 112
MEDKO
MEDKO
YOUR HEALTH SAFE
DEATH TO THE FLESHY ONES!
DRINK COKE
WERE WATCHING YOU

JUDGE DREDD: SAFE HANDS PAGE 6, 2000 AD PROG 1273, 2002
COLOURS BY CHRIS BLYTHE

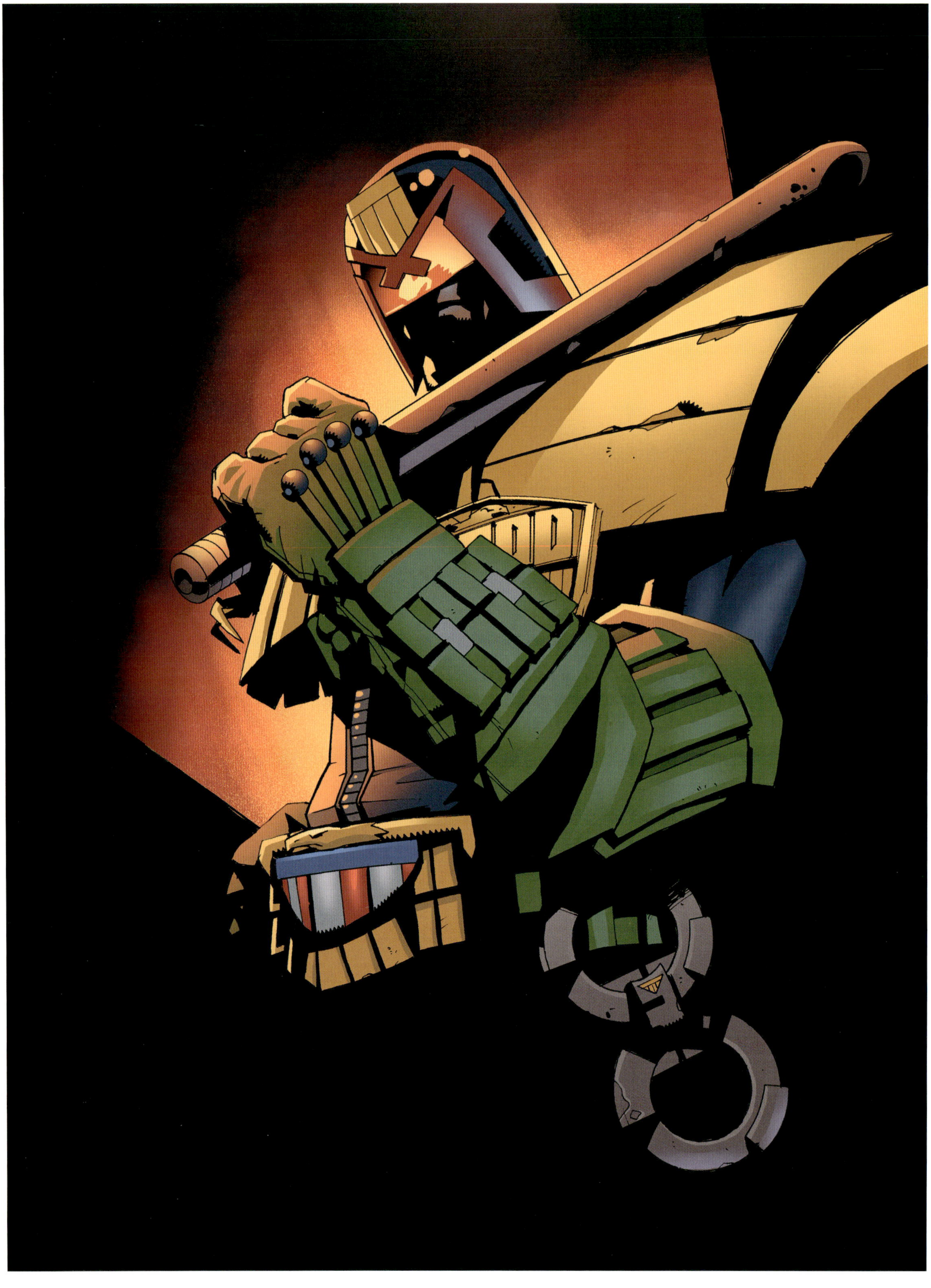

2000 AD 1304 COVER, 2002
COLOURS BY CHRIS BLYTHE

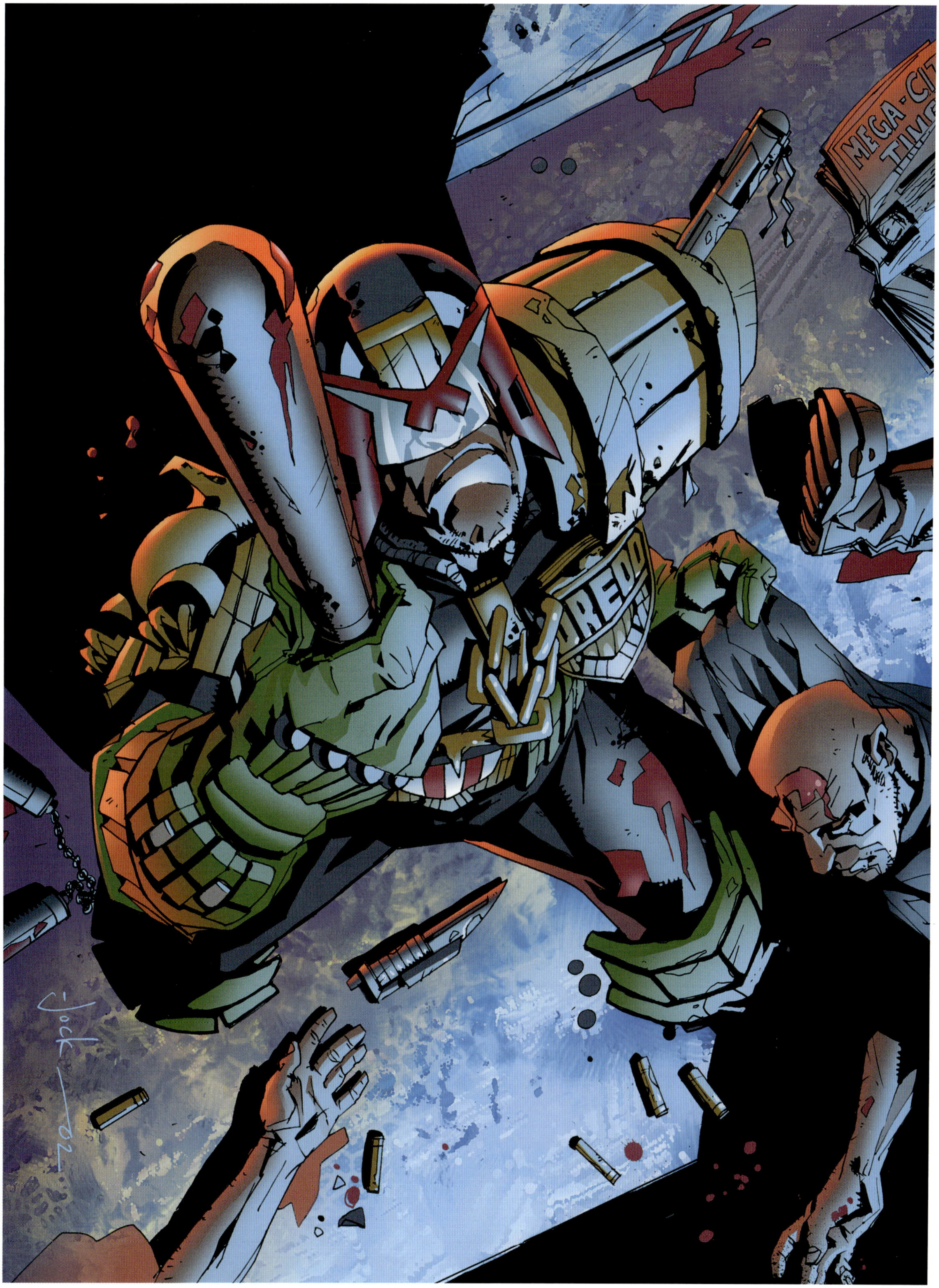
MEGA-CIT
TIM
DREDD

2000 AD PROG 1318 COVER, 2002
COLOURS BY CHRIS BLYTHE

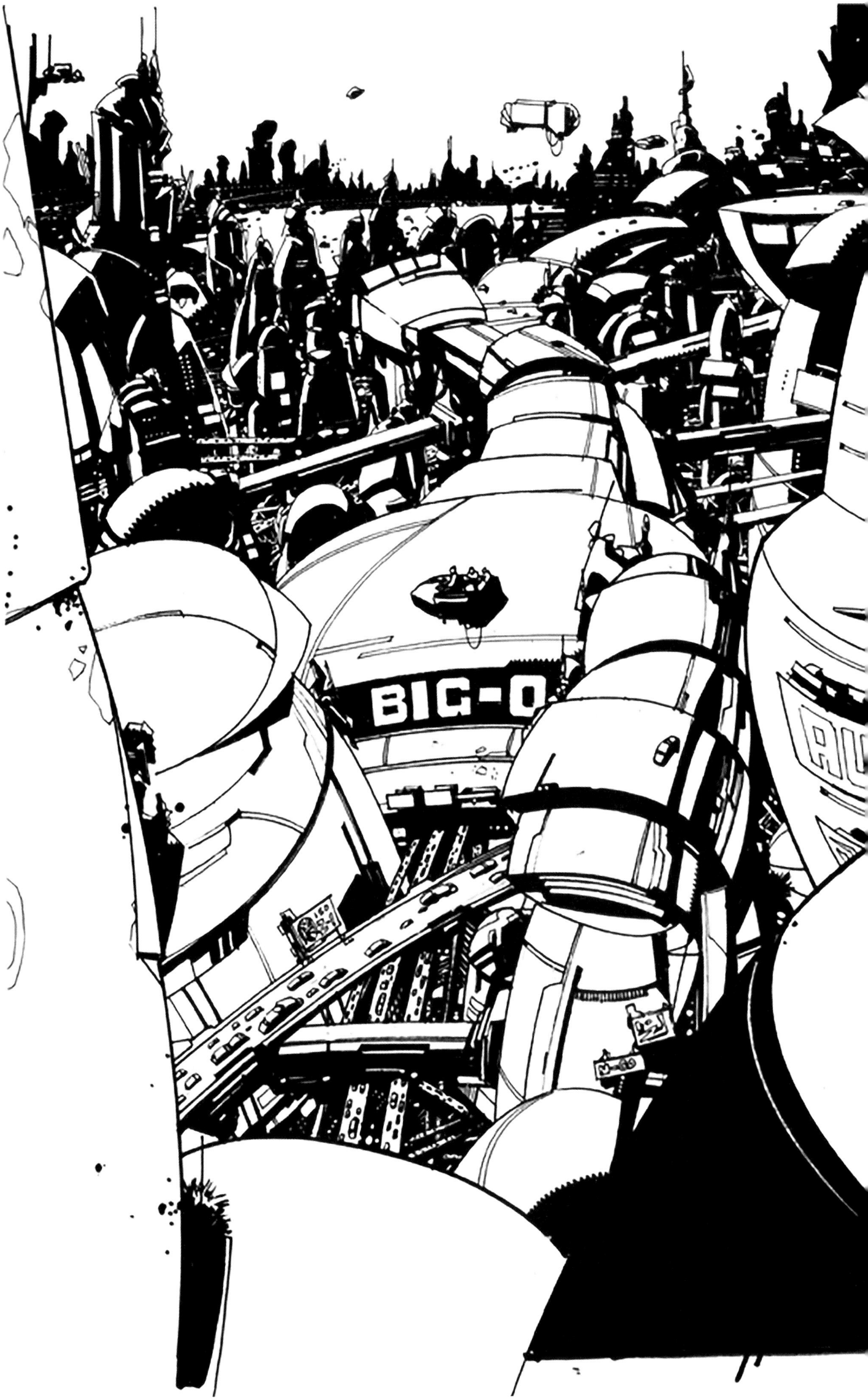
BIG-O

THIS SPREAD: 2000 AD PROG 1450 COVER INKS, 2005
OVERLEAF: 2000 AD PROG 1450 COVER, 2005

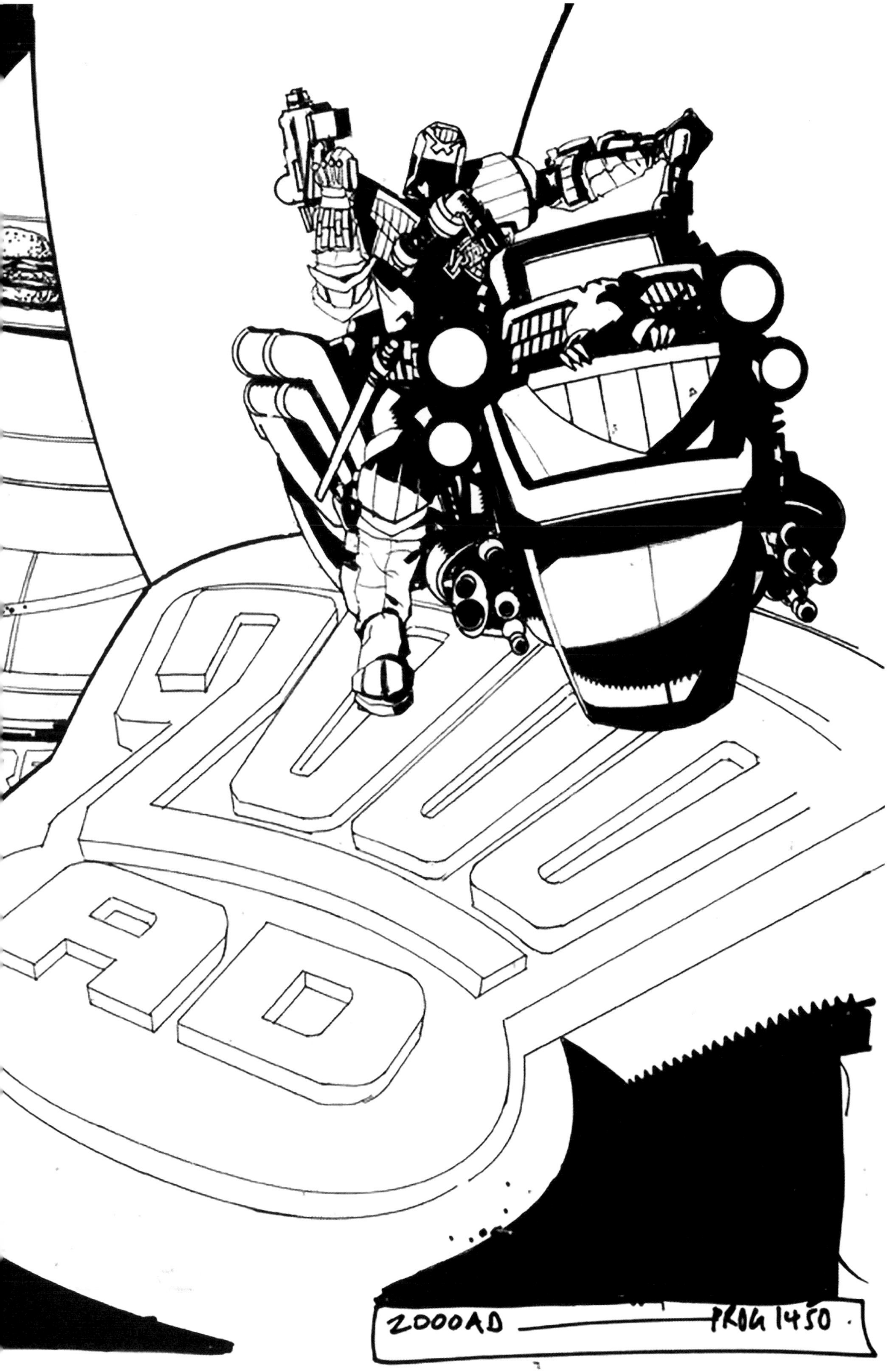
2000 AD
PROG 1450

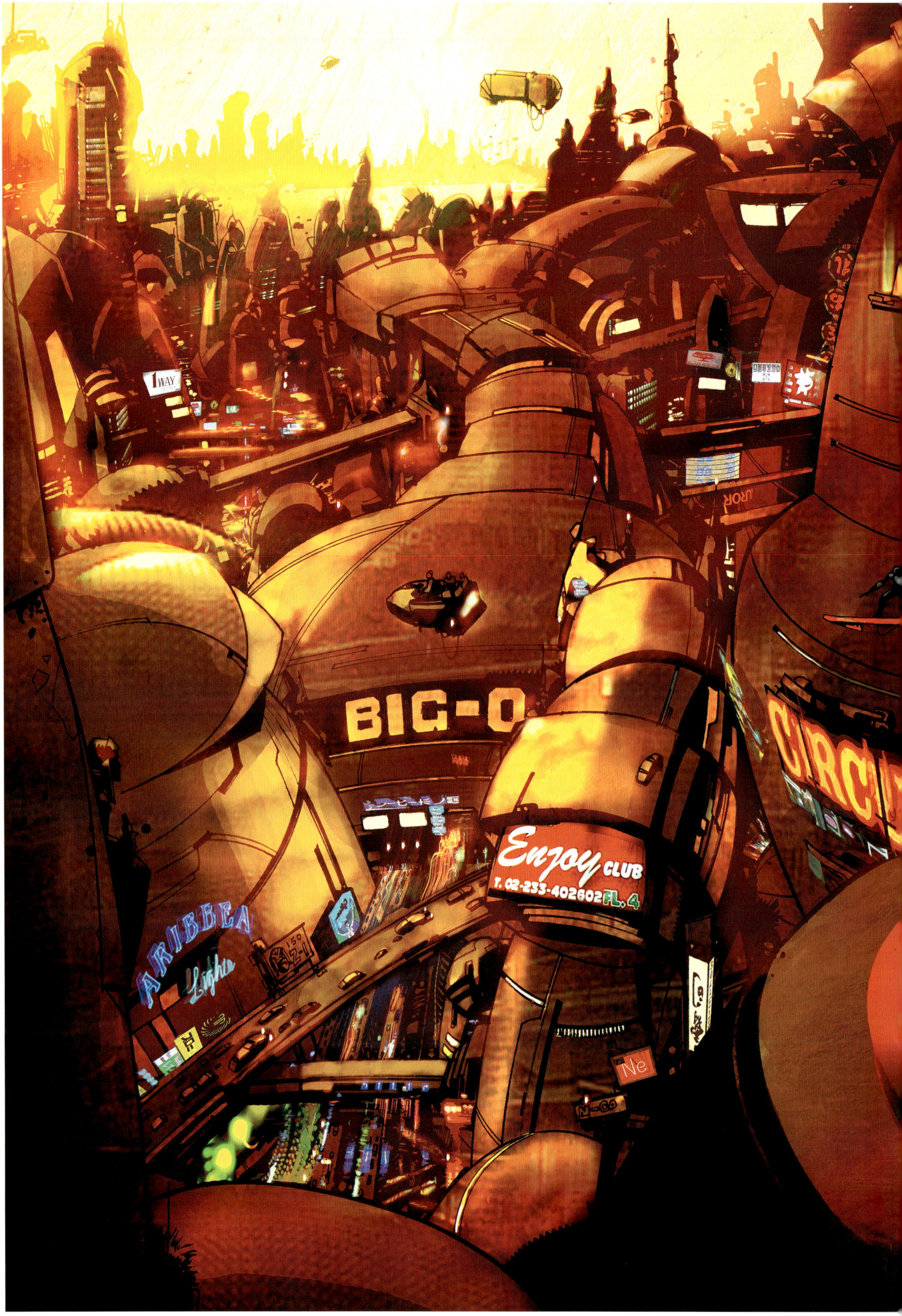
1WAY
BIG-O
Enjoy CLUB
T. 02-233-402602 FL. 4

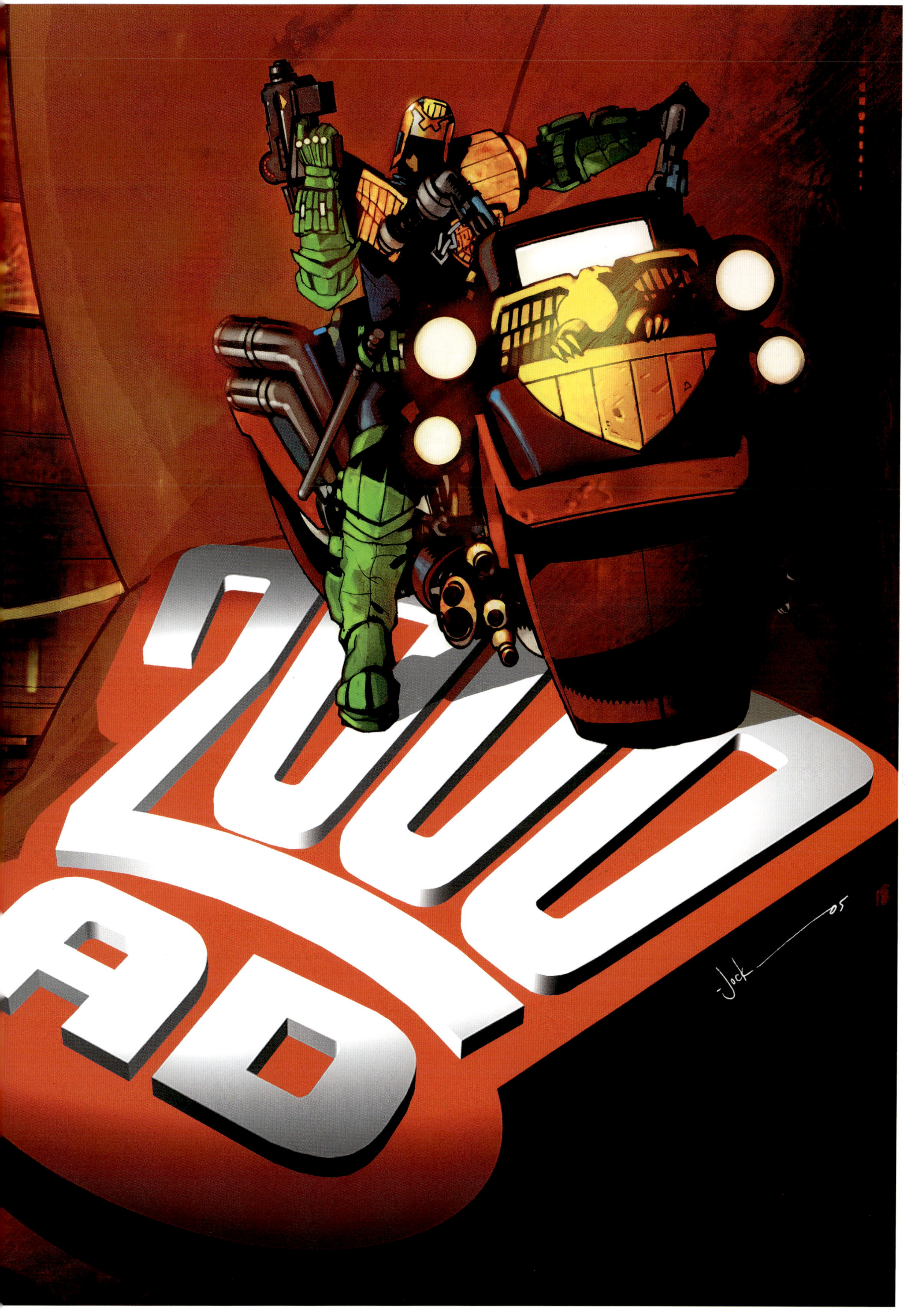
2000 AD
-Jock 05

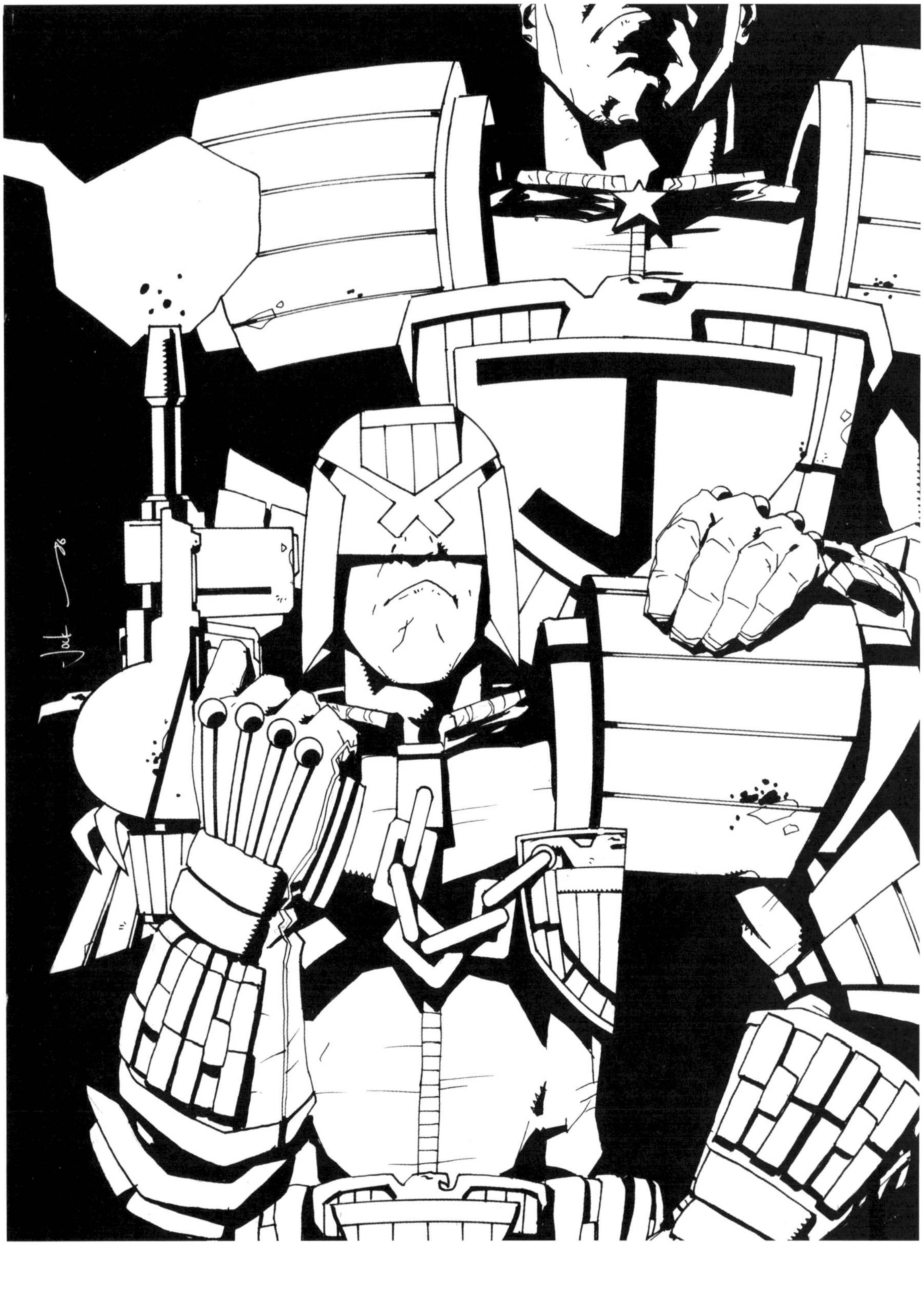

 2000 AD PROG 1503 COVER, 2006

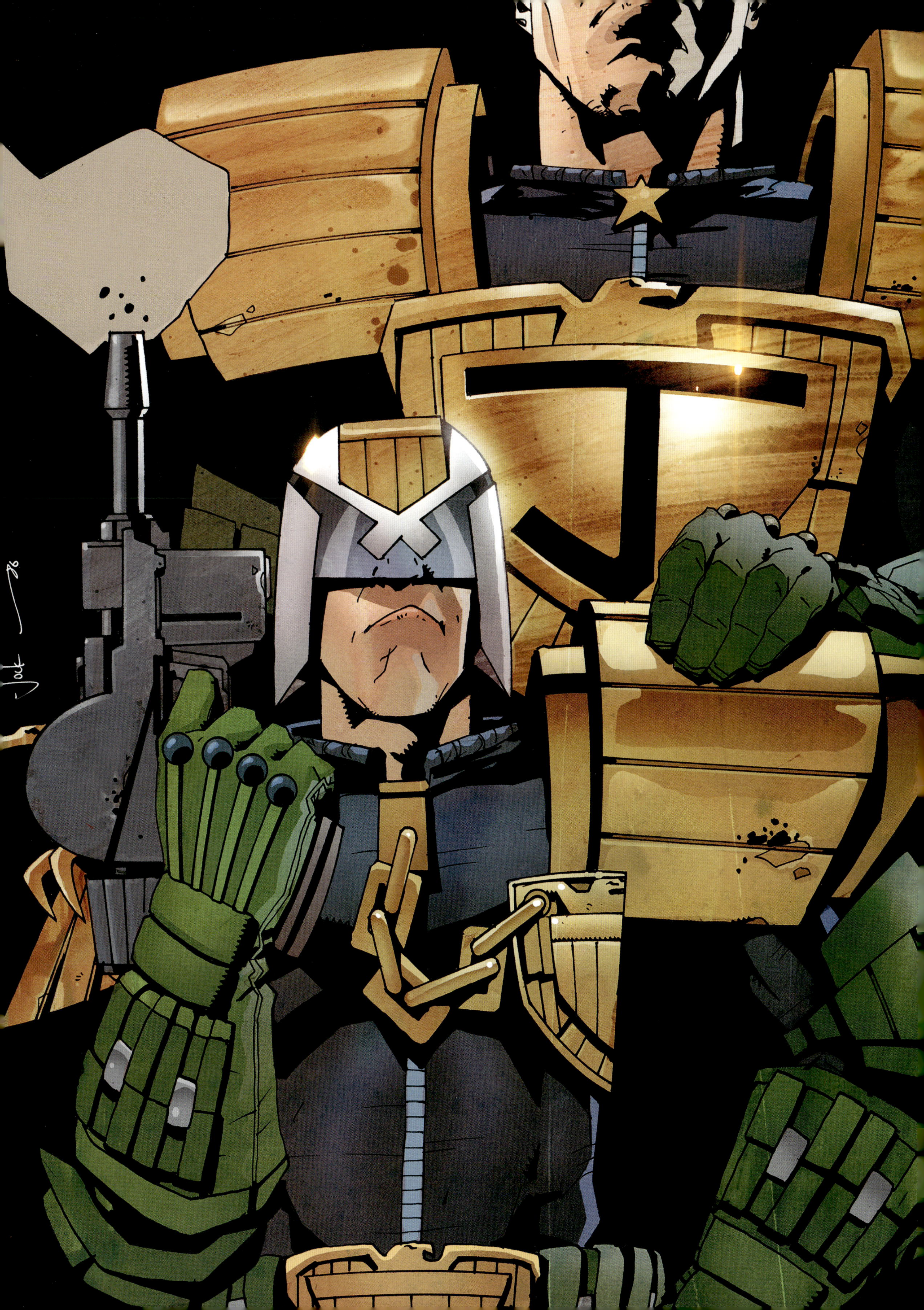

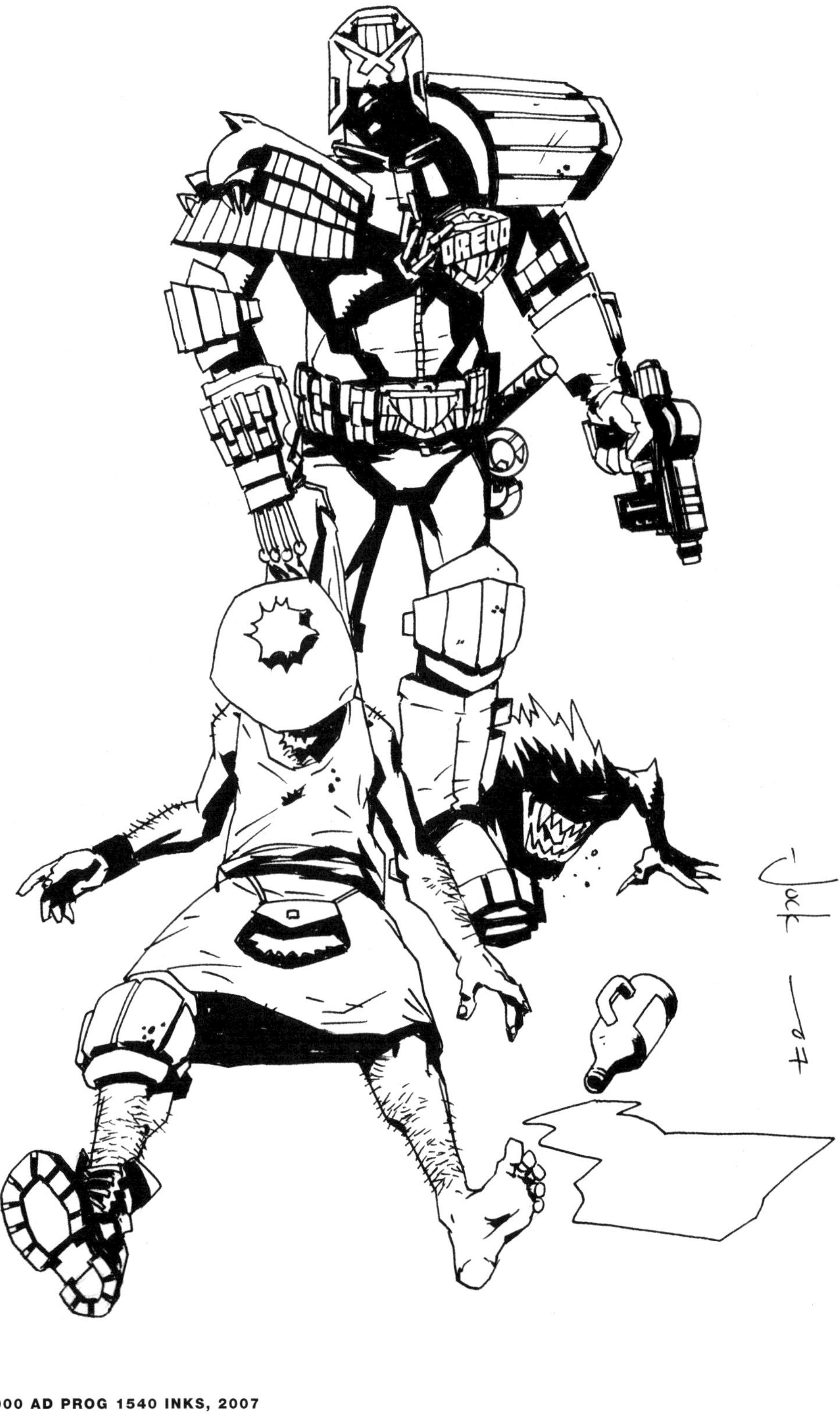
DREDD

 2000 AD PROG 1540 INKS, 2007

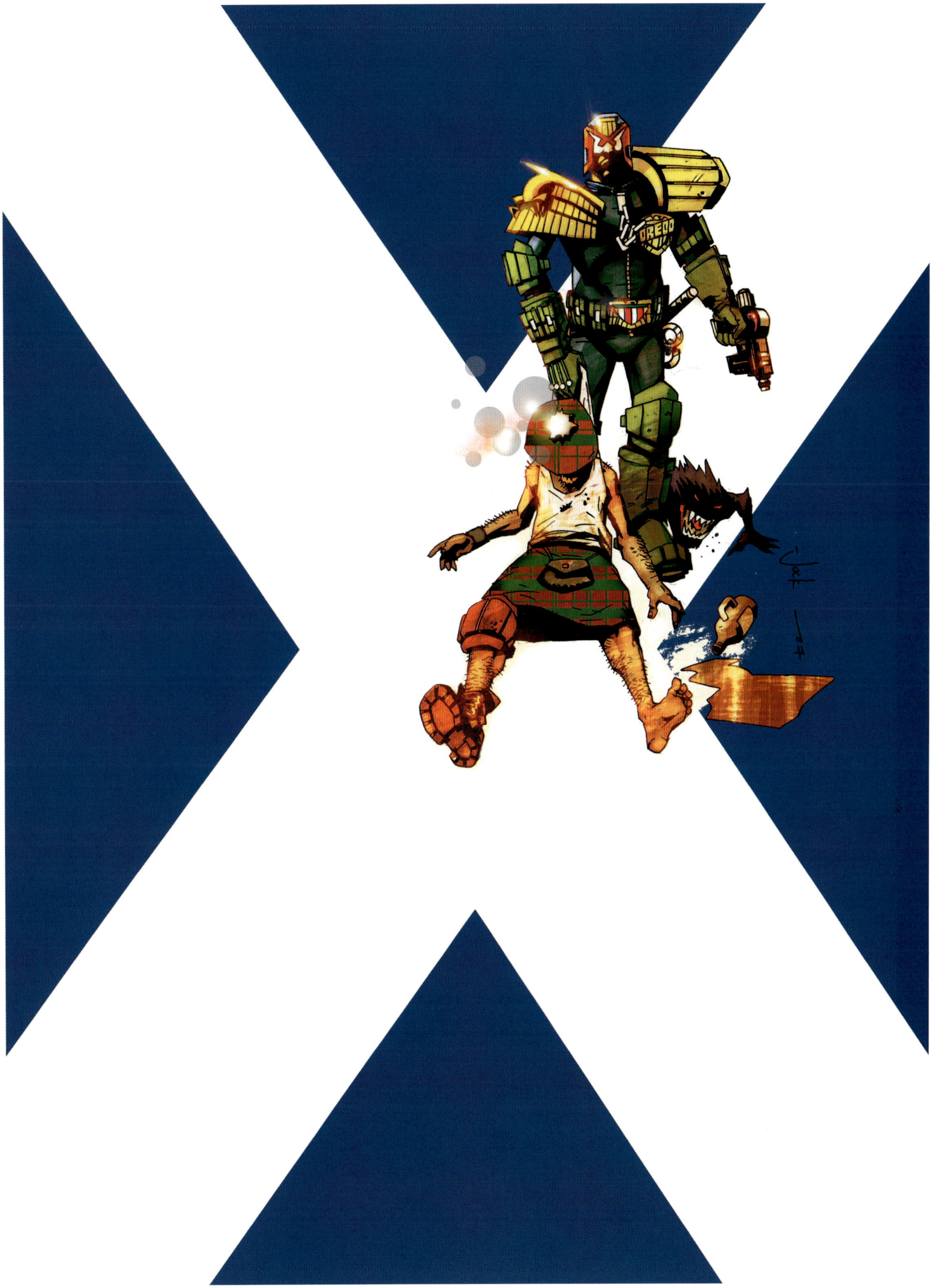
DREDD

2000 AD PROG 1540 COVER, 2007

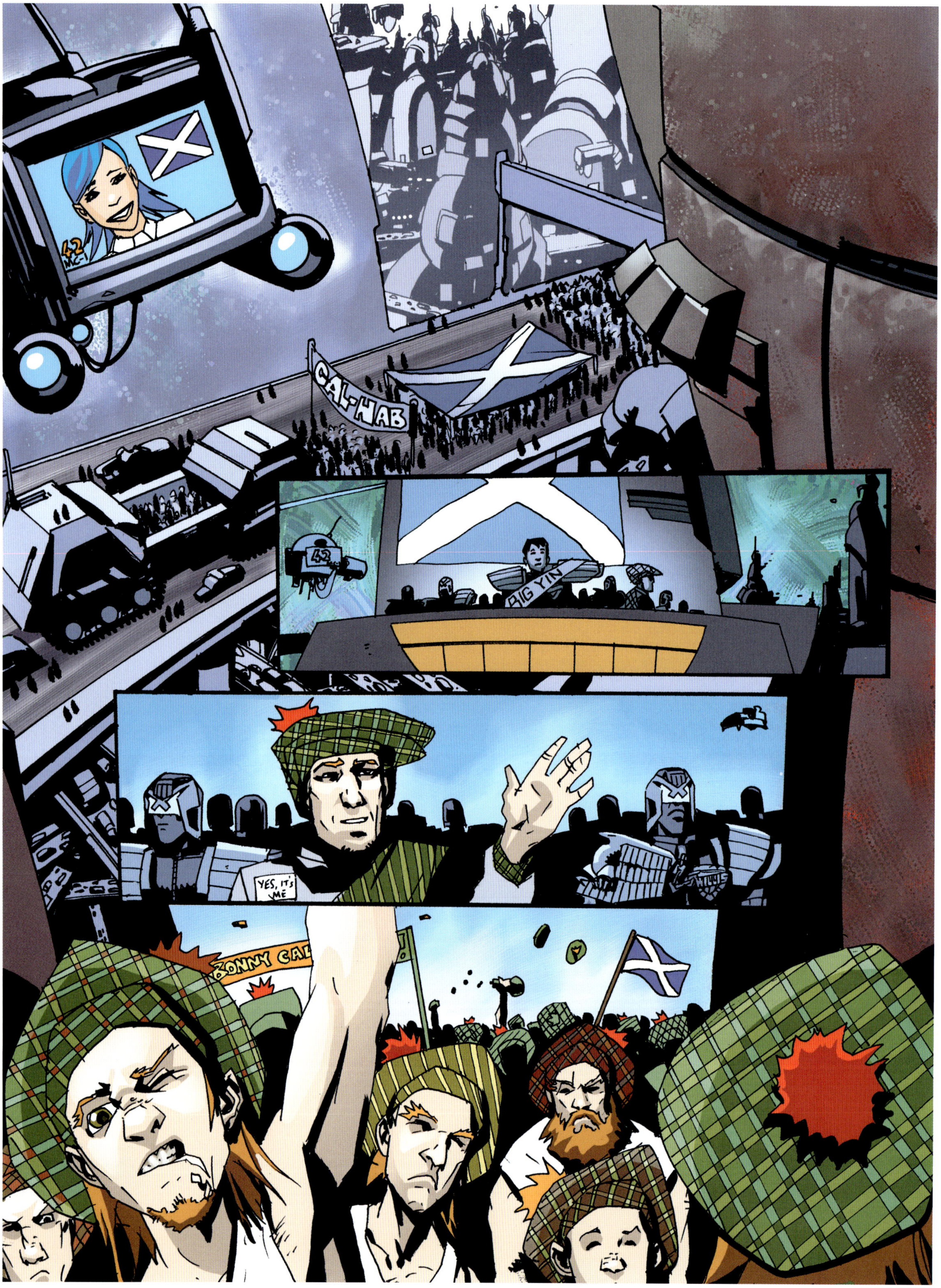
CAL-HAB
BIG YIN
YES, IT'S ME
BONNY CAL

JUDGE DREDD: TARTAN TERRORS PAGE 1, 2000 AD PROG 1540, 2007
COLOURS BY CHRIS BLYTHE

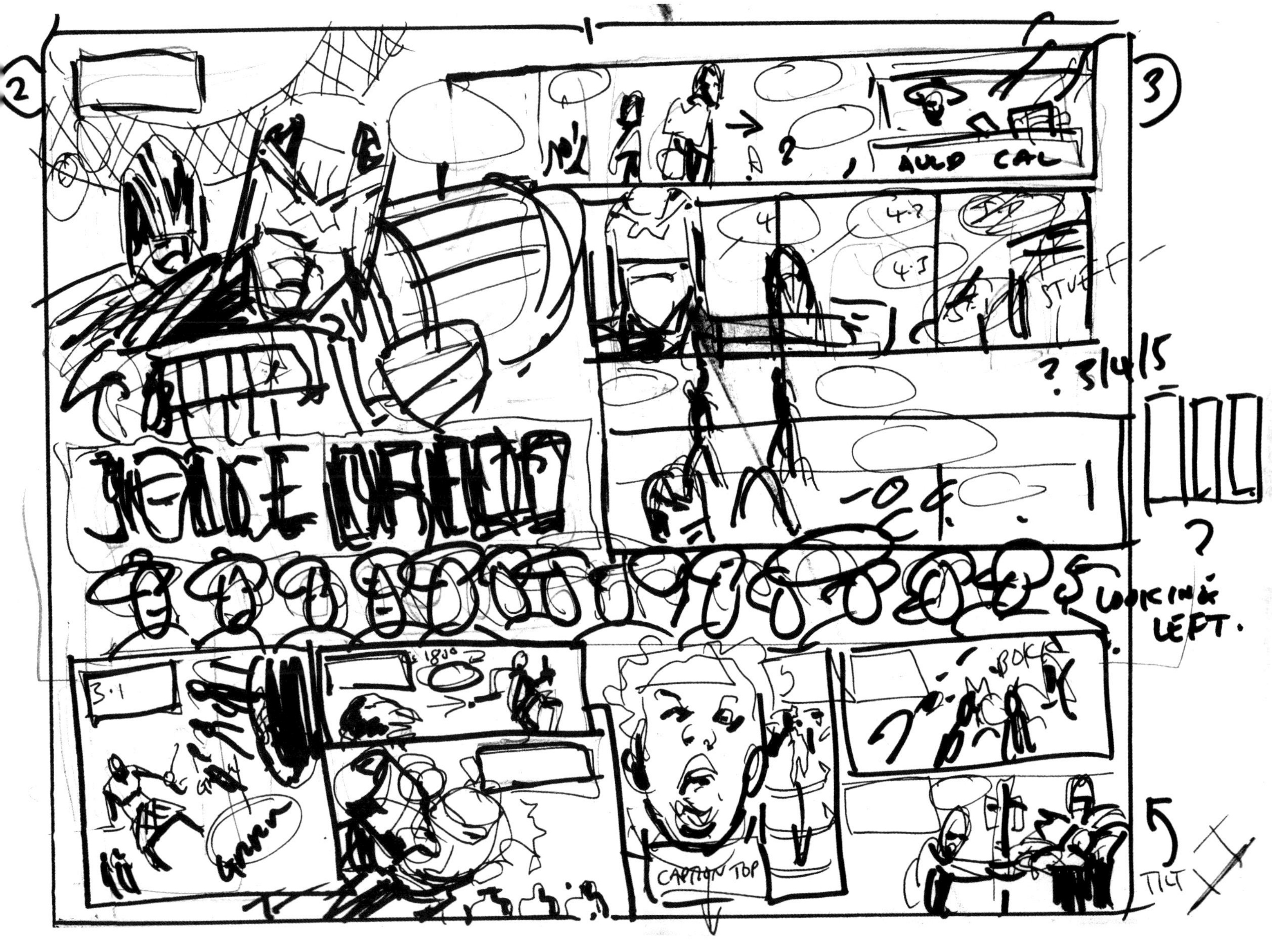
2
3
AULD CAL
STUFF
? 3/4/5
?
LOOKING LEFT.
3.1
CAPTION TOP
TILT

JUDGE DREDD: TARTAN TERRORS LAYOUTS, 2000 AD PROG 1540, 2007

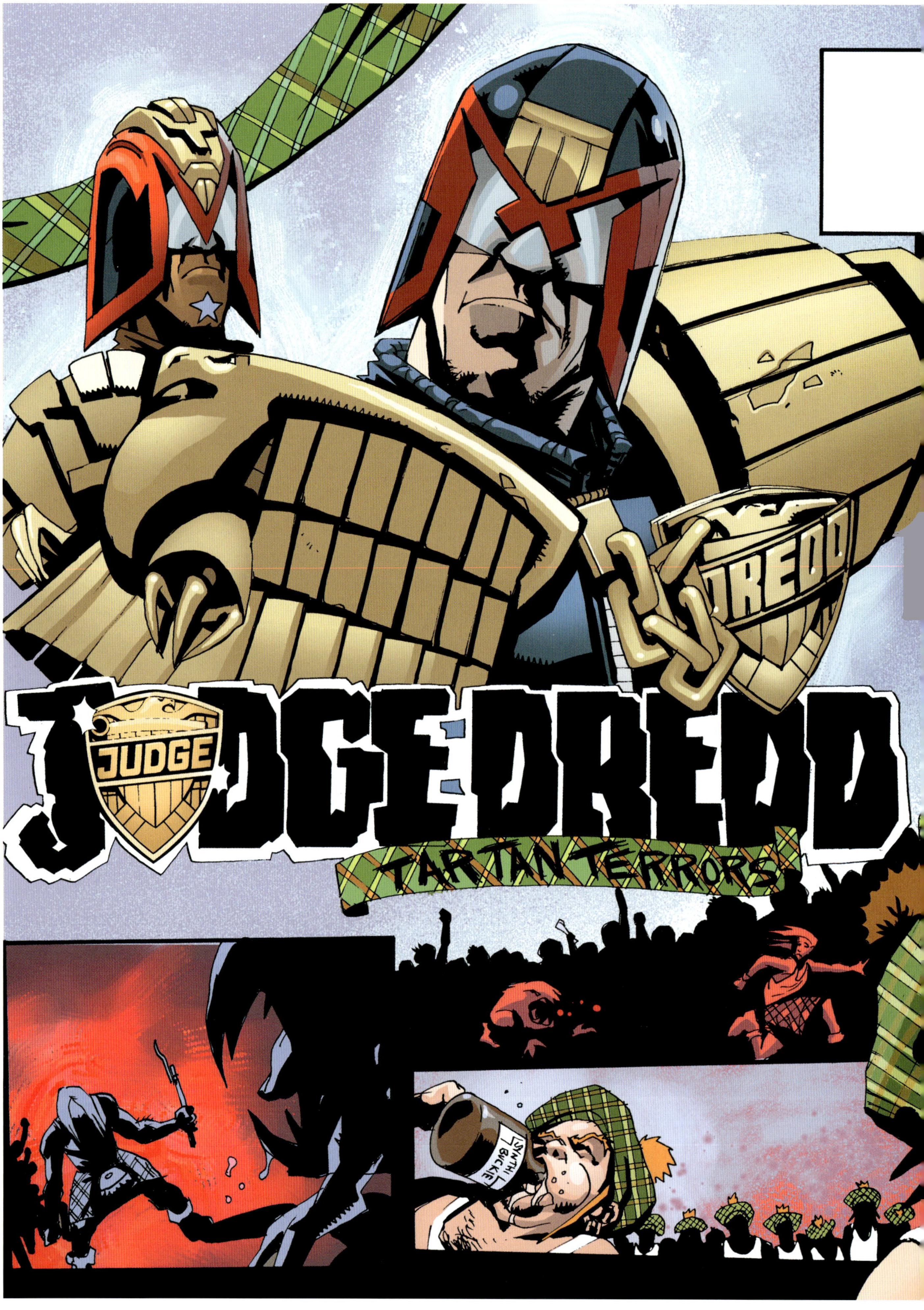
DREDD
JUDGE
JUDGE DREDD
TARTAN TERRORS
SYNTHI BUCKIE

 JUDGE DREDD: TARTAN TERRORS PAGES 2 & 3, 2000 AD PROG 1540, 2007
COLOURS BY CHRIS BLYTHE

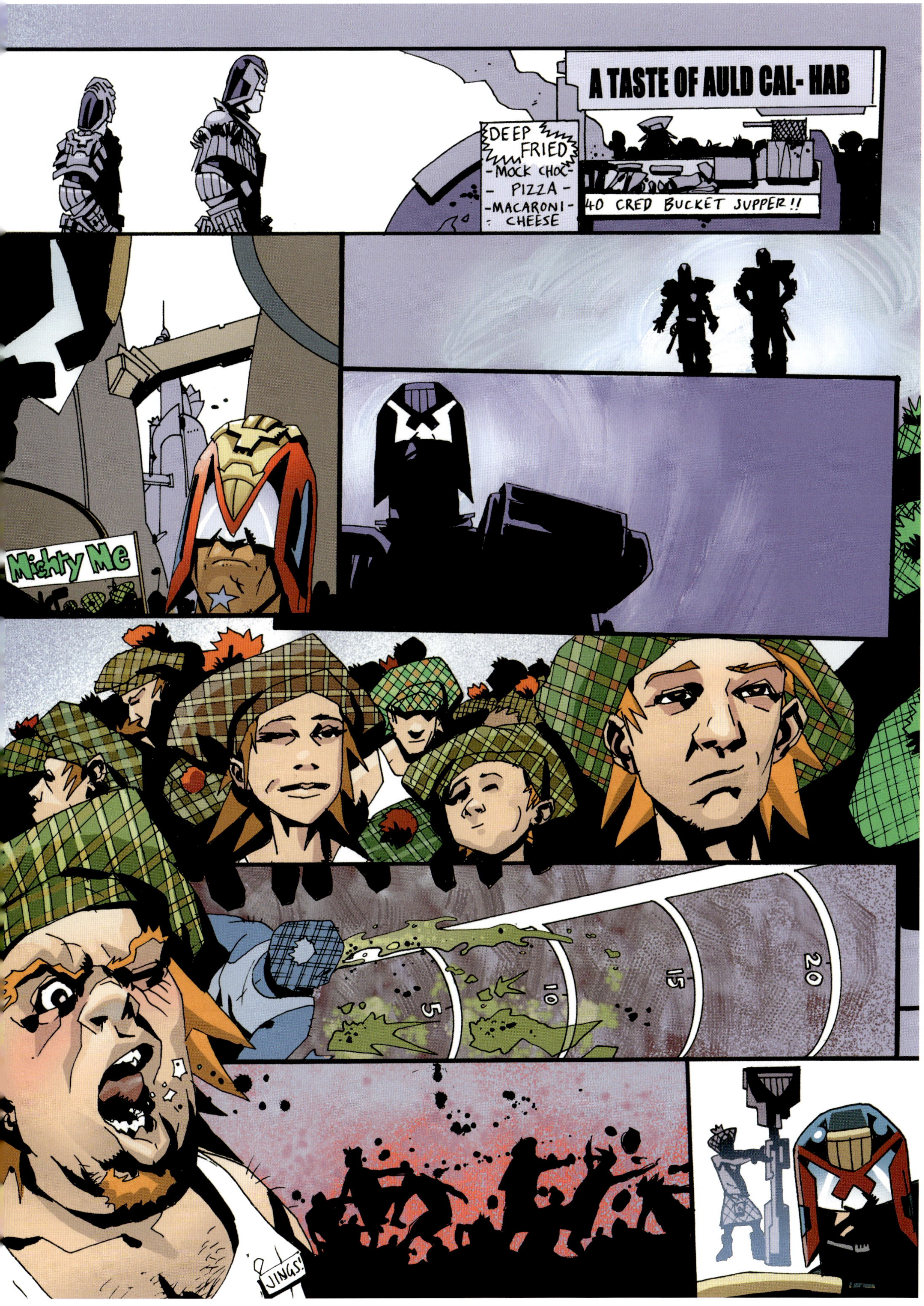
A TASTE OF AULD CAL- HAB
DEEP FRIED
-MOCK CHOC-
- PIZZA -
-MACARONI-
: CHEESE
40 CRED BUCKET SUPPER!!
Mighty Me
5
10
15
20
JINGS!

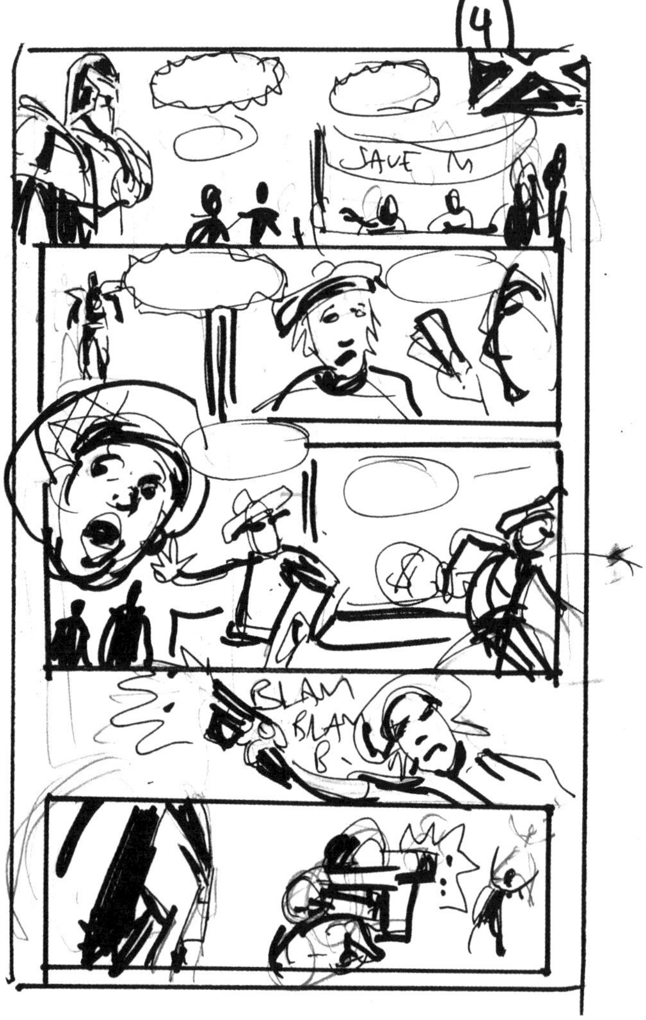
4
SAVE M
BLAM
BLAM
B

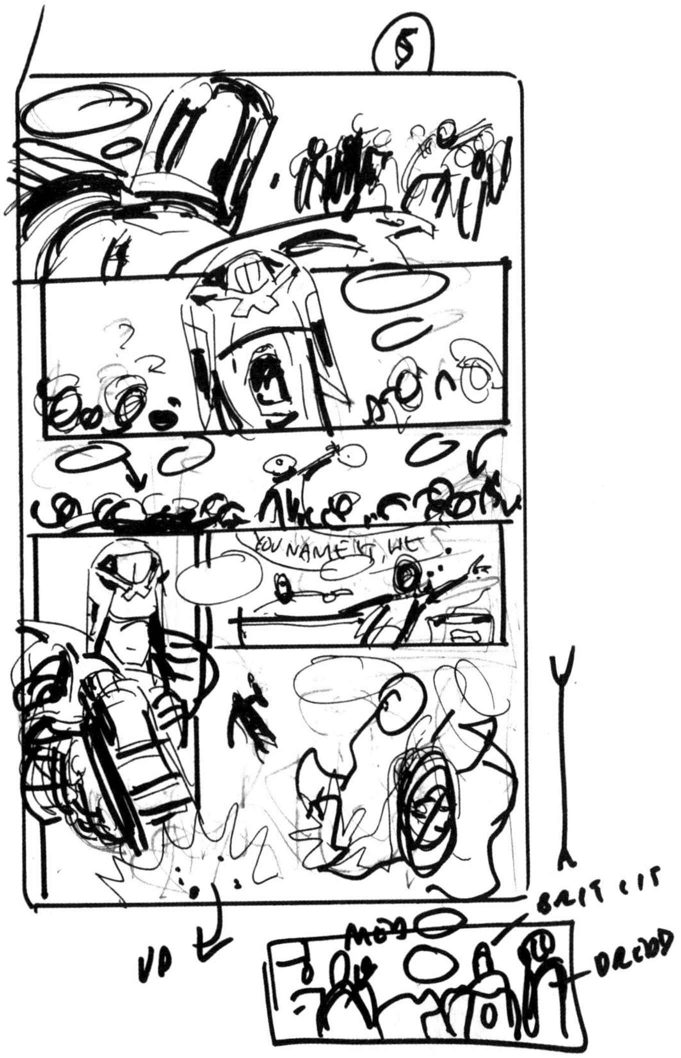
5
YOU NAME IT, WE
UP
MOB
BRIT CIT
DREDD

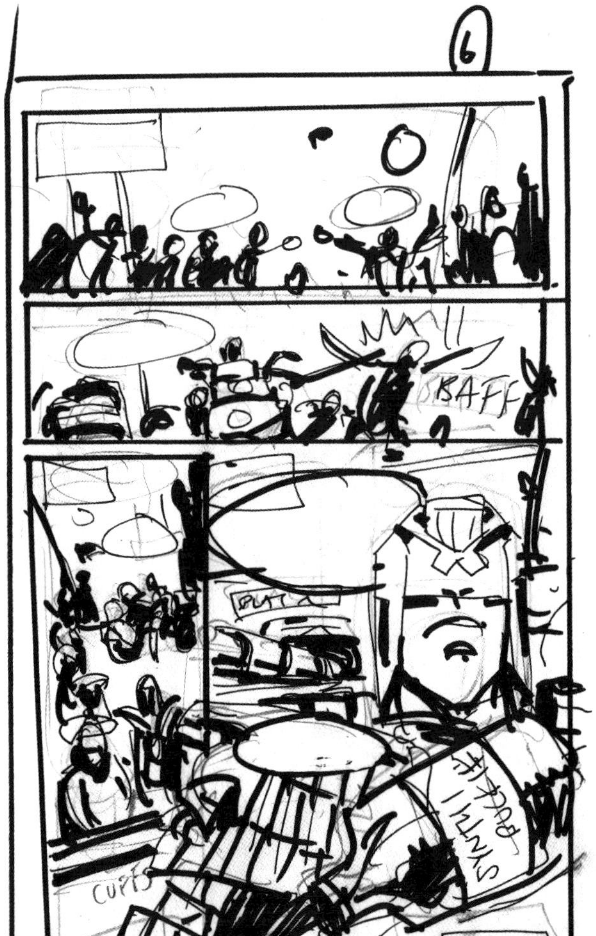
6
BAFF
CUPS
THE END

 JUDGE DREDD: TARTAN TERRORS LAYOUTS, 2000 AD PROG 1540, 2007

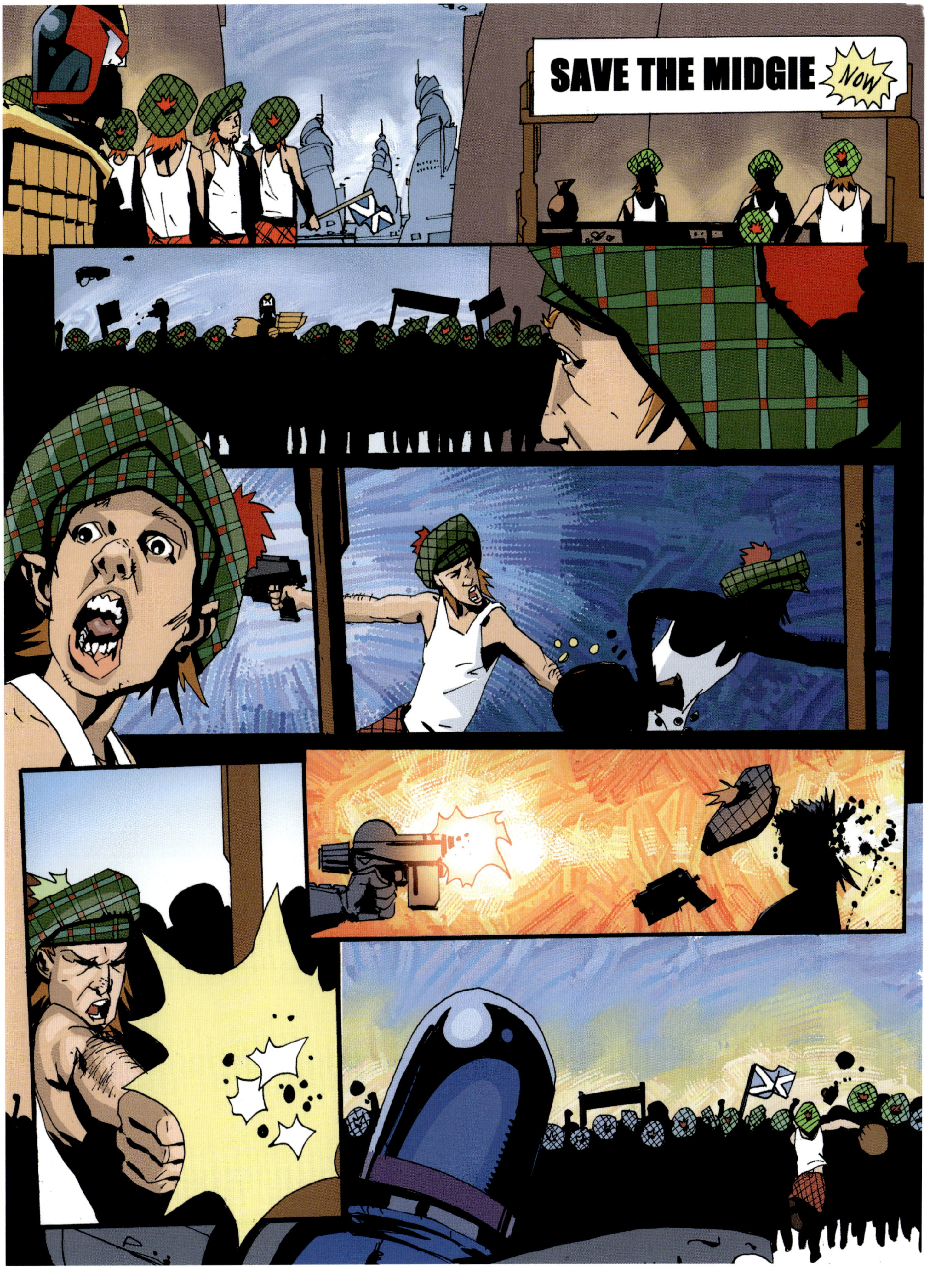
SAVE THE MIDGIE NOW

JUDGE DREDD: TARTAN TERRORS PAGE 4, 2000 AD PROG 1540, 2007
COLOURS BY CHRIS BLYTHE

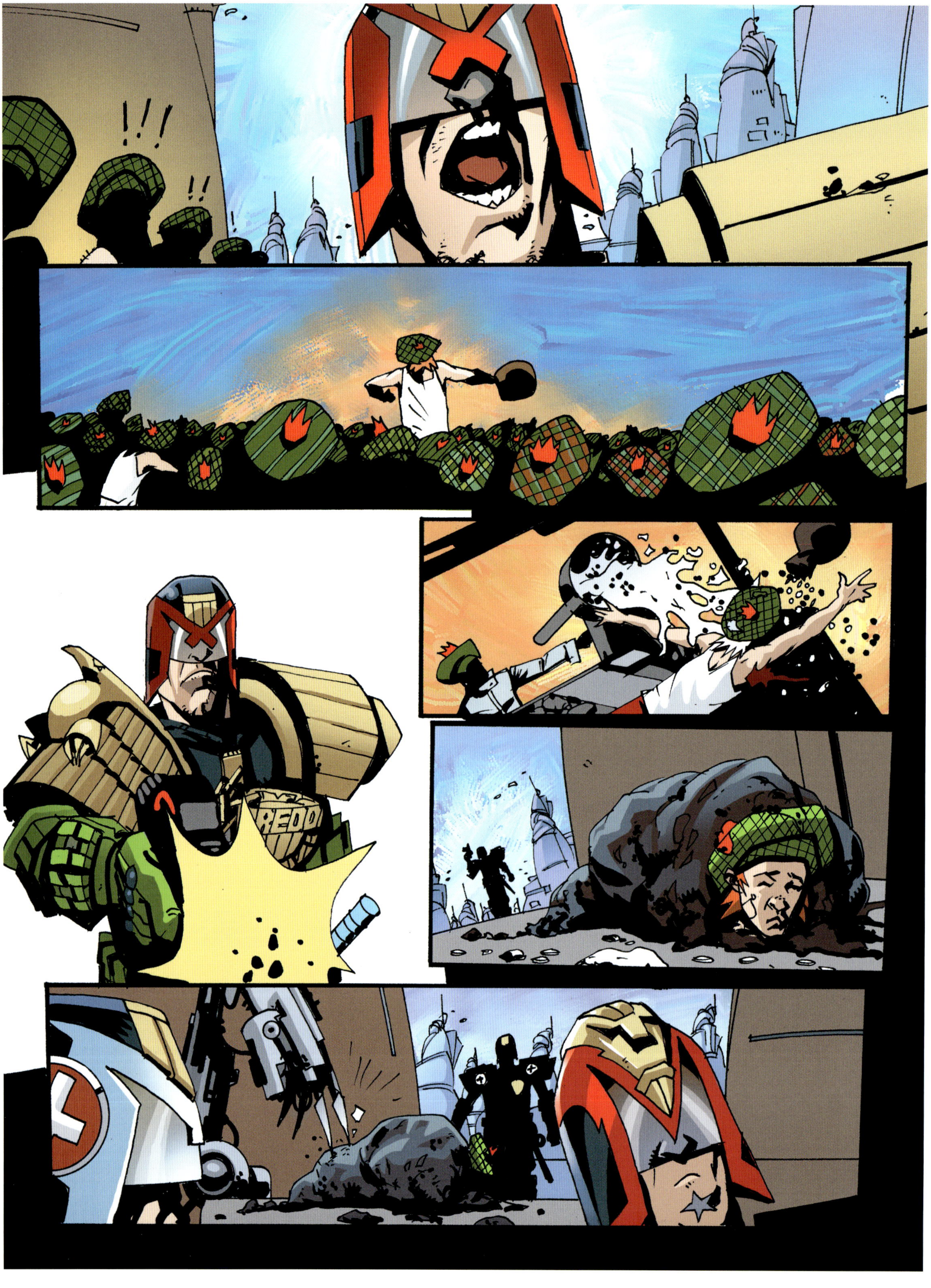
!!!
!!

JUDGE DREDD: TARTAN TERRORS PAGE 5, 2000 AD PROG 1540, 2007
COLOURS BY CHRIS BLYTHE

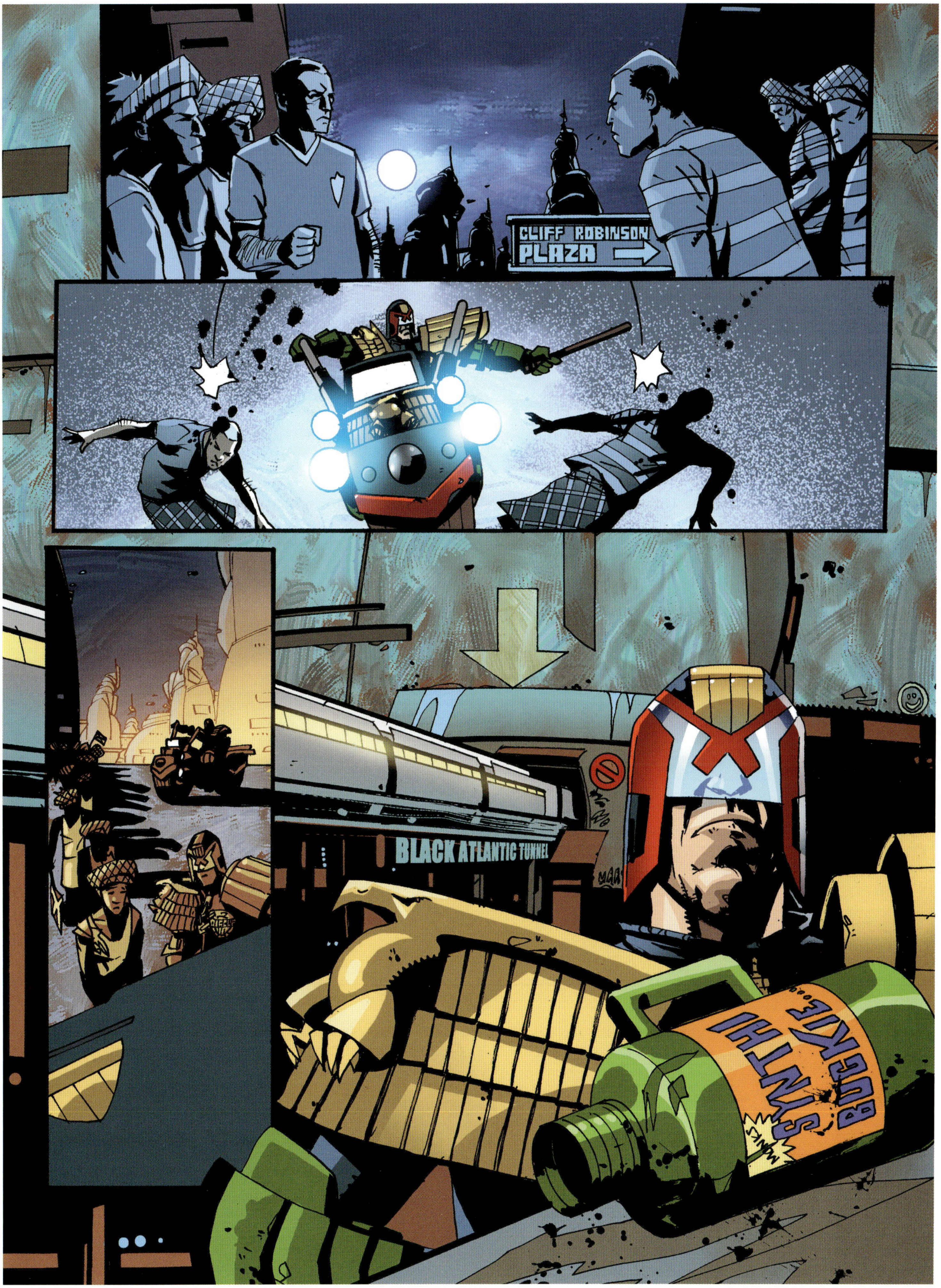
CLIFF ROBINSON
PLAZA
BLACK ATLANTIC TUNNEL
MONKS
SYNTHI
BUCKIE

JUDGE DREDD: TARTAN TERRORS PAGE 6, 2000 AD PROG 1540, 2007
COLOURS BY CHRIS BLYTHE

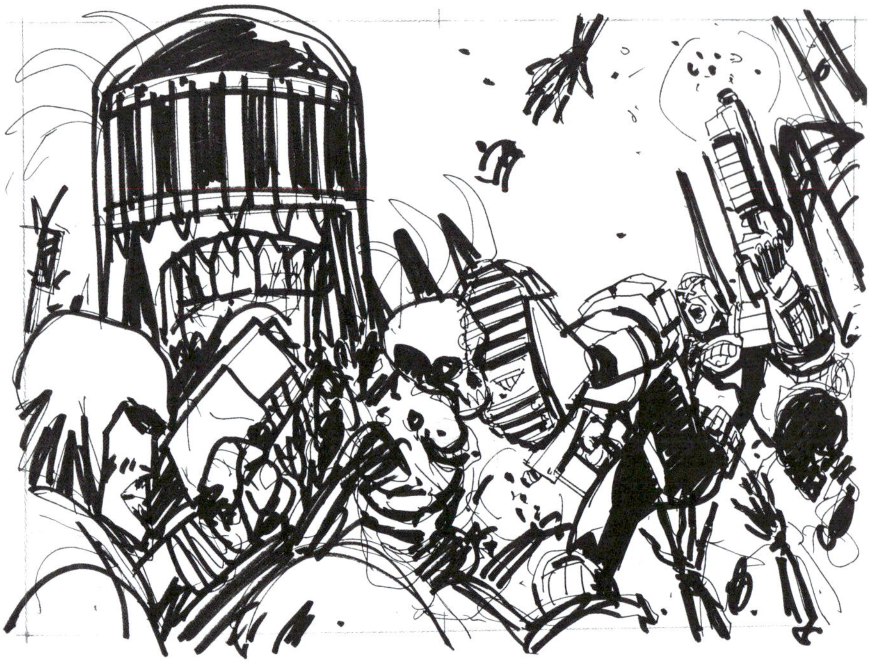

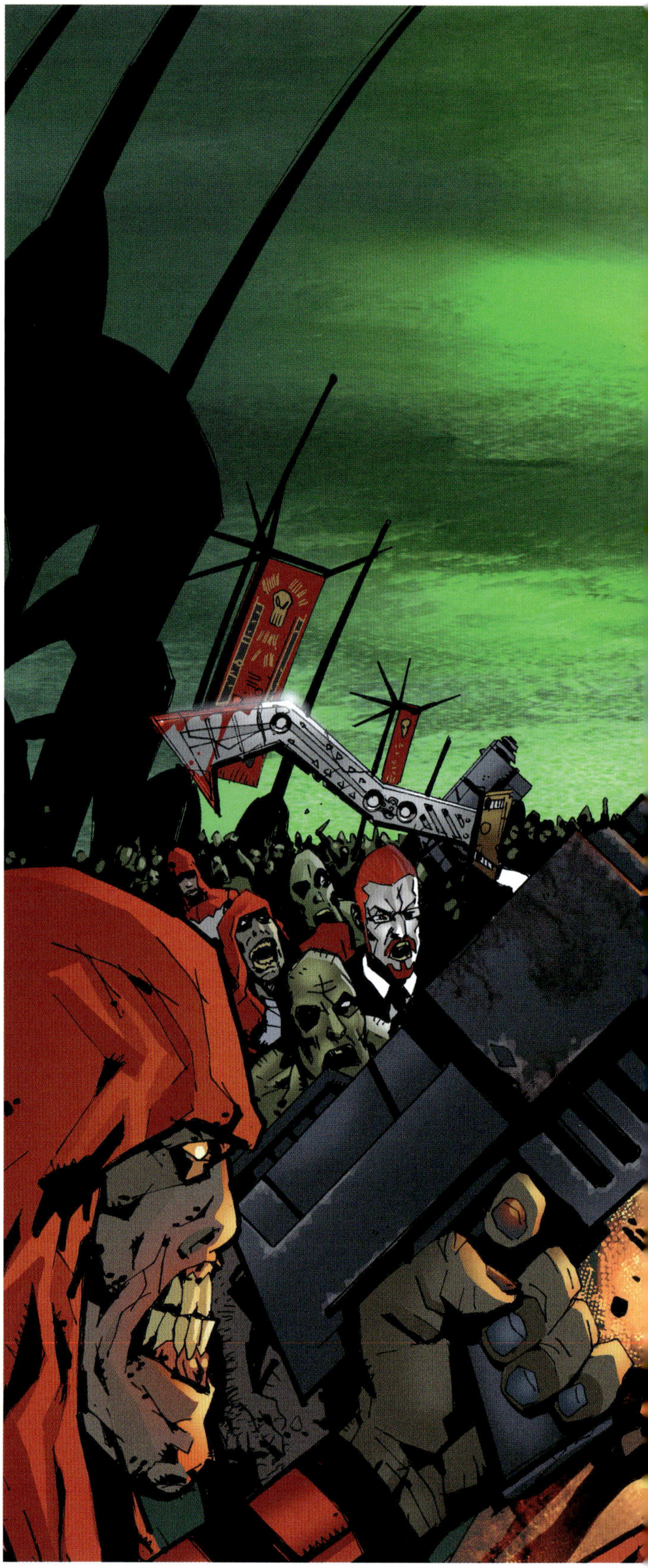

 2000 AD EXTREME EDITION #1 COVER SKETCH & FINAL ART, 2003

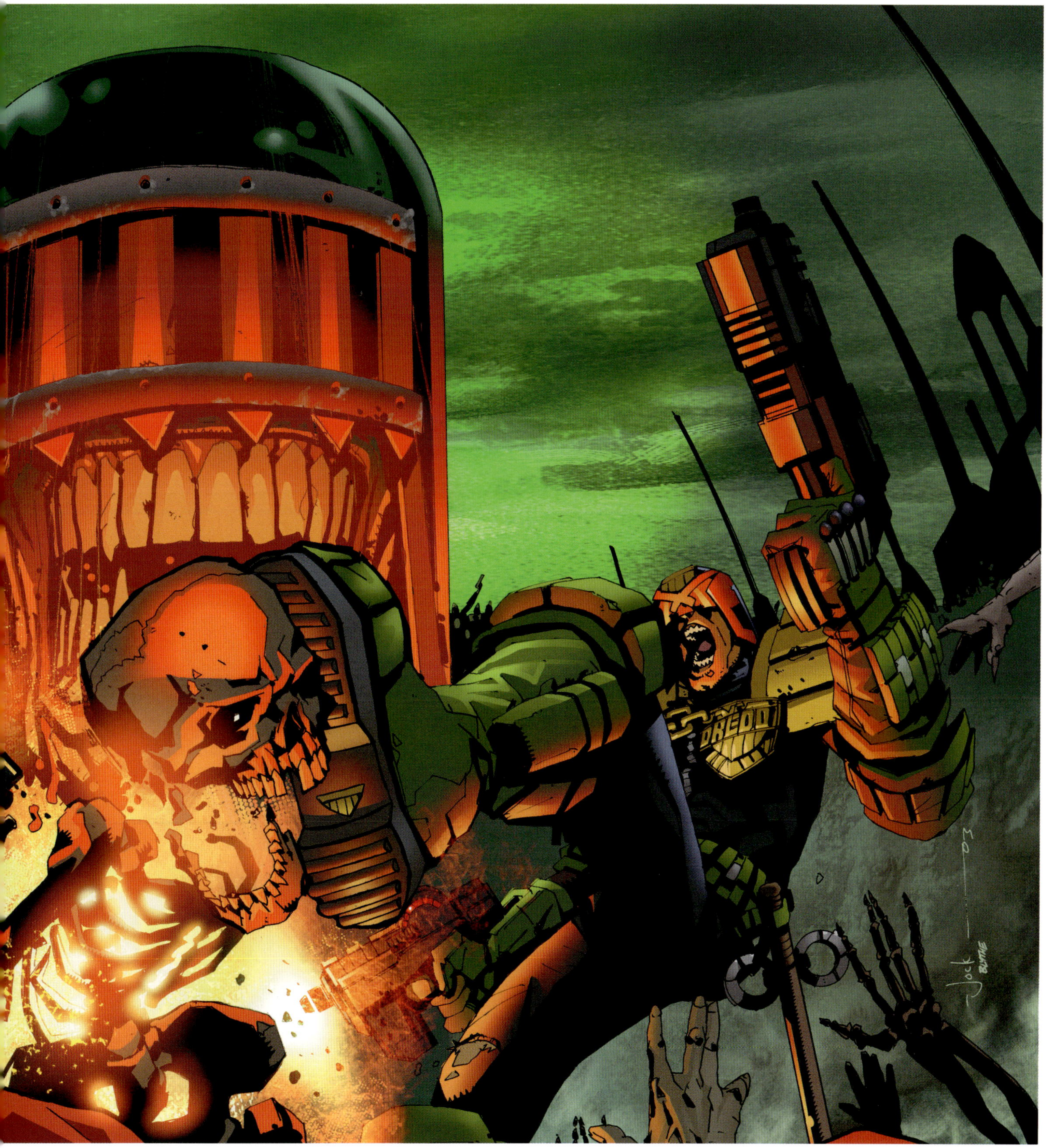
DREDD

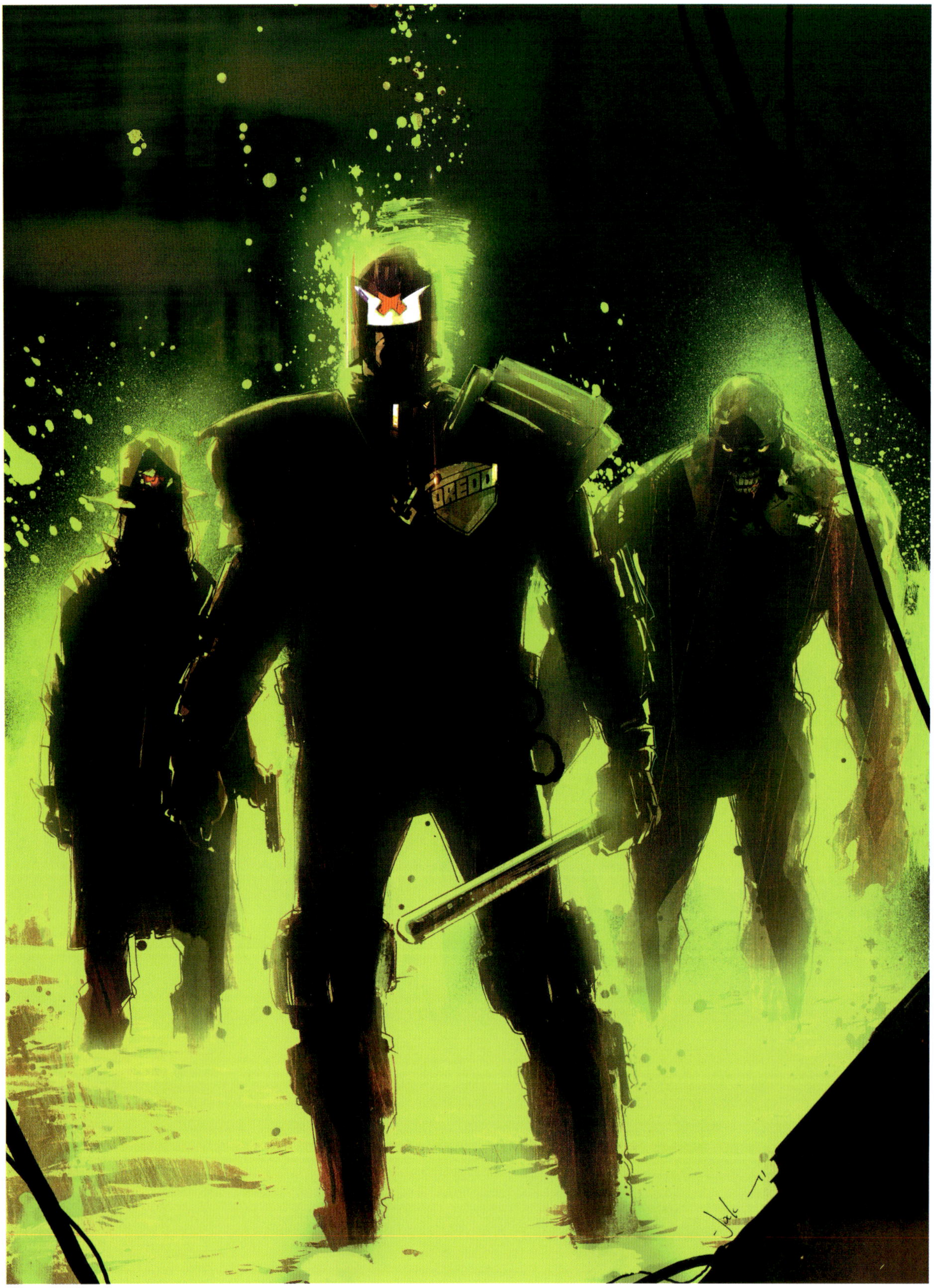
DREDD

 2000 AD FREE COMIC BOOK DAY COVER, 2012

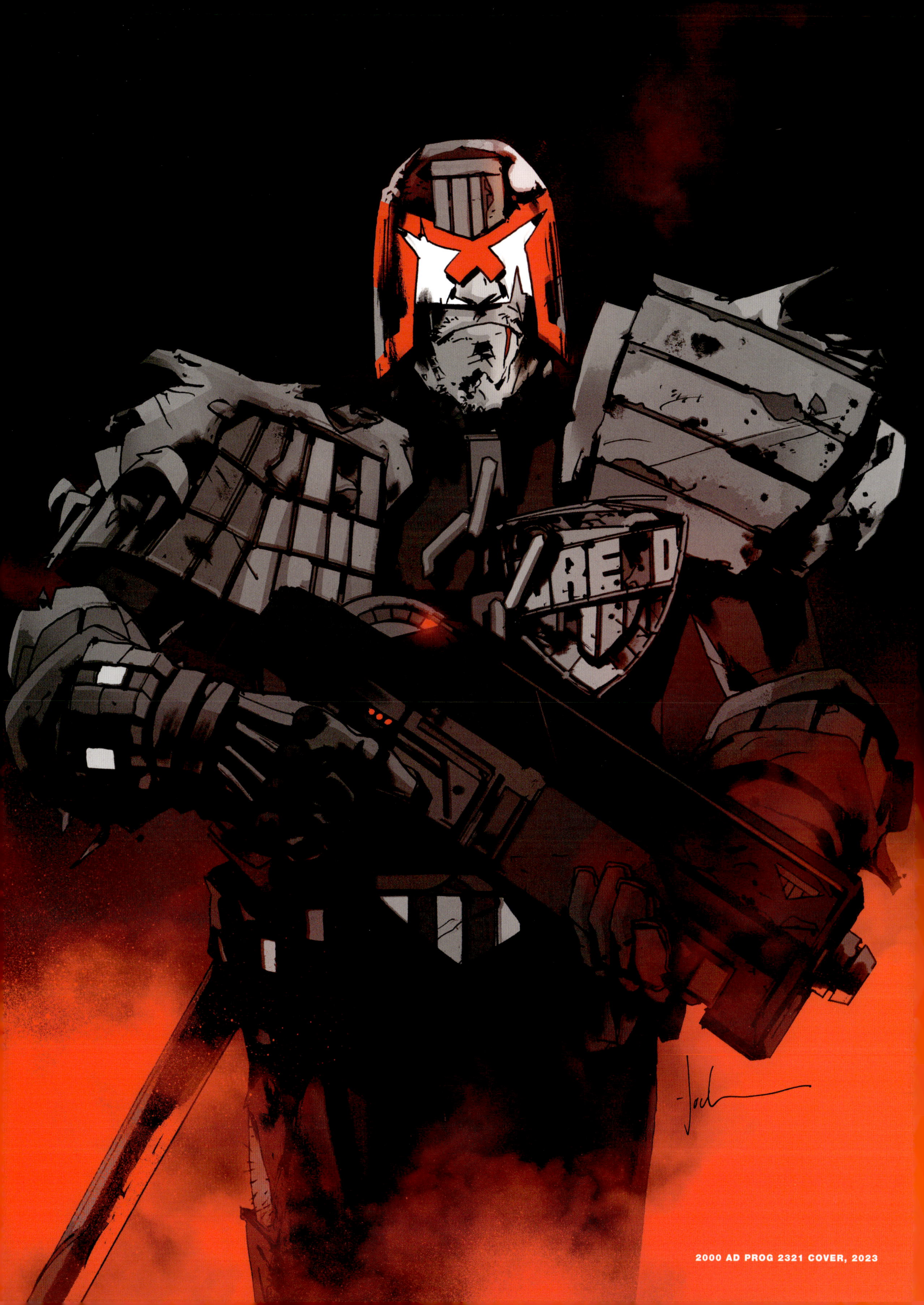

2000 AD PROG 2321 COVER, 2023

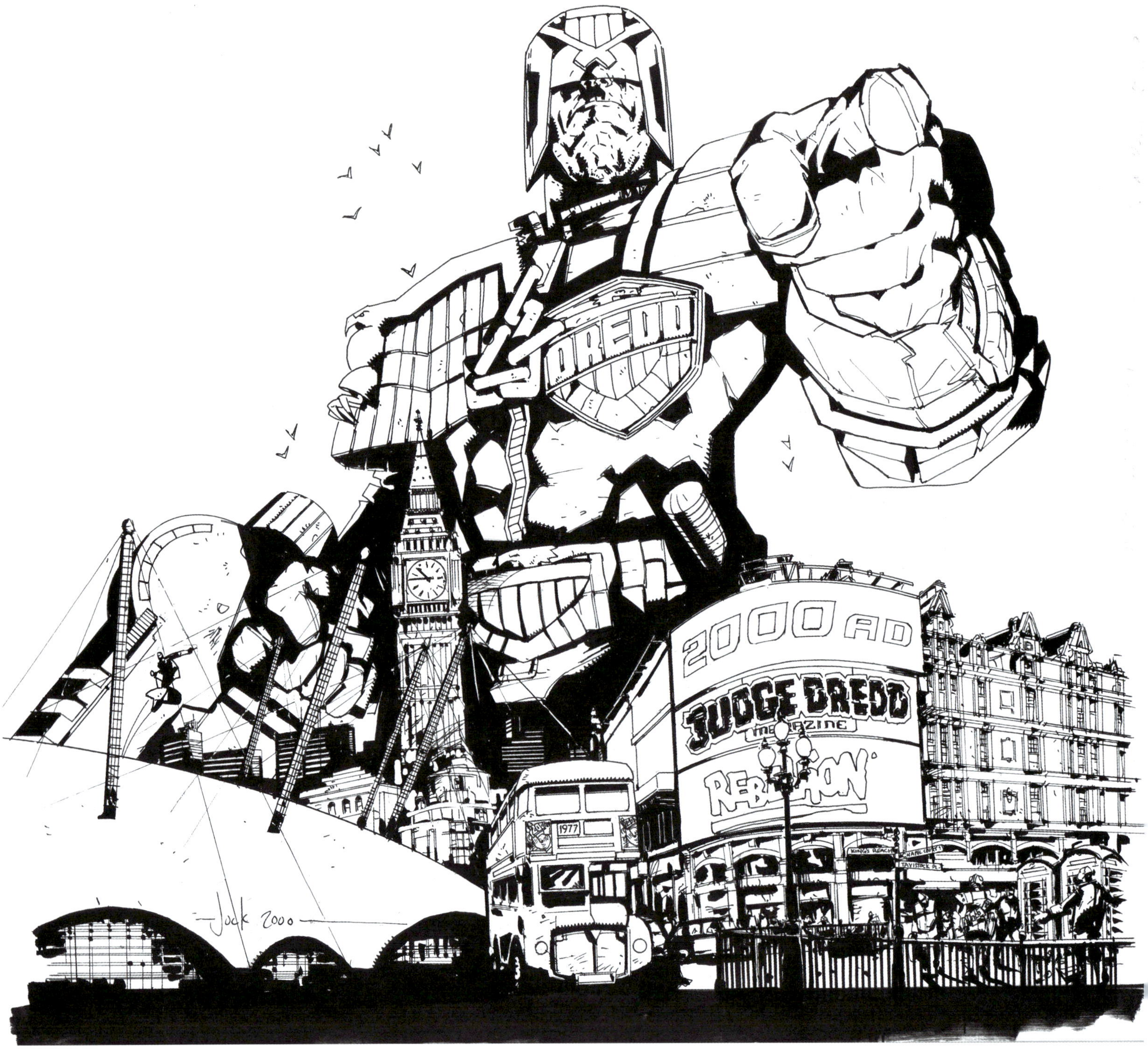
DREDD
2000 AD
JUDGE DREDD
MEGAZINE
REBELLION
1977
Jock 2000

ANNIVERSARY

'From early on I tended to be offered all these extra things, from skate decks to a **British Airways** magazine illustration, these **Dreddcon** images and mugs. And the truth is I loved it, I relished it, I was proud that I was getting to do it. It felt good that my take on Dredd was working for people. These two drawings are 20 years apart! By the looks of it, the earlier piece was drawn larger as there's more detail in it, but it's interesting to see how two very similar drawings were handled with so much time apart.'

—JOCK

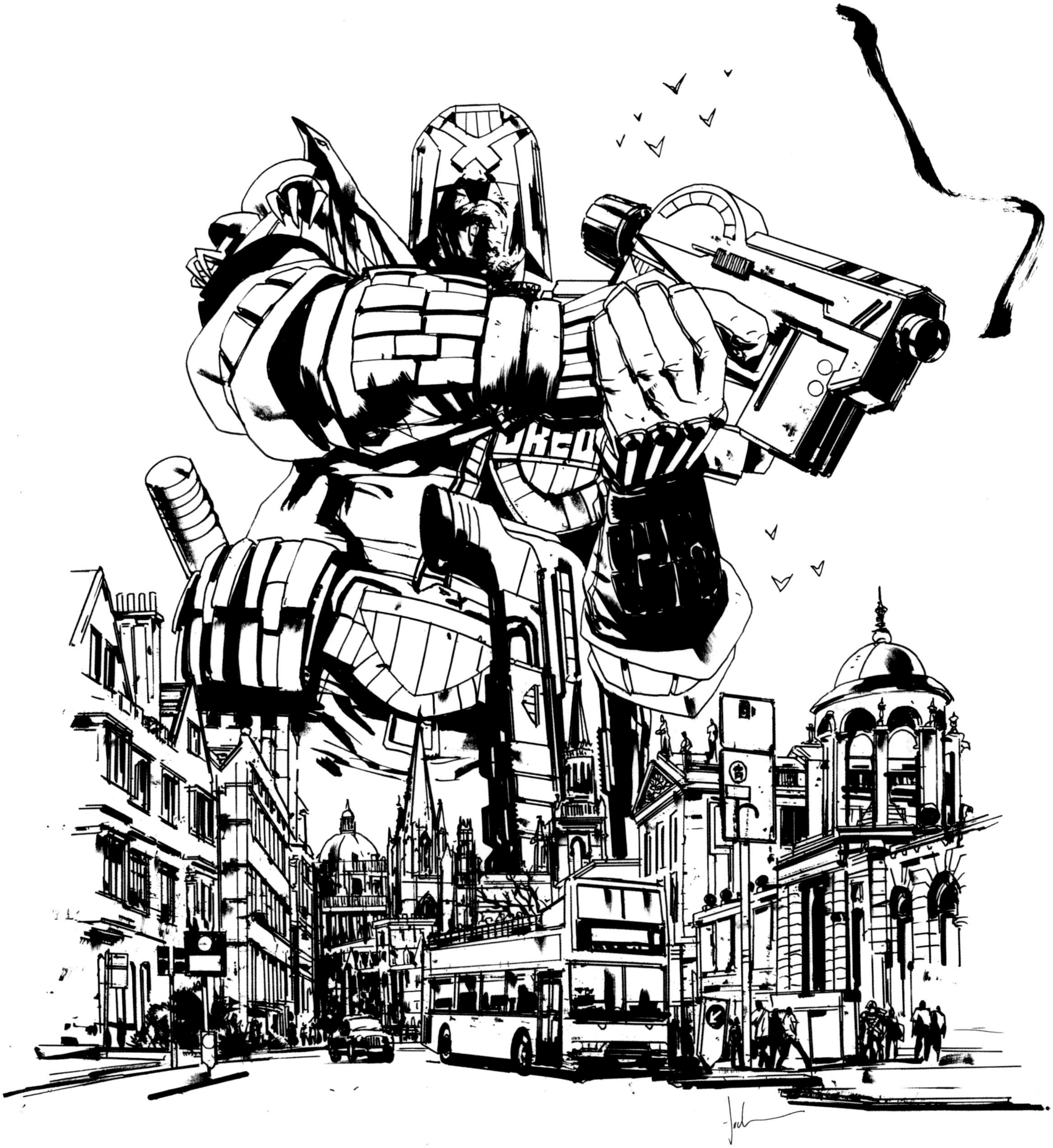

2000 AD SCI-FI SUMMER SPECIAL ILLUSTRATION, 2020

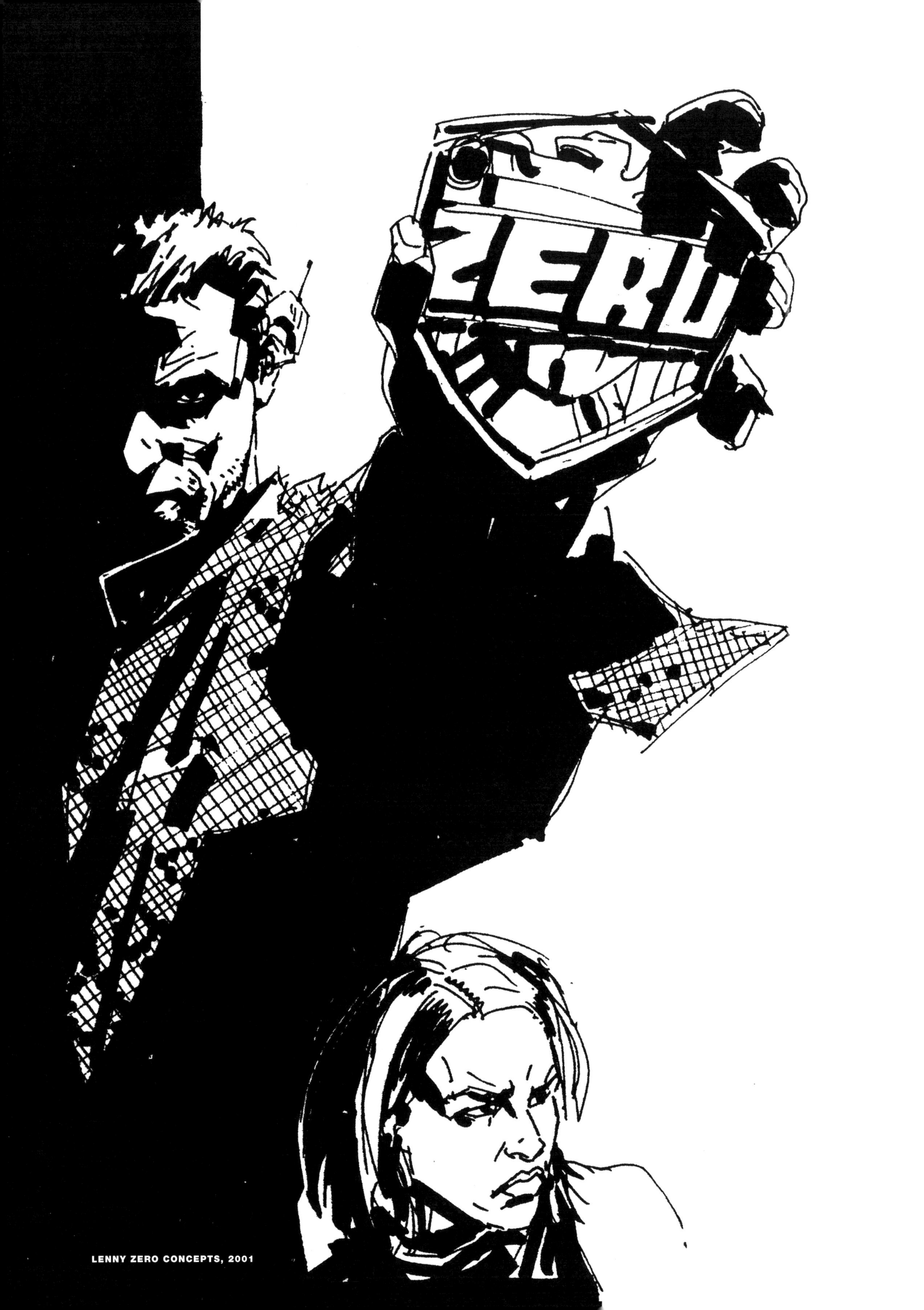
ZERO

LENNY ZERO CONCEPTS, 2001

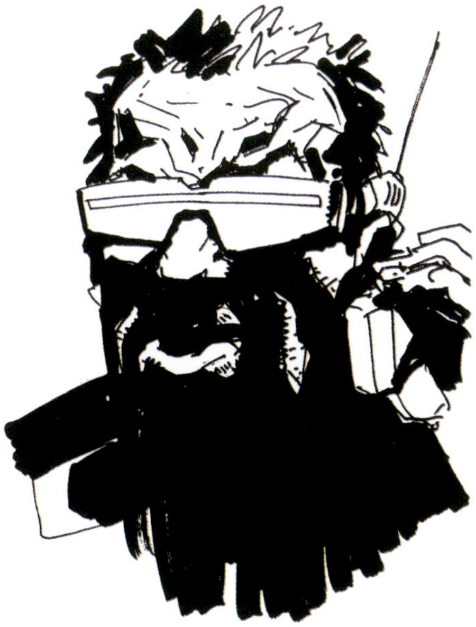

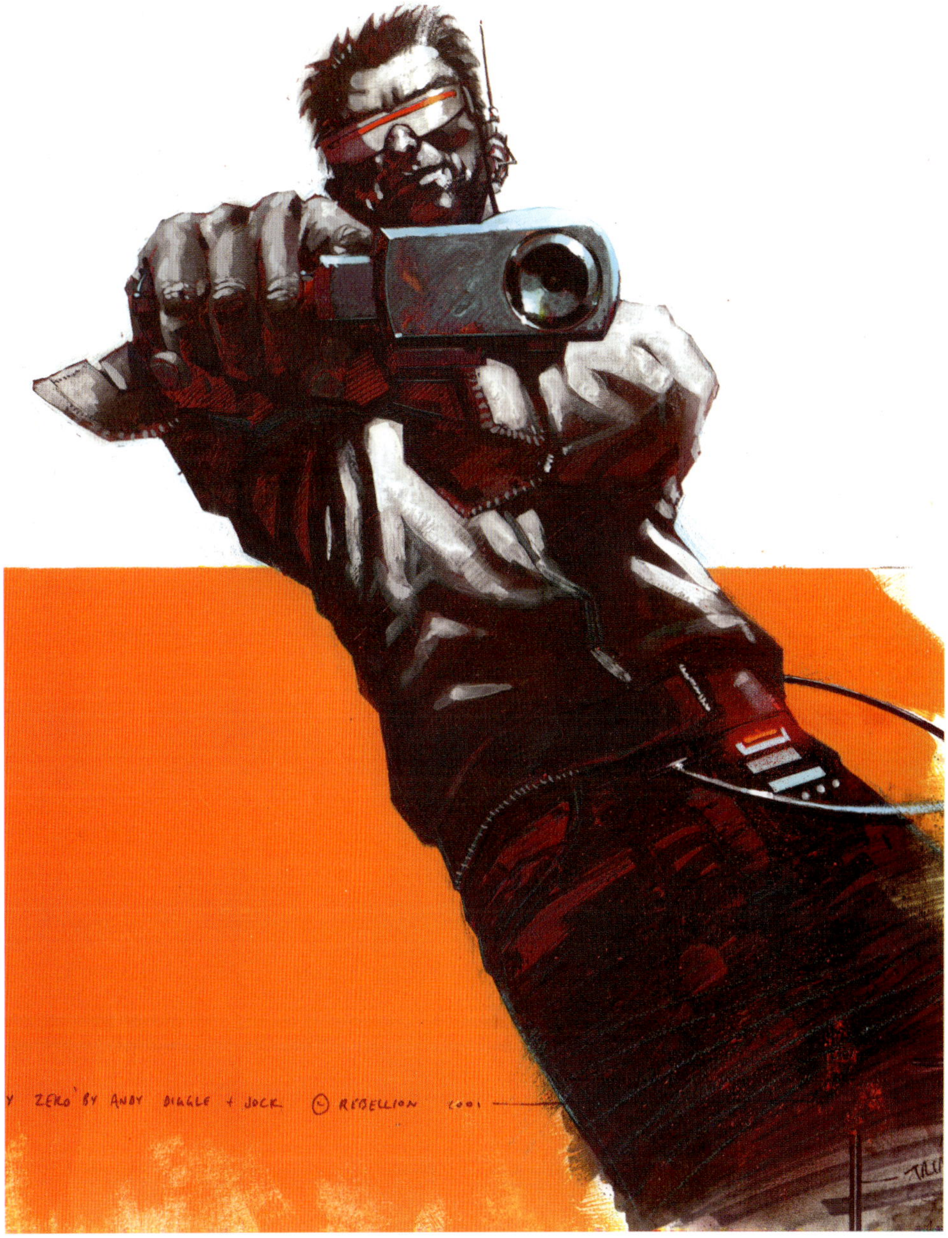
ZERO' BY ANDY DIGGLE + JOCK © REBELLION 2001

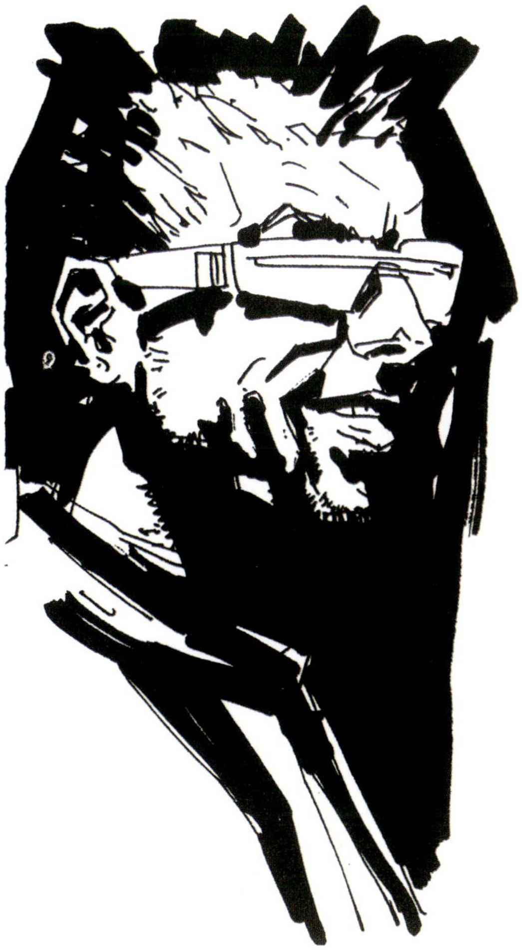

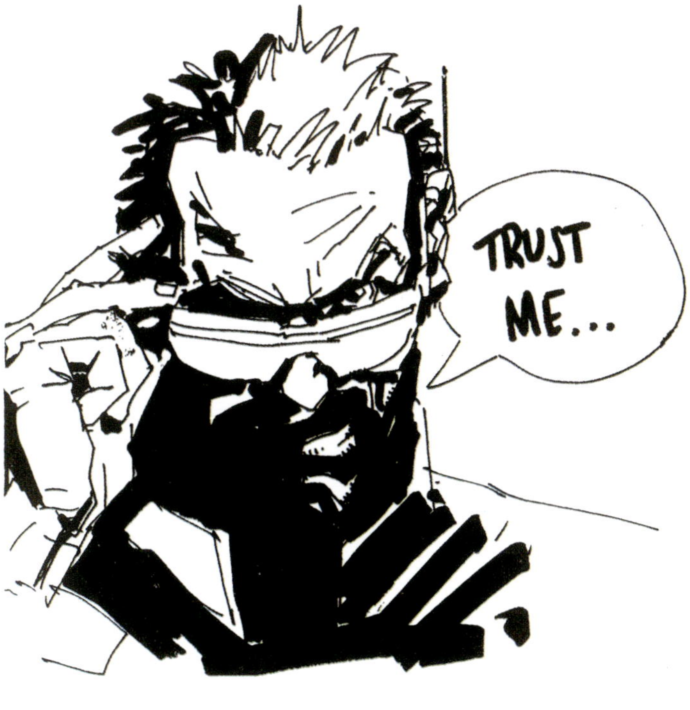
TRUST ME...

LENNY ZERO CONCEPTS, 2001

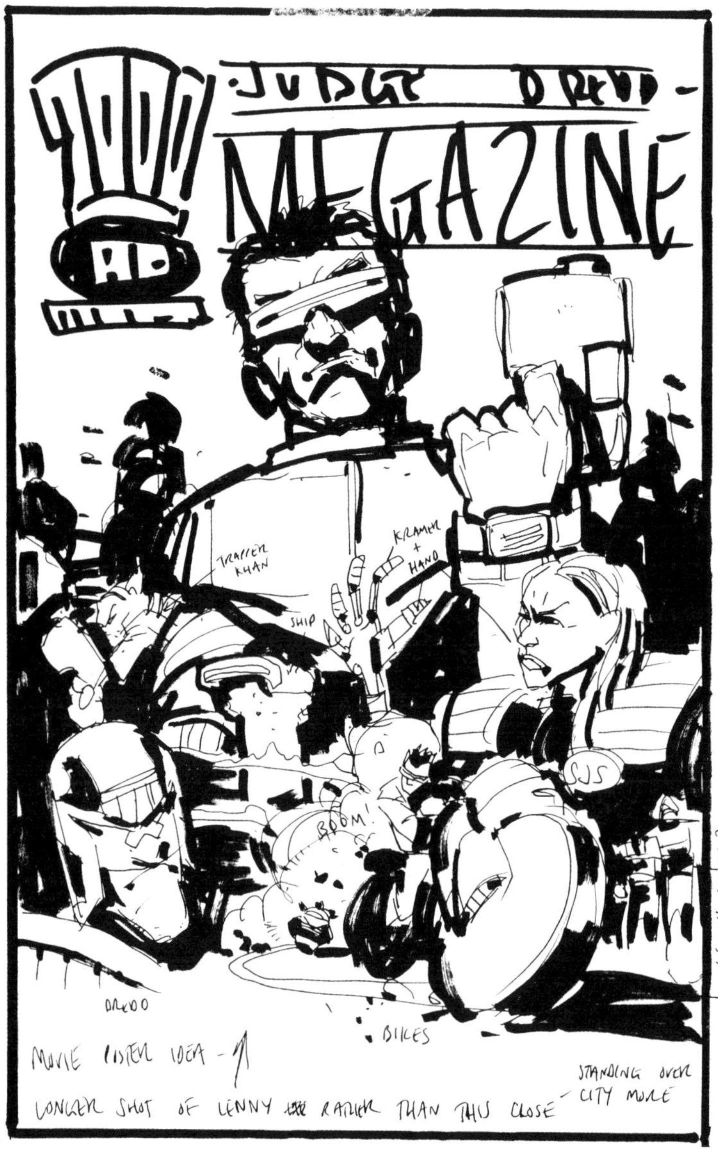
JUDGE DREDD
MEGAZINE
TRAPPER KHAN
KRAMER + HAND
SHIP
BOOM!
DREDD
BIKES
MOVIE POSTER IDEA
LONGER SHOT OF LENNY RATHER THAN THIS CLOSE
STANDING OVER CITY MORE

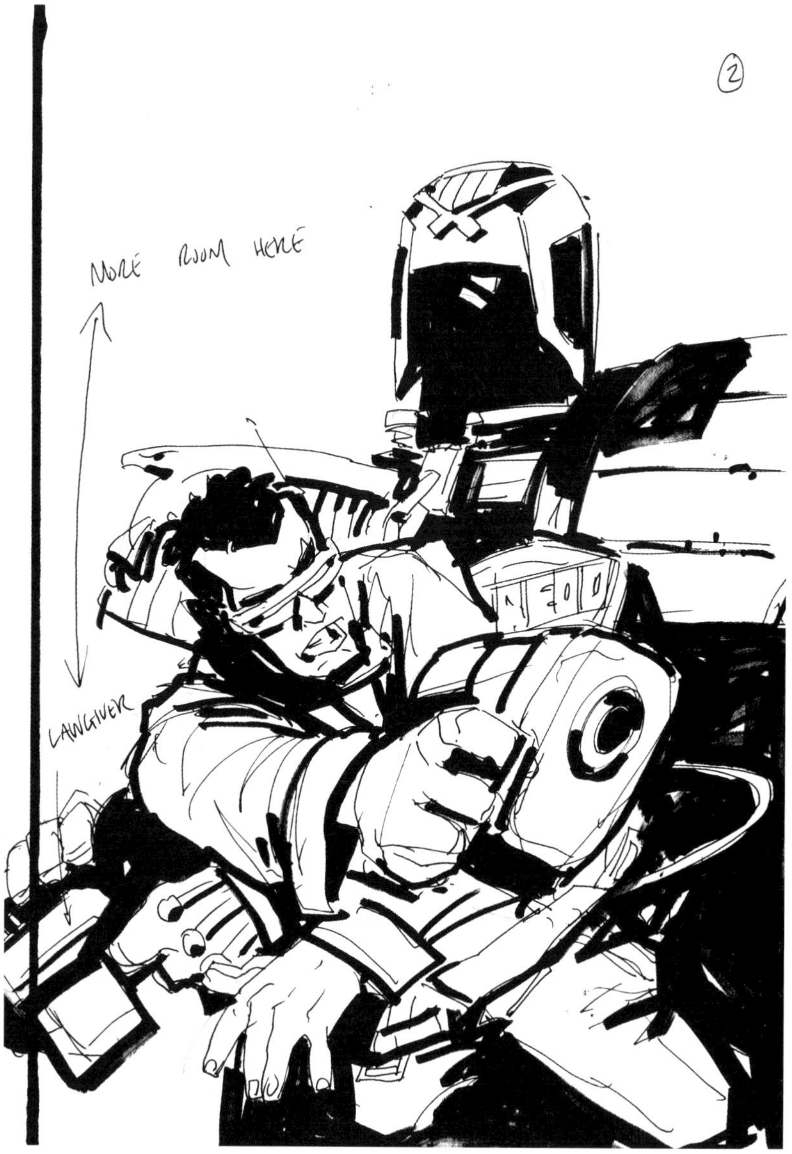
2
MORE ROOM HERE

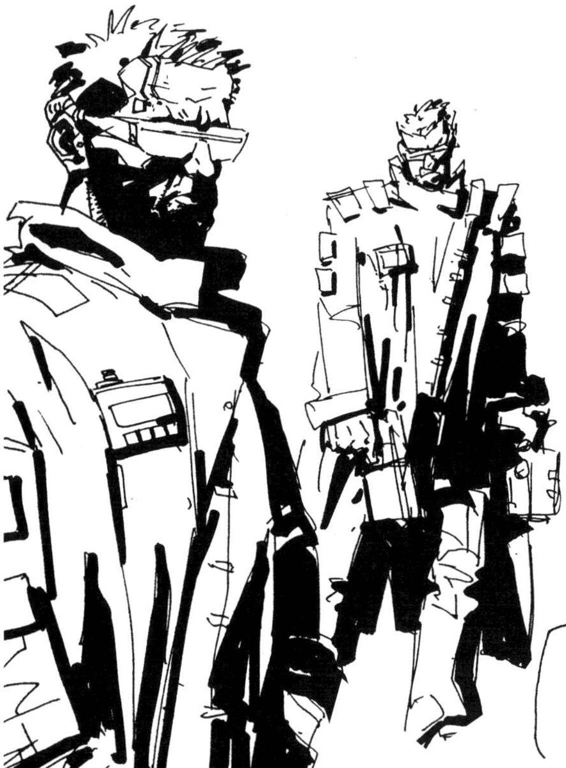

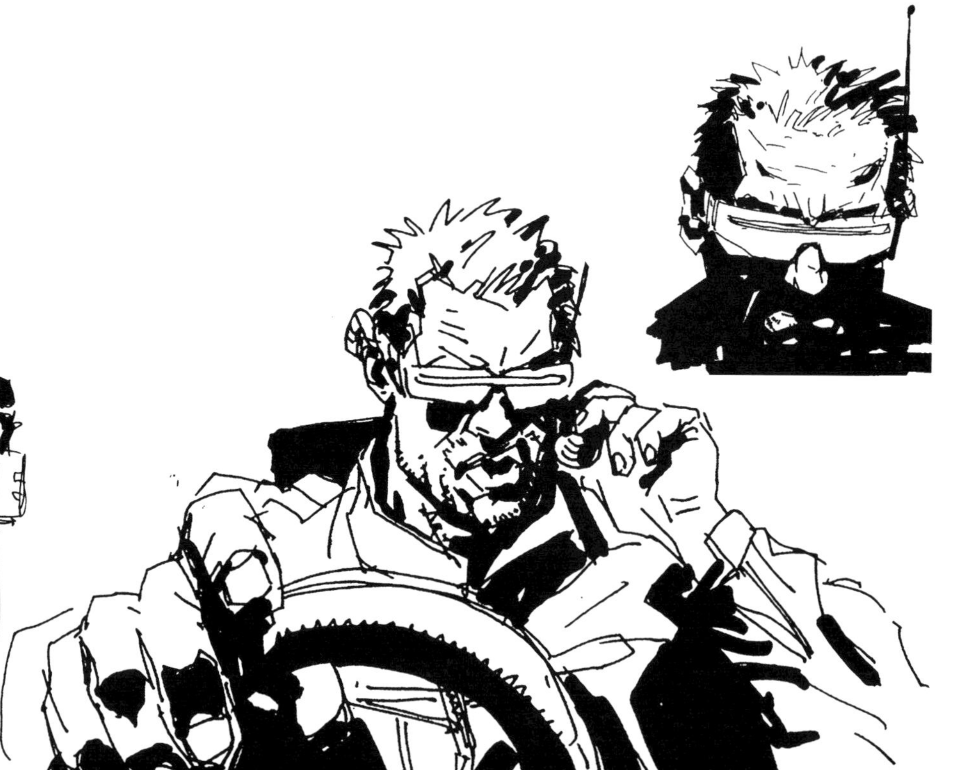

LENNY ZERO

'I still use a lot of photo reference in my work but back then, even with 'Shirley Temple of Doom', I cast friends and my wife Jo as different characters – and this was back in the day when I had to use a traditional camera, take the photos, get them processed at the local shop with, hopefully, a quick turnaround of an hour. It was a pretty laborious process. But Lenny Zero is my old friend John Spelling. And I still have the photos.

With Lenny Zero, one thing I tried to do, or rather one thing I felt I had the freedom to do, was to make it more noir-y than a regular Dredd strip. And John has great bone structure in his face and it was the first time I really got to play with large, hard shadows. When I took reference photos of him, I deliberately lit his face with hard top light to get really strong shadows. That set a tone that I still use to this day - using heavy shadow to bring out the character. I really figured that out on Lenny. In the panel where he's putting his iconic glasses on, you can see the way the light drops across his nose and a little touch on his lip and his chin. Just tiny pinpoints of highlights on the face. And that's the way the light fell on John. I loved discovering that.'

—JOCK

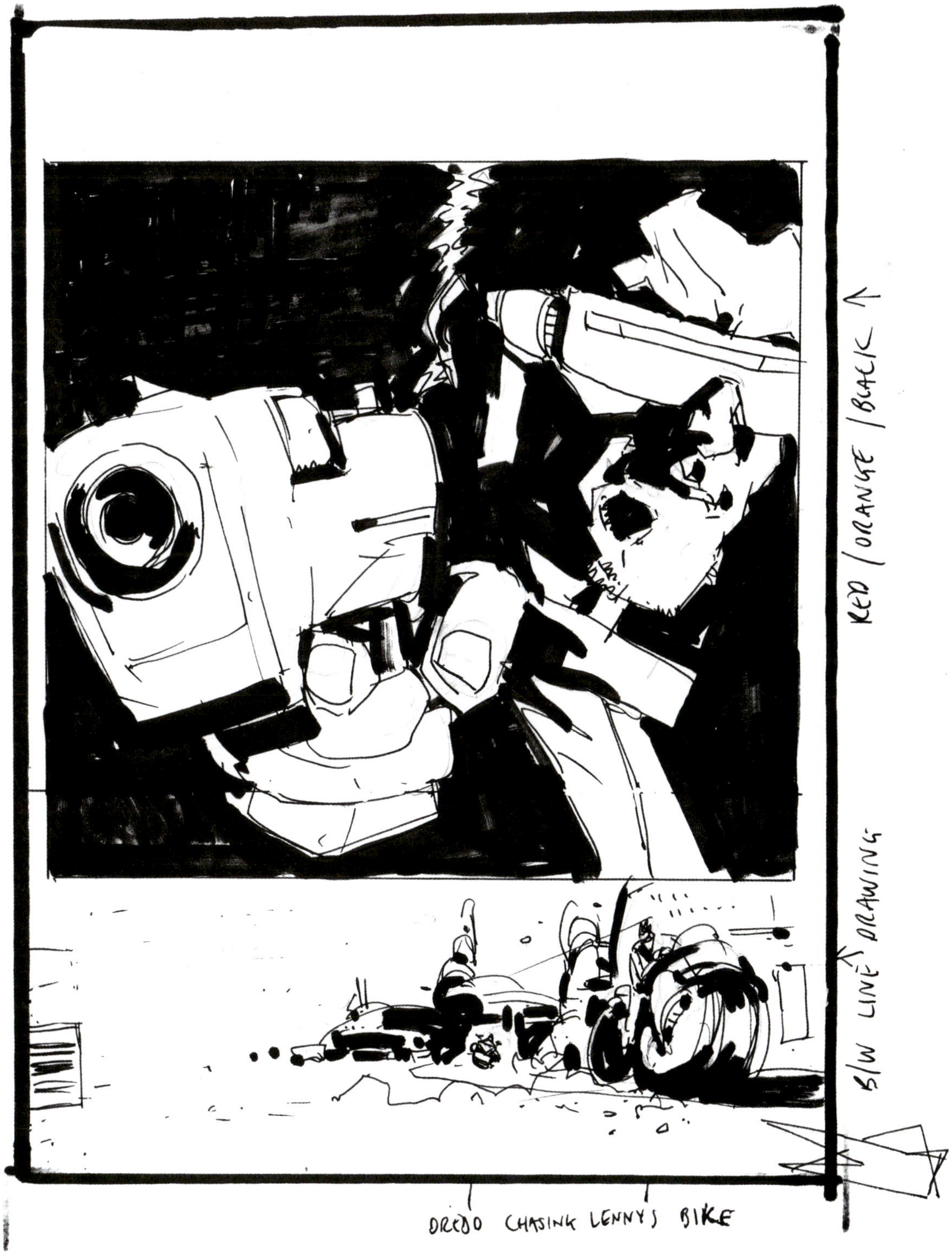
RED / ORANGE / BLACK
B/W LINE DRAWING
DREDD CHASING LENNY'S BIKE

LENNY ZERO

PAGE ONE

1) Start on a left-hand page with a full-figure establishing shot of LENNY ZERO, a mid-echelon Mega-City criminal with the effortlessly cool manner of Steve McQueen or George Clooney. He stands casually with a shuggy cue in hand. He's a tough-guy, but lean and rangy rather than overly muscular. He has short, spiky-cropped hair, wears wraparound slit-lens NightShades, a dinosaur-skin jacket and Kalvin Kleen jeans. He's playing shuggy in a dark and dingy bar, but this image may work best with no background, to establish Lenny.
   CAPTION: FIFTEEN YEARS I'D BEEN BUSTIN' MY BALLS ON THE STREETS OF THE BIG MEG. IN MY LINE OF WORK, THAT'S WAY BEYOND LIFE EXPECTANCY.
   CAPTION: I PUT IT ALL DOWN TO TRUST. THE JUDGES, THEY DON'T TRUST NOBODY... BUT THAT'S 'CAUSE THEY DON'T KNOW A THING ABOUT LOVE.
   DTP TITLE: LENNY ZERO

2) Lenny leans over the shuggy table, lining up a shot towards us. (Shuggy is the 22nd century version of pool, with the holes atop 'hills' on an uneven, round table). Sitting at the bar behind Lenny is a FAT LOSER with a shuggy cue in his hand. Next to him is MONA, Lenny's girlfriend - a dark-haired, flint-eyed beauty in a sleek black microdress.
   CAPTION: BUT I COULD ALWAYS COUNT ON MONA TO COUNT ON ME. WE WERE ONE HELL OF A TEAM. TRUST, Y'SEE?
   FAT LOSER: FIFTY CREDS SAYS YER BOYFRIEND CAN'T MAKE THAT SHOT.
   MONA: GOT YOURSELF A DEAL.

3) Close-up of the ball rolling up into the '100' hole atop a particularly difficult rise.
   FX: PLOK
   FAT LOSER (OFF): AW, MAN...
   CAPTION: SURE, I COULD'VE MADE THE SHOT WITHOUT THE HEADS-UP DISPLAY IN MY NIGHTSHADES, BUT WEARIN' 'EM MEANS PEOPLE CAN'T READ MY EYES.

4) Close profile of Lenny; somebody off-panel behind him is holding a gun to the back of Lenny's head. Lenny shouldn't be able to see it, but he can. Perhaps we can just make out tiny rear-view lenses on Lenny's NightShades.
   CAPTION: BESIDES, SOMETIMES IT PAYS TO HAVE EYES IN THE BACK OF YOUR HEAD.
   LENNY: HEY MARV, WHAT'S UP? YOU PUT MONEY ON THE FAT GUY OR SOMETHIN'?

5) Lenny turns to see a gang of futuristic mob enforcers standing behind him. Front and center is MARV, a brutal Mafia thug, holding a blaster on Lenny.
   CAPTION: MARV WAS NAMED AFTER HIS RAP SHEET - "MULTIPLE ARMED ROBBERY WITH VIOLENCE", YEAH?
   CAPTION: A NASTY PIECE OF WORK WHO TOOK A LITTLE TOO MUCH PLEASURE IN CARRYIN' OUT WHACK JOBS FOR LITTLE CAESAR PICCANTE'S MOB.
   MARV: DITCH THE BITCH, BUDDY. DA BOSS WOULD LIKE A WORD.

6) Mona has come over to Lenny, concerned. Lenny holds her back gently, gripping her upper arms - holding her back from them, not wanting her to get hurt. She refers to Lenny as "Buddy" - his assumed name.
   MONA: BUDDY? WHO ARE THESE GUYS - ?
   LENNY: JUST BUSINESS, BABY. HEAD ON HOME, I'LL CATCH UP WITH YOU LATER.
   CAPTION: I'D BEEN DOIN' SOME LAUNDERIN' WORK FOR CAESAR'S OUTFIT, SUPPLYIN' USED CRED-CARDS FOR RE-CHIPPING.
   CAPTION: SOMETHING TOLD ME I WAS ABOUT TO START LOOKIN' FOR A NEW LINE OF WORK...

PAGE TWO

1) Change of scene. Lenny, now sans shades, is ushered at gunpoint into a bright and spacious lux-apt penthouse. Riding around in a kiddie's hover-buggy is LITTLE CAESAR, a ten year-old kid in a sharp black suit and a paper party hat. His assorted goons wear party hats too. Caesar looks like an extra from Bugsy Malone, but his eyes are very old and very cruel. NOTE: there's a lot of dialogue over this next couple of pages, so leave plenty of room.
   CAPTION: LITTLE CAESAR WAS BARELY INTO HIS THIRD BIO-CHIPPED CLONE BODY, SO HE WAS PRETTY SPRY FOR A GUY HIS AGE.
   CAESAR: I'M TELLIN' YA, IT'S AMAZIN' WHAT THEY GOT FOR KIDS THESE DAYS!
   LINK: HEY THERE, BUDDY, GLAD YOU COULD JOIN THE PARTY. YOU KNOW WHAT TODAY IS? MY 200TH BIRTHDAY.

2) Lenny's POV. Close on Caesar, now looming over us with cold fury in his eyes.
   CAESAR: I WAS RUNNIN' ERRANDS FOR AL CAPONE WHEN I WAS TEN YEARS OLD. I SEEN TWO NUCLEAR WARS, THE BIG NEC, JUDGEMENT DAY... AN' I'M STILL HERE.
   LINK: AFTER ALL'A THAT, YOU REALLY THINK I'M GONNA LET MYSELF GET SHAFTED BY SOME TWO-CRED STREET PUNK ON THE MAKE?
   LINK: DO YA?

3) We're looking down over Caesar's shoulder at Lenny, kneeling now, acting innocent. Marv has a gun to Lenny's head.
   LENNY: GRUDSAKE, CAESAR - WHY DON'T YOU TELL ME WHAT THE HELL YOU'RE TALKIN' ABOUT?
   CAESAR: YOU DON'T KNOW WHAT I'M TALKIN' ABOUT. OKAY, WISEGUY, LET ME KNOW WHEN THIS STARTS SOUNDIN' FAMILIAR.

4) Flashback - we are inside a mob safehouse, maybe an old warehouse or underground bunker. ALVIN KEYES, a nerdy accountant with glasses, is typing frantically at a flatscreen computer. Behind him, a team of armed Judges are bursting through the door, blasting startled goons. The lead Judge is pointing at Keyes and shouting.
   CAPTION: "SOMEBODY TOLD THE JUDGES WHERE TO FIND ALVIN KEYES, MY CHIEF ACCOUNTANT.
   CAPTION: "NOW KEYES AIN'T NO DUMMY. MOMENT THE JAYS BUSTED IN, HE CHANGED THE ACCESS CODE TO MY ACCOUNT BEFORE THEY COULD SEIZE IT."

5) Caesar leans close into Lenny's face, screaming with rage. This kid is scary. Lenny's hands are spread open in a gesture of innocence.
   CAESAR: NOW THEY'RE GIVIN' HIM THE TREATMENT IN SOME CUBE, AN' I CAN'T EVEN GET AHOLD OF MY OWN MONEY!
   LINK: THAT'S THIRTY-THREE MILLION CREDS, YOU SON OF A BITCH!
   LENNY: WHOA, CAESAR - TIME OUT! WHY THE HELL WOULD I SELL YOU OUT? I AIN'T GOT NO DEATH WISH!

6) Caesar reaches in from off-panel, holding a photo in front of Lenny's crestfallen face. This photo is Lenny's death warrant, and his icy cool finally fails him. In fact, he looks like he's just swallowed a lemon.
   CAESAR: THAT A FACT? THEN MAYBE YOU CAN EXPLAIN HOW COME I GOT VID FOOTAGE OF YOU AN' YOUR JUDGE PAL COSYIN' UP IN SHAPIRO'S?
   LINK: HOW MUCH DID THEY PAY YOU FOR RATTIN' ME OUT, HUH?

7) Caesar turns away from Lenny with a dismissive wave. In extreme foreground, Lenny is holding the photo so we can just about make out a couple of blurry figures - Lenny and a uniformed Judge in an eaterie.
   LENNY: L-LISTEN, YOU GOT IT ALL WRONG--
   CAESAR: YOU'RE DEAD. AN' THAT PIECE OF SKIRT YOU HANG WITH, SHE'S DEAD TOO - AT LEAST, ONCE MARV HERE'S HAD HIS FUN WITH HER.
   LINK: OKAY MARV, I'M DONE TALKIN'. SHOOT THIS RAT FINK.

PAGE THREE

1) Extreme close-up on Lenny, grim. He's making the most difficult decision of his life, about to betray everything he believes in.
   LENNY: ... YOU CAN'T KILL ME, CAESAR. YOU NEED ME.
   LINK: I CAN GET HIM BACK FOR YOU.

2) Caesar has turned his back on Lenny, hands behind his back. But now he turns his head in Lenny's direction, contemptuous.
   CAESAR: THAT A FACT? YOU'RE GONNA SPRING KEYES FROM A SECTOR HOUSE INTERROGATION CUBE, DEAD MAN?
   LINK: WHAT ARE YOU, SOME KINDA MAGICIAN?

3) BIG. This is the money shot - it needs real impact. Medium close on Lenny, standing now, grim, holding out a Judge name-badge labeled "ZERO".
   LENNY: NO.
   LINK: I'M A JUDGE.

4) Wider now, taking in Lenny, Caesar and the others. Now that Lenny is standing, he's much taller than Caesar, and somehow seems to be the most powerful figure in the room.
   CAESAR: SON OF A BITCH... ALL'THIS TIME, YOU WAS WALLY SQUAD*... ?
   LINK: YOU WAS ALREADY DEAD, BUDDY. YOU'RE DOUBLE DEAD NOW.
   LENNY: LEAVE MONA OUT OF IT. SHE DOESN'T KNOW ABOUT THIS, SHE AIN'T INVOLVED.
   LINK: PLEASE, JUST... LET HER GO, AN' I'LL GET YOU THE ACCOUNTANT.
   CAPTION BELOW: * WALLY SQUAD: MEGA-SLANG FOR JUSTICE DEPARTMENT'S UNDERCOVER DIVISION.

5) Closer on Lenny, looking down on Caesar. Lenny's playing hardball for his life here.
   LENNY: SOONER OR LATER, KEYES IS GONNA CRACK. AND WHEN THE JAYS GET AHOLD OF THAT ACCOUNT CODE, YOU CAN KISS YOUR THIRTY-THREE MIL GOODBYE.
   LINK: CLOCK'S TICKIN', CAESAR.

PAGE FOUR

1) Caesar sits back. Suspicious, sizing Lenny up, one finger to his lips in a pensive gesture.
   CAESAR: YOU'RE EITHER LOOKIN' FOR A BULLET OR A ONE-WAY TICKET TO TITAN. I JUST CAN'T FIGURE WHICH.
   LINK: OKAY, YOU DO WHAT YOU GOTTA DO. BUT YOU REMEMBER, THERE AIN'T NOWHERE IN THIS CITY YOU CAN HIDE FROM ME.
   LINK: YOU TRY ANYTHIN', YOU GET TO SEE WHAT RESYK LOOKS LIKE FROM THE INSIDE, CAPICE?

2) Close-up. Lenny, back to his old self-confidence, slips his shades back on. The merest hint of a wry smile plays across his lips.
   LENNY: CAESAR...
   LINK: TRUST ME.

3) Big establishing shot - the clearly-labelled SECTOR HOUSE 24 towers before us, pedways and access ramps radiating out from it, roads spiraling around it. A bustle of citizens, Judges and Justice Department vehicles in the plaza.
   FROM BUILDING: CAESAR'S GETTIN' JUMPY, WANTS TO KNOW WHO SOLD HIM OUT.
   FROM BUILDING: SOUNDS LIKE YOU SHOULD KEEP A LOW PROFILE 'TIL THIS WHOLE THING BLOWS OVER, ZERO.

4) In a darkened observation room, Lenny and uniformed Judge CLAYTON are watching the interrogation chamber through one-way glass. Inside the interrogation chamber we can see the accountant Alvin Keyes, stripped to his vest and U-fronts, strapped into a big dentists-type chair, being grilled by two more Judges.
   LENNY: I RUN FOR COVER, THEY KNOW IT WAS ME.
   LINK: SO WHAT'S THE WORD ON KEYES HERE - HE GIVEN UP THE ACCESS CODE YET?
   CLAYTON: NOT YET. SEEMS HE WAS IMPLANTED WITH SOME KIND OF POST-HYPNOTIC MIND LOCK, HELPS HIM RESIST THE TRUTH SERUM.
   LINK: WE'VE REQUESTED A SPECIALIST FROM PSI DIVISION, SEE IF THEY CAN CRACK HIM.

5) Closer on Lenny, turning to Clayton in the gloom.
   LENNY: YOU START MESSIN' WITH A MIND LOCK, YOU'RE LIABLE TO TURN HIS BRAIN TO MUNCE - AN' THEN YOU'LL NEVER LINK HIM TO CAESAR.
   LINK: YOU GOTTA MAKE HIM WANT TO GIVE YOU THE CODE.

6) Closer still on Lenny, over Clayton's shoulder.
   CLAYTON: AND I SUPPOSE YOU HAVE SOME IDEA HOW WE DO THAT?
   LENNY: SURE I DO. LISTEN...

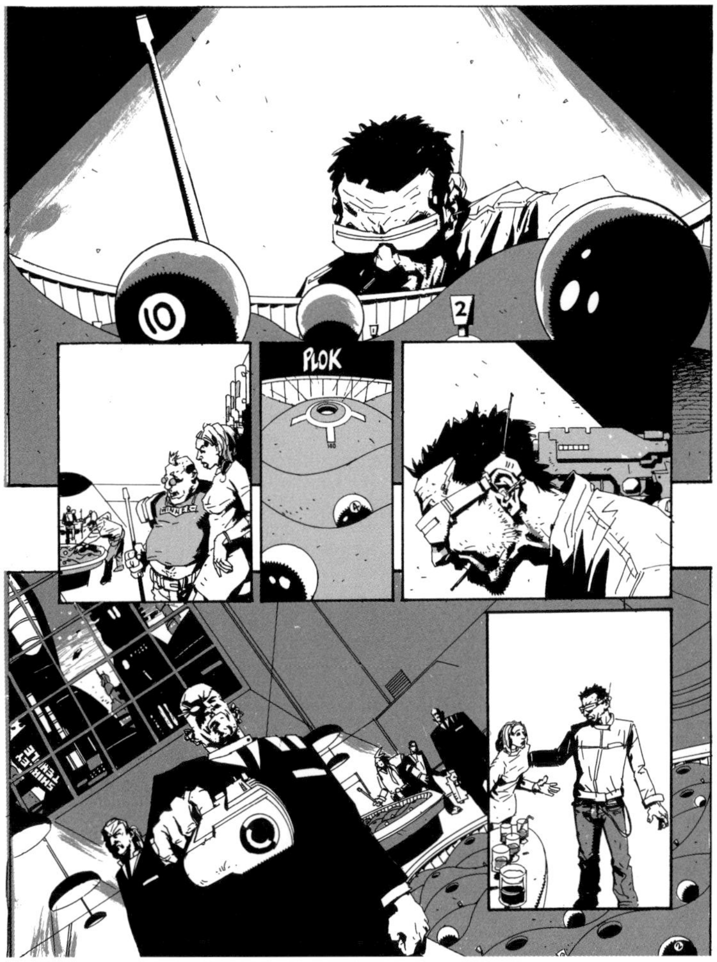
PLOK

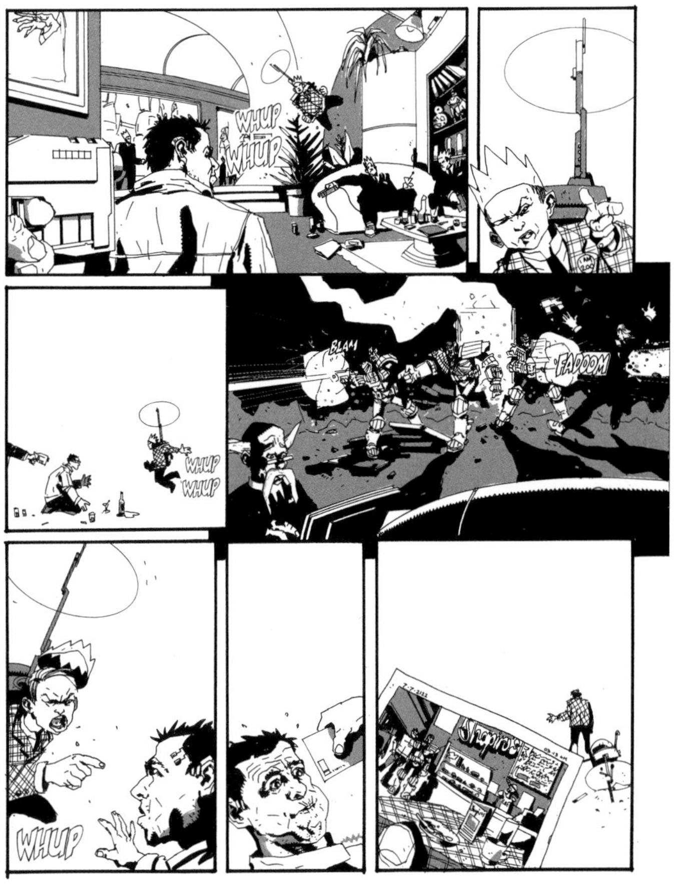
WHUP
WHUP
BLAM
FADOOM
WHUP
WHUP
WHUP

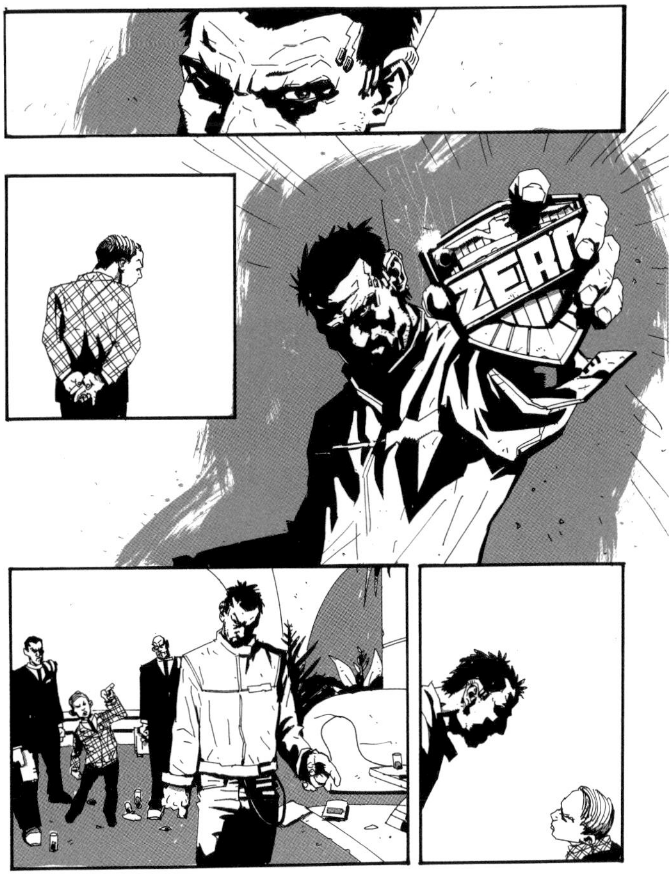
ZERO

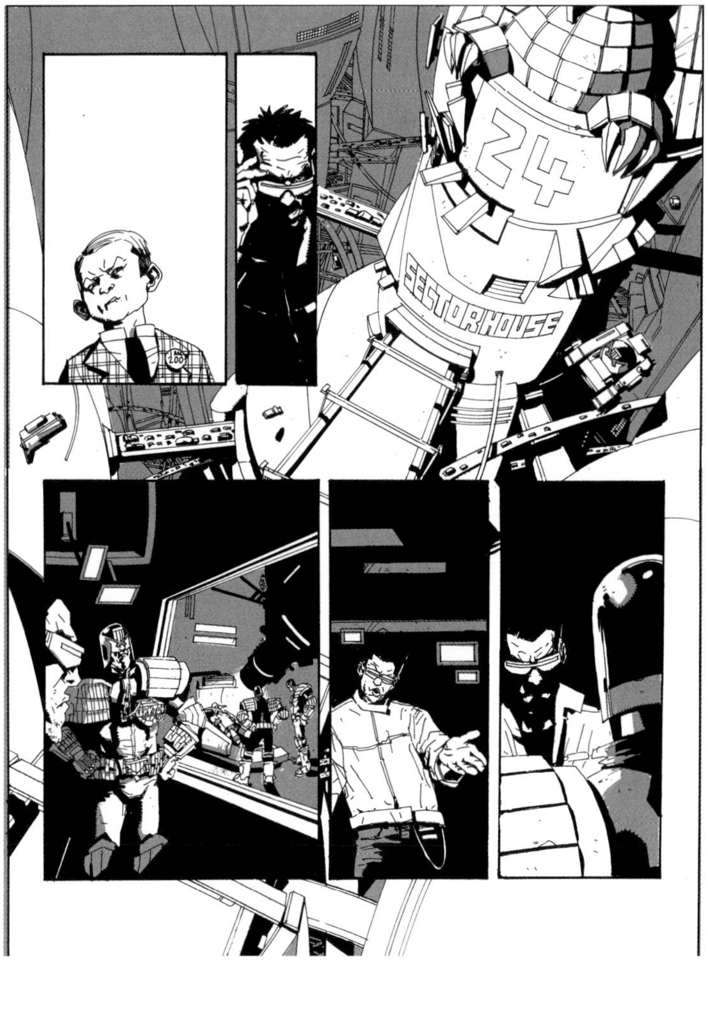
24
SECTORHOUSE

PAGE FIVE

1) Inside the interrogation chamber, Judges BALL and FLACK are leaning over Keyes, giving him the third degree. Keyes sweats under a spotlight, wired up to lie detectors and other scary-looking devices. Keyes is exhausted but defiant.
   BALL: GIVE IT UP, KEYES. YOU THINK LITTLE CAESAR WOULD SPEND THE REST OF HIS LIFE IN A CUBE FOR YOU?
   FLACK: GIVE US HIS ACCOUNT CODE AND WE'LL SUSPEND YOUR SENTENCE. YOU CAN WALK OUT OF HERE.
   KEYES: GO... GO POLISH YOUR HELMET, JUDGEY BOY...

2) From behind Lenny, who is suddenly silhouetted in the open doorway, we see the startled Judges turning to face him.
   LENNY: I GOT A MESSAGE FOR YOU GUYS.
   BALL: WHO - ?

3) One or two small inset panels. Compact energy-pistols pop out of Lenny's dino-skin sleeves on quick-draw rigs into his waiting outstretched hands.
   FX: K-CHICK! K-CHAK!

4) BIG. In a John Woo moment, Lenny blasts with both guns. He may even have his arms crossed, shooting the Judge on the left with his right hand, and vice versa. He looks mean.
   FX: BZAM! BZAM!
   LENNY: CAESAR SAYS KISS MY ASS.

5) Both Judges are blasted back by Lenny's non-lethal stun shots.
   BALL: AAAAH!
   FLACK: UNNH!

6) Lenny frees Keyes from his restraints. Keyes is flustered and confused.
   KEYES: WHA... ? WHAT IS THIS - ?
   LENNY: WHAT DOES IT LOOK LIKE, LAMEBRAIN? I'M BUSTIN' YOU OUTTA HERE!
   LINK: NOW GET DRESSED BEFORE WE'RE UP TO OUR NECKS IN ANGRY BADGES!

PAGE SIX

1) Lenny and Keyes (now dressed) stand in a clearly-labeled ELEVATOR, waiting for the doors to close. Judges bustle along the corridor, ignoring them. A bald, oriental Psi Judge is just stepping into the elevator with them.
   CAPTION: UNDERCOVER 101 - IN THE LION'S DEN, MAKE LIKE YOU OWN THE PLACE AN' YOU WON'T GET BIT.
   PSI: HOLD THE DOORS, PLEASE!
   LINK: THANKS.

2) Inside the elevator, from a low angle, close on the Judge's "PSI" badge (leave room around it for dialogue). Above and behind him, Lenny is stony-faced. The Psi is in his early 20s and, unlike regular street Judges, has a cheerful and open manner.
   CAPTION: AT LEAST, THAT'S THE THEORY. IN REAL LIFE, THINGS TEND TO GET A LITTLE MORE COMPLICATED.
   PSI: IS EVERYTHING ALL RIGHT, MY FRIEND? I HOPE YOU DON'T MIND MY SAYING SO, BUT YOU'RE BROADCASTING AN AWFUL LOT OF STRESS AND NEGATIVE ENERGY.
   LENNY: NO KIDDIN'. THIS UNDERCOVER WORK'S PLAYIN' HELL WITH MY NERVES.

3) The Psi half-turns to Lenny, smiling but concerned.
   PSI: PERHAPS YOU SHOULD THINK ABOUT TRANSFERRING OUT OF THE DIVISION. JITTERS LIKE THAT COULD GET YOU KILLED.
   LENNY: FUNNY YOU SHOULD SAY THAT, PAL...

4) Close-up on Lenny, his expression unreadable behind his NightShades.
   LENNY: I'VE BEEN THINKIN' THE SAME THING MYSELF.

5) Wide shot - the Sector House basement car park. Lenny and Keyes approach Lenny's battered old Foord (sic) roadster, which is flanked by row upon row of Lawmasters, Pat Wagons, even a Manta or two. Lenny's car is the 22nd century equivalent of a '57 Chevy - retro-futuristic, all tail-fins and chrome bulges, with an ugly supercharger intake sticking up through the hood.
   LENNY: WE GOT MAYBE TWO MINUTES MAX BEFORE THEY REALISE YOU'RE MISSIN' AN' LOCK DOWN THE BUILDING.
   LINK: GET IN THE FOORD, AN' KEEP YOUR HEAD DOWN 'TIL WE'RE CLEAR.
   KEYES: W-WHATEVER YOU SAY...

6) Aerial shot. Lenny's car cruises out to freedom down a long, curved aerial roadway.
   FROM CAR: PIECE O' CAKE.

PAGE SEVEN

1) Cut to a Sector House control room. Judge Clayton and Judge Ball peer down at a monitor screen manned by a CONTROL JUDGE. The screen displays a complex road-map marked with a flashing blip - Lenny's car.
   CONROL JUDGE: GOOD SIGNAL FROM THE TRACER. HE'S HEADING NORTH ON ROCKATANSKY OVERZOOM, APPROACHING THE SUPERSLAB FEEDWAY.
   BALL: SHOULDN'T WE AT LEAST PUT A MOBILE UNIT ON HIS TAIL?
   CLAYTON: TOO RISKY. IF KEYES SMELLS A DOUBLE-CROSS, THIS WHOLE PLAN IS BLOWN.
   LINK: ZERO KNOWS WHAT HE'S DOING.

2) On the massive multi-lane highway known as the Superslab, Lenny's car barrels towards us, the angle of the panel raked dynamically to suggest tremendous speed. Lenny is at the wheel, a nervous Keyes beside him.
   LENNY: NOW LISTEN GOOD, MONEY MAN. WE'RE ON A TIGHT SCHEDULE HERE, AN' I'M ONLY GONNA SAY THIS ONCE.
   LINK: CAESAR'S MOVIN' ALL HIS ASSETS OFF WORLD. HE SAID TO GIVE YOU THIRTY SECONDS TO GIMME THE ACCOUNT CODE.
   KEYES: WHAT? I-I'M ONLY SUPPOSED TO GIVE IT TO CAESAR HIMSELF--

3) Inside the car now, Lenny driving with one hand on the wheel. In the foreground, Lenny's blaster is aimed casually at the terrified Keyes.
   LENNY: HE ALSO SAID THAT IF YOU DON'T GIMME THE CODE, I'M SUPPOSED TO BLOW YOUR BRAINS OUT.
   LINK: TWENTY SECONDS.
   KEYES: B-BUT... BUT--

4) Reverse angle - we're with Keyes in the foreground, Lenny's blaster pointing at us.
   KEYES: I M-MEAN, CAESAR WAS ALWAYS VERY PARTICULAR ABOUT SECURITY... M-MAYBE IF I COULD JUST TALK TO HIM--
   LENNY: I ALREADY TOLD YOU, CAESAR'S OFF WORLD. HE AIN'T TALKIN' TO NOBODY 'TIL THIS HEAT DIES DOWN.
   LINK: TEN SECONDS, PAL.

5) Closer on Keyes, Lenny's gun leveled on him. He's sweating in terror.
   LENNY: FIVE. FOUR. THREE. TWO. ONE--
   KEYES: O-OKAY, OKAY! CHEEZ LOUISE...
   LINK: IT'S ACCOUNT NUMBER 779144, FIRST MEGAPOLITAN BANK. ACCESS CODE ALPHA 55 BLUE NINE.

6) Close-up on Lenny, a grim smile of satisfaction.
   LENNY: GRAVY.

PAGE EIGHT

1) Lenny's car pulls up the on-ramp of a massive multi-lane vehicle - a TOM FUELERY mobile refueling station/rest stop. Its company mascot is a friendly cartoon tom-cat in mechanic's overalls.
   FROM CAR: OKAY, THIS CAR'S HOTTER THAN HESTIA. I GOTTA DITCH IT.
   LINK: YOU BAIL OUT HERE.

2) We're in the car with Lenny. Keyes stands outside the car on the Fuelery forecourt, pleading with Lenny through the car window. Lenny leans over to hand Keyes a small object - a tracer bug.
   LENNY: TAKE THIS TRACER.
   LINK: SIT TIGHT, AN' ONE OF CAESAR'S BOYS'LL PICK YOU UP AN' TAKE YOU TO THE SPACEPORT.
   KEYES: W-WAIT A SECOND...

3) Now we're behind Keyes, still pleading with Lenny through the car window.
   KEYES: I DON'T UNDERSTAND--
   LENNY: FORGET ABOUT IT.
   LINK: SEE YA 'ROUND. PLEASURE DOIN' BUSINESS WITH YA.

4) Keyes stands there like a dumb shit with the tracer in his hand as Lenny's car burns rubber onto the Superslab. A mechanic droid approaches Keyes with a dripping oil can.
   FX: SCREEEEEEEE - !
   DROID: LUBE, SIR?

5) Wide through-the-windshield panel. Lenny drives with one hand on the wheel, speaking into a compact mobile phone.
   LENNY: ... YEAH, WORKED LIKE DREAM. LEFT HIM STANDIN' ON THE FORECOURT WITH HIS HOTTIE IN HIS HANDS.
   LINK: OKAY, BABY, TIME TO FOCUS. WE'RE ON DANGER TIME.
   LINK: TRANSFER CAESAR'S MONEY INTO MY LUNA-1 ACCOUNT AN' MEET ME AT JFK. HERE'S THE ACCESS CODE...

6) Back in the Sector House Control Room, Clayton and Ball still peer at the flashing blip.
   CONTROL JUDGE: HE'S STILL AT THE TOM FUELERY, CRUISING CLOCKWISE ON THE CENTRAL SPIRAL.
   CLAYTON: IF ZERO HASN'T GOT THE CODE YET, HE ISN'T GOING TO GET IT.
   LINK: SEND A PAT-WAGON TO THE FUELERY PICK THEM UP.

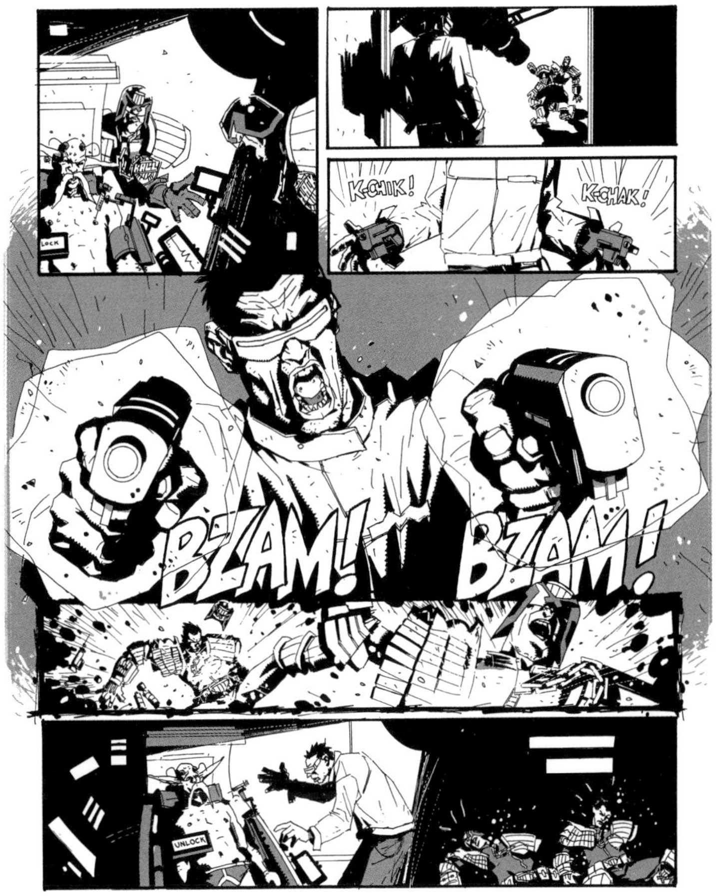
K-CHIK!
K-CHAK!
BLAM!
BLAM!
UNLOCK

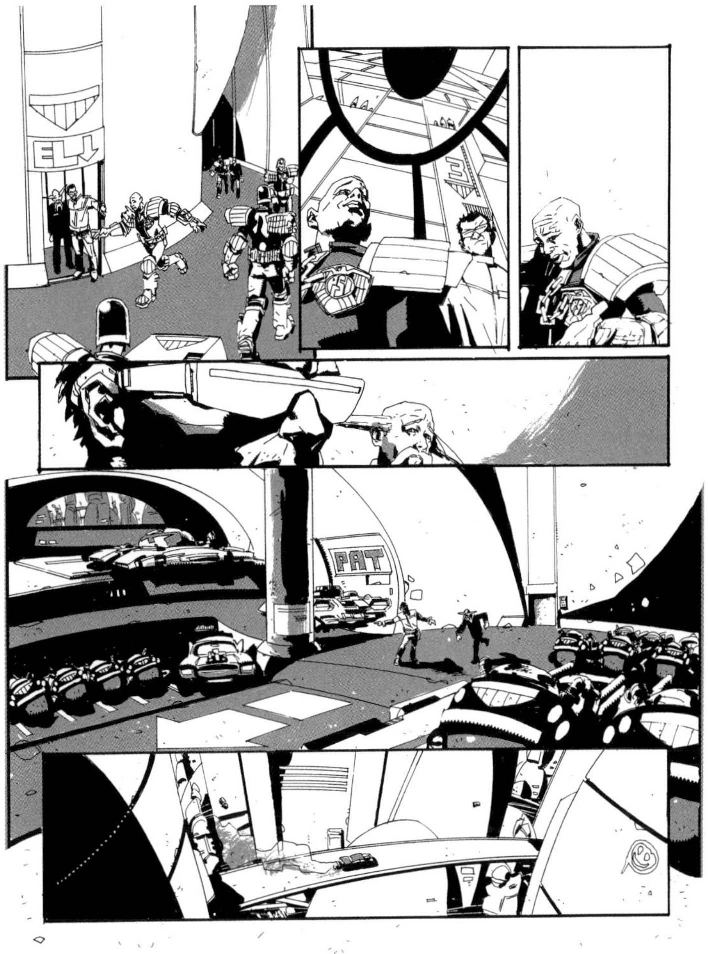
PAT

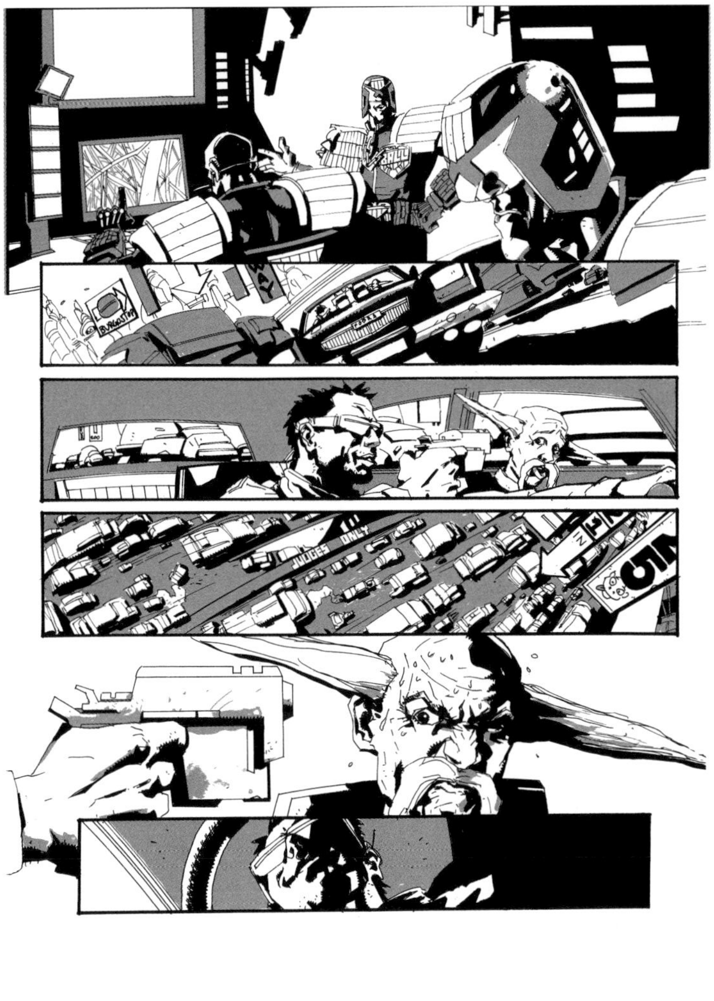
JUDGES ONLY

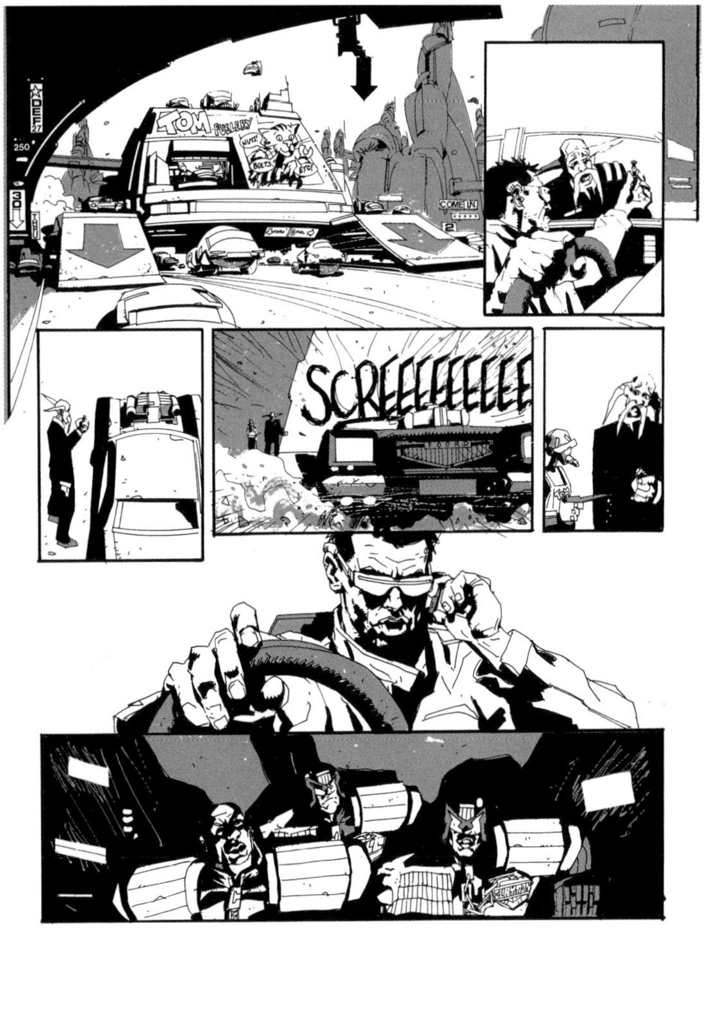
TOM

LENNY ZERO, JUDGE DREDD MEGAZINE 3.68, 2000

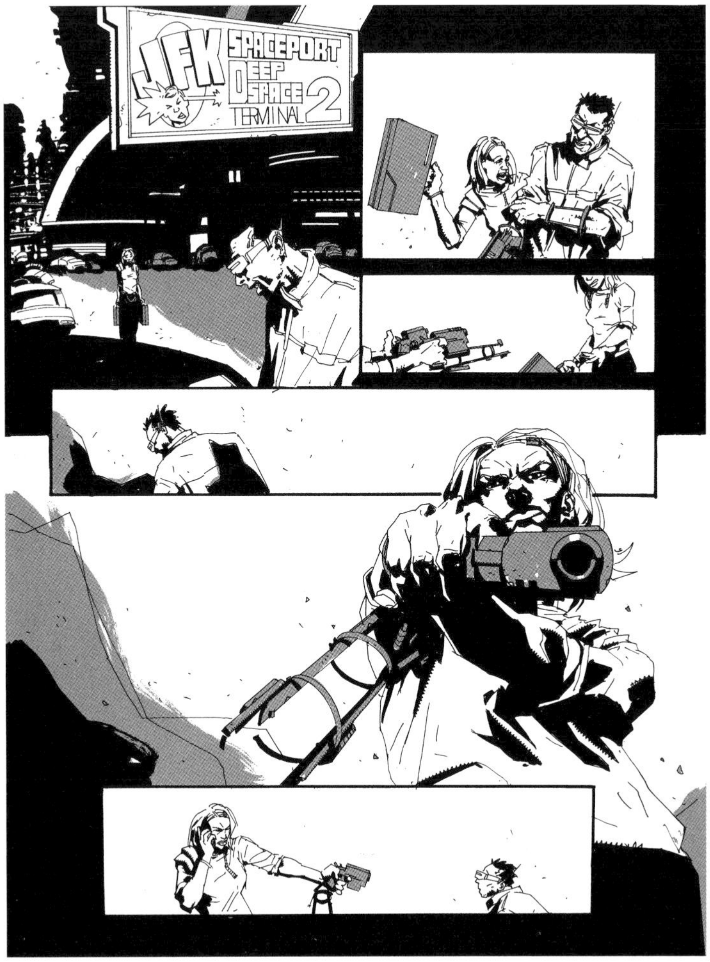
JFK SPACEPORT DEEP SPACE TERMINAL 2

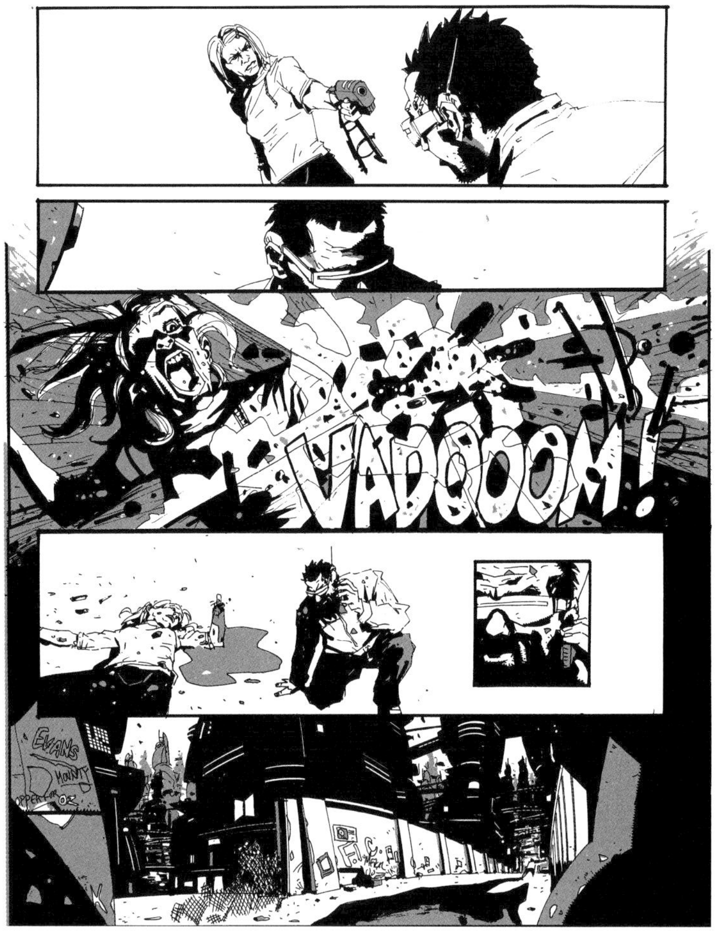
VADOOOM!

PAGE NINE

1) Lenny is getting out of his Foord in a huge car/hov-pod park, turning to see Mona approaching with two small suitcases. A large sign on the wall clearly reads "JFK SPACEPORT: DEEP SPACE - TERMINAL 2".

MONA: HUSTLE THAT TUSH, TOUGH GUY. OUR FLIGHT LEAVES IN FIFTEEN MINUTES.
LENNY: MAN, I COULD KISS MYSELF.
LINK: BY THE TIME CAESAR AN' THE DEPARTMENT FIGURE OUT WE SCREWED 'EM BOTH, WE'LL BE ON OUR WAY TO A NON-EXTRADITION PLANET...

2) Lenny, smiling, has rolled up his jacket sleeves, unbuckling his pop-out pistol rigs. Mona slides her arms around his shoulders, admiringly.

MONA: FIRST CLASS ALL THE WAY, COURTESY OF LITTLE CAESAR'S THIRTY-THREE MIL...
LENNY: MAN, I JUST WISH I COULD SEE THE LOOK ON KEYES' FACE WHEN THE JUDGES PICK HIM UP WITH A JUSTICE DEPARTMENT TRACER IN HIS HAND!

3) Lenny, still smiling, hands Mona his pistols.

LENNY: BUT FIRST THINGS FIRST - I AIN'T GETTIN' THESE BABIES THROUGH CUSTOMS. DITCH 'EM IN A GRINDER, WILL YA?

4) Lenny has turned his back on us, but his head is just beginning to turn. Mona is behind him, off panel.

MONA (OFF): FORGET ABOUT CUSTOMS, LENNY - THE ONLY TRIP YOU'RE TAKING IS TO TITAN.
LENNY: WHAT... ?

5) BIG, dramatic panel. Mona stands there with an ice-cold sneer, aiming Lenny's pistol dead at him/us.

MONA: HANDS WHERE I CAN SEE THEM, ZERO.
LINK: YOU'RE UNDER ARREST.

6) With the gun still leveled at Lenny, "Mona" speaks into her mobile phone. Lenny is crumbling.

MONA: CONTROL, THIS IS KRAMER, SJS*.
LINK: I NEED BACK-UP AND A CATCH-WAGON TO JFK POD PARK, UPPER LEVEL.
LENNY: No... No, baby, no...
CAPTION BELOW: * SJS: SPECIAL JUDICIAL SQUAD, JUSTICE DEPARTMENT'S INTERNAL INVESTIGATION DIVISION.

PAGE TEN

1) Lenny is destroyed, pleading. He loved this woman. Mona sneers contemptuously, without a shred of pity.

MONA: WE'VE HAD YOU UNDER OBSERVATION SINCE YOU FELL FOR A ROUTINE HONEY TRAP, ZERO.
LINK: WHEN A JUDGE CAN'T KEEP IT IN HIS PANTS, MAKES YOU WONDER WHAT ELSE HE'S CAPABLE OF. AND NOW WE KNOW.
LENNY: PLEASE, BABY, NO... I DID THIS FOR YOU--

2) Close on Lenny, crushed, head bowed. Mona looms over him, semi off-panel.

MONA: DON'T MAKE ME SICK. YOU BROKE THE LAW, AND NOW YOU'RE GOING TO PAY FOR IT.
LENNY: THEN... I'M SORRY.
LINK: VOICE DESTRUCT CODE GAMMA ZERO.

3) The gun EXPLODES, blowing Mona's hand completely off.

FX: VADOOOM!

4) Unhurt except for a few minor cuts and bruises, Lenny kneels by Mona, who is lying in a pool of her own blood, in deep shock, staring at the ugly stump of her hand. Lenny speaks into her mobile phone.

MONA: Whuh... Whuh...
LENNY: CONTROL, THIS IS ZERO.
LINK: CODE 99 RED, JUDGE DOWN. URGENT MED-ASSIST REQUIRED.

5) Close on Lenny, very grim, speaking into the tiny mobile phone.

LENNY: OH YEAH, AN' ONE OTHER THING.
LINK: I QUIT.

6) Wide panel, full bleed. Lenny flees down a grimy back alley, a tiny silhouette scuttling between the looming, monolithic black shadows of the cityblocks. A rat trapped in an urban maze.

NO DIALOGUE.

THE END

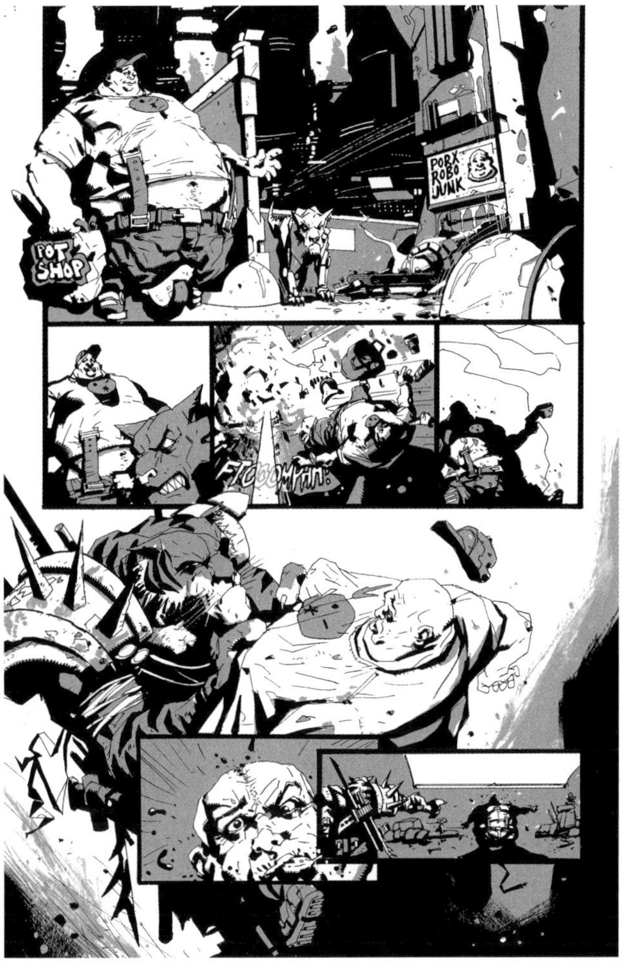
POT SHOP
PORX ROBO JUNK

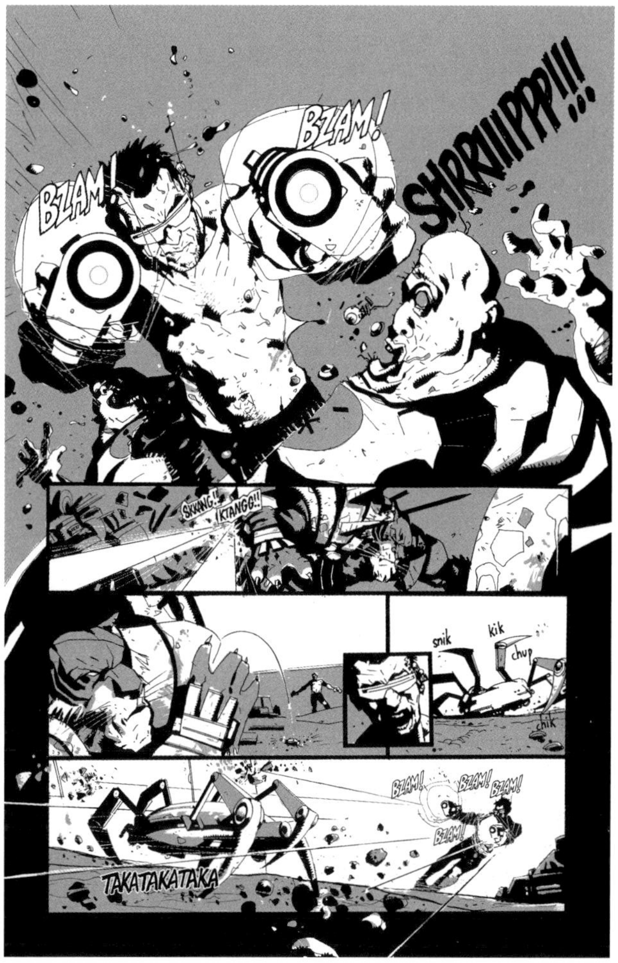
BZAM!
BZAM!
SHRIIIIPPP!!!
SKKANG!!
KTANGG!!
snik
kik
chup
chik
BZAM!
BZAM!
BZAM!
BZAM!
TAKATAKATAKA

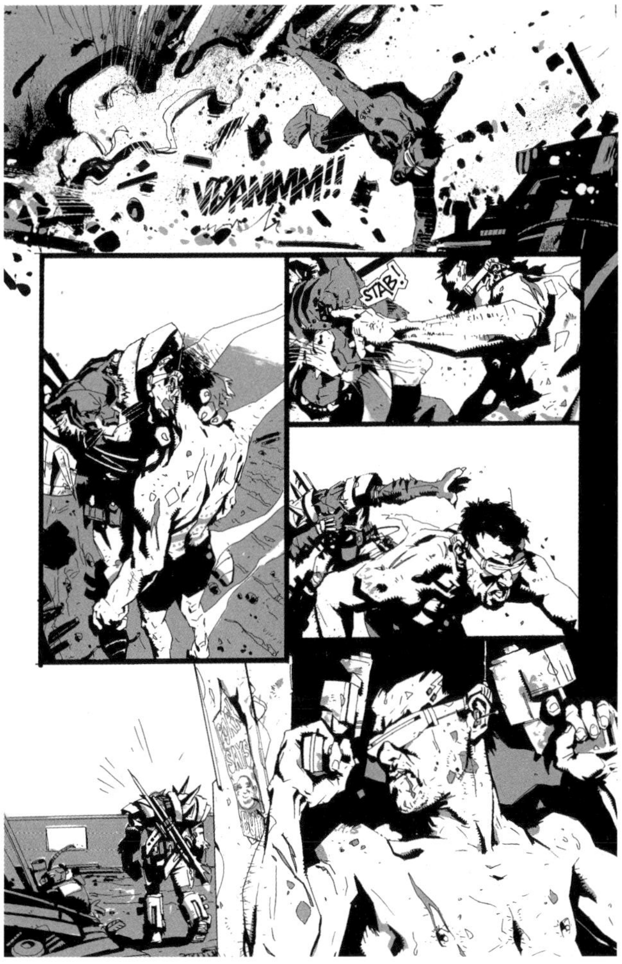
VDAMMM!!
STAB!

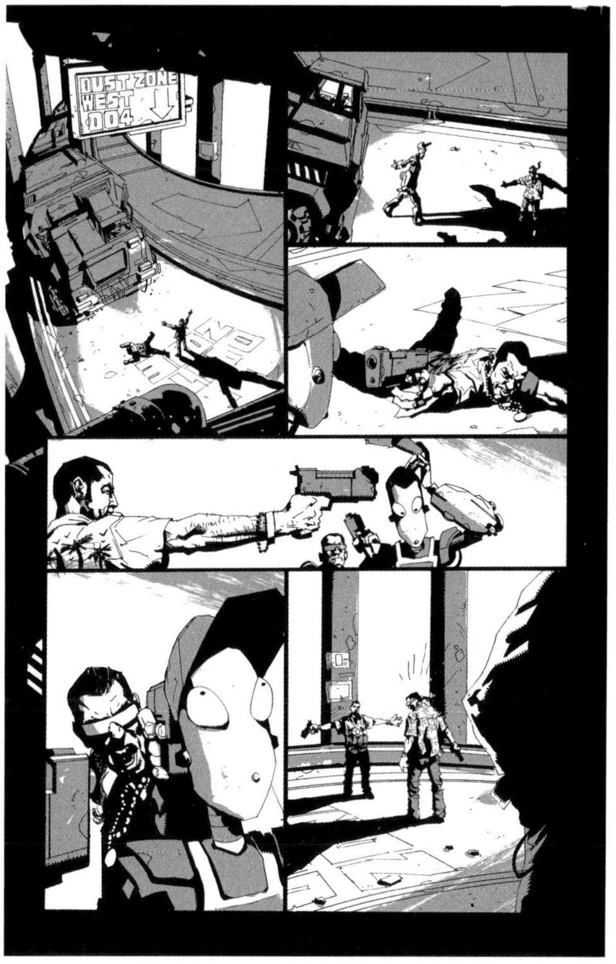
DUST ZONE WEST D04

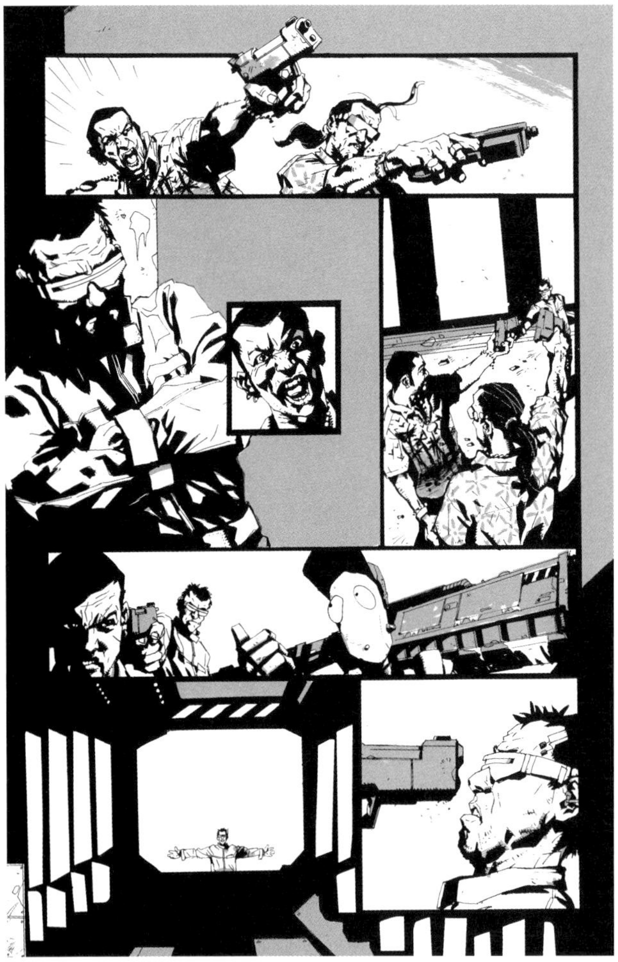

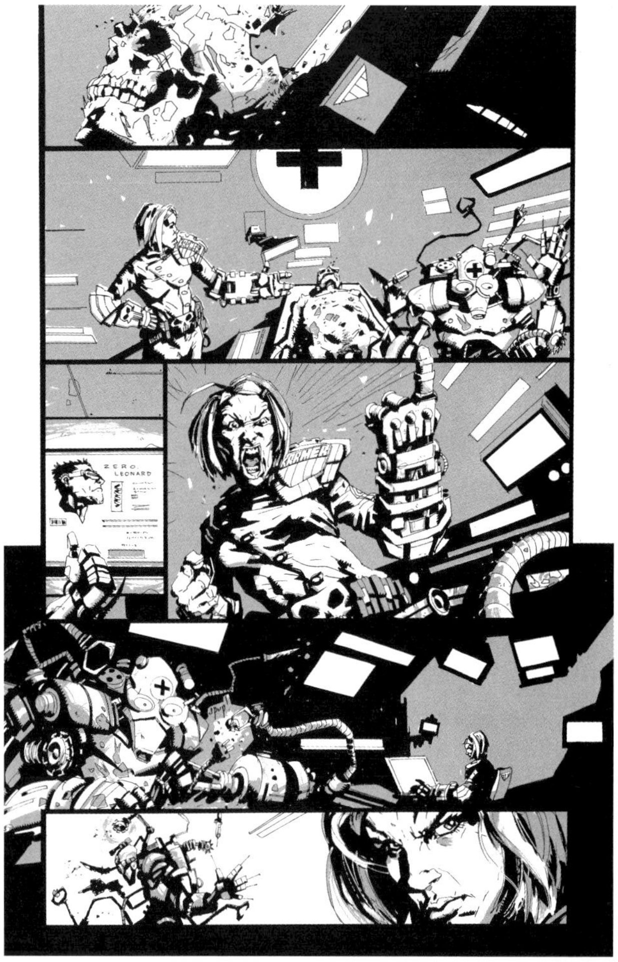

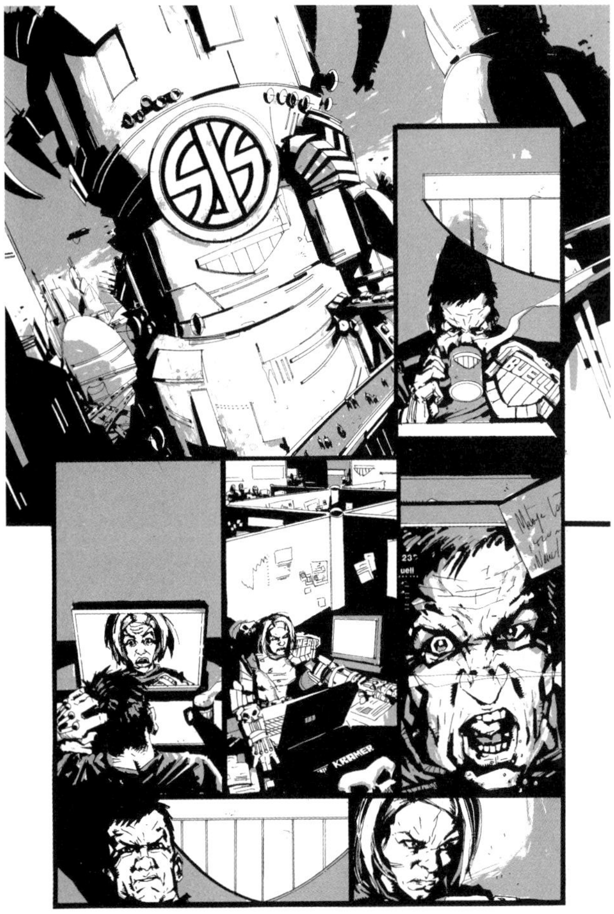

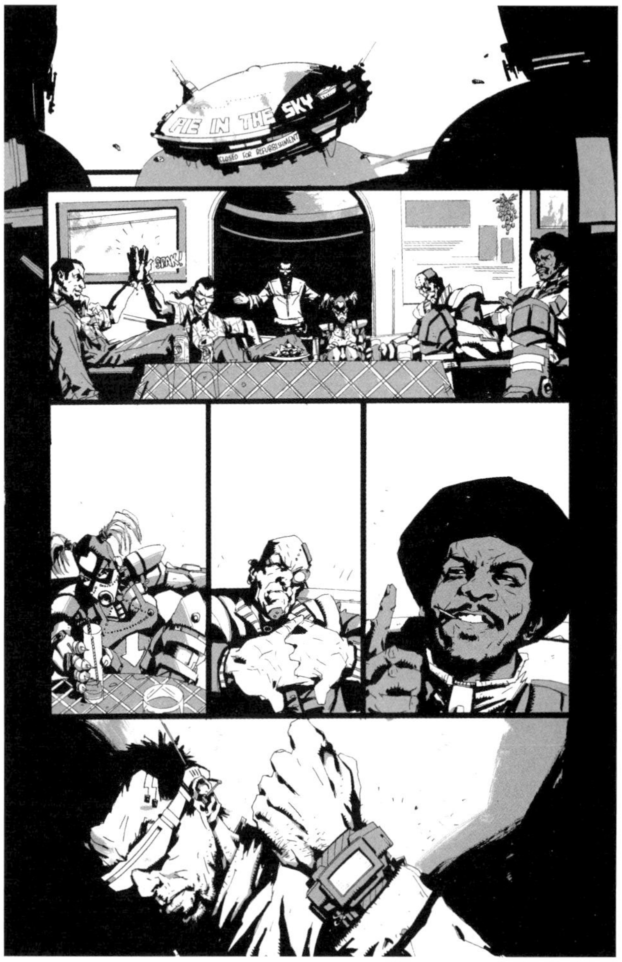
PIE IN THE SKY

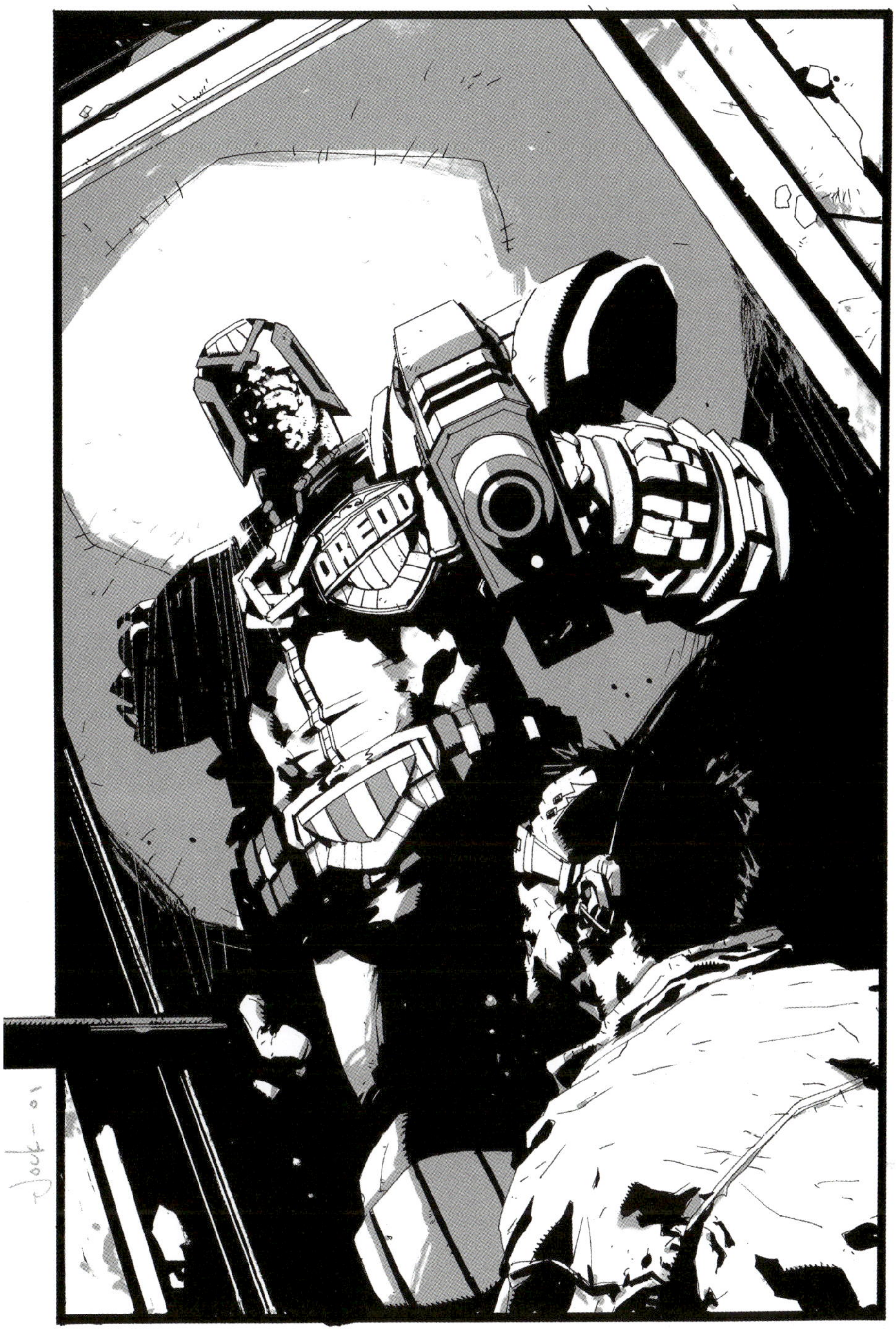
DREDD

DEAD ZERO

'When Dredd appears in the doorway in 'Dead Zero', it was a real moment… an unexpected story beat - the kind of thing Andy does so well. A badass character moment and a cliffhanger all in one – it's Dredd. I laughed when I read that in the script, I really enjoyed drawing those stories. That pose does crop up again and again. It's my synonymous Dredd shot I guess, from a low angle with the Lawgiver pointed straight at the reader. He feels monolithic. It's something I repeated with the first cover of **The Losers**. So, you know, there's a theme going on there. I was definitely trying to introduce a definitive graphic quality to my work, and Lenny Zero let me do that. It was the beginnings of ideas that I took forward with full force going into The Losers (DC Comics imprint Vertigo). I think I wanted to do something new with it too. It would be too easy, when you have utter reverence for a subject, like I had for Dredd, to try and repeat what's gone before. But, of course, it's really your job to bring your stamp to it. That's one of the reasons why he's such a good character. He's been handled so many different ways you can bring an individual stamp to him and he carries it.'

—JOCK

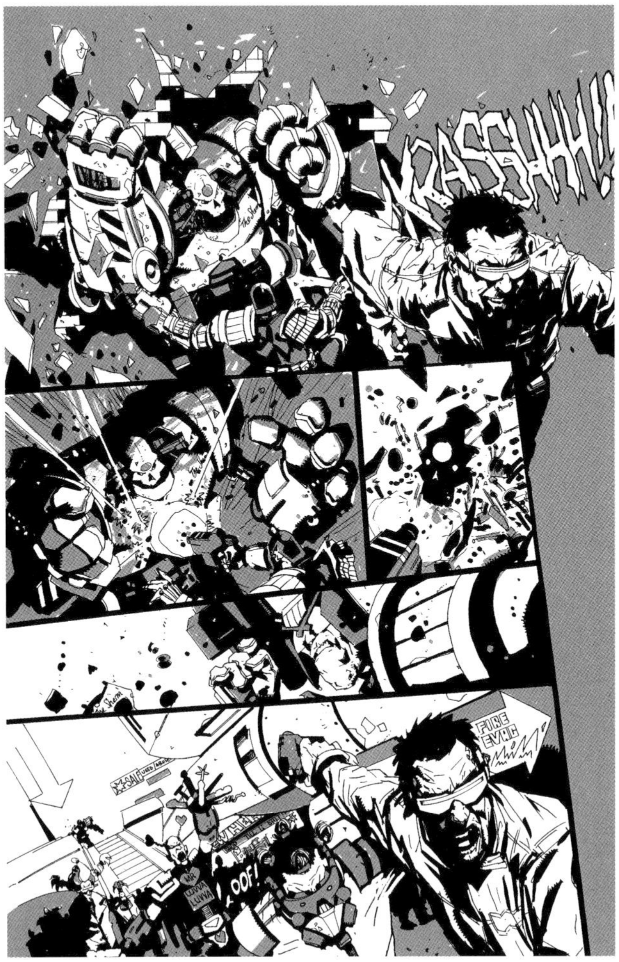
FIRE EVAC
OOF!

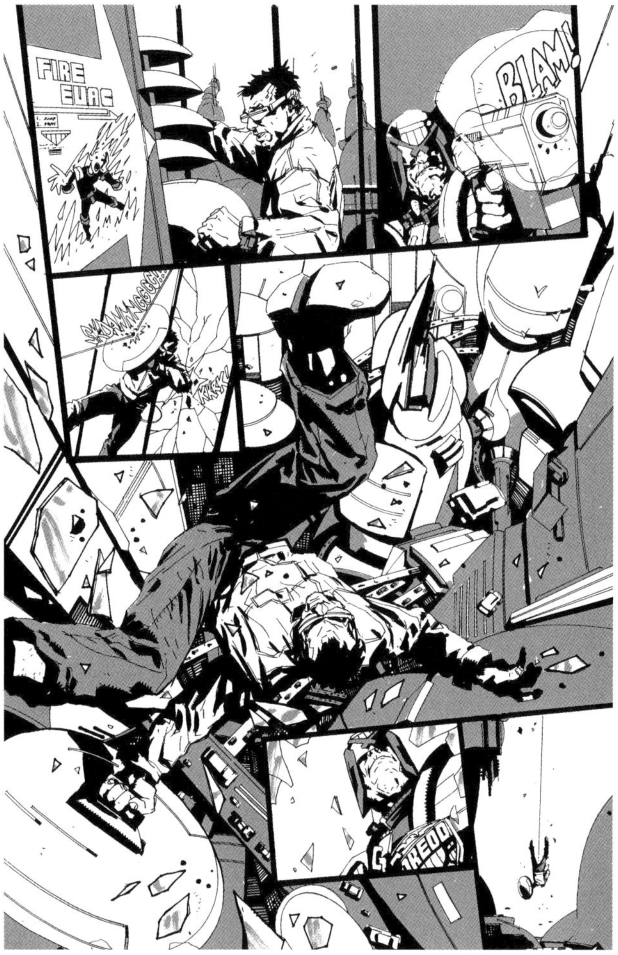
FIRE EVAC
BLAM!

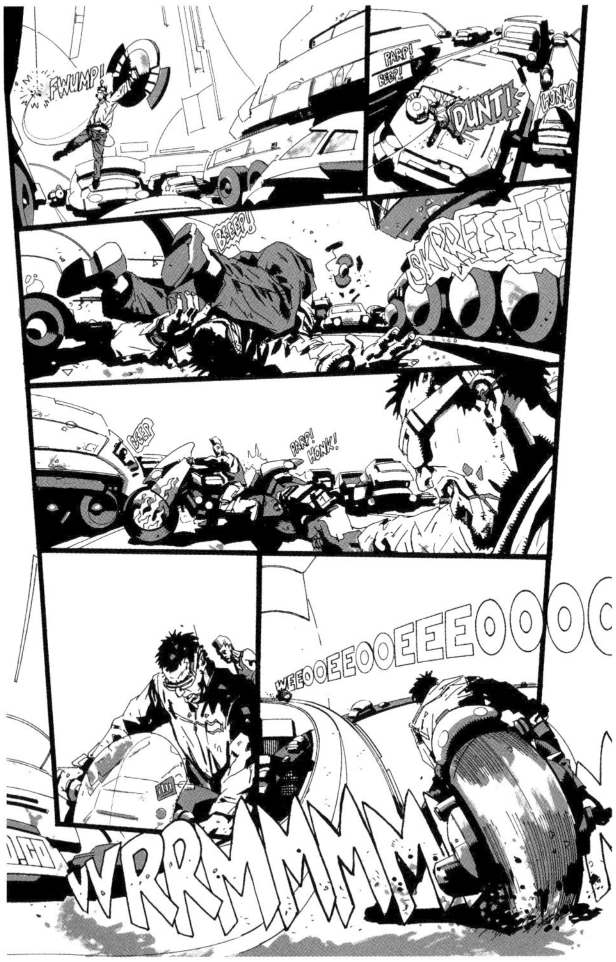
FWUMP!
DUNT!
PARP! HONK!

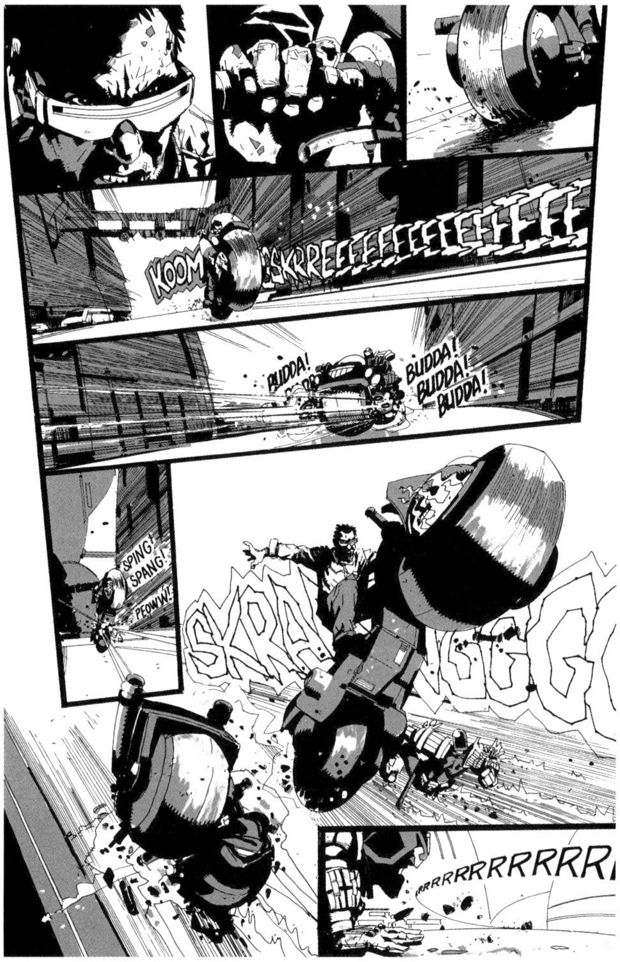
KOOM
BUDDA!
BUDDA!
BUDDA!
BUDDA!
SPING!
SPANG!
PEOWW!

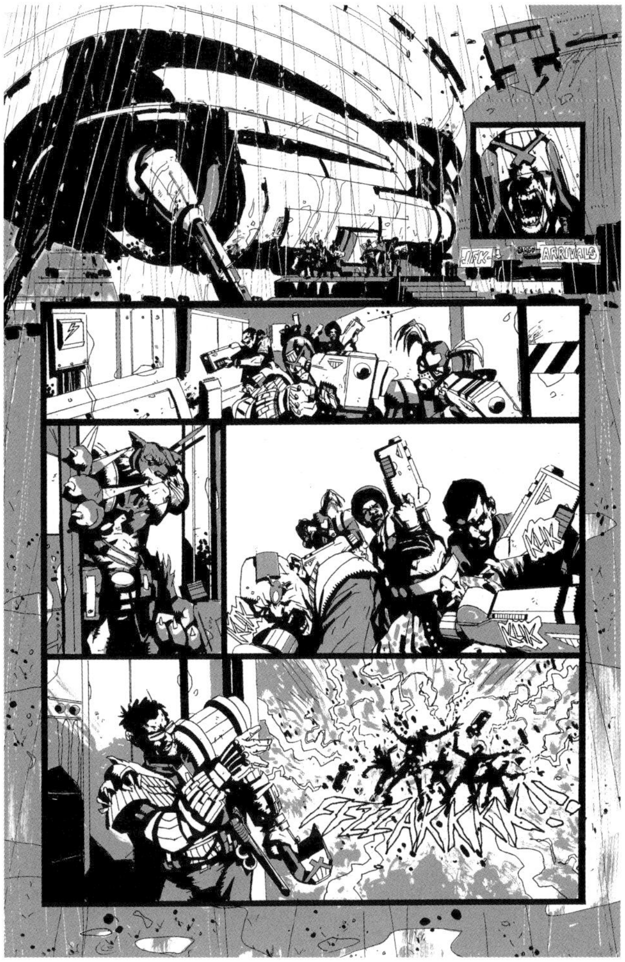
JFK
ARRIVALS

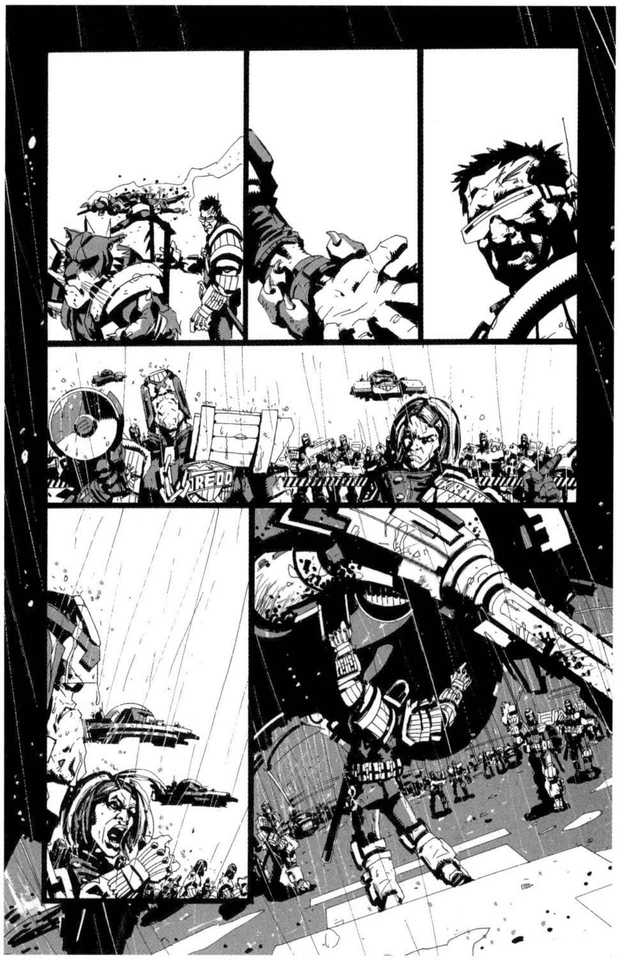
DREDD

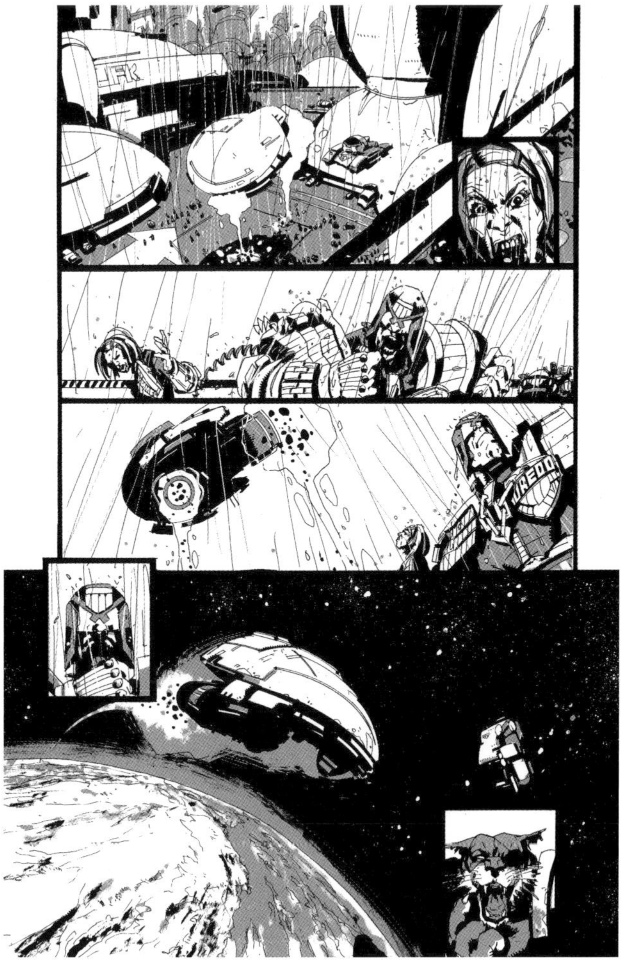
JFK
DREDD

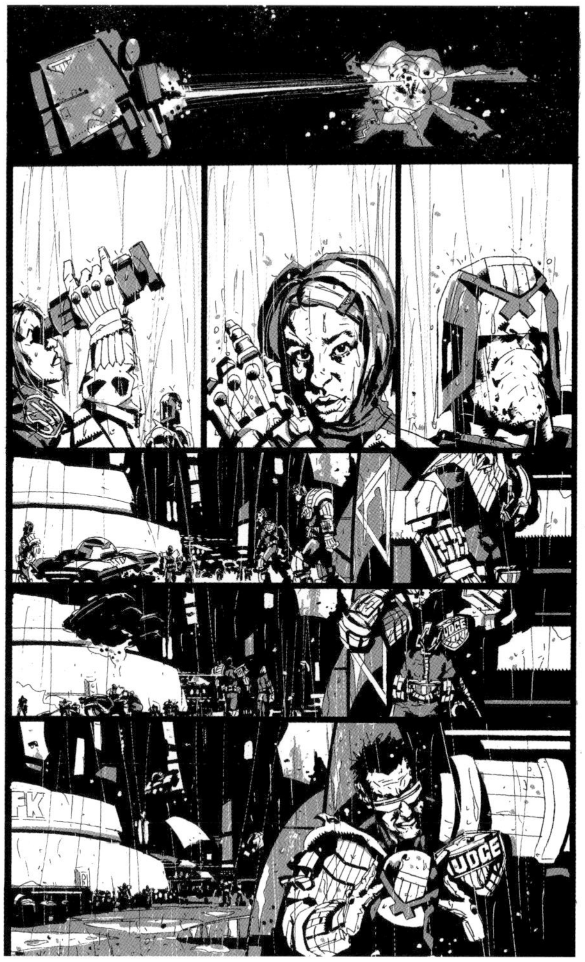
JFK
JUDGE

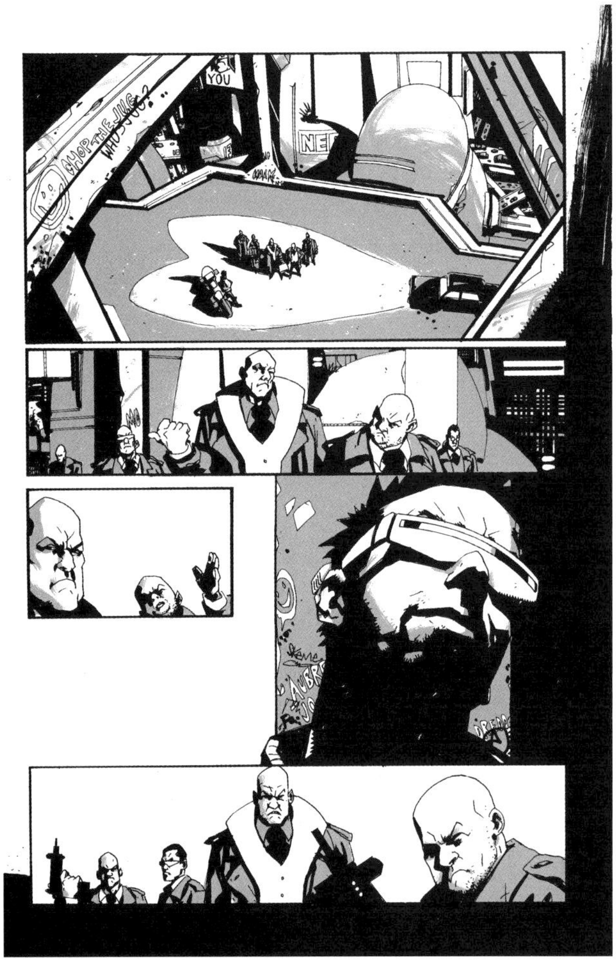

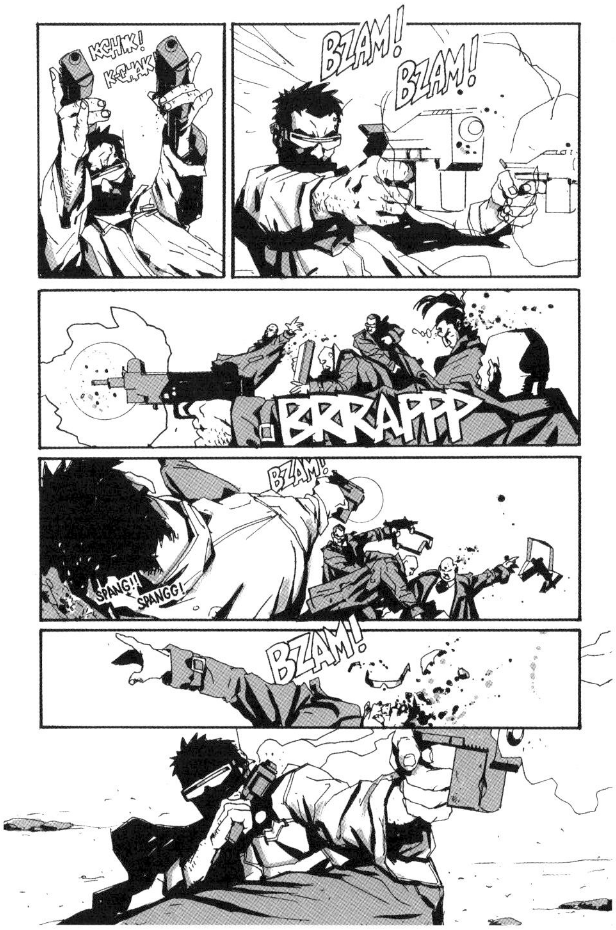
K-CHAK!
K-CHAK!
BZAM!
BZAM!
BRRAPPP
BZAM!
SPANG!!
SPANGG!
BZAM!

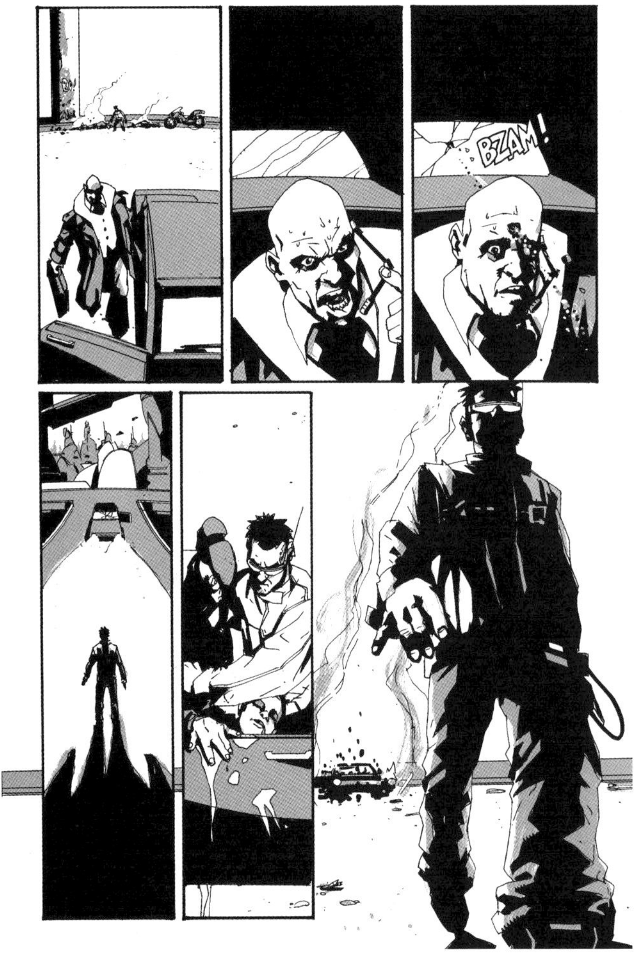
BZAM!

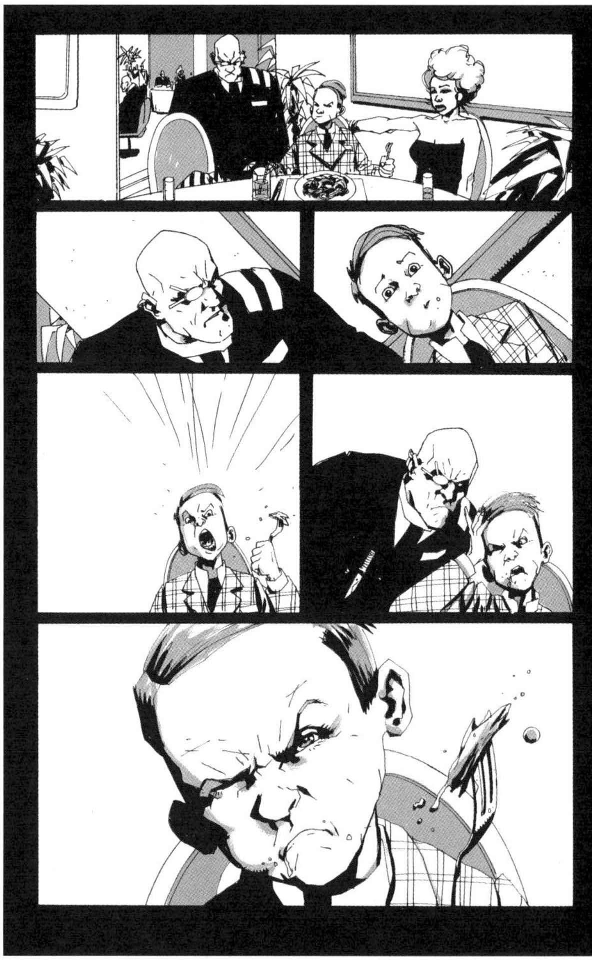

 LENNY ZERO: WIPEOUT, JUDGE DREDD MEGAZINE 4.14-4.15, 2002

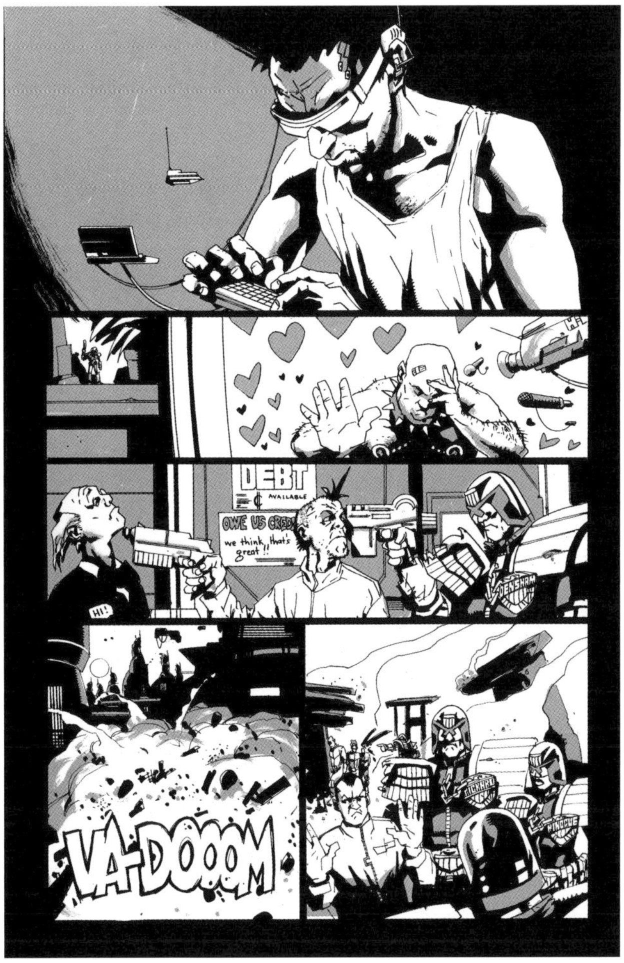
DEBT
AVAILABLE
OWE US CREDS
we think that's great!!
HI!
VA-DOOOM

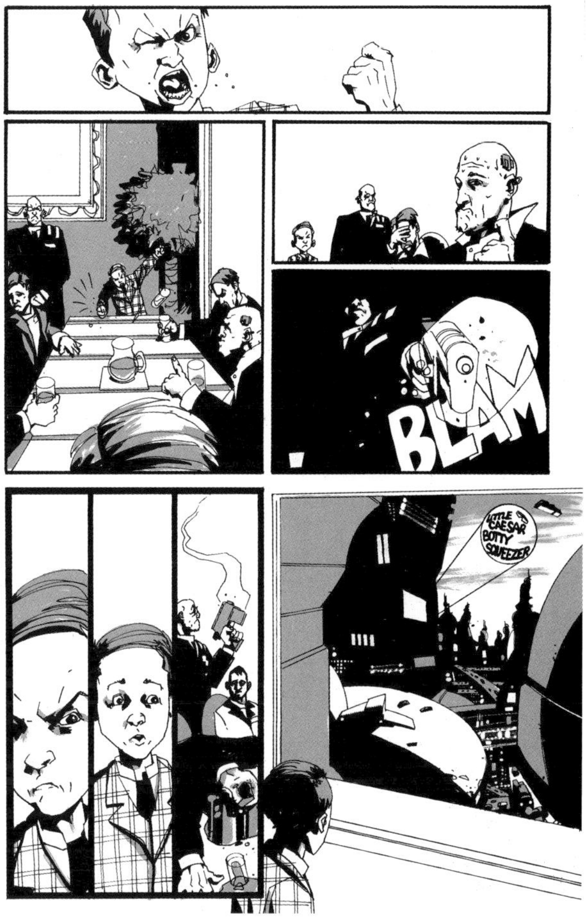
BLAM
LITTLE CAESAR BOTTY SQUEEZER

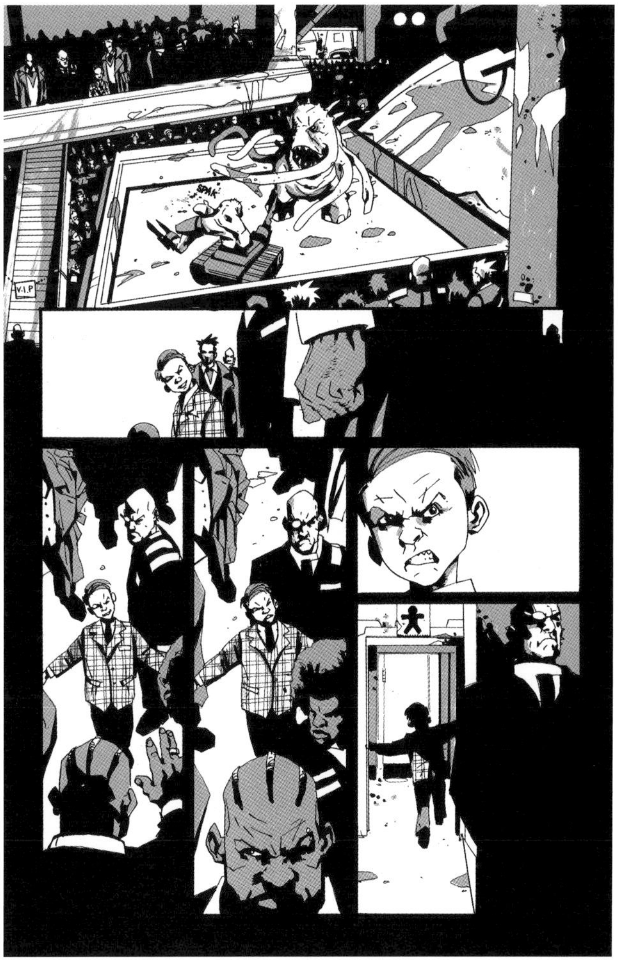
V.I.P

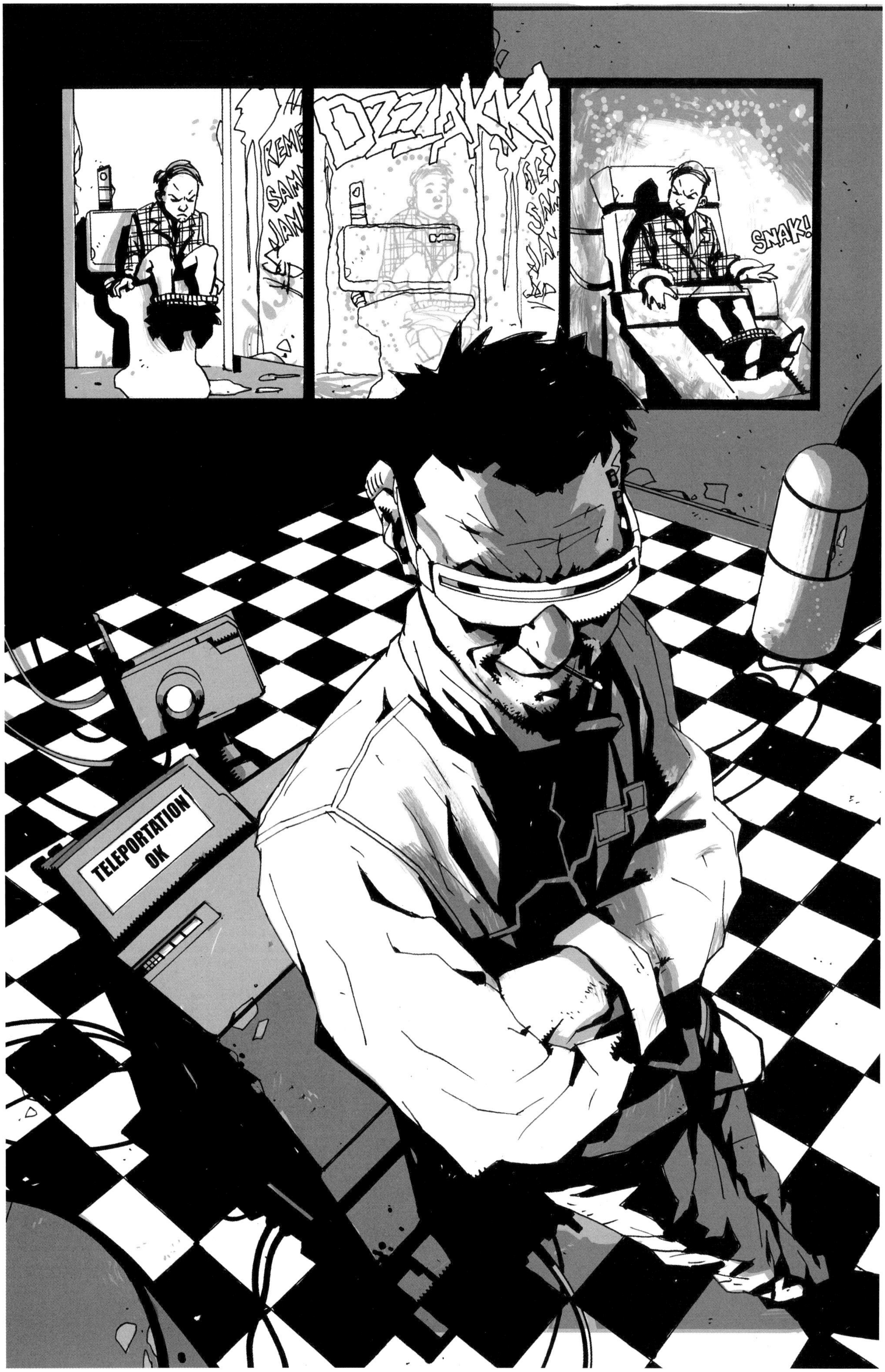
DZZAKK!
SNAK!
TELEPORTATION OK

 LENNY ZERO: WIPEOUT, JUDGE DREDD MEGAZINE 4.14-4.15, 2002

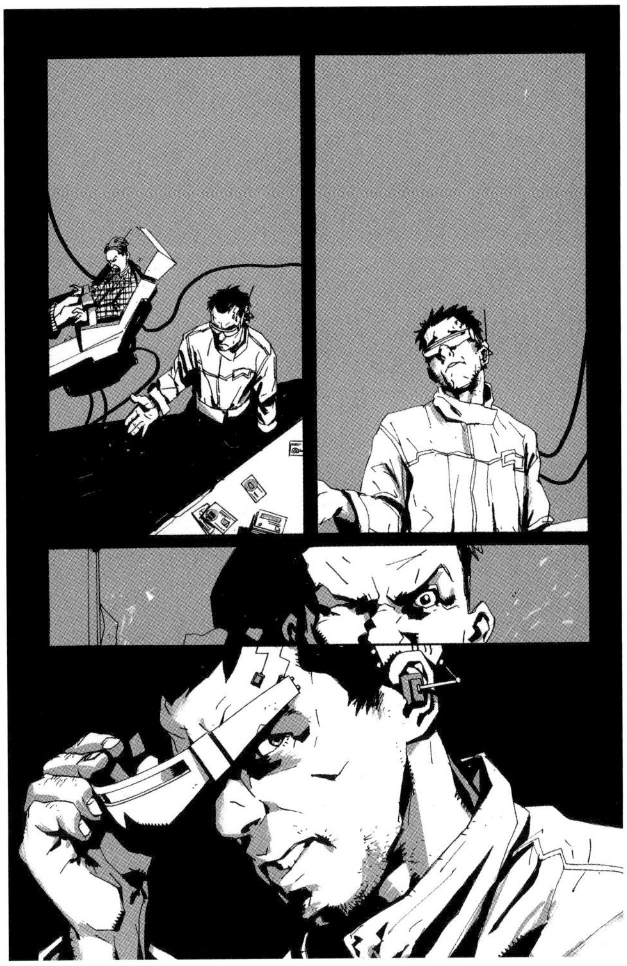

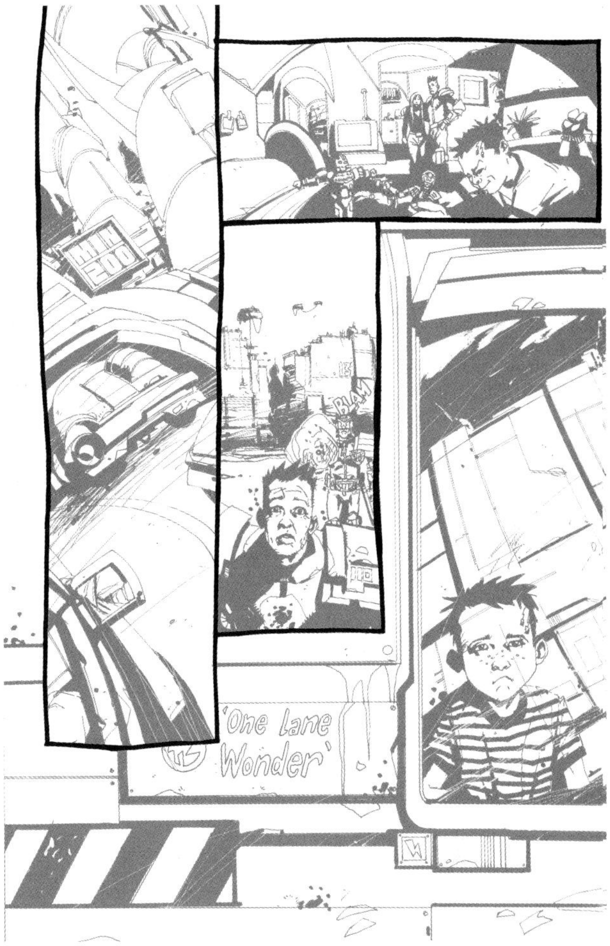
'One Lane Wonder'

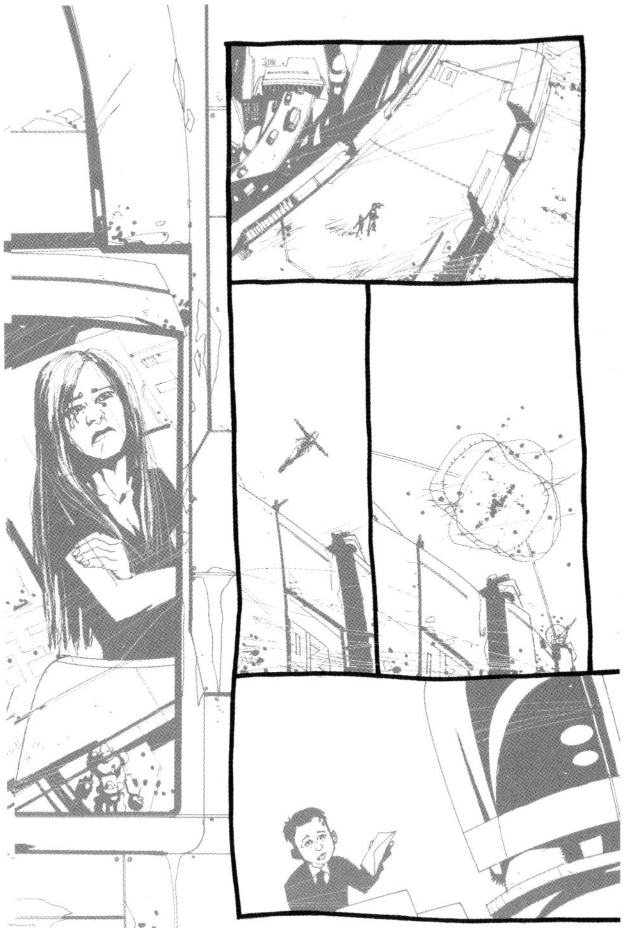

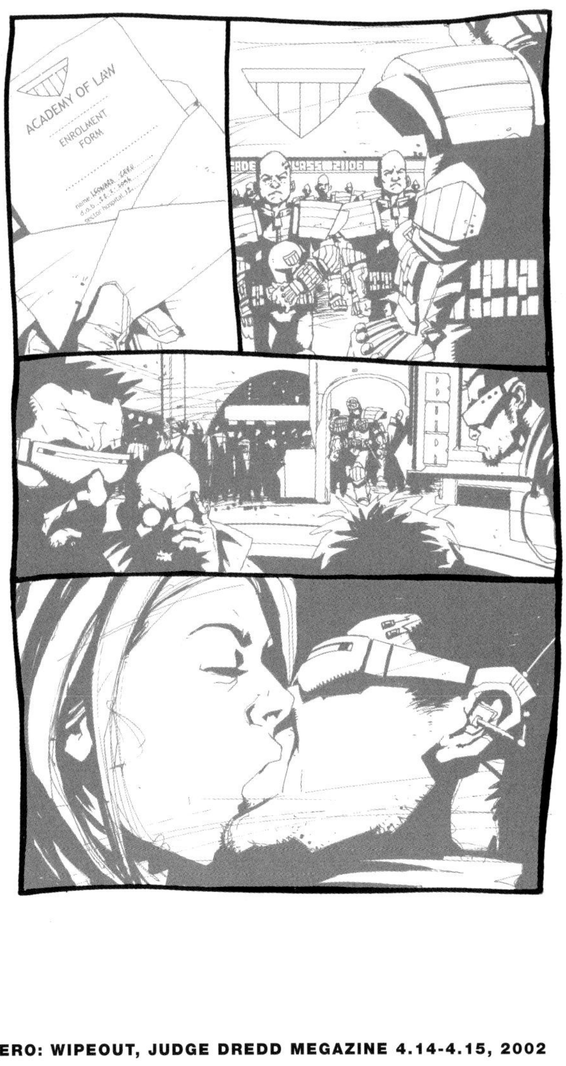
ACADEMY OF LAW
ENROLMENT FORM
BAR

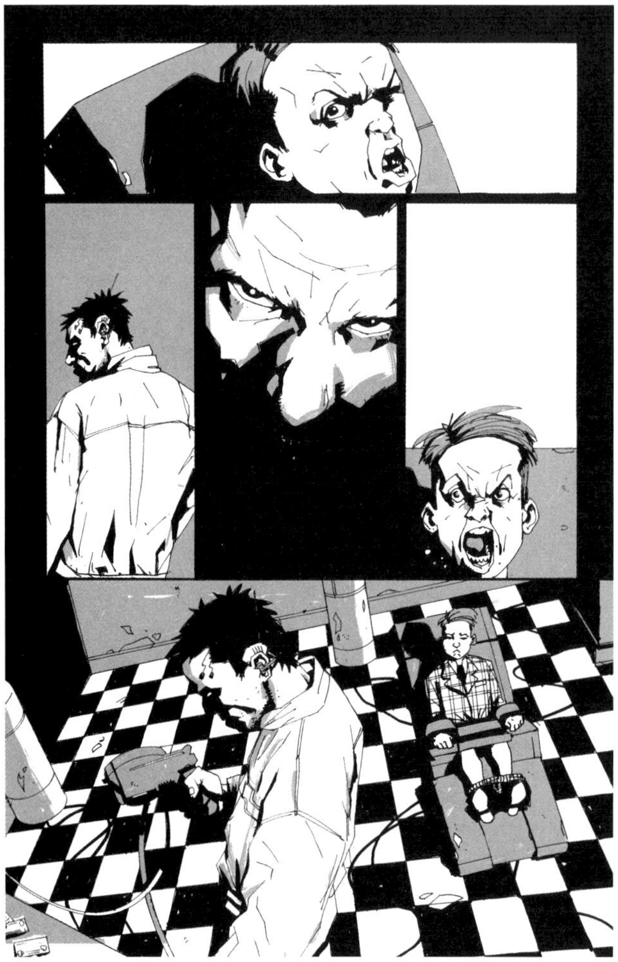

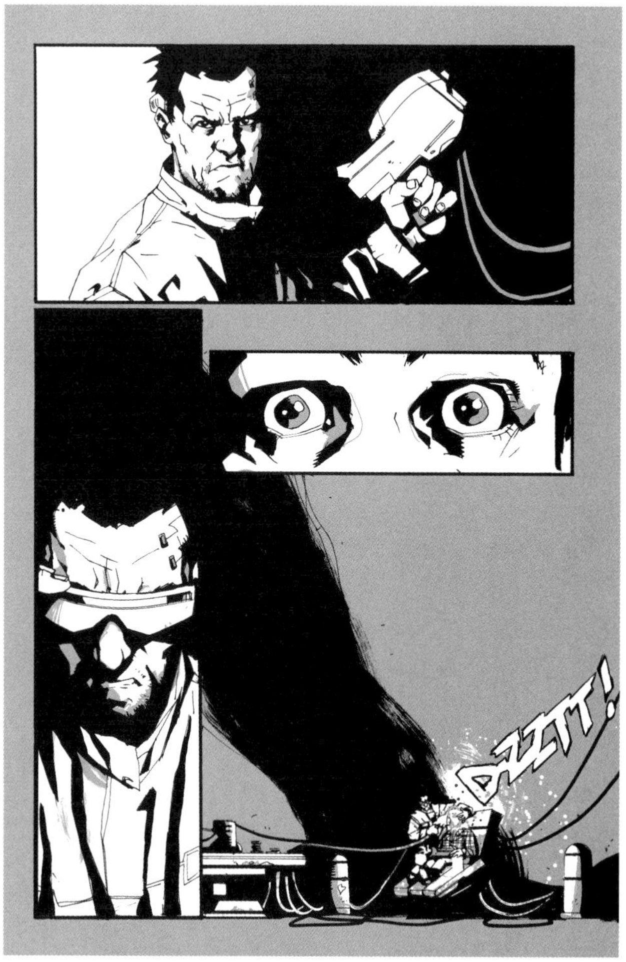

DZZTT!

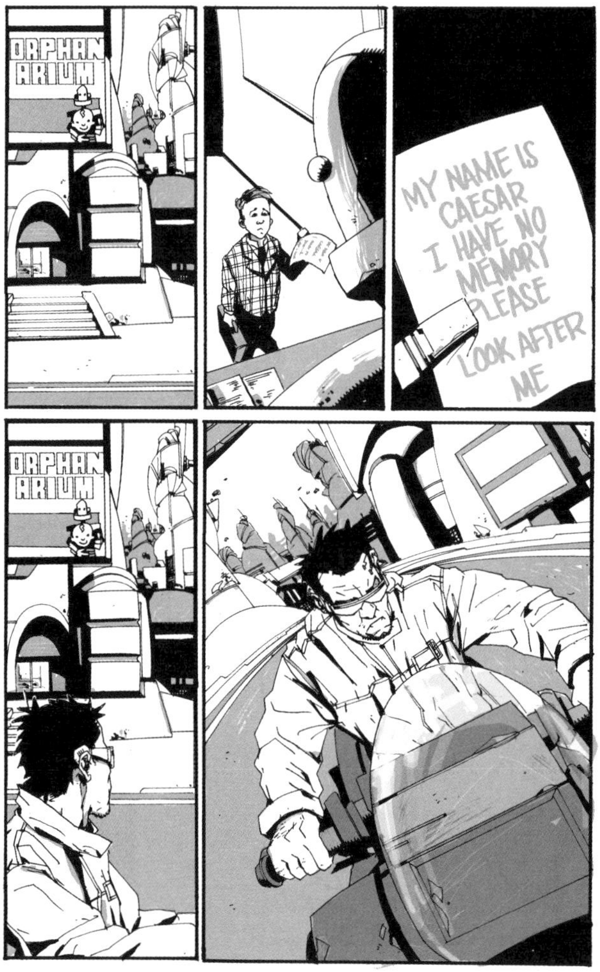

ORPHAN ARIUM
MY NAME IS CAESAR I HAVE NO MEMORY PLEASE LOOK AFTER ME
ORPHAN ARIUM

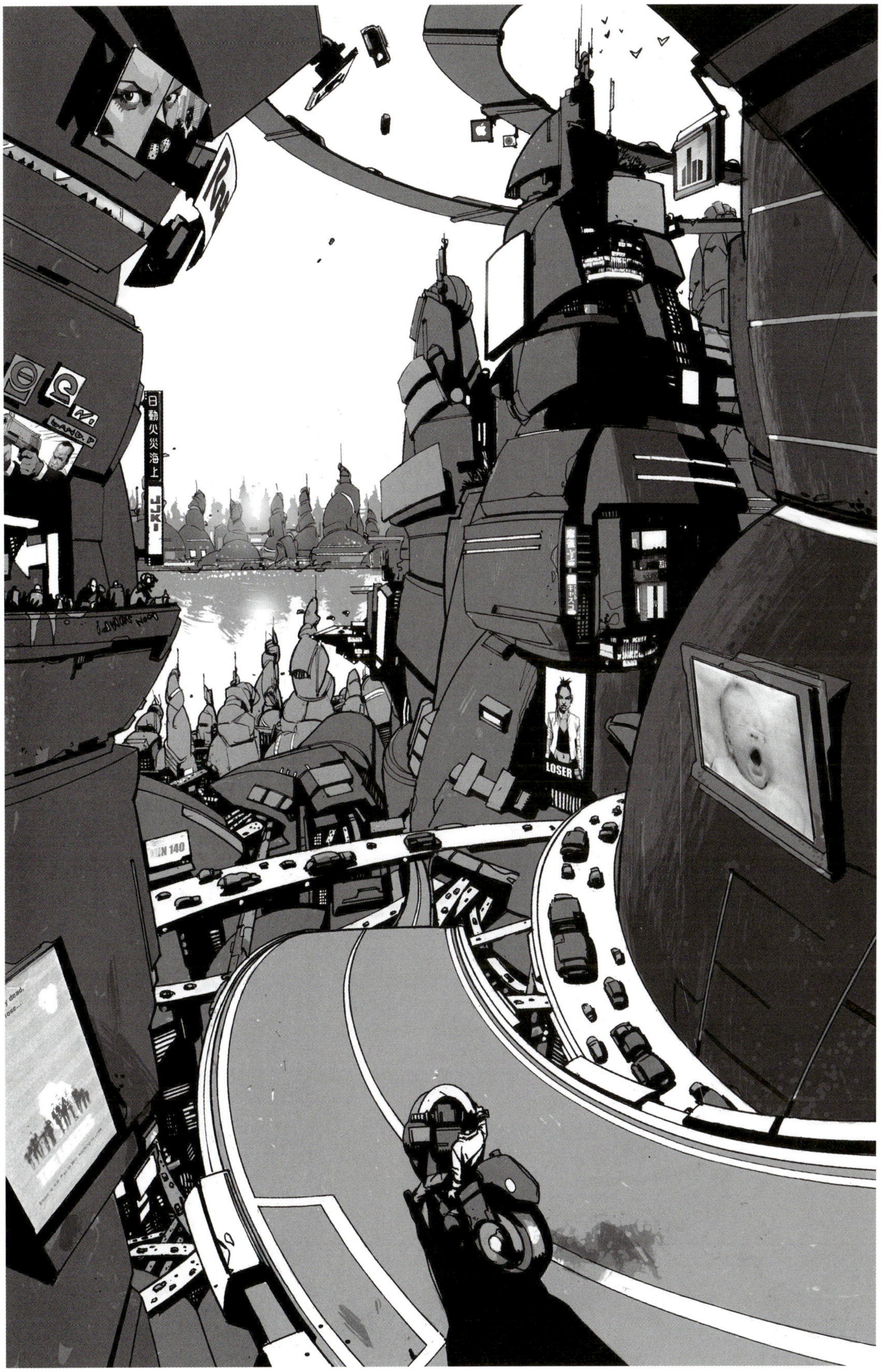
LOSER

WIPEOUT

'That yawning baby is my son, and, I really shouldn't have done it, but there's the **Elevator Suite** logo in there… there's Aisha from **The Losers**, next to Dredd, and a kind of bleached out **Ocean's Eleven** poster because that was an influence on **The Losers**. I just put them in, hoping it would fly under the radar. So this was my last page on Lenny Zero and it was telegraphing that I was about to embark on **The Losers** with Andy at Vertigo.'

—JOCK

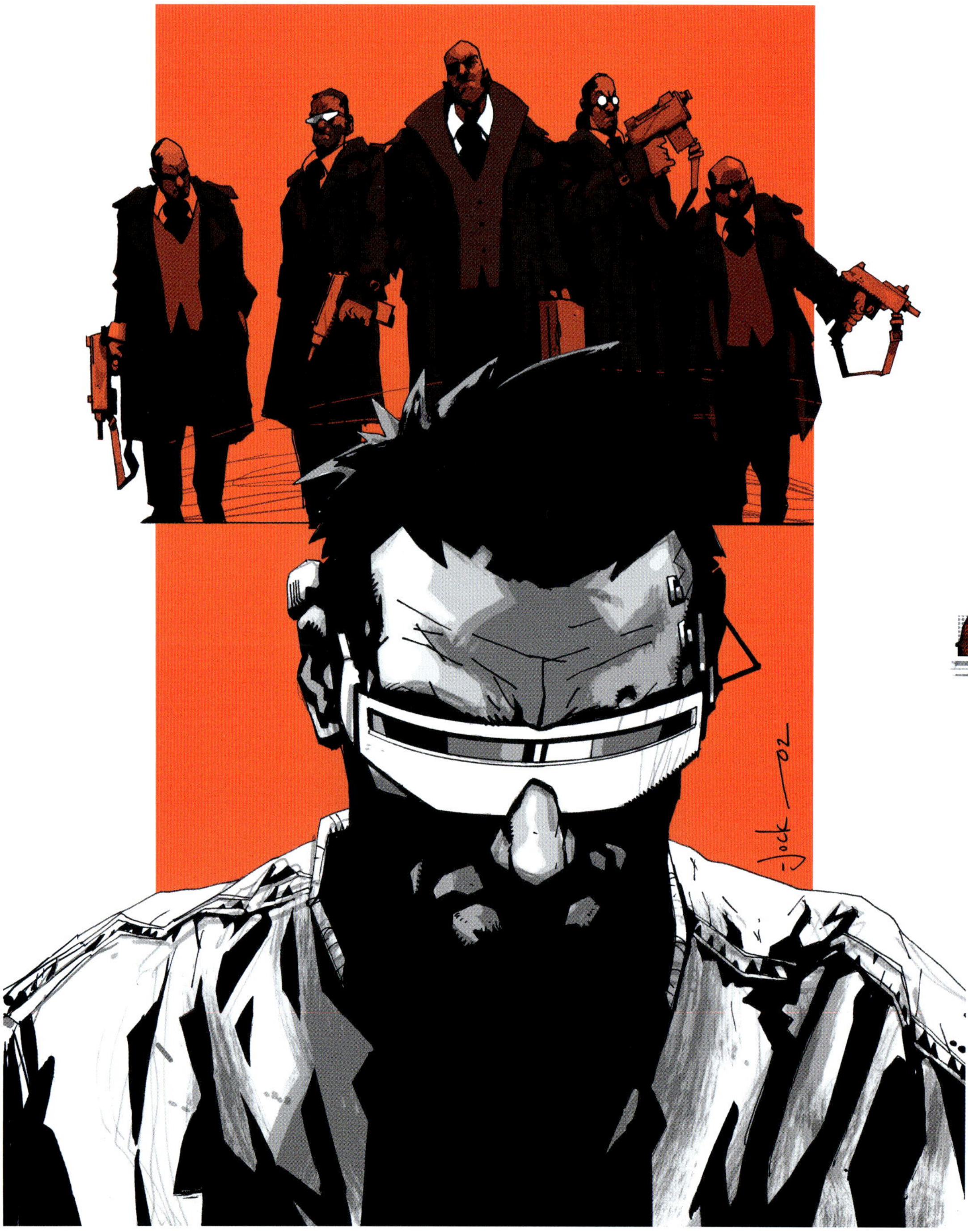

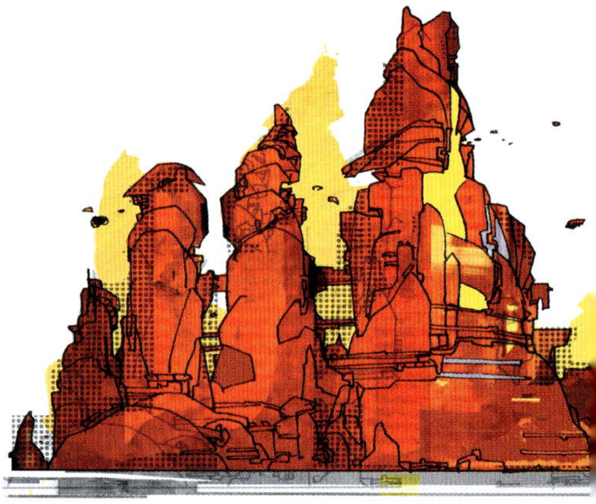

 LENNY ZERO GRAPHIC NOVEL COVER, 2011

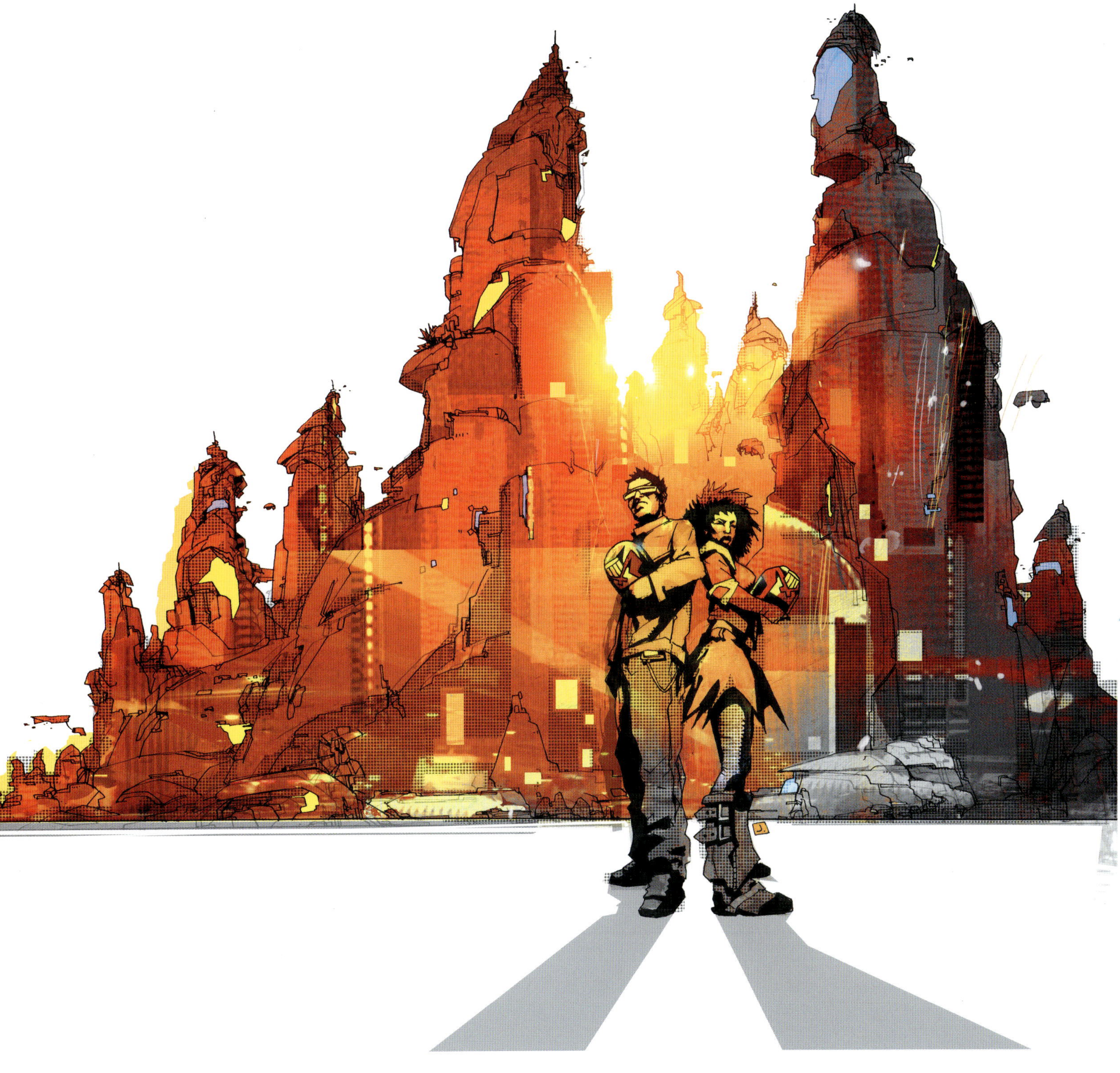

MEGA-CITY UNDERCOVER GRAPHIC NOVEL COVER, 2008

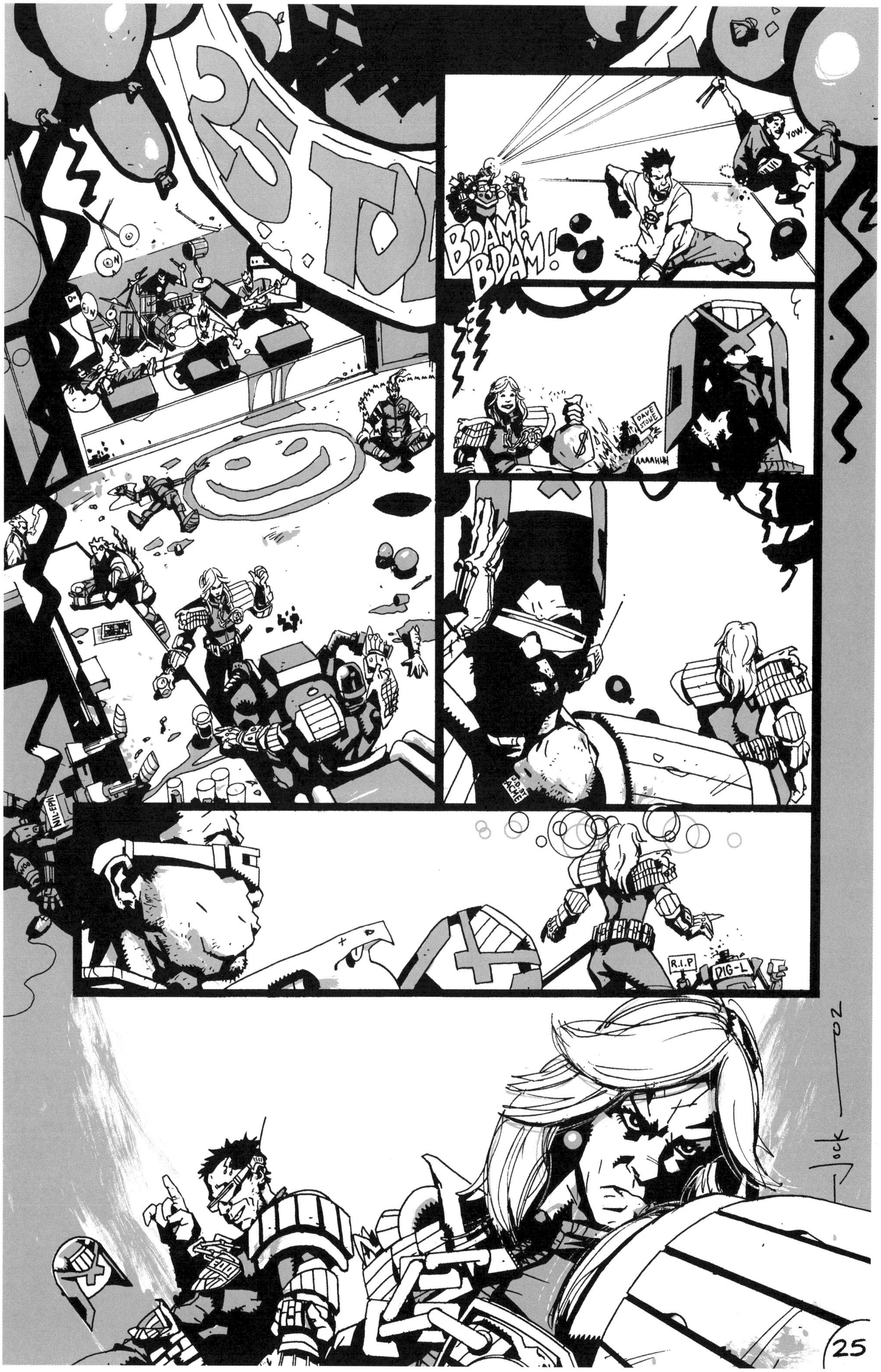
YOW!
BDAM! BDAM!
DAVE STONE
AAAHHH
NIL-EPH
R.I.P
DIG-L
25

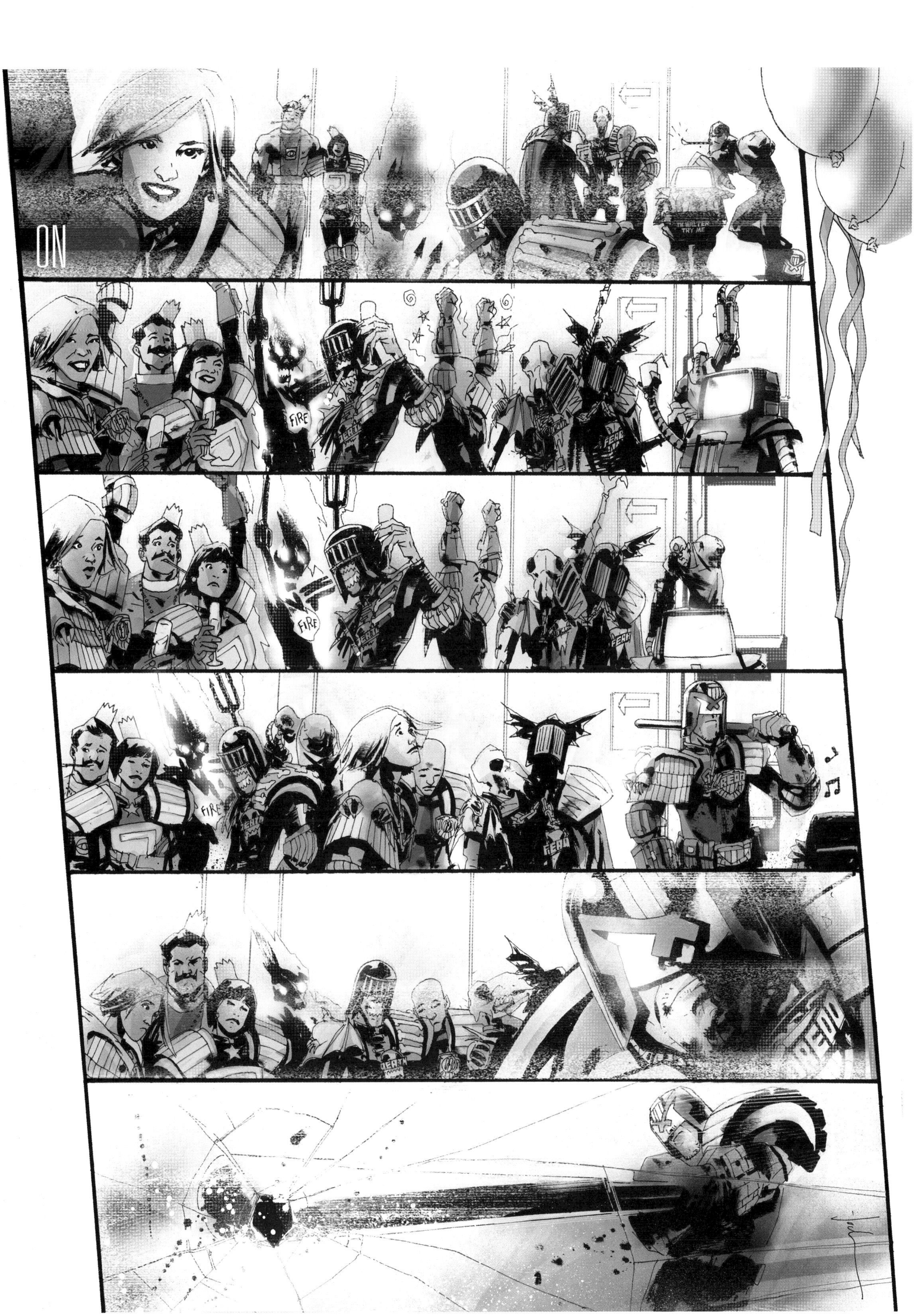
ON
FIRE
FIRE
FIRE

DREDD

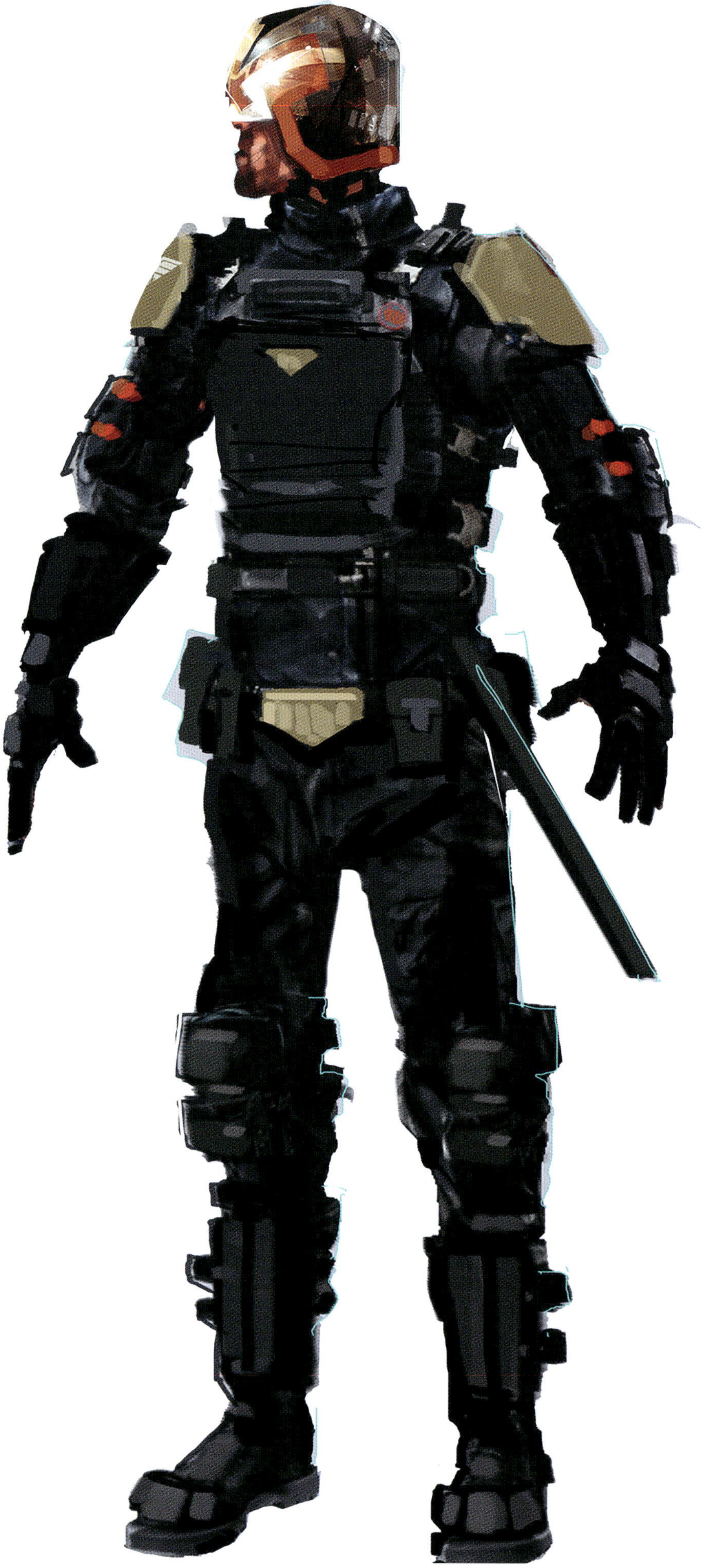

DREDD CONCEPT ART, 2010

DREDD CONCEPT ART, 2010

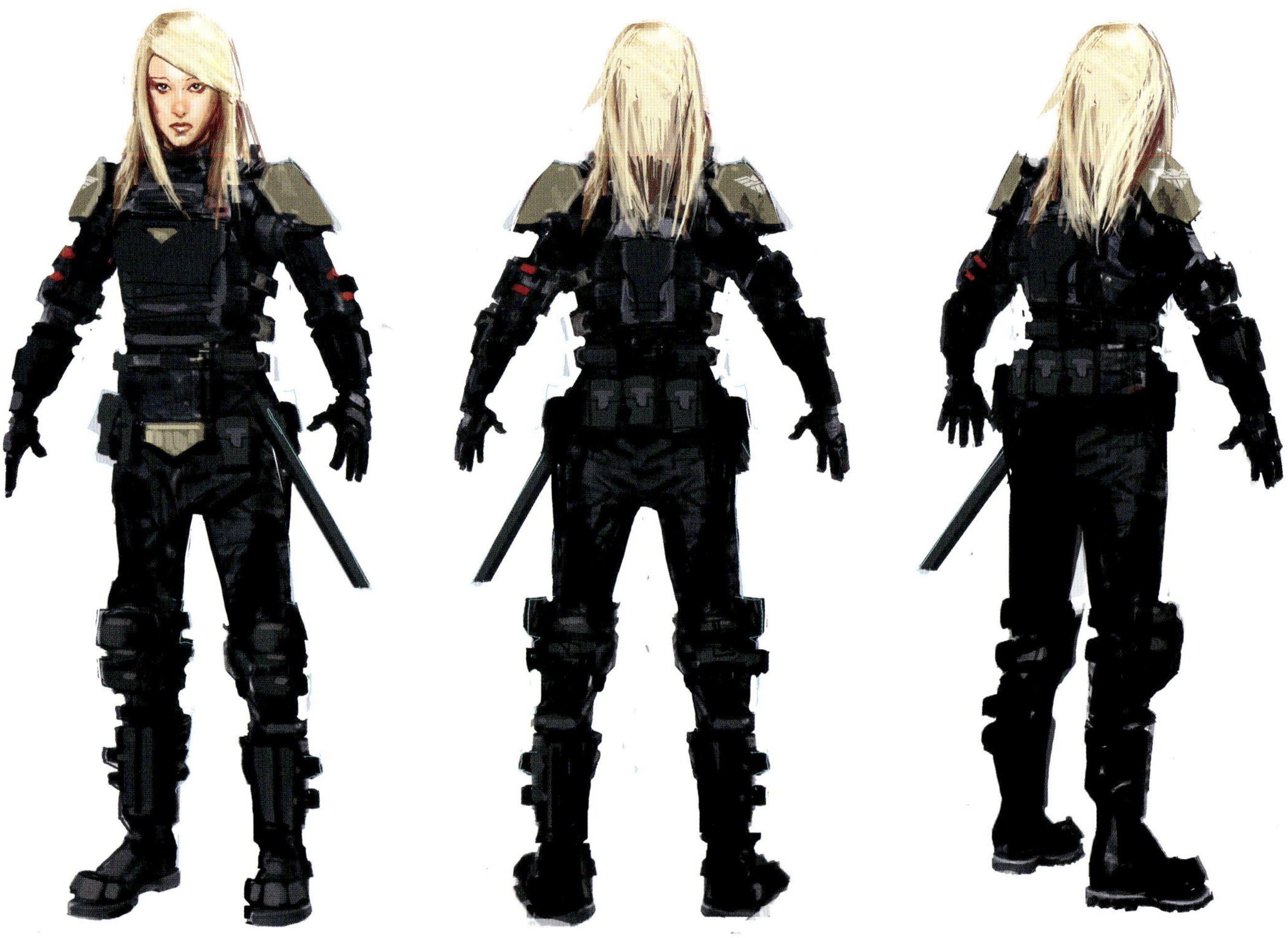

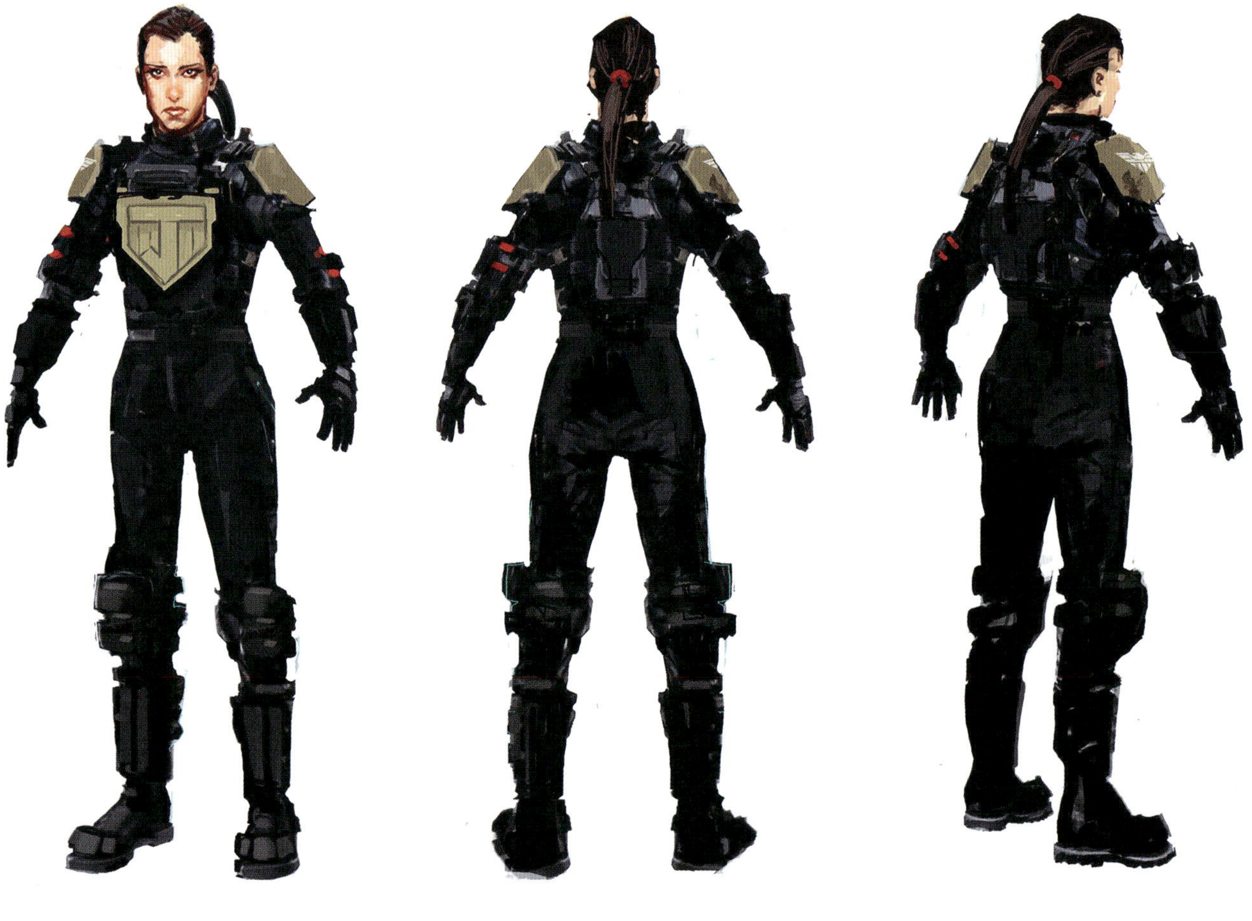

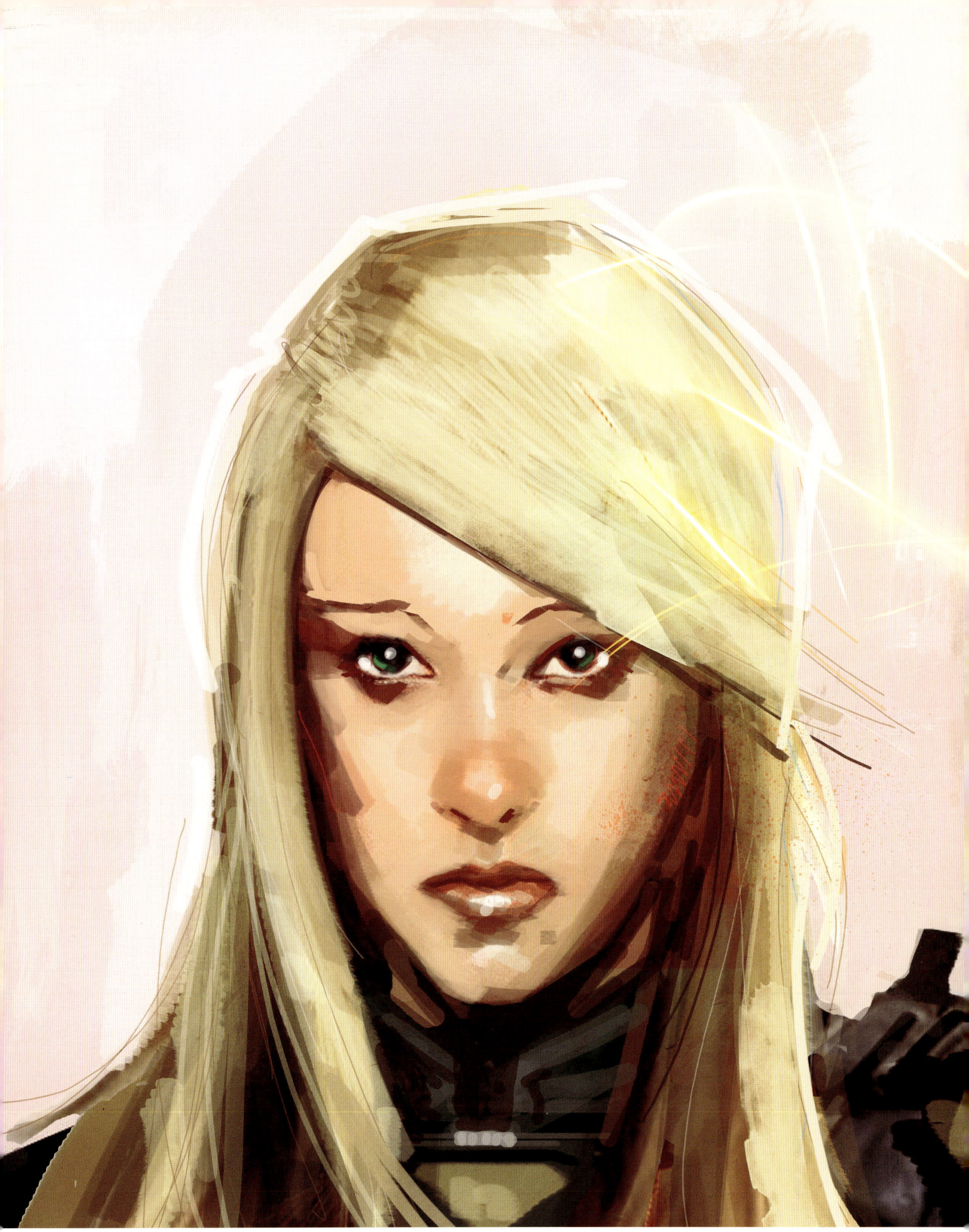

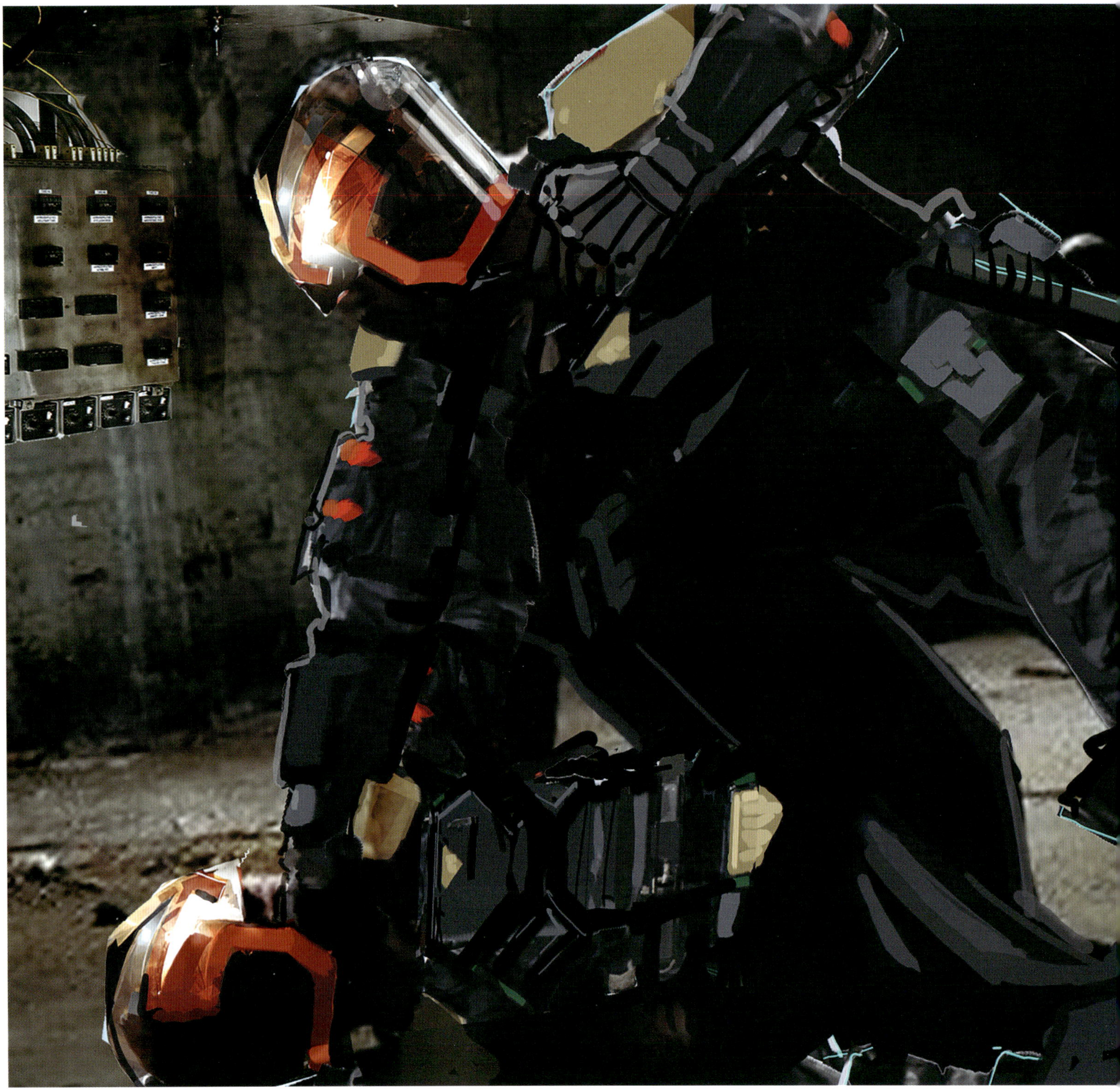

HELMETS

'The one thing the filmmakers were very keen on keeping authentic – which I was very pleased about – was the helmets. There'd been some early concept work where the helmets were nicely battle-worn but the shape was all wrong – the sides were too close and cut off his profile. I made a point of saying that "No **2000 AD** fan will like that helmet, but does that matter?" and Alex Garland just said "Yes, that really matters – why isn't it right?" So, I think they saw the value in having me on board as I was able to vocalise some of those concerns but also have an answer for them.'

—JOCK

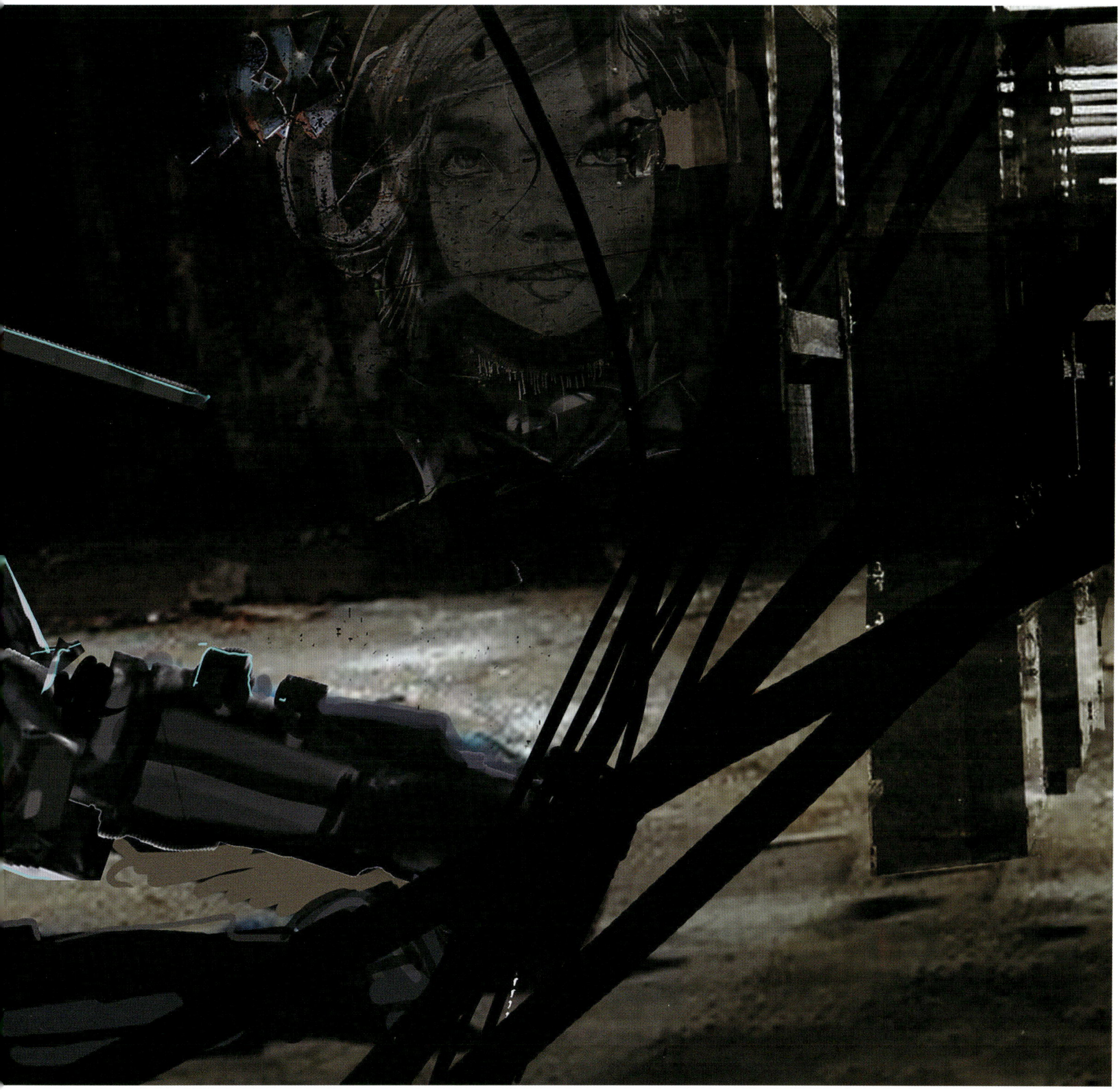

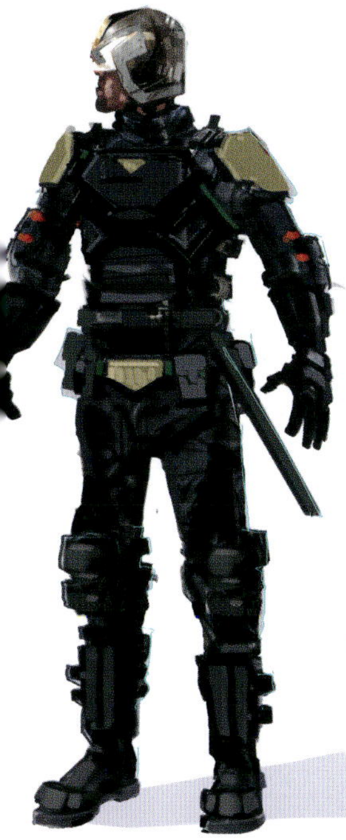

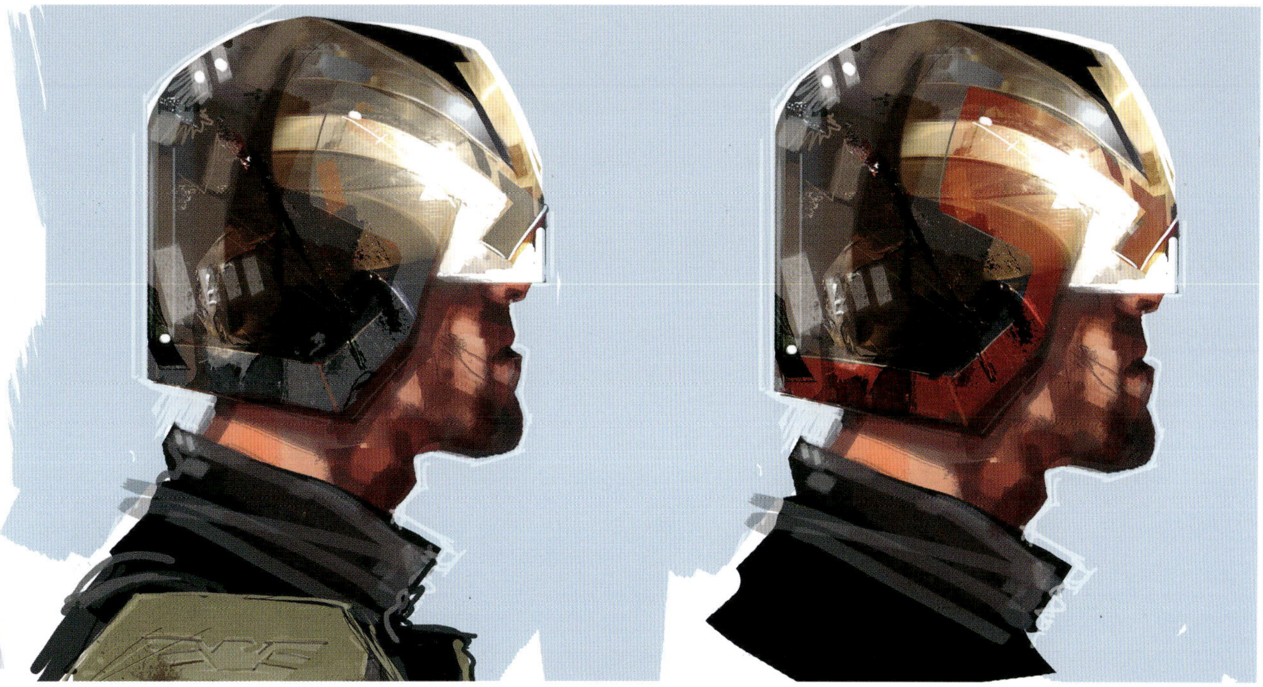

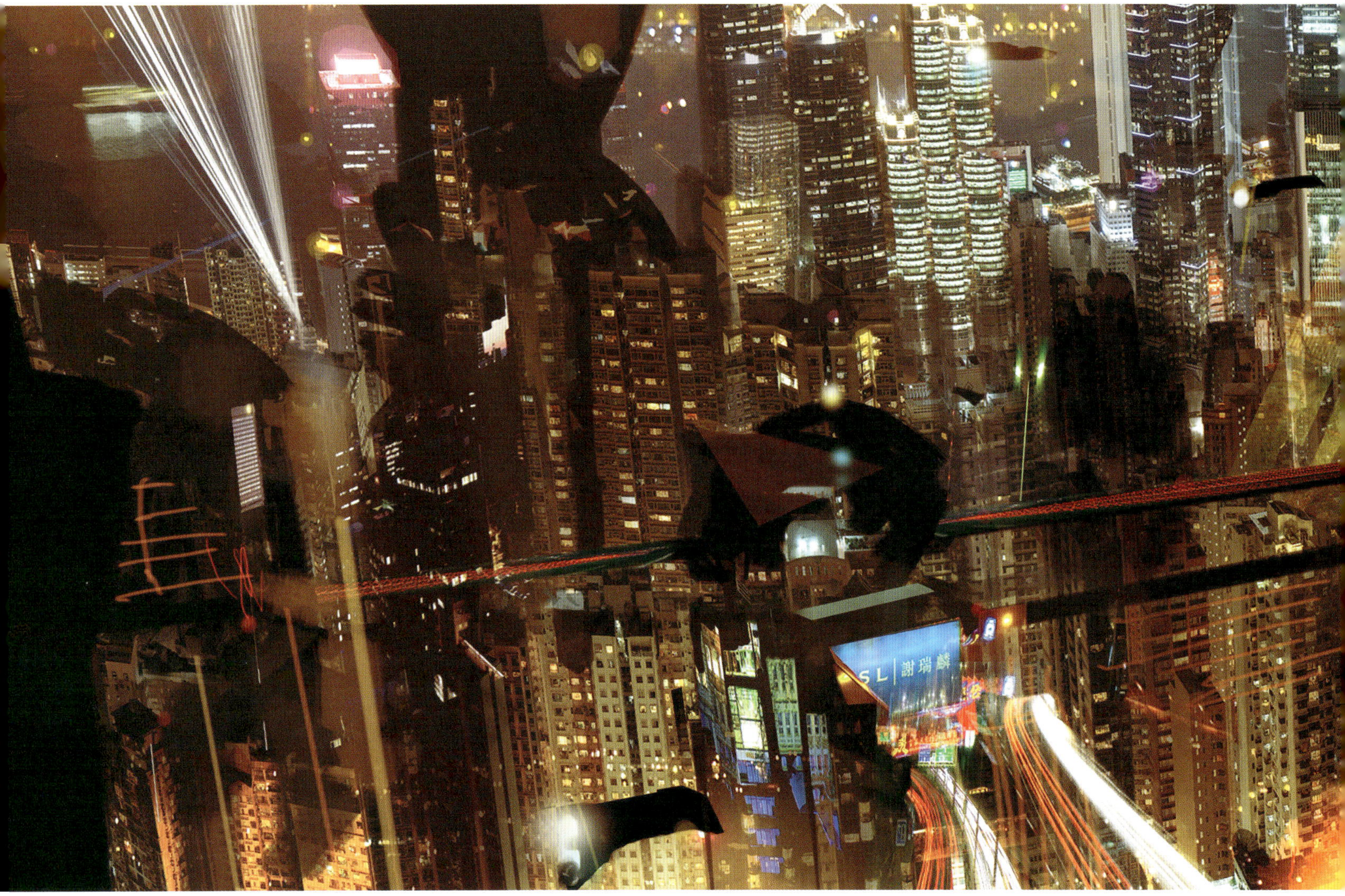
SL 謝瑞麟

 DREDD CONCEPT ART, 2010

MEGA-CITY ONE

'This was one of the pieces drawn before I was hired. It is a much more fantastical Mega-City One—sprawling neon and chaos. A contrast to the actual approach in the final film which was stripped back, brutalist, and urban.'

—JOCK

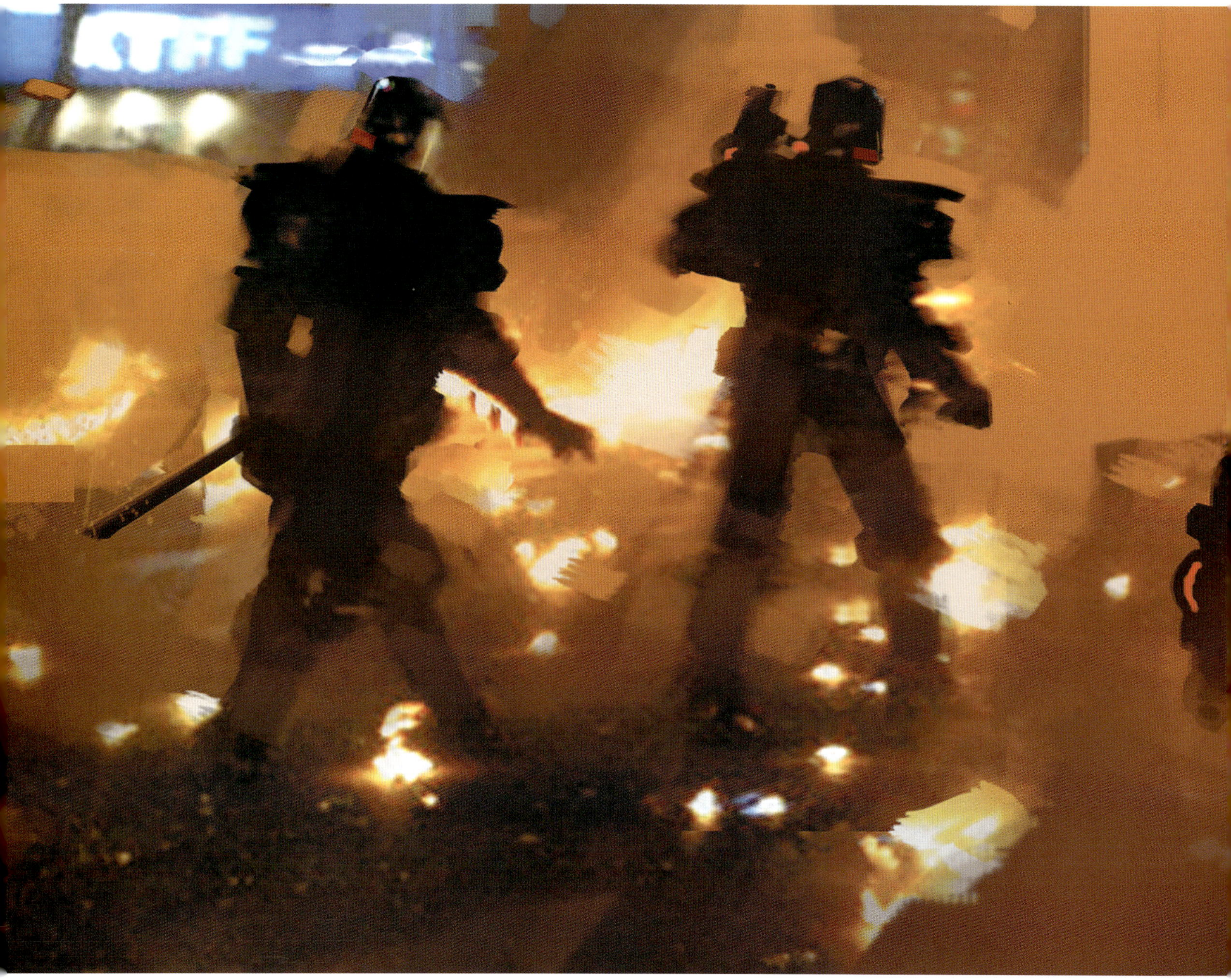

JUDGES

'This image essentially got me the job on the film. When I met Alex Garland and the team at DNA for the first time, he commented that the use of light in this was the tone they were looking for. I love finding interesting ways to handle light and shadow, using silhouettes and mood, so this really resonated with me. We see this kind of image in the real world, but here it's Mega-City One... the exaggerated profile of the Judges.. a little neon… it's close enough to our current world to make the world of Dredd feel tangible.'

—JOCK

DREDD CONCEPT ART, 2010

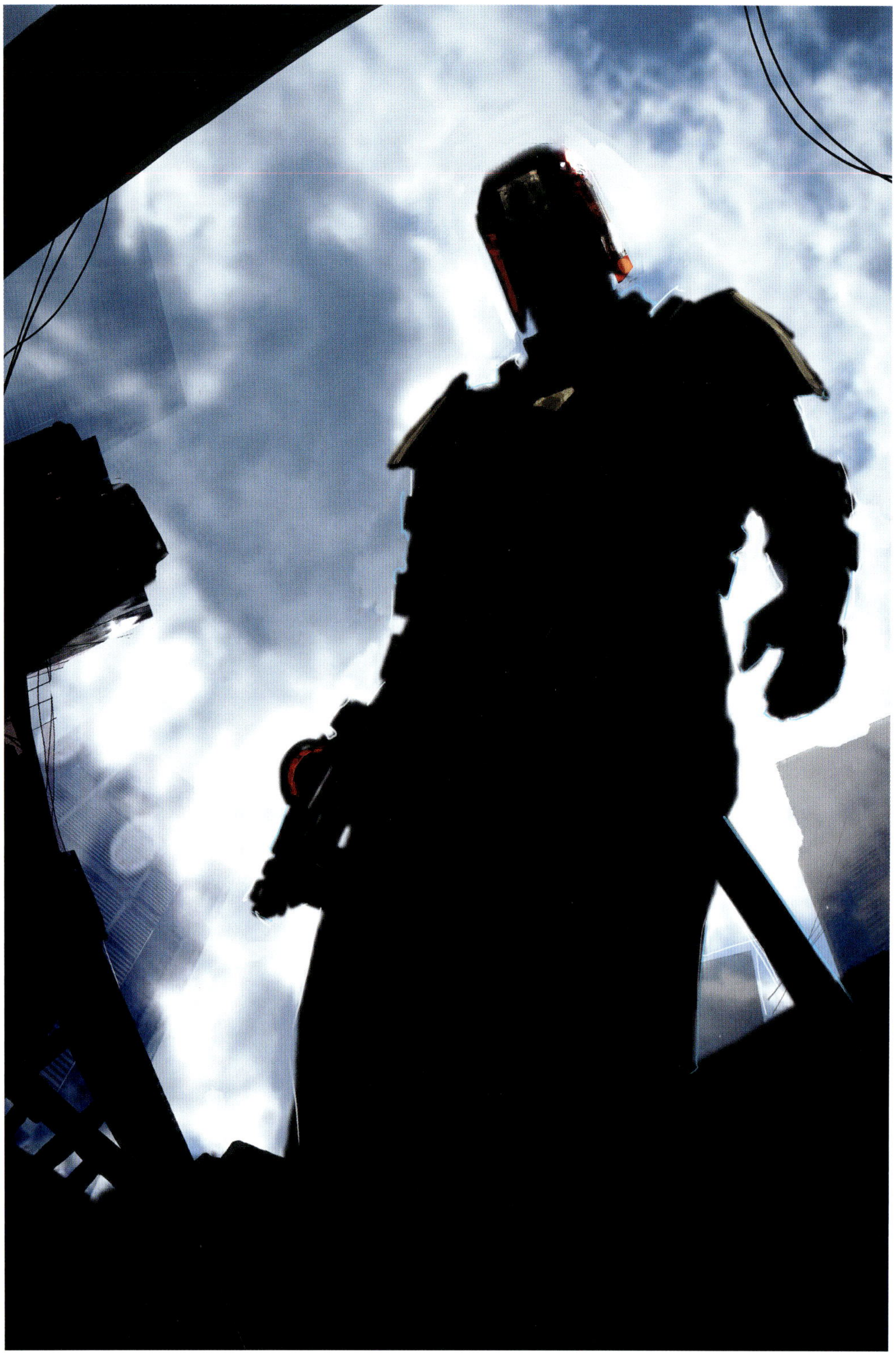

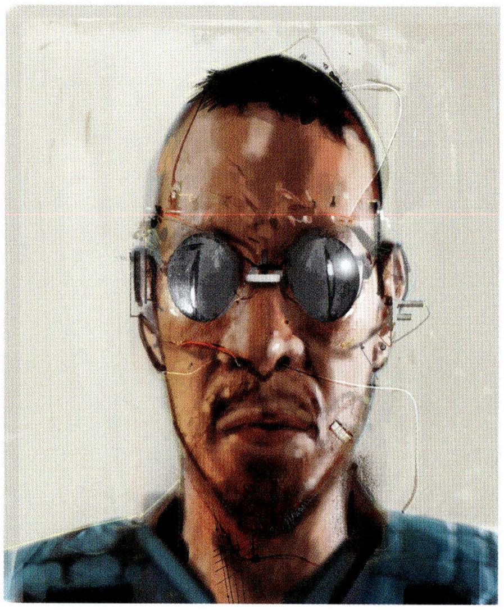

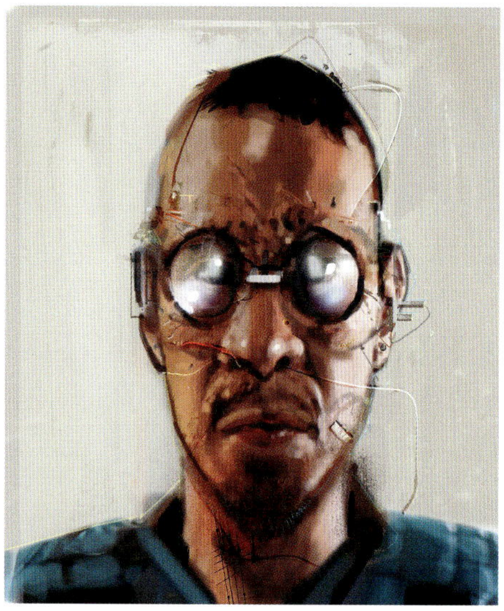

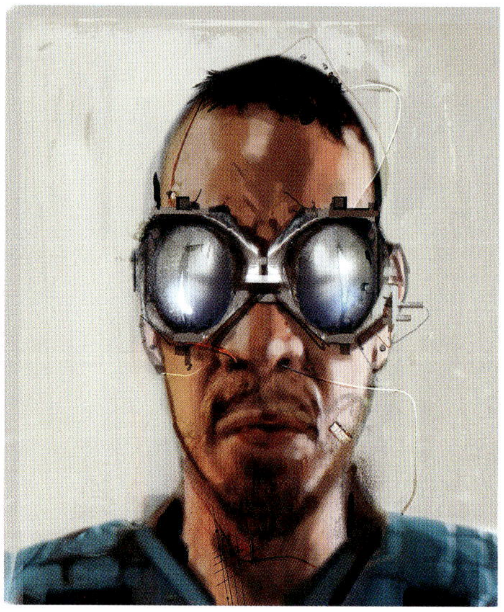

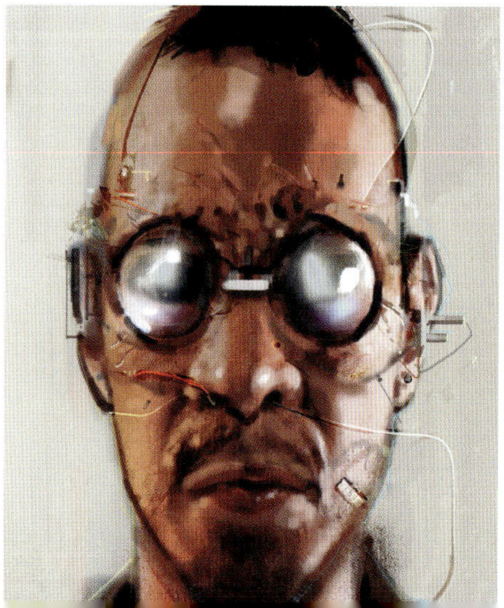

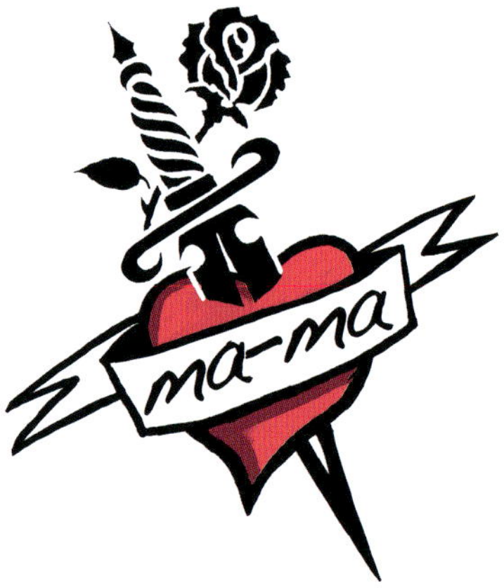
ma-ma

DREDD CONCEPT ART, 2010

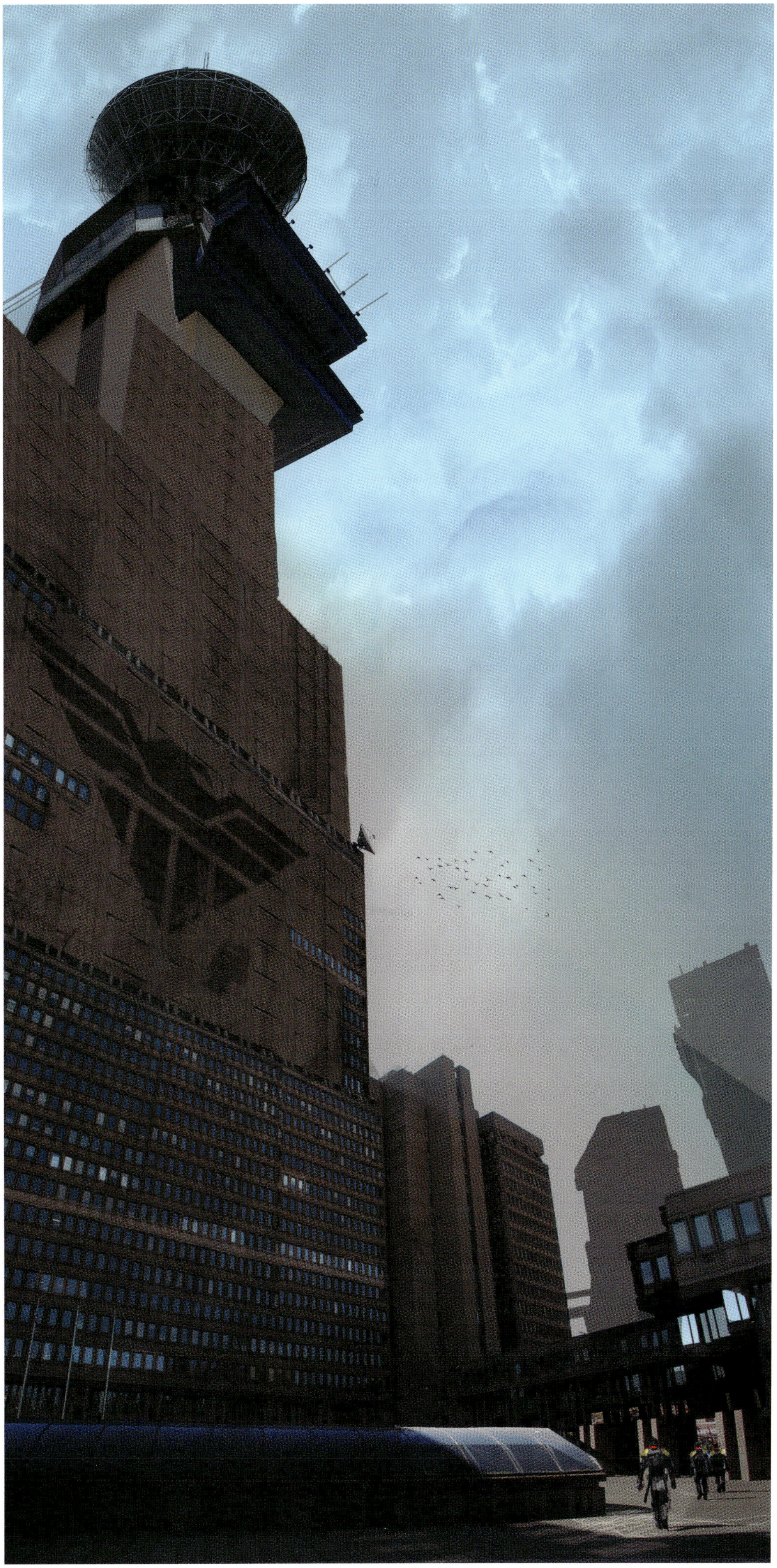

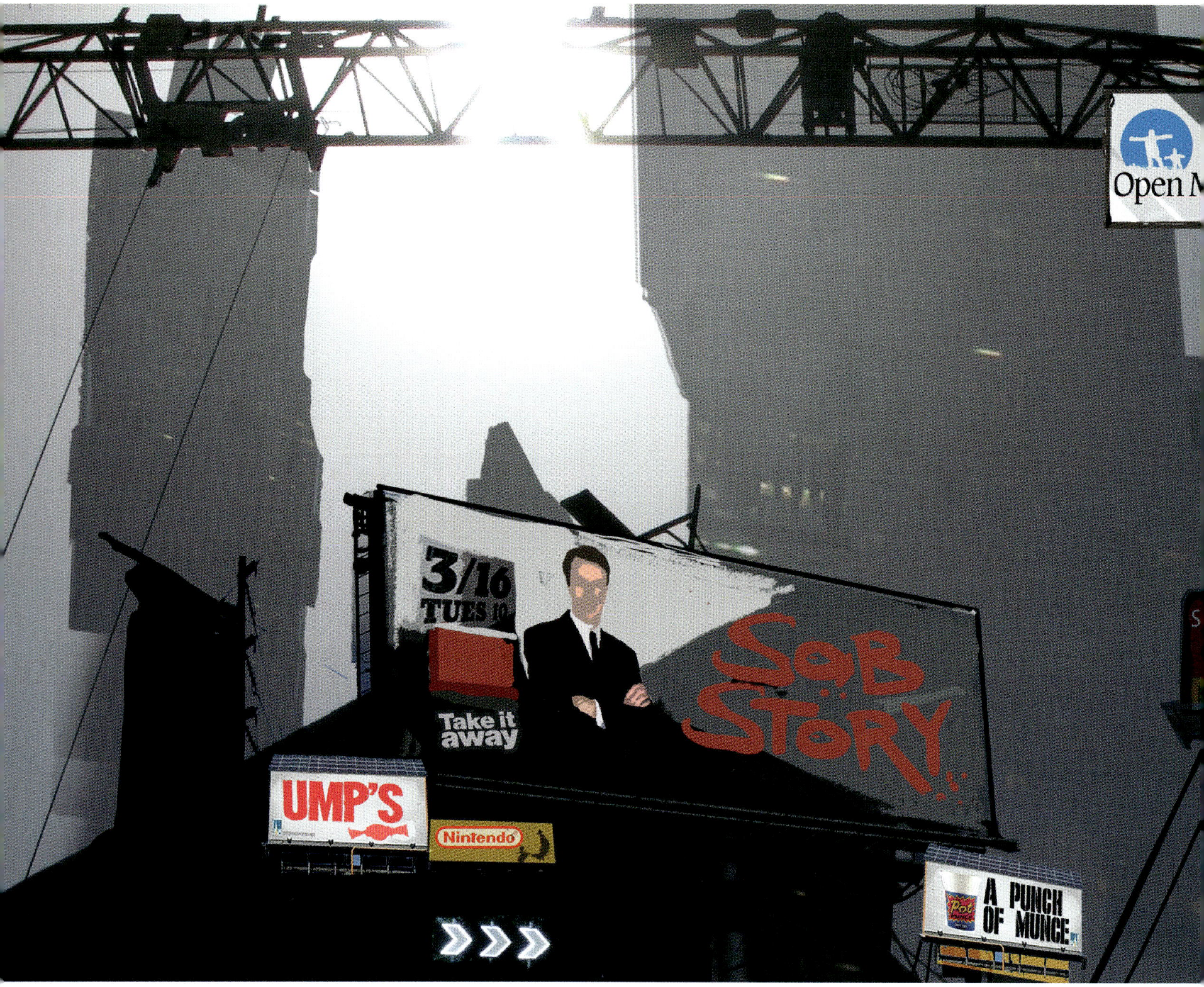
Open
3/16
TUES 10
Take it away
SOB STORY
UMP'S
Nintendo
A PUNCH OF MUNCE

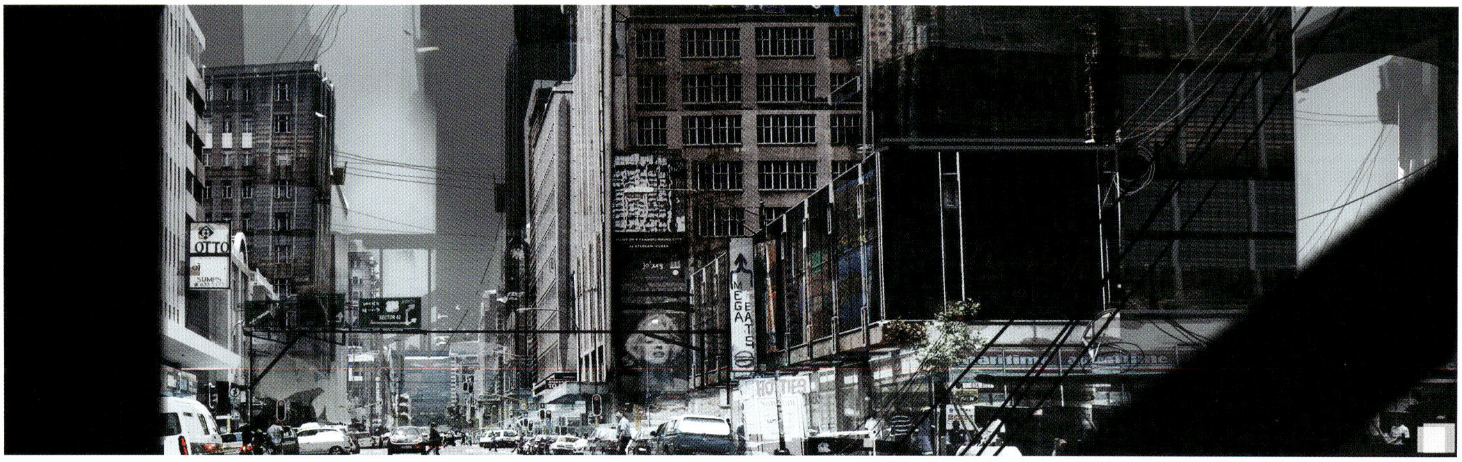
OTTO
MEGA EATS
HOTTIES

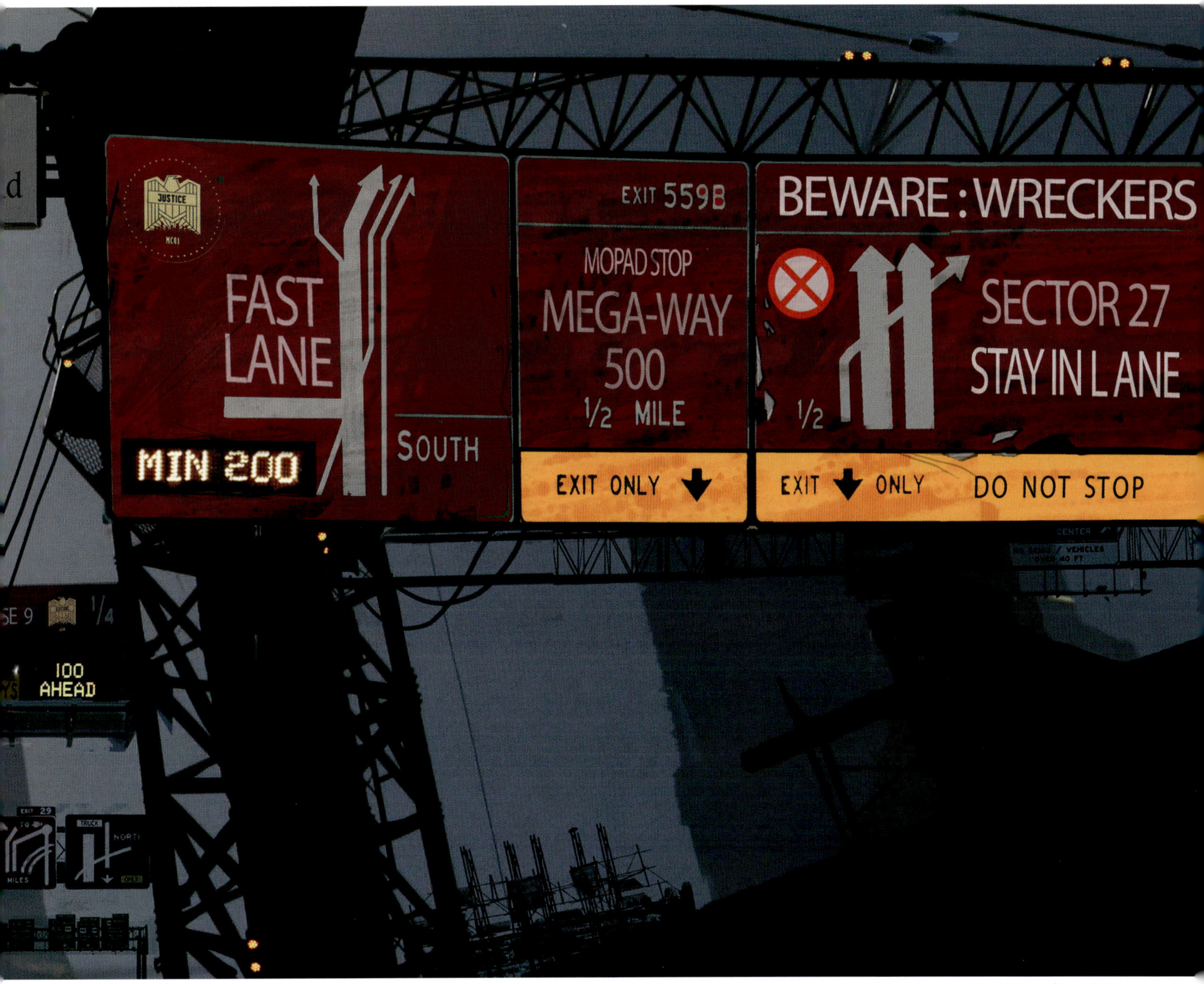
JUSTICE
FAST
LANE
MIN 200
SOUTH
EXIT 559B
MOPAD STOP
MEGA-WAY
500
1/2 MILE
EXIT ONLY
BEWARE : WRECKERS
SECTOR 27
STAY IN LANE
1/2
EXIT ONLY
DO NOT STOP
100
AHEAD

HIGHWAYS

'The number of Easter eggs in this shot is ridiculous. I absolutely loved trying to show how the world of Dredd might work in reality, incorporating things like a sign warning about Wreckers (a reference to the 1984 story 'The Wreckers') and Otto Sump. I was in heaven doing this stuff, getting to draw my Dredd world and trying to make it feel real.'

—JOCK

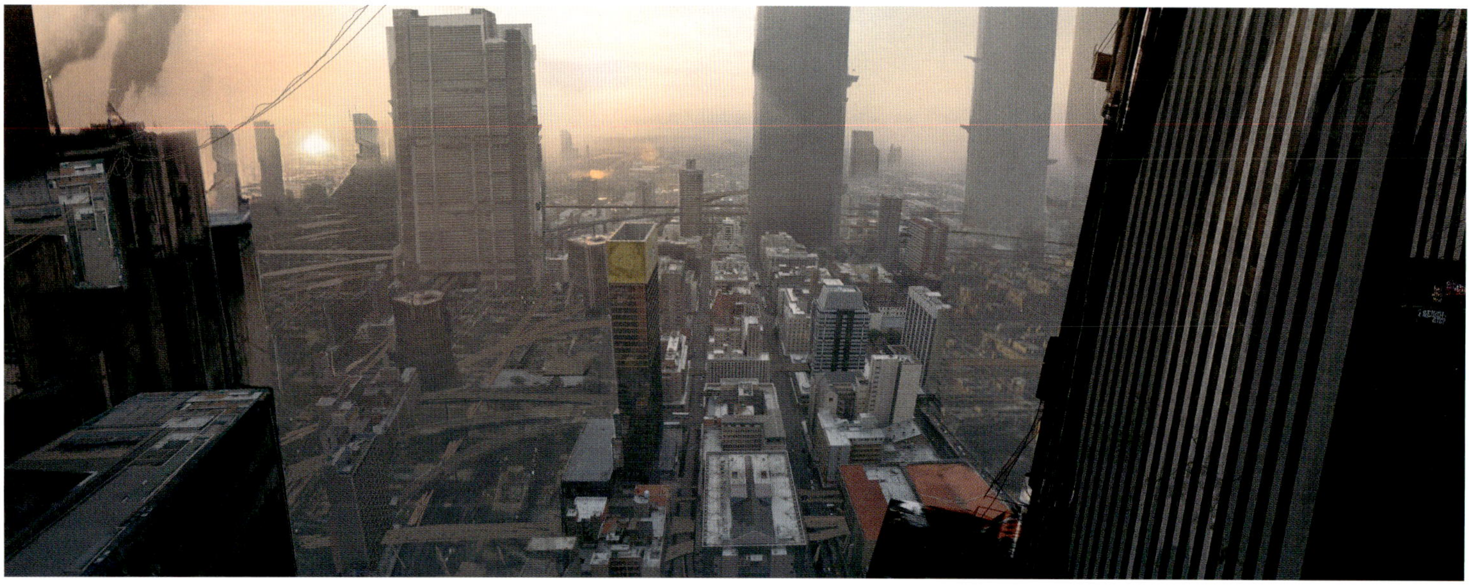

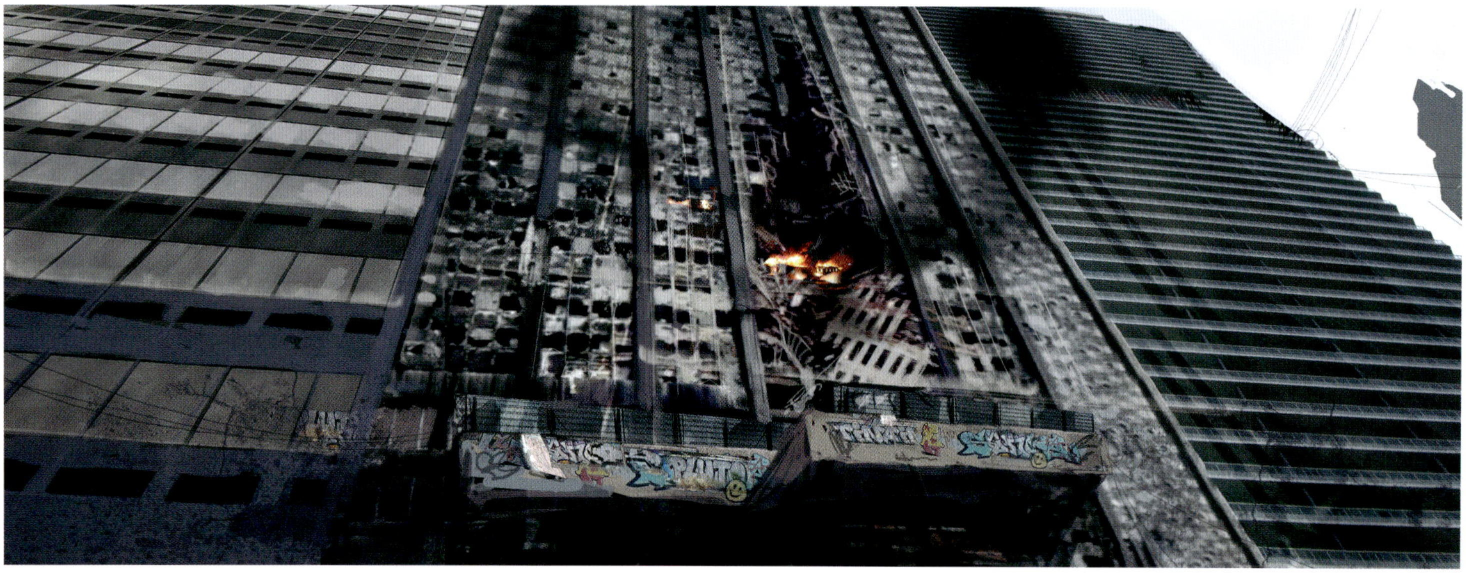

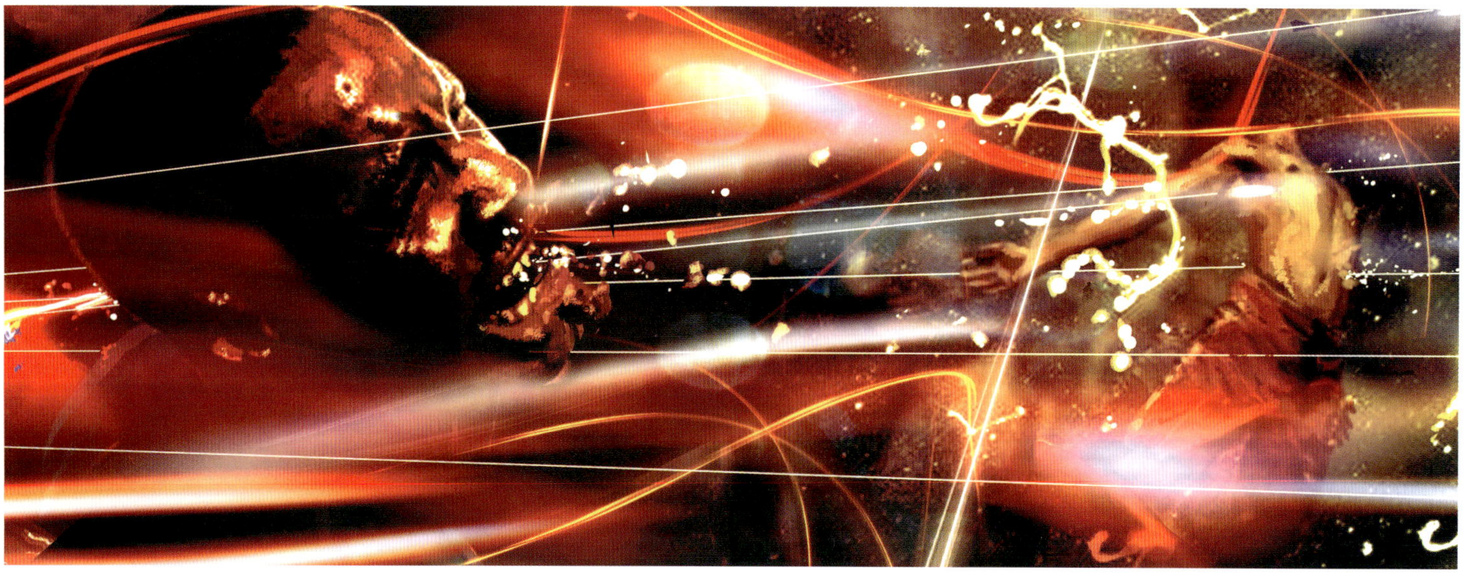

DREDD CONCEPT ART, 2010

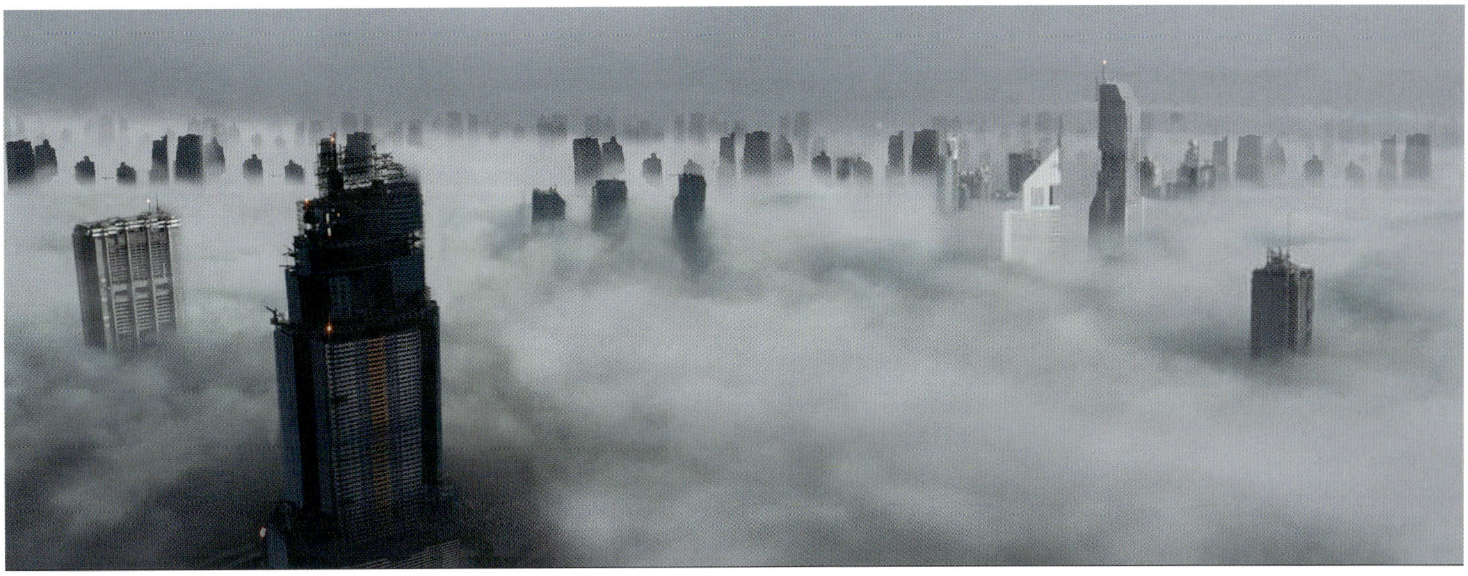

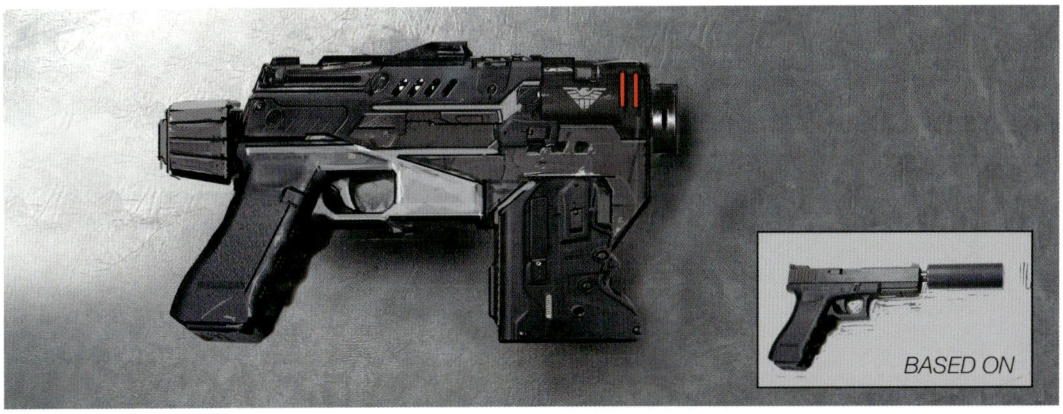
BASED ON

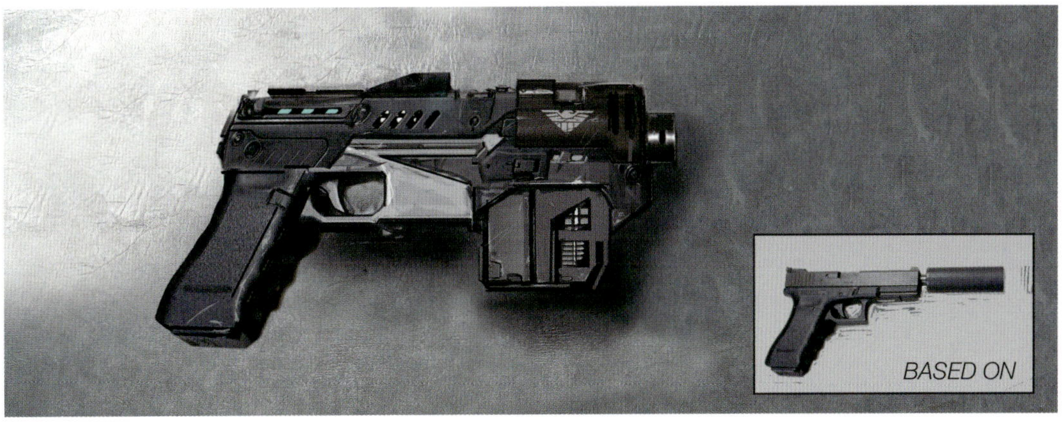
BASED ON

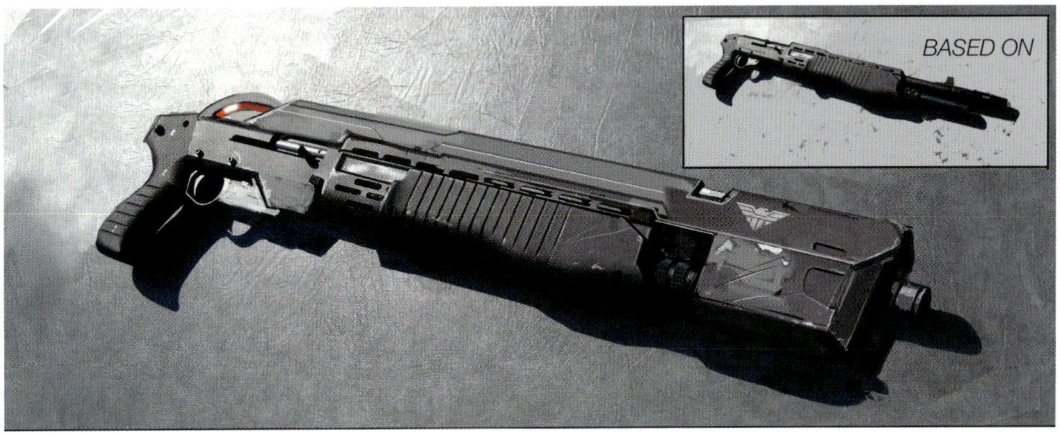
BASED ON

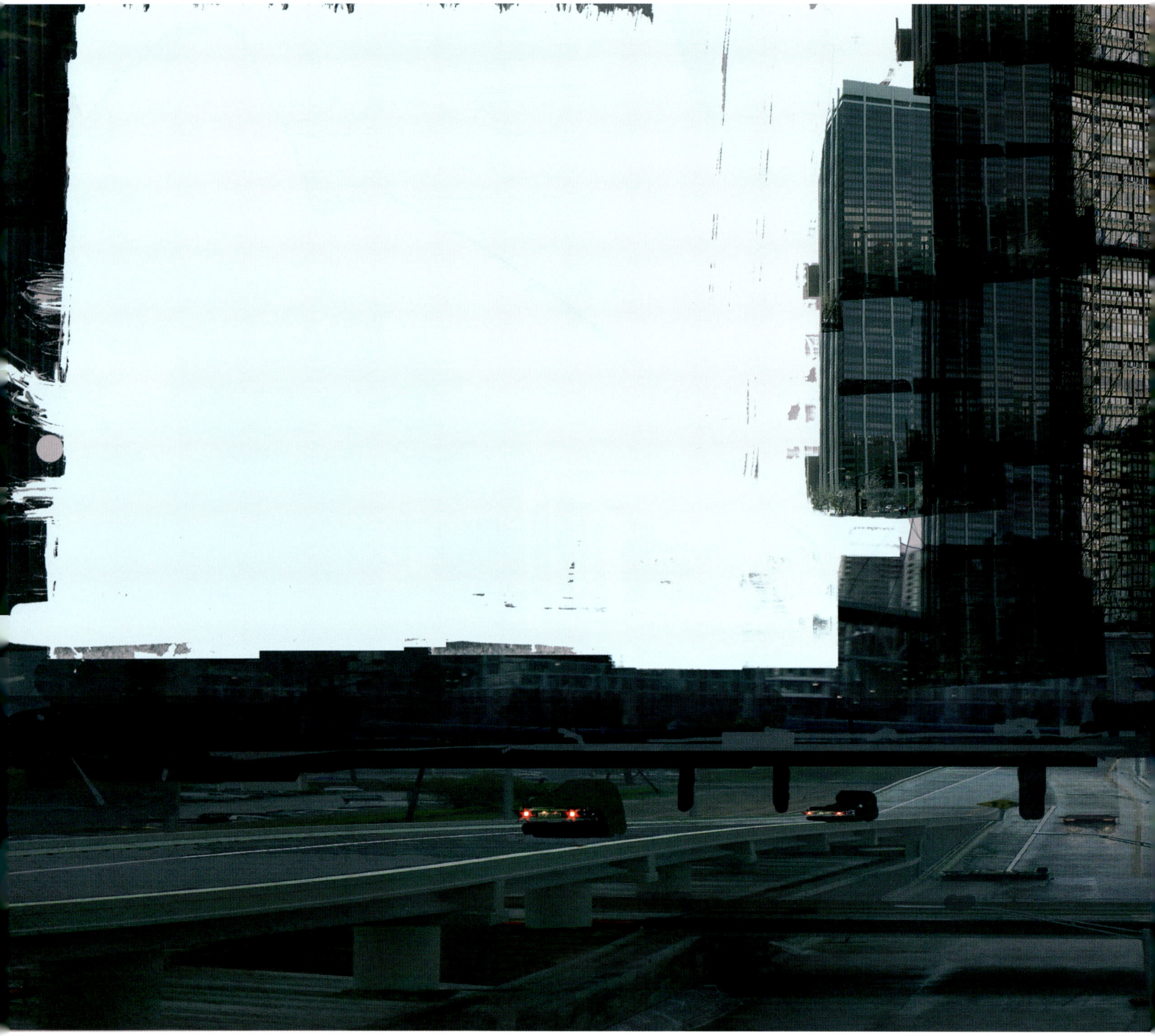

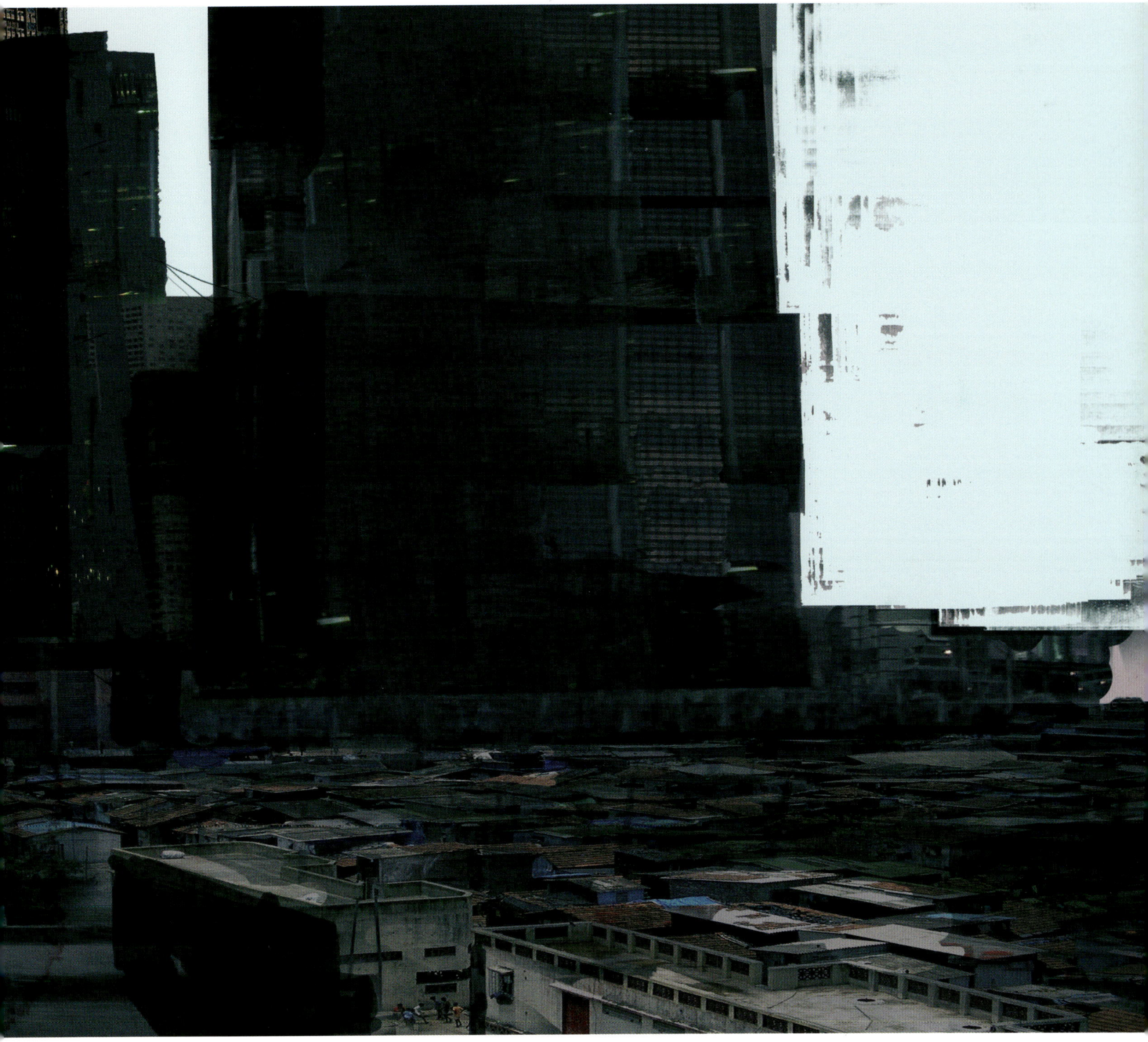

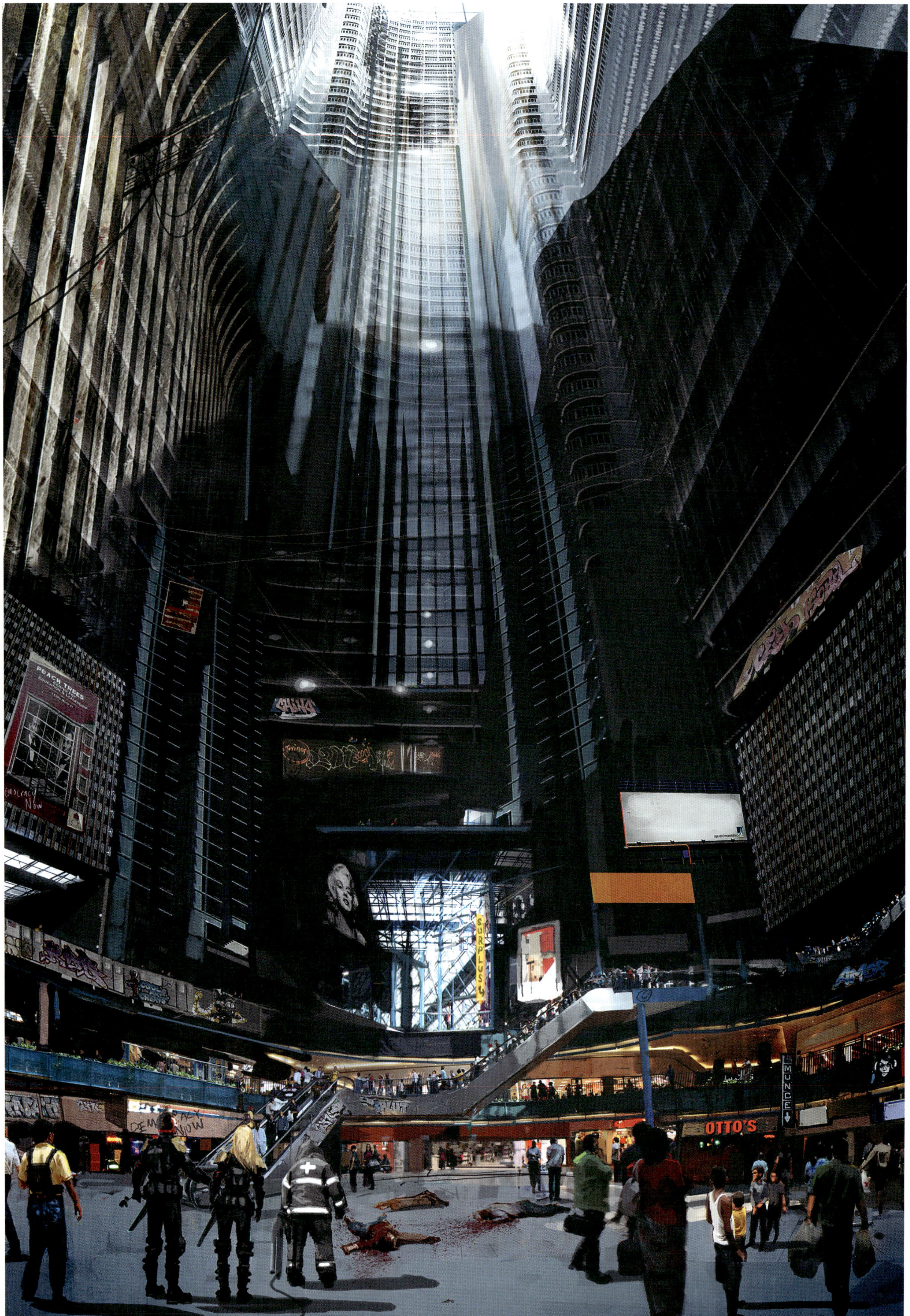
PEACH TREES
SURPLUS
OTTO'S

 CHOPPER

'This was going to be the first scene in **Dredd 2** – a carbon copy of the opening of 'Midnight Surfer' (**2000 AD** #424-#429, 1985), but in the world of the first film. He would have tipped out of the window and flown down into the city where low-level sky-surfing is illegal. And then we'd start to see the Judges noticing him. What I would have given to have seen that realised…'

—JOCK

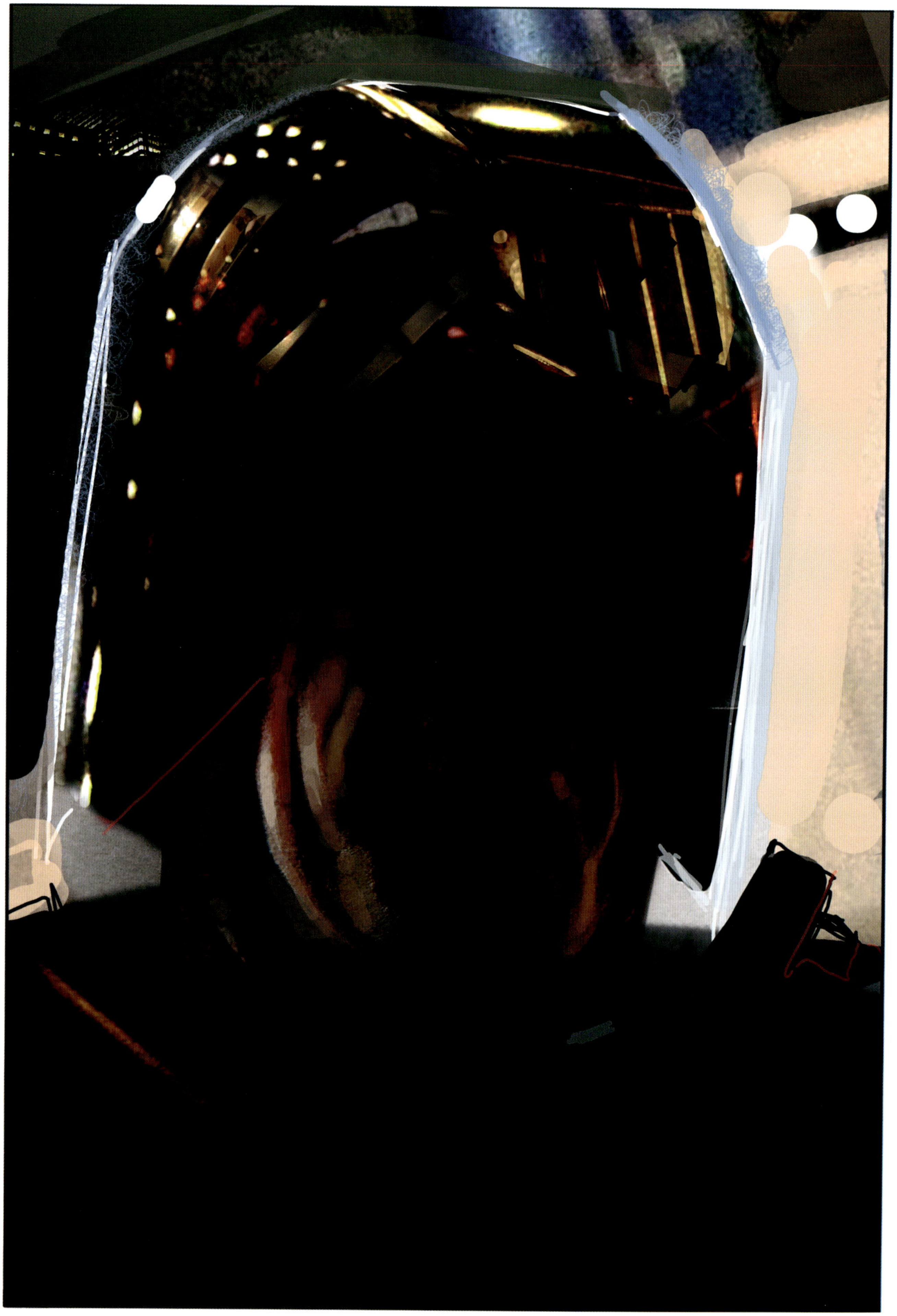

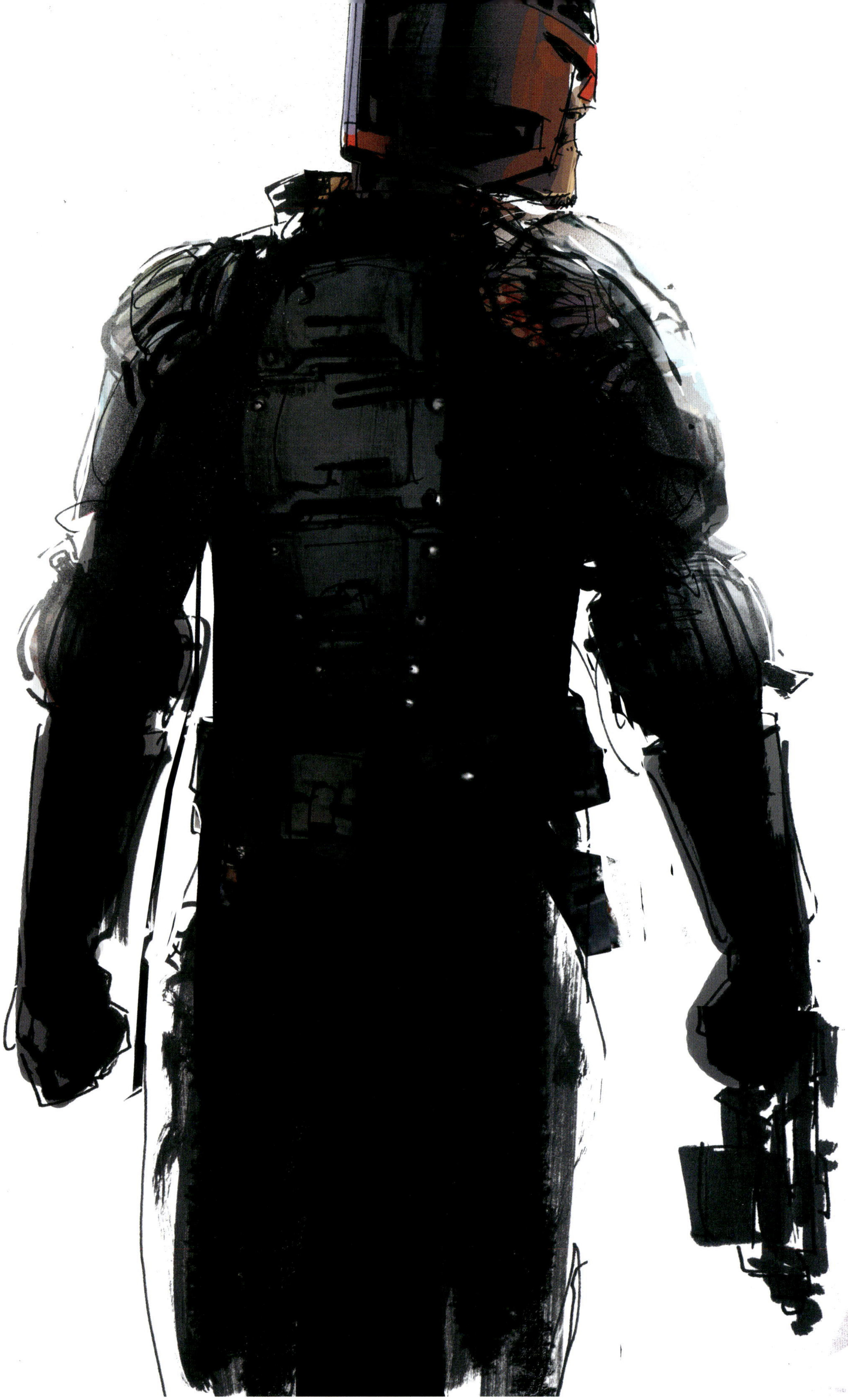

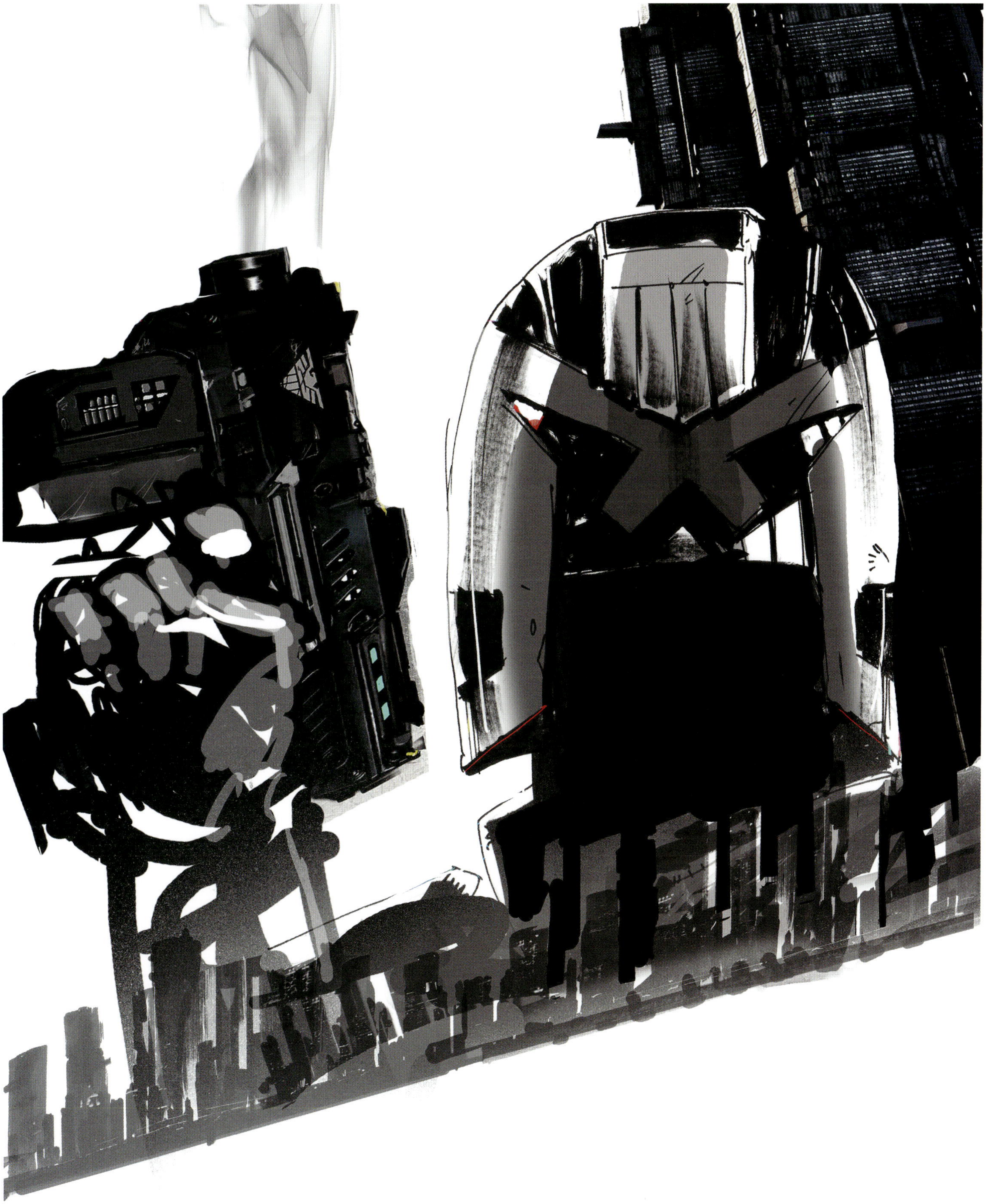

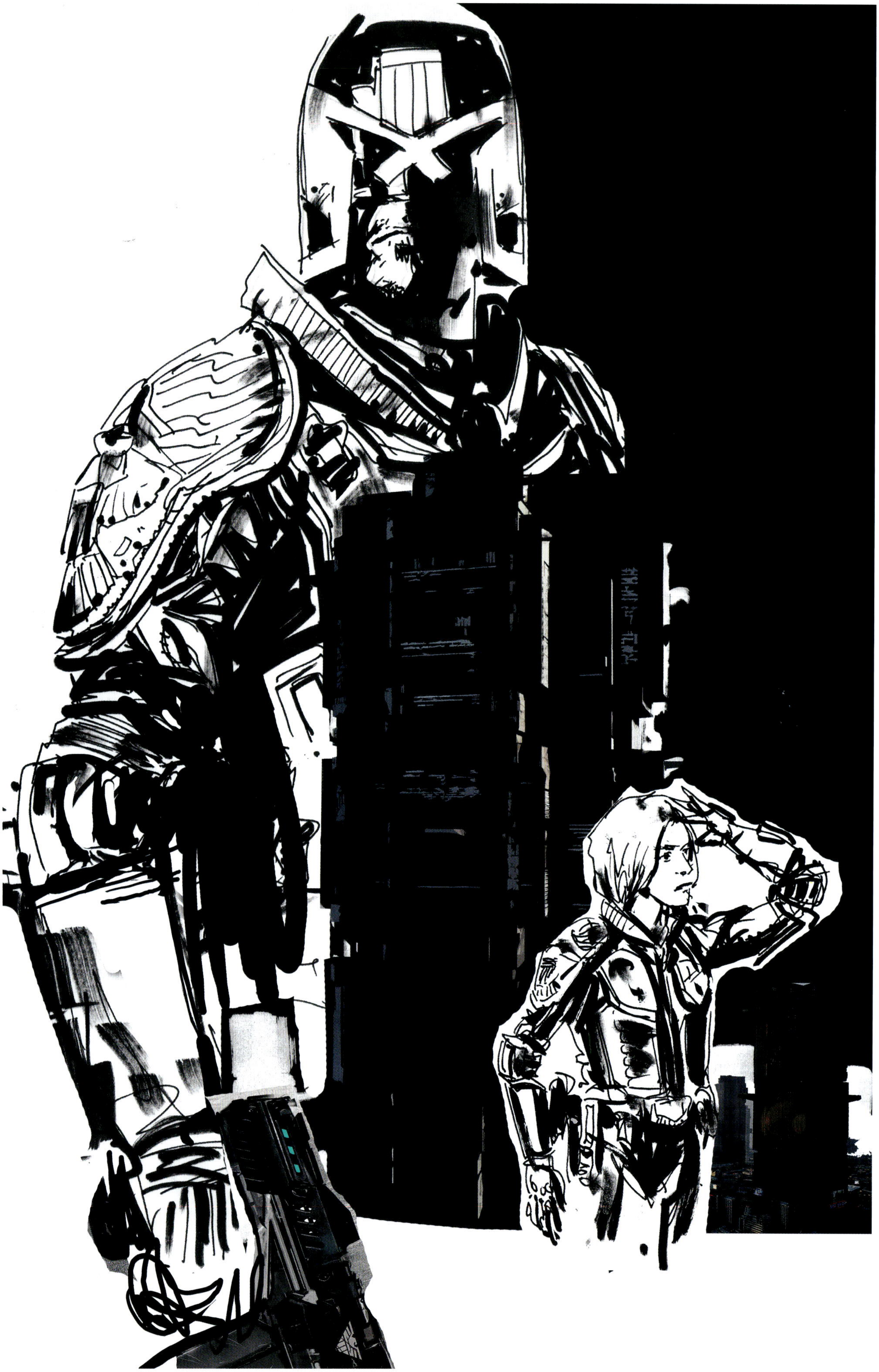

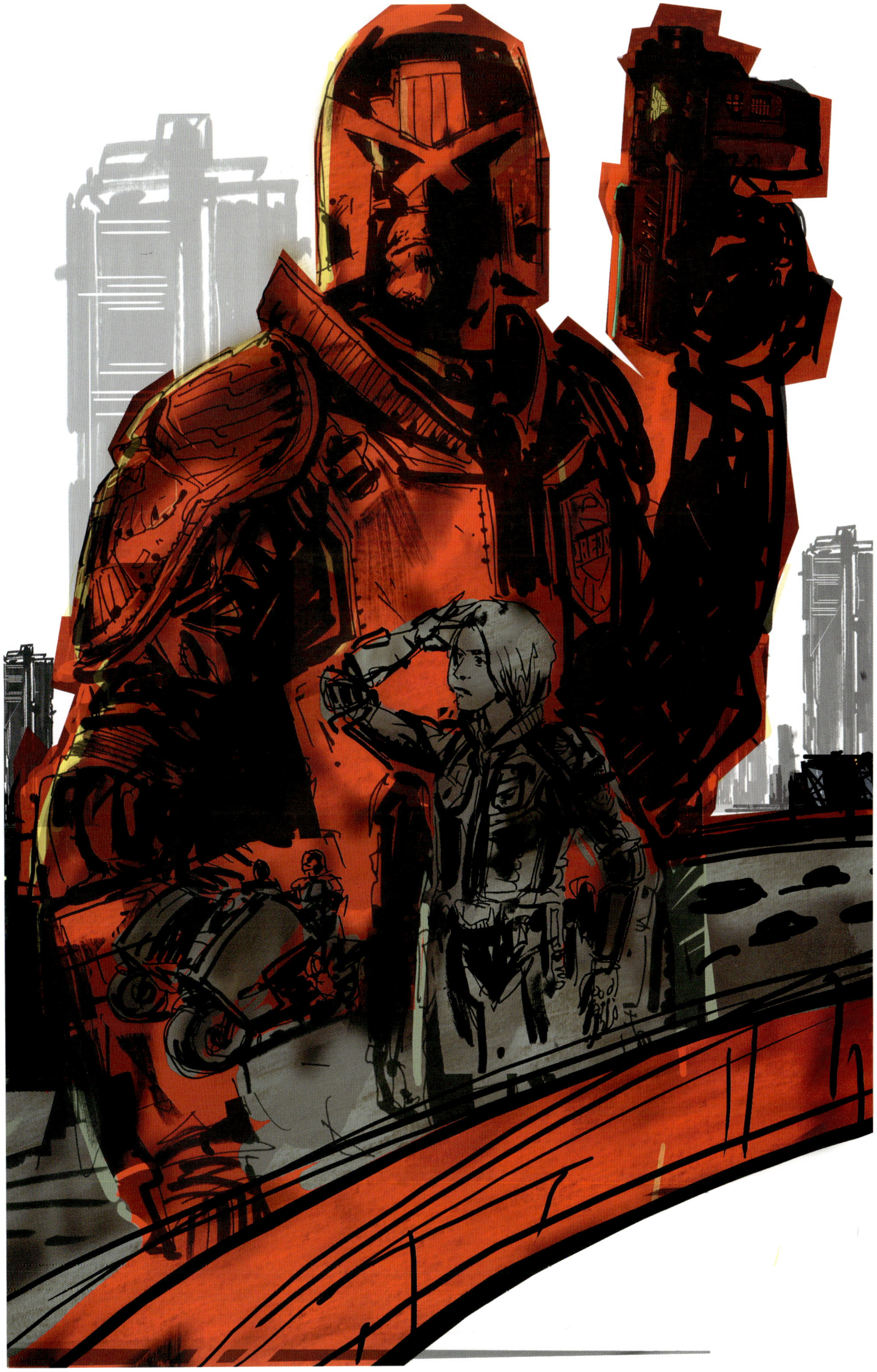

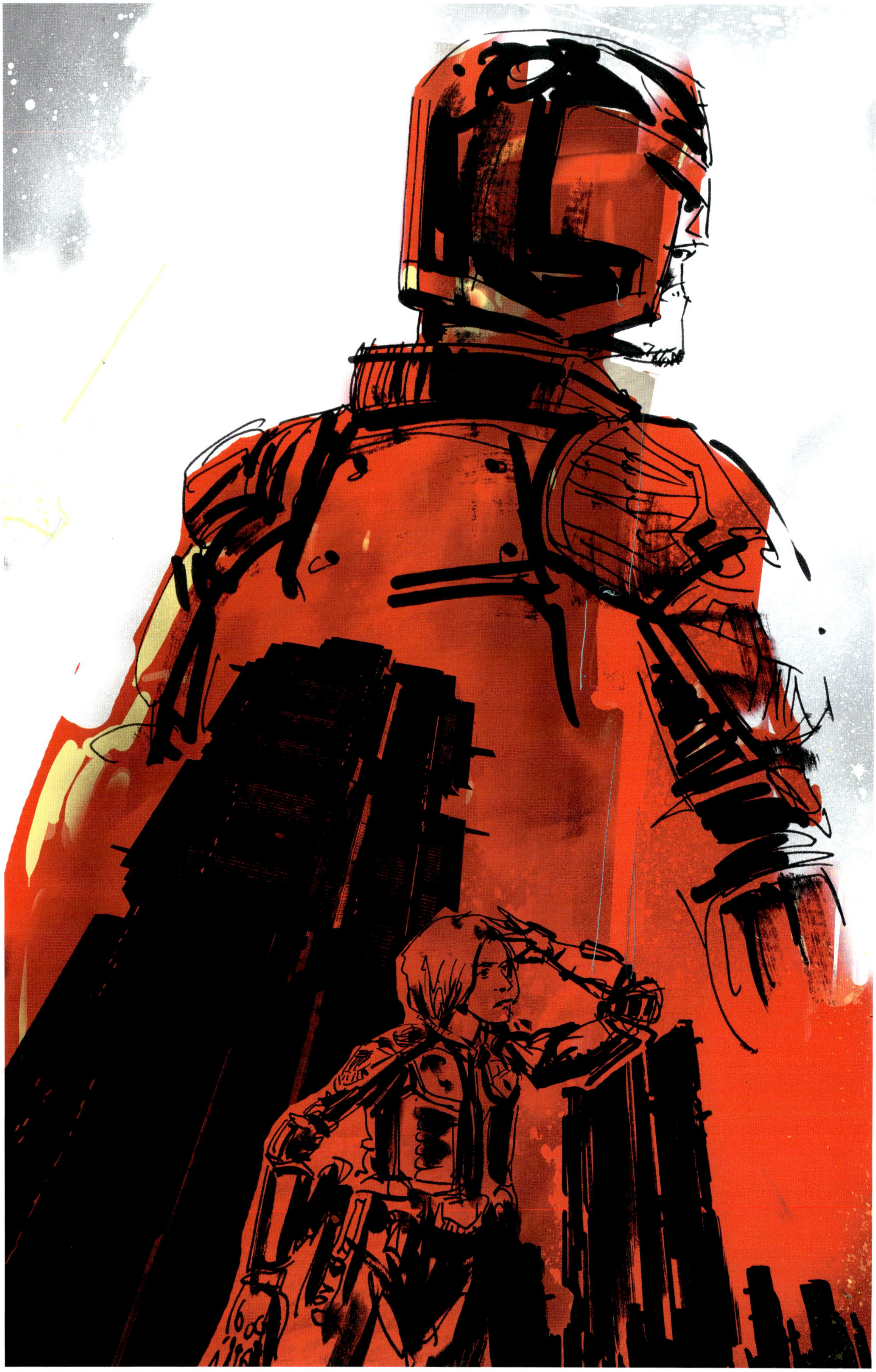

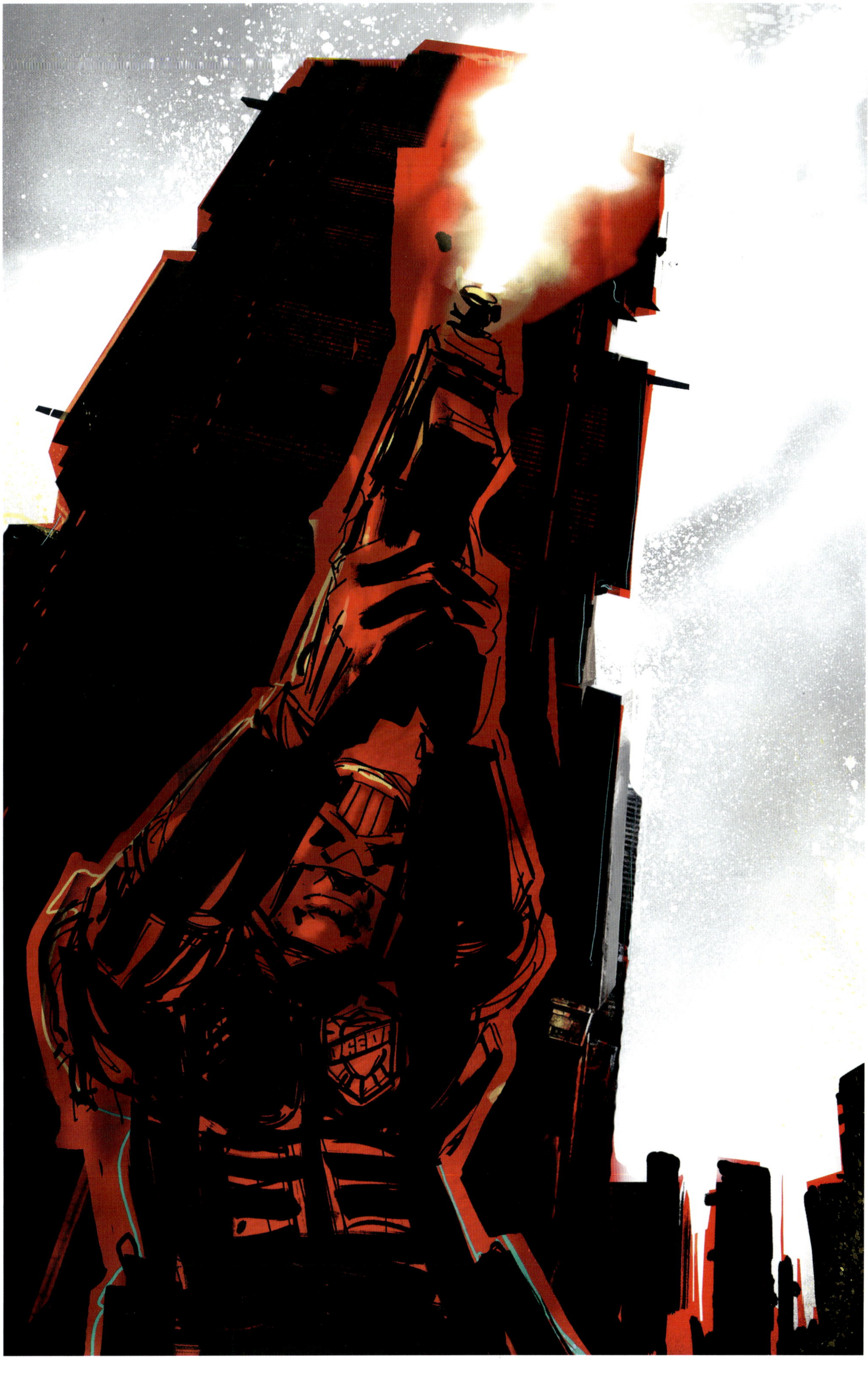

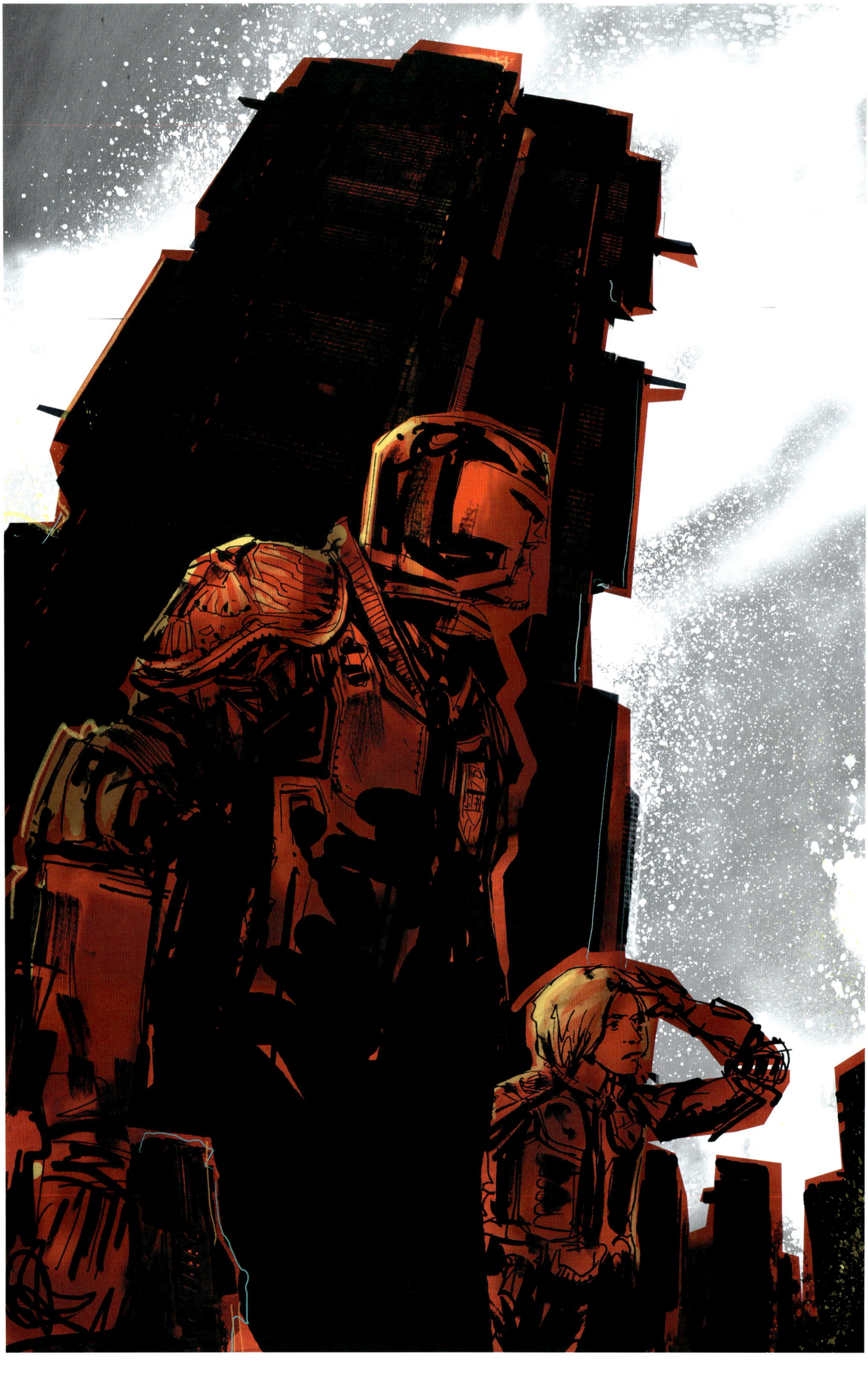

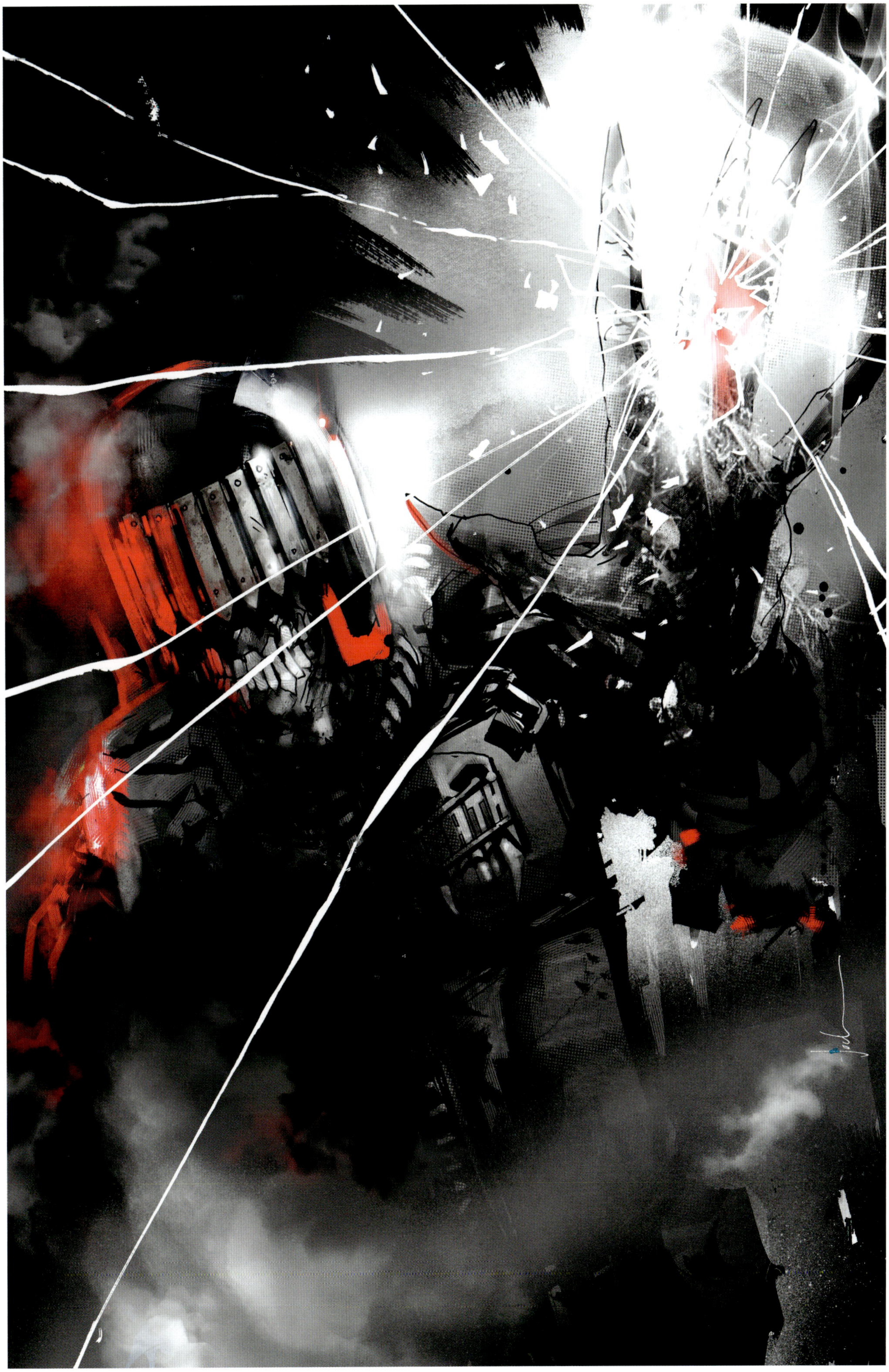

DREDD: FINAL JUDGEMENT ISSUE 1 COVER, 2018

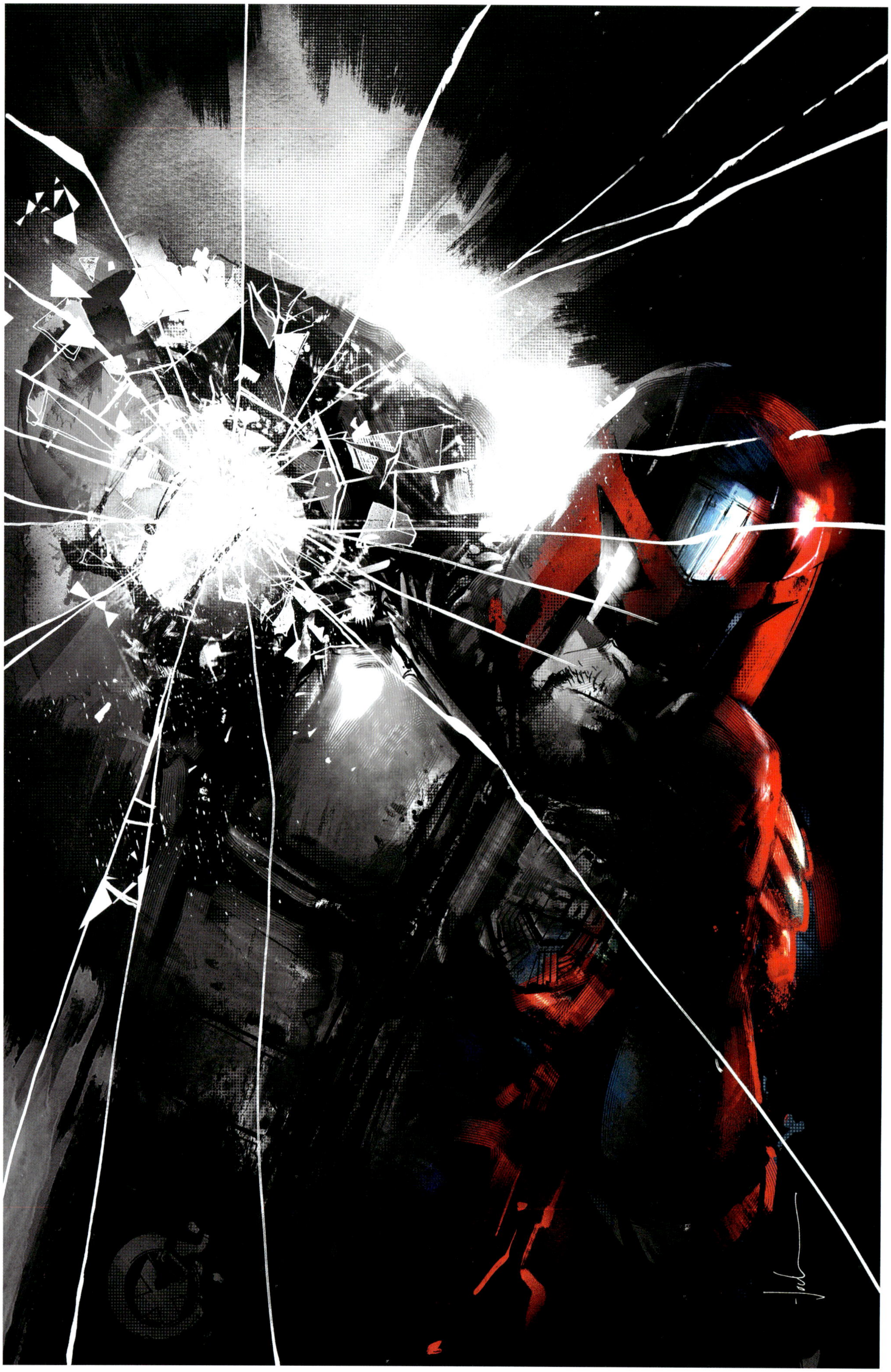

 DREDD: FINAL JUDGEMENT ISSUE 2 COVER, 2018

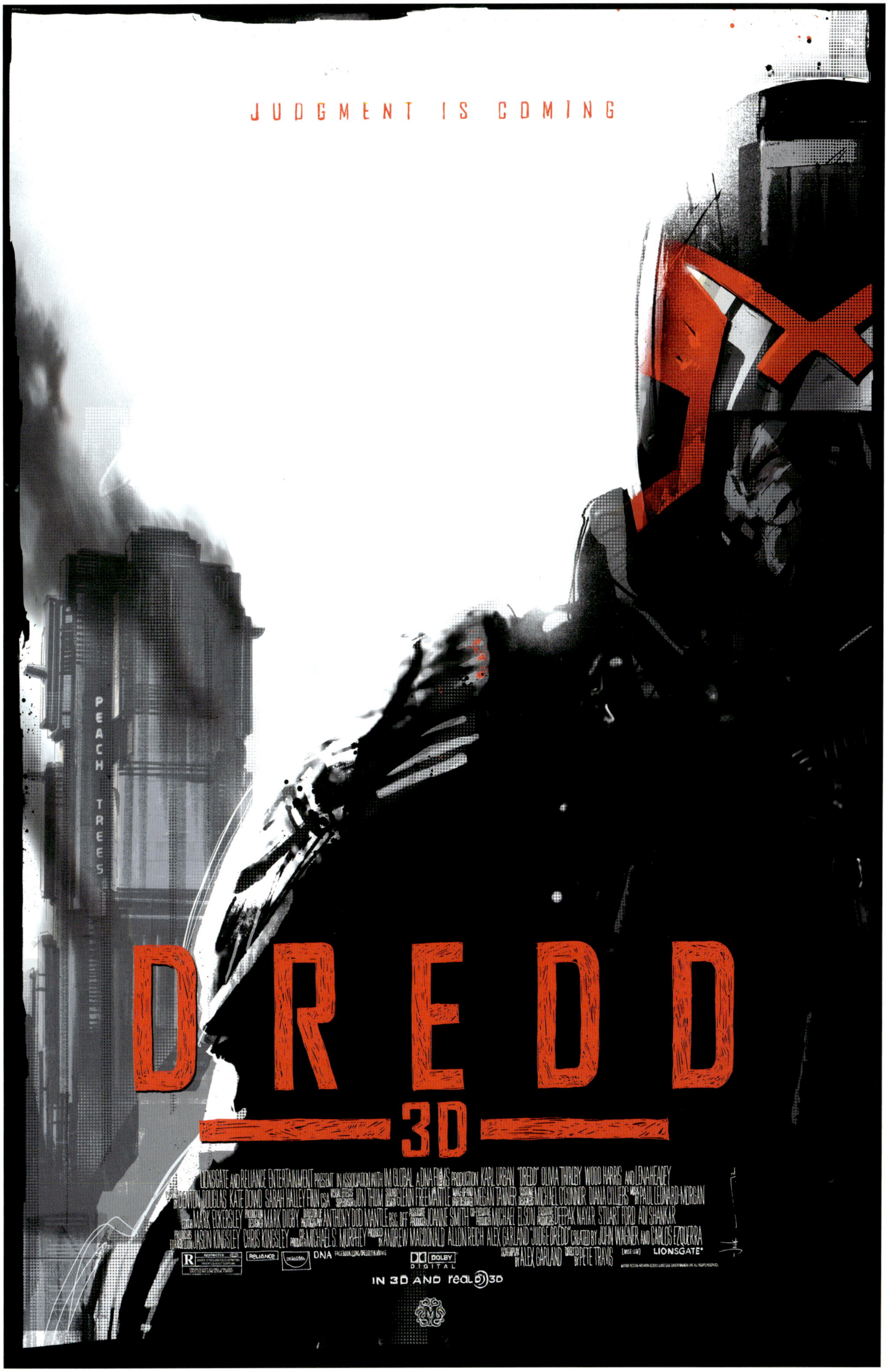

JUDGMENT IS COMING
PEACH TREES
DREDD
3D
LIONSGATE AND RELIANCE ENTERTAINMENT PRESENT IN ASSOCIATION WITH IM GLOBAL A DNA FILMS PRODUCTION KARL URBAN "DREDD" OLIVIA THIRLBY WOOD HARRIS AND LENA HEADEY
DENTON DOUGLAS KATE DOWD SARAH HALLEY FINN CSA JON THUM GLENN FREEMANTLE MEGAN TANNER MICHAEL O'CONNOR DIANA CILLIERS PAUL LEONARD-MORGAN
MARK ECKERSLEY MARK DIGBY ANTHONY DOD MANTLE BSC, DFF JOANNE SMITH MICHAEL ELSON DEEPAK NAYAR STUART FORD ADI SHANKAR
JASON KINGSLEY CHRIS KINGSLEY MICHAEL S. MURPHEY ANDREW MACDONALD ALLON REICH ALEX GARLAND "JUDGE DREDD" CREATED BY JOHN WAGNER AND CARLOS EZQUERRA
SCREENPLAY BY ALEX GARLAND DIRECTED BY PETE TRAVIS
LIONSGATE
FACEBOOK.COM/DREDDTHEMOVIE
IN 3D AND REALD 3D

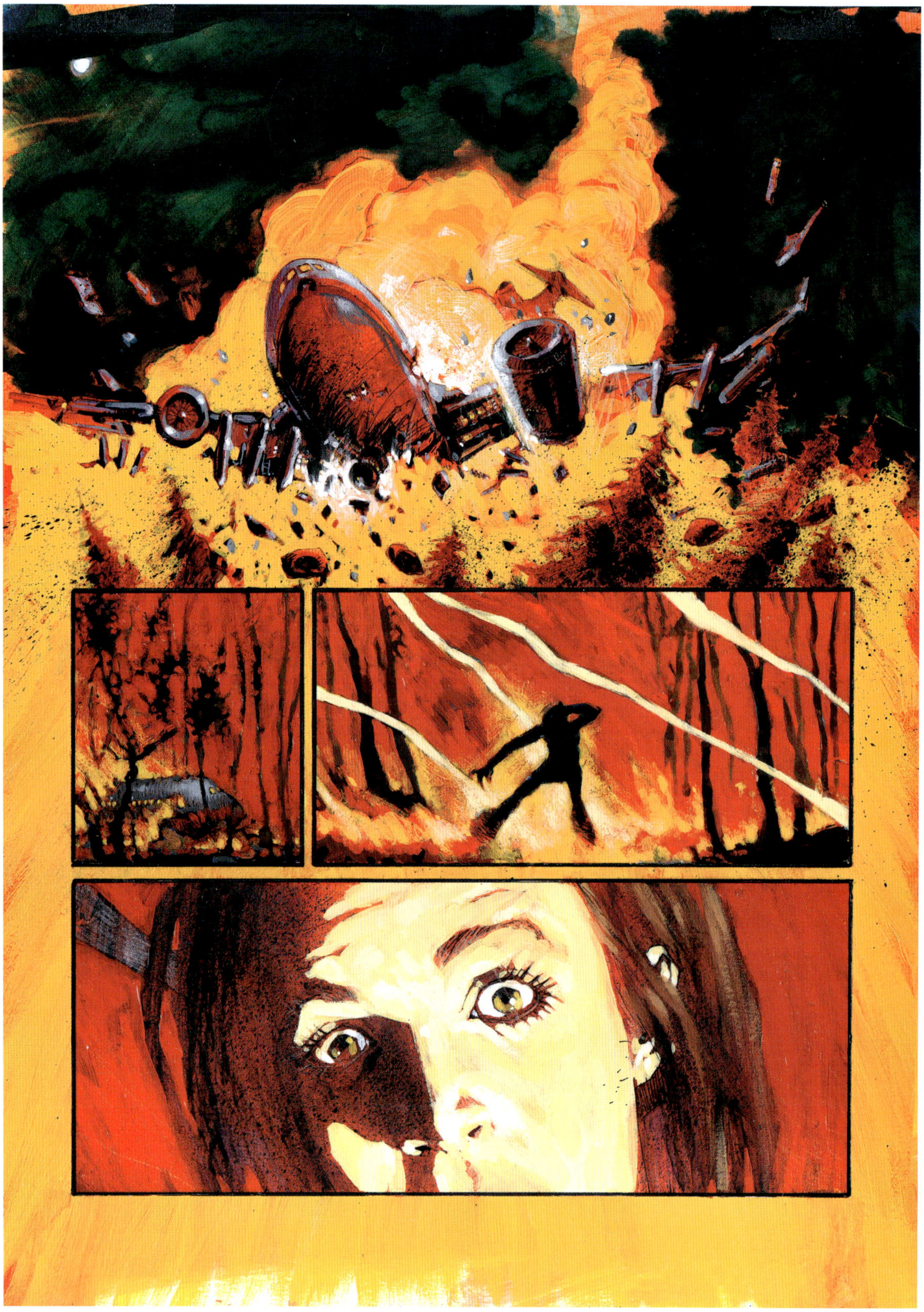

 PULP SCI-FI: REAPERMEN PAGE 1, 2000 AD PROG 1170, 1999

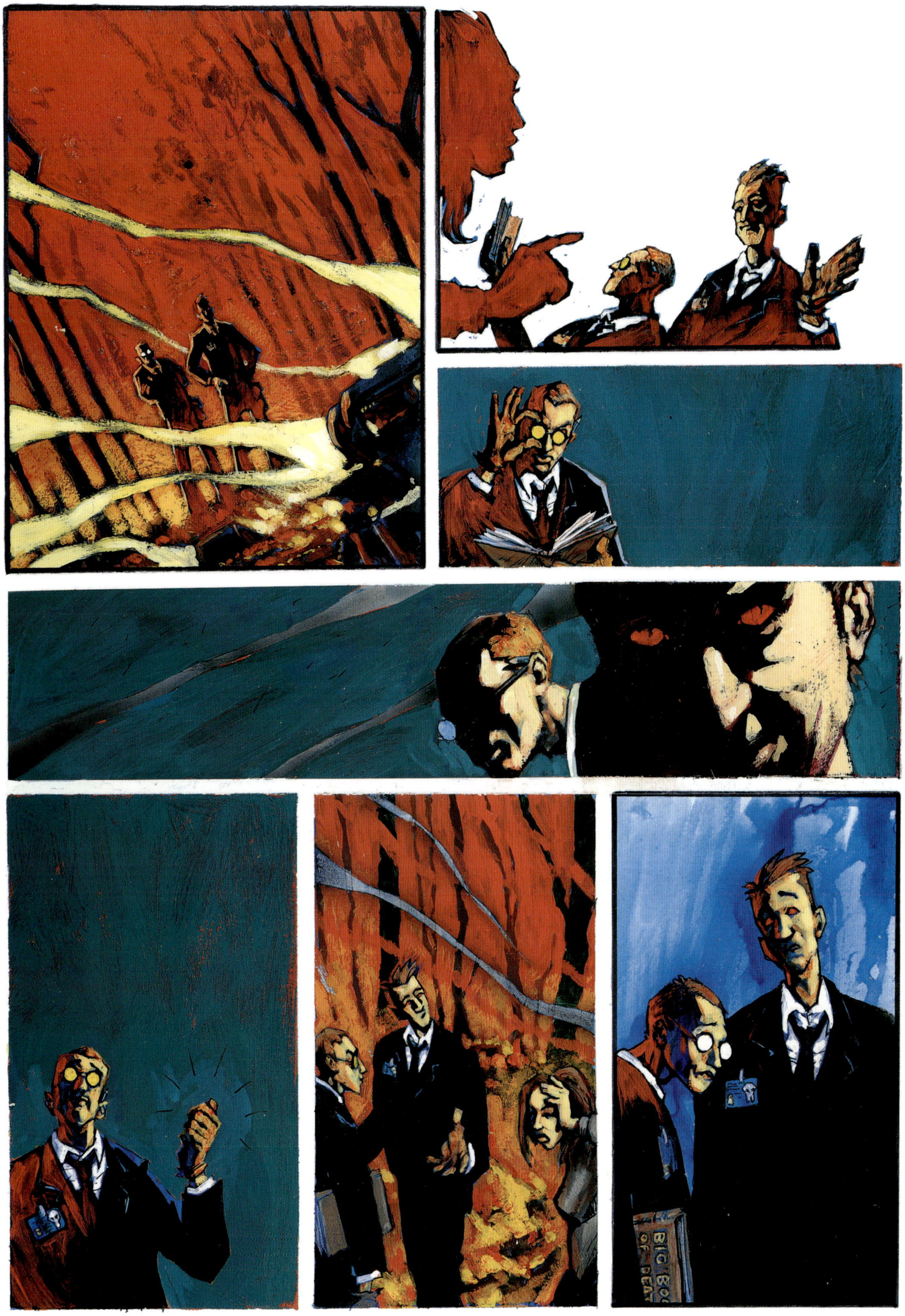

PULP SCI-FI: REAPERMEN PAGE 2, 2000 AD PROG 1170, 1999

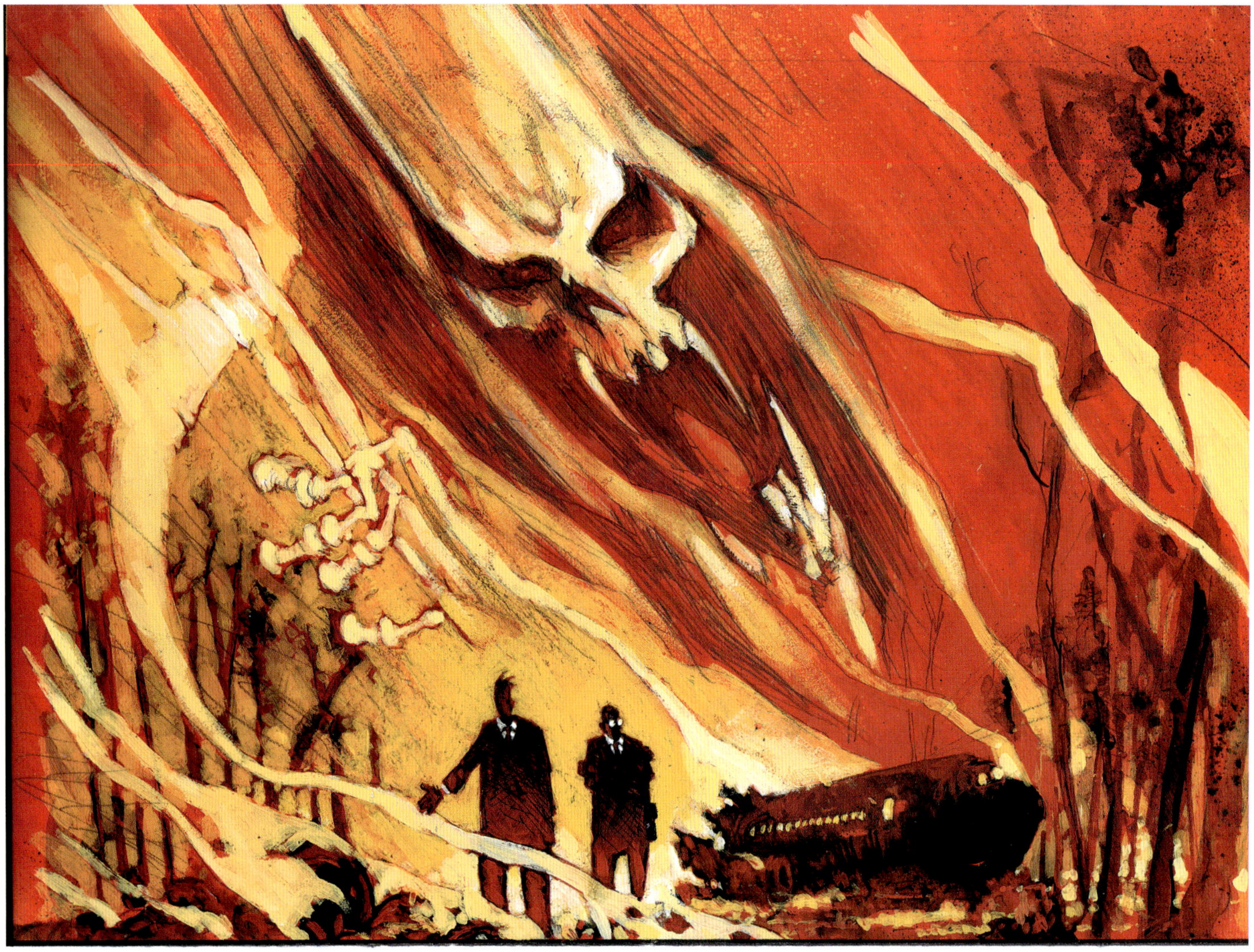

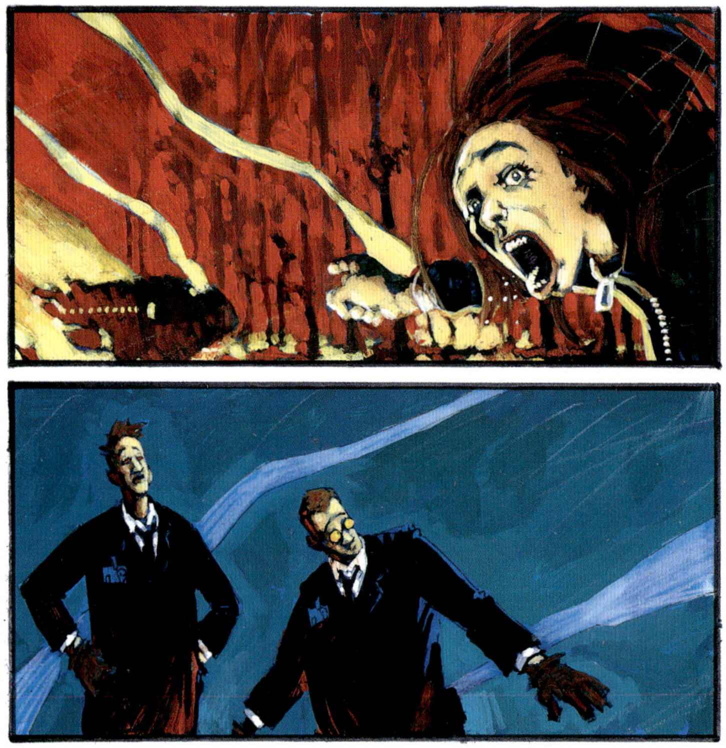

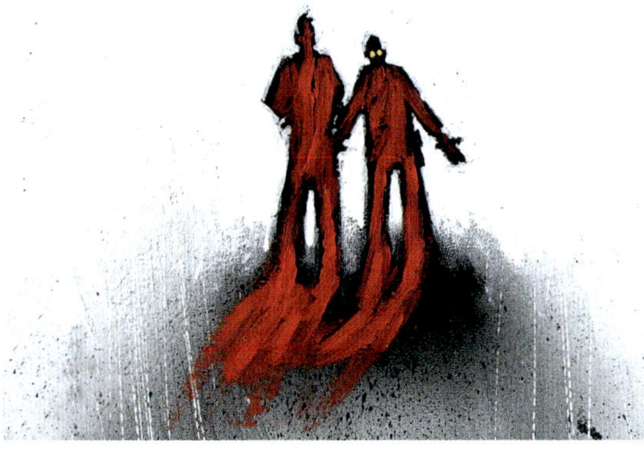

PULP SCI-FI: REAPERMEN PAGE 3, 2000 AD PROG 1170, 1999

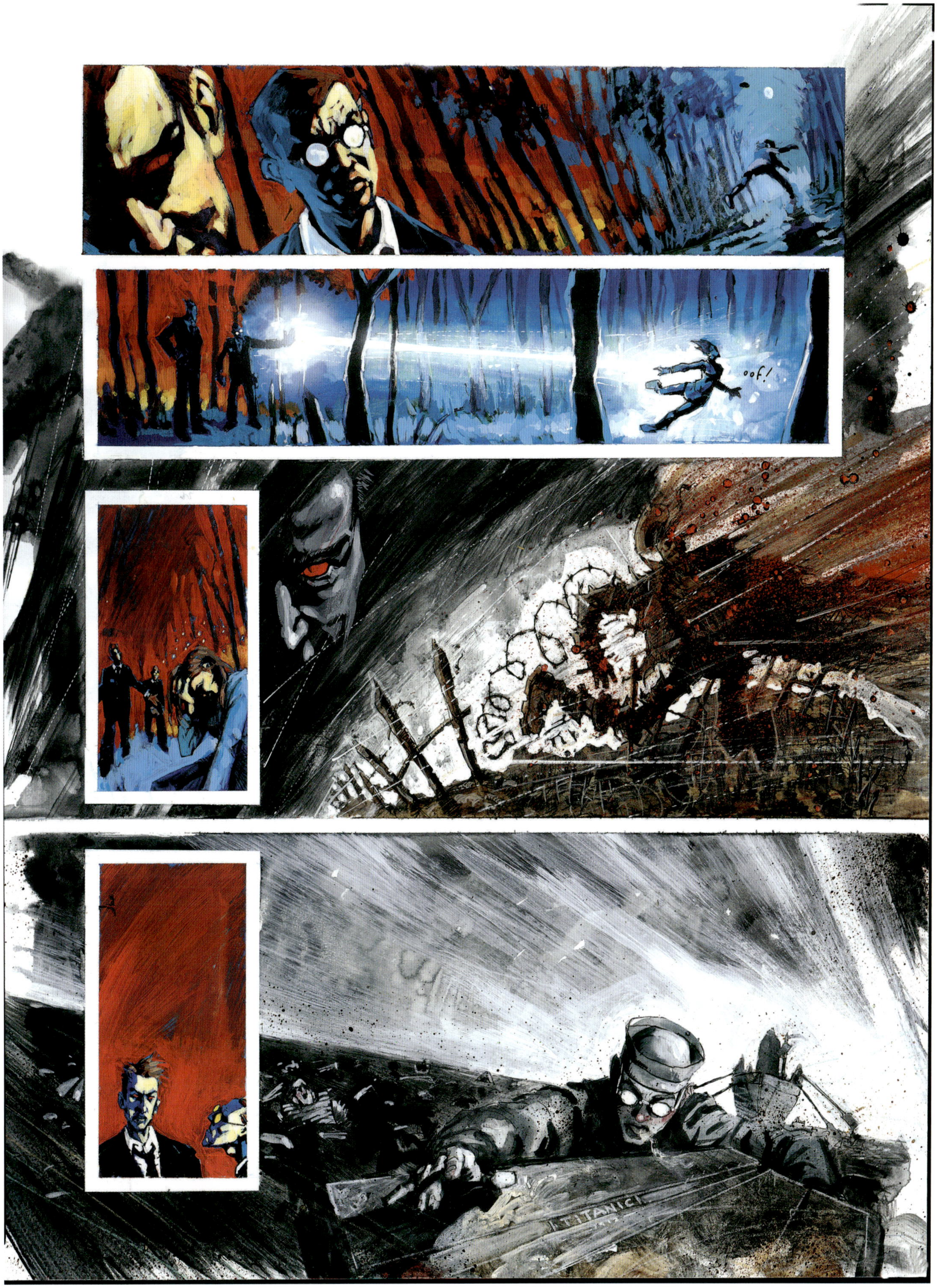
oof!
TITANIC

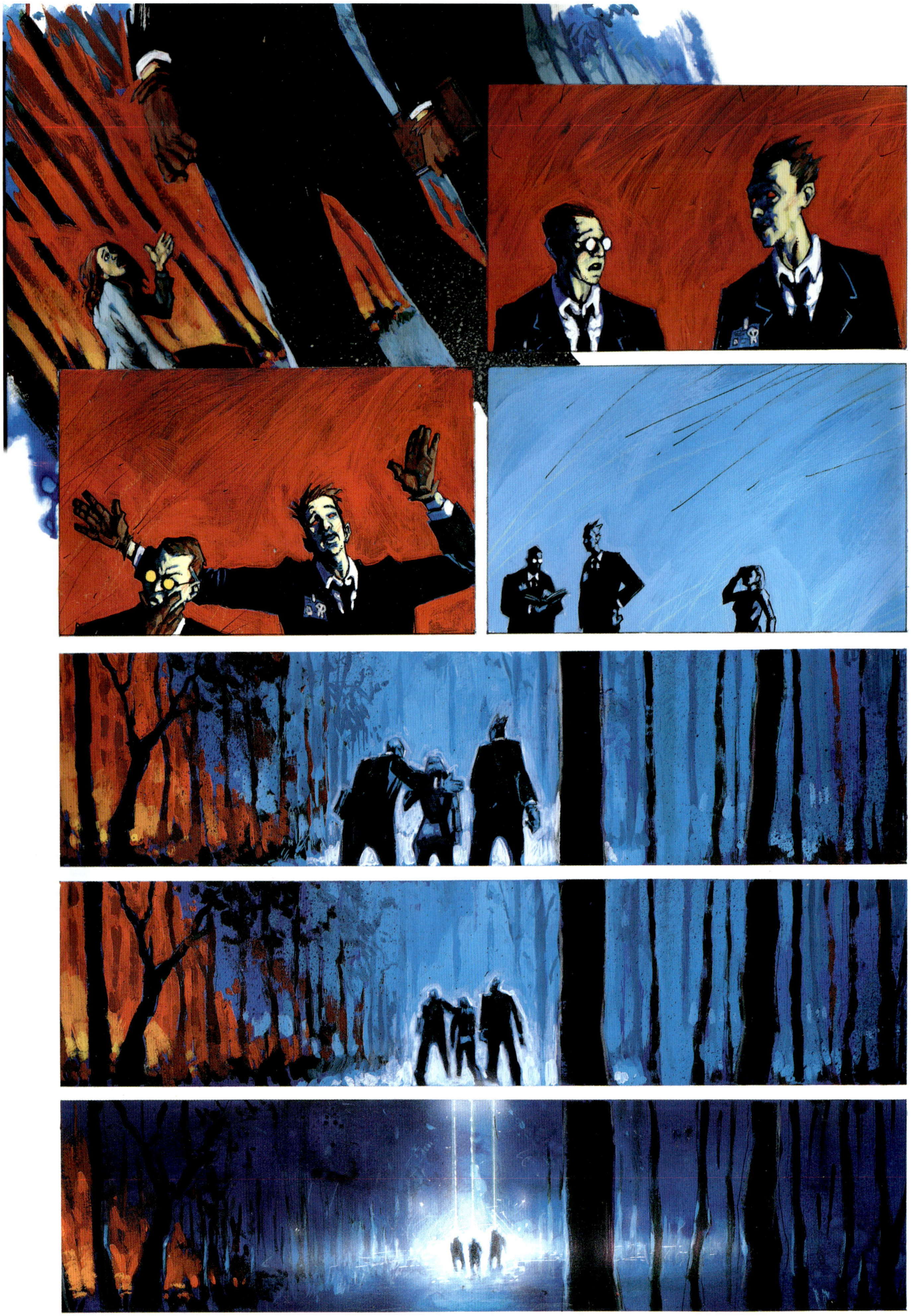

 PULP SCI-FI: REAPERMEN PAGE 5, 2000 AD PROG 1170, 1999

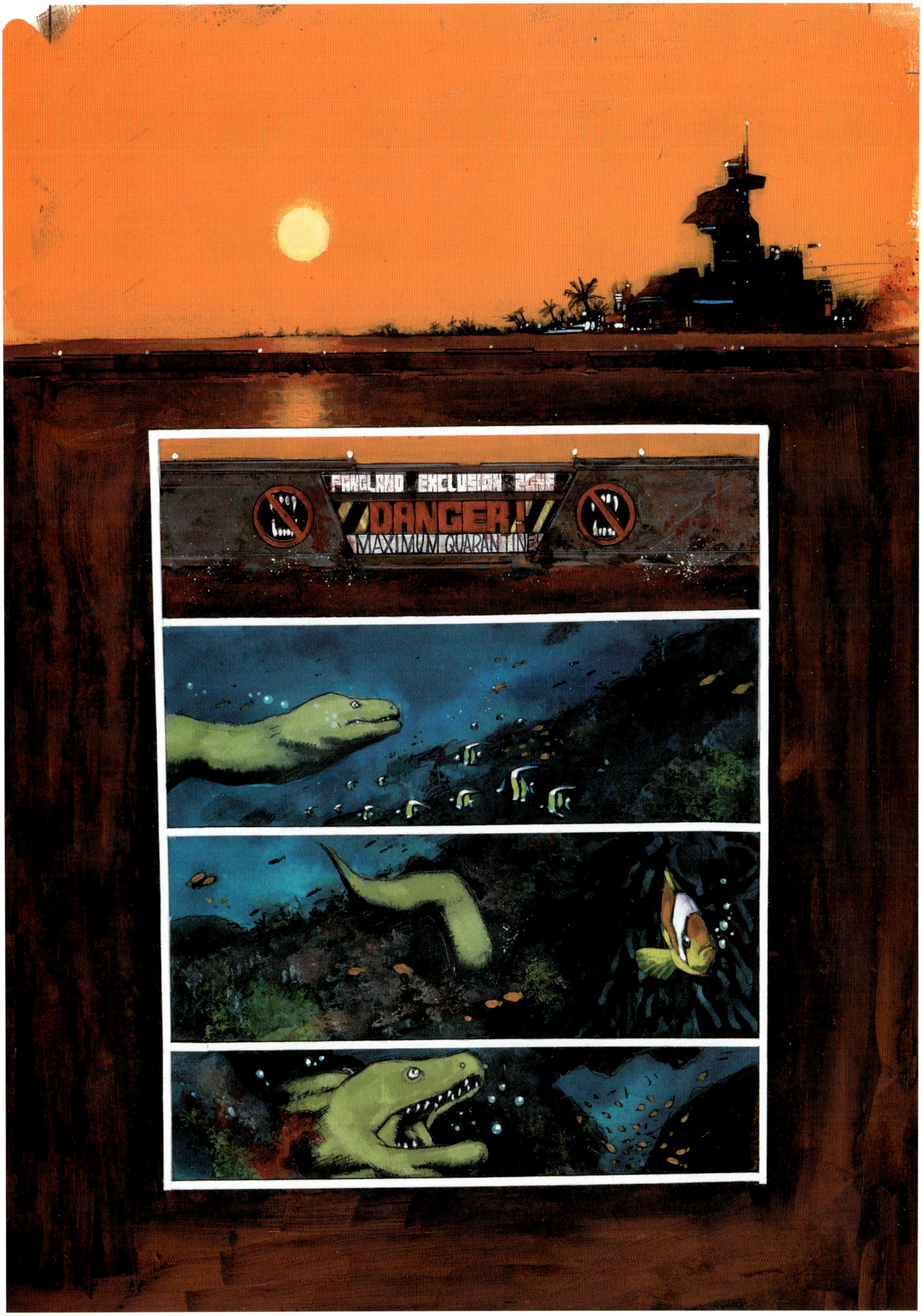
FANGLAND EXCLUSION ZONE
DANGER!
MAXIMUM QUARANTINE

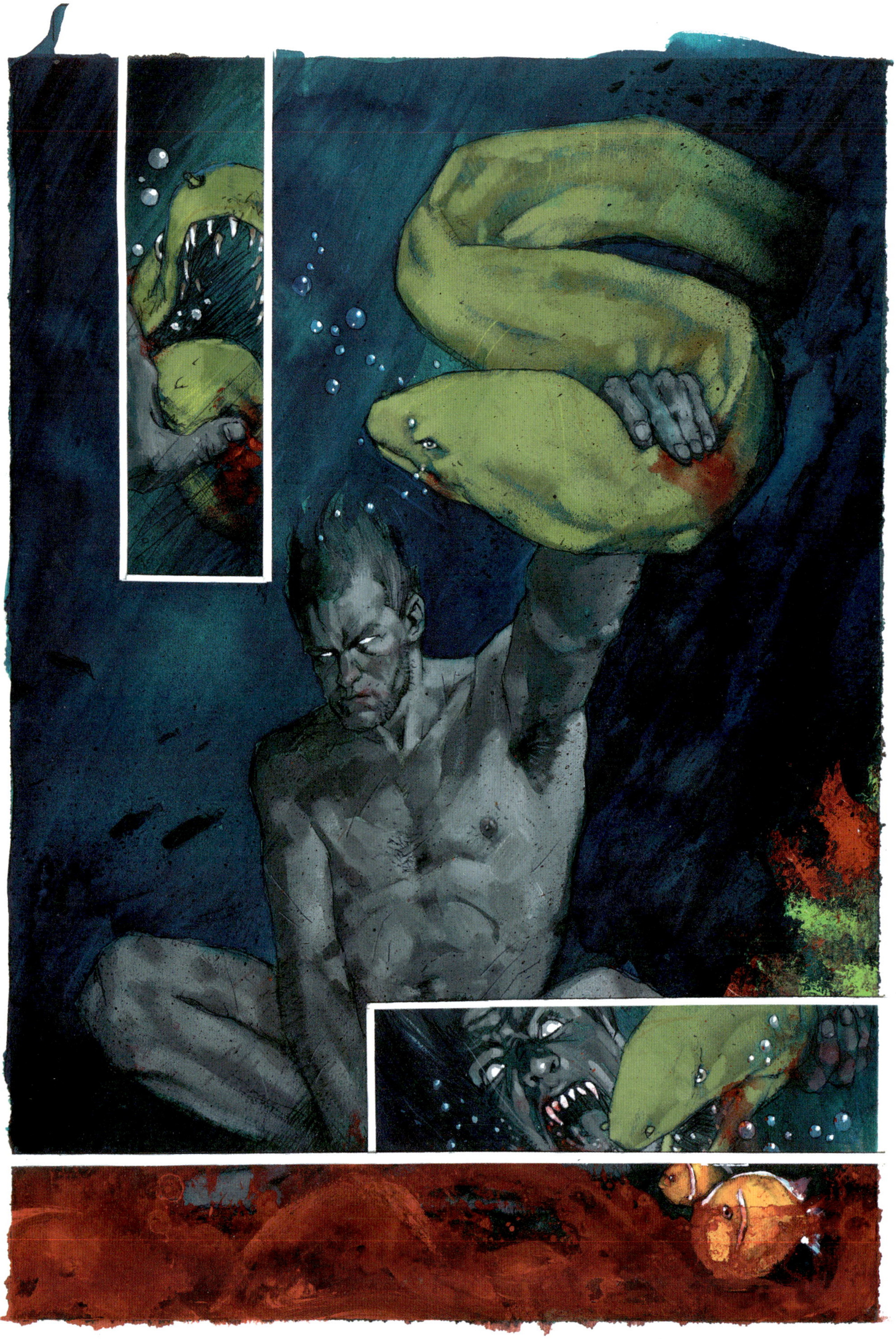

 DEVLIN WAUGH: RED TIDE PROLOGUE – UNUSED ARTWORK, 2002

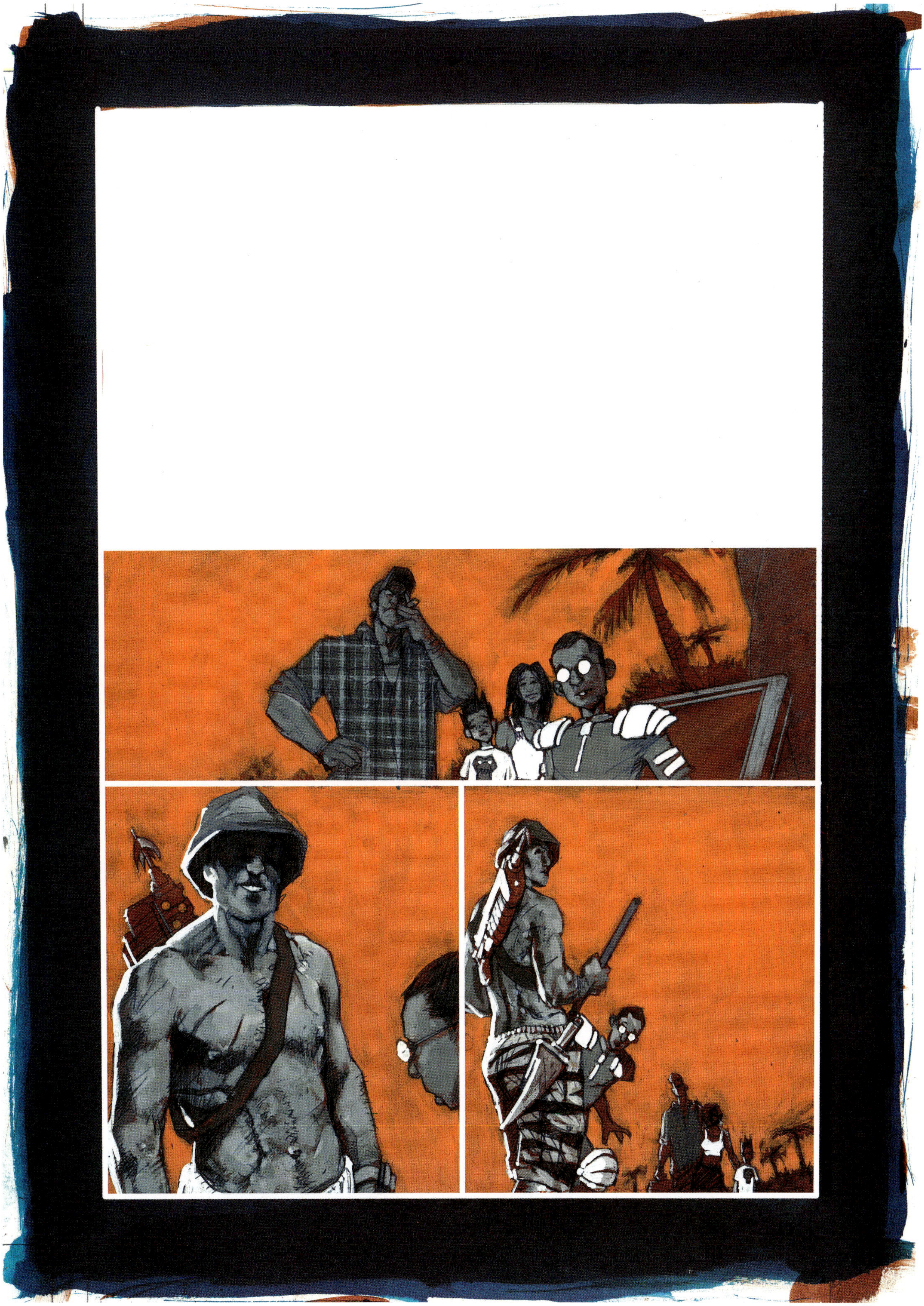

DEVLIN WAUGH: RED TIDE PROLOGUE – UNUSED ARTWORK, 2002

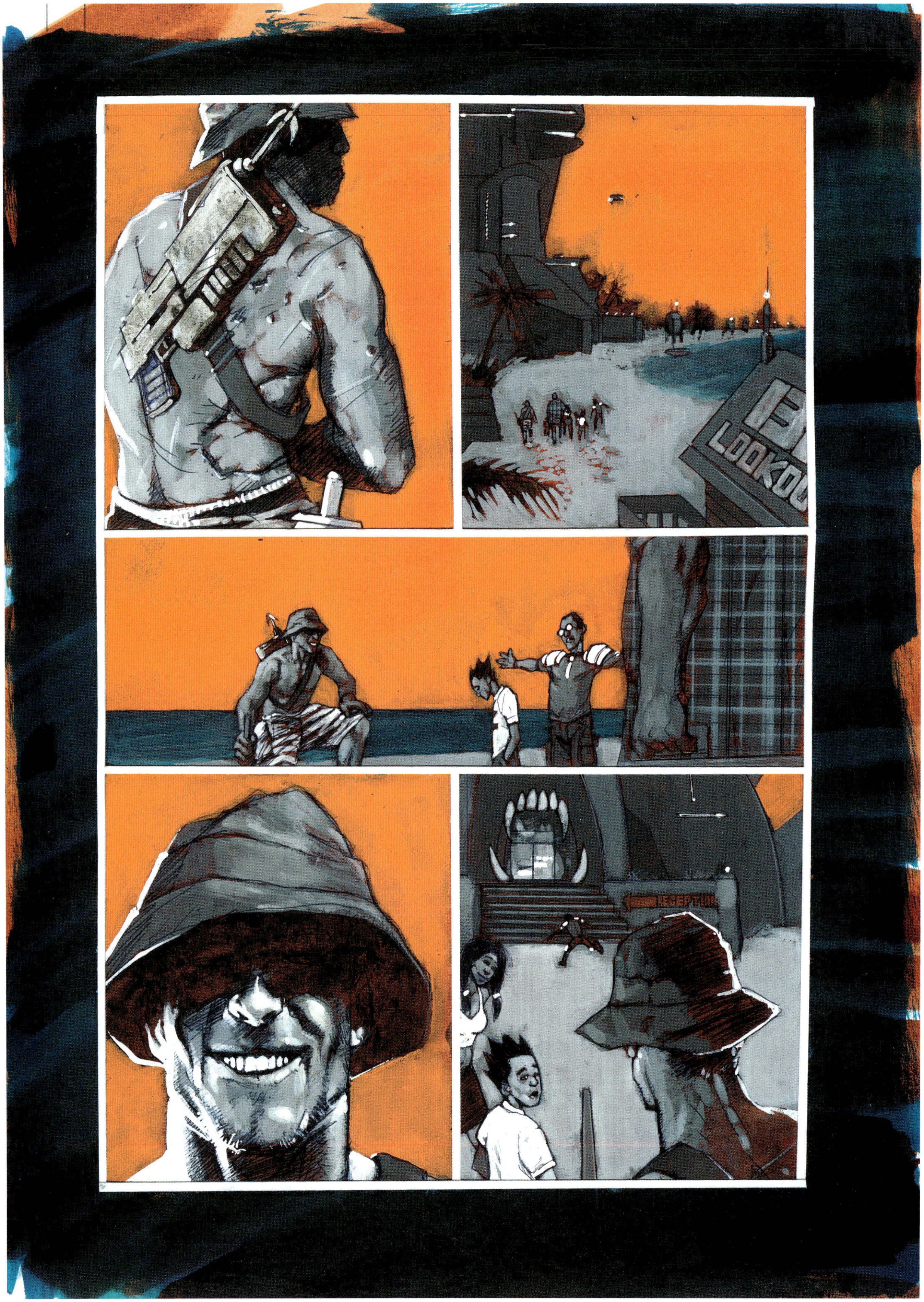
LOOKOU

 DEVLIN WAUGH: RED TIDE PROLOGUE – UNUSED ARTWORK, 2002

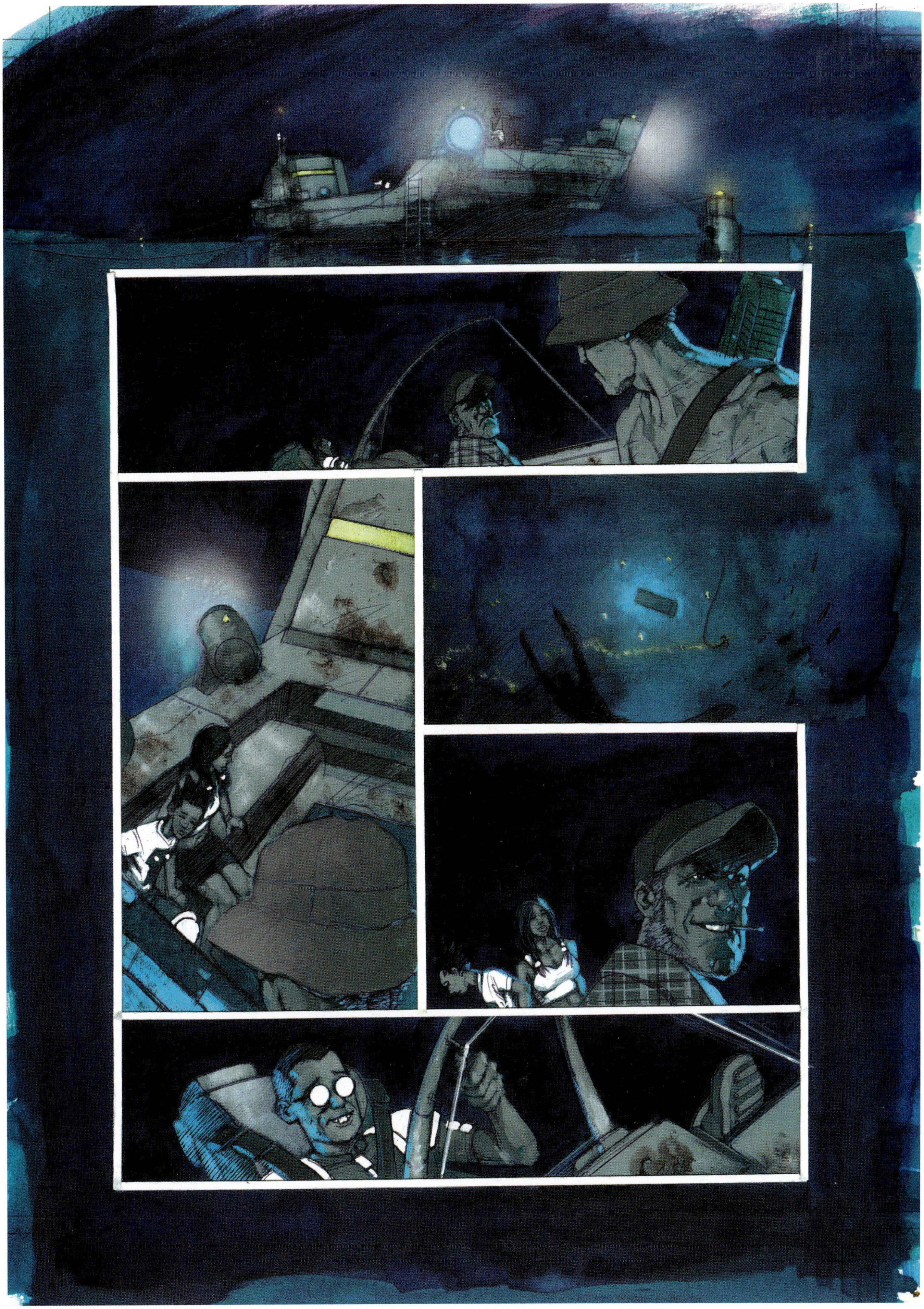

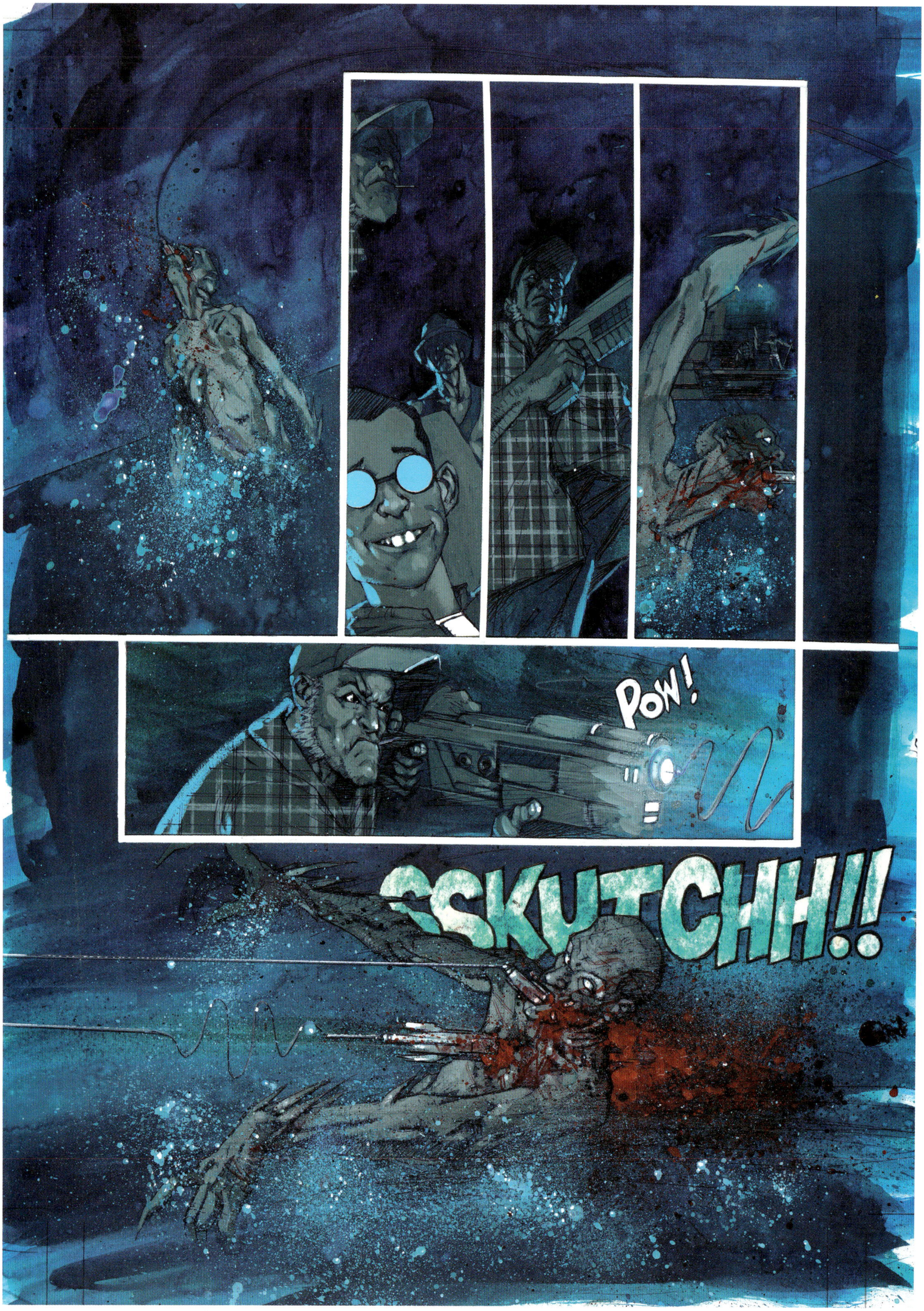
POW!
SKUTCHH!!

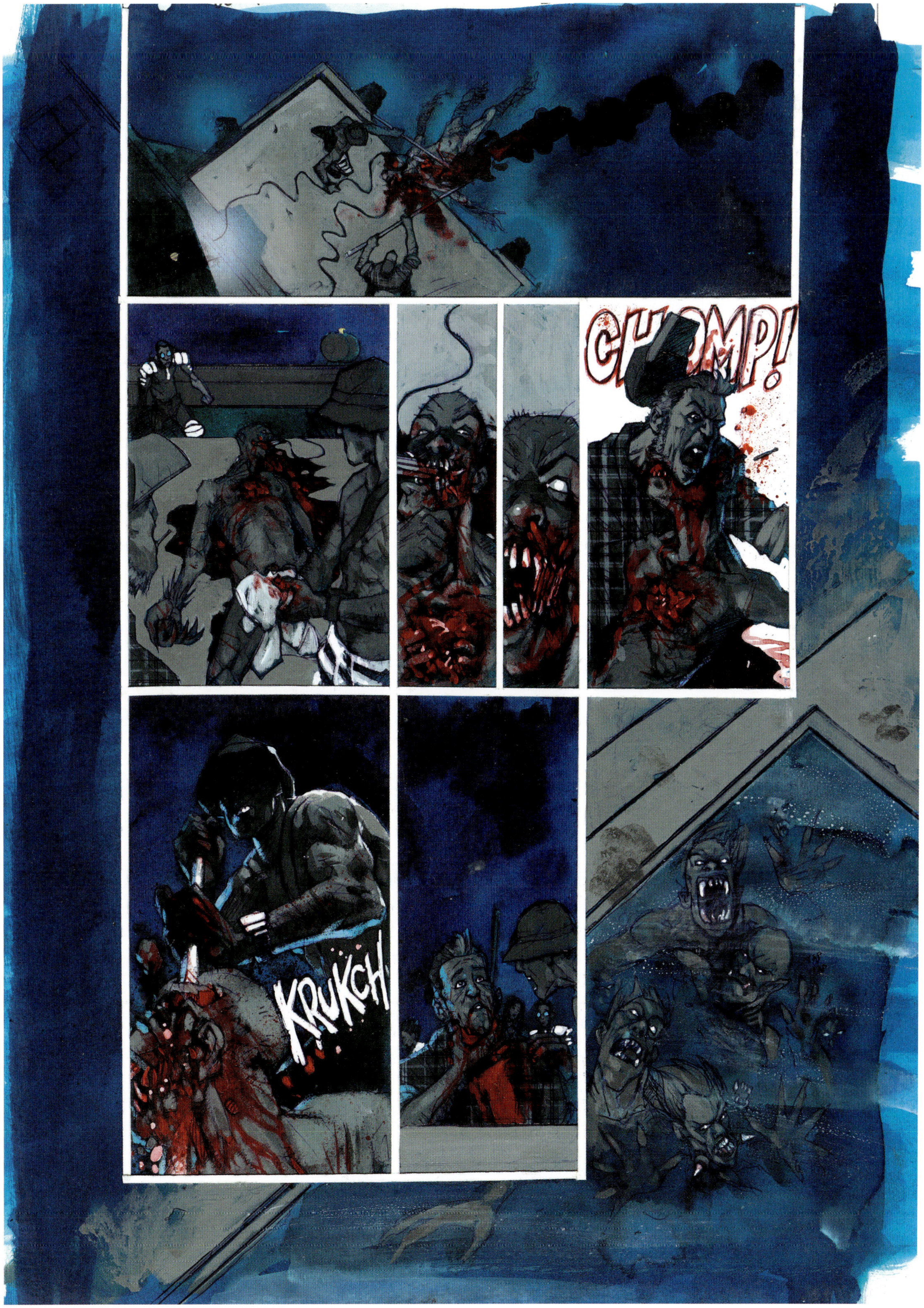
CHOMP!
KRUKCH

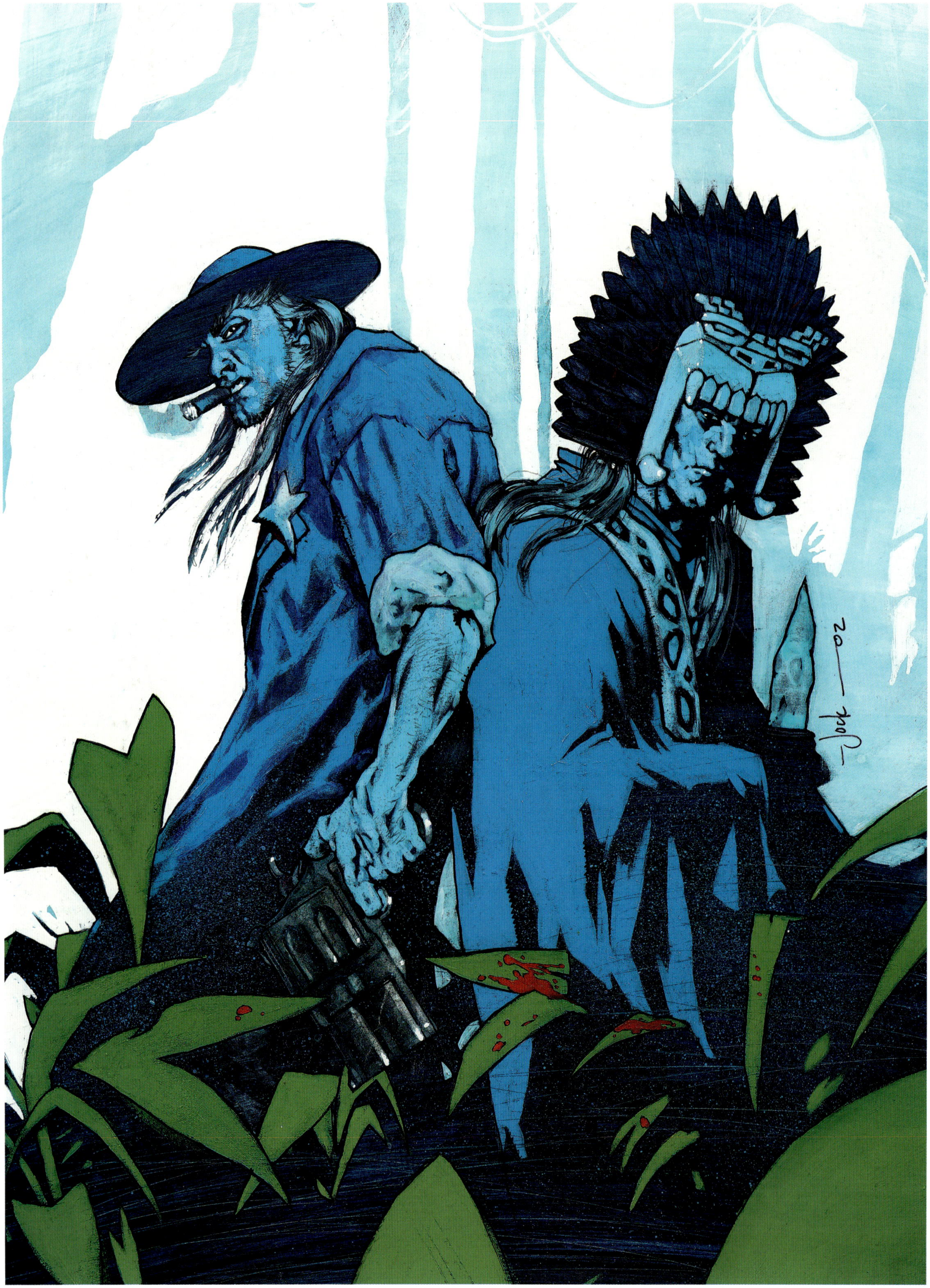
Jock 02

 JUDGE DREDD MEGAZINE 4.11 COVER, MISSIONARY MAN, 2002

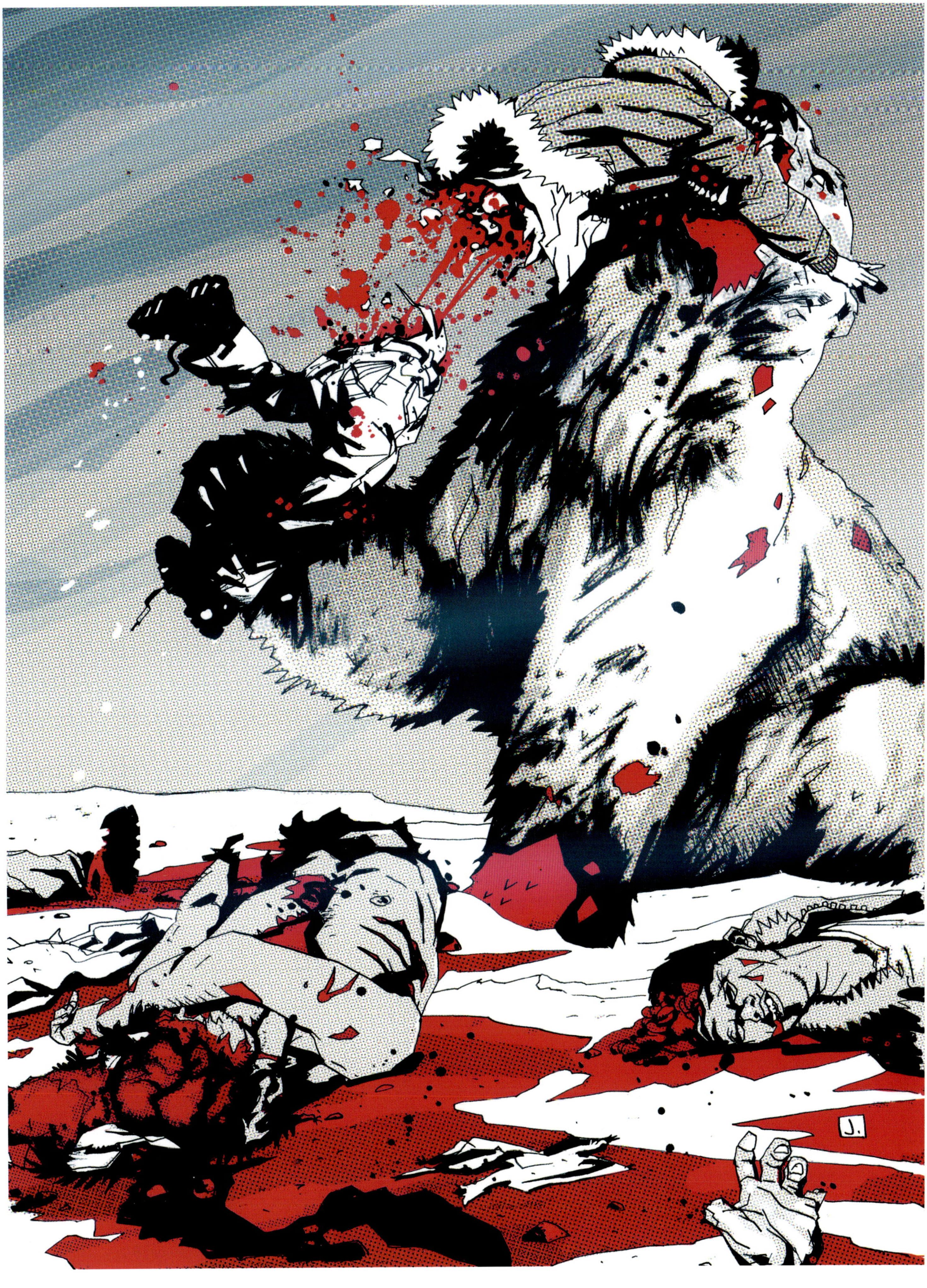

2000 AD X-MAS PROG 2004 STAR SCAN, SHAKO

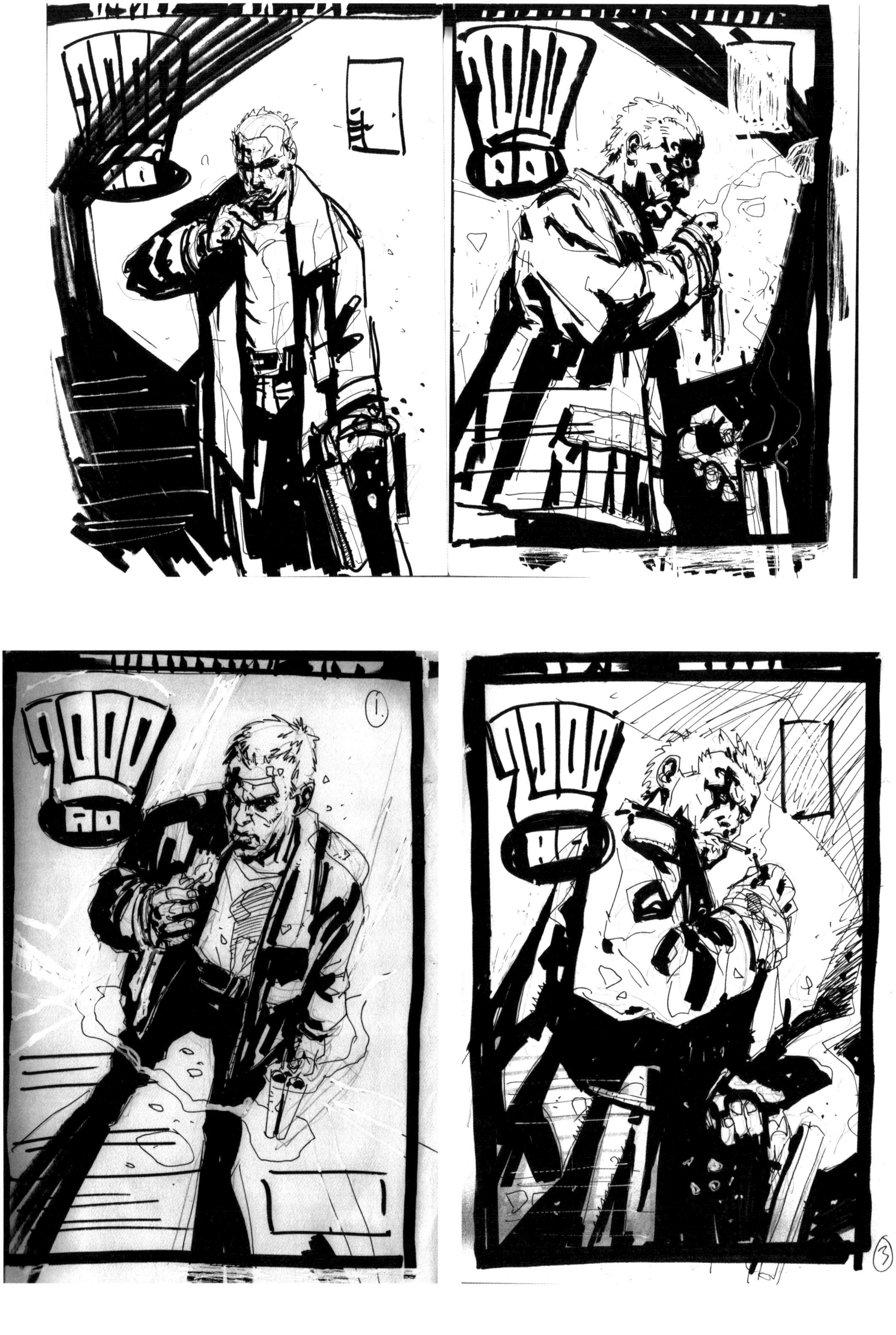

 2000 AD PROG 1236 COVER ROUGHS, CARVER HALE, 2001
OPPOSITE: FINAL CARVER HALE COVER ART

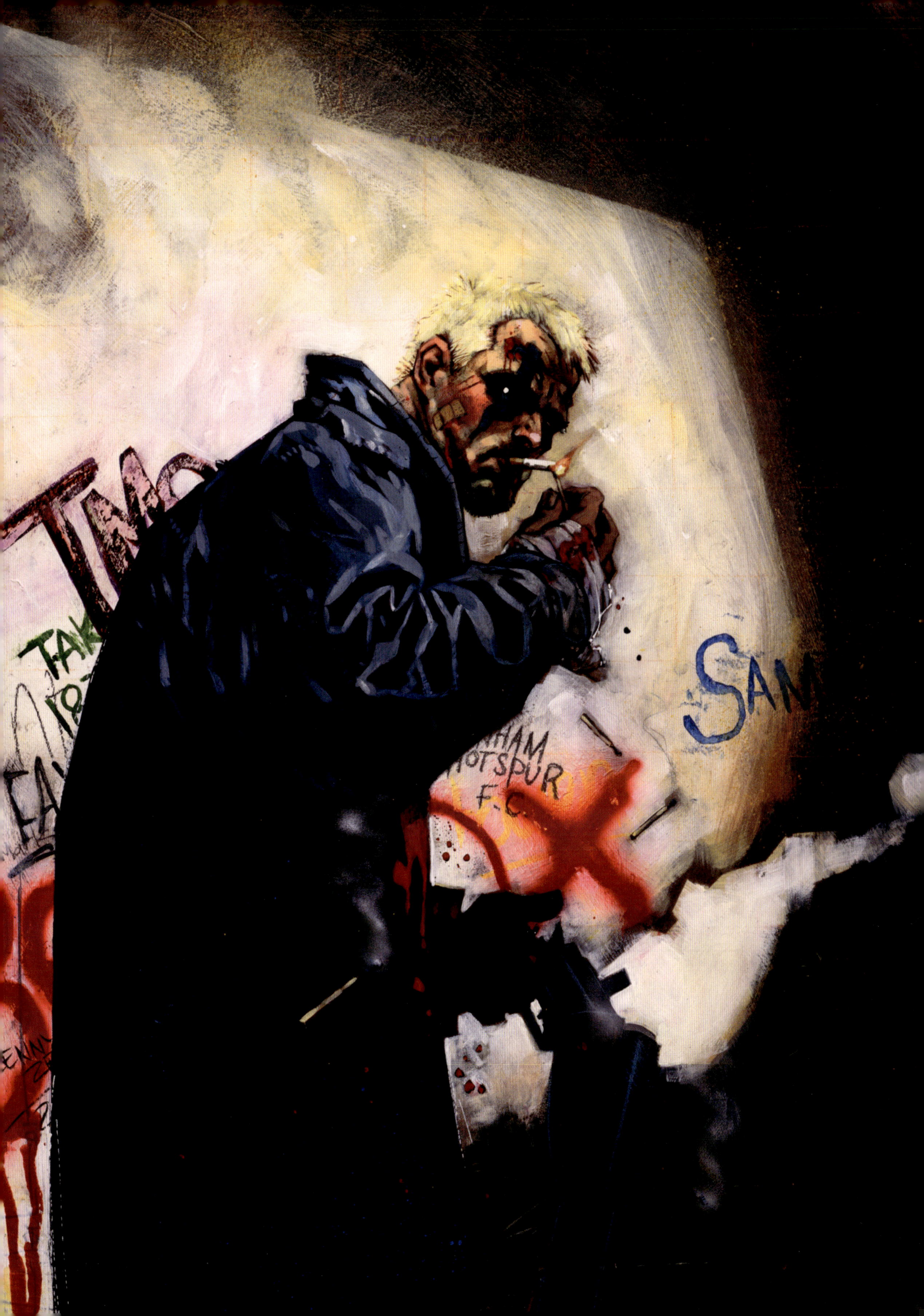
SAM
HAM
HOTSPUR
F.C

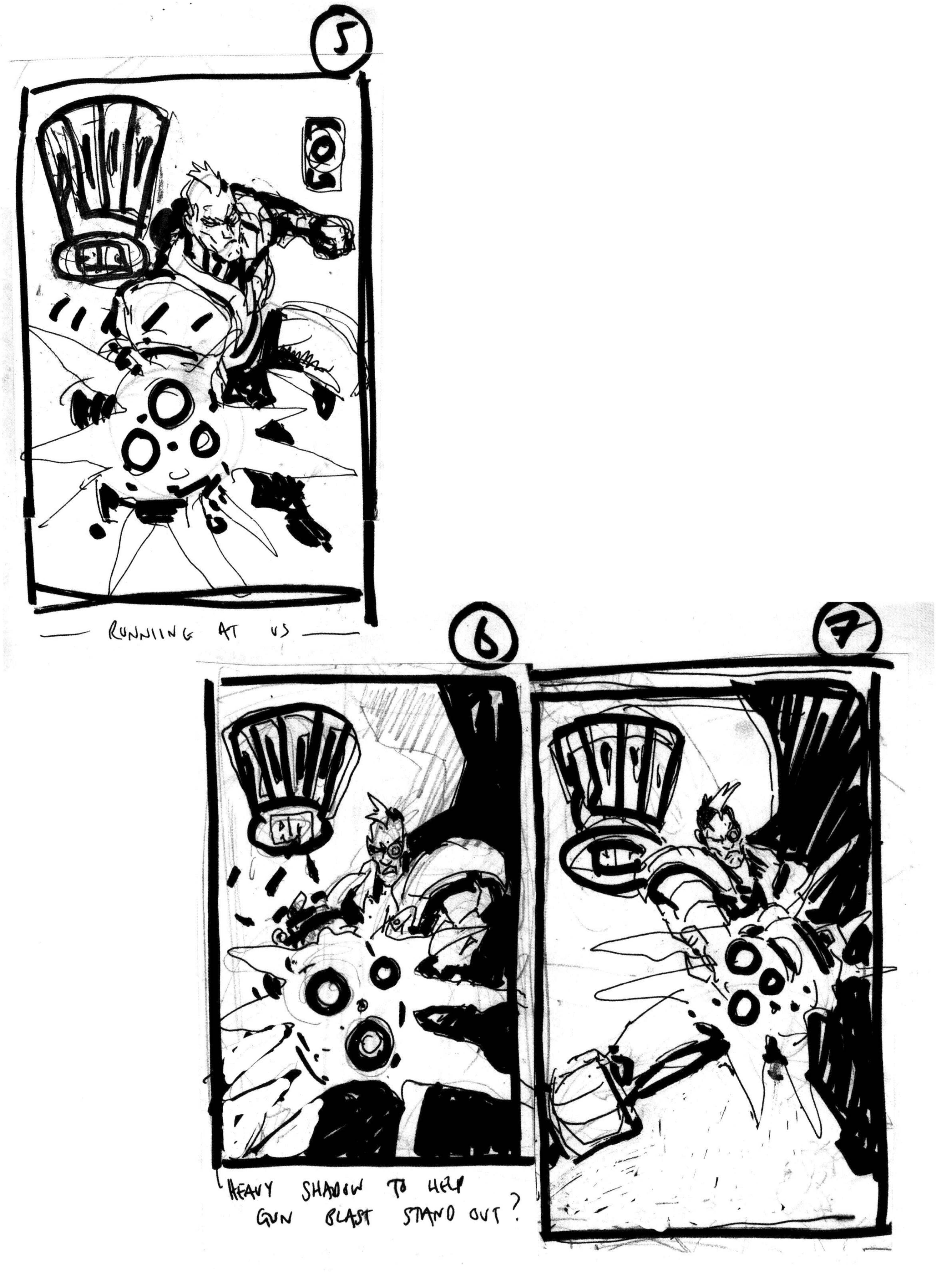
5
RUNNIING AT US
6
7
HEAVY SHADOW TO HELP GUN BLAST STAND OUT?

2000 AD PROG 1254 COVER ROUGHS, TOR CYAN, 2001
OPPOSITE: FINAL TOR CYAN COVER ART

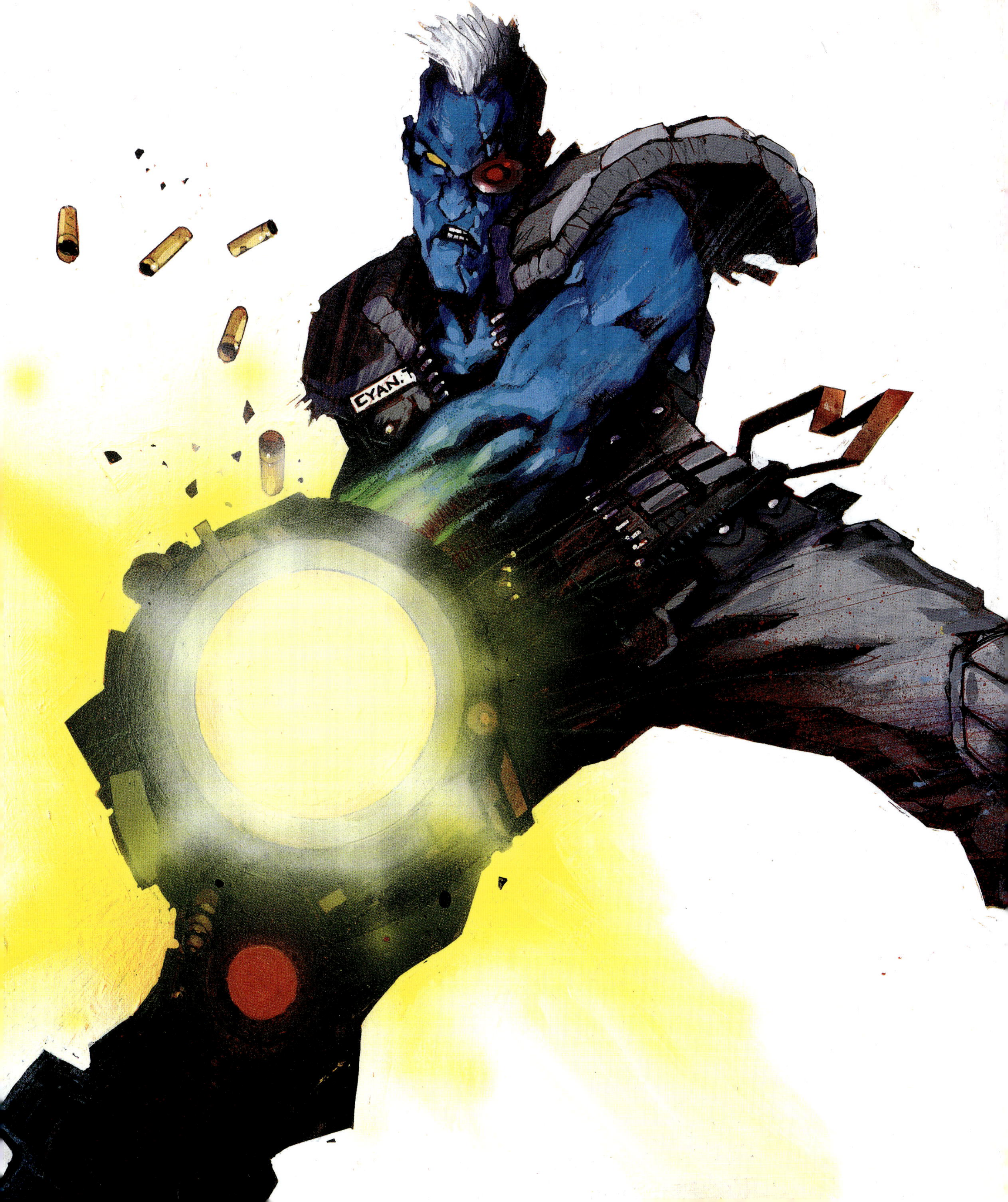
CYAN.

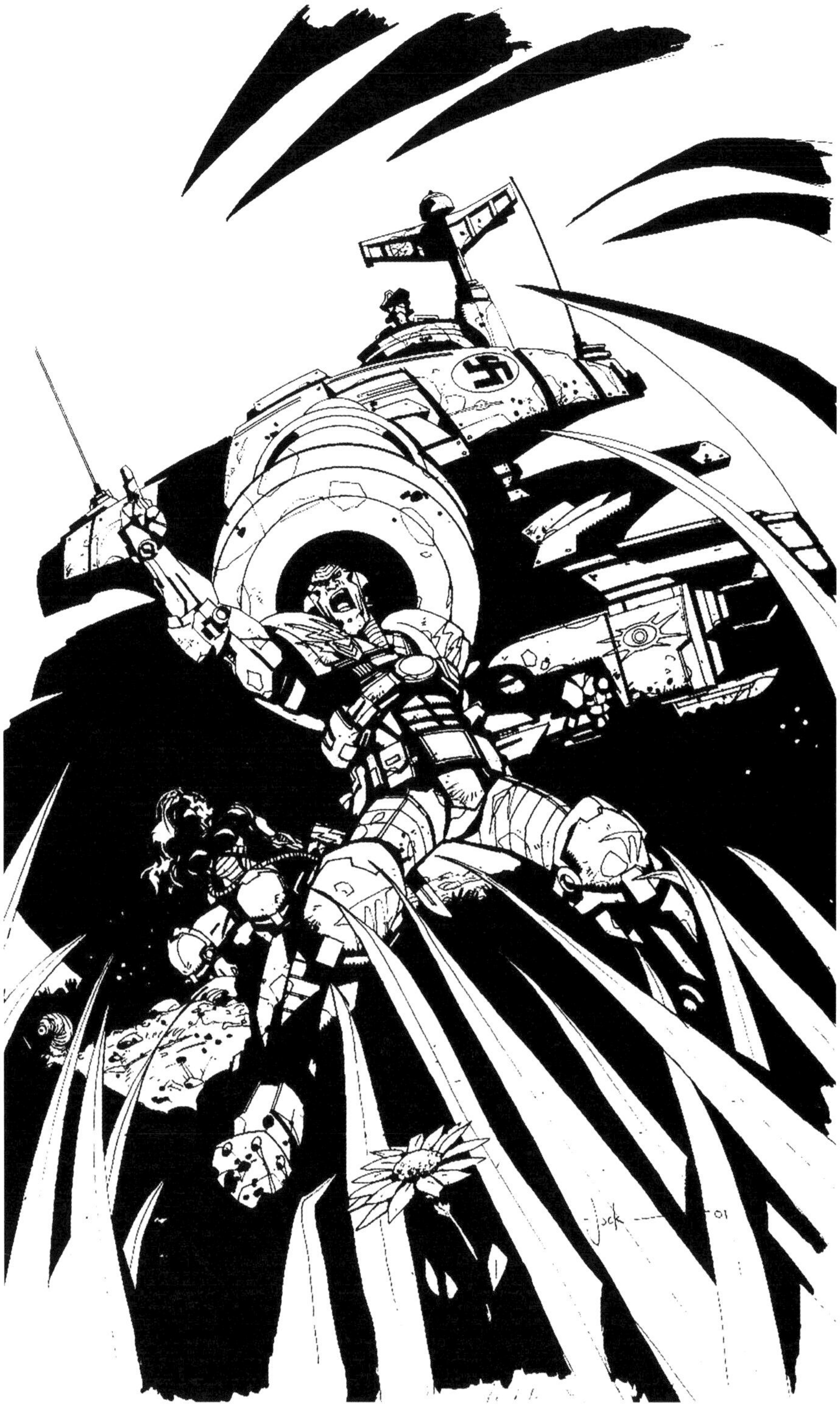

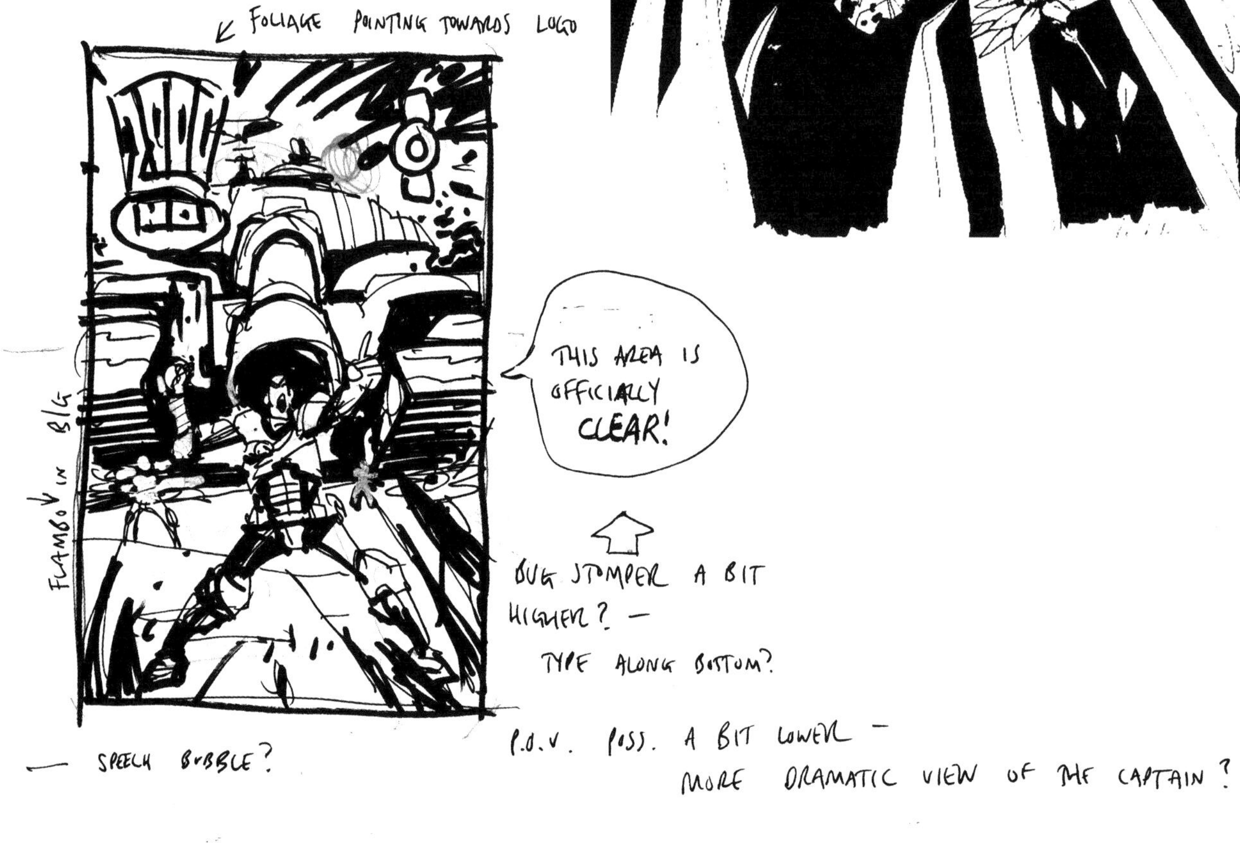
FOLIAGE POINTING TOWARDS LOGO
FLAMBO IN BIG
THIS AREA IS OFFICIALLY CLEAR!
BUG STOMPER A BIT HIGHER? -
TYPE ALONG BOTTOM?
- SPEECH BUBBLE?
P.O.V. POSS. A BIT LOWER -
MORE DRAMATIC VIEW OF THE CAPTAIN?

2000 AD PROG 1260 COVER SKETCH AND LINE ART, BANZAI BATTALION, 2001
OPPOSITE: FINAL BANZAI BATTALION COVER ART WITH COLOURS BY CHRIS BLYTHE

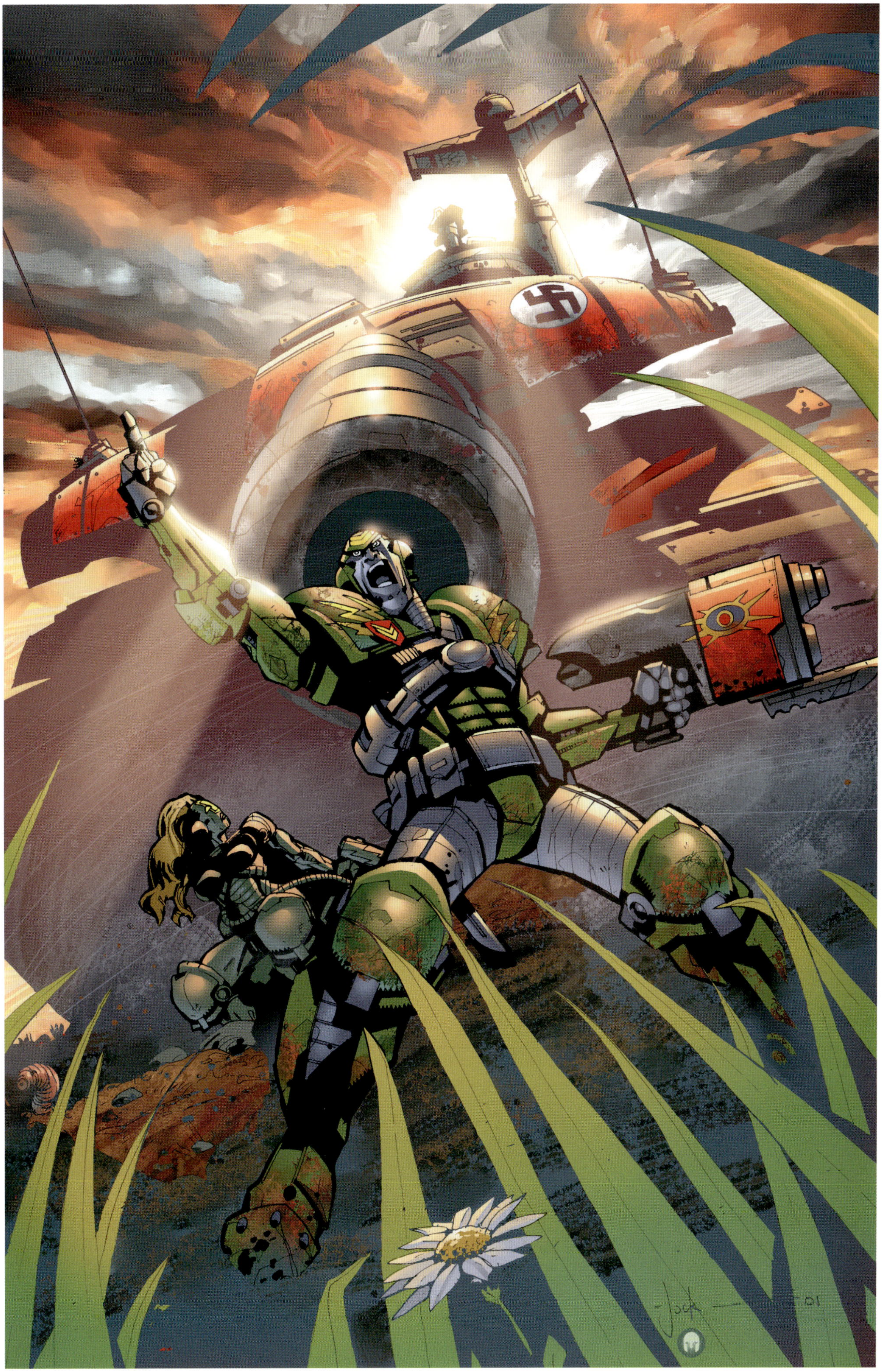

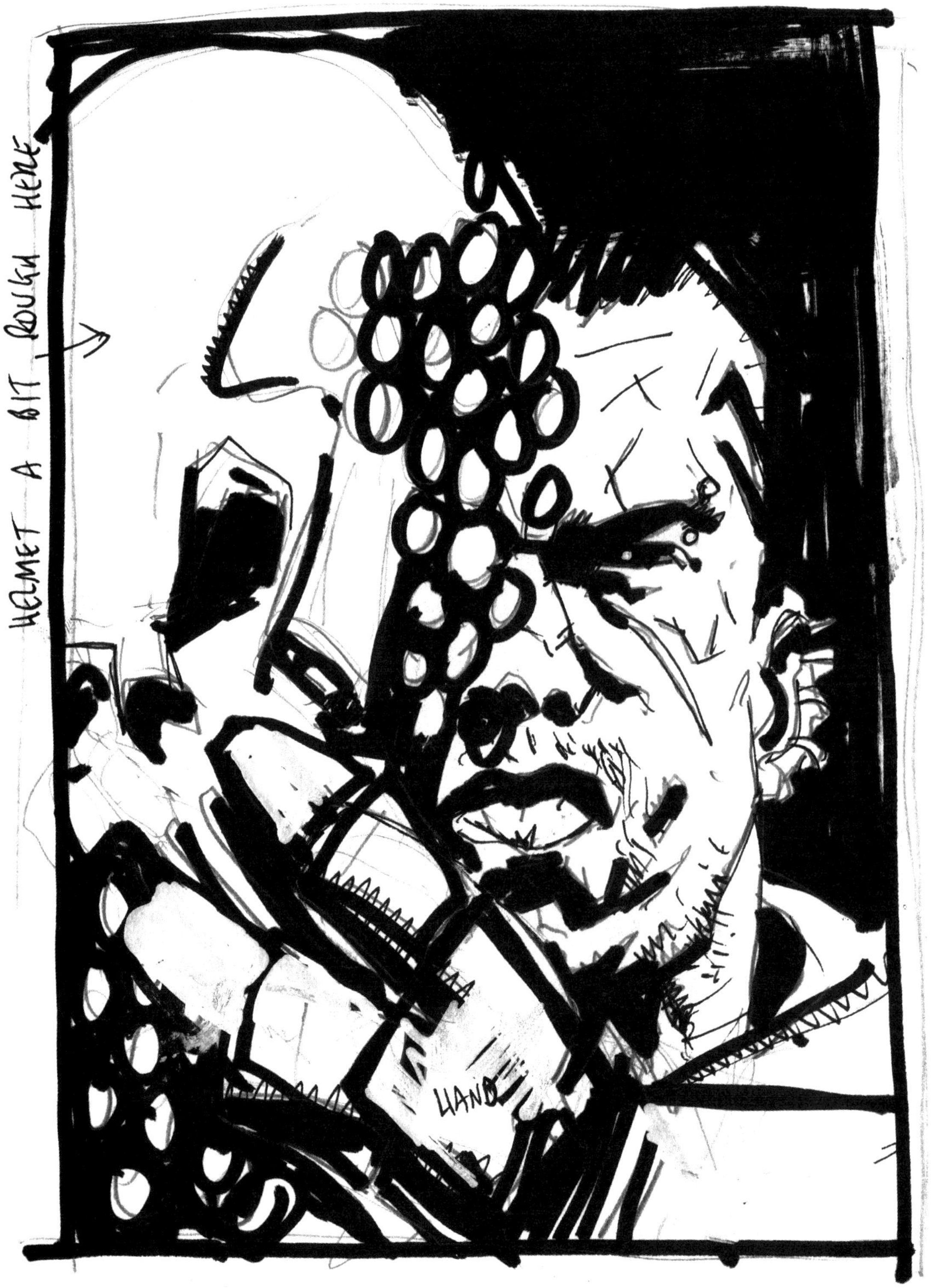
HELMET A BIT ROUGH HERE
HAND

2000 AD PROG 1266 COVER ROUGH, KILLER, 2001
OPPOSITE: FINAL KILLER COVER ART

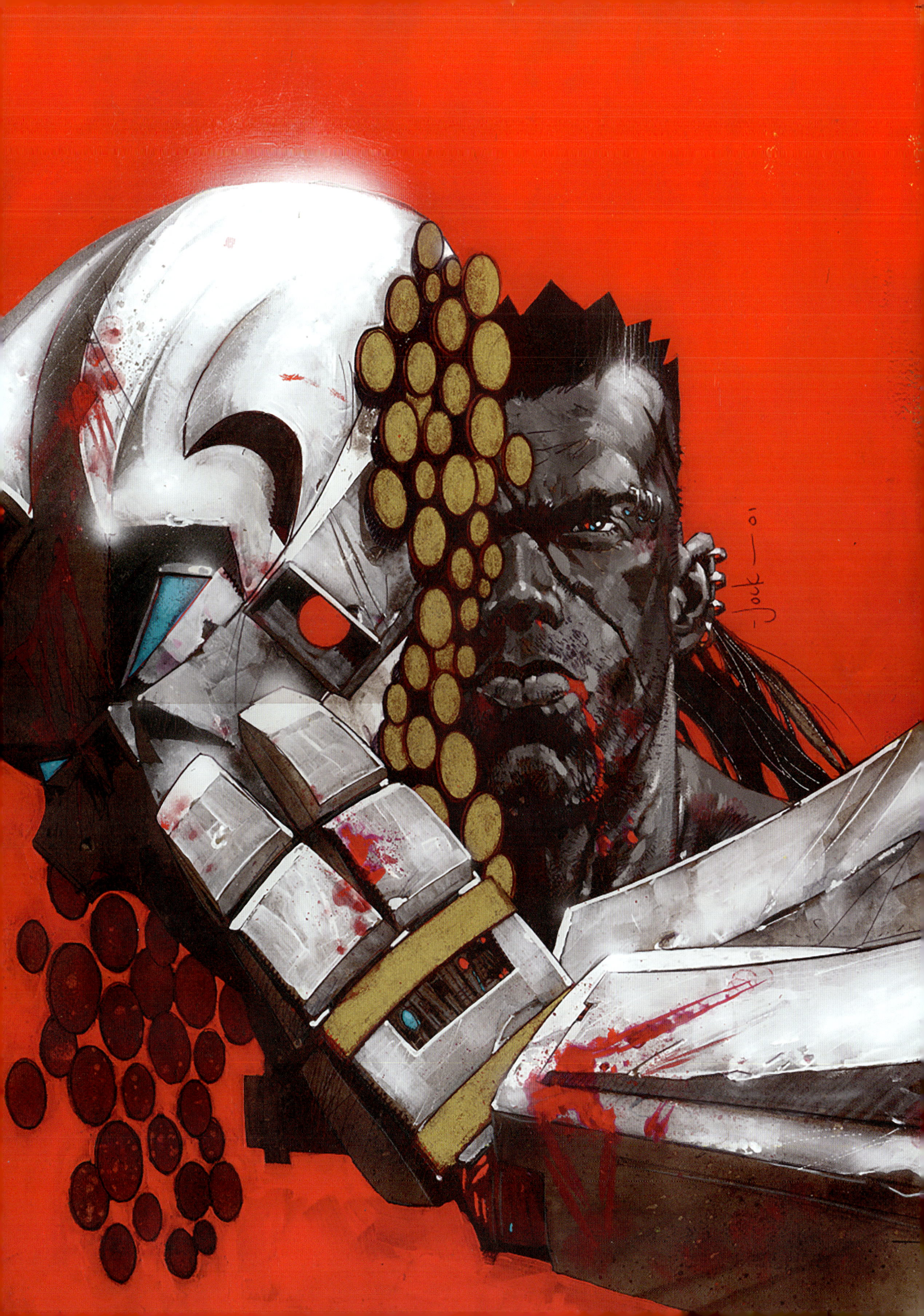

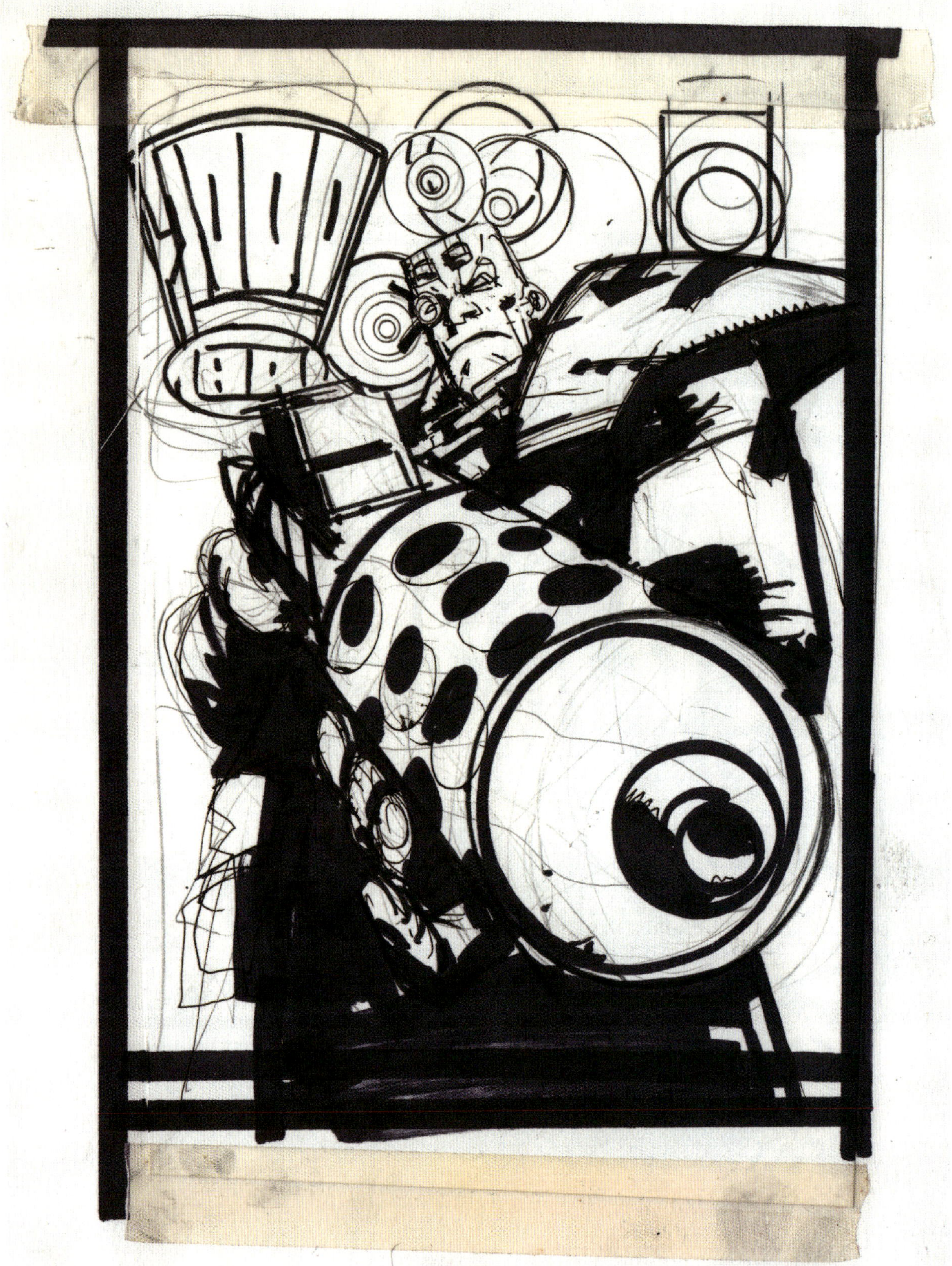

2000 AD PROG 1274 COVER ROUGH, BAD COMPANY, 2002
OPPOSITE: FINAL BAD COMPANY COVER ART WITH COLOURS BY CHRIS BLYTHE

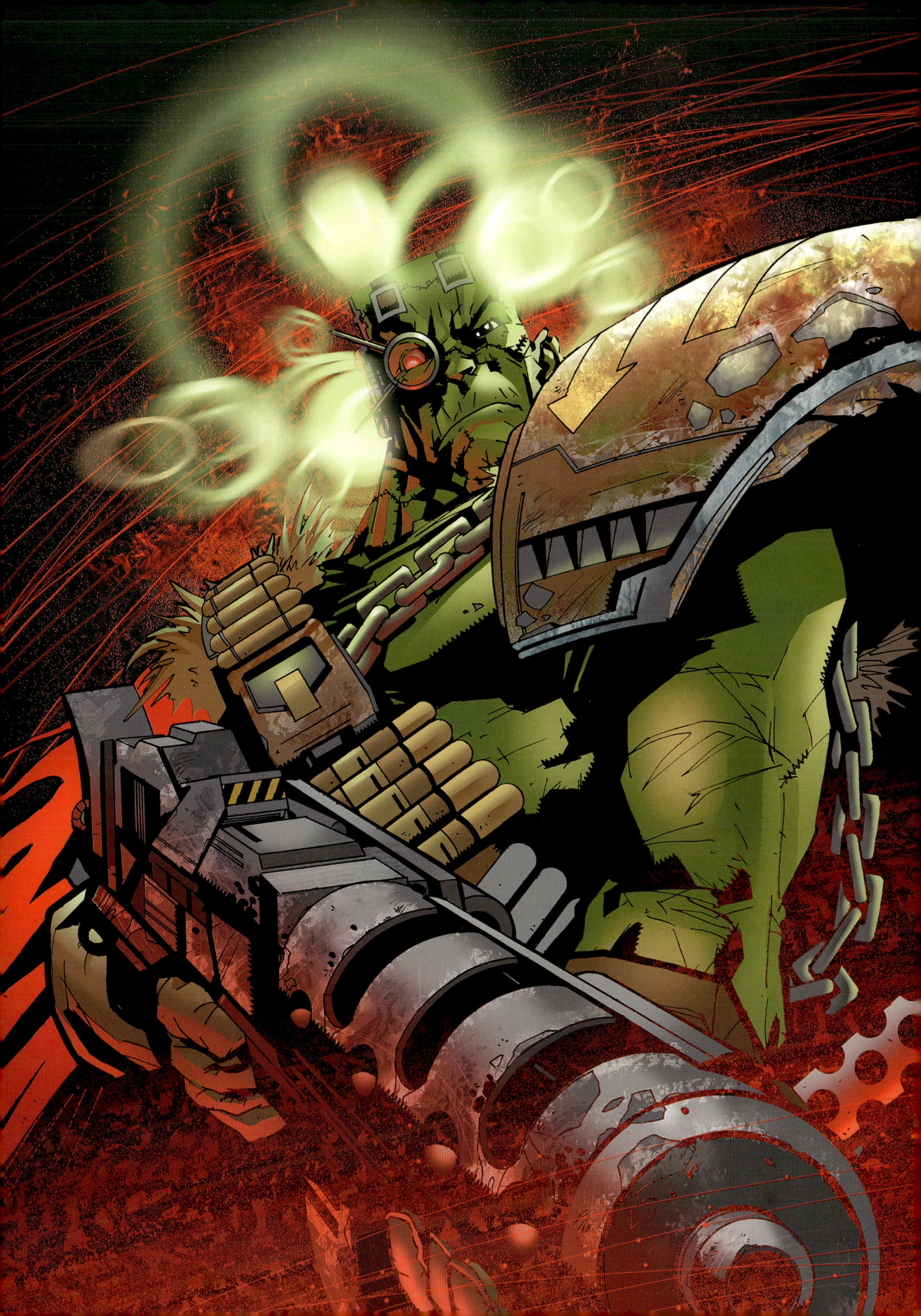

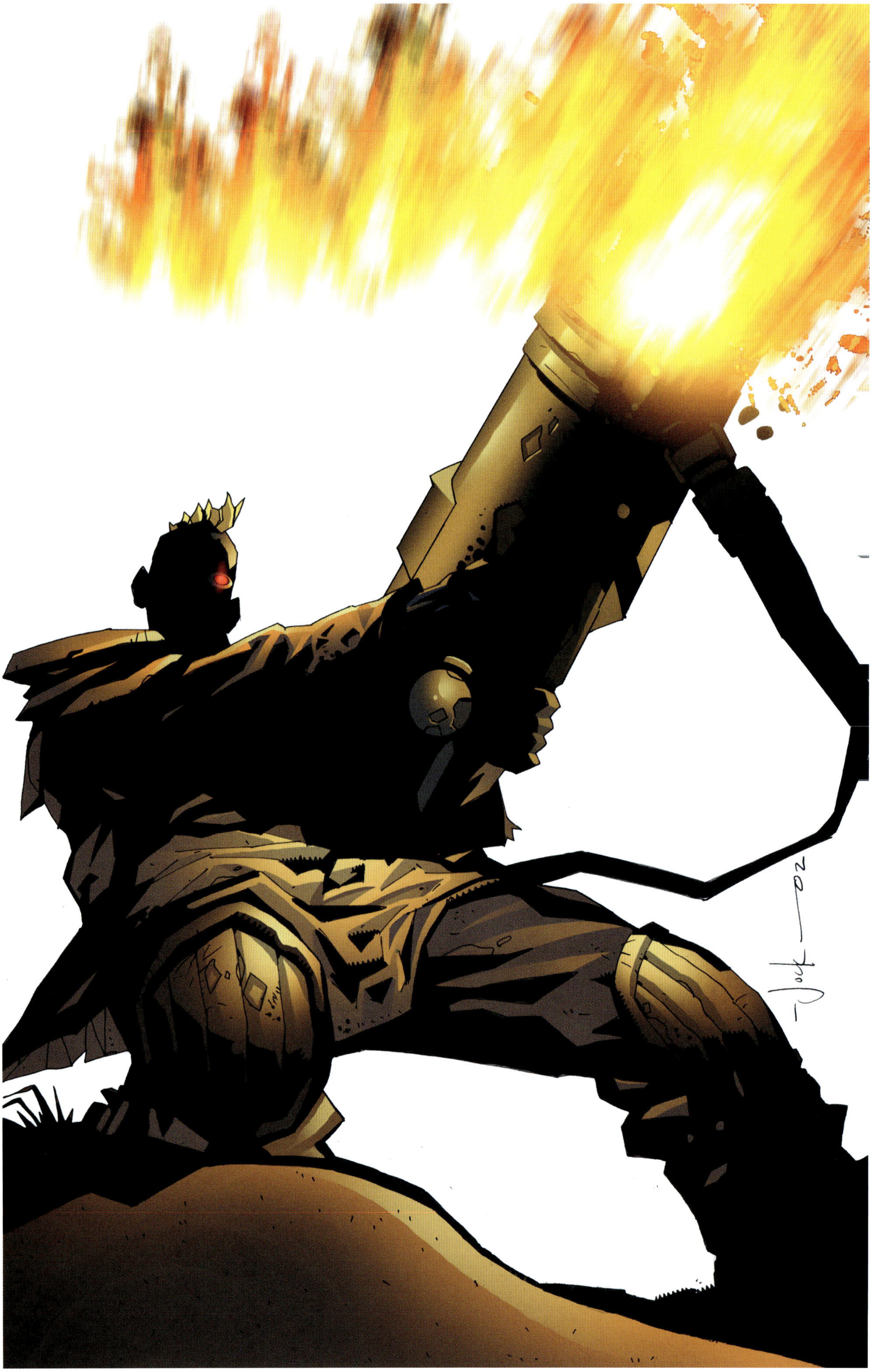

2000 AD PROG 1295 COVER, TOR CYAN, 2002
COLOURS BY CHRIS BLYTHE

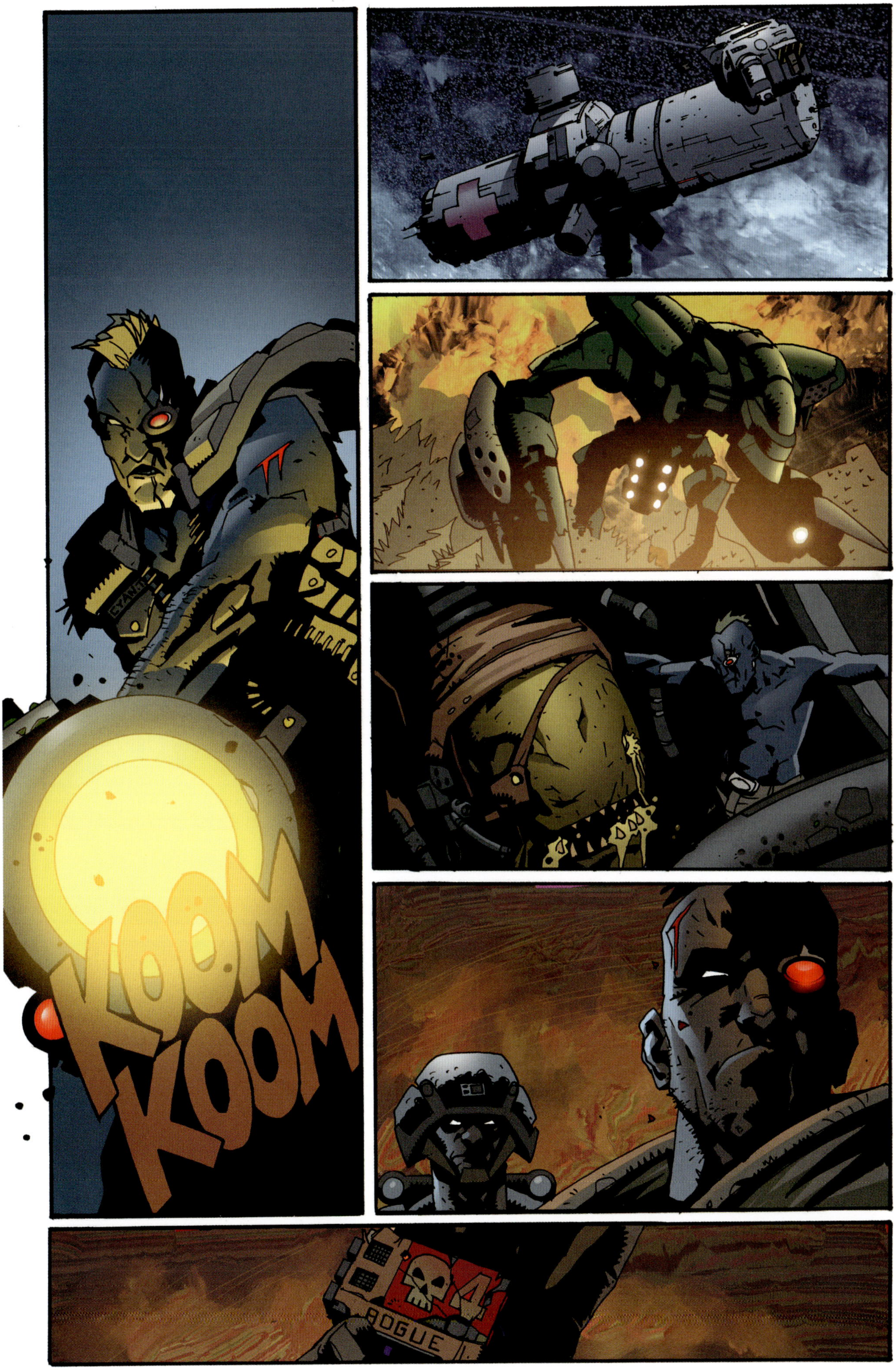
KOOM
KOOM
ROGUE

TOR CYAN: RAHAB PAGE 1, 2000 AD PROG 1295, 2002
COLOUR BY CHRIS BLYTHE

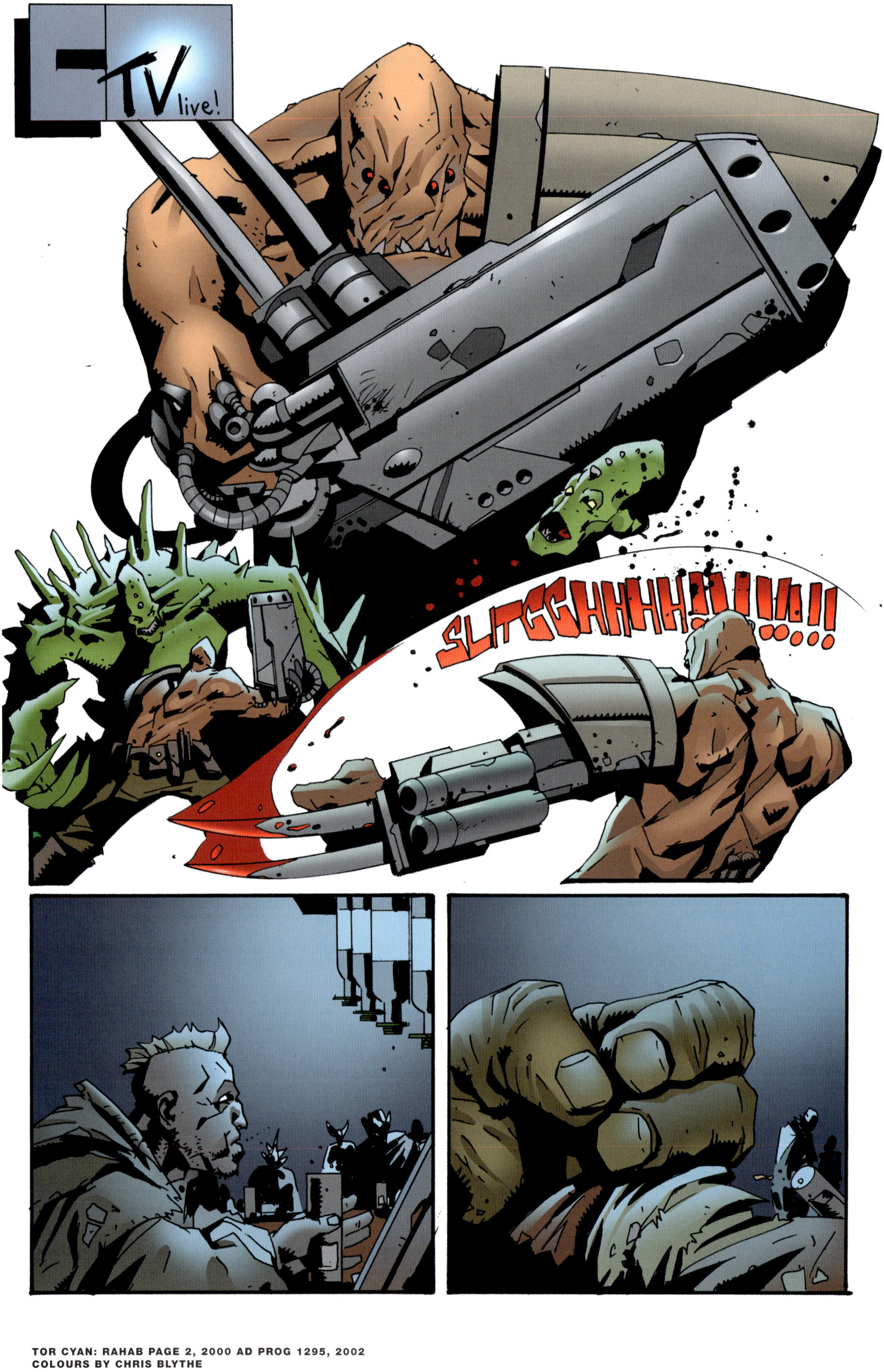
TV live!
SLITCGHHHH!!!!!!

TOR CYAN: RAHAB PAGE 2, 2000 AD PROG 1295, 2002
COLOURS BY CHRIS BLYTHE

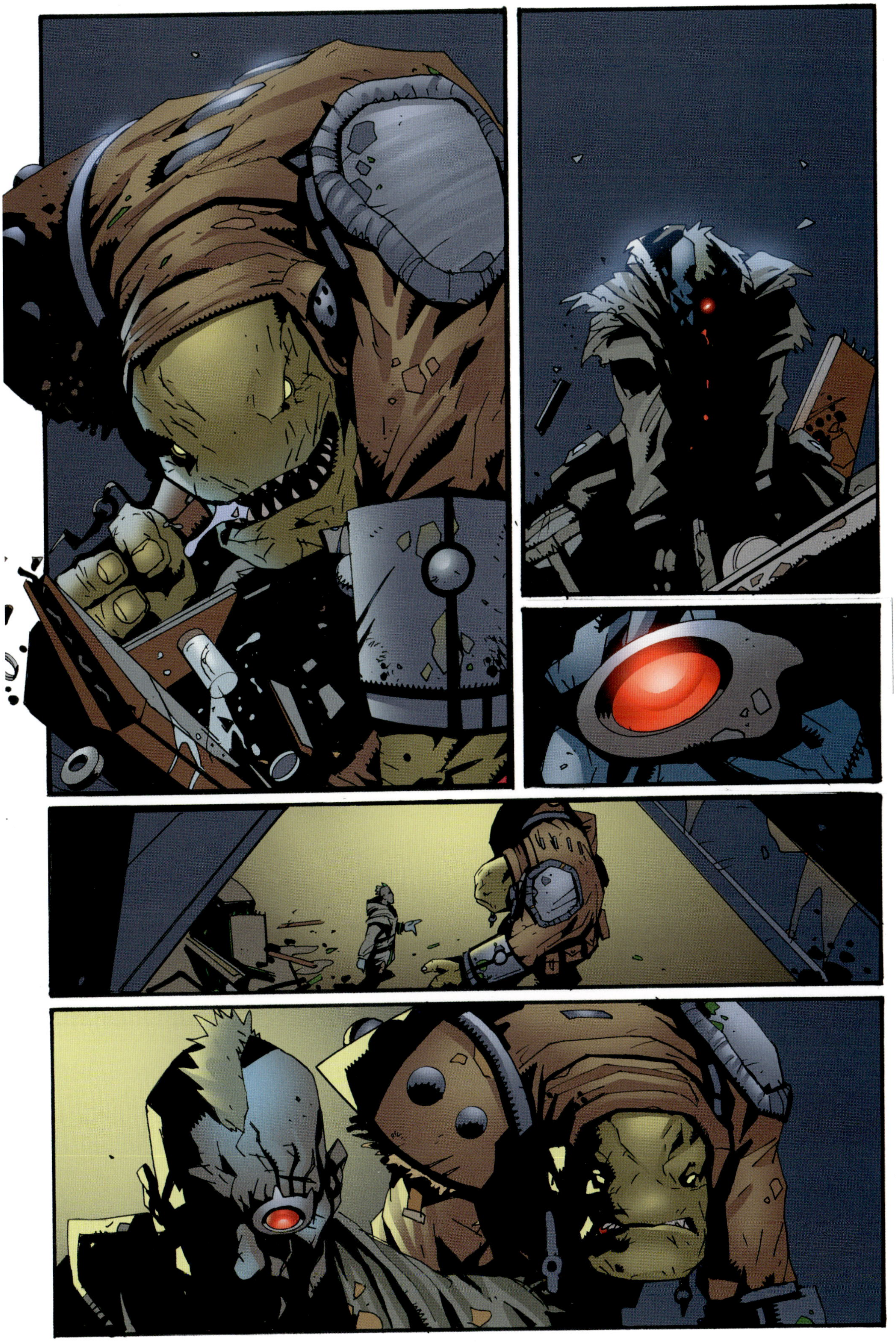

TOR CYAN: RAHAB PAGE 3, 2000 AD PROG 1295, 2002
COLOUR BY CHRIS BLYTHE

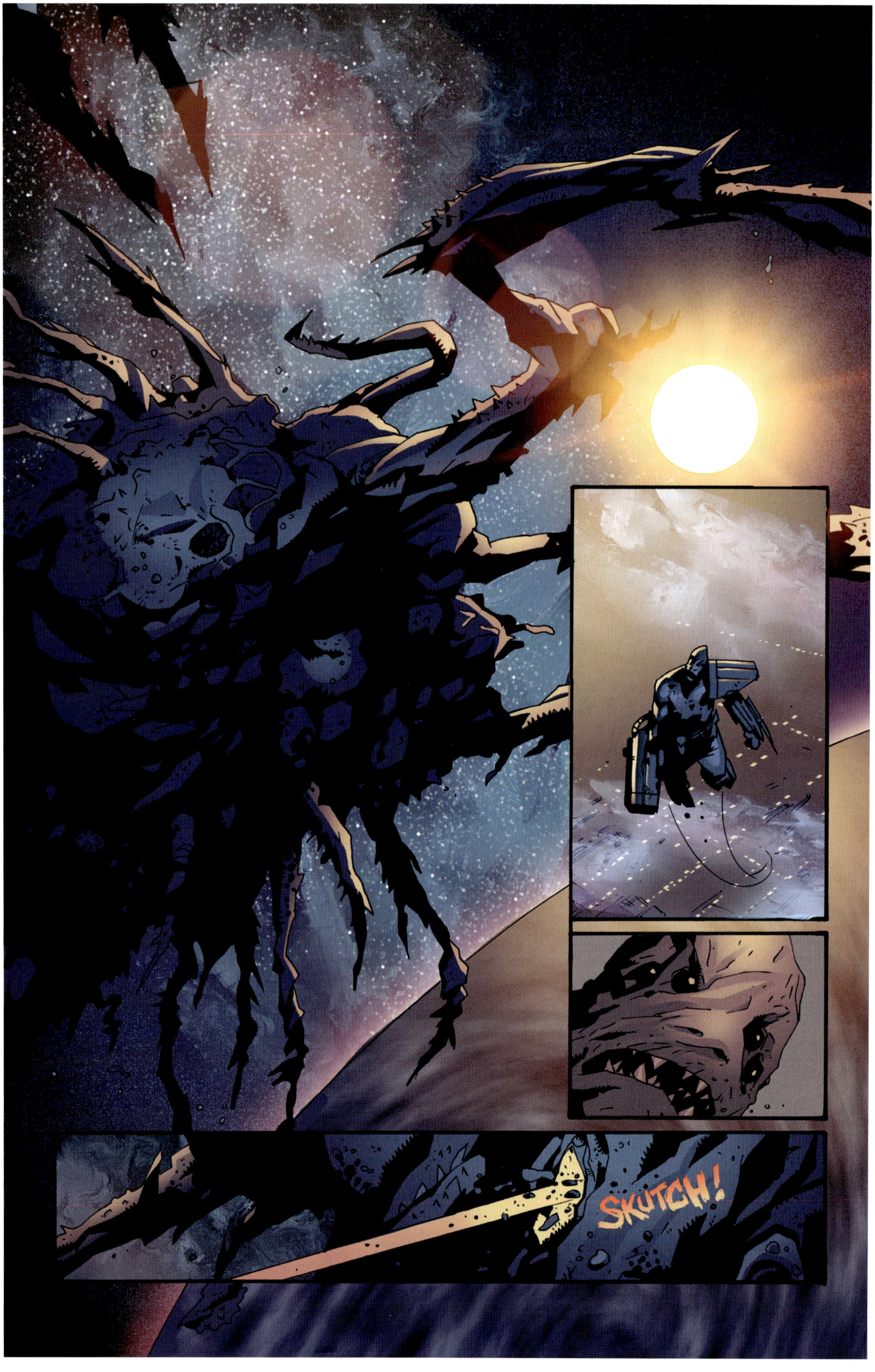
SKUTCH!

TOR CYAN: RAHAB PAGE 4, 2000 AD PROG 1295, 2002
COLOUR BY CHRIS BLYTHE

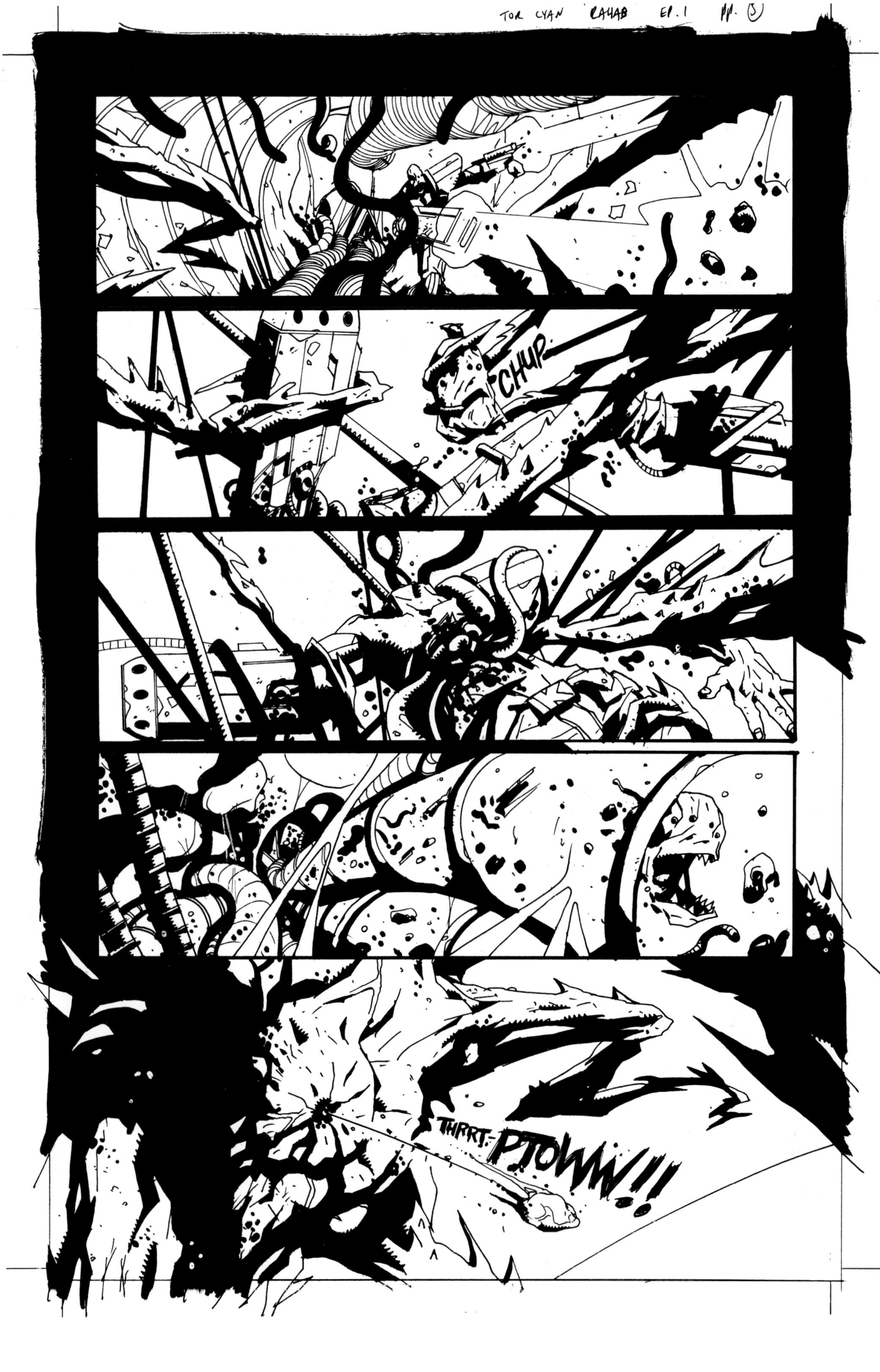
TOR CYAN RAHAB EP. 1 PP. 5
CHUP
THRRT-PTOWW!!!

TOR CYAN: RAHAB PAGE 5 INKS, 2000 AD PROG 1295, 2002

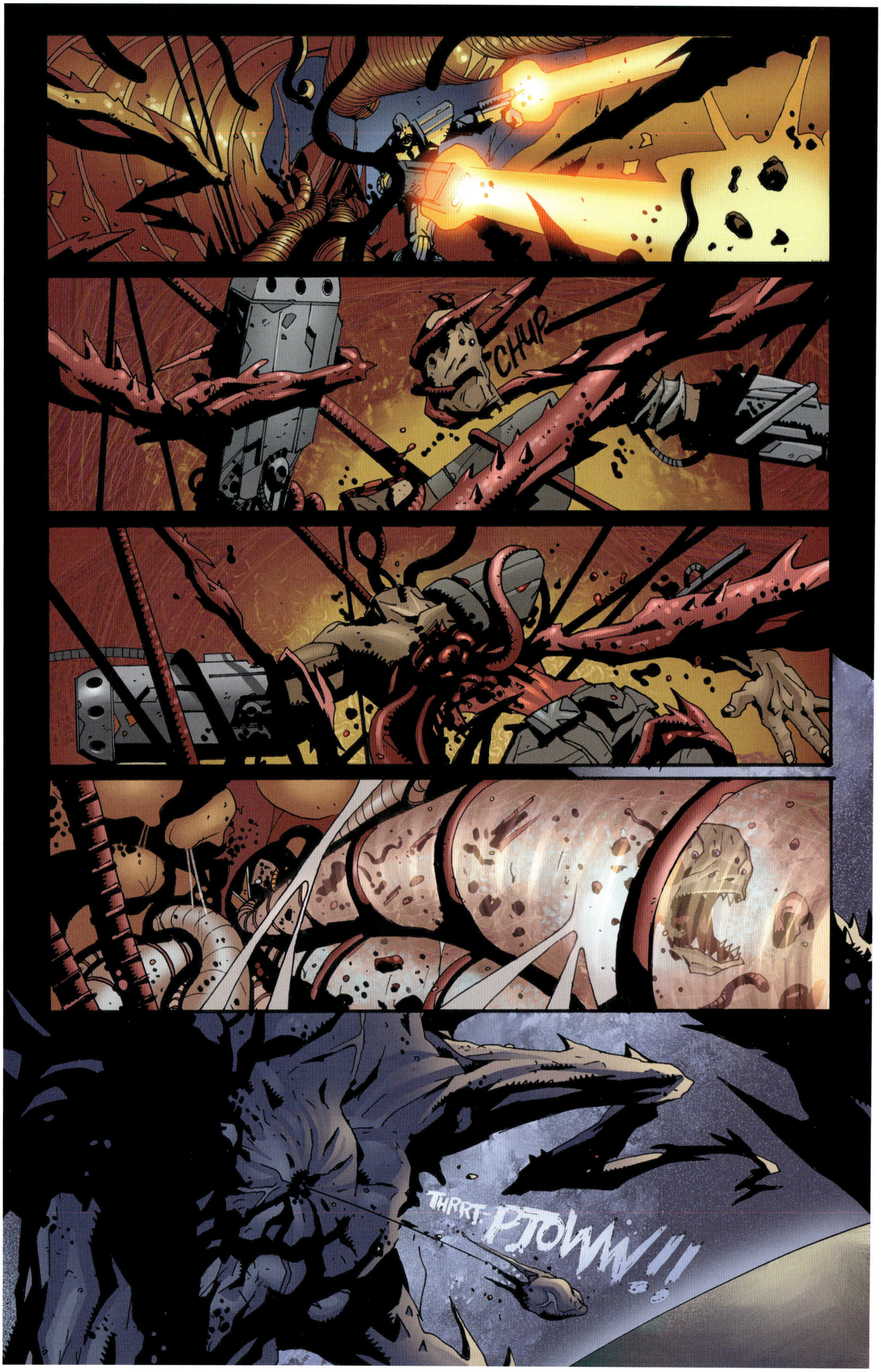

CHUP
THRRT-P'TOWW!!

TOR CYAN: RAHAB PAGE 5, 2000 AD PROG 1295, 2002
COLOUR BY CHRIS BLYTHE

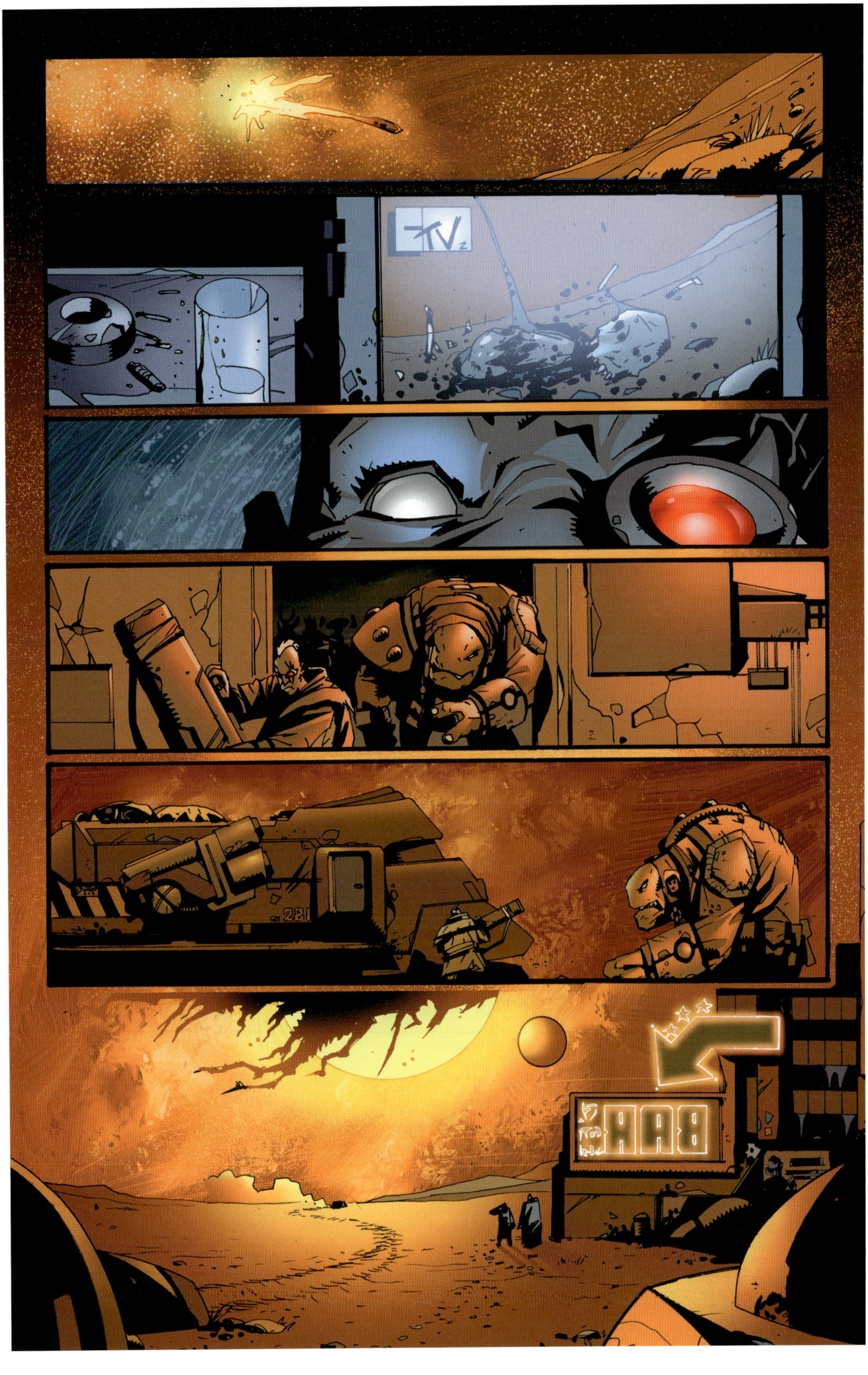

TOR CYAN: RAHAB PAGE 6, 2000 AD PROG 1295, 2002
COLOUR BY CHRIS BLYTHE

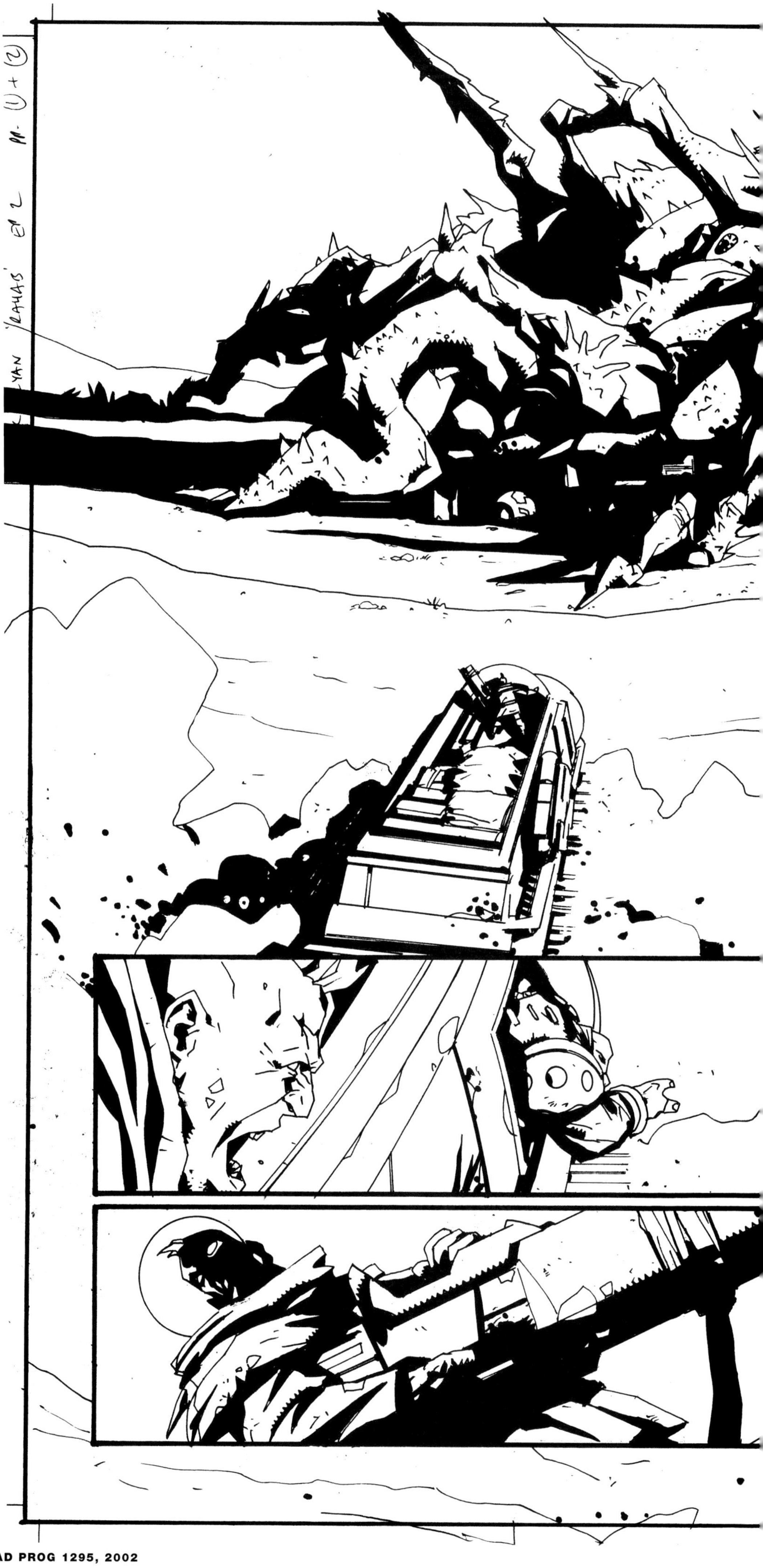

 TOR CYAN: RAHAB PAGE 7 & 8 INKS, 2000 AD PROG 1295, 2002

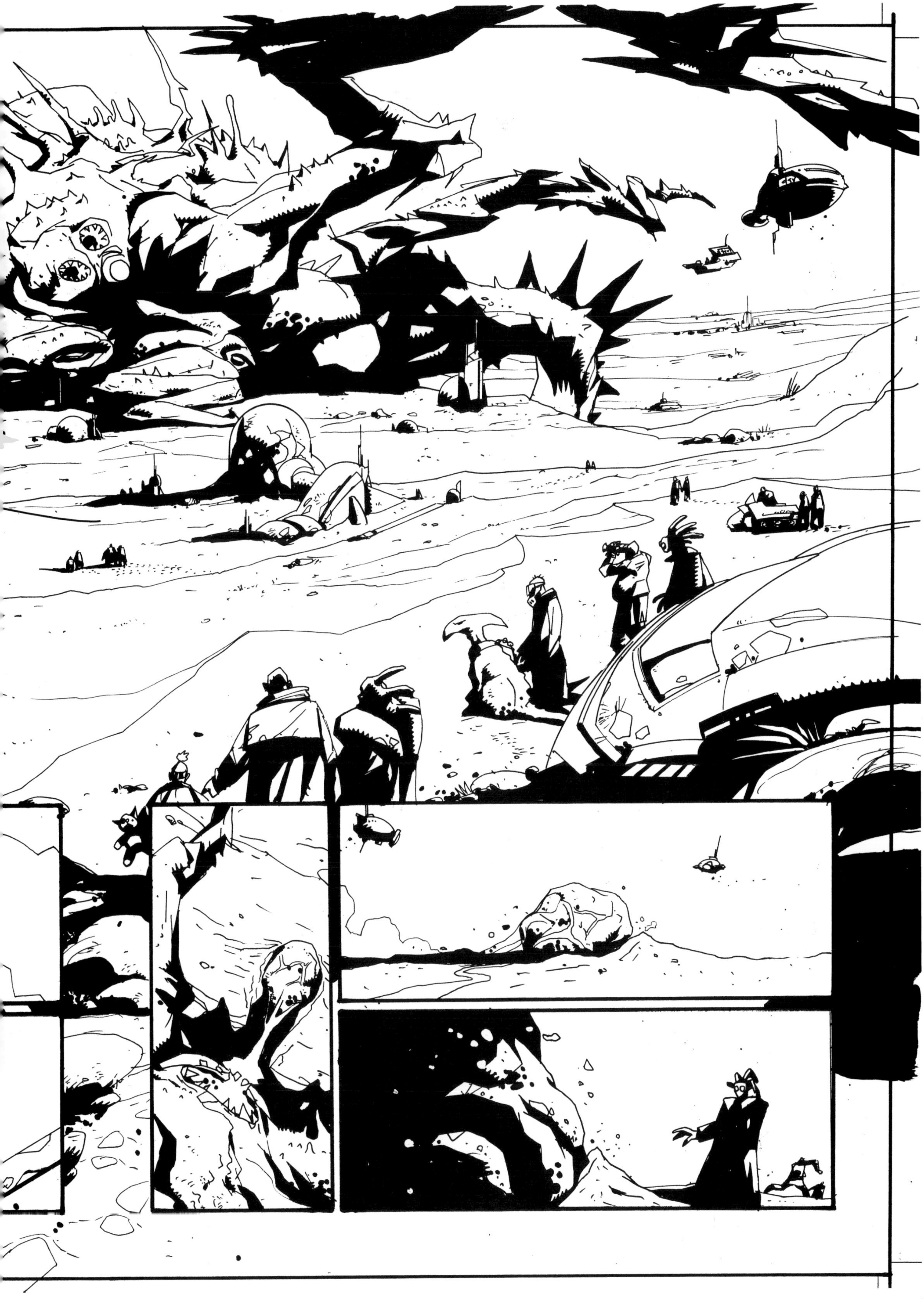

OVERLEAF: TOR CYAN: RAHAB PAGES 7 & 8, 2000 AD PROG 1295, 2002
COLOUR BY CHRIS BLYTHE

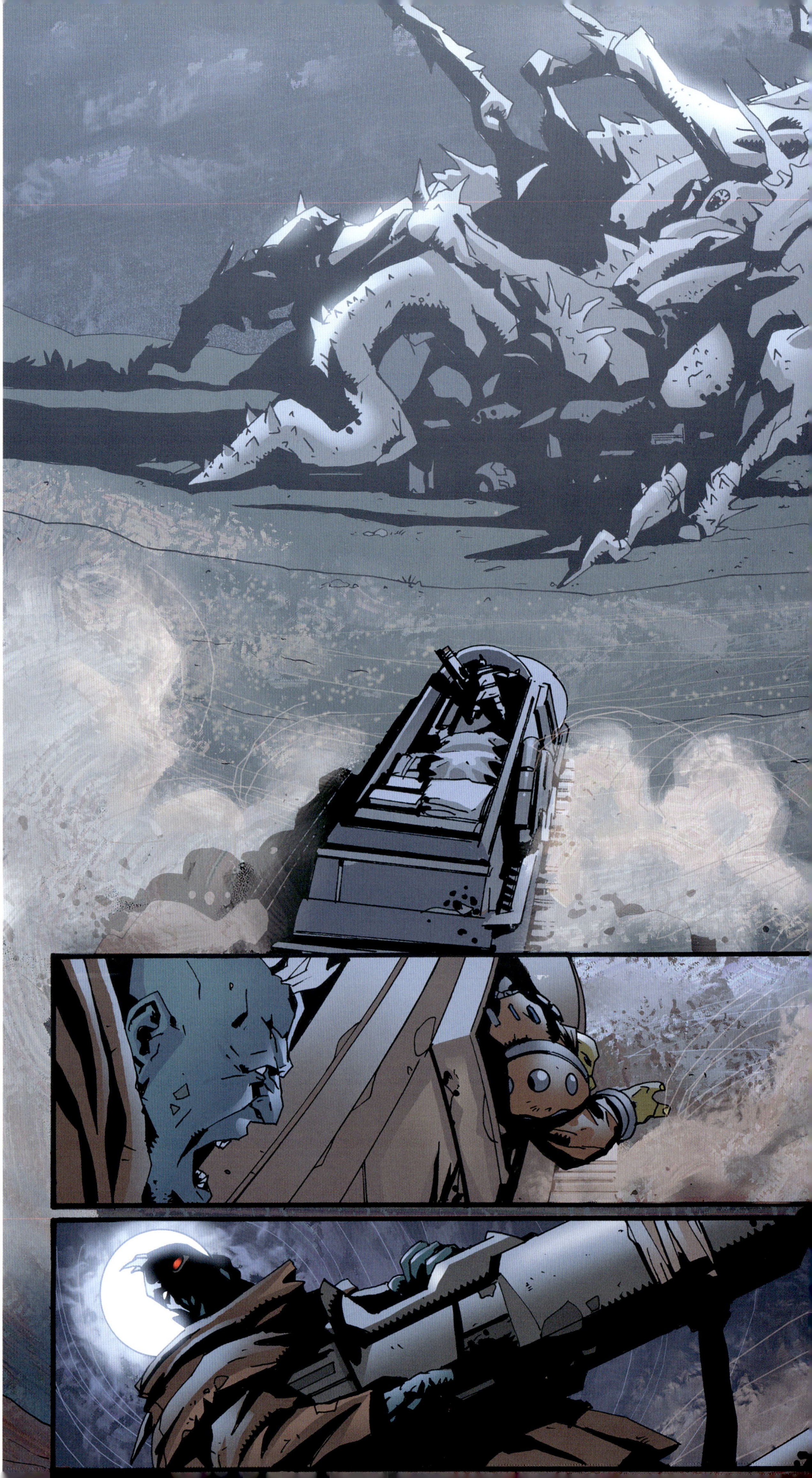

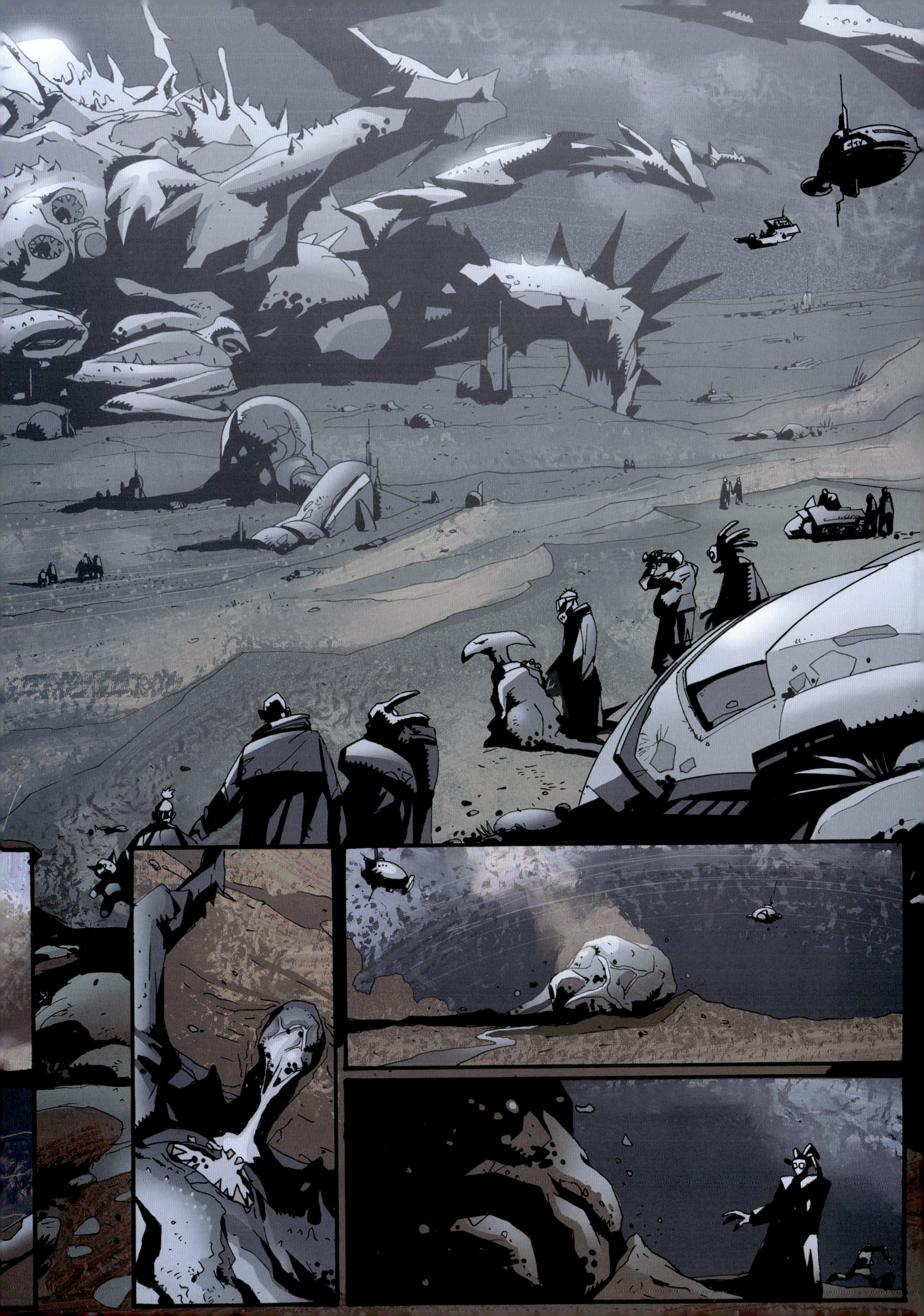

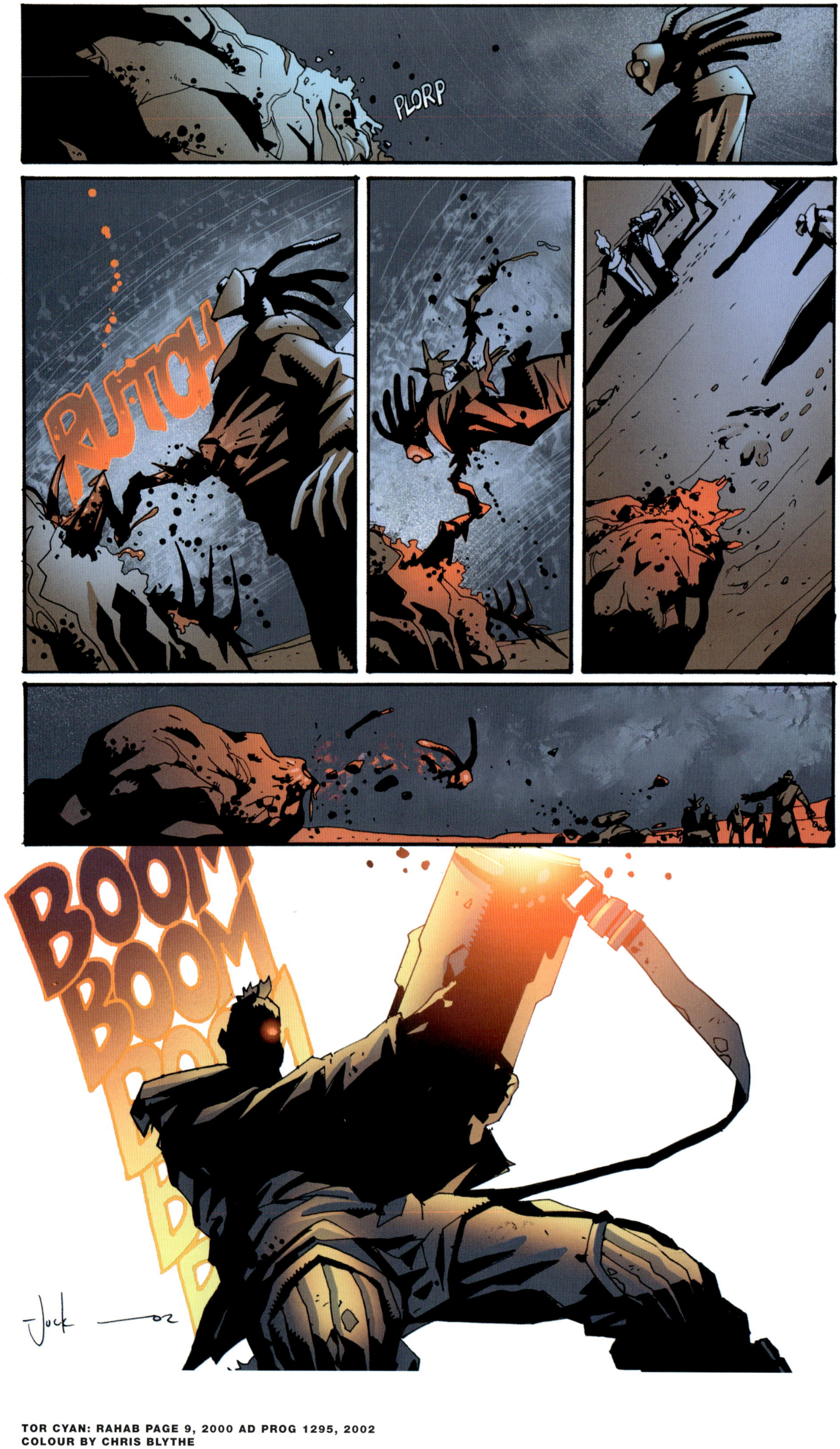
PLORP
RUTCH
BOOM
BOOM
Jock —02

TOR CYAN: RAHAB PAGE 9, 2000 AD PROG 1295, 2002
COLOUR BY CHRIS BLYTHE

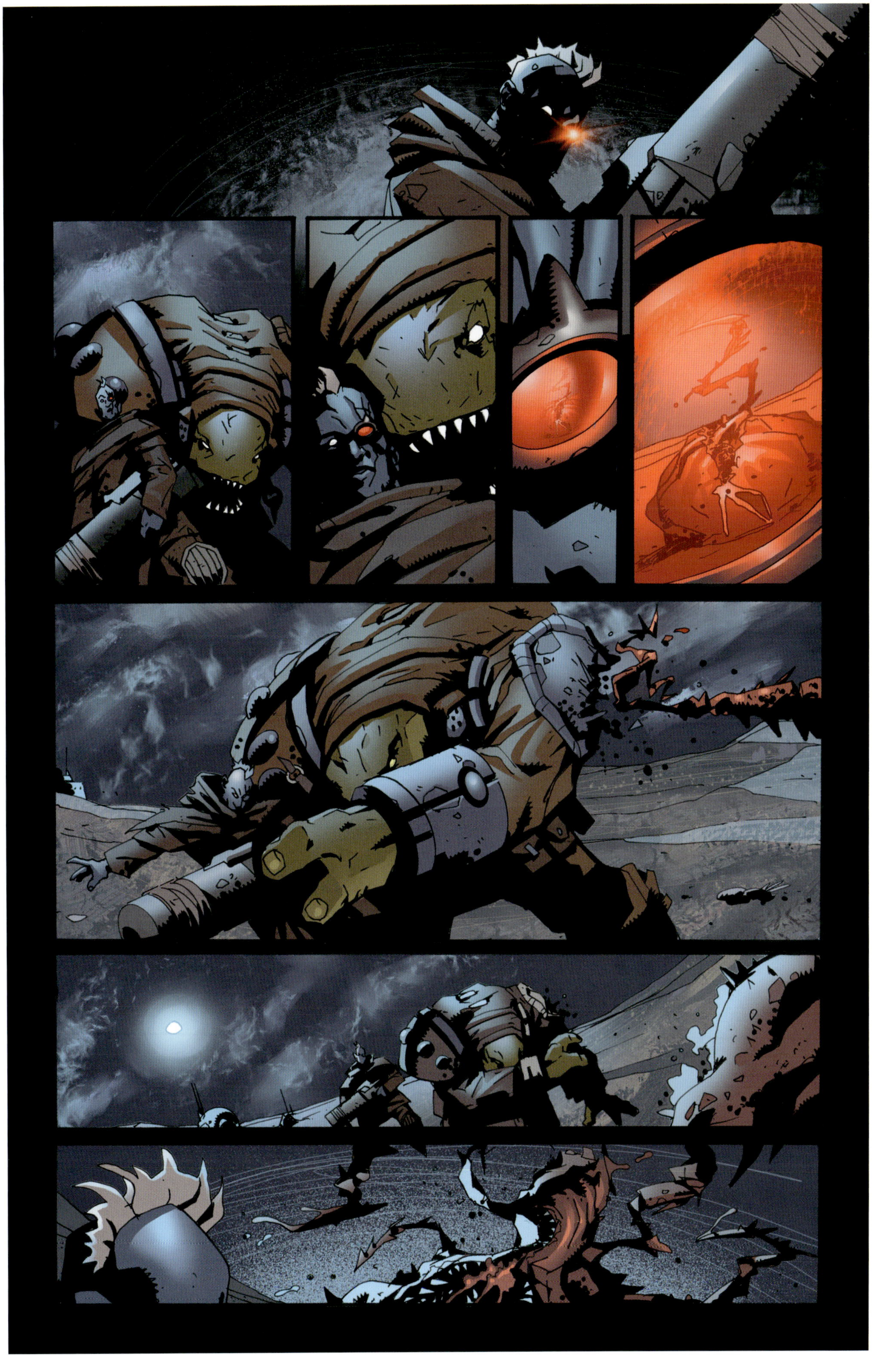

TOR CYAN: RAHAB PAGE 10, 2000 AD PROG 1295, 2002
COLOUR BY CHRIS BLYTHE

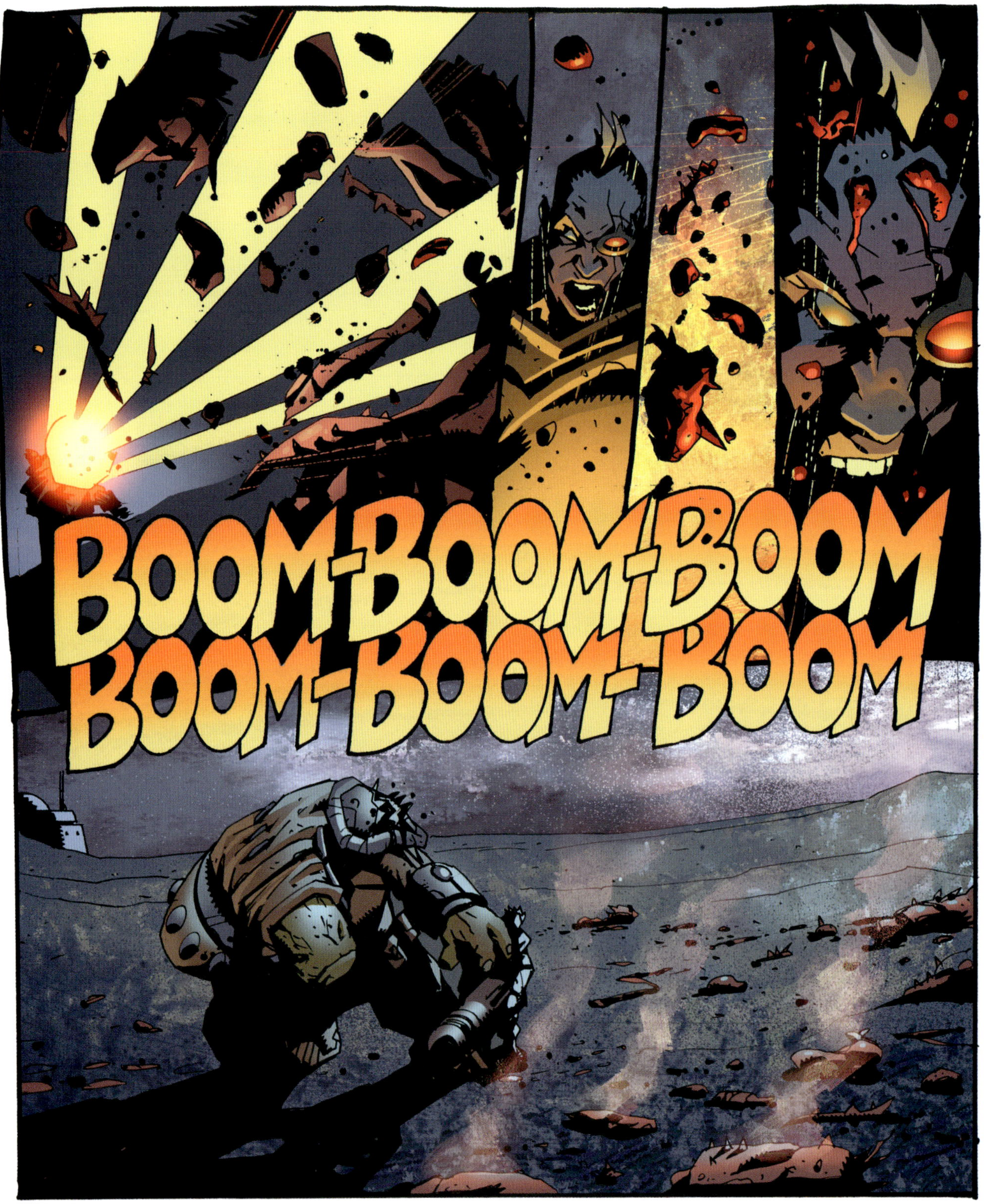
BOOM-BOOM-BOOM
BOOM-BOOM-BOOM

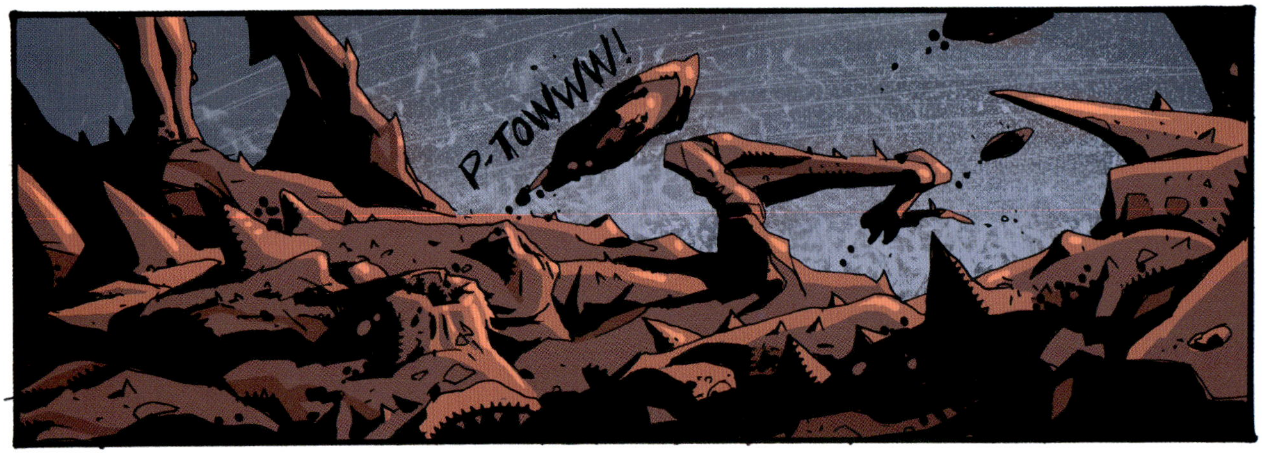
P-TOWWW!

TOR CYAN: RAHAB PAGE 11, 2000 AD PROG 1295, 2002
COLOUR BY CHRIS BLYTHE

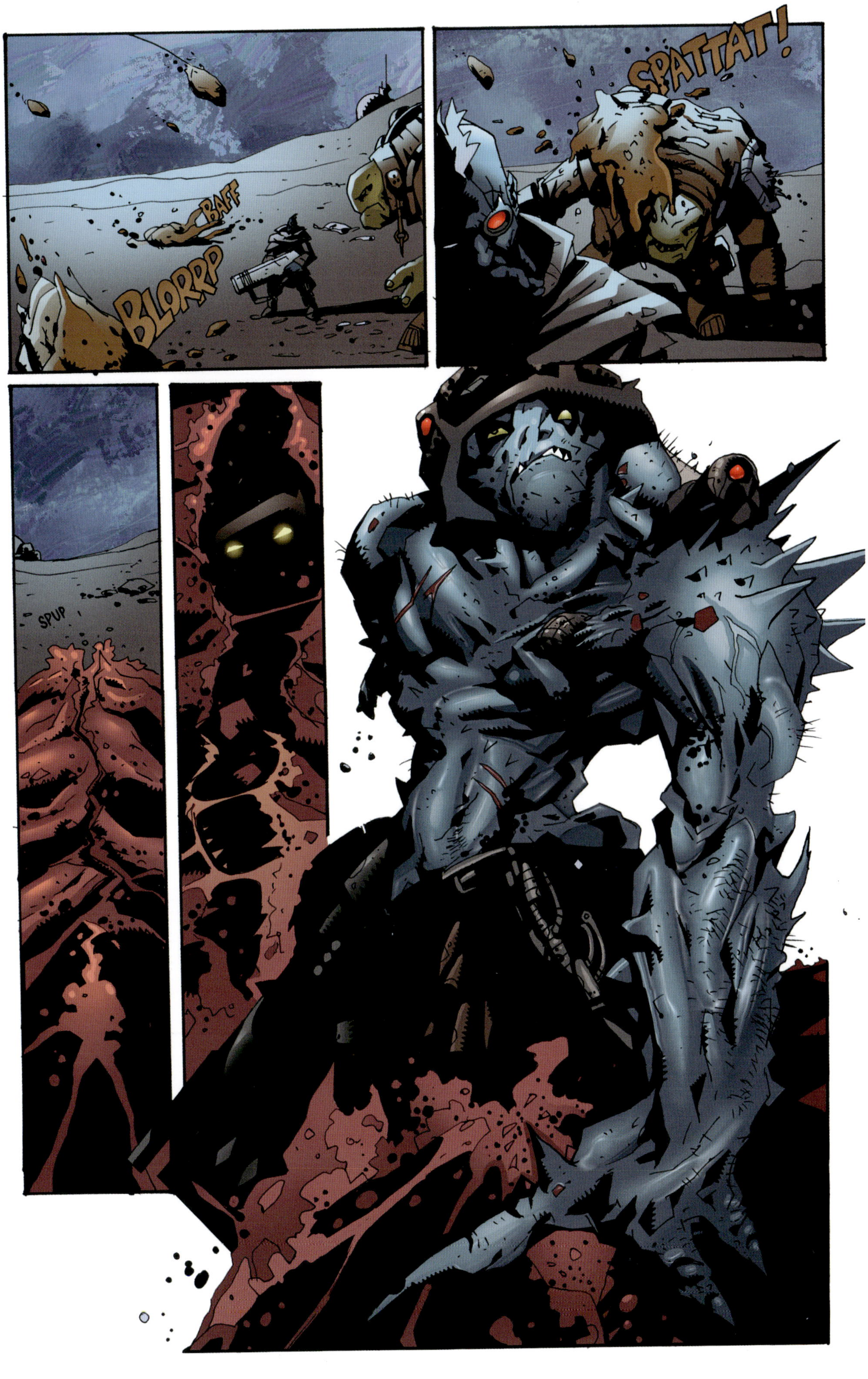
BAFF
BLORRP
SPATTAT!
SPUP

TOR CYAN: RAHAB PAGE 12, 2000 AD PROG 1295, 2002
COLOUR BY CHRIS BLYTHE

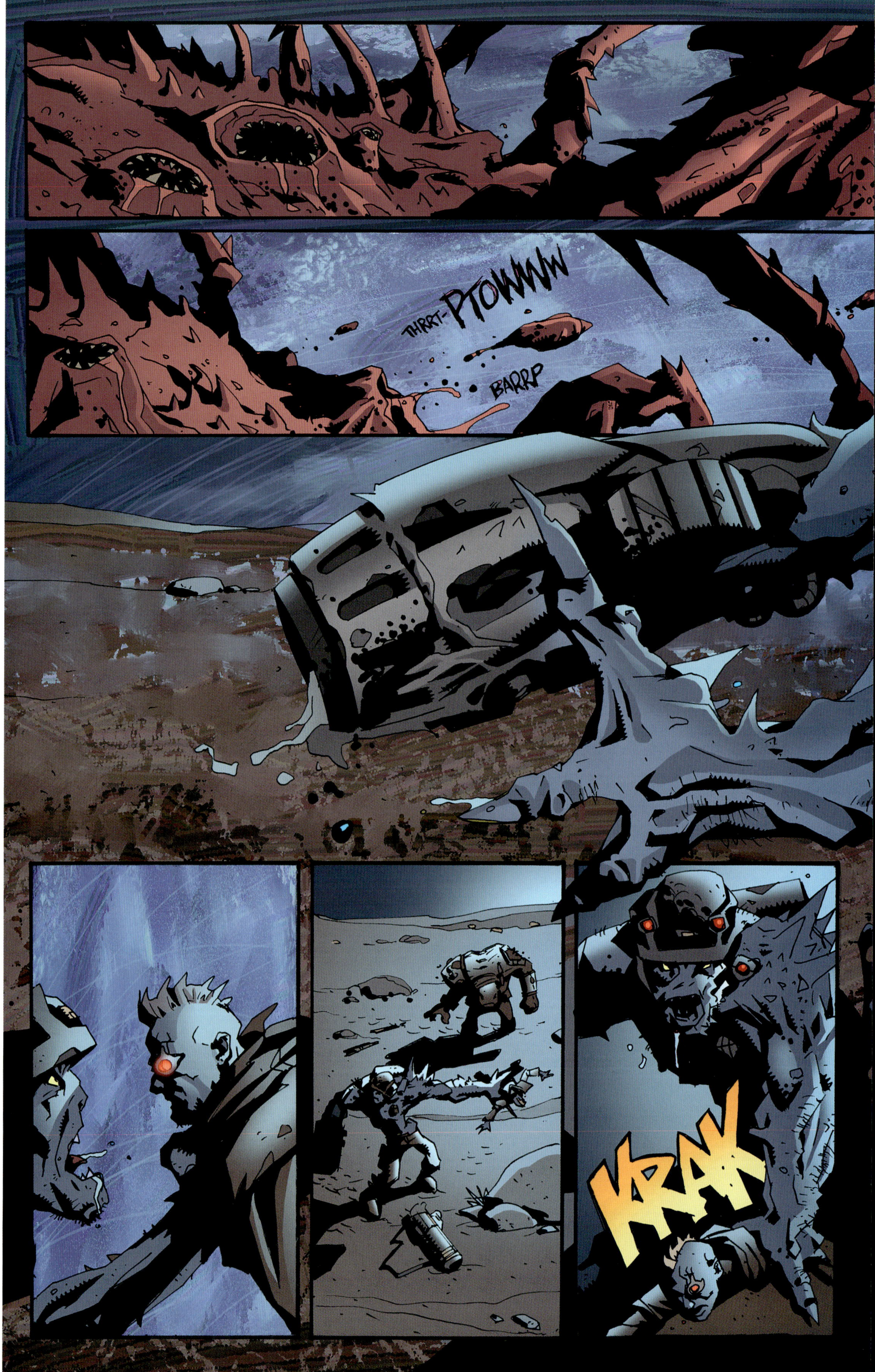
THRRT-PTOWWW
BARRP
KRAK

TOR CYAN: PHAGE PAGES 1 & 2, 2000 AD PROG 1296, 2002
COLOUR BY CHRIS BLYTHE

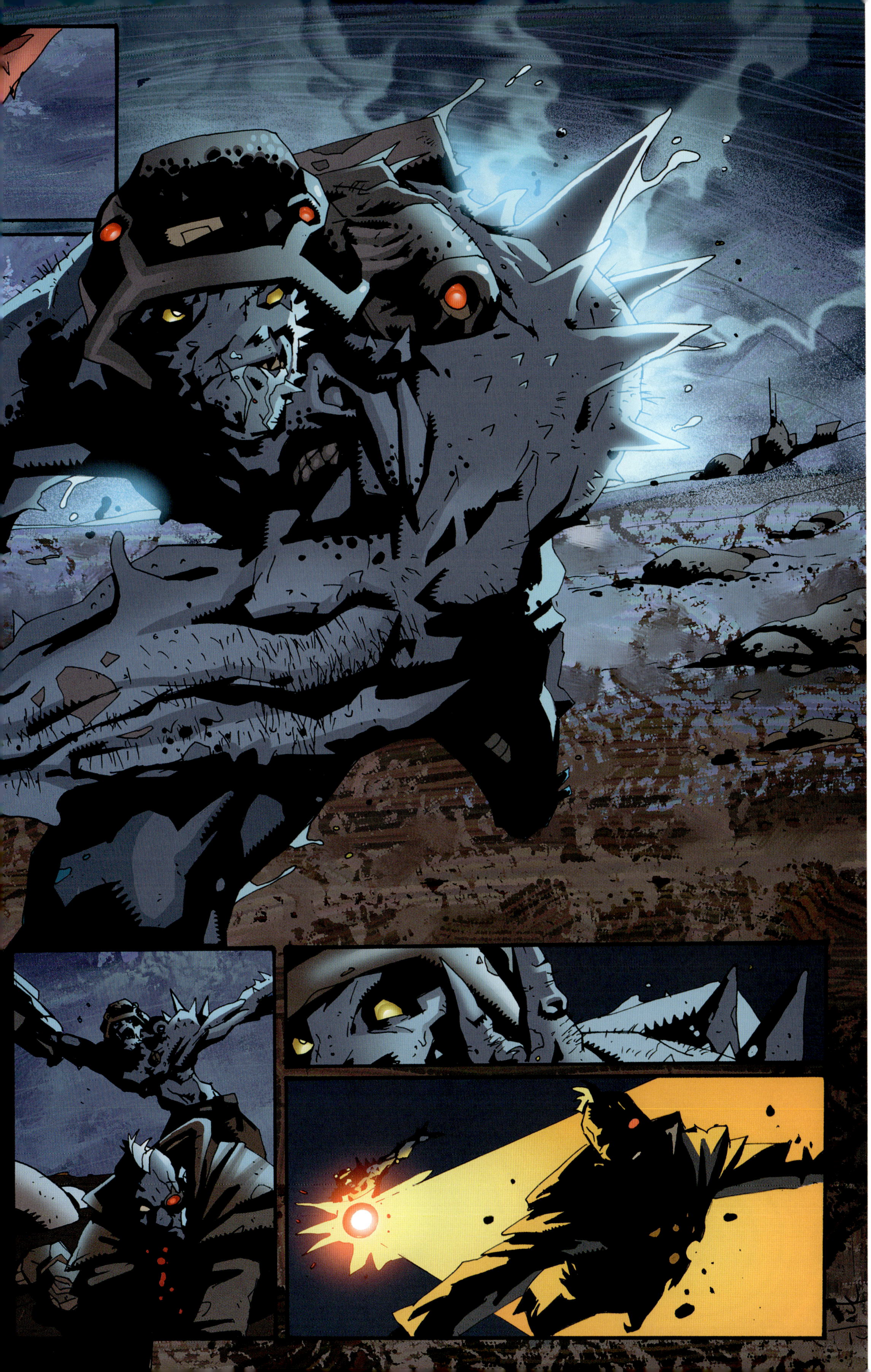

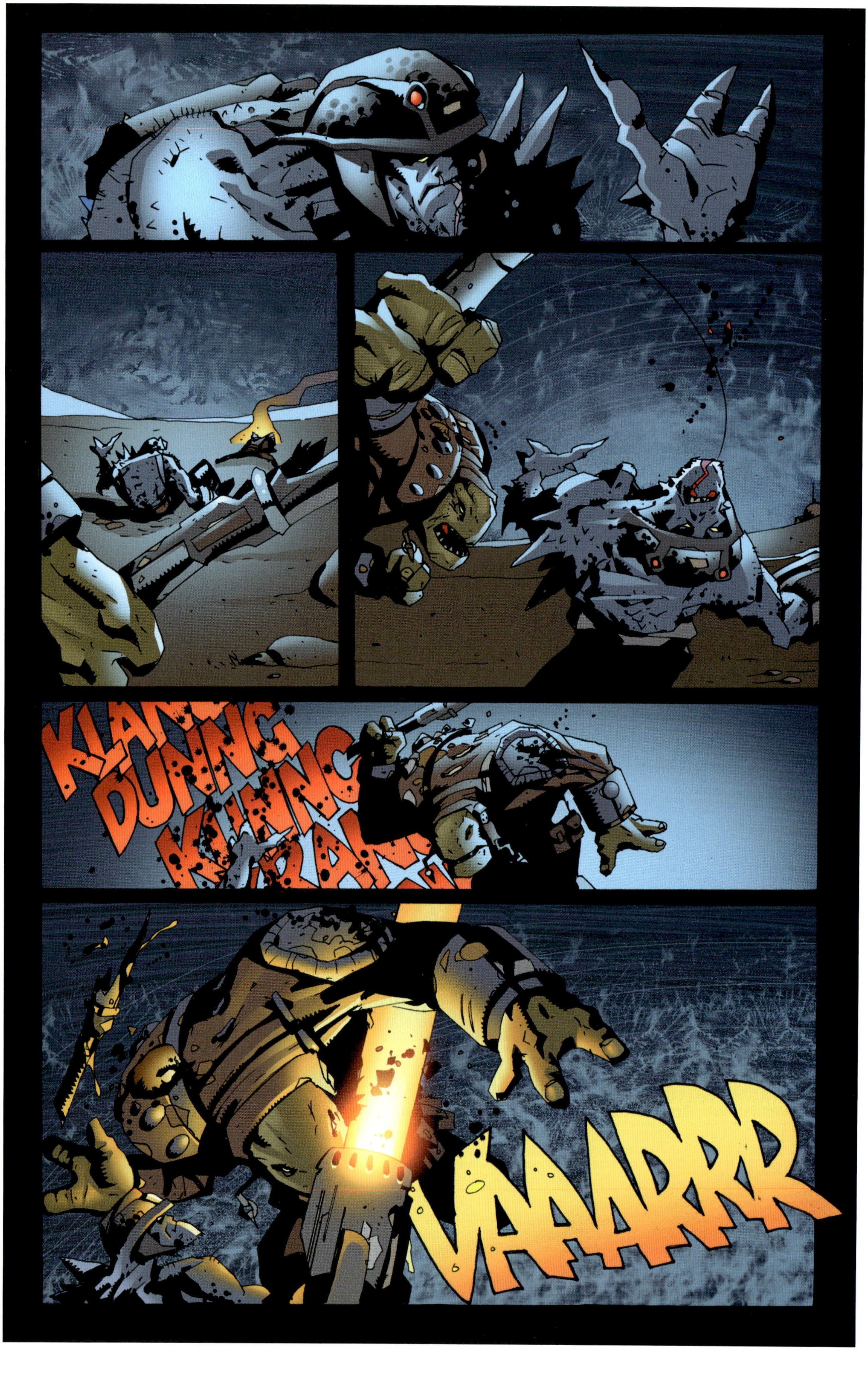
KLANG
DUNNG
VAAARRR

TOR CYAN: PHAGE PAGE 3, 2000 AD PROG 1296, 2002
COLOUR BY CHRIS BLYTHE

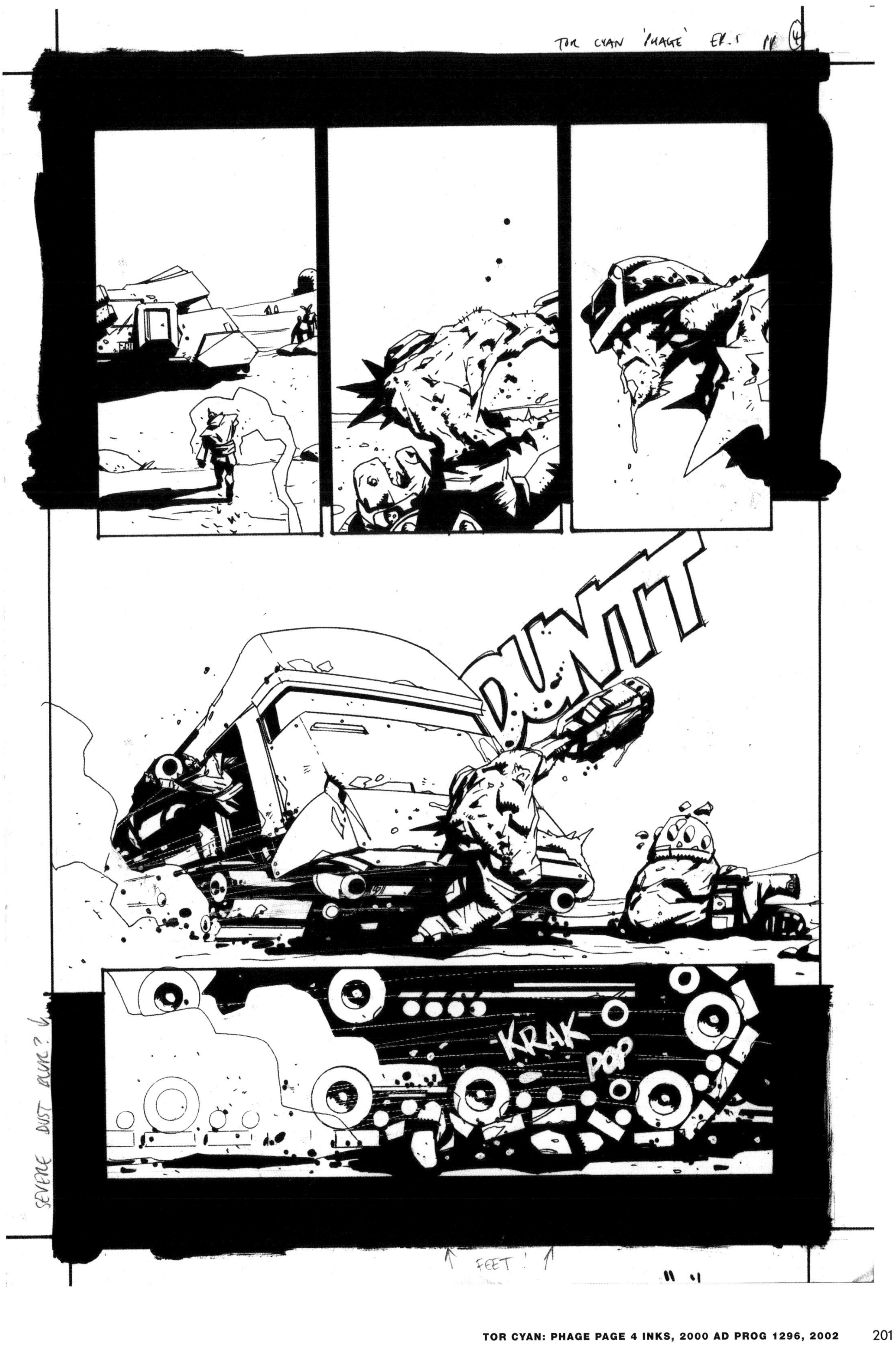
KRAK
POP

TOR CYAN: PHAGE PAGE 4 INKS, 2000 AD PROG 1296, 2002

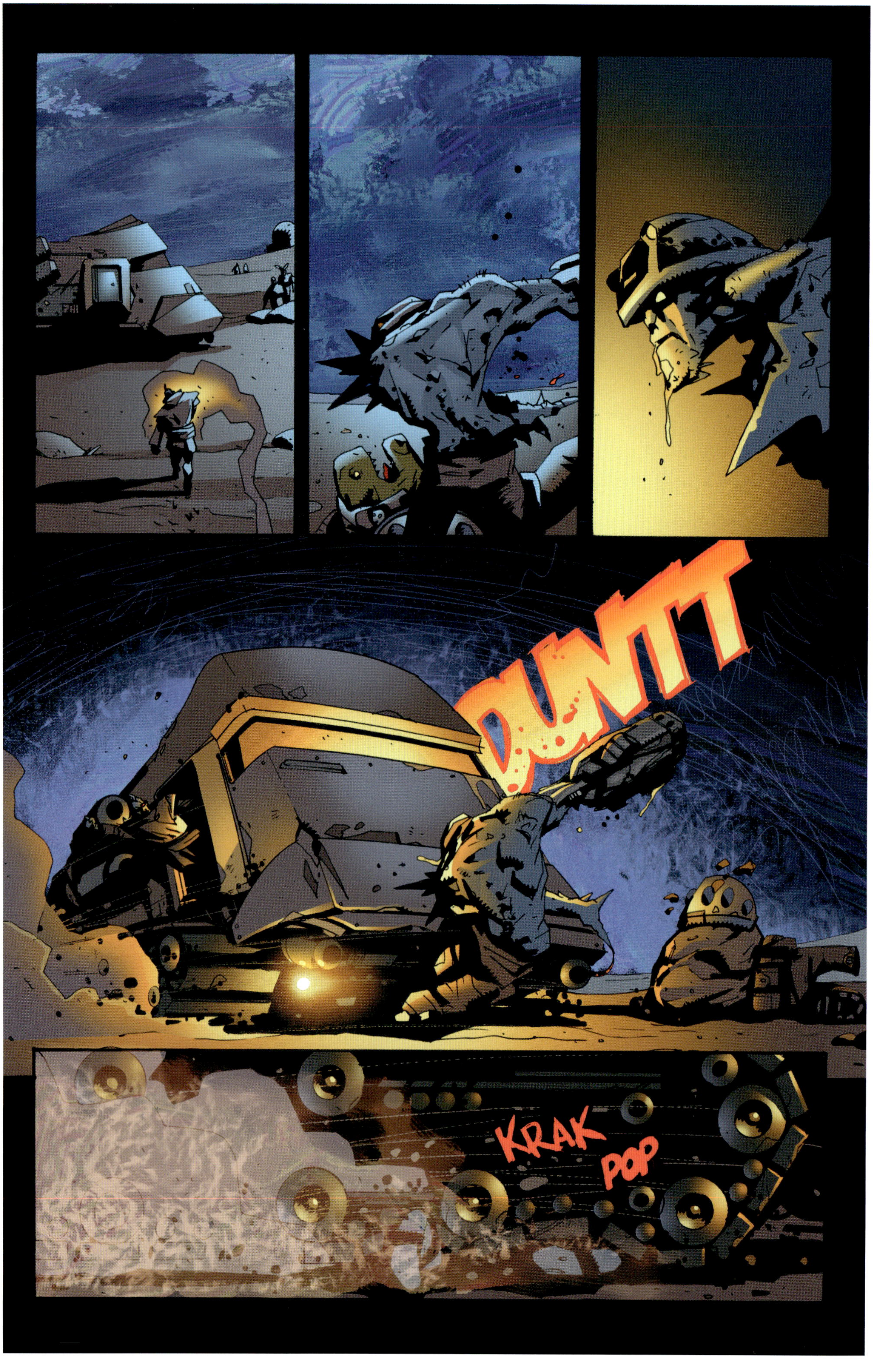
DUNTT
KRAK
POP

TOR CYAN: PHAGE PAGE 4, 2000 AD PROG 1296, 2002
COLOUR BY CHRIS BLYTHE

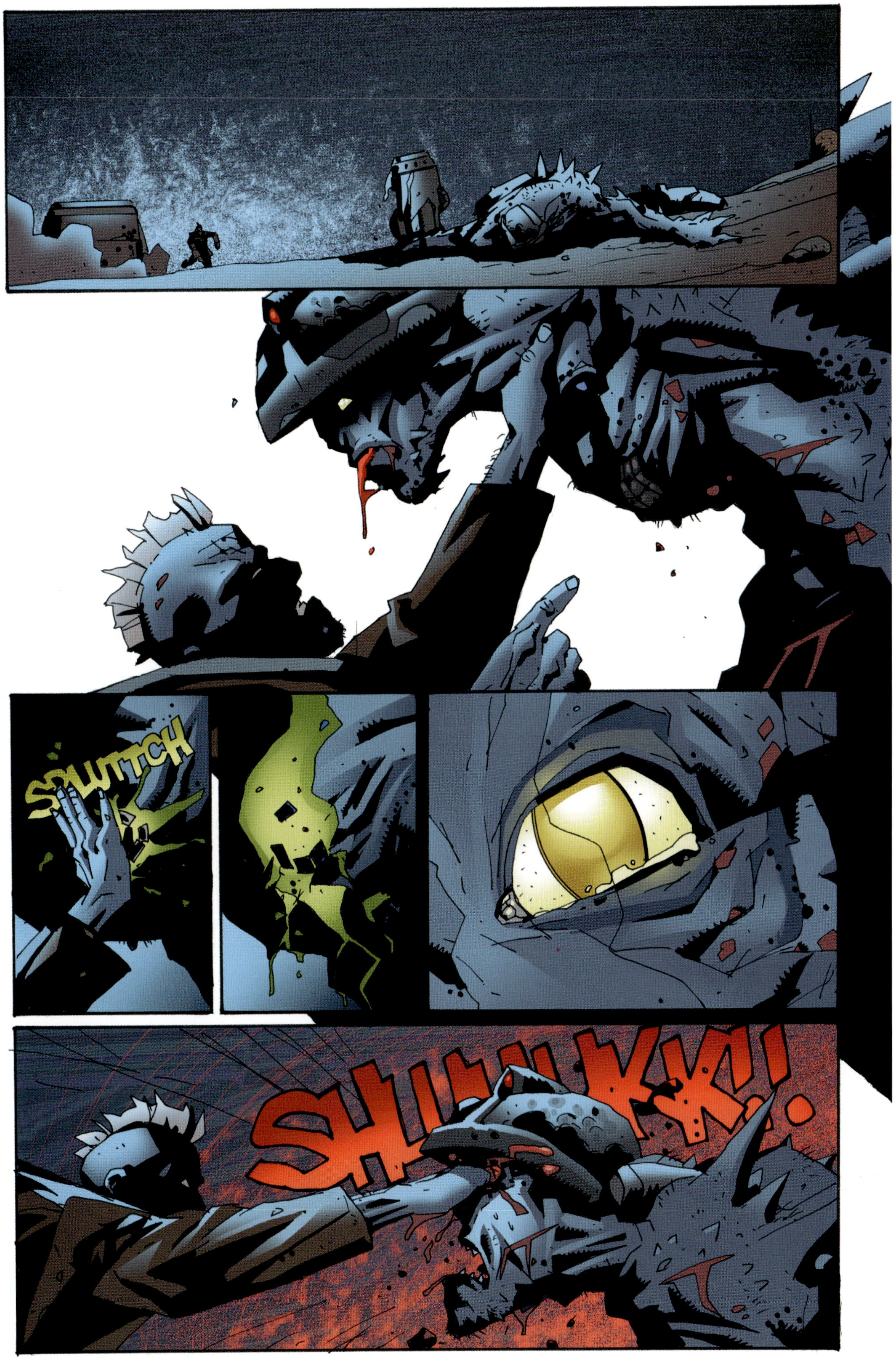
SPLUTTCH
SHLUNKK!!

TOR CYAN: PHAGE PAGE 5, 2000 AD PROG 1296, 2002
COLOUR BY CHRIS BLYTHE

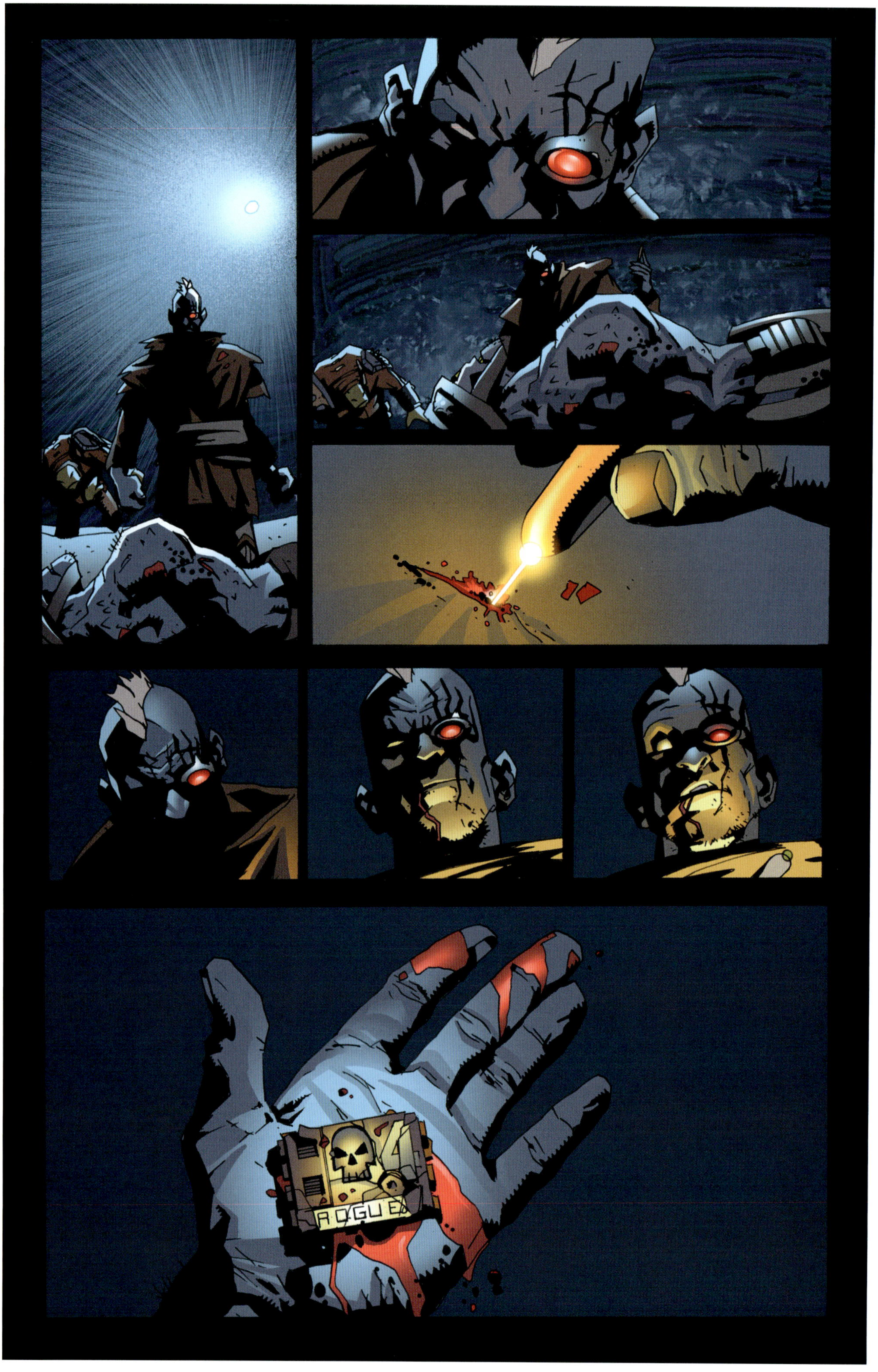
ROGUE

TOR CYAN: PHAGE PAGE 6, 2000 AD PROG 1296, 2002
COLOUR BY CHRIS BLYTHE

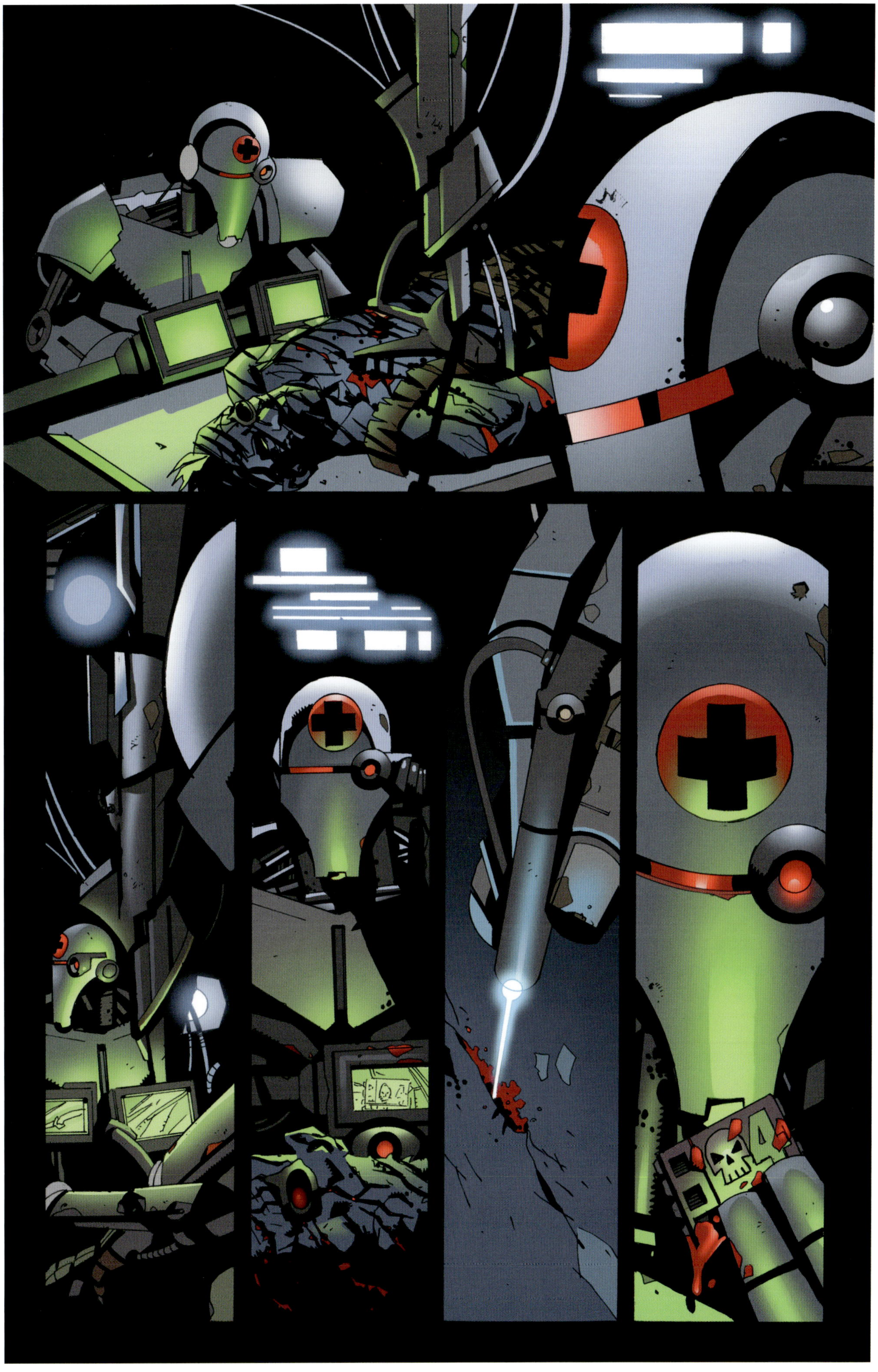

TOR CYAN: NO SUCH PLACE PAGE 1, 2000 AD PROG 1297, 2002
COLOUR BY CHRIS BLYTHE

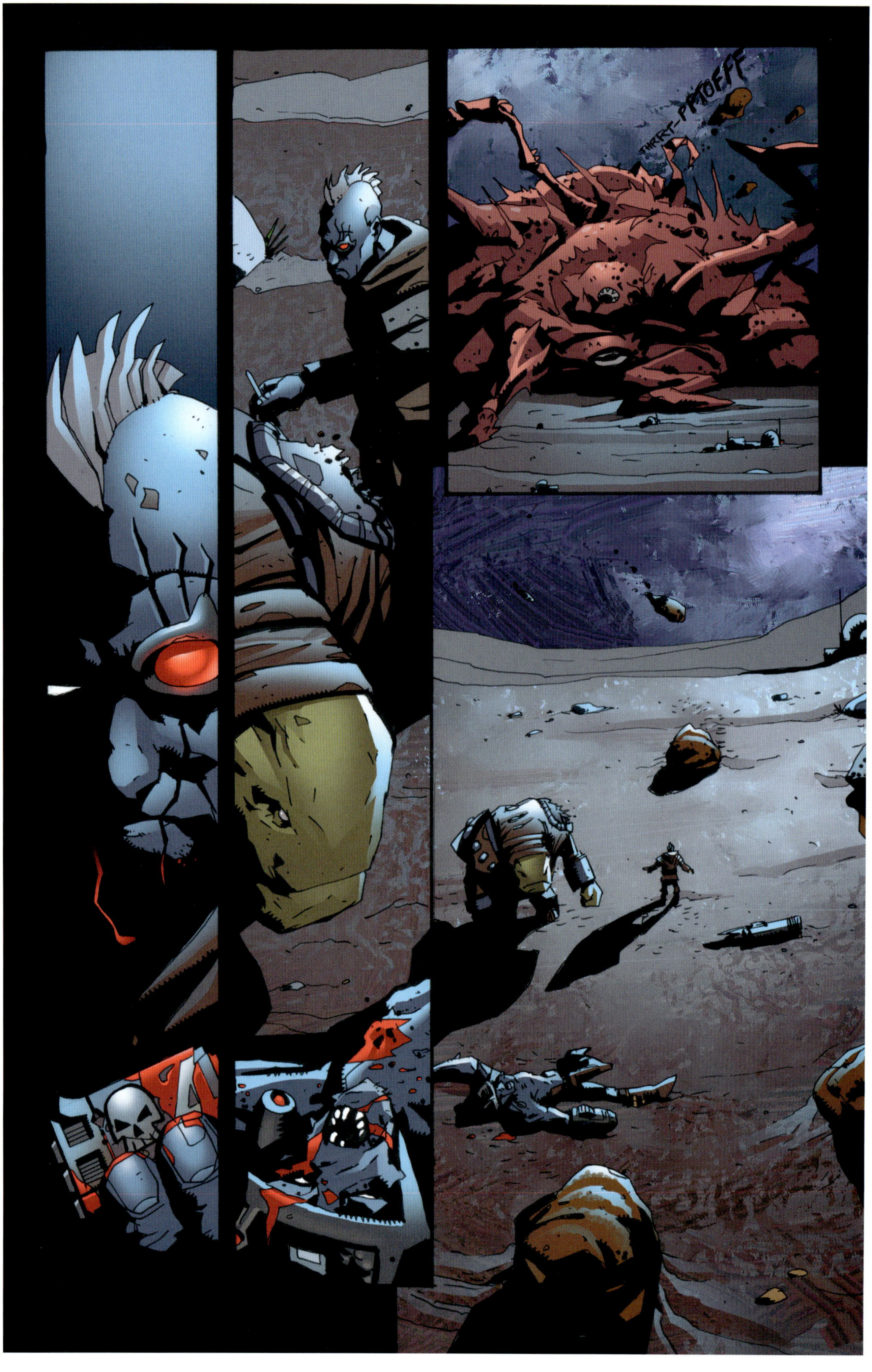
THRRT-PPTOEFF

TOR CYAN: NO SUCH PLACE PAGE 2, 2000 AD PROG 1297, 2002
COLOUR BY CHRIS BLYTHE

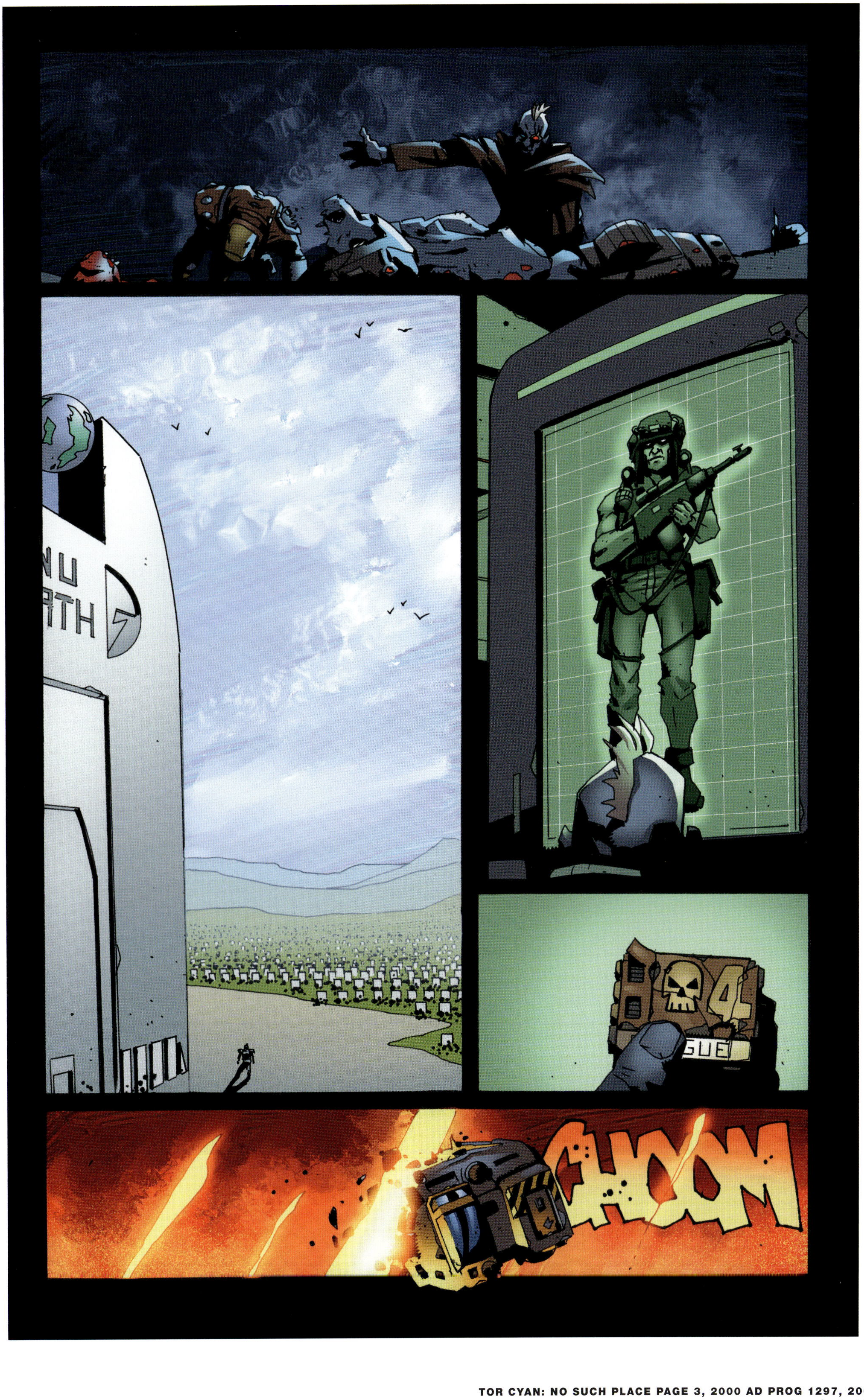
NU
RTH
GUE
CHOOM

TOR CYAN: NO SUCH PLACE PAGE 3, 2000 AD PROG 1297, 2002
COLOUR BY CHRIS BLYTHE

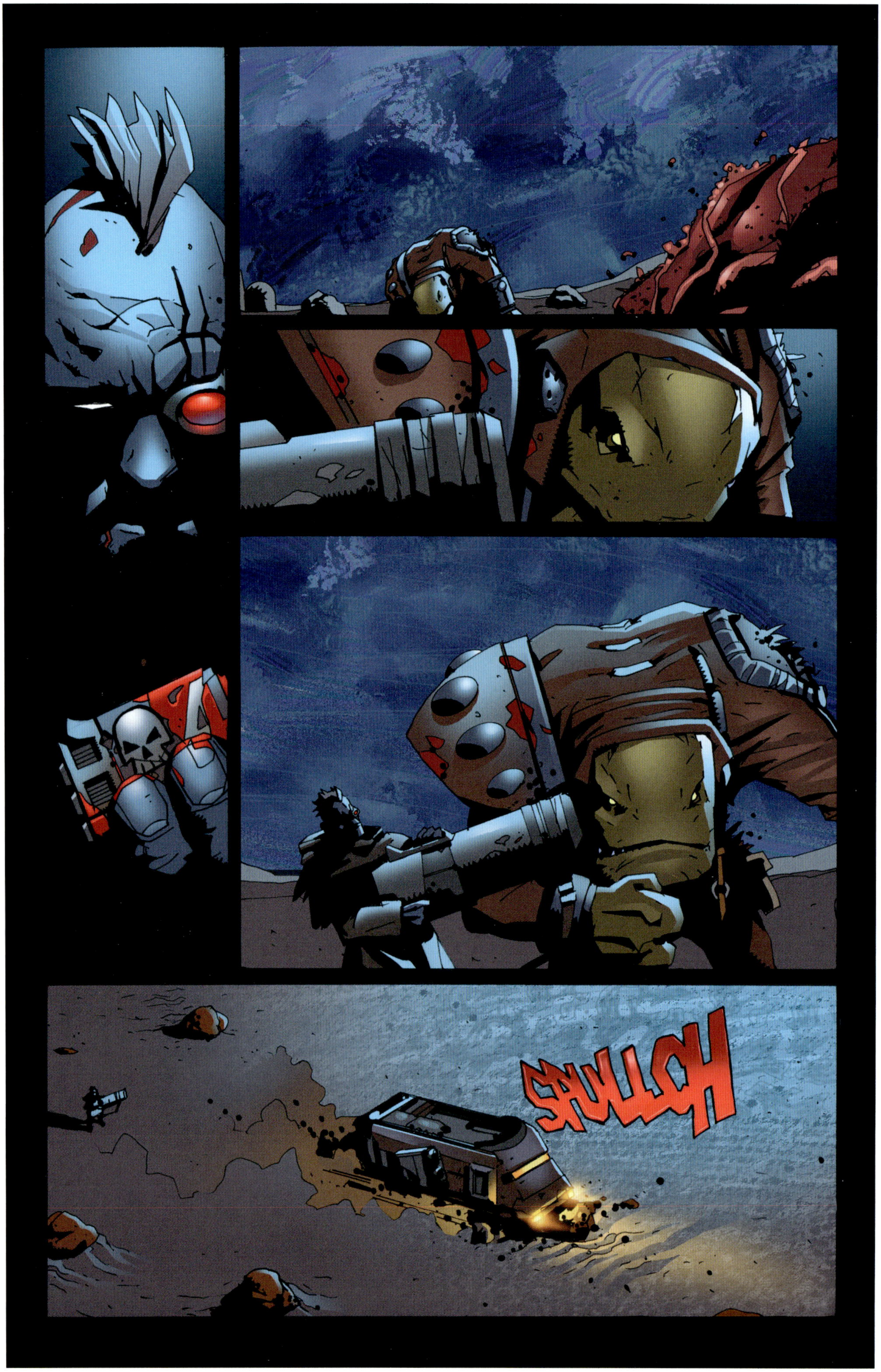
SPULLCH

TOR CYAN: NO SUCH PLACE PAGE 4, 2000 AD PROG 1297, 2002
COLOUR BY CHRIS BLYTHE

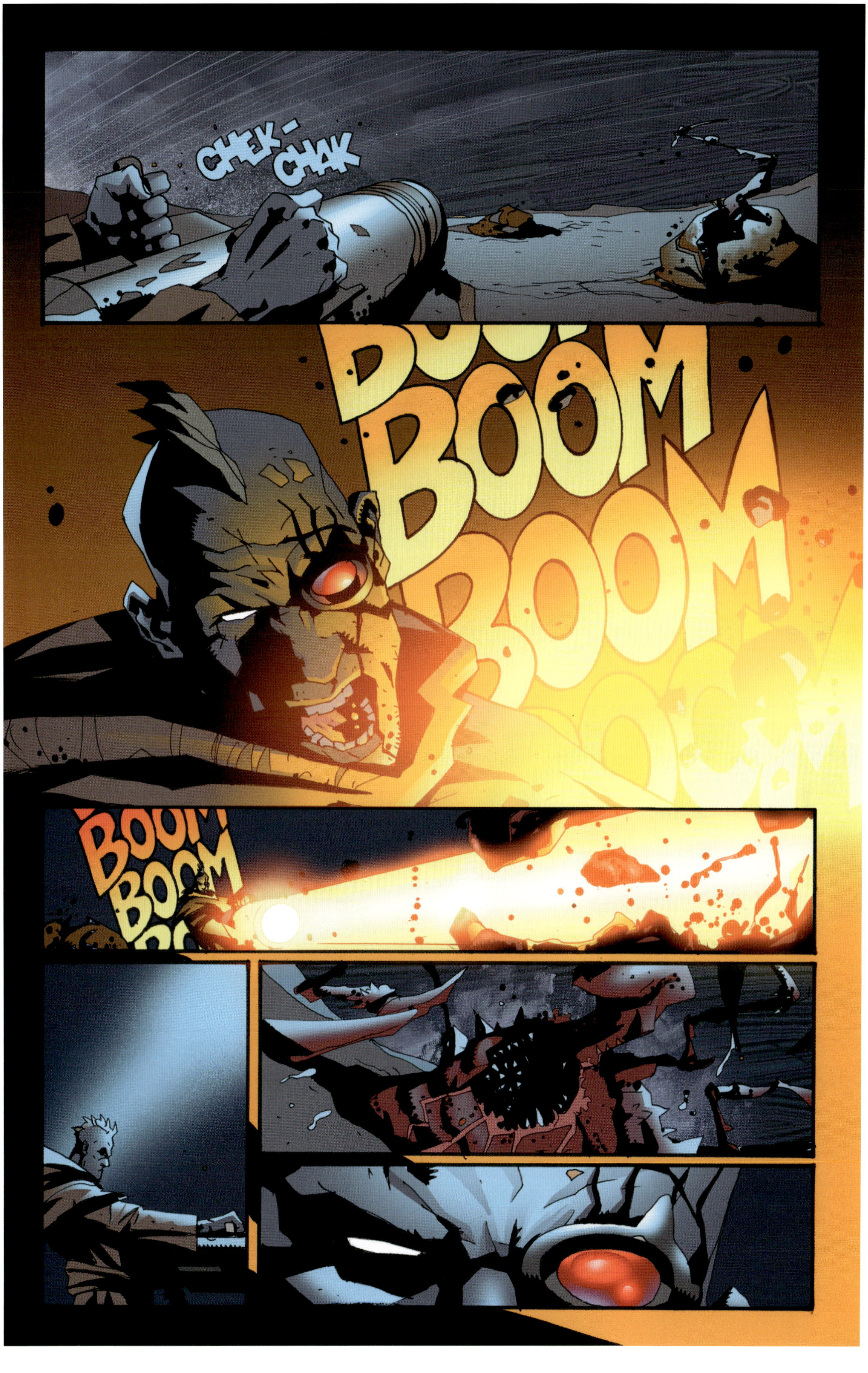
CHEK-CHAK
BOOM
BOOM
BOOM
BOOM
BOOM

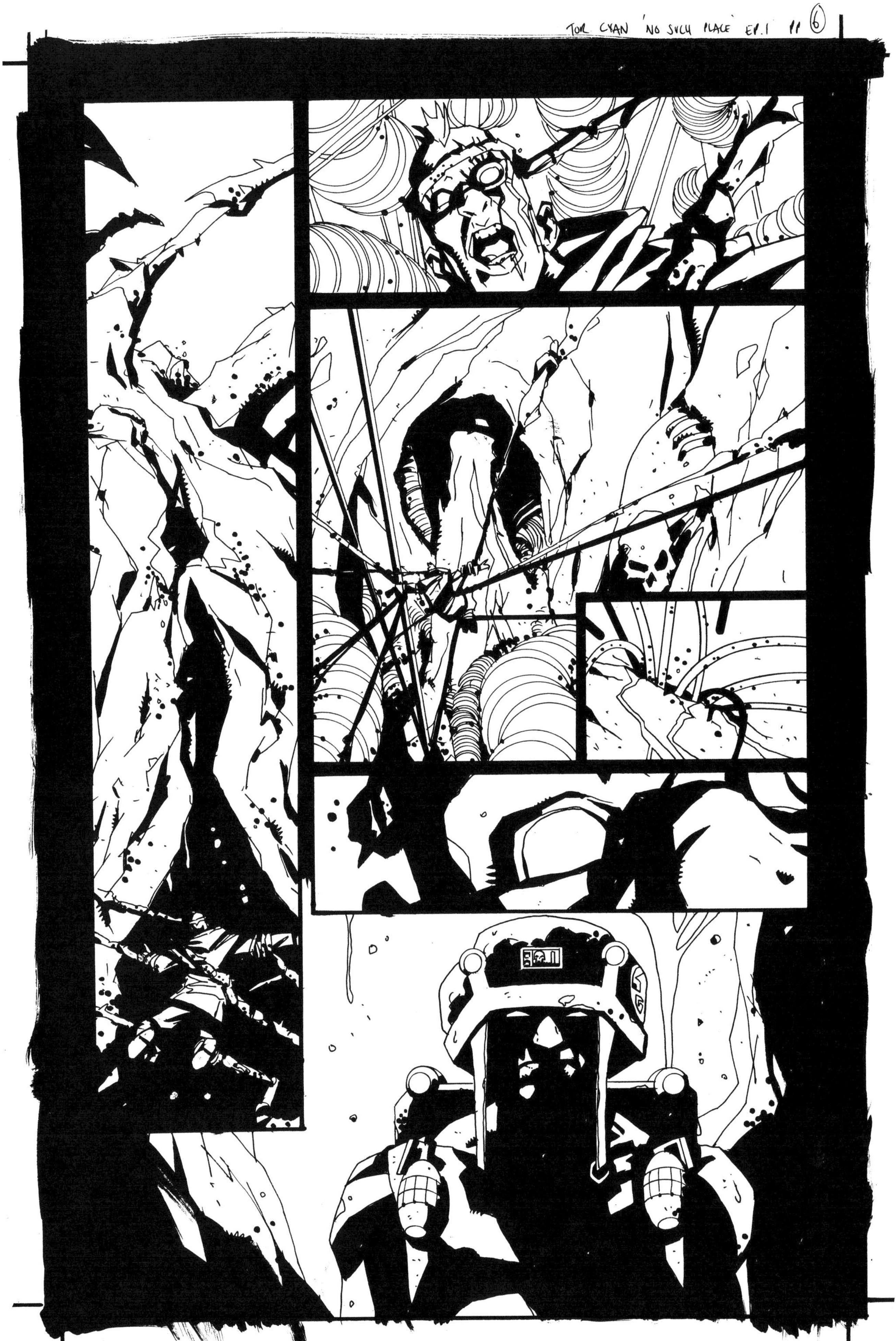
TOR CYAN 'NO SUCH PLACE' EP.1

TOR CYAN: NO SUCH PLACE PAGE 6 INKS, 2000 AD PROG 1297, 2002

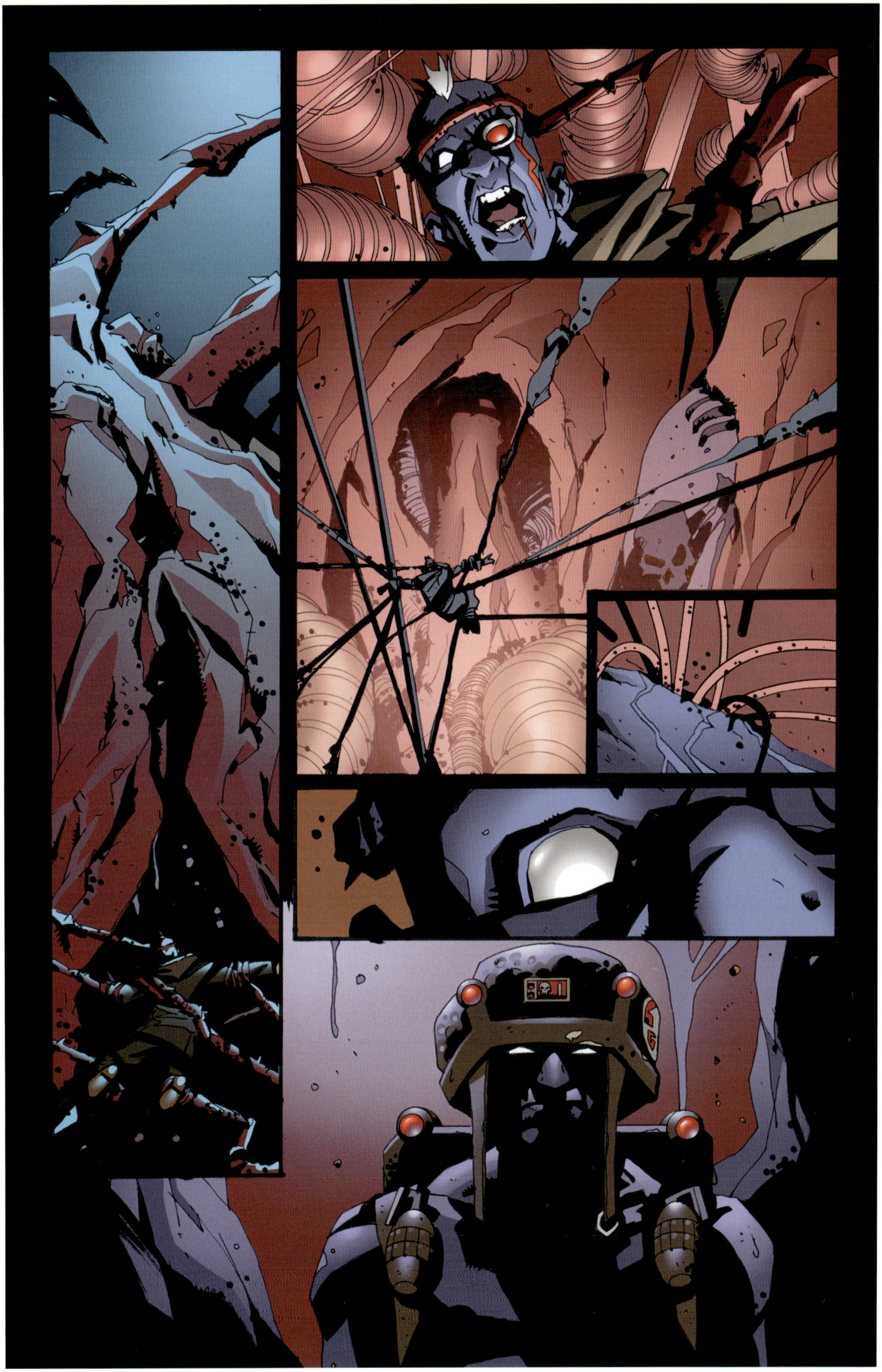

TOR CYAN: NO SUCH PLACE PAGE 6, 2000 AD PROG 1297, 2002
COLOUR BY CHRIS BLYTHE

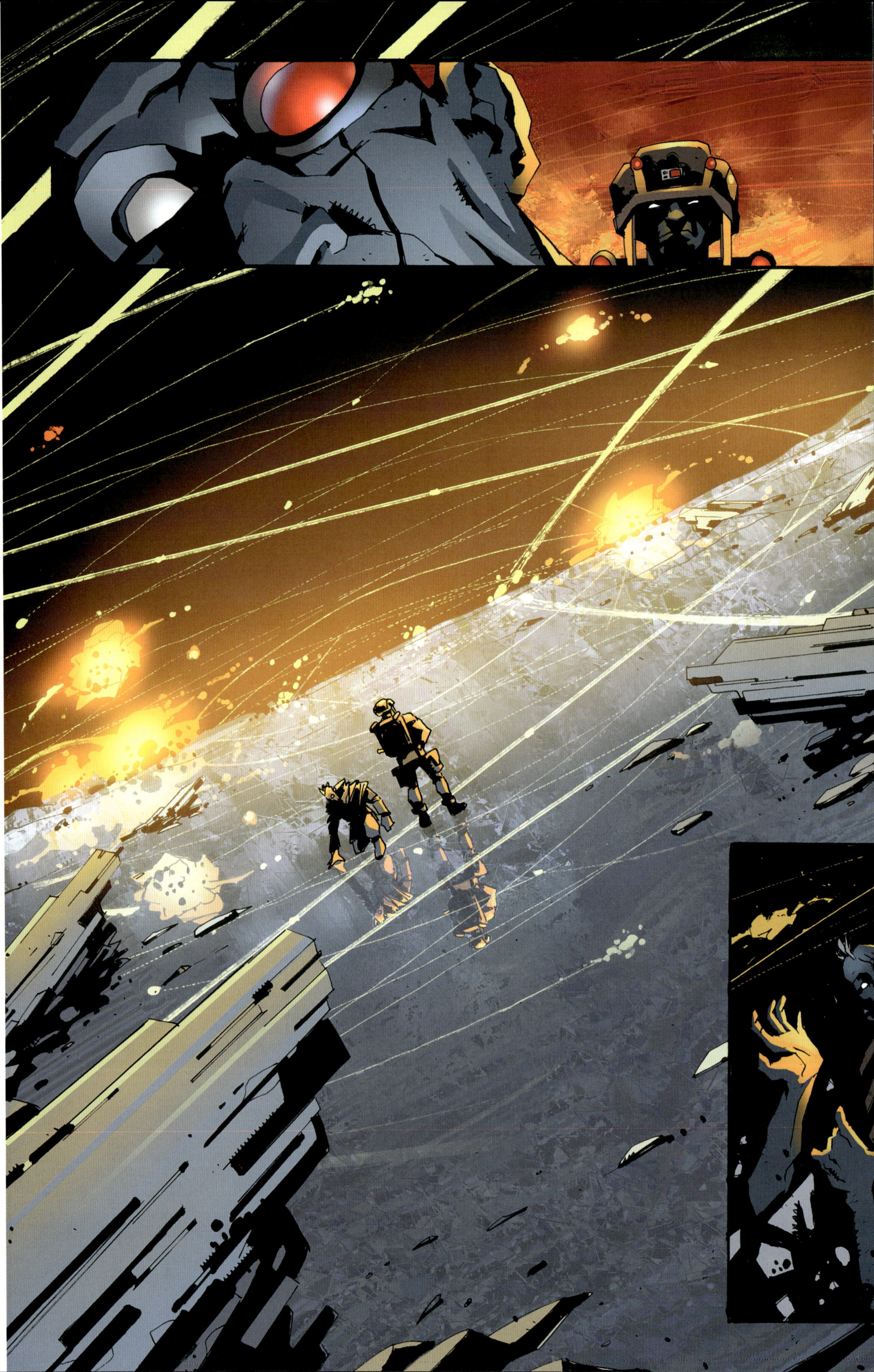

TOR CYAN: NO SUCH PLACE PAGES 7 & 8, 2000 AD PROG 1298, 2002
COLOUR BY CHRIS BLYTHE

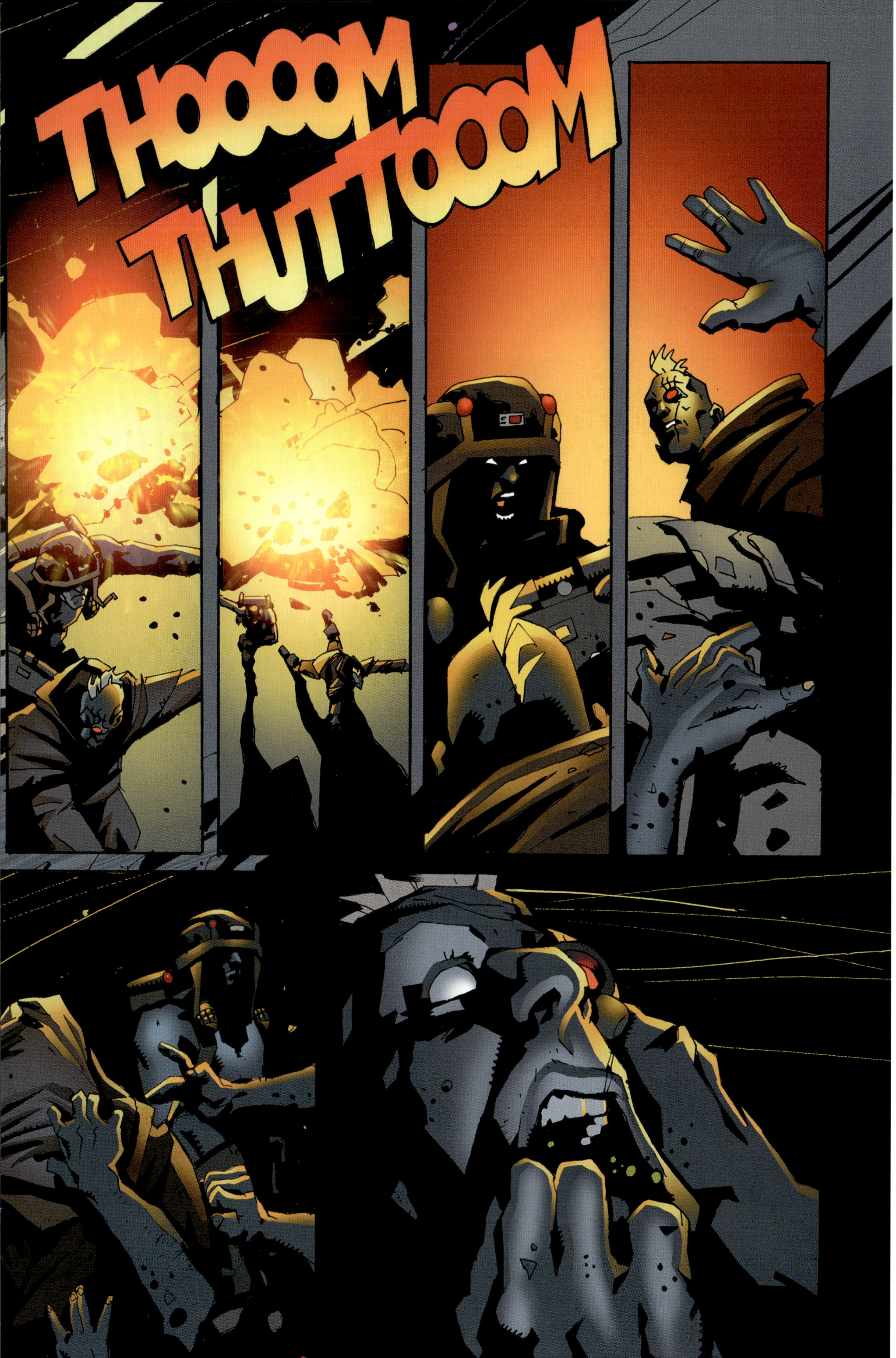
THOOOM
THUTTOOOM

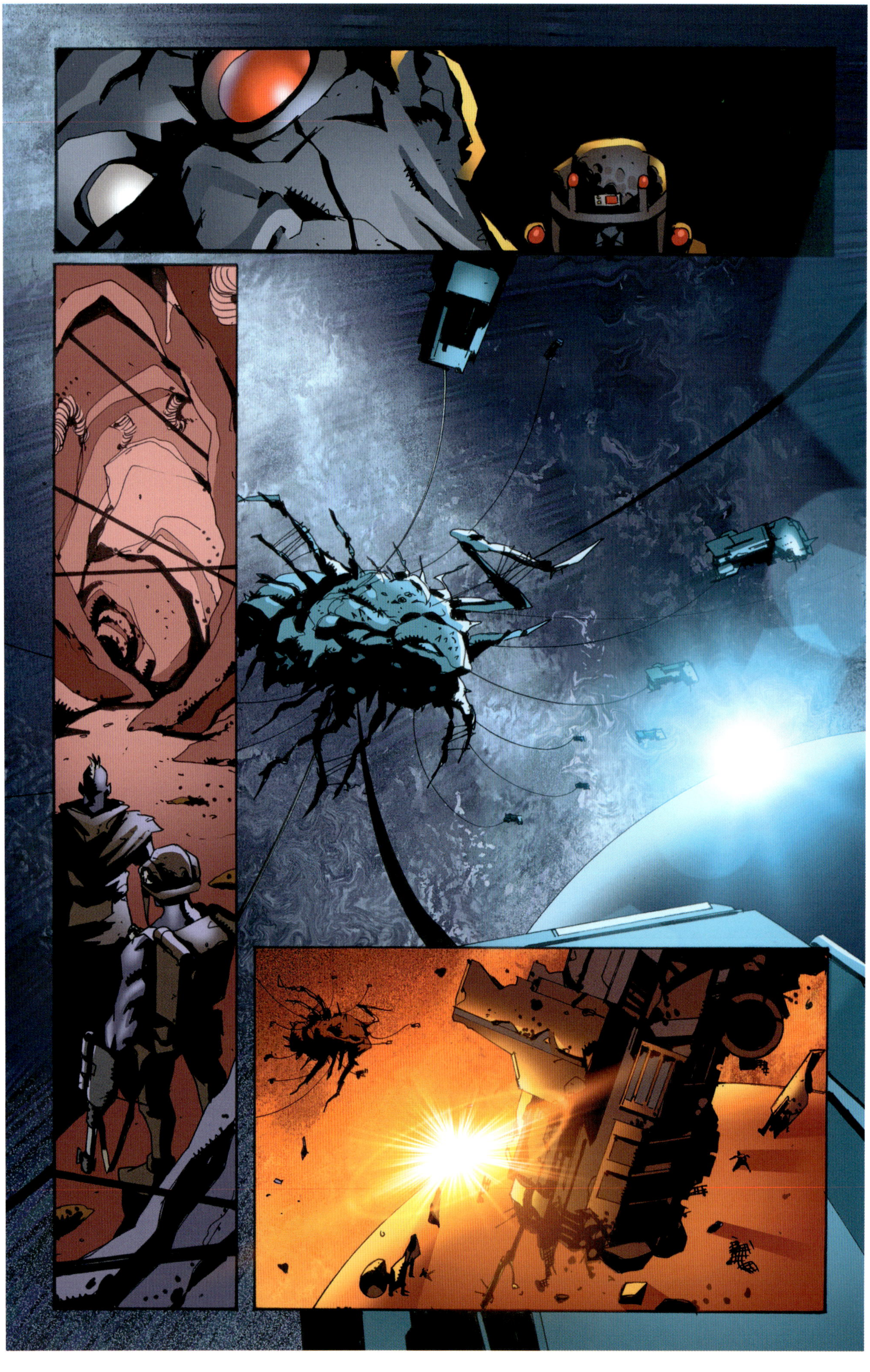

TOR CYAN: NO SUCH PLACE PAGE 9, 2000 AD PROG 1298, 2002
COLOUR BY CHRIS BLYTHE

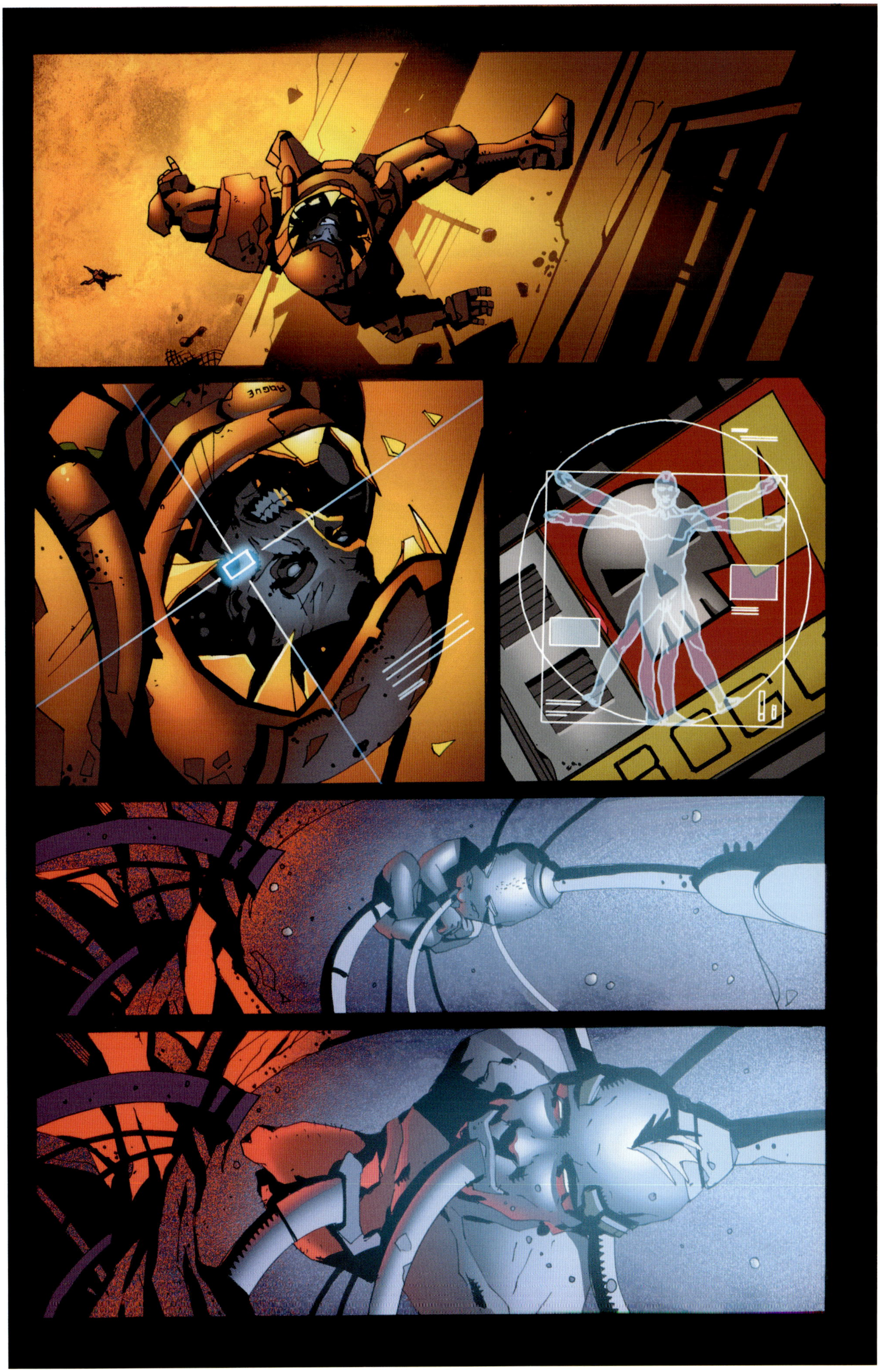
ROGUE

TOR CYAN: NO SUCH PLACE PAGE 10, 2000 AD PROG 1298, 2002
COLOUR BY CHRIS BLYTHE

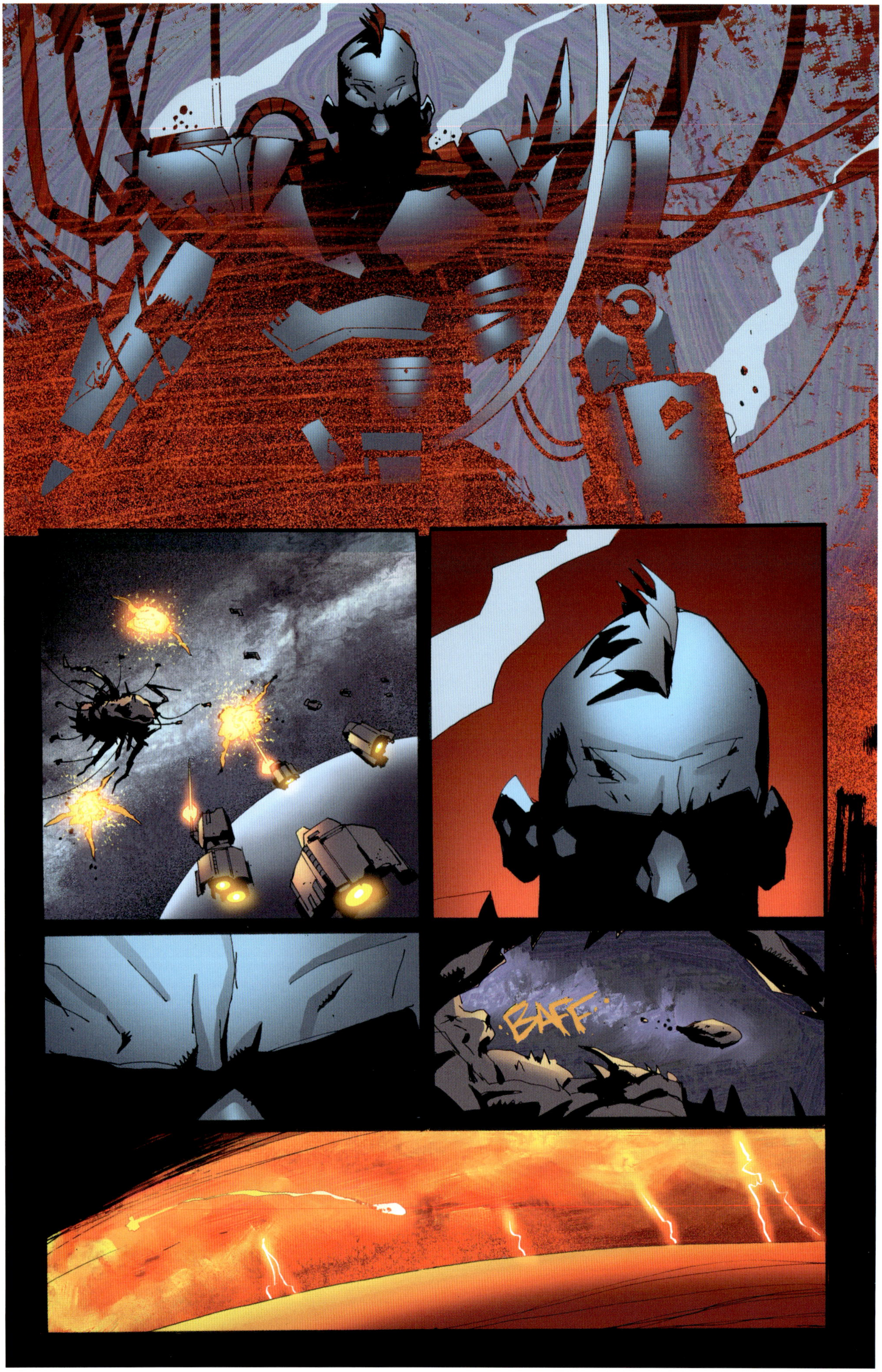
BAFF

TOR CYAN: NO SUCH PLACE PAGE 11, 2000 AD PROG 1298, 2002
COLOUR BY CHRIS BLYTHE

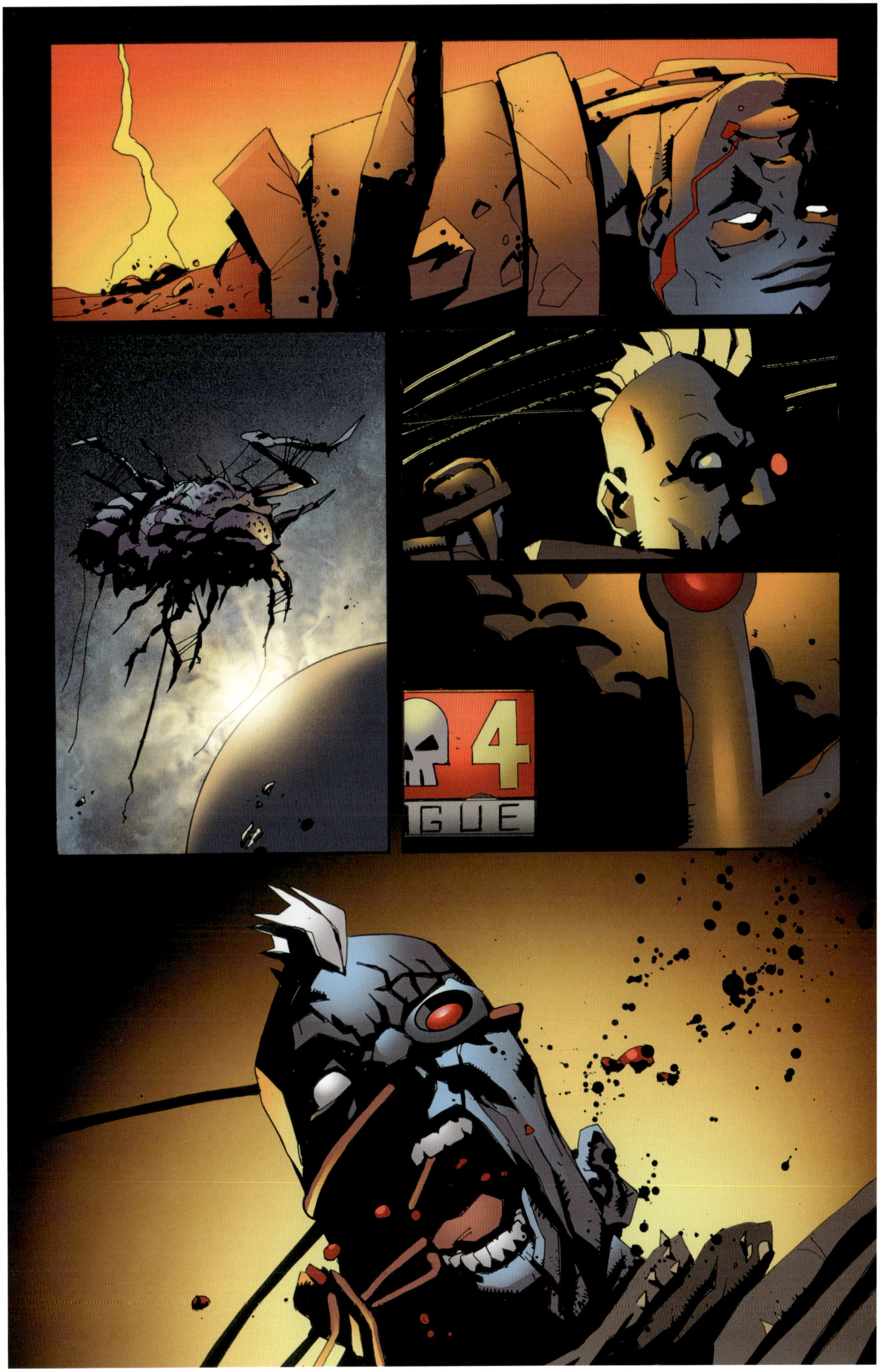
4
GUE

TOR CYAN: NO SUCH PLACE PAGE 12, 2000 AD PROG 1298, 2002
COLOUR BY CHRIS BLYTHE

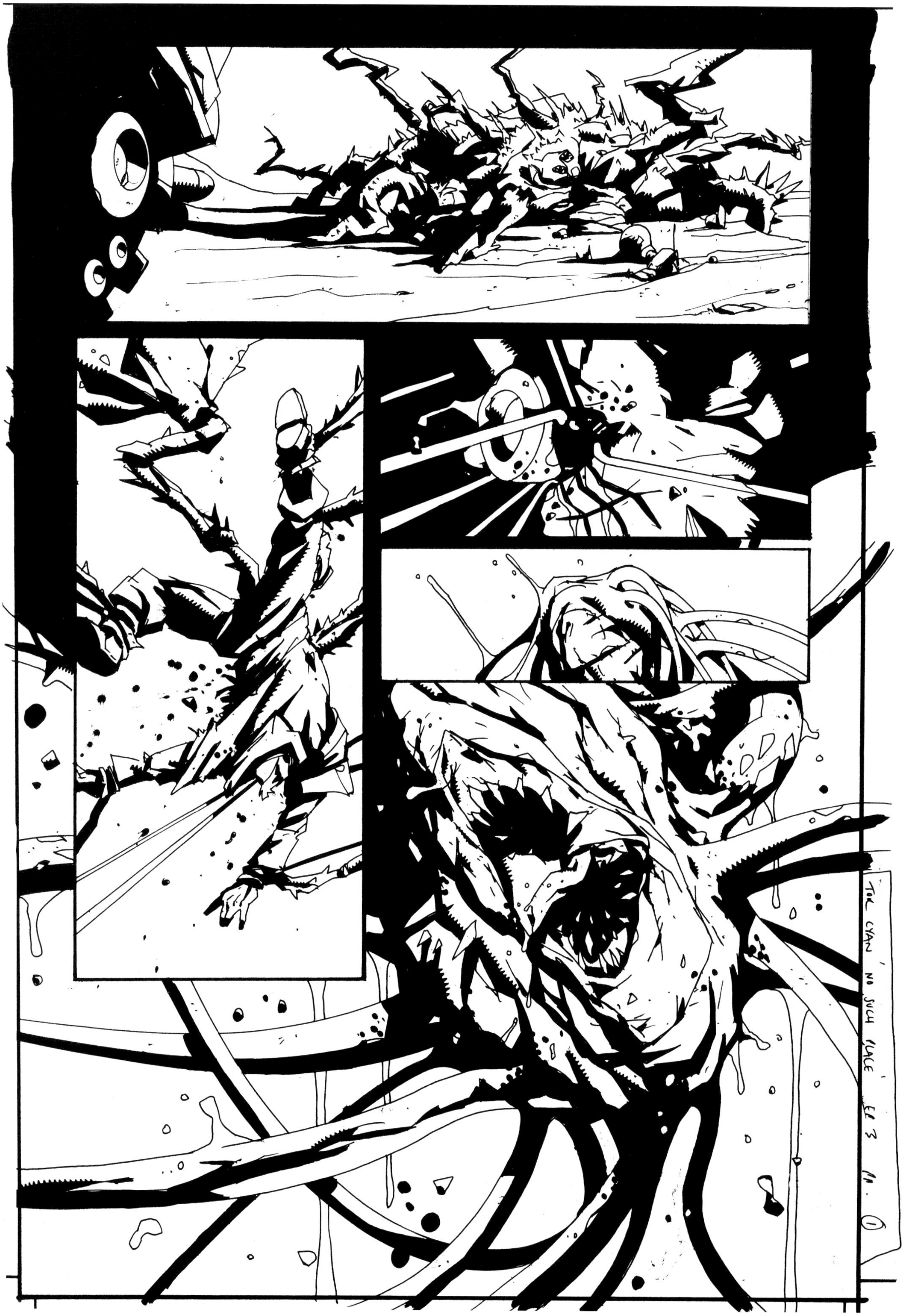
TOR CYAN 'NO SUCH PLACE' EP 3

 TOR CYAN: NO SUCH PLACE PAGE 13 INKS, 2000 AD PROG 1299, 2002

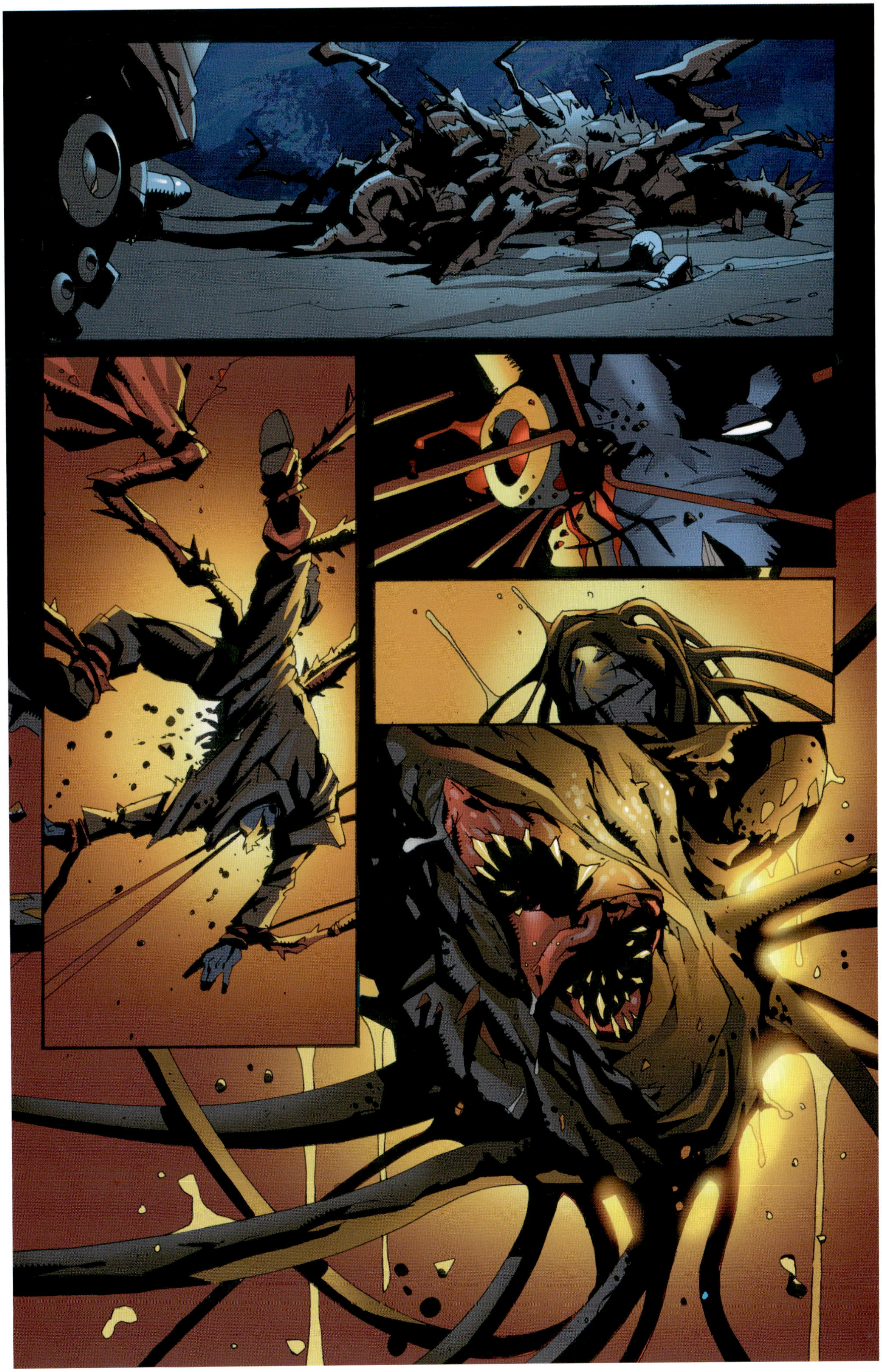

TOR CYAN: NO SUCH PLACE PAGE 13, 2000 AD PROG 1299, 2002
COLOUR BY CHRIS BLYTHE

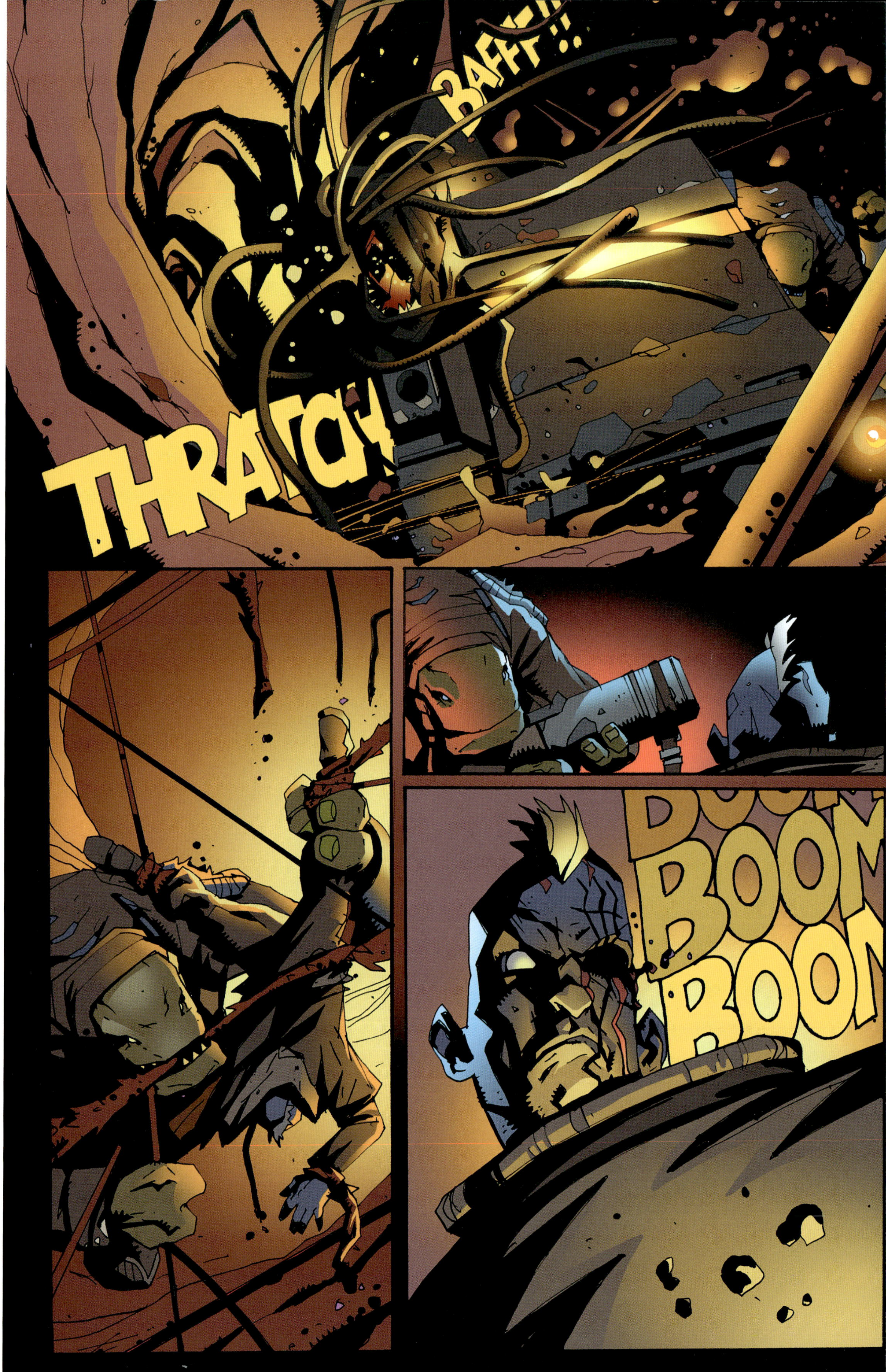
BAFF!!
THRATCH
BOOM
BOOM
BOOM

TOR CYAN: NO SUCH PLACE PAGES 14 & 15, 2000 AD PROG 1299, 2002
COLOUR BY CHRIS BLYTHE

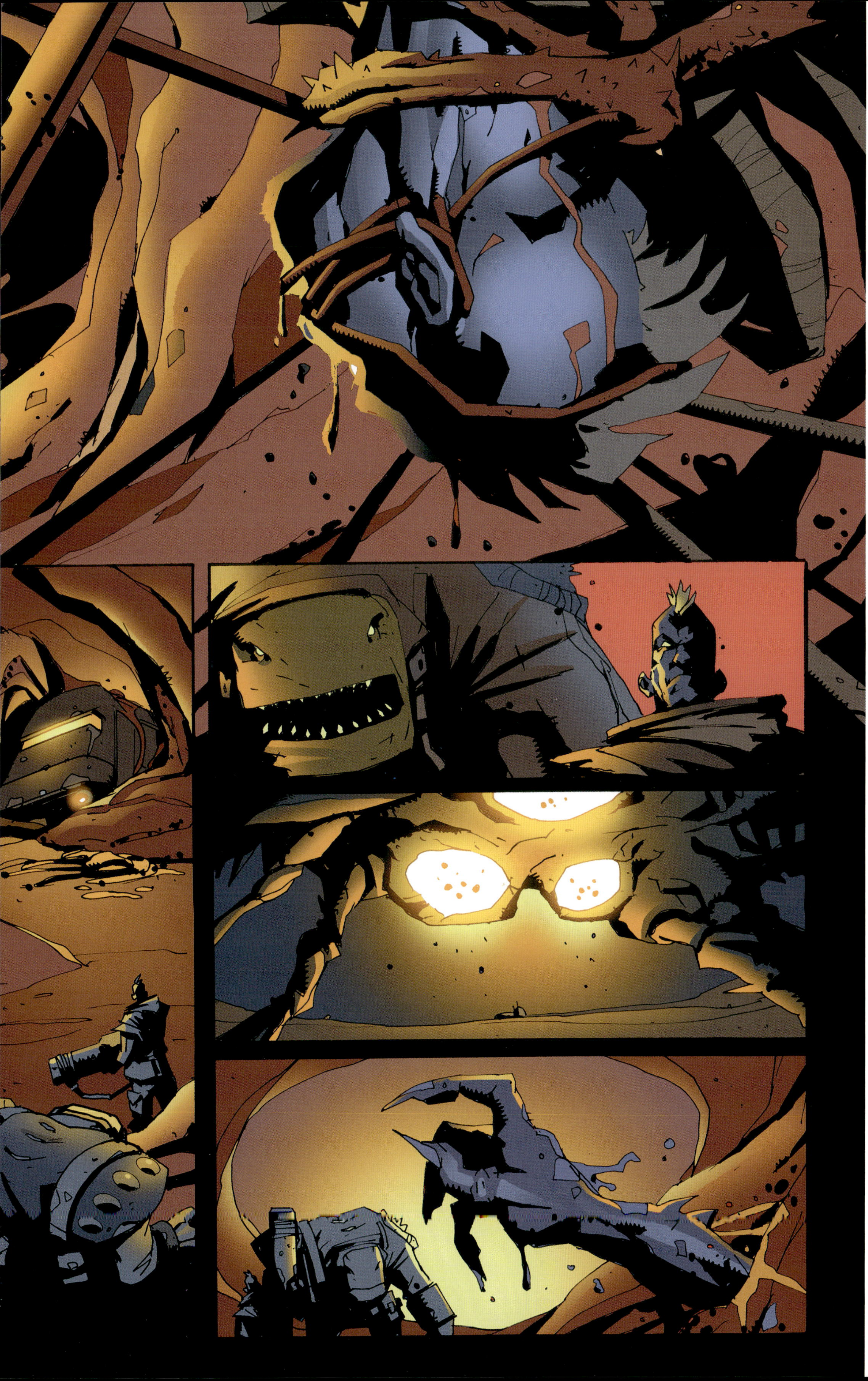

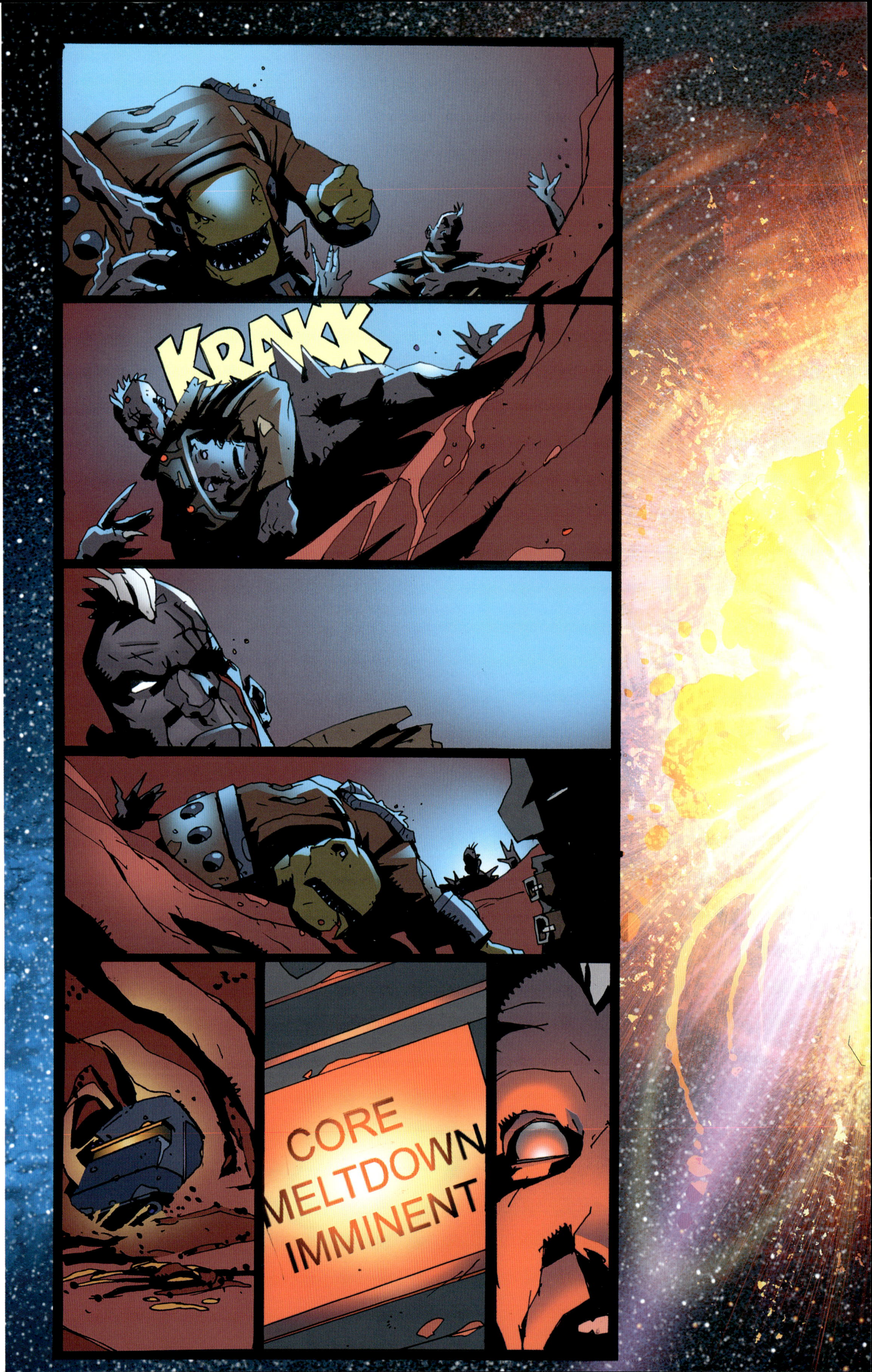
KRAKK
CORE
MELTDOWN
IMMINENT

TOR CYAN: NO SUCH PLACE PAGES 16 & 17, 2000 AD PROG 1299, 2002
COLOUR BY CHRIS BLYTHE

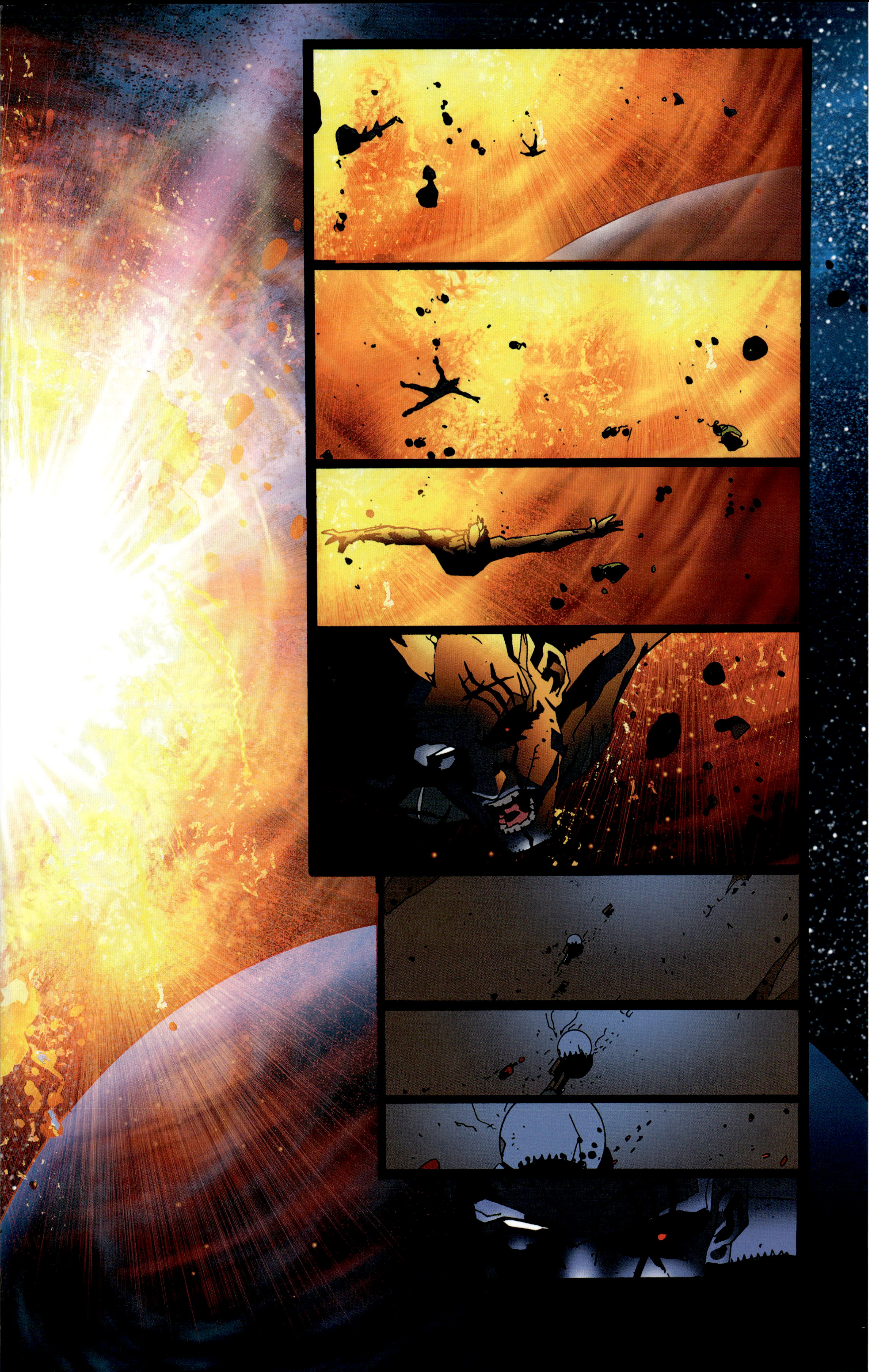

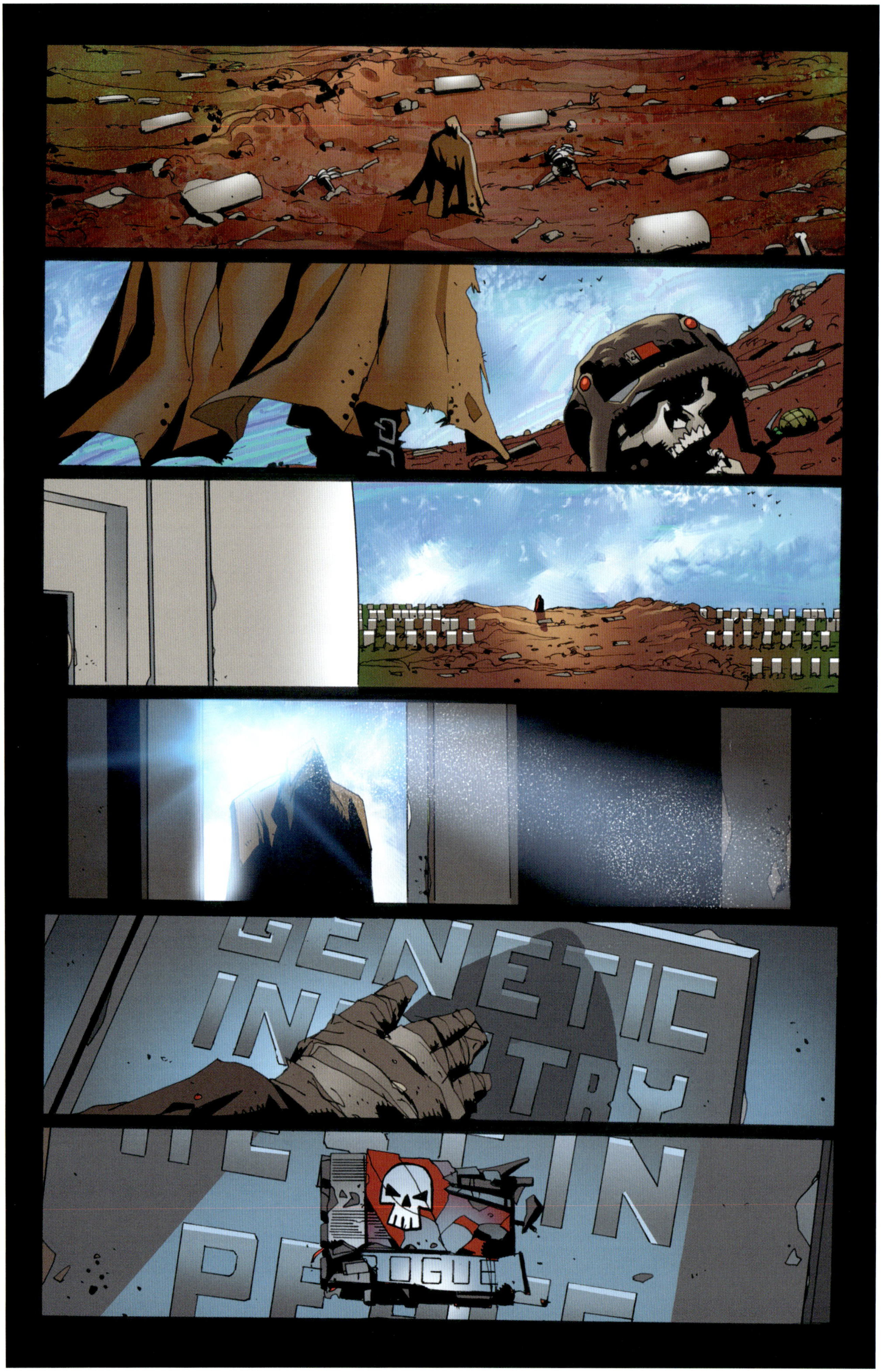
GENETIC

TOR CYAN: NO SUCH PLACE PAGE 18, 2000 AD PROG 1299, 2002
COLOUR BY CHRIS BLYTHE

Special thanks goes to Dom Reardon and my old friend Joe Craddock. Without our time spent together, this book wouldn't exist. - Jock

Jock is one of **2000 AD**'s finest creators. As well as illustrating *Judge Dredd*, *Pulp Sci-Fi*, and *Tor Cyan*, Jock co-created *Lenny Zero* with ex-**2000 AD** editor Andy Diggle, and has produced work for every major comic publisher. Among these projects are the Eisner award-nominated **The Losers** and **Green Arrow: Year One**, also with Diggle, **Batman: The Black Mirror** and **Wytches** with writer Scott Snyder, and the Eisner-winning **Snow Angels** with Jeff Lemire. Outside of comics, Jock has produced key art and concept design on films including **Ex Machina, Annihilation, Batman Begins, Star Wars: The Last Jedi**, and the 2012 **Dredd** movie. His most recent work has been as the writer/artist for **Batman: One Dark Knight** for DC, and on **Gone** for DSTLRY. Born in Glasgow, he now lives and works in Devon, England.

PEACH